The First Descent of the Matterhorn

Douglas Hadow
1846-1865

Young Peter Taugwalder
1843-1923

Edward Whymper
1840-1911

Old Peter Taugwalder
1820-1888

Charles Hudson
1828-1865

Michel Croz
1828-1865

Lord Francis Douglas
1847-1865

The first climbers of the Matterhorn *(from a photograph in the possession of the Alpine Club)*

ALAN LYALL

The First Descent of the Matterhorn

A BIBLIOGRAPHICAL GUIDE
TO THE 1865 ACCIDENT
& ITS AFTERMATH

GOMER

First Impression—1997

ISBN 1 85902 457 2

Printed in Wales at
Gomer Press, Llandysul, Ceredigion

CONTENTS

ILLUSTRATIONS

PREFACE

My object in writing this bibliographical guide to the mass of material relating to the 1865 Matterhorn accident has been twofold. Firstly, to bring together as many as possible of the contemporary documents, particularly the correspondence relating to the accident and its aftermath, to consider their implications and try to view them in their proper perspective and, secondly, to highlight and correct the erroneous and misleading statements of fact and comments that have appeared in so many of the articles and books written in the 80 years or so since the death of Edward Whymper. At the same time I have endeavoured to provide a comprehensive guide or index to the documentary evidence and to the numerous books and articles dealing with the subject, and to encourage further reading and even perhaps some further research.

Relevant letters and documents are scattered far and wide in Britain, Switzerland and elsewhere and I have where possible recorded their present location. I have discovered much previously unpublished material in the course of my research and I have been impressed by the way it almost invariably confirms precisely the account that Whymper gave. I have also been able to draw certain new conclusions from what Whymper wrote and then trace the supporting evidence, as in the case of his reference to M.Vecqueray in a letter to James Robertson of 29th September 1866, when he was seeking help in translating into French an inscription for Croz' tomb. Whymper's 'lively recollection' of his kindness, and his reference to it being 'scarcely becoming for myself, almost a stranger, to prefer the request', suggested that Vecqueray had been in Zermatt and had given him some help with translation in connection with the Enquiry. The first sign of confirmation came from a copy made by Graham Brown of extracts from Adams Reilly's 1865 Zermatt diary, of which there seems now to be no other trace. 'Mr.Vicary went' appears in Reilly's entry for the 22nd July, and some further research established that a document Whymper retained setting out his answers to the questions he was later asked at the Enquiry was almost certainly in Vecqueray's handwriting, that Vecqueray had an interest in mountaineering and that he had previously visited Zermatt in July 1863.

The errors of the critics have often been factual, sometimes merely adopting or repeating what had been written before, but there has also been misleading comment with considerable distortion of the context or contemporary perspective and even the occasional major blunder. Translation has introduced mistakes, some of which appear in the evidence given at the Enquiry and others in the official French and German editions of *Scrambles*, whilst foreign critics have at times misunderstood an English phrase. I have translated certain documents into English, including most of those relating to the Enquiry, so that they can be appreciated by the English speaking reader, and this has given rise to occasional problems, such as whether or not to retain an error made by the Clerk to the

Enquiry in transcribing Whymper's evidence, when there can be no doubt whatever, from Whymper's own record and from the Vecqueray document already mentioned, as to what he actually stated in his written answer. I have therefore also included the full original German version of the Enquiry Report so that those who understand it can see for themselves what was actually recorded by the Clerk. Translating from one language to another and then back to the original one seems to be particularly fraught with risk and I hope I have managed to avoid anything as inappropriate as the phrase that crept into a recent official Zermatt booklet with a text in four languages. Whymper wrote in *Scrambles* that his experience with guides up to 1861 had not been fortunate and that they represented to him 'pointers out of paths, and large consumers of meat and drink, but little more'. Intending to quote Whymper's same words, but after they had been translated into German and then back into English, the English text in the booklet states that 'he described them as boy scouts with huge appetites and given to heavy drinking'!

I have noticed that although in 1966 Dangar & Blakeney challenged in the *Alpine Journal* what Arnold Lunn had been writing and repeating for 25 years, and dismissed the idea that Whymper had made 'attacks' and 'accusations' against the Taugwalders, they had ten years earlier in their article on Young Peter's Narrative been more inclined to accept that Whymper's remark about 'the very ugly look' was uncalled-for. But as they became more familiar with Whymper's account their attitude seems to have changed, and although they never had the opportunity of reading Whymper's scrapbook and learning the circumstances under which the Cowell memorandum came to be made or how Whymper had gone out of his way to avoid giving pain to the relatives of Hudson, Hadow and Douglas, they began to realise that Whymper had simply been recording the facts. It seems to me that the more one studies the details and understands the background to what Whymper wrote – how, for example, he wrote of his letter to *The Times* 'I scrupulously abstain from offering observations and casting blame on anyone, and also from taking notice of the remarks that have been made on my personal capability for the expedition we undertook' – the more obvious it becomes that he was not voicing his own suspicions when he wrote about such things as Taugwalder's use of the weakest rope but was merely recording the facts and the contemporary reaction.

There is such a wide range of fresh evidence available that it is not practicable to single it all out for comment, and in any event the errors and distortions of the critics need looking at so closely that the whole subject requires a complete review. It is too complex to start at the beginning and consider all the relevant points as and when they crop up in the course of relating the full story, and I have therefore divided it into almost one hundred different parts, dealing firstly with the sixty people most directly involved with the early history of the Matterhorn and the events of July 1865 and secondly with various specific subjects. I have, where appropriate, looked at matters from the different points of view of the various individuals involved in order to try and put them back into their proper perspective. This inevitably leads to some duplication but, as this is a guidebook and is not primarily intended to be read through from beginning to end, it seems to me that repetition is the lesser of two evils and that it is preferable to deal as fully as possible in one place with a particular individual or with a particular aspect and reduce to the minimum the need to keep referring elsewhere. For example, Whymper's reference in the *Graphic* in 1894 to the guide Franz Andenmatten being ejected from the Zermatt church the next time he tried to attend Mass is detailed at least four times; under Whymper himself because he wrote it, under Robertson because he must have been Whymper's informant twenty years or more after the event, under Andenmatten because it is relevant to his achievement in leading Whymper's successful search party when the guides of Zermatt refused en masse to search on Sunday morning, and also under the subject heading 'The excommunication threat' because it seems to have been a sequel to the authorities' failure to prevent Whymper's Sunday search from taking place after the first search party led by the President had failed to reach the glacier.

I am indebted to the late D.F.O.Dangar and T.S.Blakeney, whose bold criticism of Arnold Lunn, on the basis that he was allergic to Whymper, drew attention to so many of the distortions he had introduced into the Matterhorn history, and also to T.Graham Brown, whose copious notes on the Matterhorn accident have proved most useful in checking some of the facts, even though I have been unable to share many of his conclusions and seemingly unfounded suspicions. There have been occasions when I thought initially that there might well be some substance in a point made by an anti-Whymper critic, only to discover soon afterwards some fresh evidence or something that I and others had previously overlooked, which completely undermined the critic and exonerated Whymper altogether. I have not read all Whymper's climbing diaries and now and again I have relied on extracts quoted by Frank Smythe or recorded by Graham Brown, but I have every reason to accept the comment Frank Smythe made about Whymper in 1939 in a letter to Herbert Cooke (4.67): 'Having read all Whymper's diary through his life it is not possible to come to any conclusion other than that he was an absolutely honest and scrupulous man'.

I leave it to someone else to supplement and update Smythe's biography of Whymper and correct one or two serious errors and distortions, such as taking the Cowell memorandum out of its context, and to judge the significance of the fresh evidence I have discovered. Nevertheless, after comparing what Whymper wrote in *Scrambles* with the other contemporary evidence, I can say that it all rings remarkably true and that I have only been able to find a few very minor if not trivial errors in what he wrote. His honesty, his powers of observation, his attention to detail and consequently his accuracy were all quite remarkable and it is very doubtful whether anyone else who might have had the misfortune to find himself in his position would have been able to do such justice to the truth and to the memory of Charles Hudson, Lord Francis Douglas, Douglas Hadow, Michel Croz and, last but not least, Old Peter Taugwalder.

I have received help and encouragement from many quarters, particularly from Whymper's great-nephew Timothy Woodgate, who has allowed me to quote and reproduce documents now in the Whymper Archives at the Scott Polar Research Institute at Cambridge and has read and given advice in relation to the section on Edward Whymper; also from the late Jack Baines, from Peter Ledeboer, Bob Lawford and Trevor Braham, as well as from Jon Mellor and Jerry Lovatt who read most of the manuscript and made a number of helpful suggestions. I am grateful to the former and present librarians at the Alpine Club Library, Pat Johnson and Margaret Eccleston, and to the honorary archivist, Livia Gollancz, for help in tracing books and archives; also to Gustav Anthamatten the archivist of Seiler Hotels Zermatt AG, Willy Hofstetter the custodian of the Zermatt Museum, Robert Headland the archivist of the Scott Polar Research Institute and Elgan Davies of the Welsh Books Council. Monsieur Gilles Martin of Geneva, the fourth generation of the family of Alexandre Jules Martin and holder of the family archives, has kindly provided relevant copies from the pages of the original diary of his forebear.

Finally I wish to acknowledge the invaluable assistance of the Alpine Club, in granting permission to quote and reproduce various articles from the *Alpine Journal* as well as archives from the Library, and in providing illustrations 12, 21, 23, 26, 31, 32 and 39 as well as the photograph for the frontispiece. I am also grateful to John Murray for permission to quote from several 'Whymper' letters in their archives, including Edward Whymper's letter to his father of 1st August 1862; the Trustees of the National Library of Scotland for permission to quote from the manuscripts in the Graham Brown Papers in their collection; Robert Smart, Keeper of the Muniments at the University of St Andrews, for permission to quote several letters in their collection of the papers of James David Forbes, and finally the Scott Polar Research Institute for permission to quote and reproduce documents in the Whymper Archives and for supplying photographs for illustrations 4, 25, 28, 29, 35, 36, 40 and 45.

1
INTRODUCTION

Two hundred years ago the Matterhorn was virtually unknown to the outside world, whereas Mont Blanc and the Jungfrau could be clearly seen from such places as Geneva and Interlaken and had already attracted considerable interest long before they were first climbed. The Matterhorn was one of the many peaks that could be seen from the top of the much frequented Gemmi pass, but it was hardly any more prominent than its neighbours on the skyline, such as the Weisshorn, Zinalrothorn, Obergabelhorn and Dent Blanche and few people would have known of it or even have recognised it.

The great 18th century Swiss landscape artists like Aberli and Caspar Wolf met the demand of both Swiss and foreign travellers for pictorial souvenirs of such places as Grindelwald and Lauterbrunnen, as did their successors the two Lorys, father and son. The Lorys' views of the scenery around Chamonix were second to none, but, although they travelled from Geneva to Milan via the Simplon pass in the course of producing some 35 illustrations for a fine book published in 1811, they seem not to have known of the Matterhorn. Even William Beattie's comprehensive work *Switzerland Illustrated*, which with its 106 fine steel engravings drawn by W.H.Bartlett still provides many a modern tourist with a framed print of some well known resort or mountain landscape, did not include a view of the Matterhorn. The author had certainly heard of it but in his travels he seems to have got no further up the Nikolaital than the vicinity of Stalden where Bartlett took a view which, in the original part XVIII published at the end of 1835, was entitled 'Mount Cervin (from near Stalden)'. The text referred to 'the magnificent pinnacles of Mont Cervin, or the Matterhorn' but the Matterhorn was nowhere to be seen, the southernmost peak in the picture probably being the Brunegghorn.

The very earliest painting of the Matterhorn as an individual peak seen from the Zermatt side, as opposed to its appearance in a general panorama, is probably the watercolour of Conrad Escher taken from Winkelmatten on 14th August 1806, which he followed up two days later with another one taken from Breuil. Escher was a man of great enterprise and he had no doubt read what de Saussure had written about his visit to Zermatt in 1789, even though the original 1793 edition of Ebel's Swiss guidebook mentioned neither the place nor the mountain. The first English guidebooks to Switzerland seem to have been those by Daniel Wall and by Henry Coxe, which were both first published in 1816. Coxe got no closer to mentioning Zermatt or the Matterhorn than to state of Viège that it 'is situated at the entrance of the vallies of Saas and St.Nicholas'. Coolidge wrote of Wall just mentioning Zermatt and the Matterhorn in his second edition in 1818, but the first edition did not even go that far, and merely referred to Praborgne, one of the ancient names for Zermatt:

> 'A place which may perhaps interest the tourist is THE VALLEY OF PRABORGNE, which communicates with that of St.Nicholas. It is bounded by enormous glaciers, which descend to the bottom of the valley. The village of Praborgne is very lofty, it overlooks these glaciers from an immense height; its climate is nearly as warm as that of Italy; even plants of the warm countries are gathered at a considerable height above the glaciers, which is a rare occurrence in Switzerland; they are often gathered below the glaciers, but seldom above.'

Zermatt and the Matterhorn in 1865

Another measure of the remoteness of Zermatt until about 1850, so far as both tourists and mountaineers are concerned, is the 'Topographical Section' in de Beer's book *Travellers in Switzerland*. This lists the names of visitors to various resorts in the early years as recorded in literature, and serves to emphasise the late development of Zermatt compared with such places as Grindelwald and Chamonix. It was not until 1839 that Zermatt acquired its Lauber Inn, travellers having previously been accomodated at the house of the curé or of the village doctor. But before long the increasing number of botanists, geologists and rudimentary mountaineers led Zermatt's original devotee, Christian Moritz Engelhardt of Strasburg, to recommend to his friend Joseph Clemenz ofVisp that he should build a hotel in Zermatt. The Hotel Mont Cervin was opened by Clemenz in 1852 with fourteen beds, and the following year saw the arrival of

Alexander Seiler, who was destined to do more than anyone else to help bring about the transformation of Zermatt from a small and remote farming community into the world renowned summer and winter holiday resort of today.

This fundamental change has come about in stages, and it has long been the custom for succeeding generations of visitors to look back to the good old days and regret the development that has taken place in the village. Some of the more obvious staging posts are the opening of the railway line from Visp in 1891 followed by the Gornergrat railway some seven years later, the start of a winter season and the electrification of the main railway in the late 1920's, the replacement of the Sunegga chairlift in the 1970's by an underground railway and, worst of all, the opening of the Klein Matterhorn cablecar in 1980, followed a few years later by the completion of the Furka railway tunnel linking Zermatt with St.Moritz throughout the year and bringing more and more Glacier Expresses to Zermatt, their latest Pininfarina styled Panorama carriages packed full of first class passengers. Zermatt continues to change rapidly and those who do not travel on a package or in a scheduled flock shepherded by a courier, but wish to come and go as they please other than on a Saturday, may soon find themselves regarded as too much of a nuisance and no longer welcome in some hotels.

But the event that was destined to have the most immediate and far-reaching effect on the small number of Burger families that ruled Zermatt, revolutionise their lives and rapidly increase the number of tourists and mountaineers in their midst, was the first descent of the Matterhorn. Had the Matterhorn's first ascent been accomplished without incident, it would only have been of interest to the small yet slowly increasing band of serious mountaineers, but the attention paid to the accident by the press and by the public, who seem hitherto to have regarded mountaineering as an eccentricity, focussed attention on both Zermatt and the Matterhorn, compensating almost overnight for the surprisingly late recognition by the general public of both the village and the mountain. The accident also helped indirectly to make the attractions and benefits of mountaineering more widely known.

Most of the major peaks around Zermatt were first climbed in the period of exactly ten years that started with the Dufourspitze of Monte Rosa on 31st July 1855 and ended with the Matterhorn on 14th July 1865. Almost all these ascents were made by 'Englishmen' and the majority of them were made with at least one guide from Zermatt. Guides, porters, horses and mules had long been necessary for ordinary tourists travelling in the remoter mountain valleys and as more and more tourists took to the mountains the demand for high mountain guides, or glacier guides as they were known, increased and provided a valuable source of additional income in the community. Instead of earning three francs for a half day excursion to the Findelen glacier or eight francs for an ascent of the Mettelhorn, a competent Zermatt guide could earn 50 francs, or a porter 25 francs, for an ascent of Monte Rosa. In about 1868 a guide's fee for the Matterhorn was 100 francs, and a porter's 50 francs, which was a lot of money when it is considered that a day's board and lodging at a hotel cost only about eight francs.

The publicity that Zermatt derived from the 1865 accident led to an immediate increase in visitors and although the Zermatt guides were to refuse to attempt the Hörnli ridge of the Matterhorn for the next six years, they must have enjoyed an increased demand for other tours. The village of St.Niklaus on the other hand benefitted directly and almost immediately from the first ascent of the Matterhorn, as no less than seven of its guides accompanied Birkbeck on his unsuccesful attempt in 1866 and they soon developed a monopoly in the valley for ascents from Zermatt, and this was to last for five years. But when Whymper's book *Scrambles amongst the Alps* was published in 1871, including a full account of the Hörnli ascent, there was an almost instant rise in the demand for guides for the Matterhorn, in which the men of Zermatt soon began to play their proper part.

In England the news of the Matterhorn catastrophe had a considerable impact, as is shown by the extraordinarily large number of readers' letters published in *The Times*. The generally hostile and unsympathetic attitude of the public towards mountaineering in 1865 is apparent from these letters and from the *Times* leading article of 27th July. This attitude seems to have been based largely on ignorance, but Whymper's own letter giving a detailed account of the accident and of the events surrounding it probably did a lot to educate the public, although it was to take another hundred years before mountaineering was to gain any general acceptance as a normal sort of recreation.

The earliest recorded attempt to climb the Matterhorn was made in 1857 from Breuil by a local party including J-A Carrel and Amé Gorret that got as far as the Tête du Lion. Other early attempts were detailed by Whymper and by Guido Rey, and it is significant that all the serious attempts were made from Breuil rather than from Zermatt. The three Parker brothers from Liverpool attempted the ascent from Zermatt without any guides at all in 1860 and again the following year and in 1862 T.S.Kennedy implemented his extraordinary idea that the apparently insuperable difficulties presented by glazed rocks on the upper Hörnli ridge in summer might be overcome in winter when covered in snow. But otherwise there is no record of anyone attempting the Hörnli or East face route as it was then called, although it is probable that some local men had previously explored at least as high as the Parkers managed to climb. But there is an intriguing entry in the first volume of the *SAC Jahrbuch* in 1864, in which the Editor Abraham Roth a leading Swiss mountaineer and journalist published the principal achievements of the leading Oberland glacier guides, and it suggests that Melchior Anderegg had at that time climbed the highest on the Matterhorn. Both Heinrich Dübi and Charles Gos considered such further evidence as they could find, which suggested a solo reconnaissance of the Zmutt ridge for some unknown employer, but Gos concluded that it must have been fictitious. Yet doubts about the reliability of specific details in evidence that did not appear for another 50 years and then only after Anderegg's death, hardly justify rejecting the general terms of the record made by Roth, which he must presumably have learnt direct from Anderegg himself late in 1863. Nevertheless we may never know for sure which route he took nor the circumstances in which he or his party decided to turn back. (see *SACJ1* (1864) 575; Gos, *Le Cervin* 1, 58–63; Dübi, *SACJ50* (1914–15), 218–19 and *AJ30*, 184)

The other unsuccessful attempts from Breuil were made principally by Whymper and/or Carrel, but included two attempts by John Tyndall. In all, Whymper made some eight attempts, his failures being attributable to a variety of causes, but there was one underlying reason why he was never going to succeed with J-A Carrel, which was that Carrel himself wanted to be the first to climb his native mountain and was never going to allow a foreigner to take or even share the honour. It was a feature of the several attempts from Breuil that they involved siege tactics, including the use of ladders by both Tyndall and Whymper. By the end of 1863 ropes or chains had been fixed at most of the difficult places up to the foot of the final peak and further work was carried out in 1865. By contrast the Zermatt route, which had generally been supposed to involve far greater difficulties above the shoulder, was climbed at the first really serious attempt without the need to fix any ropes at all.

The Matterhorn tragedy was not complete by 3.45p.m. on Friday 14th July 1865, when Charles Hudson's watch stopped ticking, or when three of the first four victims' lifeless bodies reached the glacier some 4,000 feet below. Frank Smythe once wrote of Edward Whymper being 'of a hard and unsympathetic type' but, even if this should perhaps have been true of his last twenty years or so it can hardly have been appropriate for 1865. Had he been as hard hearted as Young Peter Taugwalder Whymper might well have emerged equally unscathed, but he took upon himself such a burden from the moment he got back to the Monte Rosa hotel that he seems ultimately to have been overcome by it. He never referred later to the failure of the first search party to achieve its object, but it cannot have been the intention of its leader, the President of the Zermatt Commune, that as many as twenty men should merely ascend the Hohlicht heights in order to gain a view of the plateau of the Matterhorn glacier, nor would this have taken such a body of men as long as six hours. There is in fact some evidence of their attempting to reach the glacier via the Stöckli but failing, and there is little doubt that it was this lost opportunity that spurred Whymper to set out in the early hours of the Sunday morning, 'though exhausted by upwards of 60 hours work', as McCormick wrote in his initial letter to *The Times*, refusing to accede to the request of the Zermatt guides to defer the expedition. It seems as though Whymper's success, or rather that of the Saas guide Franz Andenmatten, in finding the way onto the glacier and reaching the three bodies, followed by the recovery of their valuables and other belongings prior to burying the bodies in the snow, caused such ill feeling amongst the authorities in Zermatt that in the case of Andenmatten it found vent in his being ejected from the church when he next tried to attend Mass. But, despite having had to organise his own search party and undergo the terrible ordeal of having to identify the mangled remains of the dismembered bodies of his companions amidst showers of falling stones, Whymper managed a few days later to compose his written answers to the questions to be put to him at the Enquiry with such skill that he was able to retain and incorporate many of them almost word for word in his letters to von Fellenberg and to *The Times* and later in *Scrambles*. He seems to have given invaluable assistance to the Examining Magistrate Joseph Clemenz by drafting questions for him to put to Taugwalder and it may be asked why someone in his unfortunate position should have had to relieve the authorities of their official duties. His generosity and humanity extended to many other things as well, including paying for Croz' burial, giving the Taugwalders a tip out of his own pocket and even paying Lord Francis Douglas's hotel bills and other debts.

Whymper went to considerable lengths not only to recover the bodies of his companions but subsequently to avoid giving pain to their relatives, and in so doing he created for himself all sorts of problems, which a less conscientious person might have avoided. It would have been so easy to have given interviews to the press and to have emphasised the incompetence of Hadow, the slack rope between him and Hudson or the misuse of the weakest rope to secure Lord Francis Douglas to Old Peter Taugwalder, and he might then have been spared the ordeal of having to write his letter to *The Times* – 'a more difficult and more painful task it is impossible to imagine' he later wrote to Hadow's father. It was a most remarkable letter for a twenty five year old to have written in such circumstances, giving an exceptionally clear account of the ascent and of the subsequent accident whilst at the same time avoiding any direct criticism of Hadow or of Hudson, confining himself to the facts and making but one observation. Documents retained by Whymper, which clearly do not constitute all his correspondence but only a fraction of it, show how conscientious and prompt he was in dealing with the letters that almost overwhelmed him in August 1865. He later found time to design and commission the memorial to Michel Croz that still stands so prominently in the Zermatt graveyard to-day, with its simple yet moving inscription. But it was the week he spent in Zermatt immediately following the accident which made such demands upon his initiative and compassion that he seems never to have recovered fully from the experience, but to have been haunted in later life by the sight of his helpless companions sliding to their death.

There is no question of rewriting Whymper's graphic and remarkably accurate account of the events, which he later included in *Scrambles* with hardly any alterations, but there is a need to take a much closer look at some of the other contemporary evidence in view of the many distortions and errors that have been published in the eighty years or so since his death. Whymper's accounts were intentionally silent on certain points in order to spare the families of Hadow and Hudson, and there were other matters as well to which he deliberately did not refer. He undoubtedly had a lot of further evidence which he did not reveal or emphasise – as John Tyndall learnt to his cost when, in the second edition of *Hours of exercise in the Alps*, he sought to take issue over some details of his own attempt with Carrel in 1862 as they appeared in *Scrambles*, little realising that before publication Whymper had read the passage to Carrel, who had expressed himself perfectly satisfied with its accuracy. Some critics have wrongly assumed when Whymper did not expressly make some positive assertion of fact, that it was open to them to conclude and assert the contrary. There is furthermore no question of Whymper having suppressed any fundamental evidence about the happening of the accident, as has sometimes been supposed from what Bishop Browne wrote in his memoirs fifty years later. There are two classes of previously unpublished documents that have survived in archives, which supplement and almost invariably confirm the accuracy of what Whymper himself wrote. Firstly, there are the documents that he himself retained, including newspaper cuttings, correspondence, memoranda and such things as his own record of the evidence he gave to Clemenz at the Enquiry and his original list of questions to be put to Taugwalder. Secondly, there are those documents that he himself never saw but which relate to matters of which he knew, such as entries in the diary of Adams Reilly and the Enquiry records of the composition of the search and recovery paties, as well as those relating to matters of which he knew nothing, such as the questions actually put to Taugwalder and the answers that were given by him.

The Official Enquiry Report documents released in 1920 reveal far more than J.P.Farrar published in volume 33 of the *Alpine Journal*, but even now it is not possible to determine to what extent the 'Coroner' Clemenz deliberately used Whymper in order to help solve his own personal problems arising out of the conflict between his interests as Examining Magistrate and his interests as the resident owner of Zermatt's largest hotel and, doubtless, its largest employer. There can be no question of Whymper having conspired with Clemenz but he seems to have allowed himself to be used by him, having perhaps little option to do otherwise. There was clearly a difference between what Whymper revealed to his friends on certain aspects of the accident and what he was prepared to publish but, apart from brief mention in a letter to McCormick, there is no record of his ever saying anything about Clemenz beyond what he wrote in a footnote in *Scrambles* and what appeared in the *Journal de Zermatt* article in 1895. It is doubtful whether Whymper knew that (with one minor exception) Clemenz was not going to put to Taugwalder on his first examination any question of substance other than those questions that Whymper himself had drafted, unless Clemenz had perhaps first handed him a list of general questions for Taugwalder and asked him to supplement it with some questions about the rope. But he obviously knew, yet did not reveal to his readers, that the questions Clemenz wanted him to answer himself had been given to him in advance of the hearing with time to prepare his written answers in French and that Taugwalder was almost certainly given a similar opportunity to prepare his answers.

Much of the erroneous criticsm in recent years has related to what Whymper wrote about Old Peter Taugwalder, as if he had gone out of his way to make 'accusations', 'attacks' and 'charges' against him, when he was merely recording the contemporary facts. There are several signs of Whymper having dealt as sympathetically with Old Peter as he did with the relatives of those who were killed. He never revealed that Old Peter was unfit to go on either the search or the recovery party, whereas Young Peter and his brother Joseph both went on the latter, nor did he reveal Old Peter's dissatisfaction with the fee of 100 francs for the Matterhorn despite it being 'the highest price ever given for mountain ascents'. He never revealed the reason why Old Peter went to America, although he must have learnt this from Seiler and, most significant of all, he never published anything about the heartless conduct of the two Taugwalders after the accident, as recorded in the Cowell memorandum. He was prepared to forgive Old Peter and, apart from brief mention in the long Taugwalder footnote in *Scrambles* of his being 'now nearly incapable for work—not absolutely mad, but with intellect gone and almost crazy', he revealed nothing of the most prolonged and perhaps the saddest tragedy to result from the first ascent of the Matterhorn – the tragedy of Old Peter Taugwalder. Whymper displayed no lack of sympathy for Old Peter, despite the erroneous beliefs of some of his twentieth century critics, and he did not heed the advice he was given in August 1865 to publish all he knew about the Taugwalders. But there was nothing more that he could do to help Old Peter beyond pressing for Clemenz to reveal his answers about the rope, and there was nothing that he said in evidence to the Enquiry or that he wrote in his letter to *The Times*, or even in *Scrambles* when it was published some six years after the event, that could have caused or even contributed to Old Peter's problems with his comrades and neighbours at Zermatt, or could have rendered him incapable of leading any successful ascents after 1865.

The present book takes a detailed look at all these issues and many others as well. It is not primarily intended to be read from start to finish, but, as a bibliographical guide to the accident and its aftermath, it is more in the nature of a reference book. There are seven principal sections, the longest one covering some sixty people involved in the early history of the Matterhorn, the accident and its aftermath. The next one deals with a wide range of subjects relating to the accident, to the Matterhorn and to Zermatt, including an Introduction to the somewhat complicated subject of the Official Enquiry and its shortcomings. There then follows a wide variety of contemporary documents such as items of correspondence, most of it Whymper's own, together with memoranda that he retained. Several leaders in *The Times* are also included as well as the original

German version of the Enquiry Report. The next section deals with the Enquiry in detail and includes an English translation of the evidence as well as the verdict. This is followed by short reviews of most of the principal books and articles written by the critics, drawing attention to many of the errors either when they originate or when they are adopted and repeated. The final main section lists the sources or references for each one of the people and subjects dealt with in sections two and three. The sources have been collected together in order to avoid the text of the book becoming cluttered up with footnotes and references. The text is also free from superscript numbers indicating the presence of some form of note, which may have the disadvantage of the reader not knowing for certain that a source is quoted but, hopefully, this should be outweighed by the absence of something that might otherwise unnecessarily interrupt the reading of the principal text. The sources are intended to provide the origin of, or the authority for, any significant, dubious or obscure facts and statements, to draw the attention of historians to other documents and publications that may be relevant and to make known the whereabouts of original or copy correspondence and other archives.

The following account of 'Who was who' provides a brief introduction to the sixty people included in section two, illustrating at least one aspect of each one's participation in the early history of the Matterhorn. This is followed by a 'Sequence of events', which takes the overall view one stage further, after which there is no better way to introduce the most famous accident in the history of mountaineering than to set out the account that Whymper himself gave in chapters 20 to 22 of *Scrambles amongst the Alps*.

1.1
WHO WAS WHO

The first recorded attempt to climb the Matterhorn was in 1857, when J-A Carrel and Amé Gorret and other natives of the Val Tournanche got as far as the Tête du Lion. In 1860, and again in 1861, the Parker brothers made a guideless attempt from Zermatt; also in 1860, John Tyndall made the first of his two unsuccessful attempts from Breuil. 1862 saw the extraordinary attempt by T.S.Kennedy to overcome the potential problem of ice on the upper rocks of the Hörnli ridge in summer, by climbing it in January with the guides Peter Perren and Old Peter Taugwalder, but they got little higher than 11,000 feet.

It was in August 1861 that Edward Whymper, with an Oberland guide, made the first of his seven or eight attempts from Breuil. The next year he and a companion made two unsuccessful attempts with guides and then he made a solo excursion in which he fell nearly 200 feet. Despite sustaining quite serious head injuries and fainting, he managed to make his way down to Breuil in the dark and within four days he was back on the mountain with guides, making two further attempts that year. In 1864 he had been going to attempt the ascent from Zermatt with ADAMS REILLY, when a letter from home caused him to have to return immediately on account of his business.

In 1865 a number of new contenders appeared on the Matterhorn scene. The Rev CHARLES HUDSON, considered by many of his contemporaries to be the best amateur of the day, had been planning an ascent from Zermatt with JOHN BIRKBECK as well as T.S.Kennedy, but they both had to return home unexpectedy before even reaching Zermatt. The Rev JOSEPH MCCORMICK was also included in Hudson's plans, but his duties as English summer chaplain required him to spend his first two Sundays at Grindelwald before moving on to Zermatt for the last three in July, and bad weather delayed his arrival there. Charles Hudson was travelling with a pupil, A.J.CAMPBELL, and a former pupil, DOUGLAS HADOW, the latter accompanying him, Kennedy and McCormick up Mont Blanc on the 7th July. They met F.A.Y.BROWN on or about the summit, and he later made his way to Zermatt via the High Level route with a party that included three Rugby schoolmasters, the Rev JAMES ROBERTSON, J.S.PHILLPOTTS and KNYVET WILSON and also FRANZ ANDENMATTEN, the greatest character amongst the early Alpine guides. They reached Zermatt on the Saturday afternoon, after encountering the first search party looking for the victims of Friday's accident.

Meanwhile, at the beginning of that week, Whymper had arrived in Breuil only to find that J-A Carrel was not available, having been engaged by 'a person of distinction', who turned out to be FELICE GIORDANO, who had in mind making the first ascent of the Matterhorn for the honour of the Italian Alpine Club. So finding himself without guides, Whymper decided to cross to Zermatt and make an attempt from there. He was waiting at Breuil with the Rev A.G.GIRDLESTONE, whom he did not name in *Scrambles* but referred to only as the Englishman lying sick at Valtournanche, when at about midday on Tuesday 11th a large party hove into sight from Zermatt, including LORD FRANCIS DOUGLAS and his guide JOSEPH TAUGWALDER. Before long it was agreed that Douglas should take part in Whymper's Hörnli expedition, and the following day they and Girdlestone crossed to Zermatt. Upon their arrival they engaged Joseph's father Old Peter Taugwalder, asking him to engage another guide, and he duly engaged his eldest son, YOUNG PETER TAUGWALDER. At the Monte Rosa hotel, Whymper was surprised to find his old guide MICHEL CROZ sitting on the wall opposite and to discover that he had arrived in Zermatt with Charles Hudson, with the same object of climbing the Matterhorn.

On 14th July Whymper and Croz in particular, together with Hudson, Hadow, Douglas and the two Taugwalders, were seen on the summit from Zermatt by a number of people including those lunching at the Hotel Monte Rosa. The landlord ALEXANDER SEILER announced the event to his guests and they rushed out to look, including CHARLES LONG's party of climbers from Geneva. About two hours later the accident was actually witnessed from Zermatt by FRIEDRICH TAUGWALDER, Old Peter Taugwalder's youngest son – the sharp-eyed lad mentioned by Whymper in *Scrambles*. Another Geneva party, on its way to Zermatt for the weekend led by A.J.MARTIN the Professor of Law at the University, met the Long party near Randa that afternoon and learnt of the ascent, and the entries in Martin's diary for the Saturday and Sunday contain the most accurate contemporary record yet discovered.

When Whymper and McCormick were looking for volunteers to join the second search party with a view to setting off early on the Sunday morning, GILES PULLER lent them his two guides JOSEPH-MARIE and ALEXANDER LOCHMATTER and two Chamonix guides FRÉDÉRIC PAYOT and JEAN TAIRRAZ also volunteered. On about Tuesday 18th July, two English chaplains resident in Switzerland, W.P.PRIOR and H.DOWNTON, also arrived in Zermatt, the former on holiday with family and friends – the latter despatched by the British Consul in Geneva. The Swiss authorities decided that an Enquiry should be held, and the Zermatt hotelier, J.A.CLEMENZ was appointed to preside over it in his separate judicial capacity. Whymper was helped to overcome the problem of giving his evidence in French to a German speaking tribunal by the Rugby School modern languages master, J.W.J.VECQUERAY. Although Old Peter Taugwalder obviously had no such language problem, there are several reasons for supposing that he also received some assistance and that his interests at the Enquiry were looked after by the Zermatt district judge ALOIS JULEN, who as well as being a mountain guide was also one of his cousins.

When Whymper finally got away from Zermatt on Saturday 22nd July, he headed for Interlaken where he spent a couple of nights at the Pension Schlössli owned by PETER OBER. Whilst there he completed his lengthy account of the accident to VON FELLENBERG, the secretary of the Swiss Alpine Club, and asked him to pass it on to the members and also to the Swiss press. The Rev W.H.HAWKER who had climbed with Whymper the month before, helped with the arrangements for Peter Ober to translate the letter into French and into German. Whymper had vowed in Zermatt to say nothing more about the accident but on his return to London he was pressed by many friends, including ALFRED WILLS the President of the Alpine Club, to write to *The Times*. He sought advice from the Club's former secretary J.J.COWELL and his father and from the Rev G.F.BROWNE, who became a bishop 30 years later. He was overwhelmed with correspondence, to which he nevertheless replied promptly and skilfully, his correspondence with the Rev RICHARD GLOVER disposing of any suggestion that he could not suffer fools gladly. The Rev WOOLMORE WIGRAM, who made the first ascent of the Dent Blanche, wrote saying that his guide on that occasion JEAN-BAPTISTE CROZ, Michel's brother, had written about a rumour prevalent in Chamonix that Old Peter Taugwalder cut the rope, and Whymper wrote to Croz at once to stop 'this horrible rumour'.

LORD QUEENSBERRY, the brother of Lord Francis Douglas, visited Zermatt in the last week of July 1865 and in September the young W.A.B.COOLIDGE and his aunt stayed at the Monte Rosa. That month also saw the arrival of the Prussian

PAUL GÜSSFELDT intent on repeating the ascent from Zermatt, little realising that Old Peter Taugwalder was not even prepared to contemplate it. The following July John Birkbeck engaged seven guides of St.Niklaus including the Lochmatters and PETER KNUBEL, but they got no further than he reckoned he could have got without any guides at all. LESLIE STEPHEN arrived a day or so later, as did that most enterprising Swiss pioneer FRANÇOIS THIOLY, but it was not until 1867 that the prospects for future ascents improved, following the ascents by CRAUFORD GROVE and by W.L.JORDAN. It is CANON CARREL who deserves the credit for breaking J-A Carrel's monopoly at Breuil, as he encouraged J-J MAQUIGNAZ and his brothers to make the ascent, and it was Jordan's subsequent exploration with Maquignaz and two of his brothers of the upper part of the Hörnli ridge that must have done more than anything else to open up both routes. Jordan's account of it greatly encouraged the Rev J.M.ELLIOTT to make the second ascent from Zermatt, with J-M Lochmatter and Knubel (rather than with his usual Zermatt guide FRANZ BINER), and the experience gained enabled Maquignaz and his brother in 1868 to traverse the mountain from Breuil to Zermatt with John Tyndall and also to return home a few days later by reversing the traverse with Thioly and his eccentric friend with the half metre wide hat and the clarinet, which he insisted on playing on the summit!

1.2 SEQUENCE OF EVENTS

June

Saturday 10.	Whymper leaves London
Tuesday 13.	Kennedy attempts Jungfrau with Perren
Friday 16.	Whymper makes first ascent of Grand Cornier
Saturday 17.	Kennedy and wife arrive Zermatt
Monday 19.	Whymper arrives Zermatt
Tuesday 20.	Whymper leaves Zermatt, crossing Theodule with Glover
Saturday 24.	Whymper makes first ascent of Grandes Jorasses
Sunday 25.	Kennedy and wife leave Zermatt for Sixt, staying at St.Niklaus Douglas leaves Eggishorn for Zermatt, staying at St.Niklaus
Monday 26.	Douglas arrives Zermatt Whymper arrives Chamonix

Thursday 29.	Whymper, Almer and Biner make first ascent of Aiguille Verte Kennedy arrives Chamonix

July

Saturday 1.	Whymper and Kennedy walk to Bossons glacier and dine together
Sunday 2.	Hudson, Hadow and Campbell arrive Chamonix
Monday 3.	Whymper leaves Chamonix for Courmayeur
Wednesday 5.	Hudson, Kennedy, Croz, Perren and others climb Aiguille Verte
Friday 7.	Yeats Brown climbs Mont Blanc with Devouassoud Hudson, Hadow, McCormick, Kennedy, Croz and Perren climb Mont Blanc Douglas and Old Peter Taugwalder climb Obergabelhorn McCormick leaves Chamonix for Grindelwald in evening
Saturday 8.	Douglas in Zermatt Whymper at Breuil Kennedy and wife leave Chamonix for home
Monday 10.	Douglas at Riffelhaus
Tuesday 11.	Whymper and Girdlestone at Breuil Douglas and Joseph Taugwalder arrive Breuil
Wednesday 12.	Hudson, Hadow, Campbell and Croz arrive Zermatt Whymper, Douglas and Girdlestone cross Theodule to Zermatt
Thursday 13.	Whymper/Hudson party sets off for Matterhorn, and bivouacs at 11,000 feet
Friday 14.	McCormick arrives Zermatt First ascent of the Matterhorn by Whymper and Croz, followed by Hudson, Hadow, Douglas and the two Taugwalders Carrel's party turns back on the Italian ridge Catastrophe seen by Friedrich Taugwalder from Zermatt Martin/Gautier party arrives Zermatt

Saturday 15.	Whymper and the Taugwalders return Puller and the Lochmatters arrive Zermatt First search party fails to reach glacier, but sights bodies Girdlestone climbs Monte Rosa returning to Riffelhaus McCormick and Campbell ascend Gornergrat, returning to Zermatt Martin/Gautier ascend Gornergrat, returning to Riffelhaus Robertson, Phillpotts, Wilson, Andenmatten and Yeats Brown arrive Zermatt
Sunday 16.	Whymper's search party finds and buries the three bodies on the glacier Mme. Gautier writes letter to *Journal de Genève* Martin/Gautier party leaves Zermatt Girdlestone descends to Zermatt and goes to see Whymper at about 2 p.m. McCormick writes letter to Hadow's father
Monday 17.	Carrel and Bich reach Matterhorn summit from Breuil Yeats Brown climbs Monte Rosa (?with Devouassoud) Girdlestone leaves Zermatt for Visp McCormick writes letter to *The Times*
Tuesday 18.	Whymper walks to Gornergrat and back Campbell probably left Zermatt Adams Reilly arrives Zermatt, having heard of the accident Knyvet Wilson killed on Riffelhorn in evening
Wednesday 19.	Whymper and McCormick set off to join search for Wilson
Thursday 20.	Matterhorn victims' bodies brought down to Zermatt
Friday 21.	08.30. Funeral of Michel Croz 10.00. Funerals of Hadow, Hudson and Wilson 14.00. Clemenz opens Enquiry
Saturday 22.	Robertson and Phillpotts sign for Wilson's possessions and leave Zermatt for Visp Vecqueray leaves Zermatt Whymper leaves Zermatt for Visp J-B Croz arrives Zermatt in evening
Sunday 23.	J-B Croz signs for his brother's possessions and leaves Zermatt Whymper arrives Kandersteg

Monday 24.	Whymper arrives Interlaken Queensberry and Hadow's uncle Henry arrive Zermatt
Tuesday 25.	Whymper writes letter to von Fellenberg and pays Almer the balance of his fees
Wednesday 26.	Whymper leaves Interlaken for London via Bern, Neuchâtel and Paris
Thursday 27.	Monte Rosa avalanche. Porter killed Leading article in *The Times* (?Whymper arrives London)
Friday 28.	Queensberry sets off alone for Matterhorn at 1 a.m., leaving note McCormick organizes search party, which finds him on Hörnli
Saturday 29.	Queensberry leaves Zermatt Parker brothers arrive Zermatt
Sunday 30.	Funeral of porter
Monday 31.	Henry Hadow leaves Zermatt Tyndall arrives Zermatt

August

Wednesday 2.	Whymper dines with the Cowells in London
Thursday 3.	Adams Reilly leaves Zermatt for Chamonix
Friday 4.	Parker brothers leave Zermatt for Belalp
Saturday 5.	Queensberry calls on Whymper in London
Tuesday 8.	Whymper's letter published in *The Times*

1.3
WHYMPER'S ACCOUNT IN 'SCRAMBLES'

[The following account of the ascent and of the accident was published by Whymper in 1871. It is taken from the first edition of Scrambles, omitting the many footnotes. Whymper has just described how, early on 11th July 1865 and unknown to him, his guide J-A Carrel had set off from Breuil with a large party of guides to facilitate the

way to the summit of the Matterhorn and thereafter take Signor F. Giordano and Signor Sella to the top.]

The first thing to do was to go to Zermatt. Easier said than done. The seven guides upon the mountain included the ablest men in the valley, and none of the ordinary muleteer-guides were at Breil. Two men, at least, were wanted for my baggage, but not a soul could be found. I ran about, and sent about in all directions, but not a single porter could be obtained. One was with Carrel; another was ill; another was at Chatillon, and so forth. Even Meynet, the hunchback, could not be induced to come; he was in the thick of some important cheese-making operations. I was in the position of a general without an army; it was all very well to make plans, but there was no one to execute them. This did not much trouble me, for it was evident that so long as the weather stopped traffic over the Theodule, it would hinder the men equally upon the Matterhorn; and I knew that directly it improved company would certainly arrive.

About midday on Tuesday the 11th a large party hove into sight from Zermatt, preceded by a nimble young Englishman, and one of old Peter Taugwalder's sons. I went at once to this gentleman to learn if he could dispense with Taugwalder. He said that he could not, as they were going to recross to Zermatt on the morrow, but that the young man should assist in transporting my baggage, as he had nothing to carry. We naturally got into conversation. I told my story, and learned that the young Englishman was Lord Francis Douglas, whose recent exploit—the ascent of the Gabelhorn—had excited my wonder and admiration. He brought good news. Old Peter had lately been beyond the Hörnli, and had reported that he thought an ascent of the Matterhorn was possible upon that side. Almer had left Zermatt, and could not be recovered, so I determined to seek for old Peter. Lord Francis Douglas expressed a warm desire to ascend the mountain, and before long it was determined that he should take part in the expedition.

Favre [the landlord] could no longer hinder our departure, and lent us one of his men. We crossed the Col Theodule on Wednesday morning the 12th of July, rounded the foot of the Ober Theodulgletscher, crossed the Furggengletscher, and deposited tent, blankets, ropes, and other matters in the little chapel at the Schwarzsee. All four were heavily laden, for we brought across the whole of my stores from Breil. Of rope alone there was about 600 feet. There were three kinds. First, 200 feet of the Manilla rope; second, 150 feet of a stouter, and probably stronger rope than the first; and third, more than 200 feet of a lighter and weaker rope than the first, of a kind that I used formerly (stout sash-line).

We descended to Zermatt, sought and engaged old Peter, and gave him permission to choose another guide. When we returned to the Monte Rosa Hotel, whom should we see sitting upon the wall in front, but my old *guide chef*, Michel Croz. I supposed that he had come with Mr.B—, but I learned that that gentleman had arrived in ill health, at Chamounix, and had returned to England. Croz, thus left free, had been immediately engaged by the Rev. Charles Hudson, and they had come to Zermatt with the same object as ourselves—namely, to attempt the ascent of the Matterhorn!

Lord Francis Douglas and I dined at the Monte Rosa, and had just finished when Mr.Hudson and a friend entered the *salle à manger.* They had returned from inspecting the mountain, and some idlers in the room demanded their intentions. We heard a confirmation of Croz's statement, and learned that Mr.Hudson intended to set out on the morrow at the same hour as ourselves. We left the room to consult, and agreed it was undesirable that two independent parties should be on the mountain at the same time with the same object. Mr.Hudson was therefore invited to join us, and he accepted our proposal. Before admitting his friend—Mr.Hadow—I took the precaution to inquire what he had done in the Alps, and, as well as I remember, Mr.Hudson's reply was, "Mr.Hadow has done Mont Blanc in less time than most men." He then mentioned several other excursions that were unknown to me, and added, in answer to a further question, "I consider he is a sufficiently good man to go with us." Mr.Hadow was admitted without any further question, and we then went into the matter of guides. Hudson thought that Croz and old Peter would be sufficient. The question was referred to the men themselves, and they made no objection.

So Croz and I became comrades once more; and as I threw myself on my bed and tried to go to sleep, I wondered at the strange series of chances which had first separated us and then brought us together again. I thought of the mistake through which he had accepted the engagement of Mr.B—; of his unwillingness to adopt my route; of his recommendation to transfer our energies to the chain of Mont Blanc; of the retirement of Almer and Biener; of the desertion of Carrel; of the arrival of Lord Francis Douglas; and, lastly, of our accidental meeting at Zermatt; and as I pondered over these things I could not help asking, "What next?" If any one of the links of this fatal chain of circumstances had been omitted, what a different story I should have to tell!

THE ASCENT OF THE MATTERHORN

We started from Zermatt on the 13th of July, at half-past 5, on a brilliant and perfectly cloudless morning. We were eight in number—Croz, old Peter and his two sons, Lord F. Douglas, Hadow, Hudson, and I. To ensure steady motion, one tourist and one native walked together. The youngest Taugwalder fell to my share, and the lad marched well, proud to be on the expedition, and happy to show his powers. The wine-bags also fell to my lot to carry, and throughout the day, after each drink, I replenished them secretly with water, so that at the next halt they were found fuller than before! This was considered a good omen, and little short of miraculous.

On the first day we did not intend to ascend to any great height, and we mounted, accordingly, very leisurely; picked up the things which were left in the chapel at the Schwarzsee at 8.20, and proceeded thence along the ridge connecting the Hörnli with the Matterhorn. At half-past 11 we arrived at the base of the actual peak; then quitted the ridge, and clambered round some ledges, on the eastern face. We were now fairly upon the mountain, and were astonished to find that places which from the Riffel, or even the Furggengletscher, looked entirely impracticable, were so easy that we could *run about.*

Before twelve o'clock we had found a good position for the tent, at a height of 11,000 feet. Croz and young Peter went on to see what was above, in order to save time on the following morning. They cut across the heads of the snow-slopes which descended towards the Furggengletscher, and disappeared round a corner; but shortly afterwards we saw them high on the face, moving quickly. We others made a solid platform for the tent in a well-protected spot, and then watched eagerly for the return of the men. The stones which they upset told that they were very high, and we supposed that the way must be easy. At length, just before 3 p.m., we saw them coming down, evidently much excited. "What are they saying, Peter?" "Gentlemen, they say it is no good." But when they came near we heard a different story. "Nothing but what was good; not a difficulty, not a single difficulty! We could have gone to the summit and returned to-day easily!"

We passed the remaining hours of daylight—some basking in the sunshine, some sketching or collecting; and when the sun went down, giving, as it departed, a glorious promise for the morrow, we returned to the tent to arrange for the night. Hudson made tea, I coffee, and we then retired each one to his blanket-bag; the Taugwalders, Lord Francis Douglas, and myself, occupying the tent, the others remaining, by preference, outside. Long after dusk the cliffs above echoed with our laughter and with the songs of the guides, for we were happy that night in camp, and feared no evil.

We assembled together outside the tent before dawn on the morning of the 14th, and started directly it was light enough to move. Young Peter came on with us as a guide, and his brother returned to Zermatt. We followed the route which had been taken on the previous day, and in a few minutes turned the rib which had intercepted the view of the eastern face from our tent platform. The whole of this great slope was now revealed, rising for 3000 feet like a huge natural staircase. Some parts were more, and others were less, easy; but we were not once brought to a halt by any serious impediment, for when an obstruction was met in front it could always be turned to the right or to the left. For the greater part of the way there was, indeed, no occasion for the rope, and sometimes Hudson led, sometimes myself. At 6.20 we had attained a height of 12,800 feet, and halted for half-an-hour; we then continued the ascent without a break until 9.55, when we stopped for 50 minutes, at a height of 14,000 feet. Twice we struck the N.E. ridge, and followed it for some little distance,—to no advantage, for it was usually more rotten and steep, and always more difficult than the face. Still, we kept near to it, lest stones perchance might fall.

We had now arrived at the foot of that part which, from the Riffelberg or from

Zermatt, seems perpendicular or overhanging, and could no longer continue upon the eastern side. For a little distance we ascended by snow upon the arête—that is, the ridge—descending towards Zermatt, and then, by common consent, turned over to the right, or to the northern side. Before doing so, we made a change in the order of ascent. Croz went first, I followed, Hudson came third; Hadow and old Peter were last. "Now," said Croz, as he led off, "now for something altogether different." The work became difficult, and required caution. In some places there was little to hold, and it was desirable that those should be in front who were least likely to slip. The general slope of the mountain at this part was less than 40°, and snow had accumulated in, and had filled up, the interstices of the rock-face, leaving only occasional fragments projecting here and there. These were at times covered with a thin film of ice, produced from the melting and refreezing of the snow. It was the counterpart, on a small scale, of the upper 700 feet of the Pointe des Ecrins,—only there was this material difference; the face of the Ecrins was about, or excceded, an angle of 50°, and the Matterhorn face was less than 40°. It was a place over which any fair mountaineer might pass in safety, and Mr.Hudson ascended this part, and, as far as I know, the entire mountain, without having the slightest assistance rendered to him upon any occasion. Sometimes, after I had taken a hand from Croz, or received a pull, I turned to offer the same to Hudson; but he invariably declined, saying it was not necessary. Mr.Hadow, however, was not accustomed to this kind of work, and required continual assistance. It is only fair to say that the difficulty which he found at this part arose simply and entirely from want of experience.

This solitary difficult part was of no great extent. We bore away over it at first, nearly horizontally, for a distance of about 400 feet; then ascended directly towards the summit for about 60 feet; and then doubled back to the ridge which descends towards Zermatt. A long stride round a rather awkward corner brought us to snow once more. The last doubt vanished! The Matterhorn was ours! Nothing but 200 feet of easy snow remained to be surmounted!

You must now carry your thoughts back to the seven Italians who started from Breil on the 11th of July. Four days had passed since their departure, and we were tormented with anxiety lest they should arrive on the top before us. All the way up we had talked of them, and many false alarms of "men on the summit" had been raised. The higher we rose, the more intense became the excitement. What if we should be beaten at the last moment? The slope eased off, at length we could be detached, and Croz and I, dashing away, ran a neck-and-neck race, which ended in a dead heat. At 1.40 p.m. the world was at our feet, and the Matterhorn was conquered. Hurrah! Not a footstep could be seen.

It was not yet certain that we had not been beaten. The summit of the Matterhorn was formed of a rudely level ridge, about 350 feet long, and the Italians might have been at its farther extremity. I hastened to the southern end, scanning the snow right and left eagerly. Hurrah! again; it was untrodden. "Where were the men?" I peered over the cliff, half doubting, half expectant. I saw them

"CROZ! CROZ!! COME HERE!"

immediately—mere dots on the ridge, at an immense distance below. Up went my arms and my hat. "Croz! Croz!! come here!" "Where are they, Monsieur?" "There, don't you see them, down there?" "Ah! the *coquins*, they are low down." "Croz, we must make those fellows hear us." We yelled until we were hoarse. The Italians seemed to regard us—we could not be certain. "Croz, we *must* make them hear us; they *shall* hear us!" I seized a block of rock and hurled it down, and called upon my companion, in the name of friendship, to do the same. We drove our sticks in, and prized away the crags, and soon a torrent of stones poured down the cliffs. There was no mistake about it this time. The Italians turned and fled.

Still, I would that the leader of that party could have stood with us at that moment, for our victorious shouts conveyed to him the disappointment of the ambition of a lifetime. He was *the* man, of all those who attempted the ascent of the Matterhorn, who most deserved to be the first upon its summit. He was the first to doubt its inaccessibility, and he was the only man who persisted in believing that its ascent would be accomplished. It was the aim of his life to make the ascent from the side of Italy, for the honour of his native valley. For a time he had the game in his hands: he played it as he thought best; but he made a false move, and he lost it...

The others had arrived, so we went back to the northern end of the ridge. Croz now took the tent-pole, and planted it in the highest snow. "Yes," we said, "there is the flag-staff, but where is the flag?" "Here it is," he answered, pulling off his blouse and fixing it to the stick. It made a poor flag, and there was no wind to float it out, yet it was seen all around. They saw it at Zermatt—at the Riffel—in the Val Tournanche. At Breil, the watchers cried, "Victory is ours!" They raised 'bravos' for Carrel, and 'vivas' for Italy, and hastened to put themselves *en fête*. On the morrow they were undeceived. "All was changed; the explorers returned sad—cast down—disheartened—confounded—gloomy." "It is true," said the men. "We saw them ourselves—they hurled stones at us! The old traditions *are* true,—there are spirits on the top of the Matterhorn!"

....We remained on the summit for one hour—

"One crowded hour of glorious life."

It passed away too quickly, and we began to prepare for the descent.

DESCENT OF THE MATTERHORN

Hudson and I again consulted as to the best and safest arrangement of the party. We agreed that it would be best for Croz to go first, and Hadow second; Hudson, who was almost equal to a guide in sureness of foot, wished to be third; Lord F. Douglas was placed next, and old Peter, the strongest of the remainder, after him. I suggested to Hudson that we should attach a rope to the rocks on our arrival at the difficult bit, and hold it as we descended, as an additional protection. He approved the idea, but it was not definitely settled that it should be done. The party was being arranged in the above order whilst I was sketching the summit, and they had finished, and were waiting for me to be tied in line, when someone remembered that our names had not been left in a bottle. They requested me to write them down, and moved off while it was being done.

A few minutes afterwards I tied myself to young Peter, ran down after the others, and caught them just as they were commencing the descent of the difficult part. Great care was being taken. Only one man was moving at a time; when he was firmly planted the next advanced, and so on. They had not, however, attached the additional rope to rocks, and nothing was said about it. The suggestion was not made for my own sake, and I am not sure that it even occurred to me again. For some little distance we two followed the others, detached from them, and should have continued so had not Lord F. Douglas asked me, about 3 p.m., to tie on to old Peter, as he feared, he said, that Taugwalder would not be able to hold his ground if a slip occurred.

A few minutes later, a sharp-eyed lad ran into the Monte Rosa hotel, to Seiler, saying that he had seen an avalanche fall from the summit of the Matterhorn on to the Matterhorngletscher. The boy was reproved for telling idle stories; he was right, nevertheless, and this is what he saw.

Michel Croz had laid aside his axe, and in order to give Mr.Hadow greater security, was absolutely taking hold of his legs, and putting his feet, one by one, into their proper positions. As far as I know, no one was actually descending. I cannot speak with certainty, because the two leading men were partially hidden from my sight by an intervening mass of rock, but it is my belief, from the movements of their shoulders, that Croz, having done as I have said, was in the act of turning round to go down a step or two himself; at this moment Mr.Hadow slipped, fell against him, and knocked him over. I heard one startled exclamation from Croz, then saw him and Mr.Hadow flying downwards; in another moment Hudson was dragged from his steps, and Lord F. Douglas immediately after him.

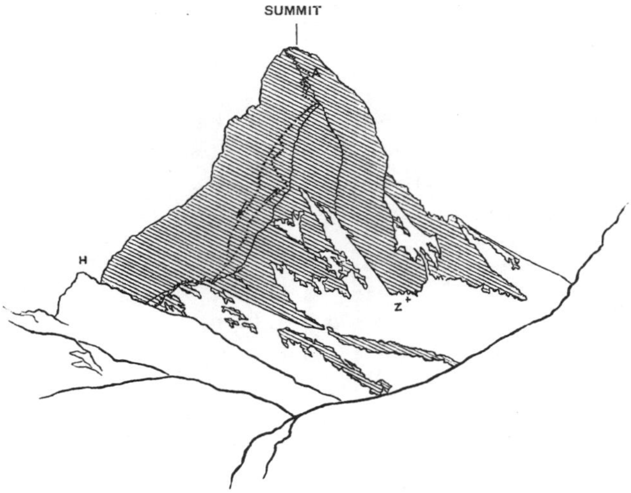

H. THE HORNLI. A. PLACE WHERE HADOW SLIPPED.
Z. PLACE WHERE THE BODIES WERE FOUND.

Whymper's diagram of the Matterhorn

All this was the work of a moment. Immediately we heard Croz's exclamation, old Peter and I planted ourselves as firmly as the rocks would permit: the rope was taut between us, and the jerk came on us both as on one man. We held; but the rope broke midway between Taugwalder and Lord Francis Douglas. For a few seconds we saw our unfortunate companions sliding on their backs, and spreading out their hands, endeavouring to save themselves. They passed from our sight uninjured, disappeared one by one, and fell from precipice to precipice on to the Matterhorngletscher below, a distance of nearly 4000 feet in height. From the moment the rope broke it was impossible to help them.

So perished our comrades! For the space of half-an-hour we remained on the spot without moving a single step. The two men, paralysed by terror, cried like infants, and trembled in such a manner as to threaten us with the fate of the others. Old Peter rent the air with exclamations of "Chamounix! Oh, what will

Chamounix say?" He meant, Who would believe that Croz could fall? The young man did nothing but scream or sob, "We are lost! we are lost!" Fixed between the two, I could neither move up nor down. I begged young Peter to descend, but he dared not. Unless he did, we could not advance. Old Peter became alive to the danger, and swelled the cry, "We are lost! we are lost!" The father's fear was natural—he trembled for his son; the young man's fear was cowardly—he thought of self alone. At last old Peter summoned up courage, and changed his position to a rock to which he could fix the rope; the young man then descended, and we all stood together. Immediately we did so, I asked for the rope which had given way, and found, to my surprise—indeed to my horror—that it was the weakest of the three ropes. It was not brought, and should not have been employed, for the purpose for which it was used. It was old rope, and, compared with the others, was feeble. It was intended as a reserve, in case we had to leave much rope behind, attached to rocks. I saw at once that a serious question was involved, and made him give me the end. It had broken in mid-air, and it did not appear to have sustained previous injury.

For more than two hours afterwards I thought almost every moment that the next would be my last; for the Taugwalders, utterly unnerved, were not only incapable of giving assistance, but were in such a state that a slip might have been expected from them at any moment. After a time, we were able to do that which should have been done at first, and fixed rope to firm rocks, in addition to being tied together. These ropes were cut from time to time, and were left behind. Even with their assurance the men were afraid to proceed, and several times old Peter turned with ashy face and faltering limbs, and said, with terrible emphasis, "*I cannot!*"

About 6 p.m. we arrived at the snow upon the ridge descending towards Zermatt, and all peril was over. We frequently looked, but in vain, for traces of our unfortunate companions; we bent over the ridge and cried to them, but no sound returned. Convinced at last that they were neither within sight nor hearing, we ceased from our useless efforts; and, too cast down for speech, silently gathered up our things, and the little effects of those who were lost, preparatory to continuing the descent. When, lo! a mighty arch appeared, rising above the Lyskamm, high into the sky. Pale, colourless, and noiseless, but perfectly sharp and defined, except where it was lost in the clouds, this unearthly apparition seemed like a vision from another world; and, almost appalled, we watched with amazement the gradual development of two vast crosses, one on either side. If the Taugwalders had not been the first to perceive it, I should have doubted my senses. They thought it had some connection with the accident, and I, after a while, that it might bear some relation to ourselves. But our movements had no effect upon it. The spectral forms remained motionless. It was a fearful and wonderful sight; unique in my experience, and impressive beyond description, coming at such a moment.

I was ready to leave, and waiting for the others. They had recovered their appetites and the use of their tongues. They spoke in patois, which I did not understand. At length the son said in French, "Monsieur." "Yes." "We are poor men; we have lost our Herr; we shall not get paid; we can ill afford this." "Stop!" I said, interrupting him, "that is nonsense; I shall pay you, of course, just as if your Herr were here." They talked together in their patois for a short time, and then the son spoke again. "We don't wish you to pay us. We wish you to write in the hotel-book at Zermatt, and to your journals, that we have not been paid." "What nonsense are you talking? I don't understand you. What do you mean?" He proceeded—"Why, next year there will be many travellers at Zermatt, and we shall get more *voyageurs*."

Who would answer such a proposition? I made them no reply in words, but they knew very well the indignation that I felt. They filled the cup of bitterness to overflowing, and I tore down the cliff, madly and recklessly, in a way that caused them, more than once, to inquire if I wished to kill them. Night fell; and for an hour the descent was continued in the darkness. At half-past 9 a resting-place was found, and upon a wretched slab, barely large enough to hold the three, we passed six miserable hours. At daybreak the descent was resumed, and from the Hörnli ridge we ran down to the chalets of Buhl, and on to Zermatt. Seiler met me at his door, and followed in silence to my room. "What is the matter?" "The Taugwalders and I have returned." He did not need more, and burst into tears; but lost no time in useless lamentations, and set to work to arouse the village. Ere long a score of men had started to ascend the Hohlicht heights, above Kalbermatt and Z'Mutt, which commanded the plateau of the Matterhorngletscher. They returned after six hours, and reported that they had seen the bodies lying motionless on the snow. This was on Saturday; and they proposed that we should leave on Sunday evening, so as to arrive upon the plateau at daybreak on Monday. Unwilling to lose the slightest chance, the Rev. J.M'Cormick and I resolved to start on Sunday morning. The Zermatt men, threatened with excommunication by their priests if they failed to attend the early mass, were unable to accompany us. To several of them, at least, this was a severe trial, and Peter Perrn declared with tears that nothing else would have prevented him from joining in the search for his old comrades. Englishmen came to our aid. The Rev. J.Robertson and Mr.J.Phillpotts offered themselves, and their guide Franz Andermatten; another Englishman lent us Joseph Marie and Alexandre Lochmatter. Frédéric Payot, and Jean Tairraz, of Chamounix, also volunteered.

We started at 2 a.m. on Sunday the 16th, and followed the route that we had taken on the previous Thursday as far as the Hörnli. From thence we went down to the right of the ridge, and mounted through the *séracs* of the Matterhorngletscher. By 8.30 we had got to the plateau at the top of the glacier, and within sight of the corner in which we knew my companions must be. As we saw one weather-beaten man after another raise the telescope, turn deadly pale, and pass it on without a word to the next, we knew that all hope was gone. We approached. They had fallen below as they had fallen above—Croz a little in advance, Hadow near him, and Hudson some distance behind; but of Lord

F. Douglas we could see nothing. We left them where they fell; buried in snow at the base of the grandest cliff of the most majestic mountain of the Alps.

All those who had fallen had been tied with the Manilla, or with the second and equally strong rope, and, consequently, there had been only one link—that between old Peter and Lord F. Douglas—where the weaker rope had been used. This had a very ugly look for Taugwalder, for it was not possible to suppose that the others would have sanctioned the employment of a rope so greatly inferior in strength when there were more than 250 feet of the better qualities still remaining out of use. For the sake of the old guide (who bore a good reputation), and upon all other accounts, it was desirable that this matter should be cleared up; and after my examination before the court of inquiry which was instituted by the Government was over, I handed in a number of questions which were framed so as to afford old Peter an opportunity of exculpating himself from the grave suspicions which at once fell upon him. The questions, I was told, were put and answered; but the answers, although promised, have never reached me.

Meanwhile, the administration sent strict injunctions to recover the bodies, and upon the 19th of July, twenty-one men of Zermatt accomplished that sad and dangerous task. Of the body of Lord Francis Douglas they, too, saw nothing; it is probably still arrested on the rocks above. The remains of Hudson and Hadow were interred upon the north side of the Zermatt church, in the presence of a reverent crowd of sympathising friends. The body of Michel Croz lies upon the other side, under a simpler tomb; whose inscription bears honourable testimony to his rectitude, to his courage, and to his devotion.

So the traditional inaccessibility of the Matterhorn was vanquished, and was replaced by legends of a more real character. Others will essay to scale its proud cliffs, but to none will it be the mountain that it was to its early explorers. Others may tread its summit-snows, but none will ever know the feelings of those who first gazed upon its marvellous panorama; and none, I trust, will ever be compelled to tell of joy turned into grief, and of laughter into mourning. It proved to be a stubborn foe; it resisted long, and gave many a hard blow; it was defeated at last with an ease that none could have anticipated, but, like a relentless enemy—conquered but not crushed—it took terrible vengeance. The time may come when the Matterhorn shall have passed away, and nothing, save a heap of shapeless fragments, will mark the spot where the great mountain stood; for, atom by atom, inch by inch, and yard by yard, it yields to forces which nothing can withstand. That time is far distant; and, ages hence, generations unborn will gaze upon its awful precipices, and wonder at its unique form. However exalted may be their ideas, and however exaggerated their expectations, none will come to return disappointed!

...The recollections of past pleasures cannot be effaced. Even now as I write they crowd up before me. First comes an endless series of pictures, magnificent in form, effect, and colour. I see the great peaks, with clouded tops, seeming to mount up for ever and ever; I hear the music of the distant herds, the peasant's jodel, and the solemn church-bells; and I scent the fragrant breath of the pines: and after these have passed away, another train of thoughts succeeds—of those who have been upright, brave, and true; of kind hearts and bold deeds; and of courtesies received at stranger hands, trifles in themselves, but expressive of that goodwill towards men which is the essence of charity.

Still, the last, sad memory hovers round, and sometimes drifts across like floating mist, cutting off sunshine, and chilling the remembrance of happier times. There have been joys too great to be described in words, and there have been griefs upon which I have not dared to dwell; and with these in mind I say, Climb if you will, but remember that courage and strength are nought without prudence, and that a momentary negligence may destroy the happiness of a lifetime. Do nothing in haste; look well to each step; and from the beginning think what may be the end.

2
THE PRINCIPAL CHARACTERS

2.1
ANDENMATTEN, FRANZ (1823 – 1883)

Andenmatten's connection with the Matterhorn accident began on the afternoon of Saturday 15th July 1865 when he was approaching Zermatt with Robertson, Phillpotts and others and encountered the first search party looking for the victims. He was one of four guides who volunteered to accompany Whymper, who intended to set off for the Matterhorn glacier in the early hours of Sunday morning, after the Zermatt guides had been threatened with excommunication if they failed to attend the early morning Mass. Andenmatten also took part in the third search party, which brought down the three bodies on the 19th/20th July and he was the only one who went to the scene on both occasions. Conway wrote of his going with Whymper, 'Franz's curé was fortunately the other side of the Mischabelhörner, but, Curé or no curé, he would have gone, as in fact he went. There was a fund of humanity in him that could not be bound in by any conventionalities when it was firmly roused.'

He gave evidence at the Enquiry on Friday 21st July, the Official Report noting where he would otherwise have signed his deposition that he could not write, and it is probable that he remained in or around Zermatt that week. In his article published in the *Graphic* in 1894, Whymper wrote of the search

> 'First to offer himself was Franz Andenmatten, a first rate mountaineer, who lived at Saas, beyond the jurisdiction of the priests of Zermatt; and under his leading the bodies were recovered and buried. Next Sunday Franz Andenmatten went to Mass, and this was his reward. "I saw him", said my informant (who is now Head Master of one of our public schools), "turned out, *ejected*, from the church at Zermatt!"'

There is little doubt that Whymper must have been referring to the Rev James Robertson as his informant, as he had been headmaster of Haileybury from 1884 until 1890, the only other possibility J.S.Phillpotts being headmaster of Bedford Grammar School. But we know that Whymper kept in touch with Robertson until at least 1895. One detail, however, cannot be quite accurate in as much as Robertson left Zermatt on Saturday 22nd July and could not have seen Andenmatten being ejected from the church on the next Sunday. But there is no reason to conclude from this that such an event was not witnessed by Robertson, as it could have occurred any day between the 16th and the 22nd July. Whymper prefaced this report in the *Graphic* with, 'Two incidents in connection with this Matterhorn catastrophe have recently come to my knowledge'. The other incident quoted by him makes express reference to 'Mr. R–', who was almost certainly Robertson, and the probability is that, sometime in the late 1880's perhaps, Robertson told Whymper of the two incidents.

In his letter to *The Times* written on 17th July and published on 22nd, the Rev J.McCormick referred by name to Franz Andenmatten and the other guides who 'generously offered their services for the [search] expedition. We hope that their names will not be forgotten'.

Andenmatten was born in Almagell, where he ultimately became President of the Gemeinde after an apprenticeship with the Saas priest J.J.Imseng both in the mountains and as Knecht and general factotum in his hotel. Carl Egger has written a ten page biography of him giving details of his early expeditions, including those with Imseng. 'He had a happy disposition and as he went along he could chatter, tells stories, sing or jodel to his heart's content.' Martin Conway wrote how

> 'He had none of the local or class jealousies common amongst guides. He was as ready to climb with a Zermatt or St.Niklaus colleague as with one from his own village. He liked to see foreign guides in his own district. When climbing without guides began, Franz was almost the only guide to express pleasure at the movement.'

He seems to have been one of the great characters amongst the early Alpine guides and few can have received so much praise from their employers. Cecil Slingsby wrote of him: 'All who have climbed with Franz Andenmatten have a very rich store of happy memories of his delightful personality, his winsome smile, his great skill, and his indomitable perseverance.'

2.2
BINER, FRANZ (WEISSHORN) (1835 – 1916)

This Zermatt guide, son of Johann Biner and not to be confused with another Franz Biner who went on the search party on 15th July and the recovery party on 20th July, became known as 'Weisshorn' Biner. He appears to have taken up serious guiding at a relatively late age. By 1864 he had climbed the Weisshorn four times but the SAC glacier guides article otherwise lists only several traverses of the Trift and Evolena passes as well as tours to Val Pellina and Chamonix. However it was in 1864 that his career seems to have taken off with a trip to the Bernina and Ortler groups with Tuckett. In 1865 he was with Whymper as second and sometimes third guide on the Grand Cornier, Dente Blanche, Aiguille Verte, Ruinette etc and he took part with Almer and Croz in Whymper's extraordinary attempt on the S E face of the Matterhorn in June 1865. On 15th July 1865 he accompanied Girdlestone up Monte Rosa and it seems as though he would have been available for the Matterhorn ascent as it was only on the 13th that Girdlestone engaged him, walking up to the Riffelberg on the 14th. Girdlestone did not make the entry in Biner's Führerbuch until the 16th. His subsequent career is described by Farrar in the obituary he wrote in the *Alpine Journal.*

Biner's career did not include the first ascent of the Weisshorn in 1861 and Kronig is wrong to credit him with this on two occasions. Not only is Tyndall's account of the first ascent inconsistent with the presence of a fourth person in the party but as Farrar pointed out Biner's Führerbuch does not start until 1863 when he climbed the Weisshorn as porter and a few days later climbed it again as guide. He seems to have acquired the name Weisshorn in mid-July 1865. Biner climbed with J.M.Elliott a lot and was with him on the Schreckhorn in 1869 when after taking the rope off Elliott missed his footing and fell to his death, through no fault of Biner's. After a long engagement in 1868 Elliott wrote in his Führerbuch: 'But most of all I like to mention his genuineness, his extreme simplicity, his diffidence, his perfect straightforwardness, his candour, his trustworthiness and his kindness of heart.' In the light of this testimonial it is hard to believe that Biner could have been responsible for the appalling incident at the Stockje in 1876, and it seems that Young Peter Taugwalder must have been the sole culprit, with Biner acquiescing at the very most. See section 2.30 (Knubel).

In 1868 Biner was still unmarried and seems to have been supporting his 68 year old mother, two unmarried sisters and a deaf and dumb brother, as well perhaps as a 71 year old father. It is hardly surprising therefore that in the aftermath of the Matterhorn accident when Elliott tried to persuade Biner to accompany him on the Hörnli as far as the shoulder, 'A shrug of the shoulders was at first his only answer...Presently he said "I will speak again to my mother." In the afternoon he returned with a sad and wistful look, and said "No sir; I cannot go. My mother cried much when I spoke of it and said, Do not go, Franz, I entreat thee. Do not go." '

In 1866 Whymper engaged Biner to help him in his research into the stratification of snow and formation of glacier ice, having written in his Führerbuch on 7th July 1865 'I have little doubt [he] may in time become a first rate guide'. There is no reason to suppose that Whymper sought to re-engage Biner on 12th July 1865, although it seems that he was probably available to join the Matterhorn party, rather than that he looked straightaway for Old Peter Taugwalder, having presumably heard from his son Joseph that he was at home. Whymper wrote in *Scrambles* of discharging Almer and Biner at Breuil on 7th July 1865: 'no two men ever served me more faithfully or more willingly'. Biner did not climb the Hörnli until August 1872 and not again until August 1875. He went with Whymper in 1892 to visit the 1865 tent platform and he is probably the one shown in Whymper's photograph in *AJ32*, 28.

2.3
BIRKBECK, JOHN (1842 – 1892)

Birkbeck's chief claim to mountaineering fame was in 1861 when at the age of 19 he was with Charles Hudson, Leslie Stephen and others on the Col de Miage:

> 'Birkbeck had occasion to leave us for a few minutes though his departure was not remarked at the time. When we discovered his absence Melchior followed his footsteps and I went after him, and, to our dismay, we saw the tracks led to the edge of the ice slope, and then suddenly stopped...He had fallen an immense distance.' [1767ft. perpendicular height]

Undeterred he was back in the Alps by 1863 climbing Mont Blanc and the Weisshorn, the latter with Franz Biner and Young Peter Taugwalder. He wrote in Taugwalder's Führerbuch 'Pierre Taugwald junr. has accompanied me to the top of the Weisshorn. I think him strong and likely to make a very good guide'. In 1864 he made a further ascent of Mont Blanc with Adams Reilly and Michel Croz, which no doubt led to his engaging Croz for six weeks in 1865 and to the misunderstanding between Croz and Whymper, a causa sine qua non of the Matterhorn accident.

On 10.6.65 Reilly wrote to Whymper, who had in fact already departed for Switzerland and did not see the letter until his return: 'I have just heard from Birkbeck. He starts with Charles Hudson on the 26th and Thomas Kennedy joins them at Chamonix. They attack the Verte at once, and the Matterhorn afterwards. He says, "I have engaged Michel Croz for some weeks".'

Birkbeck was taken ill as soon as he arrived in Geneva and had to return home. He therefore played no further part in the events of 1865, but on 14th July 1866 he attempted to climb the Matterhorn by the Hörnli, not realising that it was actually the anniversary of the first ascent. There can be little doubt that Birkbeck would have approached Young Peter Taugwalder with whom he had climbed the Weisshorn in 1863 and probably his father as well and that neither was willing to accompany him. The only known contemporary published account, in the *Journal de Genève* of 26th July 1866, seems to have escaped the attention of the mountaineering world or to have been forgotten until Montagnier rediscovered it in about 1917, although Whymper, Adams Reilly and others did learn of the attempt in 1866.

The belated account in the *Journal de Genève* stated: 'On Thursday 12th July an Englishman Mr.Birkbeck with seven guides failed even to reach the shoulder of the Matterhorn; we should add that since last year's accident the Zermatt guides have a real fear of engaging in an enterprise of this nature.' This brief account, referring to the wrong date, reveals very little and may have been based on a third or fourth hand report, as despite the size of the party there was a certain element of secrecy about the expedition. The most important feature, which was to have far reaching consequences, was that all seven guides came not from Zermatt but from St.Niklaus. The expedition did in fact reach the shoulder, although Birkbeck found it impossible to persuade the guides to go any further. However, most of the guides of St.Niklaus obtained some useful experience of the Hörnli ridge and thereby a major advantage over their fearful rivals in Zermatt, who effectively boycotted it for six years. The subsequent bitterness and resentment displayed by the Zermatt guides, which reached its peak in about 1876, is considered elsewhere. See section 3.6.3 (Guides).

Farrar published the Geneva report in *AJ32*, stating that Montagnier had found it after Peter Knubel had told him the previous summer that in 1866 he had made an attempt with Birkbeck to repeat the ascent of the Matterhorn. But Gos relates that Montagnier first found the report and then subsequently interviewed Knubel. The inconsistency is of no great significance, but as the report did not mention St.Niklaus, one would hardly expect Birkbeck to have engaged guides other than from Zermatt, particularly as it infers that they failed even to reach the shoulder because the Zermatt guides had no heart in the matter. In addition to the two Lochmatters the other guides probably included two more Knubels and one or two Imbodens.

Farrar seems then to have carried out further research and to have corresponded with Peter Knubel and with Birkbeck's widow Rachel. She sent him a copy of a note roughly written by Birkbeck for a lecture, which from the contents would appear to have been written and delivered in about 1882. It is a lengthy document referring to many of his climbs and it includes a description of his 1866 attempt on the Matterhorn. It refers to the guides coming to him on the eve of the climb, before he went to sleep, saying that

> 'they had been talking about the mountain and that they did not wish anyone who was nervous to be of the party, would I agree not to mention afterwards which of them went with me to the top so that any one of them might have no hesitation in remaining behind if he found himself at all afraid. I did not like the arrangement but agreed. The next morning when we started I noticed that the guides carefully crossed themselves. This did not look to me a very healthy sign...'

Birkbeck then goes on to refer to not finding the climbing at all difficult but to it being impossible to persuade the guides to go beyond the shoulder. 'In fact I could have ascended the mountain to that point without any guides at all.'

Other contemporay documents referring to Birkbeck's attempt include Girdlestone's letter journal, a letter from Hodgkinson to Reilly, one from Seiler to Thioly and an entry in Whymper's diary immediately before another entry dated 31.7.66: 'Found that Birkbeck had been here and had engaged 7(!) men of St.Niklaus for the Matterhorn. Had tried and had failed not even getting over the easy part. Heard that he had again failed to ascend the Verte in an attempt made this year.' Birkbeck 'did not try the mountain again for various reasons until 1874' when he had the original idea of ascending from Breuil, descending to the Hörnli and returning to Breuil by what he called the Petit Col Cervin, all of which he completed inside nineteen hours.

Another letter from Rachel to Farrar, reproduced in part in *AJ70*, refers to Birkbeck engaging Croz for six weeks in 1865 and to his proposed attempt on the Matterhorn with Hudson. She goes on to say that Hadow would not have been of the party, being no mountaineer, and that he had visited them in Settle with Hudson in about 1864 when, 'we walked up our small hill "Pennyghent"; on one side there is a small piece of rock which has to be descended with care, but most of our party could walk down it with ease. Poor Mr.Hadow found it very difficult and had to be helped down. Later, we were not surprised to hear he had slipped on the Matterhorn.'

2.4
BROWN, FREDERIC AUGUSTUS YEATS (1837 – 1925)

There has been some inconsistency in the spelling of his surname, which should not have the 'e' appended by Mumm. His father, who had attempted the Jungfrau from the Roththal in 1828, was British Consul in Genoa during most of his childhood, which accounts for his becoming a partner in a Genoa banking house and for his memoirs being privately printed in Genoa in 1917.

In 1865 his travels brought him into contact with all the tourists involved in the Matterhorn ascent, apart from Lord Francis Douglas. He ascended Mont Blanc on 7th July and met Hadow on the summit. Hudson and McCormick reached the top an hour after Hadow, and Brown may have started his descent before meeting them. Brown made the ascent with Michel Devouassoud and subsequently walked from Chamonix to Zermatt via the High Level route in company with Robertson, Phillpotts and Knyvet Wilson, arriving at Zermatt on the afternoon of Saturday 15th July after encountering the first Matterhorn search party on the way. He and Devouassoud did not accompany Whymper on the second search early on the Sunday morning, but Devouassoud was a member of the third party, which recovered the three bodies on the 19th/20th July, and which Brown went to meet on its return. On Monday 17th July Brown climbed Monte Rosa, his entry in the Riffelhaus guestbook reading 'Fred A.Y.Brown of Genoa. Mt Rosa. Splendid weather and view'.

His book, *Family Notes*, not written until about 1916, is rather disappointing so far as the 25 pages of mountaineering are concerned. It gives the impression that he wrote it from memory and did not rely on a diary or other contemporary record, and his recollections may therefore be little more reliable than those of G.F.Browne. He was certainly wrong when he wrote of his climbs in 1866 with Tuckett and Christian Almer, stating that the other guide was a man from St.Niklaus, as there is no doubt from Tuckett's journal that Brown's guide was Franz Andenmatten, who had been with the Robertson party on the High Level route in 1865.

Brown wrote of climbing Mont Blanc in 1865 with an unqualified guide

4e Année. — N° 10.

Dimanche 23 juillet 1865.

ABONNEMENTS

France (un an) . . . Fr. 11 »
Italie, Suisse et Angleterre. 13 »

On reçoit des abonnements pour la saison d'été, du 15 mai au 15 octobre, au prix de 5 fr. pour la France, 6 fr. pour l'étranger.

Un numéro, 25 centimes.

ON REÇOIT LES ABONNEMENTS

A Chamonix : Bureau du Guide-chef et au Bureau de Tabac. — A Annecy : Imprimerie du *Mont-Blanc*. — A Genève : *A. Mabbut*, Grand-Quai, 40.

Tout ce qui concerne la rédaction et les communications diverses doit être adressé *franco* au Directeur de l'*Abeille*, à Annecy.

L'ABEILLE DE CHAMONIX

ÉCHO DES STATIONS THERMALES DE LA SAVOIE

Revue littéraire, scientifique, artistique et industrielle

Paraissant le Dimanche.

SOMMAIRE. — Nouvelles ascensions au Mont-Blanc. — Chronique, par Stéphen d'Arve. — Recherche des cadavres de la catastrophe du 14 juillet au Malter-Horn, par M. G. Loppé. — Première ascension de l'Aiguille-Verte, par M. Edward Whymper. — Nouvelles locales. — Petit courrier des Bains de Saint-Gervais, par Des Thermes. — Courrier d'Aix-les-Bains, par A. Dessaix. — Petits échos. — Rébus non illustré et logogriphe. — Indicateur du touriste.

L'ABEILLE DE CHAMONIX *se trouve, par voie d'échange, d'abonnement ou d'envoi gratuit, dans tous les casinos d'Europe. Les listes de voyageurs de toutes les stations thermales lui sont également adressées; la direction les tiendra avec plaisir en communication au service de tous les intéressés.*

CINQUIÈME ASCENSION AU MONT-BLANC.

Le 7 juillet 1865.

M. Frédéric G. Brown, Anglais.
Guide : Devouassoux Michel.

SIXIÈME ASCENSION.

Le 7 juillet 1865.

Sir Thomas Kennedy, lord Douglas, Rd J. Cormik et C. Hudson, Anglais.
Guide : Cros Michel-Auguste.

SEPTIÈME ASCENSION.

Le 15 juillet 1865.

Rd Robert Dées, Anglais.
Guide : Simond Ambroise.

HUITIÈME ASCENSION.

Le même jour.

Miss Walker, MM. Horace Walker, G.-S. Mathews et A.-W. Moore.
Guides suisses.

NEUVIÈME ASCENSION.

Le 17 juillet 1865.

M. John Thom, de Liverpool.
Guides : Jean Carrier et Jean Balmat.

DIXIÈME ASCENSION.

Le 18 juillet.

MM. J. Stnytermann van Loo, Hollandais; J. Simpson Jay, Frédéric W. Ellis et Graham, Anglais.
Guides : Folliguet Joseph et Capelin Edouard.

ONZIÈME ASCENSION.

Le 19 juillet 1865.

Miss Lewis Lloyd, Anglaise.
Guides : Michel Charlet et Jean-Pierre Cachat.

Chronique.

Chamonix, 19 juillet 1865.

Encore une sinistre page dans les annales du tourisme.

Nous avions, dimanche dernier, cédé la place et les premières colonnes de cette feuille à l'un des valeureux touristes qui avaient les premiers foulé la cime de l'Aiguille-Verte, jusqu'à ce jour réputée inaccessible.

M. Hudson racontait lui-même les péripéties de cette audacieuse tentative et terminait sa relation en déclinant modestement l'honneur d'avoir eu de trop grandes difficultés à surmonter. Cette conquête ne suffisait pas à cette

L'Abeille de Chamonix (23rd July 1865)

named Payot, whereas *L'Abeille de Chamonix* of 23.7.65 recorded his ascent as being made on 7th July with Michel Devouassoud as guide. As Devouassoud was in Zermatt on 19th July, there is no reason to suppose that he did not accompany Brown to Zermatt and also climb Monte Rosa with him, particularly as Brown wrote of Payot accompanying him to Zermatt with the Robertson party yet did not even mention climbing Monte Rosa that year. His ascent of Monte Rosa 'with two good young local guides' appears much later in the book with no indication of the year. He wrote of seeing Whymper at Chamonix in 1865, which seems unlikely, as Whymper left four days before Brown climbed Mont Blanc, and after referring to Robertson and Phillpotts at Zermatt, but without naming the latter, he continued:

> 'I don't know why they did not attend Hudson and Hadow's funeral; I suppose they were bound to be elsewhere, to meet friends, or letters from home. At all events Whymper and I and the Rev. Mc.Cormick who officiated, were the only Englishmen present. Whymper, that strong, hard man whom I had admired at Chamonix, was of course, deeply moved.'

But Adams Reilly attended the funeral and he recorded in his diary how 'The service was read at the grave by Mr.McCormick assisted by Mr.Downton' (the English chaplain at Geneva). Even more significantly he referred to Michel Croz being interred at 8.30 and to 'Hudson, Haddo & Wilson at 10'. It seems therefore inconceivable that Robertson and Phillpotts, who had been holidaying with Knyvet Wilson until he fell to his death on the Riffelhorn, should not have been present at the funeral, when the three coffins of Hudson, Hadow and their friend and colleague Wilson were carried to the grave by the guides.

As for the Matterhorn accident Brown referred in his book to several aspects of it and to those involved. He commented on the descent of Mont Blanc, on how 'Mr.Hadow was evidently a novice, he kept floundering into crevasses, and having to be hauled out again', on Whymper showing him the rope that had parted, 'It had been *broken*, not cut; and was not a new rope', and on how 'It is absurd to say Taugwald cut the rope'. He described the piece of summit rock Whymper brought back as 'a bit of syenite, ½ the size of a cricket ball'. There is further evidence of Brown's poor and at times muddled recollection in his reference to Seiller's [sic] hotel at Zermatt being the only one in 1865, and it is not, therefore, possible to attach any importance to his statement that the rope 'parted, because Taugwald père placed an old rope in front of himself, as a safety valve'.

2.5
BROWNE, REV GEORGE FORREST (1833 – 1930)

G.F.Browne took Holy Orders in 1858 and was a Fellow and Lecturer at St. Catherine's College, Cambridge 1863–5 and Chaplain 1866–83. He played a prominent part in the life of the University until 1891, when he became Canon of St. Pauls. He became Bishop of Stepney in 1895 and from 1897 until 1914 he was Bishop of Bristol. He joined the Alpine Club in 1864, resigned in 1875, was re-elected in 1895 and became President in 1905.

Browne's connection with the Matterhorn accident stems from his friendship with Whymper, who on his return to London sought his advice and visited him in Cambridge some time between 3rd and 16th August 1865. Uncertainty surrounds the meeting, which is not recorded by Whymper and for which there is no entirely reliable evidence and in 1932 Lord Conway added some further mystery when he wrote, 'The late Dr.G.F.Browne...told me not many years ago that he was the only living man who knew the truth about the accident and that that knowledge would perish with him as it has perished.' Conway went on to refer (inaccurately) to Browne being in Zermatt at the time of the accident, 'Whymper came to him for advice as to how much of the true story he should tell. There was a danger of it leading to an unpleasant international debate.' Conway's conversation with Browne was mentioned by Coolidge to Charles Gos in a letter in 1921, although Coolidge was primarily telling him that he had just learnt from Conway that the rope had been cut. 'Conway related to me the other day a conversation he had quite recently with an English priest, to whom Whymper had told everything – as early as 1865!!!'

Yet further confirmation of Browne revealing something to Conway comes from the Editor of the *Alpine Journal* in 1949, Graham Brown, who inserted at the end of a review of Gos' book *Le Cervin* the following:

> 'Note. In 1932 the late Lord Conway told me that what Whymper is supposed to have told Bishop G.F.Browne was as follows (I quote from a note made at the time) "On their descent after the accident, Whymper heard the Taugwalders plotting together to kill him – as the only remaining evidence as to the real cause of the accident. Whymper drove them down in front of him." As Lord Conway said, Whymper cannot have understood the patois of the guides, but it is now known that he did commit this absurd story to paper, although that had not yet come to light in 1932. There was no substance in Whymper's suspicions, and his accusation is mentioned here only because it has been published elsewhere—Editor.'

Graham Brown is referring to the Cowell memorandum which did not come to light until Smythe discovered it and quoted from it in his 1940 biography of Whymper. But he is wrong when he states that Whymper 'did commit this absurd story to paper' as it was Cowell senior who created this second memorandum in order to supplement the first one which Whymper had written on 17th August 1865 and had sent to Cowell on the advice of the AC President, Alfred Wills. Whymper's own memorandum made no mention of the Taugwalders 'plotting to kill him'.

Before publishing *Le Cervin* Gos sought Geoffrey Winthrop Young's comments on Coolidge's letters. His reply included: 'If you are publishing something about the Coolidge letters, you ought to know this: Conway did not know the nature of the secret...Conway whom I saw a lot of in his last years and with whom I discussed thousands of things confirmed this to me...As far as I know the role played by Bishop Browne in this affair was absolutely correct and discreet.' There is however no reason to suppose that Conway had ever seen the Cowell memorandum or that there was any reference elsewhere to 'the Taugwalders plotting to kill Whymper'. In these circumstances there is no alternative but to conclude that Browne did reveal to Conway the nature of the 'secret', namely, the Taugwalders' threatening behaviour on the descent, and that Young was wrong to conclude otherwise.

In 1915 Browne published *The recollections of a bishop* from which H.E.Cooke has quoted the material passage in the *Alpine Journal*. Browne refers to his being at Geneva (in mid-July 1865) with John Tyndall at a meeting of the Helvetic Natural Science Societies, although Charles Gos' research has revealed that the meeting did not in fact start until 21st August.

> 'While we were thus engaged, the terrible accident which accompanied the first ascent of the Matterhorn took place. It was well that Tyndall at least was safe in Geneva. Charles Hudson the leader of the party was a schoolfellow of mine, about four years my senior, our very best athlete...Whymper had become a friend for a curious reason. He was marvellously clever with his pencil, and he was quite sure he could graphically 'square the circle'. He used to come to Cambridge now and again on Alpine matters, and always used to put in a little visit to me on this hopeless quest of his. I had only by chance missed meeting Douglas at breakfast on the day when he started for the Alps.
>
> When the news came down to Geneva that all the party except Whymper and the two Taugwalders were lost, and that the remains of Douglas could not be found, Tyndall was sure that he knew a ledge of rock on which the body must have caught no great distance below the lip of the precipice. He borrowed my club rope, and all the other club ropes he could borrow in Geneva, and made off with them in a sack to Zermatt, determined to be lowered down to the ledge to recover the body. The Syndic of Zermatt fortunately found out what was going on, and sent him and his ropes away; they had had plenty of Englishman killed there; they didn't want any more.
>
> As Whymper had got into the way of consulting me about matters other than Alpine, I was the first person to whom he gave a full account of what really took place. He came to see me in Cambridge. He had sealed up the bag in which he had the remains of the rope. He came to consult me on two questions of casuistry, on at least one of which he did not take my advice. Often and pleasantly as I met him through many years, he never returned to the subject with me.'

In 1936 H.E.G. Tyndale included the following note in his edited 6th edition of *Scrambles*:

> 'There is the rumour, which has found its way into print, that the full story was told by Whymper in confidence to Dr.G.F.Browne, Bishop of Stepney (later of Bristol). In this connection I may quote from Whymper's diary of 1895. "Aug 30...At dinner (at Riffelalp) Browne, Bishop of Stepney, came up and spoke to me. Said he could recognise me, although he hadn't seen me for 31 years." Apart from a note that they attended a funeral together five days later the diaries from 1895 to 1911 contain no further reference to Bishop Browne.'

Tyndale refers again to this entry in Whymper's diary in a footnote in *AJ53* in his capacity as Editor. 'The entry in Whymper's diary for August 30, 1895, states that he and Dr.Browne had not met each other for 31 years. See *Scrambles*, 1936 edition, p. vii, footnote—Editor.' But this is somewhat misleading, as Whymper was merely recording that Browne 'said he could recognise me, although he hadn't seen me for 31 years' and there is nothing to suggest that they had not met in 1865.

The first two of the three paragraphs quoted above from Browne's book are completely inaccurate in so far as they advance the Natural Science meeting by five weeks, place Browne and Tyndall in Geneva in mid-July and refer to Tyndall borrowing ropes from Browne and others before making off with them to Zermatt. Browne was over 80 when his book was published and as Ronald Clark has said in relation to him 'The trouble, of course, is not that old men forget but that they are apt to remember, with the best will in the world, slightly out of focus'. It may be said in Browne's defence that he wrote in the Preface in mitigation of possible inaccuracies, 'It should be borne in mind that these are Recollections, not Notes from a Diary, – a thing I never kept'.

There is however nothing impossible about the third paragraph quoted above and no scope there for Browne involving himself in an event that really concerned another. Whymper had spent the evening of Wednesday 2nd August with the Cowells, father and son, and taking account of his delay in replying to a note from the Editor of *The Times* dated 2nd August and of his other letter writing commitments in the first half of August, it is quite possible that he visited Browne in Cambridge on 3rd August. There does not seem to be any question of Whymper having disclosed to Browne any 'secret' beyond what he told the Cowells. He seems to have received advice on this aspect from three main sources, Cowell, Browne and Wills and it may well be that his memorandum of 17th August, recorded on the advice of Cowell senior, deliberately omitted those additional matters that appear in the Cowell memorandum, as a result of his heeding the advice of Browne. Browne's reference to Whymper not taking his advice on at least one question may relate to some of the details of the Taugwalders' behaviour included in Whymper's letter to *The Times*, to the extract from the memorandum of 17th August quoted in *Scrambles* or to something in the long footnote in *Scrambles* about the Taugwalders.

It seems that Conway's accounts of the Whymper/Browne meeting add little but further inaccuracies, although they do tend to confirm that such a meeting did take place within a month of the accident and to exclude Tyndale's inference that their first encounter after the accident was not until 1895.

2.6
CAMPBELL, A.J (c.1848 – ?)

In 1865 Campbell was a pupil of Charles Hudson and on 26th June they together with Hadow, a former pupil, and the Rev J.McCormick left London for Paris from where they were to continue to Chamonix and later Zermatt, McCormick travelling via Grindelwald on both occasions. At Chamonix on 6th July Campbell accompanied the rest of the party including T.S.Kennedy and his wife as far as the Pierre Pointue, where they all spent the night, but neither he nor Mrs.Kennedy took part in the ascent of Mont Blanc the following day and there is nothing to suggest that he did any serious mountaineering.

He accompanied Hudson and Hadow to Zermatt, probably spending the night of the 11th July at St.Niklaus. They had expected to meet McCormick in Visp on the way but he was delayed by bad weather. When Hudson set off for the Matterhorn with Hadow at 5 a.m. on the 13th, the note he left for McCormick included 'Please give an eye to Campbell as long as you are with him, and take him to the Riffel in case you go there'.

On 15th July 'before ten, Campbell and [McCormick] set off with a party for the Gornergrat' and when they were returning they learnt of the accident. Campbell appears to have left Zermatt on about Tuesday 18th July, judging from the date of the entry he made in the Monte Rosa guestbook. McCormick mentions him briefly, but otherwise he does not feature in Alpine literature and there is no reason to suppose that he ever took up mountaineering. However any diary of his that might have survived could well throw light on Hudson's original intention on the Matterhorn so far as Hadow was concerned. Had McCormick arrived in time to join Hudson in a serious attempt on the Matterhorn, as they had planned, Hadow could well have been left in Zermatt with Campbell. There is also a possibility that Campbell recorded in his diary the reason why Hadow was taken on the combined expedition, as well as some of the immediate post-accident events in Zermatt.

2.7
CARREL, CHANOINE GEORGES (1800 – 1870)

Canon Carrel of Aosta

Canon Carrel of Aosta played a very important part in the early history of climbing the Matterhorn and in the development of tourism in Breuil, as well as in the Valtournanche and Aosta regions. He himself may have been more of a walker than a climber, unlike his nephew Amé Gorret, but he was of an earlier generation and in 1842 had studied the movement of glaciers with James Forbes. He was mentioned by Ball in his *Guide to the Western Alps* in connection with the Becca di Nona, of which the Canon published a fine lithographed panorama of the summit view. Ball wrote of the chalets of Comboë, 'These belong to the Chapter of Aosta, and travellers are indebted to the Chanoine Carrel for having had one of them fitted up with a good room, clean straw, and a fireplace, and furthermore for the good path which leads from hence to the summit of the mountain'. The Canon was no hotelier, but just as Alexander Seiler was largely responsible for opening up the Zermatt side of the Matterhorn to climbers, so he provided for the needs of climbers attempting the ascent from Breuil.

Tuckett wrote of the Canon in 1862,

> 'I had long wished to make the acquaintance of this gentleman, distinguished alike for his scientific attainments, his courtesy to all who seek his society or advice, and the fine enthusiasm for his beloved Alps, which renders him so congenial a companion to younger mountaineers. This is not the place to dilate upon individual character, but I cannot forebear expressing my grateful sense of the many kindnesses received both then and since at his hands.'

Guido Rey wrote of him, how

> 'By talking with [the English] and hearing them express their curiosity concerning the Cervin and their admiration for it, he had perceived before anyone that the mountain at whose foot he had been born might become the glory and the blessing of his valley, and he had imparted his opinion to his fellow-villagers, who were unaware of their hidden treasure'.

It seems that he inspired the two Carrels and Amé Gorret to make the first attempt in 1857, of which Rey wrote, 'He was the spark which kindled a great fire; he was the creator of the idea, the others merely carried it out'.

The Canon took a keen interest in photography including stereoscopic views, and he sent Gastaldi, the President of the Italian Alpine Club, some photographs he had taken of the Matterhorn in late September 1865. He pointed out how in one the south face appeared almost completely free of snow, and as no one in the valley could remember ever seeing it so black they ought to preserve it carefully in their archives. One of his photographs was marked by Leighton Jordan in 1867 to show the various stages in his ascent, and this is reproduced in Bernardi's book.

Much of the Canon's contribution to climbing the Matterhorn, an ambition that he himself shared but could not fulfil, is found in his book *La Vallée de Valtornenche en 1867*, which appeared originally in 1868 in a quarterly number of the Italian Alpine Club bulletin. It is apparent that he had some sympathy for the comment said to have been made by Whymper when he left the Giomein for Zermatt on 12th July 1865, in so far as it related only to J-A Carrel, 'You will never get anywhere with the guides of Valtornenche, they don't work for the honour, they are only looking for a day's wages'. The Canon was directly responsible for breaking Carrel's monopoly of climbing the Matterhorn from

Breuil, when in 1867 the Maquignaz brothers made the ascent, finding a new direct route which avoided the gallery on the west face.

He intervened when in 1867 John Tyndall was met with the exorbitant demand from Carrel that he take four guides and pay them each 150frs. He wrote to him in September apologising, telling him of the new route by the Maquignaz and assuring him that it would be a pleasure for them to accompany him, without asking him to make a great financial sacrifice. He referred in his book to Tyndall having written in the Hotel du Mont-Cervin visitors book about the guides' excessive demands and pointed out that Tyndall had pioneered the route, fixed the rope [that now bears his name], been the first to reach the Pic Tyndall and also contributed 50frs towards the cost of building the hut on the Cravate. The Canon was instrumental in having the hut built and he published a list of the contributors, amongst which he himself appears as the 'promoter' with a donation of 50frs. He took a very close interest in the extraordinary explorations on the Matterhorn which Jordan carried out with the Maquignaz brothers in 1867, and he subsequently discussed with him such matters as guides fees, and recorded Jordan's donation of a dozen sheepskins for the hut and of a sum sufficient to purchase a fixed rope, which was in fact used to acquire the original Jordan ladder. His book was a complete up to date guide containing everything a climber could want to know about the Matterhorn in 1868. The 73 page book deserves to be better known.

Charles Gos has published some of the Canon's correspondence, which includes letters from Chasseur the Curé of Valtournanche and from Gorret, informing him of the first ascent from Breuil, as well as the Canon's own lengthy account of it to Gastaldi, the President of the Italian Alpine Club, based on what he had learnt from the three guides. A batch of five letters in 1866–7 relates to the hut on the Cravate and there is a curious one from J-J Maquignaz reporting an attempt by Giordano in July 1866, in very badly spelt French.

2.8
CARREL, JEAN-ANTOINE (1829 – 1890)

The Italian ridge of the Matterhorn will aways be associated with Carrel. Not only did he make its first ascent on 17th July 1865 with J.B.Bich, via the 'Galerie' that bears his name and which has not often been repeated, but he had taken part in most of the earlier attempts. These are fully detailed by Whymper and by Rey, as well as by the other participants such as Tyndall and Gorret. Much has been written about the arrangements Whymper made with Carrel on about 7th July and his subsequent discovery that Carrel had been engaged by Giordano 'who had just dispatched the party to facilitate the way to the summit, and who, when the facilitation was completed, was to be taken to the top along with Signor Sella'. Whymper wrote how he 'had been bamboozled and humbugged', and Gorret recorded how when Whymper was leaving the Giomein for Zermatt on 12th July he had said 'You will never get anywhere with the guides of Valtornenche, they don't work for the honour, they are only looking for a day's wages'.

This remark seems to have been made known in Breuil, and Gos has quoted a document relating to it, which appears to be incomplete and unsigned, in which 'the undersigned declare' that they were acting under the orders of J-A Carrel and were not themselves responsible for the fact that they did not reach the summit on 14th July; 'they therefore protest against Mr. Whymper's remark...' Gorret's account of the successful ascent on 17th July, in which he and J-A Meynet also took part although they did not go to the summit, refers to Whymper's remark when recounting the guides' response to Giordano asking them on 15th July to try again after turning back on the 14th; 'That which appeared to me at first to be nothing but a sudden outburst of spite, could now appear to be true'. But Canon Carrel in his book seems to have been able to put the remark into its proper perspective and this may well account for the document published by Gos never having been completed: 'These words are too general; the guides would have challenged the person who had pronounced them, had it not been common knowledge in the parish that they applied only to a single guide, the one who had for several years led him on the flanks of the Mont-Cervin without ever leading him to the top.'

It is interesting in the light of this responsible comment to note how Whymper bore no long term ill feeling towards Carrel and how he was able to write about their sighting the Italian party from the summit on 14th July

> 'Still I would that the leader of that party could have stood with us at that moment, for our victorious shouts conveyed to him the disappointment of the ambition of a lifetime. He was *the* man, of all who attempted the ascent of the Matterhorn, who most deserved to be the first upon its summit. He was the first to doubt its inaccessibility, and he was the only man who persisted in believing that its ascent would be accomplished. It was the aim of his life to make the ascent from the side of Italy, for the honour of his native valley. For a time he had the game in his hands: he played it as he thought best; but he made a false move, and he lost it.'

In December 1865 Elijah Walton, the artist, wrote to Whymper from Piedmont 'Enclosed is the photograph of your guide Carrel. He came to see me and wished me to say he was sorry he could not write to you knowing not your address.' This suggests that the two men were still well disposed towards each other, although there does not appear to be any other evidence of contact between them until 1869, when they were together in the Dauphiné for eight days. Although in 1866 Carrel led two other guides and five porters trying to get Giordano to the summit, they had to retreat from the foot of the final peak on account of much fresh snow, spending a total of five nights in a tent at the Cravate. In 1867 Tyndall planned to traverse the Matterhorn from Zermatt to Breuil. He corresponded with Carrel for some time 'and from his letters an enthusiastic desire to be my guide might be inferred', but when Tyndall crossed over the Theodule to Breuil on 21st July 'His demands were excessive, and he also objected to the excellent company of Christian Michel. In fact my good friend Carrel was no longer a reasonable man.' It is not entirely clear what happened then, but Grove seems to have engaged Carrel and they and Tyndall and Michel crossed the Trift pass from Zermatt to Zinal and then went on to Evolène, whilst waiting for the weather to improve. Tyndall eventually left Switzerland, but Grove managed to make the third ascent of the Matterhorn, with Carrel, Bich and S.Meynet. It was not until September 1868 that Carrel made his next ascent, with Giordano and J-J Maquignaz, followed by another ascent five days later.

In 1867 Canon·Carrel was anxious to avoid Carrel gaining a monopoly of climbing the Matterhorn, and so he was instrumental in the Maquignaz brothers making their ascent without a tourist and a subsequent ascent with Jordan, as well as Tyndall's traverse from Breuil to Zermatt in 1868, and the potential problem was thereby resolved. Whymper's employment of Carrel in 1869 is recorded in his Führerbuch in an entry made on 3rd August,

> 'Jean-Antoine Carrel has been with me as guide during the last eight days and shown that he has not lost the ability for which he is so remarkable. I have known J-A Carrel during the last eight years and consider him the finest rock climber I have seen. He possesses the highest courage and whether for one who wishes to make difficult excursions, or for one who wishes to make ordinary ones, he will be found a first rate guide.'

Jean-Antoine Carrel (1869)

It appears from a letter Whymper sent the Editor of the *Alpine Journal* at about the end of 1871, after Tyndall had taken issue with what he had written in *Scrambles* about his 1862 attempt, that in 1869 Whymper had actually checked with Carrel the accuracy of what he had written about the Tyndall expedition and he had expressed himself perfectly satisfied with its accuracy. In 1874 Carrel accompanied Whymper when he repeated his ascent of the Hörnli ridge and a couple of days later they, together with Louis Carrel, became the first to reach the Arbenjoch. In 1880 Carrel was with Whymper in the Andes, where they made the first ascents of Chimborazo and Cotopaxi as well as several lesser peaks. It was Carrel, and not Joseph Maquignaz who has erroneously been given the credit on more than one occasion, who made the first winter ascent of the Matterhorn with Vittorio Sella in 1882, when they made the traverse from Breuil to Zermatt.

Carrel, who climbed the Matterhorn fifty three times, died from exposure after leading his party safely down from the hut at the foot of the Great Tower in very severe weather conditions. His employer, Sinigaglia, wrote an account of the tragedy, much of which was reproduced in the obituary Whymper wrote for the *Alpine Journal*. He also quoted from it in the fifth edition of *Scrambles* and added,

> 'Such was the end of Jean-Antoine Carrel – a man who was possessed with a pure and genuine love of mountains; a man of originality and resource, courage and determination, who delighted in exploration. His special qualities marked him out as a fit person to take part in new enterprises and I preferred him to all others as a companion and assistant upon my journey amongst the Great Andes of the Equator...In his latter years, I am told, he showed signs of age, and from information which has been communicated to me it is clear that he had arrived at a time when it would have been prudent to retire – if he could have done so. It was not in his nature to spare himself, and he worked to the last. The manner of his death strikes a chord in hearts he never knew. He recognized to the fullest extent the duties of his position, and in the closing act of his life set a brilliant example of fidelity and devotion. For it cannot be doubted that, enfeebled as he was, he could have saved himself had he given his attention to self-preservation. He took a nobler course, and, accepting his responsibility, devoted his whole soul to the welfare of his comrades, until utterly exhausted, he fell staggering on the snow. He was already dying. Life was flickering, yet the brave spirit said, "It is *nothing*." They placed him in the rear to ease his work. He was no longer able even to support himself; he dropped to the ground, and in a few minutes expired.'

2.9
CLEMENZ, JOSEPH ANTON (1810 – ?)

Clemenz was groomed for public office and he became a member of the Valais Legislature for the district of Visp and also President of the Council, but by about 1850, on the recommendation of his friend Engelhardt of Strasburg – 'the father of Zermatt' – he began to build the Hotel Mont Cervin in Zermatt and he opened it in 1852. Alexander Seiler acquired the Lauber Inn in 1855 and renamed it the Hotel du Mont Rose and two years later Clemenz enlarged the Mont Cervin to 68 beds.

It seems that Clemenz' public duties did not interfere too much with his private enterprise during the summer months. In September 1858 J.Llewelyn Davies was staying at the Mont Cervin and he was considering attempting the first ascent of the Weisshorn with Johann Zumtaugwald

> 'but, happening to talk about it to Mr.Clemenz, the landlord of the Mont Cervin hotel, I found that he strongly recommended us to substitute the Dom for the Weisshorn. The worthy landlord was also President of the Council of his canton, and took a zealously patriotic view of an ascent of the highest Swiss mountain, assuring me that such an achievement would have "a quite other significance" for the traveller himself and for the village of Zermatt, than would belong to the ascent of any other mountain.'

Whymper was to write in his *Zermatt Guide* more than 30 years later how the Mont Cervin 'was not popular and was never full and people used to leave it to come to the Mont Rose'. He went on to refer to the number of visitors to Zermatt increasing rapidly in the late fifties and early sixties 'though all who came could be accomodated in the two hotels'. But after 1865 and the publicity resulting from the Matterhorn accident the number increased again and, as Hallenbarter has written of Clemenz, 'In 1867 he seems to have grown weary of playing host and paying compliments, and he sold his Hotel Mont Cervin to his honourable competitor Alexander Seiler'. Whymper wrote how 'in 1867 Mons. Seiler was able to make himself master of both hotels, and under his able management the Mont Cervin lost its old reputation'.

There is no reason to doubt that Clemenz was still running the Mont Cervin on about 26th June 1865 when Lord Francis Douglas arrived for a stay that was to last some two weeks. His last night there was probably the 8th but might have been Sunday 9th July as he definitely seems to have spent the night of the 10th at the Riffelhaus, where he wrote in the hotel guestbook, 'Remained here a fortnight and found everything quite perfect.' This wording has caused some confusion and the word 'here' must mean 'at Zermatt' rather than at the Riffelhaus. It has been wrongly assumed that Douglas spent a fortnight at the Monte Rosa hotel, but it seems that he stayed there only on the night of 12th July. It is unfortunate that the Mont Cervin guestbook seems not to have survived, as the entry Douglas made in it would have been interesting and could well have been in similar terms, unless the explanation is that he had forgotten to make any entry in it. The Official Report of the Enquiry into the Matterhorn accident and into the deaths of Lord Francis Douglas and the other victims has attached to it an inventory of Douglas's belongings 'zu Zermatt im Gasthof H.Staatsrat J.A.Clemenz, Hotel Mont Cervin'. They consist of a haversack, of which the contents are then detailed, as well as a wallet containing money and hotel bills. As Lord Francis Douglas had climbed from Zermatt for four consecutive years and seems not yet to have been won over by Seiler's Monte Rosa hotel despite several stays at the Riffel, it is probable that he had stayed with Clemenz before and that Clemenz would have known him and would have taken an interest in his mountaineering activities, even, perhaps, to the extent of recommending a guide. It ought therefore to have been a cause of some embarrassment to landlord Clemenz when the Cantonal Government in Sion appointed him to preside over the Official Enquiry into the accident on the Matterhorn in his capacity as judge or Examining Magistrate.

The extent of the conflict of interests between Clemenz' roles as hotelier and as President of the Enquiry may in fact have been far greater than it appears at first sight. For Clemenz the hotelier must have been about as unwelcome in Zermatt as Alexander Seiler. Theodore Wundt wrote of Seiler's 'lifelong fight with the Zermatters who continually looked upon him as a stranger, indeed as an enemy of the whole valley'. Clemenz' problems would not stem only from the fact that he was an outsider, judging from the Zermatters' jealousy at the success of the Riffelhaus, which had been built on the initiative of one of their own number, the priest Joseph Ruden. As Coolidge wrote in his 'Notes on the history of Zermatt': 'By 1854 the curé owned three-fourths of the house. The Zermatt people were jealous at the success of the inn, and created such disturbances that in 1862 the house was sold to the commune, which gave a fresh lease for fifteen years to M.Seiler.'

But how could any outsider, dependent on a number of locals for the efficient day-to-day running of the hotel, stand in judgment over those same people or members of their families when it came to deciding whether anyone was guilty of criminal negligence? The full circumstances of such an accident would never be known before the Government appointed a President, as otherwise there would be no need for an Enquiry, but what if there were an accident involving several guests in Clemenz' hotel as well as local guides, and a possibility of manslaughter? Would Clemenz have risked his hotel business or even the hotel itself, with the arrest of a guest, or a guide being tried, for manslaughter? Fortunately for Clemenz he was not faced with such a serious situation in 1865 and his only guest was dead. Subsequently, having survived the Matterhorn accident, Clemenz seems to have had the good sense to try and avoid a recurrence by selling the hotel to Seiler in 1867, no doubt prompted by the enquiries of some of his guests, and even perhaps from Whymper himself in August 1866, about the Taugwalder answers he had promised. It was indeed lucky for Clemenz that he was no longer a Zermatt hotelier when he presided over the Enquiry into the Lyskamm fatality in 1869, when the guides really do seem to have been at fault, or again when *Scrambles* was published in 1871.

Zermatt was still a very remote and close community in the nineteenth century, and knowing how a few years later the inhabitants defied all the courts in the land when they found in Seiler's favour on his application to become a Burger of Zermatt, it would not be very surprising if they had reacted to Clemenz' business venture in their midst with nothing but contempt for his official status. May it be therefore that in July 1865 he realised how vulnerable his own position was and with rumours rife in Zermatt of Old Peter having cut the rope, he decided to play safe and not ask him any questions about the happening of the accident, but rely on Whymper to do it for him by drafting Questions 22-35, with the additional precaution of allowing Old Peter's cousin Alois Julen, the Zermatt judge, to vet the questions in the course of translating them into German?

The accident had occurred on 14th July but it was not until 20th July that the three bodies were brought down and they were buried on the morning of Friday 21st July. Not until the Friday morning did Clemenz summon Whymper to appear before the Enquiry at two o'clock that afternoon. Whymper in a letter to McCormick of 25th July expressed his displeasure at having been detained so long in Zermatt 'merely, as it seems to me, to suit M.Clemenz' pleasure'. Whereas it might be thought that Clemenz was awaiting the recovery of the bodies before opening the Enquiry and could not therefore have taken Whymper's evidence any sooner, this does not stand up to close scrutiny. Firstly he did not question any of the 21 men who were in the recovery party, which included the Zermatt President Joseph Welschen, apart from the Saas guide Franz Andenmatten, but the questions put to him related only to his search with Whymper the previous Sunday. Secondly the principal ground for Whymper's complaint would seem to be that Clemenz had put his questions to Whymper several days earlier and as he added only two trivial further questions on the Friday afternoon, which the Court clerk did not even bother to record, he could have formally processed Whymper's written answers much earlier in the week.

There cannot be many tribunals in the civilised world that open an Enquiry at 2 p.m. on a Friday afternoon, continue briefly on the Saturday and finally complete the evidence on the Sunday by recalling one of the Friday witnesses. May part of the explanation be that Clemenz also held an Enquiry into Wilson's death and that it took place on the Friday morning, and that he in fact gave Taugwalder until the Saturday morning to prepare his answers to the questions handed in by Whymper?

The manner in which the Enquiry was conducted is considered fully elsewhere, but mention must be made of the way in which Clemenz appears to have prepared the evidence by dividing it into separate self-contained lots. Close consideration of the questions put to Whymper on the Friday afternoon and of those put to Taugwalder either then or the following morning suggests a parrot-like recital of pre-arranged questions without regard for any of the earlier answers. This can only be explained by the fact that the witnesses were handed their questions in advance and given time to prepare their answers in writing. In the case of Whymper this meant that he was able to have his answers translated in advance into French by the Rugby School modern languages master Vecqueray. How else could Whymper have given evidence in a foreign language, often in long sentences and in the very same terms that he was to repeat in future letters and published accounts, and how else on a Friday afternoon could Clemenz and the Court clerk have taken and recorded such lengthy evidence in French from an Englishman, who could not speak or understand their own mother tongue of German? The preparation of Taugwalder's evidence is even more pronounced when one realises that Questions 22-35 had been handed in by and mostly, if not all, drafted by Whymper, although some minor variations were introduced in the German translation. This lack of spontaneity, at its most obvious in Q32, is not evident in the questioning of Franz Andenmatten, on the Friday afternoon, in which most of the questions relate directly and expressly to previous answers. It may even be that Taugwalder did not formally recite his prepared answers until the Saturday.

It seems as though Clemenz or one of his helpers only looked closely at the written answers from Whymper and from Old Peter on the Saturday, possibly on the Saturday afternoon. By then Whymper had been allowed to leave Zermatt, Young Peter having apparently been allowed to leave for Chamonix as early as the Thursday, after helping to bring down the bodies that morning. The only one who could therefore possibly clarify anything was Old Peter. He was therefore further questioned on the Sunday, mainly on matters arising out of his own evidence, but it is by no means clear whether Clemenz was present at this further questioning, having regard to the reference to him in Q55. Most of the answers may once again have been prepared in writing.

It seems probable that Clemenz invited Whymper to prepare some questions to put to Taugwalder. How else could Clemenz have failed to put to Taugwalder on his first examination some questions of substance of his own about the accident? Or did Clemenz hand to Whymper a short list of questions for Taugwalder dealing generally with the accident and ask him to supplement it with some questions about the rope? In the article in the *Journal de Zermatt* in 1895, Whymper is quoted as saying,

> 'I gave Judge Clemenz, in charge of the Enquiry, all the information and details he asked me for, including amongst other things a questionnaire drafted by me and signed by me intended to clear up the accident completely, based amongst other things on the fact that the weakest rope had been used to tie Douglas to father Taugwalder. The questionnaire should have been returned to me by M.Clemenz but I have never seen it again.'

In his letter to *The Times* written on 7th August Whymper referred to handing in a number of questions to be put to Taugwalder. 'The questions, I was told, were put and answered before I left Zermatt; but I was not allowed to be present at the inquiry, and the answers although promised have not yet reached me.' In *Scrambles*, published in 1871, he wrote much the same, 'but the answers, although promised have never reached me', and he added a footnote:

> 'This was not the only occasion upon which M.Clemenz (who presided over the inquiry) failed to give up answers that he promised. It is greatly to be regretted that he did not feel that the suppression of the truth was equally against the interests of the travellers and of the guides. If the men were untrustworthy, the public should have been warned of the fact; but if they were blameless, why allow them to remain under unmerited suspicion?'

At least one Swiss newspaper, the *Sonntagspost*, drew attention to Whymper having left a list of questions to be put to Taugwalder with the President of the Enquiry and to his being still in ignorance of the answers, although their communication to him had been promised. It went on to emphasise the need for clarification about the ropes: '...the appropriate authorities in the Valais could provide the best information, by publishing the results of the examination of Mr. Whymper and of the two Taugwalders. We also consider such publication imperative for the honour of our country, in view of the malicious gossip doing the rounds of the European press.'

But Clemenz withheld Taugwalder's evidence from Whymper and from the public at large, even though he or the authorities did prepare an extract from Whymper's evidence for the British Mission in Berne, the extract concluding with the statement that the depositions of Old Peter confirmed Whymper's narrative of the accident. There could in fact have been no question whatever of Clemenz ever disclosing Taugwalder's answers to Whymper, once Clemenz realised that some of Whymper's questions had been distorted and rendered worthless.

Assuming that Clemenz was in Zermatt on Sunday 16th July, he is likely to have been one of the first persons to have heard a reliable account of the accident and of the loss of his former hotel guest, whose body could not be found by Whymper's search party. Girdlestone who stayed at the Mont Cervin on the Sunday night recorded in a letter how he went to see Whymper at about 2 p.m., immediately he returned after finding the three bodies, and he heard Whymper's account of the accident. That evening Girdlestone went to bed early 'and poor Whymper paid me a visit after I was in bed. I offered to stay with him if I could be of use, but as there was nothing I could do...we settled that I should go on [to Visp] on Monday morning.' Clemenz may therefore have spoken to Whymper when he visited the Mont Cervin and may have learnt something of the accident from him or he may have heard something indirectly from Girdlestone, even if neither told him the full story. He would therefore probably already have known the cause, when he was asked to preside over the Enquiry. Clemenz the hotelier would also have spoken to Whymper when he was paying Douglas's hotel bill and reimbursing Clemenz for the 58 francs advanced to Douglas for a guide.

Amongst Whymper's papers is a note to him from Clemenz, asking him for the address of 'Madame Douglas'. There is no indication of the date but it must have been before the Enquiry took place, as Whymper said in evidence (A5) that he did not know where Douglas lived and on the 24th July the Marquess himself arrived in Zermatt. He arrived the same day as Hadow's uncle, but they may not necessarily have been travelling together, as Hadow stayed longer than Queensberry. Although Hadow's father had told McCormick in a letter that his brother would be staying at the Mont Cervin, both stayed in fact at the Monte Rosa, where prior to leaving they entered their names in the guestbook.

Clemenz made his second major intrusion into Alpine literature with the publication in the *Alpine Journal* in May 1870 of a lengthy paper on the fatal accident to Chester on the Lyskamm in September 1869. There is no need to consider here the details of the untrue story given by the two guides 'in order to cover whatever was blameable in their conduct', as the party which went to recover the body within 24 hours of the happening of the accident included two experienced English barristers, one of whom, W.E.Hall, wrote the closely reasoned paper that covers nine pages. His comments on Clemenz' failure to reveal the truth are interesting and have a close bearing on his handling of the 1865 Enquiry and his failure to honour his promise to Whymper.

> 'When we returned to Zermatt an investigation was held by M.Clemenz. Our evidence was taken...M.Clemenz promised to me – and when Mr.Chester's brother arrived at Zermatt to him also – that his decision and the grounds of it should be fully communicated to us. For a long time expectation that M.Clemenz would fulfil his promise naturally and necessarily closed our mouths. But when more than six months have gone by...it becomes necessary...that the dilatory courtesy of M.Clemenz should no longer be waited for. I have no wish to express any opinion as to the conduct of M.Clemenz. I am content that my action should be sufficiently justified by the fact that like promises were made after the accident on the Matterhorn, and that they were never fulfilled...I cannot help uttering a protest, however useless it may be, against the secrecy which the character of M.Clemenz or that of Swiss law has imparted to the judicial inquiry.'

2.10
COOLIDGE, WILLIAM AUGUSTUS BREVOORT (1850 – 1926)

Coolidge was only fifteen when the Matterhorn was first climbed, but he was in Switzerland and two months later he and his aunt Meta Brevoort went to Zermatt. Ronald Clark seems to be the only one who has made a detailed study of the voluminous Coolidge archives in Zürich. He mentioned them in his book *The Victorian mountaineers* published in 1953, but it is his biography of Coolidge, *An eccentric in the Alps*, published in 1959 which provides most of the fresh information he discovered about the early history of the Matterhorn. This includes reference by Miss Brevoort in her diary to the accident and also to her ambition to climb the Matterhorn, which was not in fact climbed by a lady until 1871, despite Felicité Carrel getting as far as her Col in 1867.

In September 1865 Coolidge and his aunt stayed at the Hotel Monte Rosa. They went to see the graves of the accident victims and made several excursions including the Gornergrat and the Cima di Jazzi, Coolidge also going on his own to the Hörnli. Clark quotes an extract from the diary, relating to a conversation with a hotel maid whilst taking tea in their room on an off-day.

> 'All think the accident was owing to want of proper precautions. More guides were needed and the party to have been divided. Also they were too elated by success and came down another way from that they came up. Said it was dreadful to have to go in the dead men's rooms full of their scattered clothes etc. Described the excitement in Zermatt the day they reached the top. No one went anywhere. All stood abt. with glasses watching the top of the haughty mtn. Then the shouts when they were seen waving the flag! She says nothing else was thought of. Then the growing anxiety as they delayed returning & then – when only 3 scared creatures appeared late on Saturday night! Then the horror next day when they went to seek for the bodies & then the arrival of the relatives & especially of poor young Douglas'

> brother. She says he would stay in the same room & bed his brother had occupied & that one morg. he started off leaving a letter on the table saying he was going to look for his brother. He was alone & without any provisions. They followed & found him near the foot of the mtn. half crazy. As to Whymper she says he neither ate nor slept but went abt. crying all the time afterwards whilst he was here.'

This account provides confirmation of the fact that Douglas spent the night of 12th July at the Monte Rosa, although he had stayed at the Mont Cervin for most of the previous fortnight. Lord Queensberry made an entry in the Monte Rosa guestbook for 24th to 29th July, whereas Lord Francis Douglas presumably had made his in the Mont Cervin book, which seems not to have survived. The incident when Queensberry went to the Hörnli on his own in the middle of the night is more fully described in the diary of Adams Reilly, who also recorded details of another incident the night before.

Coolidge wrote in his book *The Alps in nature and history* of having met Julius Elliott in July 1868 a fortnight before he made the second ascent of the Matterhorn from Zermatt.

> 'It caused a very great sensation, as it proved that the expedition was not so absolutely certain to end fatally as had been imagined by many. The charm had been broken, but it required a man of strong will to break it. Some years later, in 1871, when it fell to the turn of the present writer to ascend the Matterhorn, it was still considered a most remarkable thing that within the same week *two* ascents of the dreaded peak should have been made with complete success.'

Coolidge and his aunt seem to have decided to climb the mountain at least two years before they finally made it, no doubt influenced by her ambition to make the first ascent by a lady. On 27th July 1869 they crossed the Théodule to Breuil and the following day ascended as far as the old hut on the Cravate with Christian Almer. On the 29th the weather was poor and they returned to Breuil, whereas Heathcote with Joseph Maquignaz, Peter Perren and Young Peter Taugwalder stayed on and would have reached the summit the following day, had thunder and lightning not forced them to retreat when they were within 500 feet of it. Clark states that there had been as many as thirteen in the hut on the 28th, which suggests that there may have another party staying there as well, as it is unlikely that there would have been as many as nine in the Coolidge party. Coolidge's application to join the Alpine Club later that year was seconded by Heathcote.

Clark refers to another attempt to climb the Matterhorn in 1869, made by Miss Straton and Miss Emmeline Lewis-Lloyd, of which there does not appear to be any other record. They were turned back by stonefall but there is no indication as to their route. This seems to have made Miss Brevoort even more determined and Clark quotes Coolidge as writing subsequently of 1870, 'We hovered most of the summer round Zermatt, but the weather was always against even an attempt'. In 1871 Coolidge and his aunt finally succeeded in making the ascent from Zermatt and traversing down to Breuil, but not before Lucy Walker had managed to make the first ascent by a lady on the day they arrived in Zermatt, as a result of being tipped off by E.R.Whitwell about Miss Brevoort's intention.

Coolidge's conflict with Whymper over 'Almer's leap' on the Ecrins is beyond the scope of this book, his only other involvement with the Matterhorn issues being a couple of letters he wrote to Charles Gos in 1921 about the rope being cut in 1865. It seems that Coolidge's motive was simply mischievous and that any conversation he had recently had with Conway related solely to the general question of Whymper going to see G.F.Browne on about 3rd August 1865. It is rather pathetic that Gos should have sought the comments of Guido Rey on the Coolidge letters and, 25 years later, those of Winthrop Young on Rey's reply, only to publish all four some two years later. But Gos' chapter 'La corde maudite' appears to have been written at a time when he may have been suffering severely from the illness from which he died less than a year later, and this may have affected his judgment.

Whereas Coolidge included in his book *Alpine studies* chapters on 'The History of the St.Théodule Pass' and on 'The Matterhorn and its Names', his most readable and interesting account about the area is the 70 page chapter 'How Zermatt became a mountaineering centre' in his book *Swiss Travel and Swiss guide-books*.

2.11
COWELL, JOHN WELSFORD
COWELL, JOHN JERMYN (1838 – 1867)

It seems as though Cowell senior must have had some mountaineering experience, judging from the great interest he showed in the Matterhorn accident, although any reference there may be in Alpine literature to his exploits is hard to find! His correspondence suggests familiarity with Chamonix and with the ways of guides, but coming from an earlier generation his achievements may have been fairly modest.

J.J.Cowell was Secretary of the Alpine Club in 1863–4 and was a member of the 1864 Special Committee on ropes, axes and alpenstocks. He qualified as a barrister in 1864, but it seems that in 1861 he had contracted an illness from which he never entirely recovered; at the end of July 1865 he was unwell and he died some eighteen months later. When Whymper returned home in late July 1865 he seems to have wanted the Alpine Club to hold an enquiry into the Matterhorn accident and, in the absence of the Secretary F.C.Grove who was in the Alps, Cowell advised him as to what this would entail. Cowell wrote a letter to *The Times* on 28th July and it seems from his letter of 31st July to Whymper that he wrote to him as well at about the same time. But neither that letter nor Whymper's reply seems to have survived. It appears however from Cowell's letter of 31st July and from a letter Whymper sent the Editor of *The Times* on about 4th

August, that Whymper wanted any information the public might get from him not to come direct in the form of a letter but as the result of an enquiry on the part of the Alpine Club. Cowell suggested summoning an Extraordinary General Meeting to consider if any enquiry should be made into Hudson's death, and he referred to the possibility of appointing 'a Committee of three to make enquiries of Mr. Whymper'. He advised against the Committee commencing its enquiries before the Meeting, as it might not satisfy the public if members undertook the enquiry on their own authority. He set out a detailed timetable requiring 19 days to comply with the necessary formalities for holding a meeting. He asked Whymper to call on Tuesday 1st August if he wanted to discuss the matter, and concluded by inviting him to a quiet dinner with him and his father on Wednesday 2nd August.

There is no indication as to whether Whymper called on the Tuesday, but we know that he dined with the Cowells on the Wednesday from the opening sentence of the 'Cowell memorandum'. Although Wm. Mathews was writing to Whymper on 3rd August from Birmingham saying that he did not 'see the smallest use in having an enquiry', there is nothing further from Cowell on the subject. It seems as though no formal steps were taken to summon a meeting and that Whymper was persuaded by the Editor, Wills and others to write to *The Times*.

Cowell senior wrote to Whymper after reading his letter in *The Times*, and he, rather than his son, seems to have corresponded with Whymper thereafter. He told Whymper how he had repeatedly perused the account

> 'and find it at last impossible for me to refrain from expressing the feelings of deep respect for you with which your narrative has impressed me...I might have repressed my desire to signify my sentiments on what to you must be so very painful a subject had I not observed that you had passed over in your narrative, some points in the demeanour of the Taugwalds which I venture to think it is due to yourself that you should consign to writing exactly in the manner in which you related them to my son and myself at this house on Wednesday the 2nd of August.
>
> You do not know what relations these men may endeavour to propagate; their answers to the questions which you proposed should be put to them have been withheld from you; there will be a strong *local* feeling to support any pretensions of these men to your detriment, you know what sort of men they are, and that their first thoughts after the dreadful disaster – and when, alone and unprotected you appeared almost at their mercy – were to urge you to shape your account of it in such a manner as should turn to their pecuniary advantage.
>
> You have yet to learn what they have said, and what impression it may make.
>
> I submit to you that it would be prudent, not only as regards yourself, but also as regards the memory of those who are gone, to consign to writing exactly what you communicated to my son and myself on the 2nd of August, so that we might, if the necessity for your making it public should arise hereafter, be in a condition to certify that what you may say regarding these men is no afterthought. And I think besides that some such step as this is called for in regard to the English who may visit Zermatt, and whose generous sympathies may be otherwise enlisted in favour of very undeserving persons in all respects.

> Pardon this suggestion. My son is out of town and I cannot consult him regarding it.'

Whymper seems to have heeded Cowell's advice by creating his memorandum of 17th August, although he omitted some details from it, influenced perhaps by the advice he had received from G.F.Browne on about 3rd August. He appears then to have sent the memorandum and Cowell's letter of 11th August to Alfred Wills, with whom he was already in correspondence. His letter has not survived, but Wills' reply of 20th August implies that Whymper sought his advice and expressed some doubt about revealing the Taugwalders' conduct. Wills' reply shows that he had suspected Whymper omitted some details in *The Times*.

> 'I take a little different view from you as to the desirability of saving the Taugwalders from the natural and proper consequences of their scandalous conduct...I think myself, if you will pardon me for saying so, that you will make a great mistake if you hesitate to speak of them as they should be spoken of. As Mr.Cowell senr. has written you so kind and so judicious a letter, if you are disposed to consult him on the matter again, I should be very glad if you would show him what I have said about it – and see how it strikes him. I would suggest to you also to let him and his son write under your narrative that it is in substance – or in any way they like to put it – what you told them on 2nd August, and let me write also that I read it on the 20th.
>
> Life is a very uncertain thing with the best of us and you may be glad (though it is not likely that what you say will ever be called in question) to have it in writing that so and so knows it is what you told him at first.'

Sometime between the 21st and the 31st August, judging from Cowell's reply, Whymper wrote again to Cowell sending his memorandum of 17th August and Wills letter of 20th August. So the 'Cowell memorandum' came to be made, in circumstances somewhat different from the impression given by Smythe in his biography of Whymper. Cowell replied on 4th September, enclosing 'his and his son's certificate' as to the authenticity of Whymper's memorandum of 17th August, which he returned along with Wills' letter. His letter included 'I also hope that you will be called upon to publish all you know about the Taugwalders, and I trust that the Club will upon consideration of these matters invite you to do so.'

The Cowell memorandum, which is reproduced in full in section 4.52 and considered more fully in section 3.2, begins with the words: 'The foregoing Memorandum records the substance of a communication made to the undersigned on Wednesday August 2 1865 by Edward Whymper in answer to questions which they put to him. But it was fuller, more comprehensive and more significant than this mem. exhibits it.' It seems from the precise details recorded by the Cowells in their memorandum that they must have been taken from a very full note made at the time they questioned Whymper on 2nd August. It must be emphasised that the Cowells wrote their own memorandum, and not Whymper, and that it contains facts, which were in effect extracted from Whymper in cross examination by a barrister, as well as the comments of the Cowells. Unfortunately Smythe misled his readers and himself with regard to the Cowell memorandum which only he had seen, particularly in his fifteen page essay which forms the Introduction to the 1949 edition of Whymper's *Andes* book. It includes: 'Later, Whymper wrote an extraordinary letter to the Secretary of the Alpine Club in which he accused the Taugwalders of wanting to murder him'. This is so wide of the mark as to undermine completely the comments of Lunn and Egger and others on the subject, and such writings have been ignored in the list of authorities in section 7.2.11, although they are dealt with in section 7.3.2 in relation to the separate article on 'The Cowell memorandum'. The only sound comment on the subject was that of Dangar & Blakeney who wrote in the *Alpine Journal* in 1966: 'We think that too little is known on the latter subject [of Whymper's conversations with the Cowells] for it to be wise for anyone to pronounce upon it.'

Mention should be made here of Ronald Clark's reference in *The Day the Rope Broke* to the Cowells, and to Jermyn Cowell's close friend Oscar Browning. The date of Whymper's meeting with the Cowells is known and Clark's presumption that it was the 7th (rather than the 2nd August) is wrong. Browning's recollection was therefore not quite correct when he wrote in his memoirs some 45 years later about Whymper telling Cowell the story of the catastrophe; 'I was in London that day, and Cowell repeated the story to me. The next morning Whymper's narrative appeared in the *Times*, omitting some things which he had told Cowell.'

There has never been any doubt about Whymper omitting various details from his *Times* letter, but the only things recorded by Browning that were never published by Whymper, come after his reference to Whymper's conversation with the Taugwalders, when they asked not to be paid. 'Thinking that it might be for their interest to get rid of him altogether, Whymper kept his knife ready to cut the rope, if necessary, during the descent of the *arrête*.' Although the idea of getting rid of Whymper has something in common with the reference in his own memorandum of 17.8.65 to 'men who could view the loss of their fellow creatures with such commercial feelings as these, might not, possibly, be ill pleased if I also slipped', Browning's reference to the knife is altogether new and, therefore, open to doubt.

There is, however, no reason to suppose that the contents of the Cowell memorandum made on 1.9.65 were disclosed to anyone other than to Wills before Smythe discovered it, nor is there any basis for Clark's statement: 'But it is certain that as the unsubstantiated, if inferred, libel on the guides seeped out over the years it did Whymper no good'. Whymper's publication in *Scrambles* of the first part of his memorandum of 17th August, which he had recorded on Cowell's advice, is a separate issue and has given rise to its own controversy. Clark refers later in his book to Whymper omitting from *Scrambles* any reference to the Cowell subject matter 'no doubt having second thoughts', but this overlooks altogether the defensive nature of the memorandum. It was only ever intended for use as a shield and not as a sword.

2.12
CROZ, JEAN-BAPTISTE (182? – ?)

The elder brother of Michel Croz, Jean-Baptiste was no stranger to Zermatt, having amongst other expeditions taken part in the first ascent of Castor and of the Dent Blanche, reaching the latter from Zermatt via the Col d'Herens and Bricolla with Kennedy and Wigram. Kennedy had previously had to retreat from the Dent Blanche when Old Peter Taugwalder had lost his nerve, and Wigram recorded some 45 years later how, on Kennedy's return to Zermatt; 'We chatted over the expedition and its failure. I said that I had a man with me (Croz) who would not turn back out of fear; and there and then we agreed, before Kennedy had really finished his supper and before he learned my name, to renew the attack in the following week.'

John Ball included in the 'list of the best known guides' in the original edition of his *Guide to the Western Alps* in 1863:

> 'Jean-Baptiste Croz, and Michel Croz (of Le Tour, near Chamonix). Brothers; well known for the remarkable expeditions in which they have accompanied Messrs. W.Mathews and F.F.Tuckett through a considerable portion of the Graian, Tarentaise, Dauphiné, and Cottian Alps. Both are excellent mountaineers, but Michel is generally considered the bolder of the two.'

In 1865 J-B Croz was employed during the last two weeks of June and the first week of July by F.W.Maclean, who was a friend of Lord Francis Douglas and spent quite a bit of time with him in Zermatt whilst he was waiting for the weather to improve for the Gabelhorn. Croz had therefore already spent some days in Zermatt in July 1865 when, almost three weeks later, he returned there on the evening of Saturday 22nd July in order to collect his brother's belongings. He must have passed Whymper somewhere on the way up the valley, in the vicinity of St.Niklaus, but having never previously spoken to each other nor travelled together they would not have recognised each other, even if they did exchange greetings. In Zermatt Croz collected from Seiler the items detailed in the inventory of his brother's possessions attached to the Enquiry Report, and signed for them on the Sunday morning. These included his brother's hat, omitted from the French translation, and he promised to let Adams Reilly have it. Reilly gave him 100frs from Whymper in respect of his brother's ascent of the Matterhorn, but Whymper paid nothing on account of the work he had done previously, as he had no means of learning what was due. Croz left Zermatt on the Sunday morning.

Adams Reilly had arranged to call on him in Chamonix on his way home early in August and he duly collected the hat in order to take it home for Whymper. On 2nd August *The Times* published a report quoting from an Annecy paper, which seems to be based on an article by Gabriel Loppé in *L'Abeille de Chamonix* of 23rd July, referring to Whymper finding Croz' hat at the scene of the catastrophe. Reilly passed the hat to Whymper, who at some later date seems to have given it back to Seiler, who added it to his collection of relics, eventually taken over by the Zermatt Museum.

Before Reilly returned to London on 12th August and went to see Whymper on the 14th, the latter had corresponded with Woolmore Wigram about a letter J-B Croz had sent to Wigram. Wigram referred to Croz' letter,

> 'in which he speaks of a suspicion prevalent in the Valley of Chamonix, and I fear shared by himself that Taugwald *cut the rope* on the Matterhorn. The grounds for this dreadful charge are the improbability of such a rope breaking and the fact that young Taugwald had just come to Chamonix, whence it was assumed that he was escaping justice...I am writing to Croz to represent the impossibility of such a thing being done without your knowledge;...Still I can not think that anything from me is likely to have the effect in stopping this ghastly and indeed most blameworthy scandal, that a letter from yourself to Croz would have.'

Whymper's reply of 9th August included:

> 'I cannot say that I am altogether surprised at the rumour to which you refer, as there is not amiable feeling (this year particularly) between the guides of Chamounix and the German guides, but the rumour is absolutely without foundation...the rope...has not been tampered with since the accident, indeed it has hardly been handled and it is an absolute certainty that it broke fairly...I will write at once a short note to him to stop this horrible rumour...I think it would be desirable for you to write to Croz as well as myself, and pray give my most positive assurance that there is not the slightest reason for suspecting that there was any foul play.'

Young Peter Taugwalder's visit to Chamonix about a week after the accident is mentioned in an article published by E.N.Buxton in 1866 in the second volume of the *Alpine Journal*. He refers to finding

> 'Taugwald lounging outside the hotel, having just been paid off by his employer, and looking for a return job. As he is a strong lad we engaged him as porter. Just at this time Jean-Baptiste Croz had come back from Zermatt, looking emaciated and almost crazed at the loss of his brother. His grief found vent in wild tales and half-formed accusations against the men who had been with him at the time of his death. The garrulous Frenchmen who listened, sympathized, and believed, and spread these reports, and the morning after engaging Taugwald our guides came to us, and made an abominable accusation, first against him and then against his father and announced that they dare not and would not go with him.'

On the same day that Reilly called to see Whymper (14th August), Whymper received a letter from Alfred Wills referring to a letter McCormick was writing to *The Times* to propose a subscription to build a church as a memorial to Hudson. Wills' letter included: 'But it strikes me there is a subscription wanted for a need much more pressing...and that is for the family of poor Croz...Do you know anyone who would undertake to write and make a similar appeal and collect subscriptions for the family of Croz?'

Whymper himself wrote to *The Times* making the appeal, as well as Wm. Mathews, their letters being published on 19th August, and it seems probable that his action was prompted either by what Adams Reilly had told him about J-B Croz or by a further letter from Wigram. Whymper's letters of 24th and 27th August to Richard Glover and to James Robertson both acknowledge contributions to the fund with a similar comment, that to Glover stating: 'We have been mainly influenced to commence it by the fact that the brother Jean-Baptiste Croz will in all probability have to be placed in confinement as he appears to be going out of his mind'.

Charles Gos quoted in French in his book *Propos d'un Alpiniste* from what he referred to as the text of the appeal in the *Alpine Journal* of September 1865. It relies on information from Wigram, refers to the mental state of J-B Croz and states that Gabriel Loppé, who is spending some time at Chamonix, has been asked to keep an eye on him. However, no such notice was published in the September 1865 *Journal*, but in a separate leaflet, so that not many copies have survived or been bound into *AJ2*. The text included: '[J-B Croz] roams about in the most purposeless manner, moaning and muttering to himself, telling everyone whom he meets that he is Michel's brother, &c. It is to be feared that, if he goes on, he will soon squander what little money the family may possess, and all will reduced to beggary.'

A further letter to *The Times* of 21st November referred to the fund, and Wm. Mathews' letter to the Editor of the *Alpine Journal* published in December 1866 shows how the net total of £278-15s-6d was used. Mathews letter concluded:

> 'The old employers of J-B Croz will be glad to know that he appeared to me to be in good health, and that in a glacier expedition which I made with him, his ancient skill and vigour seemed entirely unimpaired. I feel bound to bear this testimony, as I have observed with much regret that in the last edition of *Ball's Alpine Guide* his name no longer appears in the list of good guides.'

His complete recovery can also be inferred from a new 'Tour round the Breithorn' which Whymper noted in his *Guide to Zermatt* was made on 21st July 1866 by Winkworth with Croz and Peter Perren.

2.13
CROZ, MICHEL-AUGUSTE (1830 – 1865)

> 'Of all the guides with whom I travelled, Michel Croz was the man who was most after my own heart. He did not work like a blunt razor, and take to his toil unkindly. He did not need urging, or to be told a second time to do anything. You had only to say *what* was to be done, and *how* it was to be done, and the work *was* done, if it was possible. Such men are not common, and when they are known they are valued. Michel was not widely known, but

those who did know him came again and again. The inscription that is placed upon his tomb truthfully records that he was "beloved by his comrades and esteemed by travellers".'

So, Whymper wrote early in *Scrambles*, when he was describing his first meeting with the guide with whom he was going to achieve so much in two short seasons. Before parting from him in 1864, Whymper had engaged him for 1865

'but upon writing to him in the month of April to fix the dates of his engagement, I found that he had supposed he was free (in consequence of not having heard from me earlier), and had engaged himself to a Mr. B— from the 27th June. I endeavoured to hold him to his promise, but he considered himself unable to withdraw from his later obligation. His letters were honourable to him...'

There is a letter Whymper sent to Adams Reilly from Breuil on 20th June 1865 which concludes with the sentence 'Croz has become awfully bumptious, not to say fractious', and there may be some other letters that have a bearing on the relations between Whymper and Croz, judging from the final paragraph of the long note with which Farrar concluded the publication of the Official Enquiry Report in 1920. Whymper had wanted to attempt the Hörnli with Croz, Almer and Biner in 1865 but they found themselves unexpectedly checked on the Furggjoch where they arrived shortly after midday on 21st June. After the other two had sought to dissuade Whymper, Croz said 'Sir, if we cross to the other side we shall lose three days, and very likely shall not succeed. You want to make ascents in the chain of Mont Blanc, and I believe they can be made. But I shall not be able to make them with you if I spend these days here, for I must be at Chamonix on the 27th.' Whymper hesitated, it began to snow, and he decided to retreat. They climbed the Grandes Jorasses in order to get a view of the upper part of the Aiguille Verte and then made the first passage of the Col Dolent. Croz now had to leave them although Birkbeck had not yet arrived, and so he missed out on the first ascent of the Aiguille Verte. Whereas Croz may well have known his new employer's plans for the Matterhorn, it seems that any idea that he persuaded Whymper to abandon the Hörnli for that reason can be excluded by the fact that he would also have

Michel-Auguste Croz (1865)

known of the plans for the Verte and by going to Chamonix instead, Whymper was able to make its first ascent before the Kennedy/Hudson party had even assembled in Chamonix.

Of the ascent of the Matterhorn after the chance meeting between Whymper and Croz at Zermatt there is little to be said, except to ask why Croz, who had been with Hadow on Mont Blanc, albeit on a separate rope, did not raise any objection to Hudson's proposal to take him as well, in view of the potential difficulties, Hadow's limited experience and his actual difficulties descending Mont Blanc. Croz would have appreciated Whymper's determination to make the ascent at all costs, particularly if, as is likely, he was told of the attempt already underway from Breuil. It seems clear that until Whymper appeared at Zermatt Hudson had no intention of actually ascending the mountain before the arrival of McCormick, and there would have been no objection to taking Hadow on the initial exploration, but once the two parties agreed to join up the situation changed fundamentally.

The Taugwalders seem to have held Croz responsible for any failure to take any necessary precautions on the descent, yet Young Peter's answer to Montagnier's Question 5 is just too absurd to be taken seriously.

> 'Did old Peter choose the rope used to attach himelf, his son and Mr.Whymper to the rest of the party?
> Old Peter also said the rope would not be strong enough but Michel Croz wanted to have it so and attached Mr.Whymper between the two Taugwalders father and son, for Michel Croz acted as commander of the party.'

As for Old Peter, he told the Enquiry (A53) that he said to Croz 'before we reached the dangerous place that one ought for greater safety to stretch a rope. Croz replied that it was not necessary.' But this was clearly an afterthought, as he had answered the earlier question (Q31) as to whether in his opinion all necessary caution had been exercised at the place where the accident occurred with a 'yes'.

There is no reason to doubt the accuracy of Whymper's belief that, after laying aside his axe in order to take hold of Hadow's legs and put his feet one by one into their proper positions, Croz

> 'was in the act of turning round, to go down a step or two himself; at this moment Mr.Hadow slipped, fell against him, and knocked him over. I heard one startled exclamation from Croz, then saw him and Mr.Hadow flying downwards; in another moment Hudson was dragged from his steps, and Lord F. Douglas immediately after him.'

In his letter to *The Times* and also in the main text of *Scrambles* Whymper did not quote all the facts available to him, and he seems to have had second thoughts later, adding some more details in footnotes including,

> 'Croz was standing by the side of a rock which afforded good hold, and if he had been aware, or had suspected, that anything was about to occur, he might and would have gripped

> it, and would have prevented any mischief. He was taken totally by surprise. Mr.Hadow slipped off his feet on to his back, his feet struck Croz in the small of the back, and knocked him right over, head first. Croz's axe was out of reach, and without it he managed to get his head uppermost before he disappeared from our sight. If it had been in his hand, I have no doubt that he would have stopped himself and Mr.Hadow.'

Old Peter's idea that Croz did not lose his footing until after the rope had broken (A30) could only make sense if Croz had already descended so far below Hadow that he could no longer place his feet for him. But as Old Peter was preoccupied with the rock round which he wound his arms or the rope, he must have looked to it immediately he appreciated there had been a slip. It is not therefore surprising that he told the Tribunal (A63) 'As Mr. Whymper was above me in a place where he could see the unfortunate course of events better than I could, his deposition may be more correct so much so that I could not insist that Croz only fell after the three tourists'. The original French translation of his evidence is incorrect!

Whymper seems to have assumed responsibility for Croz' funeral expenses at Zermatt. He recorded in his diary an item of 20 francs 'Gave for Croz interment' and subequently sent Alexander Seiler 400 francs in respect of the monument. He devoted a lot of time to the monument, as surviving letters show. His diary contains an entry for 1st August 1866 'Made design for tomb of Michel Croz in morning'. There seem to have been two main problems, the principal one being over the land on which the monument would stand, for which an exorbitant demand was made. There is a letter Whymper received from the Curé Welschen in August 1866. It is neatly written in German but virtually impossible for anyone unfamiliar with such script to read. The individual words and even the letters are indecipherable and Whymper seems to have consulted someone on it, to judge from his own handwritten note which includes, 'No doubt a place will be granted for it *if* you pay considerably (or handsomely) for it. Communicate the offer that you will make to me direct and avoid the intervention of a third person and I will see about it.' Whymper seems to have declined the Curé's plea for secrecy and to have sought help from Alexander Seiler. Seiler's letter to Whymper of 16th September suggests that the monument will cost 500 francs, whereas a further letter in April acknowledges 400 francs for the Curé. The monument to Hudson and Hadow seems to have encountered a similar problem as on 7th September 1866 the British Consul at Geneva, Mackenzie, wrote a letter to *The Times* referring to an exorbitant demand for 5000 francs (£200) by the Communal Council of Zermatt and stating his intention of paying no more than a local would pay for the same land.

Whymper's other problem was to choose a suitable inscription. He made a draft and sent it to James Robertson asking if M.Vecqueray would translate it into French. 'I have a lively recollection of the kindness of M.Vecqueray, and I do not call to mind anyone who would be likely to do it so well as he, or who would take the pains that I think he would be likely to exercise.' Robertson and Vecqueray produced three versions, the best one, which Whymper adopted, involving a couple of fundamental amendments to his original. The carving of the letters on the stone is somewhat rough and some of them appear to have been recut at least once unless the inconsistencies result from errors made when touching up photographs. The intended wording 'en témoinage de regret à la perte d'un homme brave' often appeared as 'regret *de* la perte', as in the sketch in Whymper's *Zermatt Guide*, but for the last thirty years there has been nothing between 'regret' and 'la perte'. The last letter on four of the lines has also varied over the years, as appears from a comparison of Charles Gos' record in about 1946 with the present layout, which is in fact consistent with the photograph in Cunningham & Abney's 1887 book. The present wording is:

A LA MEMOIRE
DE
MICHEL AUGUSTE
CROZ
NE AU TOUR VALLEE DE
CHAMOUNIX EN TEM-
OIGNAGE, DE REGRET
LA PERTE D'UN HO-
MME BRAVE, ET DEV-
OUE AIME DE SES CO-
MPAGNONS ESTIME DES
VOYAGEURS, IL PERIT
NON LOIN D'ICI EN HO-
MME DE COEUR ET GUIDE
FIDELE

The Croz monument inscription in 1975

Before leaving Zermatt in July 1865 Whymper gave 100 francs to Adams Reilly to pass to Michel Croz' brother in respect of his fees for the Matterhorn. He was unable to pay anything on account of the work that he had done previously, as he had no means of learning what was due. Whymper also wanted Reilly to ask J-B Croz for his brother's hat, which bore the name of its London supplier and had presumably been given to him by Whymper earlier that year. It is now in the Zermatt Museum having been mentioned by Charles Gos in his book *Alpinisme anecdotique* in 1934, and it is almost certain that Whymper must have given it to Seiler or his son at some stage to add it to his collection of relics. It is possible to trace its travels from the scene of the accident as far as Whymper. It is first mentioned by Gabriel Loppé in *L'Abeille de Chamonix* of Sunday 23rd July 1865 in a letter to the Editor describing the search for the bodies on the glacier. 'Whymper was only able to bring back his valiant guide's hat.' Although it does not feature in the French translation of the inventory of Croz' possessions in the Enquiry Report, it is in the original German, and Reilly made a note in his diary on 22nd July: 'Jean Baptiste Croz came in the evening also Albrecht, gave Croz the 100 francs – he promised to give me Michel's hat'. Reilly collected the hat a fortnight later and when he arrived back in London a note he wrote to Whymper included 'I arrived here last night, bringing for you sundry french journaux, and also poor Croz's hat which his brother gave me in Chamounix'.

Whymper also helped with the subscription raised for the family of Croz, which is referred to here under 'J-B Croz'. Many years later he got Lance Calkin to paint a portrait of Michel Croz and when he sent a copy of it to James Robertson he received in return a sonnet in Croz' memory. William Mathews drew attention in his essay on Croz in *The Pioneers of the Alps* to his appearing prominently in many of the woodcuts in *Scrambles*.

2.14
DOUGLAS, LORD FRANCIS (1847 – 1865)

According to the entry in Mumm, Lord Francis Douglas's climbing career began in 1863 when at the age of 16½ he crossed from Zinal to St.Niklaus by the Col de Tracuit and the Bruneggjoch with Matthäus Zumtaugwald. The climb is mentioned by Ball and it seems that the Bruneggjoch had never been crossed before and the Col de Tracuit had been crossed by travellers only once. Such an obscure and unknown route would make an unusual first expedition for a youngster and it is equally strange to find such a single one way expedition being made from, rather than to, Zinal with a Zermatt guide in the days when relatively few mountaineers passed between the Val d'Anniviers and the Nikolaital. The 1865 SAC article on glacier guides suggests that Zumtaugwald was particularly proud of this expedition, as it is described under his record as 'Turtmangletscher pass from Zinal, north of the Bruneckhorn, discovered by him'. It would make a lot more sense if such an experienced guide, whose climbs included Monte Rosa some 40 times, the Lyskamm three times and the Dom and Mont Blanc once, had climbed with Douglas previously and it seems as though this probably was the case.

Lord Francis Douglas

2.14.1 His climbing record

Douglas was elected to the Alpine Club on December 12th 1864 having been proposed by F.L.Latham and seconded by A.Carr, both of whom were in 1861 assistant masters at Wellington College. Mumm records that Latham had climbed Monte Atelao with Douglas in 1864 and that in 1862 Carr and Latham had done a number of passes together including the Alphubeljoch and the Weisstor with Stephan Zumtaugwald. One hesitates before concluding that Mumm made a major omission but the Alpine Club's record of candidates in the early years shows for Douglas the following far more impressive list of climbs by the end of 1864.

Monte Rosa	Breithorn	Antelao
Adler	Weissthor	Alphubel
Triftjoch	Strahleck	New pass (Zinal to St.Niklaus)

The most logical interpretation of this list seems to be that in 1863 Douglas had gone with Matthäus Zumtaugwald from Zermatt to Zinal via the Triftjoch before returning to St.Niklaus via the 'new pass' and that he had done the Weisstor and the Alphubeljoch along with Carr and Latham in 1862, when he was only 15½. Richard Glover referred in a letter to Whymper in 1865 to his brother 'having taken an excursion or two with Lord Francis Douglas two years ago', and this is supported by the fact that both Douglas and the Rev H.Glover stayed at the Riffelhaus in 1863, even though their entries in the guestbook are a few pages apart. Douglas in fact made two separate entries, the first on 16th July recording a visit with H.Sergeant and the second on 24th August for Douglas alone recording 'Ascended Monte Rosa'. Glover's entry seven pages later may have been made at the end of a long stay. Dangar's note in *AJ73* confirms that Douglas climbed the Adler pass and the Breithorn in 1864, probably in late July if he was still in the Alps on 8th September for the Antelao. Douglas seems to have had at least 7½ weeks holiday abroad in 1864, even if it was not all spent in the Alps. It is interesting to note that he did the Adler pass and the Breithorn in very deep snow with a 20 year old guide Joseph Lauber as well as 'Pierre Perren', although there is nothing to indicate whether this was *the* Peter Perren, who had been with T.S.Kennedy on his winter attempt of the Matterhorn in 1862, or another guide of the same name.

2.14.2 His climbs with Taugwalder

Assuming that Douglas had climbed with Carr and Latham in 1862, he had already climbed from Zermatt during three seasons by the time he reached St.Niklaus on 25th June 1865 and wrote in the hotel visitors book the following day 'Found this hotel as ever clean and good food to be had'. As in 1864 he was employing two guides, and had already climbed the Wetterhorn and the

Mönchjoch with Peter Egger and Peter Inäbnit. He took Inäbnit with him to Zermatt, where with Old Peter Taugwalder as first guide he spent some days trying unsuccessfully to find a way up the Obergabelhorn and in the process making the first ascent of the Untergabelhorn and of the then still nameless Wellenkuppe. Maclean and Lord Melgrund, who were staying at the Hotel Monte Rosa, spent quite a bit of time with Douglas at the Hotel Mont Cervin and learnt of his attempts on the Gabelhorn 'which proved unsuccessful, owing to his Zermatt guide, Taugwald, having led them by a circuitous route'. But they left Zermatt on 3rd July too soon to learn and tell Douglas of the plans of Moore and Horace Walker who arrived at the Monte Rosa on the 4th and on the 6th made the first ascent of the Obergabelhorn with Jakob Anderegg at their first attempt. On the same day Douglas made his second crossing of the Triftjoch from where he saw three men on the summit of the Obergabelhorn, recording in the guestbook of the Hotel Durand in Zinal that he did not know where they had ascended from, as it was not from Zermatt or Zinal. But the following day, 7th July, with Taugwalder and Joseph Viannin, he finally succeeded in his ambition by climbing the Obergabelhorn from Zinal and descending to Zermatt.

Old Peter may have been responsible (judging from what Maclean wrote) for Douglas believing initially that they had previously climbed the Trifthorn and for his including its first ascent amongst the climbs he entered in Inäbnit's Führerbuch on Sunday 2nd July, the day Inäbnit must have left Zermatt. But Dangar & Blakeney have established in an article in the *Alpine Journal* that the first ascent they had made the day before must have been that of the Wellenkupppe. The first stage in Douglas's Gabelhorn campaign seems, therefore, to have ended on the Saturday when he concluded that it was 'utterly impracticable' and we do not know his further movements prior to about the afternoon of Wednesday 5th when he and Old Peter must have set off for Zinal. We do not know what if anything they did on the Monday or Tuesday, beyond Douglas seeing off Maclean and Melgrund at about 8.30 on the Monday morning. Whereas Old Peter may have had some other prior engagement, it is unlikely that the two of them did a climb together as Douglas seems normally to have climbed with two guides. He must have reviewed his plans and decided to try the Gabelhorn from Zinal, which would exclude any idea of Old Peter having then reconnoitred the Hörnli for Douglas, quite apart from the futility and unliklihood of such a venture.

Dangar & Blakeney concluded that Douglas must have left Zermatt before Moore arrived on the evening of Tuesday 4th, as they were unaware of each other's movements, but the explanation may simply be that they were staying in different hotels. It seems probable that Douglas and Old Peter did not leave for Zinal until the Wednesday afternoon, and that as Douglas had already made the crossing in 1863 he did not need a second guide for the Triftjoch and intended to find another one in Zinal. His entry in the guestbook of the Hotel Durand is somewhat confusing and there are slight inconsistencies in the four published versions. It seems however that Farrar was wrong to construe it as meaning that Inäbnit also accompanied Douglas to Zinal, although the latter part of the entry does rather imply his presence. Inäbnit's name must relate only to the ascent of 'another peak of the Gabelhorn', as Douglas had written near the start 'I came here with Peter Taugwald'. Douglas may well have made the entry before finding his second guide Viannin later that day, which could account for the uncertainty in his final words: 'July 7 or 8. Left here to attempt the ascent of Gabelhorn'.

Douglas made an entry in Viannin's Führerbuch describing the expedition as the most laborious he had ever undertaken, but without mentioning the accident on the summit, when he and Taugwalder fell with the cornice and Viannin succeeded in holding them both on the rope. 'He would do for a leader in expeditions with which he was acquainted and makes an *excellent* second under the direction of a good guide in a difficult expedition like the one above mentioned.' His account of the climb written for the *Alpine Journal* and found among his papers in the Mont Cervin (or the Monte Rosa) elaborates further on Viannin, stating he 'makes a good *second* guide in an expedition like this; but if he had been the leader, I may safely say we never should have reached Zermatt'. This somewhat unkind remark suggests that Viannin, whose other achievements included the Weisshorn, Dom, Monte Rosa and the remarkable first ascent of the Besso in 1862 with a fellow guide but no tourist, may have been leading the descent to Zermatt until he made some error and Taugwalder succeeded in putting him right. But it should hardly have been Viannin's responsibility to find the descent route on the Zermatt side, unless Taugwalder was initially so shocked by his accident as to be incapable of doing so. Furthermore on two previous occasions on the Zermatt side, Taugwalder had been incapable of finding the ascent route on the Obergabelhorn. It is indeed strange that Douglas should have emphasised such a relatively minor lapse by Viannin, when he failed to recognise the fault of Taugwalder in choosing to sit on a cornice for lunch.

No one has ever explained or discovered what happened to Old Peter's Führerbuch and it would have been interesting to read Douglas's testimonial. It is however safe to assume that it would have been a very glowing report, judging from the references to Taugwalder in his other accounts. The inference in the Viannin entry is that Taugwalder was 'a good guide' whereas he was not, and the *AJ* article expressly states 'Peter Taugwald acted admirably, and really showed himself a first rate guide'. Certainly Old Peter had at last exercised sound judgment in deciding that the peak could be climbed from Zinal, and he exercised considerable skill in finding the way up, but to disregard the danger presented by the cornice or fail to heed the absence of any footmarks left on it from the Anderegg party the day before was surely negligence. Douglas's misjudgment of the falling cornice accident was perhaps later to cost him his life, as despite Taugwalder's earlier failures, recorded by Maclean, the successful ascent of the Obergabelhorn seems to have given him absolute faith in Taugwalder – unless there is another altogether different explanation.

The description of the accident in the *Alpine Journal* refers to their arriving at the summit:

> 'There we found that some one had been the day before, at least to a point very little below it, where they had built a cairn; but they had not gone to the actual summit, as it was a peak of snow and there were no marks of footsteps. On this peak we sat down to dine, when, all of a sudden, I felt myself go, and the whole top fell with a crash thousands of feet below, and I with it as far as the rope allowed (some 12 feet). Here, like a flash of lightning, Taugwald came right by me some 12 feet more; but the other guide, who had only the minute before walked a few feet from the summit to pick up something, did not go down with the mass, and thus held us both. The weight on the rope must have been about 23 stone, and it is wonderful that, falling straight down without anything to break one's fall, it did not break too. Joseph Viannin then pulled us up and we began the descent to Zermatt.'

It is probable that they followed the Moore/Walker route starting down the north east ridge, from where the day before Moore had found the rocks leading down to the glacier 'much more difficult than they had seemed to us on the ascent: looking from above, the passage of the snow wall on to the rocks below the ridge seemed very formidable'. Douglas described 'having been delayed an hour in leaving the arête to join the rocks where a wall of snow intervened, down which the guides cut a path while I sat on the arête and smoked'. Nevertheless his party took only one hour longer to reach Zermatt despite commencing their descent two hours later and arriving by moonlight.

Douglas probably spent Saturday 8th recuperating in Zermatt, the next record we have of his activities being the entry he made in a hotel guestbook on about 10th July. 'Remained here a fortnight and found everything quite perfect.' From the details of expenses incurred by Whymper, as recorded in his diary, it seems probable that Douglas had paid part of his Mont Cervin hotel bill previously, perhaps at the same time as he paid his guides. This would have involved 'cashing' some £10 or £5 notes, leaving him only one more of each, deposited with the hotel amongst other valuables. A pound was worth twenty five francs at that time and whatever other means Douglas may have had of drawing money in the large towns or cities, the nearest thing he had to a banker in Zermatt must have been his landlord Clemenz. Whymper appears to have settled Douglas's debts after the accident, including an item described as 'Advanced by [Cervin hotel] to him for guide 58 francs'. This suggests that Douglas with the equivalent of 375 francs still deposited with the hotel was allowed credit, with the intention of cashing one or the other of his remaining banknotes when he finally settled with the hotel on his departure.

2.14.3 His plans for the Matterhorn

It has been wrongly assumed by many writers that Douglas still intended to try the Matterhorn in 1865 after climbing the Obergabelhorn and in particular that he had planned to make the attempt some time between Wednesday 12th and

Saturday 15th July, before he ever met Whymper in Breuil on Tuesday 11th. Whereas there seems to be no reason to doubt that he had originally planned to attempt the Matterhorn in 1865, before returning home on the 19th July in time for the 21st birthday celebrations for his brother the Marquess, as subsequently recorded in the *Dumfries Courier*, he must have had to change his plans for several reasons and even the wording of his poem, written on the Sunday or Monday, is inconsistent with any intention to attempt the ascent on the Thursday or Friday. There is furthermore no reason to conclude that he had in mind trying from Zermatt rather than from Breuil, just because we now know that the Zermatt ascent proved to be much easier than had been anticipated. Indeed it may be that Whymper's description of the route from Breuil up to a height of about 13,500 feet, published in the *Alpine Journal* in March 1865, had inspired Douglas to attempt it himself. His failure to plan any route for climbing the Obergabelhorn seems to exclude any possibility of his having given any close consideration to the best route on the Matterhorn.

It may be doubted whether Old Peter Taugwalder would have been too keen to try the Matterhorn so soon after having so nearly lost his life the previous Friday, when he fell some 25 feet and the rope held. But even so, who could Douglas have taken as his second guide and how could he have afforded to pay them by Old Peter's standards, when by the Sunday he had scarcely 300 francs left? His ascent of the Obergabelhorn must have cost him three times as much as he had expected. It had also taken him far longer than he would ever have anticipated. Old Peter seems to have been dissatisfied with 120 francs for the actual ascent of the Matterhorn, telling Parker that 'he was promised a much larger sum and would never have run so much risk for the payment he received', and it will be recalled that when he offered to accompany Whymper on the Matterhorn from Breuil in 1861 he wanted 200 francs whether they reached the summit or not.

It looks as though Douglas spent Sunday 9th in or around Zermatt intending to cross the Theodule to Breuil on the Monday, return on the Tuesday, settle his bill at the Mont Cervin, collect his belongings which were already packed and make his way down the valley, probably spending another night at St.Niklaus on the way. His passage to Breuil may have been delayed for 24 hours by bad weather. He spent the Monday night at the Riffelhaus and he probably spent the Sunday night there as well, as many travellers seem to have stayed there when crossing the Theodule, but what must be certain is that he had vacated his room at the Mont Cervin either on the Sunday or the Monday, as when he stayed in Zermatt again on the Wednesday night he seems to have stayed at the Monte Rosa without disturbing his luggage at the Mont Cervin. Whymper subsequently paid 40.25 francs in respect of 'His bill at Cervin hotel' and he also 'Paid for Douglas at M.Rosa' 8.50frs, making a total outlay of 121.75frs including the advanced guides fees and Joseph Taugwalder's 15frs for the Theodule.

It has been wrongly supposed that Douglas spent a fortnight at the Monte Rosa

The Riffelhaus and the Matterhorn in 1865

hotel, although the guestbook entry 'Remained here a fortnight and found everything quite perfect' was made in a different type of book from that used at the Monte Rosa, in which seven of the columns on each page bear a heading. Furthermore the inventory of Douglas's belongings and valuables attached to the Official Enquiry Report records that they were at the Mont Cervin, whereas the other victims' belongings were all at the Monte Rosa and their valuables had been entrusted to Alexander Seiler. The misunderstanding seems to have stemmed from Douglas spending the night of the 12th July at the Monte Rosa, where his brother also stayed during the last week in July.

It would seem therefore that the guestbook entry which has been displayed in the Zermatt Museum for many years must have come from the book of the Mont Cervin, where Douglas had spent a fortnight or so, but this is not in fact so. The Mont Cervin book has been lost or mislaid and we may never know what, if anything, Douglas wrote in it. The entry in fact comes from the Riffelhaus book, which seems almost to raise more problems than it solves. Douglas did not date his entry, but the next two are dated 10th and 11th July, which fits in with his one or two nights stay on the way to Breuil. For some unaccountable reason he gives the impression that he had stayed at the Riffelhaus for a fortnight, which cannot have been the case. Maclean refers expressly to visiting him at the Mont Cervin early in his stay at Zermatt and the advance for guides fees, the deposit of cash and the outstanding bill seem to account for the later part of his stay, quite apart from the fact that no one would sensibly move his base up to the Riffelhaus in order to explore the Obergabelhorn. The word 'here' must have been referring to Zermatt rather than to the Riffelhaus, despite the fact that a guest usually pays compliments to his host in such a book. The possibility that the book was in the

Mont Cervin when Douglas made his entry can be excluded by other entries made by Seiler guests such as T.S.Kennedy on 20th June and the Parkers on 4th August, and the explanation for the wording may simply be that he had forgotten to make any entry at the Mont Cervin. There were in fact two guestbooks in use in 1865 at the Riffelhaus, the entries by Douglas, Kennedy, Bailey and the Parkers etc being in the large one, whereas Girdlestone, Yeats Brown and the Martin/Gautier party used the small one, with Prior using both! The reason for the overlap is not apparent as although the large one does contain some drawings and verses, the small one also makes occasional reference to an ascent.

One of the consequences of Douglas travelling on his own and not staying at the Hotel Monte Rosa (the Clubroom of Zermatt) must have been that he was a bit out of touch with what was going on. In the same way that Moore and Walker reached the summit of the Gabelhorn without his knowledge, although he had been trying to achieve the same thing for ten days without success, he would probably not have been familiar with all the previous attempts to climb the Matterhorn. It is easy to overlook that before 1865, and indeed before Whymper assembled details of the early attempts and included them in *Scrambles*, very little had been published about the attempts from Breuil and that mostly in the *Athenaeum*, a weekly periodical, apart from Hawkins' account of his 1860 attempt with Tyndall. Nevertheless there were channels through which Douglas could have heard of J-A Carrel as the most determined of the guides at Breuil and it is safe to assume that the purpose of his visit to Breuil was to make contact with Carrel or some other guide there, with a view to making an attempt on the Matterhorn from Breuil in 1866. The possibility of Douglas contemplating an attempt from Breuil later that week can be excluded by his having arranged to return to Zermatt the following day and by the need for him to leave Zermatt on the Saturday at the very latest in order to get home for his brother's 21st birthday. There is no reason whatever to suppose that he had in mind asking Carrel to join him in an attempt on the Hörnli. Quite apart from the question of national pride which was unlikely to allow Carrel to make the first ascent from Switzerland, although he did ultimately make the first ascent from Breuil via the upper part of the Swiss owned Zmutt ridge, there is no reason why Douglas should have rated a comparatively unknown Italian guide, who only found fame after his first ascent from Breuil, higher than the several Swiss guides already known to him or others of good reputation, who were readily available.

The weather was bad at Breuil on Sunday 9th July and also on the Monday, but Douglas was able to make his postponed trip on the Tuesday with Old Peter's second son Joseph. Whymper tells us nothing of the purpose of Douglas's visit to Breuil, but after recounting how he told him his story and how he arranged that Joseph should assist in transporting his baggage to Zermatt on the morrow he writes that 'Lord Francis Douglas expressed a warm desire to ascend the mountain, and before long it was determined that he should take part in the expedition'. Graham Brown seems wrongly to have convinced himself, although there is no evidence to support him, that Douglas was about to attempt the Matterhorn with Old Peter, who was still in his employment and had been sent to reconnoitre the Zermatt ridge before the weather broke. He guessed that the purpose of his dash to Breuil was that he might find J-A Carrel and engage 'that great guide's' services for his attempt, in addition to Old Peter.

So far as Old Peter's so-called reconnaisance is concerned, he was a reliable Monte Rosa guide of considerable experience and with over 85 ascents to his credit. Aged 45 and active in the mountains all his life, he had been guiding for many years, his earliest mention in Alpine literature being in 1851. Only three years before climbing with Douglas he had been with Kennedy on his winter attempt and it hardly seems inappropriate, that he should have told Douglas that he had 'lately' been beyond the Hörnli and thought an ascent was possible on that side, particularly if he had been trying to encourage Douglas to give him further employment. There is in fact no evidence that Old Peter was still in Douglas's employment nor that he had been sent to reconnoitre. Only Joseph Taugwalder's fees were outstanding at his death and having regard to their repeated attempts on the Gabelhorn, including retreats due to rain, there was no time for Douglas to despatch Old Peter and in any event he would surely have accompanied him on any such venture.

It has been said that Old Peter was the only one who believed all along that the Zermatt ridge could be climbed, but again there is no evidence to support this. Just assuming that he had made a reconnaissance, what might he have achieved and what did he actually achieve? Without going to the shoulder or at least far beyond the height of about 11,000 ft he had reached with Kennedy, he could not have achieved anything worthwhile as no one should ever have seriously doubted the feasibility of the ridge below the shoulder and we know in fact from Leslie Stephen that Old Peter had told him (probably in 1860) that it would be tolerably easy to climb as far as the shoulder. As for his actual achievement, there is no sign of his having learnt anything more than he learnt in 1862, as when Whymper's party reached a suitable site for a tent platform slightly higher than Kennedy's cairn, Croz and Young Peter 'went on to see what was above, in order to save time on the following morning'. This would hardly have been necessary had Old Peter been far beyond only days before, nor would their report of 'not a difficulty, not a single difficulty' have revealed anything new. It seems quite clear that no one had seen at close quarters the difficulties that lay ahead, above the shoulder. If, contrary to the evidence, Old Peter did make some sort of reconnaissance after going beyond the Hörnli in 1862 with Kennedy and Perren, it must have been a waste of time and must have achieved nothing that he had not already guessed about the likely nature of the ridge when it was free from snow.

2.14.4 His ascent of the Matterhorn

Whymper had stayed at the Hotel Monte Rosa three weeks earlier and he returned there on Wednesday 12th. Douglas clearly dined with Whymper that night at the Monte Rosa, along with Girdlestone, and there seems little doubt from indirect evidence that he also spent the night there. Whymper subsequently paid Douglas's bill of 8.50frs, as already noted, which in those days would have covered dinner, bed and breakfast, and not just dinner. But the main evidence comes from the Coolidge archives in Zürich, quoted by Clark. Coolidge's aunt Meta Brevoort may possibly have recorded that Douglas stayed at the Monte Rosa with the rest of the party on the Wednesday night, but she certainly seems to have recorded how the Marquess of Queensberry 'would stay in the same room and bed his brother had occupied', and there is no doubt that although the Marquess and Hadow's uncle seem to have intended to stay at the Mont Cervin they in fact stayed at the Monte Rosa, where they duly entered their names in the guestbook.

There is only one point to mention about Douglas's actual climbing on the Matterhorn. Whymper wrote of him, 'He was nimble as a deer, and was becoming an expert mountaineer' and, in a letter to Richard Glover of 18th August, 'A more excellent walker and promising mountaineer I never came across'. Young Peter Taugwalder on the other hand said in his 'Narrative' in 1917 in relation to climbing the shoulder: 'But Douglas in front of me had great difficulty in putting his feet down in the steps and several times he slipped. However, I held his legs firm in the steps with my hands almost all the time.' Although Dangar & Blakeney considered the evidence of Douglas's climbing ability in an article in 1957 and did not reject Young Peter's comment, it seems probable that he was confused by the presence of two Douglases in the party and that he was in fact referring to Douglas Hadow, whom Hudson at least is likely to have addressed by his Christian name. It is significant that Young Peter does not identify the person who slipped on the descent, nor does he refer elsewhere in his 'Narrative' to the real Hadow's rock climbing ability, whereas his father described Hadow at the Enquiry as 'a very bad climber'. Dangar & Blakeney in fact rejected the double Douglas theory in their review of Clark's book *The Day the Rope Broke* stating that it was unconvincing for Clark to suggest that Young Peter was referring to Douglas Hadow as the bad climber, as he had referred to Hadow by name only a few lines before.

But there is another incident which seems to be attributable to Young Peter's confusion over the two Douglases, namely the account of the accident in the *Journal de Genève* of 18th July. Without going into all the details here, it is apparent that this French report was based on an interview with Young Peter, whereas the German report in *Der Bund* of 19th July was based on Old Peter's account, neither being consistent with any information that Seiler or anyone else at the Monte Rosa might have disclosed to a reporter. *Der Bund* stated that 'the Englishman immediately behind the leading guide...slipped' (consistent with Old Peter's Answer 30 at the Enquiry), whereas the *Journal de Genève* stated they were 'climbing down...when Lord Fr. Douglas chanced to slip, and imparting a violent jerk to the rope, he dislodged in turn Messrs Haddo and Hudson and the whole party was swept down...' It is furthermore inconceivable that Old Peter should have made such a mistake after spending more than a week with Lord Francis Douglas trying to climb the Gabelhorn. Yet another example of the double Douglas confusion appears in *L'Abeille de Chamonix* of 23.7.65 which refers wrongly to Lord Douglas, and not Douglas Hadow, having climbed Mont Blanc with Hudson, Kennedy and McCormick on the 7th July. An account of the Matterhorn accident by Stéphen d'Arve in the same number refers to Lord Douglas slipping, dragging down Hudson, who was held by Croz until the third tourist Mr.Haddo fell in turn, breaking the rope etc. It is quite clear that Douglas Hadow was mistakenly being called Lord Douglas. The final words on Lord Francis Douglas's climbing ability should therefore be those of Whymper in his letter to *The Times*,

> 'Although young, he was a most accomplished mountaineer, hardly ever required the slightest assistance, and did not make a single slip throughout the day. He had only a few days before we met made the ascent of the Gabelhorn – a summit considerably more difficult, I believe, to reach than the Matterhorn itself.'

2.14.5 The sashline

No one knows for certain why Old Peter used the sashline, the weakest of the three ropes, to tie himself to Douglas, who as the fourth man on the leading rope must already have been tied by Croz with the brand-new Manilla or other equally strong rope. The answer to this question is not necessarily the same as the answer to the equally vital question as to why Douglas condoned 'the employment of a rope so greatly inferior in strength when there were more than two hundred and fifty feet of the better qualities still remaining out of use'.

A number of critics have sought to say that Old Peter would not have known one rope from another and that no one told him that the plaited rope or sashline had only been taken on the climb in order to be cut up and used as fixed rope, as it in fact was after the accident. But these critics have overlooked Taugwalder's own evidence at the Enquiry (A53 and A24) which shows that he very much had in mind the need to fix ropes during the descent and that he distinguished the plaited rope from the rope linking Croz with Douglas, which he described in A26 as 'a strong and brand-new rope', by saying that he tied himself to Lord Douglas with 'a special rope'. Whatever the original intentions of the party with regard to roping on the descent, before it was decided that Whymper and Young Peter should follow the others after leaving names in a bottle, they ended up as a rope of seven with Douglas at the centre. The contrast in the appearance of the two ropes tied to him, a well used thinner plaited rope or sashline and the almost brand-new thicker twisted rope, must have been very obvious to Douglas, particularly if, before Old Peter tied on his rope, Croz had tied his rope on to Douglas and had then tied on Hudson and Hadow before tying on himself and securing any spare length remaining. If in fact Croz tied on to Douglas after Old Peter had done the same, then Croz and possibly Hudson as well would also have been aware that the weaker plaited rope had been used.

Some critics have also suggested that Whymper made too much of the difference between the plaited and the twisted ropes, but this overlooks the publication in July/September 1864 of the Report of the Alpine Club's Special Committee on ropes etc. Whymper referred in chapter 20 of *Scrambles* to the Committee being appointed to test and to report upon the most suitable ropes for mountaineering purposes and he mentioned that the Manilla and Italian hemp ropes approved would sustain a weight of 168lbs falling 10 feet or 196lbs falling 8 feet. Unfortunately the Editor of the 6th edition of *Scrambles* in 1936 saw fit to delete Whymper's reference to the report, with the result that any reader not familiar with an earlier edition may be unaware of the report's existence. The significance of the report lies in the Committee's preliminary test in which they rejected any rope which would not bear 168lbs (12 stone) falling 5 feet. 'Under this trial, all those plaited ropes which are generally supposed to be so strong, and many most carefully made twisted ropes, gave way in such a manner as was very startling to some of our number, who had been in the habit of using these treacherous cords with perfect and most unfounded confidence.' The Report was not published in the *Alpine Journal* until September 1864, and the June 1865 *Journal* commented 'As this report was not published till late in the season it is probable that its contents were never made known to the very persons who ought to know them best, the guides, who in practice arrange the rope for a party'. It seems therefore highly probable that at the start of the 1865 season most guides were still unaware of the weakness of plaited ropes and of other details in the Report.

Douglas was a keen and ambitious mountaineer, but at the age of 18 with only three previous Alpine seasons he had not yet acquired as much experience as his rivals, as is shown by the comparative ease with which Moore and Walker beat him to the first ascent of the Gabelhorn. He joined the Alpine Club in December 1864 and would almost certainly have read the September 1864 number of the *Alpine Journal* from cover to cover. It started with the Report of the Special Committee on ropes, axes and alpenstocks and it seems inconceivable that he would not have studied it keenly and carefully and heeded it in so far as he could. In addition to the extracts quoted above, it should be noted that the Committee found that none of the ropes tested, 'the heaviest which can be conveniently carried about in the Alps', would bear 14 stone falling 10 feet.

Ball points out in his 1863 *Guide to the Western Alps* that a guide is expected 'to find himself in the articles requisite for his profession such as rope', and when Douglas engaged Taugwalder at the end of June 1865 the latter would almost certainly have provided the rope. There is no evidence as to whether the rope was a plaited one or not, but let us for the present assume that it was, as if Taugwalder had ever possessed any such rope he is unlikely to have discarded it by June 1865. Douglas would no doubt have suggested that it was inadequate, recalling the AC

Committee's Report, but if the 45 year old guide had replied to the effect that there might be some weak plaited ropes but his was a really strong one and his own practical experience was to be preferred to the secondhand reports of those whose recommendations were only based on theory and contrived tests, the keen and ambitious 18 year old would have had little alternative but to accept the plaited rope.

Amongst Douglas's belongings was found the account he had written for the *Alpine Journal* describing his ascent of the Gabelhorn with Taugwalder and Viannin on 7th July, exactly a week before the Matterhorn accident. His description of the accident has been quoted already, but it is worth looking again at what he said about the actual fall:

> 'On this peak we sat down to dine, when, all of a sudden, I felt myself go, and the whole top fell with a crash thousands of feet below, and I with it as far as the rope allowed (some 12 feet). Here, like a flash of lightning, Taugwald came right by me some 12 feet more; but the other guide who had only the minute before walked a few feet from the summit to pick up something, did not go down with the mass, and thus held us both. The weight on the rope must have been about 23 stone, and it is wonderful that, falling straight down without anything to break one's fall, it did not break too.'

Douglas's reference to the distance they fell and to the weight on the rope seems to confirm his familiarity with the Committee's Report, particularly when he expresses wonder that the rope did not break. So if the rope involved in the Gabelhorn was indeed a plaited one, Douglas would thereafter have had perfect confidence in such a rope. And so would Taugwalder. Douglas's tribute to Taugwalder in the same article reveals a certain lack of mountaineering judgment or experience, when he states 'Peter Taugwald acted admirably, and really showed himself a first rate guide'. This fails to take account of the folly of lunching on a cornice but could in fact be based, at least in part, on Taugwalder's assurance that the plaited rope was a good rope, if indeed such a rope was involved.

Extrapolating from the AC test results, it would seem as though no rope either twisted or plaited would sustain 12 stone falling 12 feet. This may have almost been the force of Douglas's own fall, which was followed immediately by the further shock on the same stretch of rope of some 12 stone of Taugwalder falling a total of 24 feet. Even if the Douglas – Viannin rope absorbed some of the initial shock by cutting into the snow slope away from the cornice and if Douglas only fell about 8 feet vertically, the force could still equal if not exceed the theoretical capacity of all the plaited and many of the twisted ropes tested by the Committee. But Taugwalder's 12 stone free fall of 20 to 24 feet seems to be beyond doubt and his half of the rope therefore sustained and withstood twice the maximum load calculated in the tests on twisted ropes, disregarding any resilience that remained in the other half after the shock load Douglas had imparted to it only a moment before.

It would be wrong to impute to Taugwalder too great an understanding of the qualities of ropes of different construction. He would however no doubt recognise a rope of the type with which he was familiar and conversely might reject the unfamiliar in favour of that of which he had experience, particularly in the case of a rope that had saved his life. The balance of probabilities seems therefore to favour his familiarity with plaited rope as if a twisted rope had saved his life on his last climb exactly a week before the ascent of the Matterhorn, he would surely have insisted on using one of the almost new twisted ropes that was readily available, rather than an elderly looking and obviously thinner plaited rope. The Gabelhorn accident should have served to remind Taugwalder that danger can present itself unexpectedly and there would be no reason for him to assume that he was immune from risks such as stonefall, so that if he had been hit and had fallen (before Douglas asked Whymper to tie on to Taugwalder) any deliberate use of a weak rope could have endangered himself. It therefore looks as though he may well have chosen to use the plaited rope on the Matterhorn because he had been carrying it ready to use as fixed rope and because he honestly believed in the light of a similar looking rope saving his life on the Gabelhorn the week before that it was the equal of, if not superior to, the brand-new twisted ropes.

Whatever went through Taugwalder's mind as he attached the special rope to Douglas, what would the situation be as far as Douglas was concerned? Croz would already have tied the end of the twisted Manilla or the stouter and probably stronger rope round his waist, when Taugwalder decided to attach the end of the special rope. The superficial contrast between the two ropes must have been blatantly obvious to Douglas. He could not have forgotten his miraculous escape on the Gabelhorn and if it had been attributable to the use of a thicker, twisted rope then no matter how great his exhilaration at having made the first ascent of the Matterhorn he would surely have objected to Taugwalder using the obviously inferior, old and thinner plaited rope, which he would know had been taken on the climb for use as fixed rope. The *Dumfries Courier* reported that he had in April 1865 come first out of 119 seeking direct commissions in the Army, gaining some 8% more marks than any other candidate, and it seems reasonable to conclude that he was exceptionally intelligent and would both have recognised and objected to a situation that involved unnecessary danger. But if it had been a plaited rope that saved his life on the Gabelhorn, it is understandable that he should have been prepared to allow Taugwalder to use a similar rope on the Matterhorn, as in such a large and for the most part competent party it would have seemed inconceivable that the rope would ever have had to sustain a load anywhere near that of a 12 stone man falling 20 feet or more.

Whereas one should be able to exclude the possibility that Douglas encouraged Taugwalder to use the plaited rope, he lost two separate opportunities of insisting on a twisted rope. His exhilaration must have worn off by the time he asked Whymper to tie on to Old Peter saying, according to Whymper, that 'he feared ...Taugwalder would not be able to hold his ground if a slip occurred'. It would have been so easy to ask Whymper to lower enough strong twisted rope for him to attach himself to it as well, if he had any doubt about the security of the 'special' rope. It seems therefore that both Taugwalder and Douglas had good reason to suppose (albeit wrongly) that the plaited rope was as strong as the others.

For the sake of completeness, mention should be made of the 1951 article by R.P.Mears 'Experience with climbing ropes', which suggests that the 1864 tests may have been unduly severe on the ropes if cast iron weights were used, as they would not be representative of the weight of a human body. This does not however mean that the Committee's findings were worthless, although it may help to explain why the rope did not break on the Gabelhorn, whether it was of twisted or of plaited construction. The real value of the Report was to draw attention to the relative strength of different climbing ropes and the need to employ the best available. It was the apparently unjustifiable use of the weakest rope, which then broke, that led those familiar with the facts of the accident to call for an explanation. As Whymper put it in a letter to Woolmore Wigram on 9th August 1865, 'How it came to pass that the weakest rope was used between Taugwald and Lord Douglas I have no idea, that is, I have no idea why he did not use the stronger ropes. Still, I have no reason to suspect even that this was done *intentionally.*'

It seems probable that, when Douglas was recovering from the exertions of the Gabelhorn climb and then waiting for the weather to improve so as to cross the Theodule pass to Breuil, composing his poem on the Matterhorn and writing his article for the *Alpine Journal*, he would also have written home to report his success and his lucky escape, particularly as it was his mother's birthday on 14th July. But it seems that we shall never know whether in his letter he commented on the remarkable rope supplied by his guide, as any such document is no longer in existence. The only hope is that he may have made some reference to the rope in Old Peter's Führerbuch, if it should still exist.

2.14.6 Other matters

A number of other doubtful references to Douglas in Alpine literature that merit comment relate to possible links between the Queensberry and Hadow families and also between Douglas and Charles Hudson, there being no possible substance in the absurd report soon after the accident that Whymper owed him money. Alfred Ceresole, the Vevey priest who wrote a Zermatt guidebook, stated that Hadow's mother came from the Douglas family, but he quoted no authority or further detail. Douglas Hadow's father was in fact Patrick Douglas Hadow, but no one seems to have suggested any possible link there. A more remarkable statement, again lacking details as well as comment, is made by Arnold Lunn in a footnote in his book *Matterhorn Centenary*. After giving some details of the Hadow family Lunn concludes, 'At the time of the accident Charles Hudson was tutoring Douglas Hadow, having previously tutored Lord Francis Douglas. The

Queensberry and Hadow families were close friends and neighbours'. All we know for certain is that by July 1865 Hadow was not a pupil of Hudson, but a former pupil, nevertheless Hadow's uncle Henry and Lord Queensberry did both arrive in Zermatt on 24th July and may have liaised together, although Queensberry and his companion Stevenson left on 29th July whereas Hadow remained in Zermatt until 31st July. If Lord Francis Douglas was a former pupil of Hudson's or if he and Hadow were friends or acquaintances, either fact might have had a considerable bearing on the question as to why Hadow was taken on the climb. But Girdlestone and even McCormick would surely have commented on such a chance encounter, even if Whymper did not. It would seem therefore as though Lunn is wrong again.

The body of Douglas was never found, but gave rise to considerable speculation even before his sister Florence Dixie wrote to the press in 1905. She was primarily concerned with the idea that the Zmutt glacier should yield up her brother's body 'in a perfect state of preservation and easily recognisable' 40 years after the accident, but her letter to the *Daily Graphic* has wider implications and helps to explain her mother's telegram to McCormick and also Ronald Clark's quotation of Newman Hall referring to John Tyndall's daring plan in August 1865 to search for the body. 'He told me that the mother of Lord Douglas had a morbid idea that her son was still alive on the rocks. He knew this to be impossible.' Florence Dixie told in great detail how on the night of the accident she and her mother were staying in London and their maid kept appearing as if she had been called. Each time she was sent away but on the fourth occasion she was in a very agitated state declaring that in a dream or vision she had seen Lord Francis lying on a rocky ledge on a great precipice, terribly wounded. A few days later news came of the accident.

There is some evidence that in August and Sepember 1867 Leighton Jordan saw some remains of the accident. In 1957 Dangar & Blakeney quoted from a letter his sister had written in 1871 to Tyndall, in which she said her brother found several vestiges of the accident, 'the ice axe of Michel Croz, I believe, and other articles, and my brother felt confident that he could distinguish the missing body hanging over a ledge of rock, but thought it would only tend to harrow the feelings of his friends did he make it known'. Dangar & Blakeney commented 'The claim to have seen Lord Francis's body was never put out by Jordan himself and must be viewed with some doubt'. There is however some additional contemporary evidence of Jordan reporting having seen something, in that Chanoine Carrel recorded in 1868 how Jordan 'had thought he saw some scraps of clothing and other things on some sort of projection on the terrible precipice, but then fresh snow covered everything and he saw nothing more'. Only Jordan's diary, should it still be in existence, could throw further light on what he thought he saw and on whether the body of Lord Francis Douglas did get caught in the upper rocks. But, if it never in fact fell as far as the glacier, it would surely have been spotted by the eight eagles seen by the Parker brothers at the end of July

1865, and mentioned in Sandbach's letter to J.D.Forbes, so that Jordan could never have seen anything more than bones.

2.15
DOWNTON, REV HENRY (1818 – 1885)

Downton was the English chaplain at Geneva, who had assisted Hudson in 1861 after Birkbeck had his 1767ft fall from the Col de Miage. Clark recounts how he was sent to Zermatt almost immediately news of the Matterhorn accident reached Geneva and he despatched his report on 20th July. He assisted McCormick with the burial service and McCormick spent a while with him and his family at Geneva on his way home from Zermatt, at the beginning of August.

2.16
ELLIOTT, REV JULIUS MARSHALL (1841 – 1869)

Unlike most of the Alpine pioneers Elliott's climbing career started in the English Lake district. His name appears in the Riffelhaus guestbook in July 1865, about a week after the Matterhorn accident, with that of C.A.Elliott of the Bengal Civil Service, who may have been a brother, but there is no indication of their having made any climb. 1866 appears to have been his first serious Alpine season, but by the time he turned to the Matterhorn at the end of July 1868 he had accomplished a great deal, mostly with Franz Biner. Like Leighton Jordan, who was the first man to tread the whole of both the Zermatt and Breuil routes on the Matterhorn but whose climbing origins are unknown, Elliott seems to have possessed remarkable self-confidence on the mountains. His death on the Schreckhorn in 1869 resulted from his foolish insistence on not being roped at the time. Coolidge met him early in July 1868 in the Gleckstein cave, and subsequently wrote of his determination to climb the Matterhorn and of how his achievement a fortnight later 'proved that the expedition was not so absolutely certain to end fatally as had been imagined by many'.

Franz Biner was not prepared to accompany him on the Matterhorn even after their ascent of the Weisshorn, about which Elliott commented, 'The work on the Weisshorn is spoken of as so hard, and I found it so easy, though the descent was very difficult, that I got a higher, perhaps vainer, idea of my powers'. The reason for Biner's refusal seems to have been his 68 year old mother, but, after Elliott had tried to persuade him to go as far as the shoulder, he said

> ' "I will speak again to my mother." In the afternoon he returned with a sad and wistful look, and said, "No, sir; I cannot go. My mother cried much when I spoke of it, and said, Do not go, Franz, I entreat thee. Do not go." I at once responded, "That settles the question; don't go on any account; you have done quite right to make that resolve." And so it

happened that I found myself, on July 24, 1868, without my own trusty guide, making arrangements with two men who knew nothing of me, and of whom I knew nothing, who had not been up the Matterhorn or any really dangerous mountain, and of whose capacity to render help when wanted, my opinion did not increase upon experience.'

This account in his *Memoir* is amplified considerably in the lengthy letter he wrote the day after his ascent to a friend, Mr. Wood. It may well be that this was the Rev R. Wood, mentioned by Long as having been lunching at the Monte Rosa hotel in Zermatt when Whymper's party was first seen on the summit, and who subsequently joined Long's party at his own request in order to climb the Dom. Elliott had read Jordan's account in the Monte Rosa guestbook;

'In this he fully bore out our view that this side is the easiest, and he found a means of ascent all the way along the arête by which he avoided the dangerous place where the accident happened. This greatly encouraged me, and – must I confess it? (you will have already guessed it) – I sanguinely hoped to find my way alone from the shoulder to the top and back. At any rate whether guides were found to try it or whether I tried alone and failed, I thought it a pity to turn back when the thing seemed feasible.'

A little later he writes 'I was alone and all Zermatt against me; not a Zermatt guide would go'. He then set off with a porter, reaching the hut in seven hours. 'So easy did the work seem I fancied I could have got up in three hours from the hut and half determined to try. But though I succeeded beyond my expectations and reached a point not 2000ft. below the summit the cries of the men in the hut to me to return were so incessant that for mere peace and quietness I returned.' He managed to persuade Peter Knubel and J-M Lochmatter, who had just completed the construction of the hut, to accompany him. 'The hut is comfortable enough, built solidly of stone and boarded inside, as solidly that is, as anything can be without mortar...They had just finished the hut; there were four lazy fellows, soon joined by three others.'

Elliott was somewhat critical of Knubel for insisting on leaving two of the three stocks at the foot of the tallest crag, despite his remonstrating saying they would want them above; 'one other complaint I had to make against Knubel – that he held the rope and would not tie it when I bade him, saying it was safer so, which, of course, was false'. After describing the view from the summit he says:

'We remained but a short time at the top, for the guides begged me at once to descend while the snow was good, and I think they began now to realise their mistake; for now we had to descend snow slopes of 45° with an abrupt descent at the end, full of the recollection of what happened at the first ascent, and with but one axe to stop the fall of three...I went first, slowly and steadily, planting my feet deep and using my hands to grasp the firm crust of frozen snow behind; the others followed, one only moving at a time. It was slow work, and their clumsiness made it slower. I really never saw men so little practised in snow and rockwork. Would you believe it, they came down all the snow, and all the rock, and all the ice backwards, with their faces turned towards the slope; long time had I again for enjoying the view as I waited for them...it was perhaps wise to take extraordinary precautions with

> such recollections as crowded one's memory. But, unfortunately the men did not know the difficult from the easy, and took as great precautions on the one as on the other.'

Elliott's letter was first published in *The Field* sometime in 1910, where the Editor added a note stating 'Mr.Whymper entirely dissociates himself from the opinion expressed by Mr.Elliott concerning the experience and capabilities of the guides, for Lochmatter was a competent mountaineer, and Peter Knubel, says Mr.Whymper, is still alive and in working order at 75 years of age, having made more than a hundred ascents of the Matterhorn'. Ronald Clark has also come to the guides' defence against Elliott's charges, but it should be borne in mind that in July 1868 Knubel in particular had very little experience of serious climbing. They soon built up experience and skill thereafter and became leading guides, but their very considerable achievement in accompanying Elliott on the first complete ascent from Zermatt since the accident was their willingness to do so, because, as Clark has described it, they thereby 'erased in a single day much of the reputation which had still clung to the Matterhorn'.

As already noted, Jordan had encouraged Elliott with his account. He described the vicinity of the accident as 'these glorious slopes' and helped to put the difficulties into their proper perspective. Elliott likewise was taking a realistic view when he commented on the chief difficulty of the expedition, 'it was not more difficult than many rocks which I have climbed alone in Cumberland', although he may have been somewhat ahead of his time. Elliott told Wood that he reached Zermatt at 4.23p.m., before anyone expected him and so avoided recognition. This was half an hour before his guides, having got tired of waiting for them perpetually stopping to eat or rest. It is not entirely consistent with what Théophile Gautier wrote of the returning caravan.

One further aspect of Elliott's account, relating to the arts, is his reference to 'turning the corner at the base of the final peak to get on to the northern side. It is as unlike Whymper's picture as anything I have ever seen.' The Editor of *The Field* noted that Whymper 'has no recollection of having shown or of having made any drawings at the point referred to by Mr.Elliott, who may possibly have had in his mind two drawings by Gustave Doré which were lithographed and circulated extensively, but had nothing to do with Mr.Whymper.' Whereas we do not know precisely what Whymper said to *The Field*, there is reason to believe that he did provide Doré with some sort of sketch in about September 1865, and it may well be that Elliott had heard of this and supposed that Whymper had drawn the base of the final peak. It seems more likely, however, that Whymper provided little more than the general shape of the upper part of the mountain, as Doré's published lithographs had to bear some resemblance to the original drawings he exhibited in Paris within a month of the accident. Whymper in a letter to Hadow's father referred to the originals as 'these drawings, which I have been informed by a friend are grossly inaccurate in almost every particular'. The subject is considered in greater detail in section 3.8 (Illustrations) where the sources are also given.

When Thioly was having difficulty in finding guides for the Matterhorn in Zermatt at the end of July 1868, he engaged Knubel and Lochmatter for the ascent, but some hours later they disappeared under the pretext that Elliott had left without paying them and that they were going to look for him, and he did not see them again for five days. There is, however, no reason to suppose that they spent five days looking for Elliott, rather than that they wanted to avoid Thioly, having changed their minds, no longer wishing to get themselves involved with Thioly's friend Hoiler. Nevertheless Elliott does seem to have had some sort of financial dispute with his guides, according to Farrar's correspondence with Montagnier in 1917.

2.17
FELLENBERG, EDMUND VON (1838 – 1902)

Elected to the Alpine Club in December 1863, von Fellenberg was a founder member of the Swiss Alpine Club and its first secretary. Whymper had never met him, but on 25th July he completed a lengthy letter to him giving most of the facts of the Matterhorn accident with a view to correcting the inaccuracies in the various published versions. He asked him to submit it to SAC members at the earliest opportunity, and if he saw fit to send a copy to the *Journal de Genève* and to *Der Bund*. In a covering letter of 26th July Whymper wrote 'I cannot bring myself to write to the newspapers respecting this sad affair, but it seems to me, there is no impropriety in addressing this letter to you, and in its being published by you'.

Whymper wrote the letters from Interlaken, where he had the assistance of W.H.Hawker with whom he had climbed in June that year. The main letter was translated into French and German by Peter Ober in whose hotel Whymper had been staying. Von Fellenberg was then already in Grindelwald and Hawker wrote to him there asking where he should send Whymper's letter or whether he would not mind calling at the Hotel Ober for it if he should shortly be passing through Interlaken.

Whymper also sent a copy of the letter to the secretary of the Italian Alpine Club, and whereas it has been suggested that only the Italian version was ever published, this is not strictly accurate. Von Fellenberg seems to have been climbing from Grindelwald from the end of July until mid August. He probably received the letter on about 4th August and sent it to his colleague Abraham Roth, another founder member of the SAC, who edited the weekly *Sonntagspost*, a Bern Sunday newspaper, having previously edited *Der Bund*. On 13th August the contents of the letter were published almost word for word, but not in the original form. An Italian translation of the letter was not published until at least the beginning of September, when it appeared in a Club bulletin. Whymper's letter to *The Times* was published on 8th August, when the *Sonntagspost* was already in the press, and the following Sunday, the 20th, the *Sonntagspost* published a further article commenting on the *Times* letter and questioning certain details about the ropes. There is no reason however to suppose that the comments were those of von Fellenberg rather than Abraham Roth.

Von Fellenberg and Roth's first ascents of the Doldenhorn and Weisse Frau in 1862 are described in a book of which there is an English edition.

2.18
GIORDANO, FELICE (18?? – 1892)

The Italian Alpine Club was founded in 1863 and Guido Rey recorded in his great book *The Matterhorn* how the founders secretly proposed to attempt some feat that would bring honour to the Club. Having been deprived of the first ascent of Monte Viso they chose the Matterhorn as their target. The founders were scientists and included Rey's uncle Quintino Sella as well as the mining engineer Giordano, who was delegated to make the necessary preparations and to lead the expedition. In 1864 Giordano visited Zermatt on his way to Breuil after an ascent of Mont Blanc, and he met J-A Carrel on the Theodule pass. An entry in his notebook records how he 'Spent a whole evening at the Jomein with Carrel and the Chanoine Carrel'. So it came about that on 8th July 1865 Giordano arrived at Valtournanche and met J-A Carrel who had just returned with other men from a reconnaissance they had carried out on his behalf. He was the 'family of distinction' with whom Carrel was engaged to travel in the valley of Aosta after Tuesday 11th July, according to what he had told Whymper, who described in considerable detail in *Scrambles* the circumstances in which he came to be 'bamboozled and humbugged'.

Rey published in his book four letters that his uncle, Sella, received from Giordano, written on the 7th, 11th, 14th & 15th July, which describe the preparations and the subsequent events on the mountain. Whilst Carrel and the other guides were making their attempt, Giordano climbed the Theodulhorn and a couple of other minor peaks with Amé Gorret. They kept an eye on the Matterhorn and towards two o'clock on the 14th they saw Whymper's party on the summit, mistaking it for that of Carrel. Giordano was so excited that he sent Sella a telegram, followed up by a letter, telling him to start immediately and saying that if he had not arrived by the following evening, 'I shall go and plant our flag up there, that it may be the first. This is essential. I will, however, do all I can to wait for you, so that you may come yourself. Whymper has gone off to make an attempt on the other side, but I think in vain.'

When Giordano learnt the truth from Carrel and how they had retreated after seeing that they had been forestalled by Whymper, he was particularly upset to discover that they had brought down the tents and other equipment. He wanted Carrel to try again, but none of the others would go and it was Amé Gorret who

Valtournanche Matterhorn Guides (1867)

came to the rescue and agreed to accompany Carrel. Giordano wanted to go himself, but Carrel insisted that they should not have any traveller with them. In July 1866 Giordano returned to attempt the ascent himself, make a geological study of the mountain and inspect the site of the proposed refuge on the Cravate. The weather was stormy with three inches of snow on the tent the first morning. 'Giordano lay encamped for five days and five nights, alone with his three guides, with a single rug for all of them, and with a temperature that sank as low as -9° C. inside the tent.' They got no further than the foot of the final peak and when they returned to the Cravate for the night he found amongst the post that the porters had brought up for him telegrams summoning him back to town.

In September 1868 he finally succeeded in making the ascent with Carrel and J-J Maquignaz and descending to Zermatt, so repeating the traverse that Tyndall had first made some five weeks earlier. Tyndall quoted, from a letter Giordano sent him, his comments on the difficulties and on the danger from stonefalls, including, 'One of my two guides had his haversack cut in two by a block and I myself was somewhat contused'. Whymper published in *Scrambles* in 1871 Giordano's geological section of the Matterhorn as well as his note on the subject. He also included in the 4th edition a paragraph about Giordano's tragic death.

It is fortunate that the ascent of the Matterhorn proved as easy as it did and that Giordano never had the need nor the opportunity to implement the thoughts he had when contemplating the Hörnli from the Riffelalp in 1864. For he wrote in his notebook after referring to the Zermatt route having been climbed to within five hundred feet of the summit: 'In order to complete the ascent it would be necessary to cut steps and do other work in the rock for a height of about a hundred feet; eight or ten days, and three or four stone cutters at twenty francs a day would be required.'

2.19
GIRDLESTONE, REV ARTHUR GILBERT (1842 – 1908)

Girdlestone's reputation as a mountaineer seems to have been undermined by the Alpine Club's opinion on guideless climbing, as expressed in *AJ5* after the discussion by prominent members that followed the reading of a paper by Crauford Grove in June 1870 on the comparative skill of travellers and guides. The paper was based on Girdlestone's book *The high alps without guides* and one of the conclusions of the Club's discussion reads 'It was the general opinion that he had not taken proper precautions, and that, if his example should be generally followed, the result would be a frightful increase of accidents'. Yet Grove appears to have based his paper on the misconception that of 'more than seventy expeditions without guides...he has chosen the most successful ones, and that in the remaining forty-nine he did not consider himself fortunate'. Grove must have overlooked that Girdlestone wrote on page 20:

> 'The adventures without guides related in the accompanying pages are necessarily selected as the most exciting and interesting which I have met with. The dangers encountered in them might be held prejudicial to my argument, but success under such difficulties may encourage further efforts, while far more numerous successes without any difficulties at all, which are not here recounted, rebut accusations of rashness, though they would be uninteresting to relate in consequence.'

Coolidge seems to have been alone in respecting Girdlestone, although it was not until 1908 that he wrote:

> 'Now guideless climbing by competent men is no very new thing. We have mentioned above the splendid feats of Messrs Hudson and Kennedy's party on Mont Blanc as far back as 1855, while in 1870 Mr.Girdlestone devoted a whole book to the subject, illustrating it by the thrilling recital of his own exciting experiences between 1864 and 1869.'

It is beyond the scope of this book to make a fresh assessment of Girdlestone's contribution as a pioneer and advocate of guideless climbing. But even Grove referred to him as 'a gentleman of exceptionally large experience' and, disregarding his guideless expeditions, there is no reason whatever to suppose that, when climbing with guides, he was any less surefooted or competent than the best guided climbers of his day. It is therefore necessary to draw attention to the somewhat uncharacteristic and unjustifiable remark made by Dangar & Blakeney, in their centenary article on Old Peter Taugwalder in *AJ70*, in relation to Hudson having invited various others to join him in the Matterhorn attempt, 'Girdlestone says that he too might have joined the party, but luckily the expedition was spared him'.

Girdlestone was never a member of the Alpine Club and relatively little would have been known of his climbing career – apart from his book, a short obituary in *AJ24* and one or two brief mentions elsewhere – had it not been for the initiative of Graham Brown in tracing his letter journal, which the Canon's nephew subsequently presented to the Alpine Club. It consists of a copy of a substantial number of letters written to family and friends describing his climbs. The writing is not the easiest to read and detailed study would take a considerable time. Girdlestone in fact made one of the earliest guided ascents of the Matterhorn from Zermatt in September 1868, along with Kelso, J-M Lochmatter and Peter & Nicholas Knubel, as well as Crauford Grove. In August 1871 Girdlestone and Kelso climbed the Matterhorn from Breuil with the Maquignaz brothers, being second only to Grove as tourists making complete ascents from both sides.

But it is Girdlestone's involvement with the party that made the first ascent that makes his letter journal such an important historical record. Whymper refers in *Scrambles* to meeting Girdlestone at the Montanvert on July 3rd 1865 and again later the same day at Courmayeur after crossing by different passes, but he does not otherwise mention him by name apart from listing his 1868 and 1871 ascents. He does however refer to him indirectly as the sick Englishman at Valtournanche for whom he walked from Breuil to Chatillon to fetch him medicine on July 9th. Whymper returned to Breuil on the morning of the 10th and wrote 'In the evening the sick man crawled up, a good deal better'. Unaccountably Whymper makes no further mention of Girdlestone direct or indirect in *Scrambles* and one can only speculate whether this may have been in some way related to the publication of Girdlestone's book in the Spring of 1870. But perhaps it was not the Alpine Club's condemnation of Girdlestone's account of guideless climbing nor his attributing the Matterhorn accident to 'bad mountaineering – not a bad rope' that influenced Whymper, but, as Graham Brown has suggested 'rather unnecessary deference to the proprieties, for which Whymper was a stickler'. The frontispiece in Girdlestone's book bears Whymper's name.

Girdlestone's movements in July 1865, immediately before and after the accident, were as follows

9th	Ill at Valtournanche. Visited by Whymper.
10th	Arrived at Breuil in evening.
11th	At Breuil with Whymper and later Lord Francis Douglas.
12th	Crossed Theodule pass to Zermatt with Whymper and Douglas. Spent evening with them at Hotel Monte Rosa.

13th	Walked up to Gornergrat and back.
14th	Walked to Riffelberg. Saw Whymper and Croz on summit of Matterhorn. Slept at Riffelberg.
15th	Climbed Monte Rosa with Biner. Slept at Riffelberg, heard of accident.
16th	Descended to Zermatt. Went to see Whymper at Hotel Monte Rosa on his return after finding the bodies. Slept at Hotel Mont Cervin, where Whymper visited him in the evening.
17th	Walked down to Visp.

In his fourteen page article 'Girdlestone and the Matterhorn accident 1865' Graham Brown quotes most of the fresh details Girdlestone recorded in his journal and he considers the implications involved. Some of his conclusions, such as that Douglas dashed over to Breuil on the chance that he might be able to engage Carrel's services as well as Old Peter's for his own attempt, are open to so many doubts that they can almost certainly be rejected, but there is much of value in the article.

There is doubt as to whether Girdlestone stayed at the Monte Rosa on the night of the 12th. He probably stayed at the Mont Cervin, where he definitely was on the 16th. Douglas had stayed at the Mont Cervin for a fortnight before vacating his room on the 9th or 10th and moving to the Riffelhaus, and he must have spent the night of the 12th at the Monte Rosa. Girdlestone dined with Whymper and Douglas at the Monte Rosa that evening, recording in his journal how the Hudson and Whymper parties were meaning to try the Matterhorn independently but 'the two parties joined and set off on Thursday morning I having sat with them all on the previous evening whilst they arranged their plans. Indeed I should probably have joined them had not my recovery been so slow'.

On Sunday 16th July at about 2 p.m. Girdlestone went to see Whymper, immediately he had returned after discovering and burying the bodies. That evening Girdlestone had gone to bed early, when Whymper paid him a visit. He offered to stay with Whymper but as there was nothing he could do they settled that he should go the following morning. Graham Brown suggested that the account of the accident that Girdlestone wrote on or before 20th July was the first record of what Whymper believed to have been the cause of the accident, being earlier than his evidence to the Enquiry on 21st July. Whereas this may be so, it is probable that Whymper had in fact drafted his answers a day or two before the Enquiry took place, so that Vecqueray had time to translate them into French, and the Girdlestone and Vecqueray documents may therefore be contemporaneous.

Girdlestone's more controversial statements in his book relate to the payment of guides fees, the specification of ropes and the cause of the 1865 accident.

> 'There are a number of travellers who can by no means afford the luxury of carrying a guide about with them: for the ordinary charge of one is from six to ten francs a day and twenty francs for glacier days: often it is much higher.' (p19).

> 'I obtain, and use with perfect satisfaction, Buckingham's lightest club-rope. Much that is said about the necessity of very strong rope is founded on error. I use the same rope for several years in succession, although it certainly becomes weaker; because a place must be very bad where the rope cannot be kept so far taut as to prevent the chance of a sudden and tremendous strain upon it and on such a place everyone would infallibly be pulled over by the shock of the strain before an ordinary window-cord would reach its point of rupture. On this ground I think the club-rope might be made a size smaller than it is. The apparent exception to this statement presented by the fatal accident on the first ascent of the Matterhorn vanishes before the fact that, owing to the inexperience of one of the mountaineers, the rope could not be kept taut between him and his guide, and thus the rope was subjected to a sudden strain where the holding of some of the party was good. Bad mountaineering – not a bad rope – appears to have been the cause of that lamentable catastrophe.' (p167).

In conclusion a couple of biographical notes are worth quoting. In his obituary of Girdlestone W.H.Glover wrote: 'Absolutely sincere, and with a keen sense of humour, he was a charming companion.' In the course of a paper read to the Alpine Club in 1942 entitled 'First affections' H.E.G.Tyndale wrote of his guideless introduction to the Alps at Arolla by R.L.G.Irving:

> 'Fortunately for us, there were then kings in the land, and the monarch of the Mont Collon [hotel] had once been the original sinner of guideless climbing; he was none other than Girdlestone himself. Rumour breathed that he had usurped the throne by a *coup d' état* from Zinal; be that as it may, no more benevolent despot ever reigned in an Alpine hotel, and he looked with sympathy on the youngest of his subjects. I can see him now tending his beloved rock garden in a battered straw hat, perhaps the selfsame object of chaff in his salad days, and hear his deep voice on Sundays from the lectern denouncing blind guides.'

2.20
GLOVER, REV RICHARD

In 1865 Glover was Vicar of Christchurch, Dover but he was no mountaineer. It seems as though he met Whymper for the first time in Zermatt in June of that year. Whymper recorded in his diary how Glover had been talking to Seiler 'and as I found from his talk that he wanted to cross the Theodule and had not too much money I offered to take him over, which offer he accepted'. Whymper later saw him in Chamonix for half an hour, 'but beyond this I know nothing of him' he wrote to Sir T.F.Buxton in August 1865.

Glover first appeared on the scene of the Matterhorn accident on 27th July, when *The Times* published a lengthy letter he had written to the Editor two days earlier. It was an unfortunate letter, obviously written with the best of intentions, but it must have appalled Whymper, not only because of Glover's ill-judged and inaccurate assessment of the situation, his claim to have been tied to the same rope a month or so before and his attempts to exonerate Whymper from any blame, but also on account of his speculation 'It seems to me that the unfortunate slip was most likely made (as one account stated) by the youngest of the party poor Lord Francis Douglas'. This led to one of Douglas's relatives writing to Glover and to his further letter of 29th July, published on 1st August, expressing regret that anyone should have thought that he was imputing blame to Douglas. Whymper also seems to have found it necessary to intervene at this stage, with the result that *The Times* published a short note on 2nd August stating: 'We are requested to state on the best authority that Lord Francis Douglas did not make the fatal slip which caused the lamentable accident on the Matterhorn'.

On 31st July Glover wrote to Whymper stating in all innocence in relation to his first letter to *The Times*, 'I could not help writing in your absence and I hope that nothing I said was at all displeasing to you. I foresaw that there would be much discussion about your *rope* and that was the chief point to which I wished to draw attention...subsequent letters and articles in the papers convinced me that I did well to speak on them.' Whymper did not reply until 18th August, partly as a result of Glover's letter having been addressed to some club, where a friend found it and forwarded it to him. It has been said that Whymper did not suffer fools gladly, but his reply to Glover is a masterly example of restraint and tact, showing his remarkable maturity and letter writing skill. It reveals his inner feelings, perhaps more than any other letter. It led Glover to write in reply 'You are quite right in supposing that I now regret my allusion to poor Lord Francis Douglas in my letter. I do so most sincerely...I have very little leisure for such employments and I write too hastily – and so far foolishly. I have endeavoured to make the "amende honorable" but none the less regret hazarding such an unwise and useless conjecture.'

Glover's letter of 31st July 1865 contains some useful information with regard to the extent of Lord Francis Douglas's climbing experience, stating, 'My brother took an excursion or two with Lord Francis Douglas two years ago'. The Riffelhaus guestbook seems to provide confirmation of this with an entry in 1863 by 'Rev H.Glover' a few pages after Douglas noted an ascent of Monte Rosa on 24th August. Douglas had also made an earlier entry on 16th July 1863, and he probably then went elsewhere for a few weeks, meeting H.Glover after his return. There is an entry in the same book for 1865, 'June 17. Revd Richard Glover – Dover – from Zermatt to Chamonix'.

2.21
GORRET, ABBÉ AMÉ (1836 – 1907)

Gorret's account of the first ascent of the Matterhorn from Breuil, published in October 1865 in the *Feuille d'Aoste*, brought him recognition as a mountaineer and as a writer. He made a number of first ascents in 1865 and 1866 and he became a regular contributor to the bulletin of the Italian Alpine Club, with the result that in November 1869 he was made an honorary member of the Club. A book of his writings was published by Alfonso Bernardi in 1965.

Gorret was born in Valtournanche and in 1857 he took part in the first recorded attempt to climb the Matterhorn, getting as far as the Tête du Lion with J-A and J-J Carrel. In 1861 he was ordained priest, and in 1865 it so happened that he was able to take the whole of the month of July as holiday, so he set off from Cogne, where he was Vicar, for Valtournanche. On 14th July 1865 Gorret was with Giordano, who had gone to Breuil to explore and hopefully climb the Matterhorn, when they saw Whymper's party on the summit and mistook it for that of Carrel, who had been making a reconnaissance. The following morning, when the Italians had returned defeated and despondent, Giordano did not reproach them but only remarked that they ought at least to have solved the question as to whether an ascent was possible on that side, whereas they had discovered nothing; 'Up to now I have striven for the honour of making the first ascent, but fate was against me...If I now make some further sacrifice, it will be for you, for your honour, for your interest.' Gorret continues his narrative by saying that Giordano asked them if they would set off again in order to resolve the question, but he got no positive response. The situation seems to have reminded Gorret of Whymper's remark a few days earlier before leaving Breuil to go and try the Matterhorn from Zermatt,

> ' "You will never get anywhere with the guides of Valtournanche, they don't work for the honour, they are only looking for a day's wages". That which appeared to me at first to be nothing but a sudden outburst of spite, could now appear to be true. M.Giordano was making offers for my country that would never be made again. My country's honour was offended, it would lose a fortune. I would suffer.'

So Gorret said he would go and he asked who would accompany him. Carrel said he would, but none of the others; one of them not even for a thousand francs. In the evening two of the others agreed to accompany them, but Gorret imposed a condition that none of them should be rewarded, as despite the engineer having to forgo the pleasure of making the ascent himself, he was providing all the necessaries and they were going to avenge the national honour.

It seems therefore that Carrel and Bich owed it to Gorret that they were able to make the ascent on the 17th July, not least because he and Meynet were prepared to stay behind at the final col and forgo the summit, in order to safeguard their return. In his letter of 19th July to Canon Carrel reporting the successful ascent, Gorret stated that he and Carrel were off to Zermatt to have a look at Whymper's route, but the Canon subsequently noted on the letter that they did not go.

In 1877 he published his *Guide de la vallée d'Aoste* and his friendship with Victor-Emmanuel II led to another publication in 1879 after the king's sudden death. But Gorret was to enjoy only five more years before everything apart from his love of the mountains was to start to fall apart. His love of the mountains took him to France where he served as a curate for three years, during which time he climbed the Meije and the Ecrins, but when French bishops were forbidden to employ foreign clergy he was forced to return to Italy in 1884. His fame as a mountaineer was not sufficient to outweigh the unpopularity that arose from his somewhat blunt observations and sometimes caustic comments and he was sent to a poor parish in the Gressoney valley, where he remained some 20 years, ending his life in poverty and largely forgotten by the outside world, even though he continued to write articles under the name of'the mountain bear'. His latter years were tragic, and in an obituary Henri Ferrand wrote:

> 'Endowed as he was in body and soul, what a marvellous apostle of mountaineering [he] would have been if his mature years had been sustained, if he had not been constantly in the grip of need, if he had not been confined by misery in his poor hovel...We cannot refrain from experiencing a sense of injustice, when casting an eye on his life, his brilliant start, his arduous development and his miserable end.'

2.22
GROVE, FLORENCE CRAUFORD (1838 – 1902)

Grove had the distinction in 1867 of being the first to climb the Matterhorn since July 1865 and also of making the first ascent by a tourist from Breuil. He had taken part in the first ascent of the Dent d'Herens in 1863 and of the Rothorn in 1864 and there must be a possibility that he would have tried the Matterhorn in 1865 had there been no accident. In fact he was with Buxton in Chamonix at the end of July 1865, when they chanced to engage Young Peter Taugwalder as a porter, and it is possible that he learnt direct from him something of the accident and of the measure of difficulty and danger on the Hörnli ridge.

Prior to going to the Alps in 1867, he consulted Whymper about the Matterhorn and he recommended him to make the ascent from Zermatt with J-A Carrel. The same year John Tyndall had intended to make the ascent with Carrel, having corresponded with him, but when he met Carrel in Breuil his demands were so excessive that Tyndall seems to have abandoned the idea. Grove then seems to have engaged Carrel as his guide whilst Tyndall had with him Christian Michel, and the four of them crossed from Zermatt to Zinal by the Trift pass going on to Evolène the next day. Tyndall's account suggests that both he and Grove were then going to leave Switzerland on account of the bad weather, but at Visp Grove changed his mind and went to Zermatt, where the weather suddenly turned fine for a fortnight. He climbed the Rimpfischhorn with Kennedy, who seems to have lost his interest in the Matterhorn after the first ascent, and subsequently repeated Carrel's original ascent via the Galerie with Carrel, Meynet and J.B.Bich.

The following year Grove tagged himself on to Girdlestone and Kelso and the three of them made the ascent via the Hörnli with just three guides. Grove read a paper to the Alpine Club describing the two routes, and two years later he read a further paper on 'The comparative skill of travellers and guides', both being published in the *Journal*. The latter was little more than a highly critical review of Girdlestone's recently published book *The high alps without guides*, and the ensuing discussion led to the *Journal* recording that 'the neglect to take guides on difficult expeditions, and especially the neglect to take them when the party is not exclusively composed of practised mountaineers, is totally unjustifiable, and calculated to produce the most lamentable results'.

In 1865 Grove was the Secretary of the Alpine Club but was already in the Alps by the time Whymper returned to London and wanted the Club to summon a meeting to enquire into the death of Hudson. The previous Secretary, J.J.Cowell, therefore stood in for him, advising Whymper on the possible course of action although in the end nothing came of the matter. Cowell also wrote a letter to *The Times* in Grove's absence to defend the Club against the wild allegations being made about it. Grove was the Secretary of the Club's 1864 Special Committee on ropes etc.

2.23
GÜSSFELDT, PAUL (1840 – 1920)

In 1865 Paul Güssfeldt, from Prussia, was 25 years old. He already had five Alpine seasons behind him and when he heard of the Matterhorn catastrophe he never doubted for a moment that he could accomplish the ascent in safety. He therefore made his way to Zermatt in September and sought out Old Peter Taugwalder. His earliest account of the events that followed seems to have been a lecture he gave to the Berlin section of the German Alpine Club in about 1876. The lecture was reported in a rather obscure annual published in Bern *Die Alpenrosen* of which an extract translated into English appeared in the *Alpine Journal* in 1925. The same extract has been translated into French and published by Charles Gos, although in the process the report in the third person gets changed into the first person plural. It seems unlikely that Gos saw the original German, as he merely acknowledges the *Alpine Journal*, apart from confusing this account with that in Güssfeldt's book *In den Hochalpen*. It seems furthermore as though the *Alpenrosen* article was not written by Güssfeldt himself but by someone who attended the lecture as the reference to the difficulties increasing with every step and to 'steep snowfields, ice coated rocks' is hardly consistent with Güssfeldt writing in his book 'The climbing became wild and dangerous: no snow, no ice, only rock'.

Güssfeldt may have made an entry in Old Peter's Führerbuch, but there is nothing to indicate that it has survived, and the most reliable evidence must be the account published in his book in 1886. Nevertheless, the *Alpenrosen* account records how he addressed himself to Taugwalder 'but he was still too much shaken by the mishap...and it required long negotiations and ample promises to induce him and his son to try once more this dreadful enterprise'. The book refers to his sending for Old Peter immediately he reached Zermatt and 'when I informed him of my plan, he got very alarmed, tried to dissuade me and showed me the scars which the rope had left on his wrist before it broke; finally he implored me to refrain from that which could not come to good'. But Güssfeldt was in no mood to be dissuaded and resorted to what he calls 'the well tried and tested threat that I would fetch a guide from the Oberland or Chamonix in order to carry out my plan. So we then arranged with the utmost secrecy to attempt the ascent from the Italian side, because the fresh snow on the north side offered no opportunity and because even without fresh snow Taugwalder would have avoided the scene of the accident.'

He then refers to crossing the Theodule, and says that Old Peter's younger son (i.e. Joseph) who was to serve as second guide only joined them en route so as to avoid causing a stir. Farrar commented in relation to the *Alpenrosen* article 'It is certainly remarkable to find the two Taugwalders prefer to attempt the Italian side about which they knew nothing', and he would have been all the more surprised to learn that it was the second son Joseph and not Young Peter who accompanied his father. Any possibility that both sons went on the climb can be excluded for two reasons; firstly Güssfeldt refers to having to leave the frightened Italian porter on a slab of rock, where he remained in the company of a loaf of bread, and says that the *three* of them then divided up the loads and climbed on. Secondly there is little doubt from an entry by Paul Müller of Berlin in Young Peter's Führerbuch, dated 25th September, relating to Monte Rosa, the Theodule pass, Col du Géant, Grands Mulets, Mont Blanc and Tête Noir that he was engaged elsewhere when his father was on the Italian ridge on 18th September. Güssfeldt reckoned that they got to a point 500 metres below the summit when all further progress was barred by smooth walls. Shortly after they turned back, there was a rock fall at the very spot where they had been, and Güssfeldt says that on account of this the Italian guides with whom he wanted to try again right away were not willing to undertake anything more that year and put him off until the next year. But a war prevented Güssfeldt from returning in 1866 and it was not until 1868 that he reached the foot of the Matterhorn again.

He succeeded in climbing the Hörnli ridge on 9th August 1868 with J-M Lochmatter, Niklaus and Peter Knubel. His entry in Peter Knubel's Führerbuch refers to his unsuccessful attempt in 1865 and is the earliest record of it, although it gives little detail. It seems that Güssfeldt did not approach Old Peter for the Matterhorn in 1868, but instead arranged to cross to Macugnaga with him over the Old Weissthor pass. Old Peter only agreed to go 'if other company was excluded'. This seems to be the only expedition recorded for Old Peter during 1867, 1868 or 1869 and it was not a success, as they lost the way on the descent and had to spend the night out.

2.24
HADOW, DOUGLAS ROBERT (1846 – 1865)

Less is known about Douglas Hadow than about any of the other victims of the accident. McCormick described him as 'a gentle, simple-minded pious youth' and

Douglas Robert Hadow

Preston-Thomas wrote of his being a keen cricketer. Graham Brown wondered if he was short-sighted as the Enquiry Report reveals that some spectacles were found in his pocket, but the word 'conserves' qualifying 'lunettes' in the French translation means dark or tinted, and the original German states 'gefärbte' or coloured, confirming that they must have been some sort of snow glasses.

In 1865 Hadow's father Patrick Douglas Hadow was the vice chairman of the Pacific and Oriental Steam Navigation Company. Alfred Ceresole, the Vevey priest, states in the German edition of his guidebook *Führer von Zermatt*, published in about 1890, that Hadow's mother came from the Douglas (i.e. Queensberry) family, but he provides no further information nor authority for this statement. Arnold Lunn makes the even more remarkable statement in his book *Matterhorn Centenary* that the Hadow and Queensberry families were close friends and neighbours, and that 'At the time of the accident Charles Hudson was tutoring Douglas Hadow, having previously tutored Lord Francis Douglas'. But without some reliable corroboration there is little reason to suppose that this is any more reliable than many of Lunn's other pronouncements in relation to the Matterhorn accident and Whymper in particular. If it were true there would be some quite far-reaching implications for relations between Lord Francis Douglas and Hadow and also Hudson, as well as for certain parts of Whymper's narrative. But either Girdlestone or McCormick would surely have recorded something about such a chance meeting between Lord Francis Douglas and his former tutor and also his neighbour, even if Whymper remained silent.

The only suggestion of any possible connection between the two families is that Hadow's uncle, Henry Hadow, and Lord Queensberry both reached Zermatt on 24th July but that may have been little more than a coincidence, as when Lord Queensberry left Zermatt on 29th July Hadow stayed on until the 31st. But we know for certain that Hadow was a former pupil of Hudson's even though there has been a certain amount of argument and contradiction on the subject as a result of the letter from the Rev J.W.Charlton published in *The Times* on 26th July. His letter purporting to be written from Chamonix on 21st July asserted that

Hudson was neither the tutor of Hadow nor of Douglas and 'that neither...was connected with Mr.Hudson by any other ties at the time of the ascent of the Matterhorn than those of ordinary travelling companionship'. The letter appears to have been misunderstood, and whilst the sentence quoted may be strictly true it takes no account of the very different relationship between Hudson and his ex-pupil Douglas Hadow, compared with that between Hudson and Lord Francis Douglas who are unlikely to have met previously unless there is some substance in what Lunn has written.

But the oddest thing about Charlton's letter apparently written at Chamonix on 21st July is how he could possibly have been in a position to know anything about 'the report so generally believed in English circles at home, and on the Continent that the Rev Mr.Hudson was the private tutor of Mr.Hadow and Lord F. Douglas'. The accident happened on Friday 14th but the news did not even reach Zermatt until 15th and was not published in Geneva until 18th July. There was therefore no time even for the initial inaccurate reports to travel to England and gain belief 'in English circles' in time for news of that belief to travel back to Charlton waiting in Chamonix, and spur him to put pen to paper and write to *The Times* on 21st July. Charlton may therefore have been rather too keen to minimise any responsibility on the part of Hudson and may have written in anticipation of a hostile reaction, in order to dissociate Hudson from Lord Francis Douglas, in much the same way as the Rev R.Glover, whose unfortunate letter about Whymper was published in *The Times* on 27th July.

Dangar & Blakeney wrote of Douglas Hadow in a note about the Hadow family in the *Alpine Journal* how, 'prior to his visit to the Alps in 1865 he was said to have gone as a pupil to Charles Hudson. This, however, is explicitly denied by the Rev J.W.Charlton (*AJ32*, 21). No letters of Hadow's appear to exist and nothing has survived that throws any light on his character.' There is however the evidence of Hadow having accompanied Hudson to the Birkbeck home in Yorkshire in 1864, which comes in a letter Farrar received from Mrs.Birkbeck in 1918, and the overwhelming evidence from Hudson's friend McCormick contained in his pamphlet on the accident, *A sad holiday*. In addition to other references to 'master and pupil', McCormick refers to meeting Hudson in London on 26th June and continues 'Mr.Campbell (one of his pupils) and Mr.Hadow (a former pupil) were with him'.

The earliest mention or record of Douglas Hadow appears to be an entry in the guestbook of the Riffelhaus on 3rd September 1864, followed by another in the Monte Rosa guestbook later the same day. Graham Brown first noticed the latter in 1949. Hadow's name is bracketed with that of Robert Bolton, who either came from Romford or bore the surname Romford, the entry not being entirely clear. They had come from Leukerbad and the column recording where they were going states in French 'wherever the weather allows us to go'. The length of their stay and what they actually did in Zermatt are not recorded, but they seem to have had bad weather, judging from the Riffelhaus entry. The two names are again bracketed together and it looks as though Hadow's companion was another of his tutors, as the name now appears as 'Revd Robert Bolton Mansford'. The rest of the entry reads, 'Up here from 11am Sep' 2nd to 10am Sep 3rd of wh. time we have spent 14 hours in bed'. It looks therefore as though Hadow arrived at the Monte Rosa on about the 1st September after crossing the Gemmi pass, spent the night of the 2nd at the Riffelhaus and left Zermatt on about the 4th September.

Apart from the Rachel Birkbeck letter, referred to below, the only other record of Hadow's activities before reaching the Alps in 1865 is that made by Herbert Preston-Thomas, who wrote in his book *The work and play of a Government Inspector* in 1909:

> 'I was specially shocked by the news, as poor Hadow and I had played many a cricket match together, and only a day or so before he started for Switzerland he came to see me at the Privy Council office. I happened to be treasurer of a club to which he belonged, and when he told me that he was going abroad with Hudson, celebrated as an ardent mountaineer, I laughingly said to him, "Well if you're going to break your neck in Switzerland, you had better pay me your subscription before you start". To which he rejoined that I might be easy about his coming back, as Hudson was not going to take him climbing that year. In less than a fortnight the poor fellow was killed, and when the telegram came one of my colleagues recalled our conversation.'

Hudson had planned at Easter 1865 to attempt the Aiguille Verte at the end of June with Birkbeck, Kennedy and McCormick and thereafter the Matterhorn. It is significant that there was no suggestion that Hadow should join the Aiguille Verte party. Kennedy refers to Birkbeck and McCormick being too ill to join in the second ascent of the Aiguille Verte but he does not mention Hadow. From this it would seem as though Hudson did not consider Hadow competent to climb the Aiguille Verte which had already been climbed by a different route, so why did he subsequently think he was competent enough to climb the Matterhorn? But Hadow had in the meantime been up Mont Blanc where his stamina impressed Kennedy, who subsequently wrote of the descent 'The snow was very soft, and Hadow, although of wonderful pluck and strength, had not yet acquired sufficient practice to make him quite secure on his feet. So I left Perren to bring up the rear and afford Hadow support...'

The question as to why Hudson did take Hadow on the Matterhorn is a complex one and is considered in section 2.26.3 (Hudson). Nevertheless it is appropriate to mention one or two aspects. In considering the wisdom of taking Hadow on the climb it should be remembered that the climb proved to be remarkably free from difficulty. Hudson, in particular, had anticipated far greater difficulties, taking a wire-rope with him to Zermatt although he did not take it on the climb. McCormick's letter of 22nd July to *The Times* also referred to Hudson inventing and having made a kind of ladder for scaling precipices. The difficulties could have proved even greater than Whymper had anticipated and Hadow would have been a considerable liability unless he had turned back. Nevertheless, as

Graham Brown noted, even though Hadow may have been inexperienced, he was not apparently scared of the mountain.

John Birkbeck's widow wrote of Hadow in a letter to Farrar in 1918 that 'he was no mountaineer'. Old Peter Taugwalder described him at the Enquiry as 'a very bad climber' and the fact is that apart from Mont Blanc and the Buet a week before the Matterhorn, the only peak he is known to have climbed is Pennyghent. Mrs.Birkbeck wrote 'on one side there is a small piece of rock which has to be descended with care, but most of our party could walk down it. Poor Mr.Hadow found it very difficult and had to be helped down. Later we were not surprised to hear that he had slipped on the Matterhorn.'

In the *Journal de Zermatt* article of August 1895 Whymper is quoted as attributing Lord Francis Douglas's apprehension that Taugwalder would not be able to hold his ground if a slip occurred to his unease over Hadow's unsteady gait. But Hadow's fault was not that he slipped, the risk of his so doing must have been obvious to all his companions, but that he slipped at the wrong moment when his helper and foot placer Michel Croz was in the act of turning round to go down a step or two himself. Hadow fell against Croz and knocked him over at a time when even the careful and watchful Hudson seems to have expected him to keep still.

The presence in the party of two Douglases, Hadow and Lord Francis, seems to have given rise to some confusion in newspaper reports and this may well be attributable to Young Peter Taugwalder, who in his 'Narrative' in 1917 was still saying how badly Lord Francis Douglas climbed. The probability is that the only mention of the word Douglas during the climb would be to address Hadow by his Christian name and that it would not have been used in relation to Lord Francis. Old Peter had no problem, having climbed with Lord Francis for some ten days, but both Douglases were strangers to Young Peter and it is understandable that he should have regarded Hadow as Douglas, in the same way that the *Abeille de Chamonix* of Sunday 23rd July 1865 recorded that Lord Douglas (instead of Hadow) had climbed Mont Blanc on 7th July with Hudson, Kennedy and McCormick. The subject is considered in greater detail in section 2.14.4 (Lord Francis Douglas).

Quite a lot has been written about one of Hadow's boots, with the complication that someone may have confused it with a boot belonging to Lord Francis Douglas, the inference being that a somewhat worn horseshoe shaped plate on the heel may have led to the accident. But this takes no account of the fact that Hadow should have been standing still in both of his boots at the time he came unstuck. See section 3.7 (Hadow's boots).

McCormick wrote to Hadow's father on 16th July informing him of the accident but there is no reason to suppose that the letter has survived. The reply of 22nd July referred to Henry Hadow, Douglas's uncle, having left London for Zermatt the previous evening and said that he would be staying at the Mont Cervin Hotel, although he in fact stayed at the Monte Rosa, as did Lord

Queensberry. Some of Henry Hadow's activities during his week in Zermatt were recorded by Adams Reilly. About a fortnight later he wrote to Whymper from his brother's address asking for details of any expenses he had paid for his nephew and Whymper duly replied saying that there were none as McCormick had already paid his share of the general expenses for guides and provisions etc. Whymper quotes some figures and it is interesting to note that he himself seems to have borne the whole of the Taugwalder bonnemain, as it does not feature in the division of the general expenses into four.

McCormick and Whymper seem to have taken great care to avoid upsetting the families of the victims in their letters to *The Times*. Writing privately to the Editor of *The Times* on about 4th August and referring to McCormick's letters, Whymper said 'they were intentionally silent on certain points, including the exact cause of the accident, in order to spare the families of Messrs Hadow & Hudson the additional pain they must feel if it is published'. Whymper was unable to stand by his original 'firm intention to print nothing and to say nothing [when he came home]. I found this was impossible. Most injurious rumours were circulated and I was forced – most unwillingly, to write to the *Times*; a more difficult and more painful task it is impossible to imagine.' This extract comes from a letter he wrote to Hadow's father on 23rd August concerning Gustave Doré. In the same letter he said 'I have endeavoured in all that I have done since this much lamentable accident, to avoid giving pain to yourself and to the relatives of Lord Douglas and Mr.Hudson.'

Whymper's letter to *The Times* did however upset Hadow's father, who wrote to McCormick on 10th August, stating that they had been 'greatly distressed by Mr.Whymper's letter in *The Times*'. Yet by the 26th August in his reply to Whymper, father Hadow was able to say:

> 'With regard to your letter in the *Times* after Mr.McCormick's account, there were indeed some portions which caused us pain, as they appeared to enter into unnecessary details; I have however no desire to criticise these for I can well believe you had a difficult and painful task; I would much rather take the opportunity of sincerely thanking you for your gallant and successful exertions in recovering the remains of our dear boy and his companions, which at first seemed so improbable.'

Whereas twentieth century critics have sometimes taken a distorted view of Hadow's slip and of Hudson's decision to take him on the climb, there is no shortage of contemporary comment in the correspondence that Whymper retained in a scrapbook:

> 3rd August, Wm. Mathews jnr. to Whymper. 'The bosh that is being written to the *Times* by a lot of silly people is perfectly sickening, but I don't think it much matters. All sensible persons understand that the accident was caused by the preventable error of suffering a man to go with the party who was totally unfit for such an expedition and that the responsibility of having taken him rests mainly with Charles Hudson. As Hudson is one of the victims and has left a widow behind him one doesn't greatly like to put this in print.'

7th August, Wm. Longman to Whymper. '...it appears to me that the only ground on which you can possibly be open to blame is, for not more strongly opposing poor Hudson's wish to take Hadow on the expedition. But would not almost every one have yielded in like manner?'

8th August, Whymper to T.F.Buxton. 'Mr.Hadow was the sole cause of the accident.'

9th August, Buxton to Whymper. 'Mr.Hadow was apparently the cause of the accident through his inexperience of difficult climbing, but I know how extremely difficult it is to object to a companion for any such reason.'

9th August, Wills to Whymper. '...it is impossible not to see that in the first place it was a good natured mistake, but still a mistake, on Hudson's part to take Hadow.'

18th August, Whymper to R.Glover. 'I cannot feel myself in blame at all except for allowing Hadow to go.'

Whymper wrote in *Scrambles* of the last part of the ascent, 'Mr.Hadow, however, was not accustomed to this kind of work, and required continual assistance. It is only fair to say that the difficulty that he found at this part arose simply and entirely from want of experience.'

In 1965 Dangar & Blakeney commented on the question of Hadow being in the party; 'it is interesting to see how [Rachel Birkbeck] confirms what Whymper, Taugwalder, T.S.Kennedy and Yeats Brown all say about Hadow's incompetence. Farrar's attempt to justify Hadow's inclusion (*AJ32*, 28) is unconvincing.' It may be however that if Hadow had had more experience he could have become a competent climber. He was not a born climber, and he had not practised enough to achieve climbing skills before having rock climbing thrust upon him. But he seems to have been keen to learn and it may well be that his ascent of the Matterhorn was not just the result of the well intended but misguided decision of Hudson to take him on the climb, but arose in part from his own ambition to climb the Matterhorn, from having seen it on at least one previous visit to Zermatt.

In his book *Das Matterhorn und seine Geschichte*, published at the end of the last century, Theodor Wundt included a page of facsimile signatures of prominent climbers taken from the Zermatt hotel guestbooks. Amongst 'Lord F Douglas', 'Hudson', 'John Tyndall' and others, appears 'Hadow', but the handwriting seems to be that of Robert Bolton and not that of Douglas Hadow.

2.25
HAWKER, REV WILLIAM HENRY (1827 – 1874)

Hawker spent the entire summer of 1865 in Switzerland based at Interlaken, accompanying Whymper in an attempt on the Ebnefluhjoch in mid-June. When

Whymper spent a couple of nights at Interlaken on his way home from Zermatt after the accident he called at the house where Hawker was based and seems to have left him in charge of despatching his letter to von Fellenberg, after getting Peter Ober to translate it into French and German.

2.26 HUDSON, REV CHARLES (1828 – 1865)

2.26.1 His climbing career and reputation

Rev Charles Hudson

Hudson's standing as a mountaineer seems to have become somewhat distorted even before Arnold Lunn in his book *Matterhorn Centenary* purported to quote Coolidge as saying that 'Hudson was the outstanding mountaineer of the day' and that Whymper 'never attempted the obvious route up the Matterhorn till he tacked himself on to Hudson'. Lunn went on to give his own 'uninformed verdict', as even he himself would surely have called it in retrospect in the light of his subsequent retraction, that Whymper 'must have known that Hudson was a more experienced mountaineer'. As Dangar & Blakeney pointed out in their closely reasoned article in the *Alpine Journal* 'A word for Whymper: a reply to Sir Arnold Lunn'

> 'On any estimate, Whymper's record is far more impressive than Hudson's. Not that the latter's technical ability, by the standards of those days, is in question; T.S.Kennedy, Leslie Stephen, and Whymper himself all bear testimony to it. But there is no need to exaggerate; as noted above [until 1865 (the Verte) Hudson had not made a single reputable rock climb], Hudson's climbs had been almost entirely on snow peaks, so when one finds Farrar writing (*AJ32*, 22) of Hudson as "almost the sole great master and exponent" of new principles of rock climbing (!), one can only wish that he had not allowed his enthusiasm to outstrip his judgment.'

Lunn responded later, 'My critics have convinced me that Whymper's mountaineering record was far finer than Hudson's'. It should perhaps be pointed out that Hudson's contemporaries seem to have been under the impression that he had climbed more than his record now shows.

Hudson's relatively modest achievements, with 'barely a dozen completed expeditions in eight seasons' to quote Dangar & Blakeney again, seem to have been outweighed by the high regard in which he was held by his contemporaries. Whymper wrote in *Scrambles* how Hudson 'was considered by the mountaineering fraternity to be the best amateur of his time...His long practice made him surefooted, and in that respect he was not greatly inferior to a born mountaineer.' Likewise Kennedy wrote of him, 'He was almost as great as a guide'. This point also cropped up in Old Peter's evidence at the Enquiry when his answers included: 'Then came Hadow, then Hudson who regarded himself as a guide'(A55), and also, 'Hudson said he did not need a guide and that he could act as a guide'(A56). Dangar & Blakeney have pointed out how Hudson's general reliability as a climber was based largely on his activities on two mountains, Mont Blanc and Monte Rosa; he had made the first guideless ascent of Mont Blanc in 1855 and the first guided ascent of Monte Rosa the same year, with further guided ascents of both in 1859, but the prestige of both mountains was already somewhat reduced by 1865, Tyndall having made a solo ascent of Monte Rosa as far back as 1858 and Morshead having soloed Mont Blanc in 1864.

There appears to be another reason for Hudson's involvement in the Matterhorn first ascent and in the accident becoming somewhat distorted, which stems from the accounts of the accident published in *The Times*. It may be a little difficult to appreciate to-day with a thriving grief industry seizing every opportunity to portray and pursue grieving widows and parents, that in 1865 things were different. There was no proper enquiry conducted into the accident on the descent, but only that of Clemenz who seems to have had no interest in establishing the truth, and the only information that came before the public was contained in the letters of McCormick and Whymper published in *The Times* on 22nd July and 8th August 1865. The editor of *The Times* respected Whymper's confidence and did not reveal how Whymper had written to him on about 4th August in reply to his appeal,

> 'I had hoped that the letters of the Revd. J.McCormick would have been sufficient for the information of the public, although they were intentionally silent on certain points, including the exact cause of the accident, in order to spare the families of Messrs Hadow & Hudson the additional pain they must feel if it is published.'

This same wish to spare the families of Messrs Hadow & Hudson colours Whymper's account published on 8th August, despite the Hadow family being offended by it, and even *Scrambles* seems to have been inhibited by the same natural wish to avoid upsetting the victims' families. It was not until 1895 (*Journal de Zermatt*) and 1909 (the *Strand*) that Whymper publicly criticised Hudson for taking Hadow on the Matterhorn. In the former article he is quoted as saying, 'It was an incredible imprudence on the part of Hudson to let him come with us'. Graham Brown wrote of Whymper's article in the *Strand*, 'he allowed his bitterness against Hudson to appear in an unfair attack'. Lunn of course seized upon this but once again Dangar & Blakeney have put things into the proper perspective, writing in their Whymper article already mentioned above,

> 'Graham Brown's opinion...does not impress us. It seems to be completely outweighed by the opinions expressed about Hadow by Hort, T.S.Kennedy, Yeats-Brown, Old Taugwalder, Mrs.Birkbeck, and others. Naturally, at the time, and out of regard for Mrs.Hudson's feelings, the point was not laboured, and even the little said by Whymper in *The Times* was thought by Hadow's father to be too much (*AJ70*, 18). But that Hudson was too easy-going in the way he invited people to join him on the Matterhorn seems beyond dispute (see *AJ61*, 486-7).'

But there is some further evidence that excludes any question of Whymper feeling 'bitterness against Hudson'. It appears in letters written by Montagnier to Farrar in 1917, at the time when Montagnier was carrying out a lot of research into the Matterhorn accident and Farrar was shortly to publish his paper on Hudson. In one letter he wrote:

> 'The one thing that impressed me in Whymper's chats with me about the accident was his attitude towards Hudson. He spoke of him as a man many years his senior who had had vastly more experience in mountaineering than he had had. In arranging the party Whymper told me that he relied mainly on Hudson's judgment, as the oldest man in the party and the most experienced climber. But he insisted that Hudson had made a very grave mistake in admitting to the party an inexperienced youth of 18. He always described Hudson as a man of charming personality and a remarkably strong walker.'

In another letter Montagnier wrote:

> 'Whymper, whom I knew about as well as one can know a man nearly 40 years one's senior, often talked to me about the accident with the utmost frankness. I remember one evening in 1907 he came to dine with me in my little "pied à terre" in Geneva...he was in a reminiscent mood and told of his first meeting with Hudson and Douglas, of all his attempts on the Matterhorn, of the first ascent, the accident and the descent to Zermatt. He regarded Hudson as an exceptionally competent mountaineer but blamed him severely for admitting such an inexperienced youth as Hadow to the party; in fact he maintained that the entire responsibility for the tragedy fell upon Hudson and that had Hadow been left in Zermatt they would have effected the descent without the least difficulty.'

Another insight into Whymper's attitude towards Hudson comes from a letter he wrote on 8th August 1865 to Sir T.F.Buxton, expressing with masterly tact his strong disapproval of a letter Buxton had sent to *The Times* commenting on the accident. Whymper's letter includes:

> 'In my letter [in the *Times* of this day] I scrupulously abstain from offering observations and casting blame on anyone, and also from taking notice of the remarks that have been made on my personal capability for the expedition we undertook. There remains unanswered your charge of want of prudence or inexperience in myself...

> If you included the Revd. Charles Hudson in your charge of want of prudence and experience, I can only say that you could not have known him, for a more prudent and a more experienced man could not I think be found.
> Mr.Hadow was the sole cause of the accident. If any fault can be found with us it can only be for allowing him to go.'

Likewise in a letter of 23rd August 1865 to Hadow's father Whymper wrote:

> 'I have endeavoured in all that I have done since this much lamentable accident, to avoid giving pain to yourself and to the relatives of Lord Douglas and Mr.Hudson.'

Graham Brown carried out a great deal of research into the circumstances surrounding the Matterhorn accident, but published very little on the subject. One aspect which crops up in his notes on several occasions is that in *Scrambles* Whymper suppressed Hudson's part in the climb 'just as he suppressed Hudson's careful preparations for an attempt on the Matterhorn by the Zermatt arête, the details of which he certainly knew'. This quotation comes from Graham Brown's article 'Girdlestone and the Matterhorn accident 1865' and seems to be based on the dubious assumption that Hudson had been planning to climb the peak from Zermatt for some seven years. But before looking at the evidence it should be emphasised that Hudson did not in fact contribute anything vital to the success of the expedition (with the possible exception of Croz), and that Whymper and Douglas would still have made the first ascent, had they never met Hudson. The presence of Croz relates only to the avoidance of a repeat of the fiasco on the Dent Blanche, when in 1862 Kennedy had to retreat when Old Peter's nerve failed, the son sided with his father and they both refused to go on. But had the Taugwalders refused to climb beyond the shoulder, the probability is that Whymper and Douglas would have gone on alone and would have made an otherwise uneventful ascent followed by a safe descent.

2.26.2 His interest in the Matterhorn

Hudson's name is first associated with the Matterhorn in 1858, the year after the two Carrels and Gorret had made the first recorded attempt to climb it, although he had crossed the Theodule pass as early as 1852. George Barnard in his book *Drawing from nature*, published in 1865 but including one chapter based on a lecture he gave in the autumn of 1858, wrote of the Matterhorn after arriving at Breuil and the Giomein hotel, 'From this side the mountain certainly does not look quite so impossible to climb; indeed, while I was there, Mr.Hudson's guide, an old veteran, ascended alone 12,000 feet, merely, as he said, to look at it'.

Mumm does not record Hudson ever climbing from Breuil, nor is there any record of his visiting Zermatt in 1857 apart from Coleman mentioning his 'having engagements at Zermatt'. In 1858 Barnard had an article on the Matterhorn published in the *Illustrated London News*, which includes 'If ever this vast crag is climbed by Hudson, Kennedy or other brave hands, it will be from this side [Breuil]', but as Hudson was in Zermatt in 1859 and left no sign of having gone near it, it is hard to believe that he had any particular interest in climbing the Matterhorn. Graham Brown's notes indicate however that he held the contrary view, relying in particular on Barnard's two 1858 references to him. In 1861 Hudson's holiday plans were affected by the Birkbeck accident, in 1862 he visited Zermatt on his honeymoon and in 1863 & 1864 there is no record at all. In these circumstances there do not seem to be any grounds for supposing that Hudson had any serious ambition to make the ascent, before the spring of 1865. Another straw at which Graham Brown seems to have clutched, is the mention in Hudson's diary of someone of the name of Parker in Geneva, when he was there in 1852/3, but although Charles Parker was about the same age as Hudson it really does seem too far fetched to suggest that it may have been Hudson that inspired the Parker brothers to make their guideless attempts on the Hörnli seven or eight years later.

It seems therefore as though Hudson's real interest was first awakened in the winter or early spring of 1865, not long before he made his plans to attempt the first ascent of the Aiguille Verte at the end of June and then the Matterhorn. Both Kennedy and McCormick wrote subsequently of having visited him at Skillington in March 1865 and of arranging to join in the attempts, McCormick stating that 'Hudson most confidently maintained that the Matterhorn could be conquered, and that from Zermatt'. We know also from Adams Reilly's letter to Whymper that Hudson had made arrangements with both Kennedy and Birkbeck. The only other information we have of his preparations comes from the correspondence columns of *The Times*. McCormick wrote of Hudson, 'Some months ago the Rev. Charles Hudson determined to ascend the Matterhorn this season. Before leaving England he invented and had made a ladder for scaling precipices'. Some three weeks later Whymper wrote 'It has been repeatedly asked, "Why was not the wire-rope taken which Mr.Hudson brought to Zermatt?" I do not know; it was not mentioned by Mr.Hudson, and at that time I had not even seen it.'

Whymper never seems to have mentioned either the ladder or the wire-rope elsewhere, certainly not in *Scrambles*. Perhaps this was because he knew nothing of Hudson's actual intentions for them, and not just because they may have seemed so absurd in the light of the difficulties actually encountered. It might have been understandable had Hudson made a reconnaissance in previous years, particularly when we know from Leslie Stephen and Morshead that Peter Taugwalder and Peter Perren shared what must have been the common view that the ascent would be practicable, or even perhaps easy, as far as the shoulder. It should also be borne in mind that siege tactics had been adopted on the Italian ridge for many years. But the idea of preparing for an instant siege from Zermatt without any preliminary reconnaissance, with mechanical reinforcements and the necessary army of porters readily available in the village as and when required, seems to be wholly inconsistent with Hudson having brooded over the venture for many years. On the contrary it suggests a somewhat hasty decision to force a way up before anyone else.

Hudson's climbing plans for 1865 had begun to fall apart even before he met Birkbeck in Geneva, as Whymper had already made the first ascent of the Aiguille Verte. Then Birkbeck became ill and had to return home, McCormick, despite catching up with Hudson and Kennedy at the Montanvert, had to abandon the new route on the Verte on account of illness consequent on travelling almost non-stop from Grindelwald for 30 hours and missing two nights sleep, and three days later after climbing Mont Blanc Kennedy had to return home unexpectedly. McCormick had already set off on a mule for Martigny on his way back to Grindelwald to conduct the Sunday services, having arranged that he would meet Hudson in Visp the following Tuesday 11th July and they would then go to Zermatt. Hudson had therefore lost his most experienced climbing companions Kennedy and Birkbeck, but had acquired Birkbeck's guide Croz as well as Peter Perren, who had accompanied the Verte and Mont Blanc parties. He also had with him a pupil named Campbell and his former pupil Douglas Hadow. Campbell does not appear to have taken part in any major ascent, but Hadow did climb the Buet and Mont Blanc. More significantly Hadow did not take part in the second ascent of the Aiguille Verte.

Wet and stormy weather on the Monday and Tuesday prevented McCormick from keeping the appointment in Visp. He did not therefore think an attempt could be made to climb the Matterhorn and did not hurry to Zermatt, but arrived there on the morning of Friday 14th. Hudson probably spent the Tuesday night at St.Niklaus and reached Zermatt early the following afternoon with Croz, Perren, Hadow, Campbell and a number of porters ferrying a large trunk, a precipice ladder and a wire-rope. The following morning Hudson wrote a note to McCormick at 5 o'clock stating:

> 'We and Whymper are just off to try the Cervin...Follow us, if you like. We expect to sleep out to-night, and to make the attempt to-morrow. Please give an eye to Campbell as long as you are with him, and take him to the Riffel, in case you go there. We expect to be back to-morrow. It is possible we might be out a second night, but not likely.'

There is no evidence of Hudson's intentions for the Matterhorn once he reached Zermatt, other than that which appears in what Whymper subsequently wrote, and the question as to why he ever took Hadow on such a potentially difficult climb is considered below. If Campbell kept a diary and if it should still be in existence, some useful light might be thrown on the subject. As Hudson was travelling with Hadow and Campbell, his use of the word 'We' to include Hadow but not Campbell gives rise to the possibility that McCormick already knew that Hadow was going to be taken on the Matterhorn.

2.26.3 Why did he take Hadow?

A day or so before heading for the Alps in 1865 Hadow had told his friend Preston-Thomas that Hudson was not going to take him climbing that year, the reason presumably being because Hudson was going to do some serious mountaineering. He had assembled a particularly strong team, including Kennedy and Birkbeck, who had engaged Peter Perren and Michel Croz as their guides. The object was to make the first ascents of the Aiguille Verte and of the Matterhorn, both of which were regarded as formidable peaks, and for the latter Hudson had brought with him a wire-rope and a ladder specially made for scaling precipices. Why then did Hudson change his plans from one extreme to the other, and after losing Kennedy and Birkbeck opt for an attempt with Hadow, plus Croz but minus ladder and wire-rope? There are many different aspects to consider in seeking an answer, but one of the principal factors must have been the ever changing composition of his party.

By all accounts Hadow was no climber, although it may be wrong to attach too much importance to Mrs.Birkbeck's account of Pennyghent. There is no reason to suppose that he was short sighted or that he had any other physical disability that affected his performance on a mountain, particularly on a descent. He was probably just a slow learner. He must have been keen to climb the Matterhorn, having stayed in Zermatt at the Monte Rosa hotel the previous September. There is nothing to suggest that he was affected by vertigo or that he was any less able than the other members of the party to make most of the ascent unroped. There is the evidence of Old Peter Taugwalder that he was a very bad climber (A31), and Whymper said at the Enquiry (A11) that 'Hadow experienced considerable difficulty in coming down', but Whymper did not say any such thing in public. On the contrary he added a footnote in *Scrambles* to avoid any possible ambiguity in his reference to Croz 'absolutely taking hold of his legs, and putting his feet, one by one, into their proper positions'. The footnote included 'Not at all an unusual proceeding, even between born mountaineers. I wish to convey the impression that Croz was using all pains, rather than to indicate inability on the part of Mr.Hadow.'

It has been suggested that Hudson invited Robertson to join in the Matterhorn attempt when he met him in Chamonix, after losing both Birkbeck and Kennedy. It has also been suggested that the Rev R.Wood might have been in the party, although the basis for this, Long's article in the 1867 *Echo des Alpes*, is hardly reliable evidence and may add up to nothing more than that Wood regretted not having arrived in Zermatt early enough to gatecrash Hudson's party in the same way that he had invited himself to join Long's party on the Dom. Girdlestone does not really come into the same category, as although he wrote 'Indeed I should probably have joined them had not my recovery been so slow', he would essentially have been invited by Whymper and Douglas rather than by Hudson, having been in their company for some 30 hours or so before they ever met

Hudson at the Monte Rosa. But Hadow was not Hudson's only remaining hope, as McCormick was still available to carry out the original plan. The fact that he had not met them in Visp on the Tuesday was no more than a trivial hitch, particularly when the weather was so bad. He was due to stay in Zermatt for the next three Sundays and there is no reason to suppose that Hudson was not able and intending to stay there as well until the end of July, judging from his letter of the 26th April. They would have plenty of time in the next fortnight to arrange and carry out their attempt, and in the circumstances there can be little doubt that until Whymper appeared on the scene Hudson had no intention of seriously attempting the ascent of the Matterhorn in McCormick's absence.

Whymper's account in *Scrambles* suggests that he and Douglas went to the Monte Rosa hotel as soon as they reached Zermatt on the Wednesday and then went to find Old Peter Taugwalder and engage him. On returning to the Monte Rosa they found Croz sitting on the wall in front of the hotel and learnt that he had been engaged by Hudson in the absence of Birkbeck. They had come to Zermatt with the object of climbing the Matterhorn and, as Whymper learnt subsequently, Hudson and Hadow were then 'inspecting the mountain'. In the dining room Whymper and Douglas overheard Hudson confirming Croz' statement to some other guests and learned that he 'intended to set out on the morrow at the same time as ourselves'. In his letter to *The Times*, Whymper's account of the same incident referred to Hudson and Hadow's 'intention of starting to attack the Matterhorn on the following morning'.

It seems therefore probable that Hudson's intention was to set off early on the Thursday morning with Hadow and Croz and explore or examine the Hörnli ridge at close quarters, going as far as they reasonably could, but not beyond the shoulder. Then, when McCormick had arrived they could decide in the light of this reconnaissance how many guides they would require, whether any other climbers ought to accompany the two of them and how many porters would be necessary for getting the ladder or the wire-rope, or both up the mountain. The *Times* letter seems to provide some indirect confirmation of this having been Hudson's original plan, based perhaps on the understanding of the other hotel guests or even that of Campbell or Peter Perren, before Hudson changed his plan and agreed to join Whymper and Douglas. 'It was our intention on leaving Zermatt [Whymper wrote] to attack the mountain seriously – not, as it has been frequently stated, to explore or examine it – and we were provided with everything long experience has shown to be necessary for the most difficult mountains.'

The vital question as to why Hudson took Hadow therefore needs some revision or amplification as the original reconnaissance would not necessarily have been beyond his capabilities, notwithstanding his inexperience and his known difficulties descending Pennyghent and Mont Blanc. Why did Hudson still want to take Hadow on the climb after hearing Whymper's account of the rival attempt being made in Italy, knowing his determination and how he would not be turning back as soon as they encountered some real difficulties? It seems as though Hudson's own wish to take part in the first ascent overrode any commitment he might have felt towards McCormick, unless he honestly believed that there was no prospect whatever of the combined party reaching the summit without the use of his special ladder. For Whymper and Douglas to materialise as substitutes for Birkbeck and Kennedy must have seemed almost too good to be true, but Hadow the 'simple-minded pious youth' would surely have understood had his former master wanted to revert to his original plan and make a serious attempt to climb the peak, without taking him. He had been left behind on the Aiguille Verte and there is little doubt about the Matterhorn having a far greater reputation at that time as an inaccessible peak.

The potential degree of difficulty to be encountered on the Hörnli can be looked at in three ways. Firstly there is that anticipated by Hudson, which was so great as to merit the invention, construction and carriage of 'a kind of ladder for scaling precipices'. Secondly, at the other extreme, is Whymper's account of what they actually found 'The solitary difficult part was of no great extent' or his comment on the mountain's traditional inaccessibility, 'it was defeated at last with an ease that none could have anticipated'. Thirdly there is the degree of difficulty anticipated by Whymper and other leading mountaineers, which did not fall far short of that of Hudson already referred to, so that if the ascent proved possible it would probably deserve the epithet 'the most difficult climb in the Alps'. It is this third degree, rather than the actual degree of difficulty encountered, against which the justification for taking Hadow must be weighed. It is therefore quite impossible to justify Hudson's decision to take Hadow, although it may have been excusable if he firmly believed that they would not be able to get beyond the shoulder. This however gives rise to the further question as to why Hudson did not turn back or wait there with Hadow when they reached the difficult part.

There is one further consideration on the question of taking Hadow, which is why Michel Croz either agreed to his taking part or acquiesced in it. Whymper and Douglas had to rely on Hudson's judgment 'I consider he is a sufficiently good man to go with us', whereas Croz had been with Hudson and Hadow in Chamonix. Croz knew that Hadow had been left behind when he, Perren and another guide accompanied Hudson, Hodgkinson, Kennedy and his dog up the Aiguille Verte. On Mont Blanc Croz was not on the same rope as Hadow, but he would surely have heard subsequently from Perren, who could speak French, how on the descent, as Kennedy wrote, 'the snow was very soft, and Hadow, although of wonderful pluck and strength, had not yet acquired sufficient practice to make him quite secure upon his feet. So I left Perren to bring up the rear and afford Hadow support'. Although Whymper does not mention it, it is almost certain that Hudson would have conferred with Croz on the Wednesday evening after deciding to join up with Whymper and that he would not just have confronted him with a fundamental change of plan at 5 o'clock in the morning.

Graham Brown suggested in an article in *The Field* in 1932 that Hudson was justified in reversing his decision not to take Hadow on the Aiguille Verte and in taking him on the Matterhorn, as Hadow had been on a different rope when he made his fast ascent of Mont Blanc, and when Kennedy had to return home suddenly there was no one to tell him of Hadow's problems on the descent. 'Hudson and Croz were now left with the knowledge of Hadow's extraordinary feat, but with no chance of knowing anything of his actual ability.' But this overlooks Perren and also the fact that Hudson accompanied Kennedy as far as Les Ouches the following morning, providing ample opportunity to discuss the ascent of Mont Blanc as well as the prospects for the Matterhorn.

The explanation for taking Hadow seems therefore to be that neither Hudson nor Croz thought there was any prospect of getting beyond the shoulder and they therefore decided that they might as well carry out their original plan. Whymper clearly had a different idea, for as he said in his letter to *The Times* they took 'provisions amply sufficient for the whole party for three days, in case the ascent should prove more difficult than we anticipated'. It seems that Whymper and Hudson were not therefore ad idem and that when the anticipated difficulties failed to materialise Hudson failed to reconsider the wisdom of taking Hadow on such steep ground. Although Whymper did refer in *Scrambles* to Hadow having problems at the solitary difficult part during the ascent, he omitted certain details included in his *Times* letter such as, 'Still it was a place over which any fair mountaineer might pass in safety. We found, however, that Mr.Hadow was not accustomed to this kind of work, and required continual assistance; but no one suggested that he should stop, and he was taken to the top.'

Hadow's fault was not that he slipped 'at a comparatively easy part' (as Whymper wrote in a footnote in *Scrambles*), but that he slipped at the wrong moment, when he should have stood still to let Croz descend. Everyone seems to have been anticipating that he might slip, yet although Hudson approved Whymper's suggestion that they should attach a rope to the rocks at the difficult bit, this was not done. Old Peter said in evidence at the Enquiry (A53) that he made the same suggestion to Croz before they reached the dangerous place, but Croz replied it was not necessary. In the footnote in *Scrambles* Whymper gave a lot of fairly precise details of the position of the party at the time Hadow slipped, that had not appeared in his letter to *The Times*, and in relation to Hudson he wrote 'The rope was not taut from him to Hadow, and the two men fell ten or twelve feet before the jerk came upon him'. This suggests that Hudson was not paying attention at the critical moment and allowed there to be some ten feet of slack rope, something that inevitably magnified the shock load when it came upon him and reduced his chances of arresting a fall.

Finally, mention should be made of one detail in a somewhat obscure article discovered by Charles Gos and quoted in his book *Le Cervin*, although he himself seems to have regarded it as apocryphal. It is by Georges Casella and relates to a chance meeting he had with Whymper in Chamonix a few days before he died. It recounts a conversation which includes a lot of detail that Casella could hardly have learnt other than from Whymper. The article in *L'Auto* of 18.9.1911 is considered more fully in section 2.57.12 (Whymper) and only one short extract is relevant here. Casella quotes Whymper, who has had quite a bit to drink and has just referred to the weak rope and to the fact that Old Peter could not have cut the rope; 'Besides I explained all that to the *Times* on the orders of the Alpine Club. But what I can tell you, is that the Matterhorn was very easy and that we only took Hadow – a fool, I can tell you – because the guide...no, I am not going to say that...let's drink!'

2.27
JORDAN, WILLIAM LEIGHTON (1836 – 1922)

Jordan's meteoric Alpine career seems to have been confined to the years 1867 and 1868. Not only does he appear to have been the original Alpine rocknast, judging by his acrobatics at the scene of the subsequent ladder on the Italian ridge, the nonchalent way he wandered about the scene of the accident on the Hörnli ridge unroped and his emergence from a crevasse on the Adler glacier by a few pulls hand over hand on the rope, but he did more than anyone else to open up both the Italian and the Hörnli routes by his explorations and by the detailed accounts that he wrote of them.

Jordan was the first man to tread the whole of both routes and he spent a lot of time improving both routes. But the most remarkable features of his Matterhorn exploration are perhaps the goodwill he engendered in Breuil and the enthusiasm and enjoyment expressed in his contemporary accounts. In October 1867 when the Zermatt guides' fear of the Hörnli ridge had already given the advantage to the guides of St.Niklaus, who were to dominate the route for more than five years, Jordan was describing the upperpart of the Hörnli ridge as 'these glorious slopes'.

In addition to Mont Blanc, Weisshorn, Aiguille Verte and other expeditions mentioned by Mumm, Jordan also climbed Monte Rosa and many lesser peaks and passes with Joseph Maquignaz, but the Mattterhorn was the main attraction for him. His attempts on the Hörnli in August and September 1867 took him as far as the scene of the accident, and after reaching the summit from Breuil in October the same year he descended the Hörnli as far as his previous highest point and then returned to the summit and to the hut on the Cravate. He intended to climb back to the summit and descend the Hörnli ridge to Zermatt the following day, only to be frustrated by bad weather, as he was once again in September 1868 when he was about to traverse the Matterhorn from Zermatt with Maquignaz. Later that year he returned to South America and seems to have disappeared from the Alpine scene until Farrar rediscovered him in about 1916.

Although Whymper included Jordan's climb from Breuil in his list of ascents of the Matterhorn in an appendix to *Scrambles*, it seems that his two earlier attempts on the Hörnli had been forgotten until a letter, written from Zermatt in 1868 by J.M.Elliott to a friend, was published in *The Field* in 1910. The letter mentioned that he had read Jordan's accounts of his partial ascent from Zermatt the previous year and of his successful ascent from Breuil 'when he came down and joined his point of ascent, but owing to bad weather was unable to complete the passage and make the Matterhorn a col'. Farrar added a footnote to extracts from Elliott's letter published in *AJ28* in 1914, stating that no record of Jordan's partial traverse had apparently been published and that it was probable Elliott had been misinformed. But Farrar soon discovered his error and when Jordan contacted him Farrar suggested that he should write down a few notes on the expedition. These appear in *AJ30* and include a copy of the entry Jordan made in the travellers' book of the Hotel Mont Cervin at Breuil on 3rd October 1867. The entry which he made in the Hotel Monte Rosa book at Zermatt four days later was published by Montagnier in *AJ31* and Jordan's entries in Knubel's Führerbuch relating to the two Hörnli attempts are reproduced in *AJ32*.

Jordan is the third man known to have arrived in Zermatt after the accident determined to climb the Hörnli. It is interesting to compare Old Peter Taugwalder's reaction in September 1865 to Güssfeldt wanting to climb the Hörnli, when he would only accompany him on the Italian ridge, with his reaction in September 1867 to Jordan's arrival in Breuil to attempt the Italian ridge. 'The Taugwalders, father and son, were there and wanted immediately to go for the ascent with me from Zermatt.' Jordan would have been well aware of the situation that had confronted Birkbeck in July 1866 when he could find no Zermatt guide willing to accompany him on the Hörnli and had to engage seven men from St.Niklaus on most unusual terms. They had included Peter Knubel and J-M Lochmatter, who as stone masons were to become well acquainted with the lower part of the ridge in the course of building the upper hut for Seiler. It may well be that Jordan's enthusiasm and in particular his account in the Monte Rosa book encouraged Seiler to build the hut. Jordan's first attempt was with Knubel and Tobie Couttet, a Chamonix guide, but the latter gave his place to Lochmatter for the second attempt, when they reached just above the scene of the accident before snowfall forced a retreat.

Jordan then went to Breuil and engaged Joseph Maquignaz with the intention of repeating the ascent Maquignaz had just made, as soon as the weather was suitable. For the next fortnight or so he made numerous climbs with Maquignaz and Couttet, some of which are named in the entry he made in the former's book in 1868. He pointed out to Maquignaz from the Adler glacier the route they would take for their descent of the Zermatt face of the Matterhorn and realising that they should already be on the mountain in such fine weather they then crossed to Breuil, after spending the night in Zermatt. On 1st October Jordan set off with J-J and J-P Maquignaz, as well as four porters including Victor Maquignaz who were only to go as far as the hut. The following morning Victor asked if he could accompany them to the summit as a volunteer, Jordan writing in the travellers' book at the Hotel Mont Cervin at Breuil 'My companions on this trip have, in a great measure, acted as volunteers'.

Jordan's ascent is remarkable for its many diversions after reaching the summit. Bernardi in his anthology *Il Gran Cervino* has reproduced two important documents that seem to have belonged to Chanoine Carrel. The first is a photograph, said to be taken by the Chanoine on 28th September 1865, showing the Matterhorn from Leyet above the blue lake, on which Jordan has marked with the letters A to F six places, which also feature in the second document, which lists in Jordan's handwriting the times he reached or departed from the same places. It is interesting to note that Jordan marked the Col Felicité as such and also referred to it in his hotel book account. It was less than three weeks since the 18 year old Felicité Carrel had climbed as far as the col on the occasion of the first Maquignaz ascent, and according to Canon Carrel it was Jordan who gave it her name.

Jordan's timetable shows that he and the three Maquignaz would have had ample time to complete their traverse to Zermatt on the 2nd October, even with their eighty five minute stop on the summit, had they not already decided to complete the traverse the following day (apart from Victor). They found a better route on the upper part of the Hörnli, avoiding the scene of the accident, returned to the summit, spent some time repositioning the rope that was replaced by the Echelle Jordan in August 1869 and then descended to the Cravate to spend a second night at the hut, only to be frustrated by the weather the following day. Ignoring the time spent on the summit they had in fact spent three hours in Switzerland exploring the upper part of the Hörnli and this experience must have been of great value the following year to the Maquignaz brothers, and indirectly to John Tyndall, when with him they traversed the mountain from Breuil to Zermatt and again a few days later when they returned home by traversing the mountain in the opposite direction with the Swiss dentist Thioly and his eccentric companion Hoiler.

The very full accounts that Jordan recorded in the hotel books at Breuil and Zermatt must have done a lot to put the ascent of the Matterhorn into its proper perspective and to reward Seiler, Knubel, Lochmatter and the Maquignaz brothers for their enterprise. The Zermatt guides, however, seem to have preferred the negative verdict of the Taugwalders and not until 1871, when *Scrambles* was published and Lucy Walker ascended the Hörnli, did one of their number, Peter Perren, repeat the ascent, by which time the domination of the St.Niklaus guides was well established.

Jordan was not only an enterprising climber but seems to have appreciated the mountain's future. On his return to Breuil on 3rd October 1867 after his ascent he wrote; 'the longer route on the Zermatt side made by Mr.Whymper in 1865, as also the longer route on this side made by the Italian party in 1865 and by Mr.Grove this year, are not likely to be taken again by anyone simply desirous of reaching the summit of the mountain'. Four days later he wrote in Zermatt; 'As far as my experience of mountaineering in Switzerland goes, this ascent of the Matterhorn is the most glorious and enjoyable trip a mountaineer can make.' Jordan's further writings on the subject are limited to his entries in the Führerbuch of Peter Knubel on 25th August and 11th September 1867, and to those in Joseph Maquignaz' book on 14th and 18th September 1868. The 14th September entry made at Breuil includes; 'Joseph Maquignaz accompanied me on 2nd October last year to the summit of the Matterhorn...I have to-day crossed the Theodule with him an intended passage of the Matterhorn from Zermatt to [?here] having been frustrated by the weather.'

The only other references to Jordan seem to be those by Chanoine Carrel in *La Vallée de Valtornenche en 1867*. Not only does he refer to Jordan's two Hörnli attempts and to his successful ascent from Breuil, but he makes several references to discussing matters with Jordan and mentions the donations that he made for purchasing a dozen sheepskins for the Cravate hut as well as a cable, or as it transpired a rope ladder, to facilitate the final difficulty. Carrel quotes Jordan on the relative difficulties of the two routes, saying that the Valais side was easier but more dangerous and the Italian more difficult but safer. He also suggests appropriate fees for guides, saying that he has discussed the subject at length with Jordan and with Giordano.

Dangar & Blakeney referred in *AJ61* to Jordan's sister Eliza Pennell's letter of 4.9.71 to Tyndall, in which she says her brother found several vestiges of the accident; 'the ice axe of Michel Croz, I believe, and other articles, and my brother felt confident that he could distinguish the missing body hanging over a ledge of rock, but thought it would only tend to harrow the feelings of his friends did he make it known'. Dangar & Blakeney commented that 'The claim to have seen Lord Francis's body was never put out by Jordan himself and must be viewed with some doubt.' There is however some additional evidence of Jordan reporting having seen something in that Carrel wrote how, 'During his attempts on 22nd August and 10th September Mr Leighton [sic] thought he saw some scraps of clothing and other things on some sort of projection on the terrible precipice, but the fresh snow covered everything and he saw nothing more'.

Only Jordan's diary, should it still be in existence, could throw further light on what he thought he saw, which may have been some bones left by the eight eagles that Sandbach Parker mentioned in his letter to J.D.Forbes.

2.28
JULEN, ALOIS (1823 – ?)

A native of Zermatt, almost unknown in Alpine literature, Julen may have played a leading role in influencing the official attitude towards the accident and in particular towards such aspects as the breaking of the rope. Julen was one of the less well-known guides who seems to have concentrated less on peaks than on passes and glaciers. His name appears in the article on glacier guides in the 1865 volume of the *SAC Jahrbuch*. Whereas some eleven Zermatt guides are listed with details of their major ascents, Julen is one of five others mentioned as 'good guides'.

He was mentioned by Hinchliff in *Summer months amongst the Alps* as having been with him 'on many a glacier expedition in the more immediate neighbourhood of Zermatt and had always behaved like a good fellow: but he had never been as yet to the upper part of Monte Rosa, and seemed to find it more alarming than he had anticipated'. The large party, which included Old Peter Taugwalder and two of the Zumtaugwalds, reached the summit of Monte Rosa and Hinchliff went on to describe the descent.

> 'Poor Julen was not in his best trim: he was tired, and seemed to have been regularly frightened on the upper part of the mountain. I had often noticed his anxious expression, and felt many a tug at the rope behind me in the course of the day: and when during the latter part of the descent I slapped him on the back and asked how he found himself, he looked over his shoulder towards the summit which he had left, and, with a melancholy smile, said, he was very glad he could say he had once in his life been on the Höchste Spitze of Monte Rosa.'

Prior to making that ascent, Hinchliff had not long arrived at Seiler's Monte Rosa hotel when 'I was told that two of my former guides had already come to find me out, and presently I was shaking hands with Peter Taugwald and Aloys Jullen'. Whereas there may sometimes have been rivalry between guides, these two seem likely to have sought out Hinchliff together not only because they had climbed with him before but also because they were cousins and probably helped each other to find employment. But the fact that Hinchliff employed him on many occasions despite his relatively modest technical ability may well be due to their having had another common interest or qualification, in that they were both lawyers, even though Hinchliff himself never practised. Some of those who worked as glacier guides during the short summer season were carpenters, cobblers or even priests, but Alois Julen was the local judge. There appears to have been another district judge at Randa, so Julen's jurisdiction would not have been very extensive, and he probably had plenty of spare time to guide the increasing number of visitors who wanted to explore the lower glaciers and passes.

Not much else seems to be recorded about judge Julen in mountaineering literature, but he was a member of the party that went to recover the bodies of Hudson, Hadow and Croz on the 19th/20th July, and it seems probable that in the circumstances he went in the dual capacity of guide and lawyer, even if he played no official role as judge. The Enquiry Report places him second in the recovery party as 'M. le juge Louis Julen', immediately after 'M. le Président Welschen'. The questions of Julen's involvement in the recovery, his apparent non-involvement with the Official Enquiry (the Randa district judge Biner seems to have been co-opted rather than Julen to record and account for the victims' belongings) and the real nature of the part he played behind the scenes are complex and are considered elsewhere in relation to the Enquiry.

Alois Julen was the son of Old Peter Taugwalder's mother's brother, whose wife was the sister of Old Peter's wife's father. Putting it another way, Peter's wife Anna Maria was a Zumtaugwald and her father's sister Aloisia married Joseph Julen, the father of judge Alois Julen. Joseph Julen's sister Maria Katharina married Old Peter's father Johann Joseph Taugwalder. Thus judge Julen was a cousin of Old Peter Taugwalder and also a cousin of Old Peter's wife. Whereas both men had plenty of cousins, Hinchliff's account shows that these two were acting together in the mountains regularly and it seems only natural that Julen should have done his utmost to help his cousin to cope with the ordeal of giving evidence to the Enquiry. They may have had a common understanding of the skills and duties of a mountain guide, but Old Peter would have been utterly bewildered and overwhelmed by the legal formalities and questioning of the Enquiry, without the benefit of the skill and guidance of a lawyer to safeguard his interests. It seems probable, furthermore, that Julen's assistance extended to translating into German the list of questions that Whymper had prepared in French for Old Peter to answer.

The only other matter relevant to Alois Julen's involvement in the aftermath of the accident is that his elder brother Johannes seems to have been the Enquiry's ad hoc bailiff. So, whatever the extent to which Old Peter's cousin the judge may have acted behind the scenes, there is little doubt that in Johannes Julen Old Peter certainly did have a cousin at Court.

2.29
KENNEDY, THOMAS STUART (1841 – 1894)

Thomas S. Kennedy

Not to be confused with E.S.Kennedy an original member and early President of the Alpine Club and Charles Hudson's co-author of *Where there's a will there's a way*, T.S.Kennedy took an immediate interest in the Matterhorn and this led to his extraordinary idea of making a winter attempt in 1862 and subsequently to his intention to make a serious attempt on it with Hudson and Birkbeck in July 1865. In the event he was prevented from taking part in the 1865 attempt, having to return home suddenly on account of his business and he seems never to have tried the Matterhorn again, although he remained active in the Alps until 1877, when he resigned from the Alpine Club. Kennedy's writings are particularly useful in that they show us the contemporary scene and throw a good deal of light on such aspects as climbing technique in the early 1860's, the assessment of the difficulties likely to be encountered on the Matterhorn and the limitations of a less than first rate guide like Old Peter Taugwalder.

His article 'Zermatt and the Matterhorn in winter' includes the assessments he had made in the summers of 1858 and 1860;

> 'From Breuil all access to the summit appeared to me to be out of the question...the only route offering a chance of success was the northern or Hörnli ridge. The upper part is tremendously steep; a body falling from it would not be arrested until it reached the moraines of the glacier of Zmutt, 6000 feet below. But even in July and August snow lies there thickly, and black rocks jut their heads through, and where snow can lie a man may generally cut his steps and ascend. Careful examination with the telescope convinced me, however, that the greatest obstacles would be found at a point considerably below the pyramid. There are long unweathered sheets of rock, very frequently covered with thin glassy ice from the drippings from above, and presenting of all things the most insuperable difficulties to the climber. Indeed I did not see how, even with the aid of long ladders, they could be surmounted, till it struck me that in winter they might perhaps be found covered with snow.'

Kennedy engaged Peter Perren, and the following day when they were returning to Zermatt after labouring for many hours through deep dry floury snow above Furi and even setting off an avalanche, they met Old Peter Taugwalder 'evidently looking for work' and engaged him as well. The next day they got up to the Schwarzsee chapel where they spent the night, setting off shortly after 6 a.m. in an increasingly fierce north wind. After being forced off the ridge by the wind and continuing up the east face,

> 'The work was laborious: steps had to be hewn, loose gravelly couloirs to be carefully crossed, and unsafe rocks to be avoided. Presently Old Peter halted, announcing that he could not go farther; Perren looked upwards, and thought he could climb up again to the arête. [They all continued a little longer]...no one seemed to like to be the first to give in, till a gust fiercer than usual forced us to shelter for a time behind a rock. Immediately it was tacitly understood that our expedition must now end.'

In July the same year Kennedy tried the Dent Blanche with the two Taugwalders but had to turn back on account of Old Peter's inability to cope with the difficulties, less than an hour below the summit. Kennedy wrote of Old Peter:

> 'After paying out fifty or sixty feet, I heard him clattering down, and was surprised to see the weatherbeaten old fellow with a face as white as that of a frightened girl. He seized eagerly upon some spirits of wine we chanced to have, and then told me that when on the top of the rock his foot had slipped, and that for a moment he had thought himself done for. His nerve being entirely destroyed by the fright, I fixed the rope round my waist, and led the way upwards. But presently his courage failed again – he declared that he could not follow, and the son sided with his father; so it being useless to think of ascending alone, I was obliged to yield.'

It was then 1 p.m. and Kennedy wanting to be back in Zermatt the next day proposed to cross the Col d'Herens at once. 'At 8 p.m. we arrived in Zermatt, hungry, as may be imagined, and Old Peter quite blown and distressed with the speed at which we had come.'

Kennedy's third article with a bearing on the subject is his account of the second ascent of the Aiguille Verte, followed by an ascent of Mont Blanc. But mention should be made first of something that relates equally to the Italian ridge of the Matterhorn and supports the comments of Chanoine Carrel on the exploitation of foreign tourists. Of the Aiguille Verte Kennedy wrote:

> 'I may here state that the Chamouni guides have made at least twenty attempts to scale this peak, of which some were really hard tussles with the mountain, whilst others were merely sham expeditions organized to extort money from their employers, it being well understood amongst the guides that the first difficulty should stop them.'

Of the Mont Blanc ascent he wrote:

> 'I asked Hadow how he felt, telling him that this was the point where travellers usually succumbed to the might of Mont Blanc. He only laughed, adding that this was the first glacier mountain he had ever ascended, excepting the Buet; his strength and endurance were extraordinary...we started on the downward journey. The snow was very soft, and Hadow, although of wonderful pluck and strength, had not yet acquired sufficient practice to make him quite secure upon his feet. So I left Perren to bring up the rear and afford Hadow support and went on in front.'

Kennedy's final contribution to the future debate was his letter of 25th July 1865 to *The Times* with remarks directed 'not, of course, to those who are better mountaineers than myself, but to the numerous tribe of climbers who, without experience, and without the necessary powers of mountaineering, induce guides to conduct them up the most difficult summits'. He wrote that 'A large party should always be divided into threes, or, at the most, fours' and that in descending an awkward place 'the third...having no rope from above to trust to, should usually be the best cragsman of the three'.

One may ask what was Kennedy's motive in writing such a letter when Whymper had not yet returned from Switzerland and the most detailed reliable account was McCormick's letter in *The Times* of 22nd July. If he was saying that Croz should have been the last of the rope of seven, it must be pointed out that Kennedy himself did not practise what he preached, writing two years later of the Aiguille Verte ascent, the week before the Matterhorn accident, 'We left the top...all [six excluding the dog!] tied to one long rope, a mode of proceeding which was certainly not the best one...Croz led the way down...and Hudson was last of all'. If on the other hand he was saying that Croz should have descended an awkward place as last man of a rope of three or four – this has no relevance to the accident, as it did not occur when the last man was descending 'having no rope from above to trust to'. Kennedy also described in some detail how 'a long steep couloir of softened snow or ice should always be descended backwards', a mode of descent which has never subsequently been generally accepted, but which sorely tested Elliott's patience during his descent with Knubel and Lochmatter following the second ascent of the Hörnli in 1868; 'I really never saw men so little practised in snow and rockwork. Would you believe it, they came down all the snow, and all the rock, and all the ice backwards, with their faces turned towards the slope.' Kennedy was no doubt correct in his comment 'men who have succeeded in a difficult task usually become indifferent to danger, and their thoughts are wholly directed to the quickest mode of getting down again', but he was not aware of the full facts of the accident at the time he wrote it.

Perhaps his most extraordinary comment is the beginning of his last paragraph 'Finally, it is necessary to protest against the practice of inexperienced men ascending difficult peaks. A man who has spent only three or four years on the Alps is not and cannot be a first rate mountaineer.' Not only would his protest extend to Birkbeck, who had spent only two years in the Alps subsequent to his record breaking slide from the Col de Miage in 1861, yet was due to attempt the Aiguille Verte and the Matterhorn with Kennedy in 1865, but Kennedy's own qualifications for the Dent Blanche and the Aiguille Verte, as well as that of Hodgkinson for the Verte, also fall short of the same standard, judging from the details in Mumm. But having been a friend of Hudson, visiting him at Skillington at Easter 1865 to plan the Swiss tour, it seems remarkable that Kennedy should have been so tactless as to protest against the practice of inexperienced men ascending difficult peaks, when he must have had in mind Hudson's former pupil Hadow (rather than Lord Francis Douglas), having observed for himself that Hadow could not keep secure footing on Mont Blanc. Kennedy's own attempts on the Lyskamm and the Aiguille Verte in 1860, in his first major Alpine season, are no less deserving of protest by his standards. Perhaps Wm. Mathews jnr had Kennedy's letter in mind, amongst others, when he wrote to Whymper on 3.8.65, 'The bosh that is being written to *The Times* by a lot of silly people is perfectly sickening, but I don't think it much matters'.

Kennedy had met Whymper in Zermatt on 19th June 1865 and again in Chamonix ten days later. On his way from Zermatt to Sixt on 26th June 1865 Kennedy and his wife and dog stayed at the St.Niklaus Hotel Monte Rosa the same night as Lord Francis Douglas, who was on his way from Visp to Zermatt. It seems likely that Douglas would have revealed his plan to attempt the Matterhorn, but presumably Kennedy did not disclose that he was also going to attempt it with Hudson and Birkbeck, or else Whymper would probably have learned in advance of Hudson's plan, before ever meeting Croz on 12th July. Kennedy was in Zermatt again in 1866, according to an entry in the Riffelhaus guestbook, but there does not appear to be any record of his making any climbs. He seems to have abandoned any idea of climbing the Matterhorn, even though in 1867 he climbed the Rimpfischhorn with Grove a few days before Grove went to Breuil and made the third ever ascent of the Matterhorn.

2.30
KNUBEL, PETER (1832 – 1919)

A guide and stone mason in St.Niklaus Knubel did not start guiding until 1863, when his friend J-M Lochmatter recommended him to the Hotel Mont Cervin in Zermatt. His first contact or connection with the Matterhorn seems to have been on the 14th July 1866 when he was one of the party of seven guides from St.Niklaus that accompanied Birkbeck on his unsuccessful attempt to climb the Hörnli ridge. His first ascent of the mountain was in 1868, and his last exactly 40 years later in 1908 at the age of 76.

His second attempt was with Jordan in August 1867, followed by a further attempt with him in September. On this occasion J-M Lochmatter replaced Jordan's Chamonix guide and they reached just above the scene of the accident before snowfall forced a retreat. Knubel and Lochmatter deserve the credit for opening up the Hörnli route after the accident, with the support of Alexander Seiler, although it was not until Knubel's fourth attempt in July 1868 that the two guides succeeded in making the second ascent from Zermatt with Elliott. Knubel made three further ascents that year, with Foster, Güssfeldt and Girdlestone and by 1870 he had earned a reputation as 'der gewandteste und tüchtigste Führer des Matterhorns' (the most experienced and able Matterhorn guide).

With Lochmatter and with help from his own brothers, presumably Niklaus and Peter Joseph, Peter had built the upper Hörnli hut for Seiler at a height of 3818 metres. Its first use was by Elliott, who reached it with a porter on 24th July 1868 and subsequently engaged Knubel and Lochmatter, who made the ascent with him the following day. Elliott's comments on his guides and on Knubel in particular have been criticised, but it must be remembered that this was one of Knubel's earliest climbs, whereas Elliott was unusual amongst the pioneers in having started rock climbing in the English Lake District.

Mention must be made of the appalling incident described by Frederick Gardiner in 1876, as it seems likely to have arisen out of the Zermatt guides' jealousy of Peter Knubel's domination of the Matterhorn. They were at the Stockje hut when Peter Knubel's brother Hans told Gardiner that he was 'extremely ill'.

> 'He was indeed very ill, and evidently suffering horribly from cramp in the stomach...I was really very much alarmed and scarcely knew what to do...The Baron and his cousin [two other climbers at the hut] were most kind, and did all they could to assist, and as they were returning to Zermatt and did not require all the provisions, and above all the wine, they had brought with them, they most generously offered it for my acceptance. I need scarcely say how gratefully I accepted their kind offer, for I scarcely knew how long we might be detained at the hut.'

Gardiner goes on to explain how, after the Baron ordered the guides to unpack,

> 'three bottles of wine, half a bottle of brandy, and sundry eatables were made over to me by him. I then went out of the hut to say adieu to my kind friends, and saw them fairly off. Returning to the hut I immediately missed the wine and brandy which the Baron had left, and then found to my disgust that his [Zermatt] guides had actually, after having been ordered to leave us the wine for the benefit of a sick fellow-guide, when our backs were turned repacked it in their knapsacks and made off with it!'

Gardiner then refers to the difficulties Seiler had had early that season when a deputation of Zermatt guides 'suggested that he should refuse accomodation to all foreign guides, and recommend only guides connected with the commune, excluding even the guides of St.Niklaus'. It seems from this that the success of Peter Knubel and J-M Lochmatter and the other St.Niklaus guides in taking tourists up the Matterhorn at a time when their Zermatt counterparts were too frightened to go near the mountain had far-reaching effects, and it was no doubt indirectly the origin of the spiteful campaign waged against Alexander Seiler by the natives of Zermatt.

2.31
LOCHMATTER, ALEXANDER (1837 – ?)

A guide and clockmaker in St.Niklaus, Alexander Lochmatter played a somewhat lesser role in the early history of the Matterhorn than his brother Joseph-Marie. His name appears in the 1865 SAC article on glacier guides, listed under St.Niklaus as recommended for the Zermatt mountains, and also under Macugnaga as a dependable guide for Monte Rosa and other peaks and passes in the region. His elder brother Franz was the family's main presence in Macugnaga, where he married and opened the small Monte Rosa hotel in about 1860, although Joseph-Marie seems also to have worked from there. This accounts for McCormick referring to Alexander and Joseph-Marie in his letter to *The Times* as 'the brothers Lochmatter of Macugnaga'.

Alexander had climbed around Monte Rosa in 1864 with Giles Puller and Old Peter Taugwalder and it seems to have been Giles Puller who took him and his brother to Zermatt on Saturday 15th July 1865, where they arrived at about midday. He was a member of the Hohlicht search party that afternoon and was one of the guides who left Zermatt in the early hours of Sunday morning with Whymper, McCormick and others to search for the bodies on the Matterhorn glacier. He gave evidence to the Enquiry on Saturday 22nd July of having discovered the bodies the previous Sunday. He was also one of three guides accompanying the Baileys on Monte Rosa on 27th July, when a slab avalanche was released, killing one porter and injuring another.

The following year he was one of the seven guides from St.Niklaus who accompanied Birkbeck on his attempt on the Hörnli ridge on the 14th July. It seems that it was not until August 1873 that he made his first ascent of the

Matterhorn with his brother and Ewbank. He seems to have given up guiding soon afterwards and opened the Hotel-Pension Lochmatter at St.Niklaus. According to Dangar & Blakeney, his most notable expedition was probably the first passage of the Colle delle Loccie in 1862.

2.32
LOCHMATTER, JOSEPH-MARIE (1837 – 1882)

A guide and stone mason in St.Niklaus, Joseph-Marie Lochmatter has a full entry in the 1865 SAC article on glacier guides under St.Niklaus, and is also mentioned under Macugnaga as a dependable guide for Monte Rosa and other peaks and passes in the region. This link with Macugnaga, where his other brother Franz married and had a small hotel, accounts for McCormick referring in his letter to *The Times* to Alexander and Joseph-Marie as 'the brothers Lochmatter of Macugnaga'.

The two brothers had arrived in Zermatt on Saturday 15th July with Giles Puller at about midday. They both went on the Hohlicht search party the same afternoon and accompanied Whymper and others leaving Zermatt in the early hours of Sunday morning to search for the bodies on the Matterhorn glacier. It may well be that this willingness to help was recalled by Seiler when he later wanted to build a hut on the Hörnli ridge. It was Joseph-Marie who in August 1865 co-operated with John Tyndall in his ambitious plan to recover the body of Douglas, and he went to Geneva to purchase 900 metres of rope for him. He had been with the Baileys on Monte Rosa on 27th July when a slab avalanche was released, killing one porter and injuring another.

He and Peter Knubel must take the main credit for opening up the Hörnli ridge route with the support of Alexander Seiler. Although it was not until his third attempt, in July 1868, that he succeeded with Knubel and J.M.Elliott in making the second ascent of the Hörnli, his pioneering achievements included the Birkbeck and Jordan attempts, three ascents in 1868, two in 1871 and another three in 1873, as well as paving the way with the construction of the original upper hut, completed on 24th July 1868 at a height of 3818 metres. He built the hut with Peter Knubel, another guide and stone mason of St.Niklaus.

Joseph-Marie must have shared Seiler's recognition of the route as a perfectly feasible climb in the future, despite the mountain's pre-accident reputation and the subsequent reaction of the Taugwalders, which for six years seems to have deterred all the Zermatt guides from even attempting the ascent of the Hörnli, until July 1871 when Peter Perren was included in the large party in which Lucy Walker and her father made the ascent. Perren and Young Peter Taugwalder had attempted the Italian ridge in 1869, but before Taugwalder made his second ascent in 1872 Lochmatter had already made five ascents.

His first attempt on the Matterhorn seems to have been the seven guide caravan from St.Niklaus which accompanied Birkbeck in 1866. They got no further than the shoulder, due to the guides' nervousness. Peter Knubel was also in the party. In August 1867 Knubel made an attempt with Leighton Jordan and the Chamonix guide Tobie Couttet, but when Jordan made a further attempt in September that year Couttet gave his place to Lochmatter. They reached just above the scene of the accident before snowfall forced a retreat. But in July 1868 Lochmatter and Knubel accompanied Elliott to the top. Elliott was not very complimentary about his guides, but they had now overcome the psychological barrier and they repeated the climb in August and again in September the same year. In 1874 Joseph-Marie, Carrel and Bich accompanied Whymper, when he made his second ascent from Zermatt.

There has been some inconsistency over Lochmatter's year of birth, which Ruppen correctly gives as 1833, whereas a memorial card for him and his son records 1837. He was killed with his son Alexander and W.E.Gabbett on the Dent Blanche in 1882.

2.33
LONG, CHARLES

One of the many eyewitnesses of the first ascent of the Matterhorn but one of the few who left any written record of the occasion, Long had reached Zermatt on Thursday 13th July via the High Level Route with his Geneva colleagues Moise Briquet and L.Maquelin. They were forced to have a rest day in Zermatt, due to the temporary disability of one of their guides, and they lunched at their hotel the Monte Rosa the following day. Long's account was published in the *Echo des Alpes* in September 1867, which was almost two years after McCormick had published his pamphlet *A sad holiday*, describing the same scene. Long refers to McCormick without naming him, as one of the energetic climbing types sitting near them.

> 'Here amongst others the English clergyman at Zermatt. With dignity he shows the flag for his country; chapped lips and bloodshot eyes bear witness against him only too well. Representing the evangelical pulpit he challenges the roman church and the palms gathered by the Carrels and the Imsengs! Next to us at table is another reverend, Mr.R.Wood, who learning that we are to undertake the Dom asks if he can join us.'

He goes on to refer to Seiler announcing just as they are about to demolish an appetising dessert of wild strawberries and raspberries, that the climbers have been seen close to the shoulder. They all rush outside but can see nothing.

> Only 'the guides with their lynx like eyes spot the caravan's movements; they see it winding up to the highest point of the northeast arête, connecting the Hoernli with the main summit...At half past one, as far as I recall, a human silhouette (Mr.Whymper) appeared on

> the summit ridge, immediately joined by another (Michel Croz); some more arrive, we count seven, all is well...
> "Oh!" shouts one of Taugwald's sons after a few minutes search, as ardent as any to follow the course of his father and his brother: "an avalanche!"
> I look at Seiler, who has grown pale. – Taugwald speaks in his ear. – "Nonsense! an avalanche! that's often seen on a hot summer's day".'

Long's party had planned to set off for Randa at five, but seems to have left somewhat earlier, and somewhere beyond Täsch they met the Martin/Gautier party from Geneva on their way to Zermatt for the weekend. They climbed the Dom the following day, Saturday, and shortly before getting back to Randa they heard of the terrible catastrophe. 'It turned our joy to sorrow. Mr.Wood was even more moved than we were, if that were possible, not that he knew any of the gentlemen personally, but they were his compatriots and members of the same Club, and he had expressed to us his genuine regret at not having arrived at Zermatt early enough to join up with them.'

There does not appear to have been any Rev R.Wood in the Alpine Club in 1865, but it may well be that he was the friend of the Rev Julius Elliott (Mr.Wood) to whom Elliott adddressed his long letter of 25th July 1868 after making the second ascent of the Matterhorn from Zermatt that day. There are passages in the letter that suggest that Elliott and Wood had contemplated an ascent previously. The fact that he wrote such a detailed account to Wood so soon and included some specific advice for him about the hut, 'When you sleep there let me advise you...', suggests that Elliott may possibly have expected Wood to have a go at it later that year, although Whymper did not record anyone by the name of Wood ever making the ascent.

Long's reference to [Friedrich] Taugwalder, whom Whymper referred to in *Scrambles* as the 'sharp-eyed lad', is yet further confirmation of what was also recorded by McCormick and by Downton, although Long was the only writer who went so far as to identify him. Notwithstanding such corroboration of Whymper, Lunn sought persistently to denigrate him by implying that the sharp-eyed lad was 'one of Whymper's picturesque inventions'. He ultimately conceded to Dangar & Blakeney that he had been wrong.

2.34
McCORMICK, REV JOSEPH (1834 – 1914)

A friend of Charles Hudson, McCormick had visited him at Skillington in March 1865 where they made plans to attempt the first ascent of the Aiguille Verte and of the Matterhorn. He subsequently applied to the Colonial and Continental Church Society for a summer chaplaincy and was appointed to Grindelwald for the first two Sundays in July and to Zermatt for the other three. In his pamphlet *A sad holiday* he describes how he had arranged to meet Hudson at Argentière on the morning of Tuesday 4th July and therefore left Grindelwald just after midnight on the Sunday in order to walk to Interlaken from where he continued by steamer and trains to reach Martigny at 9.30p.m. An hour later he set off with a guide to walk to Argentière, where he found a note from Hudson telling him they had changed their plans and intended to start the Aiguille Verte ascent from Chamonix. Despite having travelled almost non-stop for 30 hours, including 10 hours walking, and having missed two nights sleep, McCormick set off again for Chamonix after a short rest only to arrive there 20 minutes after Hudson's party had set off. He then had something to eat and set off in pursuit 'at a great pace up a rather steep path, and under a hot sun' but although he caught them up at Montanvert he was soon so ill that he had to abandon the venture and return to Chamonix for the night with Mrs.Kennedy and Hadow. Whilst Hudson climbed the Aiguille Verte on the Wednesday, McCormick only went to the Flegère. On the Thursday he set off with Hudson, Hadow and others for the Pierre Pointue and climbed Mont Blanc the following day. After four hours rest he left Chamonix again after 9 p.m. (on the Friday) on a mule to ride to Martigny 'having to hurry to Grindelwald for [his] Sunday's duty'.

He had arranged to meet Hudson at Visp the following Tuesday 11th July, but the weather was so wet and stormy that he was unable to keep the appointment. He did not think an attempt could be made to scale the Matterhorn in view of the weather and did not therefore hurry to Zermatt, but arrived there on the Friday morning, when he was handed the note which Hudson had written for him at 5 a.m. on the Thursday.

McCormick was one of those who saw the party on the top of the Matterhorn and he recorded how the accident was seen a little later by a boy, whom Whymper subsequently termed 'the sharp-eyed lad' (Friedrich Taugwalder). The non-return of Hudson and the others on the Friday evening, and not even by 9 a.m. the following morning, did not alarm McCormick, partly perhaps because Hudson had been expected to return from the Aiguille Verte the same evening but did not in fact return until early the following morning and also because Hudson had said in his note that they might possibly be out a second night. But 'before ten' Campbell and McCormick set off with a party for the Gornergrat. It is not known who else was in the party, but it would not have included Robertson and Phillpotts who did not reach Zermatt until that afternoon nor the Martin party as it had left the Hotel Monte Rosa for the Gornergrat at 6 a.m.

As McCormick was returning from the Gornergrat, a messenger gave him a letter from Whymper informing him of the death of Hudson and asking if he could possibly return by 4.30p.m. so as to join him in a search. He ran down from the Riffel but it was too late to do anything that day, even had they started at four o'clock, and so McCormick, Whymper and others set off at one o'clock on the Sunday morning. McCormick's church duties were performed by the Rev Warr and the Rev Sanders.

McCormick seems to have given great support to Whymper during the week

The English church at Zermatt

that followed the accident and he may well have been the principal influence on him, particularly in the way he was to speak and write of the accident. McCormick's letter to *The Times* written on 17th July and published on 22nd was not just his own account of the background to Hudson's attempt, followed by what he had heard of the climb and accident from Whymper, plus details of the search and the burial of the bodies. It seems as though he and Whymper worked together and decided to publish the essential facts once and for all and in particular to avoid causing pain to the relatives of the victims. When Whymper was later being pressed to write to *The Times*, he wrote to the Editor on about 4th August 'I had hoped that the letters of the Revd. McCormick would have been sufficient for the information of the public, although they were intentionally silent on certain points, including the exact cause of the accident, in order to spare the families of Messrs. Hadow and Hudson the additional pain they must feel if it is published.'

McCormick's problems during his sad holiday in Zermatt in July 1865 were not confined to the aftermath of the Matterhorn accident and the avalanche on Monte Rosa on 27th July from which everyone except a porter was dug out alive. On 19th July, when rumour reached Zermatt that Knyvet Wilson was missing from the Riffel, McCormick set off with Whymper and others to search for him, and on 28th July he and Stephenson, who had accompanied Lord Queensberry to Zermatt, had to get a party of guides together and set off with them in search of Lord Queensberry, who had started out alone at one o'clock in the morning for the Matterhorn, leaving a letter explaining his purpose. They managed to find him on the Hörnli, where he had made his way in the dark and then, according to Adams Reilly, 'clambered up the E face, had several narrow escapes and slipped down an ice slope'. McCormick was glad to get away from Zermatt and find some rest at Geneva with the Chaplain the Rev Henry Downton and his family, before resuming his duties at home.

Dangar & Blakeney referred briefly to him in *AJ70*. There seems to be no other reference to his mountaineering record, but judging from the stamina exhibited in his travels between Grindelwald and Chamonix and the fact that he was a noted athlete at Cambridge, he may well have been equal to many of the Alpine pioneers, who served little in the way of an apprenticeship in the mountains before making notable ascents, and had he been able to join Hudson in an attempt on the Matterhorn he would probably have been a great asset.

It was McCormick who launched the appeal for the Zermatt Memorial church. The main stages in his career are noted in the *Alpine Journal*, including being Chaplain to Queen Victoria, Edward VII and George V. He officiated at Whymper's wedding in 1906.

2.35
MAQUIGNAZ, JEAN-JOSEPH (1829 – 1890)

J-J Maquignaz' climbing career seems to have started in July 1865, when he was one of the porters accompanying J-A Carrel and other guides on the Matterhorn reconnaissance on behalf of Giordano. Whymper recorded in *Scrambles* under 'Subsequent history of the Matterhorn' how when the party arrived at the base of the final peak on 14th July only Carrel and J-J Maquignaz wanted to go on. It seems likely that this is based on what Carrel subsequently told him, but the question as to why they turned back is open to doubt and Whymper was probably wrong in view of what Gorret wrote on the subject. An important factor must have been Carrel's own disappointment on seeing Whymper's party on the summit and if he had wanted to go on, as well as Maquignaz, they would surely have done so. Guido Rey wrote of Gorret having verbally confirmed to him the original version and he supports it further by quoting from Giordano's diary: 'At 2 p.m. they saw Whymper and six others on the top; this froze them, as it were, and they all turned and descended'. Be that as it may, Maquignaz did not volunteer to try again when Giordano challenged the despondent men on 15th July, and he was not therefore a member of the victorious team on the 17th July.

But Maquignaz did take part as porter in Giordano's attempt on the Matterhorn in July 1866, when he was accompanied by three guides and four porters, and he wrote a letter a few days later to Canon Carrel reporting on the expedition in very bad French spelling. They spent five nights at the Cravate when bad weather prevented their reaching the Pic Tyndall and they had to retreat. A month earlier Maquignaz had sent another letter to the Canon,

J-Joseph Maquignaz

reporting the discovery of the cave near the Cravate, but this letter appears to have been written for him by the Curé and he merely signed it.

After Tyndall wanted to climb the Matterhorn in July 1867, but refused to meet Carrel's exorbitant demand that he take four guides and pay each one 150frs, Crauford Grove succeeded in making the ascent with Carrel, Bich and a Meynet. Canon Carrel had been most upset to learn of Tyndall's set-back and he seems to have encouraged Maquignaz to make the ascent, and he subsequently wrote to Tyndall describing the new route and saying that it would be a pleasure for the Maquignaz brothers to accompany him, without asking him to make a great financial sacrifice.

Although J-A Carrel stands out as the one who first doubted the inaccessibility of the Matterhorn and was determined to make the first ascent from Breuil, which he ultimately achieved with his bold traverse of the gallery above the Tiefenmatten face that bears his name, Maquignaz in fact did more than any other guide to open up the mountain by his achievements in 1867 and 1868. In marked contrast to the guides of Zermatt, he and some of the other guides of Breuil seem to have recognised from the advice of Canon Carrel, that foreigners would want to climb the Matterhorn and in order that J-A Carrel might not acquire a monopoly after Grove's ascent, they set off on 12th September 1867 to climb the mountain. The party consisted of three Maquignaz, two new Carrels and Felicité, the eighteen year old daughter of one of the Carrels, who managed to get as far as the Col that now bears her name. Only J-J and J-P Maquignaz reached the summit, by tackling the final rocks direct and avoiding the detour into Switzerland via the Galerie Carrel. This route, which Gorret had wanted to take on the first ascent, involved some very hard climbing in the vicinity of the present Echelle Jordan.

Joseph Maquignaz' future was assured the same day by the arrival in Breuil of Leighton Jordan, fresh from his unsuccessful attempts to climb the Matterhorn from Zermatt. The weather prevented them from repeating the ascent from Breuil immediately, and during the next fortnight or so they made numerous other climbs. As Rey wrote in his great book: 'J.Joseph Maquignaz, the humble porter who had been enrolled by Carrel in 1865 to work as a stone-cutter, had suddenly become a great guide. That was the heroic age, when men lay down to sleep as private soldiers and awoke as field-marshals.'

From the Adler glacier Jordan pointed out to Maquignaz the route they would take for their descent to Zermatt. On 2nd October they climbed the Matterhorn from Breuil, descending on the Zermatt side as far as the scene of the catastrophe. They explored the vicinity, found an alternative and better route, returned to the summit, repositioned the rope that was replaced in 1869 by the Echelle Jordan and descended to the hut on the Cravate for the night. Their intention to return to the summit and descend to Zermatt the next day was frustrated by bad weather and they had to descend to Breuil. But Maquignaz had seen enough of the Hörnli ridge to be able to lead Tyndall on the first traverse from Breuil to Zermatt in July 1868, making what they must have thought would have been the first full descent of the Hörnli ridge since the accident, little knowing until they noticed footsteps that Elliott had in fact made the second ascent from Zermatt only two days before. Equally remarkable was Maquignaz' willingness the following day to agree to return home by repeating the traverse in the opposite direction with the Swiss climber Thioly. They had to wait a few days for the weather to improve before completing the traverse with the additional handicap of the eccentric Hoiler, who insisted on wearing his half metre wide hat and on playing his clarinet on the summit.

In 1868 Joseph made another traverse from Breuil to Zermatt as well as a further ascent from Breuil, and was only prevented by bad weather from making a further traverse from Zermatt with Jordan. In August 1869 he and his three brothers accompanied Heathcote, making the ascent from Breuil and fixing the Jordan ladder on the way. Only a month before he had been Heathcote's leading guide in an unsuccessful attempt from Breuil in company with Peter Perren and Young Peter Taugwalder, when they were all struck by lightning as they were retreating from the Col Felicité. By then Maquignaz had made six ascents of the mountain, two normal ascents from Breuil and back, the Jordan climb from Breuil involving three hours exploration on the upper part of the Hörnli, and a total of three traverses, two from Breuil and one from Zermatt. It is interesting to speculate whether Heathcote had intended to traverse from Breuil to Zermatt, but why else would he have taken two Zermatt guides to Breuil and then have engaged a local man? Had there been no thunderstorm, the further opening up of the Matterhorn might have been advanced by two years or so by Maquignaz showing Perren and Taugwalder the safe way down the Hörnli! Young Peter Taugwalder would surely have discovered that there was no serious difficulty on the improved route above the shoulder on the Hörnli, and yet he did not make his second ascent of the Hörnli for another three years.

Maquignaz' subsequent career is covered by writers like Clark and Cunningham & Abney. Although he continued to climb the Matterhorn fairly regularly, he seems to have been retained a good deal by the Sella family. Clark states in his book on the early Alpine guides that he led Vittorio Sella on the first winter ascent or traverse of the Matterhorn in 1882, although in his biography of Sella, *The splendid hills*, published the year before he gives the credit to J-A Carrel. There is however little doubt that Carrel was the leading guide on that occasion, and that although Maquignaz did do a number of first winter ascents with Sella he did not accompany him on the Matterhorn. It seems likely that the error originated with Cunningham's essay on Maquignaz in his book *The Pioneers of the Alps*.

Tyndall wrote, comparing the qualities of Joseph and Pierre Maquignaz on the Matterhorn, how

> 'Joseph was the leader of our little party, and a brave, cool, and competent leader he proved himself to be. He was silent, save when he answered his brother's anxious and oft repeated question, "Est-tu bien placé, Joseph?" Along with being perfectly cool and brave, he seemed to be perfectly truthful. He did not pretend to be "bien placé" when he was not, nor avow a power of holding which he knew he did not possess. Pierre is, I believe, under normal circumstances, an excellent guide, and he enjoys the reputation of being never tired. But in such circumstances as we encountered on the Matterhorn he is not the equal of his brother. Joseph, if I may use the term, is a man of high boiling point, his constitutional *sangfroid* resisting the ebullition of fear. Pierre, on the contrary, shows a strong tendency to boil over in perilous places.'

Joseph Maquignaz and J-A Carrel were both born in 1829 and they both died in 1890, Joseph having disappeared in a terrible storm on Mont Blanc less than a week before Carrel collapsed and died from exposure on the Matterhorn.

Whymper appears to have made one of his rare factual errors by including Maquignaz in 'The Clubroom of Zermatt, in 1864', as it was probably not until 1867 that he first visited Zermatt as a guide.

2.36
MARTIN, ALEXANDRE JULES (1822 – 1887)

Martin, who visited Zermatt from the 14th until the 16th July 1865 with his son Ernest and Dr & Mrs Gautier and their two sons, was Professor of law at Geneva University. They left Geneva on 13th July and Martin recorded in his diary their travels which after Zermatt took them on to Belalp, Eggishorn (after crossing the Aletsch glacier to Riederalp, their horses following more slowly) and to Oberwald; then over the Grimsel to Interlaken and Bern, returning to Geneva on 24th July.

They left Visp early on Friday 14th July, lunched at St.Niklaus and after passing through Randa met M.Briquet of Geneva and his companions who told them that the Matterhorn had been climbed by some Englishmen. Reaching Zermatt at 5.30p.m. they spent the night at the Monte Rosa. They set off at 6 a.m. on the Saturday morning for the Riffel and the Gornergrat, which they reached in 3½ hours, returning to the Riffel by midday and staying there that night. The diary entry for Saturday 15th July includes:

> 'News – as disastrous as it is unexpected – yesterday's ascent ended in disaster: four people killed, three English and a Chamonix guide. Such is the news tourists bring us from

> Zermatt: Mr.Whymper returned alone at 10.30 to-day with two Tauchwalder, Zermatt guides. Perished: Messrs Hadow, Hudson, Lord Douglas (aged 18), & Michel Croz a Chamonix guide. The accident happened on the descent quite close to the summit, at about 3 o'clock yesterday afternoon. Hadow slipped, dragged down Hudson, Douglas, and Croz; they fell into empty space; the last 3 held on with the rope that was securing all seven, but the rope broke between Douglas & Tauchwalder; & the first 4 were thrown onto the rocks, & from there onto the glacier at the foot of the Matterhorn; 4,000 feet below! This horrible news haunted us for the rest of the day...'

On the Sunday morning they leave early, reaching Zermatt by seven o'clock, where they find Seiler very upset by the tragedy. 'Mr.Whymper set off in the night with some Chamonix guides'. Martin's son Ernest is feeling tired, so Augusta Gautier stays behind with him whilst the others go up to the Schwarzsee chapel following 'the route taken by the Matterhorn climbers and by those who are looking for them'. Back in Zermatt by half past twelve they discover that during their absence Augusta has written an account of the previous day's occurrence to send to the *Journal de Genève*. The diary records that Whymper arrived at about three o'clock with a few Englishmen and some guides, having found the three almost unrecognisable bodies of Hadow, Hudson and Croz, but no sign of Douglas. At four o'clock the Martin party sets off for Randa and St.Niklaus.

Claire Engel, who first learnt of Martin's diary account from his grandson and published extracts from it in an article in *Die Alpen* in 1949, commented on it being curious that he should have recorded without comment how Whymper had set off with a party of Chamonix guides and how there would have been plenty to say about the Zermatt priest prohibiting the local guides from taking part. She also commented on the accuracy of Martin's account, which is all the more remarkable when consideration is given to the unreliability of most of the reports reaching the newspapers in the week that followed the accident. There can however be doubt as to when someone actually made an entry in a diary, as even the best routine may be interrupted from time to time with the result that several days entries are all written at the same time. It does not therefore necessarily follow that Martin recorded the names of the victims correctly on the Saturday, but the explanation may well be that he learnt them from Girdlestone who was also at the Riffelhaus. In any event Martin would have had several opportunities to learn more details on the Sunday, including during his two visits to the Monte Rosa hotel.

McCormick, together with Campbell and others whom he did not name, had set off for the Gornergrat on the Saturday morning 'before ten', and they cannot have missed seeing Whymper by very much if he reached Zermatt at half-past ten, even though their tracks would not have crossed. The messenger who carried Whymper's letter informing McCormick of Hudson's death must have brought the earliest reliable news of the accident, but unless he also carried a message from Seiler to the Riffel hotel he cannot have communicated accurate details of the

Nous avons reçu de Zermatt (16 juillet) plusieurs lettres, qui complètent sur quelques points le récit que nous avons donné de la terrible catastrophe du 14 juillet. En voici quelques extraits :

« ... En arrivant à Zermatt le vendredi 14 au soir, nous avons appris que le pic du Matterhorn, jusqu'alors inaccessible, avait enfin été atteint, et qu'avec une lunette d'approche on avait vu à 2 heures des hommes sur son sommet.

« Il était en effet parti la veille une expédition pour cette redoutable cime. Des Anglais, cela va sans dire, avaient résolu de tenter encore une fois de gravir le géant qui surplombe de sa pyramide abrupte les hautes montagnes d'alentour, et dont la hauteur est de 4482 mètres. Ils étaient quatre ; l'un d'entre eux, M. E. Whymper avait failli payer de sa vie il y a deux ans, cette même ascension ; il était décidé, dit-on, à l'accomplir ou à y trouver la mort. Trois guides, deux de Zermatt et l'autre de Chamounix, accompagnaient ces hardis fils d'Albion.

« Tout Zermatt ne parlait que de la grande nouvelle : la dernière cime de la chaîne du Mont-Rose avait été à son tour foulée par le pied de l'homme, et rien n'était impossible à l'audace et au sang-froid de la race anglo-saxonne.

« Ceux qui ont visité Zermatt et vu le gigantesque pic se dresser à une hauteur de 4000 pieds au-dessus de sa large base, peuvent seuls comprendre le péril immense de cette entreprise inouïe. Mais dans la joie du triomphe et de la victoire, on ne réfléchissait pas que tout n'était pas encore dit, et qu'il s'agissait de redescendre les flancs du rocher.

« Quoi qu'il en soit, une douloureuse nouvelle se répandit le samedi matin et parvint bientôt jusqu'au Riffel, où nous étions. Sur les sept voyageurs partis le 13 de Zermatt, trois seulement y étaient rentrés ; les autres avaient péri en redescendant. Voici les faits tels que nous les avons recueillis.

« Parvenus, après beaucoup de peine, tout en haut de la paroi verticale qui termine le Cervin, les voyageurs durent se cramponner à la cîme, large à peine de quelques pieds. Ils se préparèrent ensuite à revenir sur leurs pas et commencèrent à descendre ; le guide de Chamounix, Michel Cropt, était le premier ; puis venaient trois Anglais ; arrivés à 80 ou 100 pieds du sommet, le pied manqua à l'un de ceux-ci, qui en était à son coup d'essai et n'avait encore jamais fait de grandes ascensions. Il tombe et se trouve suspendu à la corde de sûreté. Fût-ce cette secousse ou leur propre fatigue, toujours est-il que les deux autres Anglais ne tardèrent pas à être lancés aussi dans le vide, et que ce poids soudain rompit la corde usée sans doute par le frottement du rocher. Elle se cassa, entraînant les quatre malheureux dans un abîme de 4000 pieds. Les autres durent la vie à leur présence d'esprit ; ils eurent le temps de rattacher le reste de la corde à une saillie du rocher, et, continuant leur terrible descente, ils marchèrent jusqu'à dix heures du soir, puis passèrent la nuit appuyés contre un rocher. M. Whymper, l'Anglais survivant, ne prononça, dit-on, pas une parole pendant cette affreuse nuit. Il arrivait le lendemain vers onze heures à Zermatt, avec les deux guides du pays, le père et le fils Taugwald, et dix hommes partirent aussitôt pour aller à la recherche des corps. Il paraît qu'on les a découverts sur un champ de neige entouré de crevasses peut-être infranchissables, et tout à la base du cône du Cervin, à une hauteur de 9000 pieds à peu près. Quatre Anglais, dont M. Whymper, sont repartis cette nuit avec plusieurs guides, et l'on espère ramener les dépouilles des victimes ; mais ce sera sans doute long et difficile.

« Si nous étions encore au temps des légendes, on en ferait une sur cette montagne se vengeant d'une si terrible façon de ceux qui avaient été assez audacieux pour ternir l'éclat de ses neiges immaculées.

« Mais dans notre siècle positif, je crains fort que l'avertissement ne soit perdu, et que, pas plus tard que l'an prochain, quelque aventureux membre de l'Alpine-Club ne tente encore une fois la redoutable aventure. »

Nous lisons dans une autre lettre :

« . . . Vendredi soir nous apprîmes la grande nouvelle que le Mont-Cervin était escaladé ; on avait vu à 2 heures des hommes sur la cime ; il n'y avait plus à en douter. C'était la préoccupation de toute la vallée. Hélas ! samedi matin à dix heures, un *seul* des quatre Anglais qui avaient fait l'entreprise revenait, M. Whymper ; trois Anglais ont péri avec un guide de Chamounix. Deux guides de Zermatt ont survécu aussi.

« En résumé, une heure à peine après l'arrivée au sommet, et dans la descente, à peu de distance de la cime, un des voyageurs a glissé et a entraîné successivement deux autres voyageurs et le guide de Chamounix par le fait de la corde qui les retenait tous. Les deux derniers guides et M. Whymper ont tenu bon, en enroulant la corde autour d'une pierre ; mais l'élan était donné, la corde a cassé et les quatre malheureux ont été lancés dans le vide. Ils sont tombés sur des rochers, à 4000 pieds plus bas, sur un champ de neige qui touche la face nord du Cervin. Les trois survivants ont fini par redescendre en se suspendant successivement à des fragments de corde qu'on fixait de distance en distance, mais ils sont arrivés le lendemain seulement à Zermatt. Jugez de la consternation succédant à l'exaltation de la veille. On a fait des recherches pour retrouver les corps, et hier j'ai vu revenir une compagnie de guides et d'Anglais qui avaient réussi à arriver à l'endroit où ils reposaient. Trois corps ont été reconnus, ceux de deux Anglais, MM. Hudson et Haddo, et du guide de Chamounix. Le corps du troisième Anglais, le jeune lord Fr. Douglas, n'a pu être retrouvé. On les a ensevelis provisoirement dans la neige, en attendant de savoir comment on pourra les transporter.

« L'entreprise était folle, et pourtant elle avait réussi à moitié. La cime avait été gravie, mais la catastrophe a été terrible ! »

Mme Gautier's letter extract in *Journal de Genève* of 20th July 1865

(see first two columns)

names etc, as it was only when McCormick arrived in Zermatt that 'the appalling truth was made known that he was but one of four who had fallen'. McCormick's party enjoyed the splendid view from the Gornergrat and was returning when the messenger 'came in haste' and gave him the letter. He then ran down from the Riffel, presumably starting at around three. It therefore looks as though Martin did not learn the news any earlier than McCormick and that if tourists brought it, as he stated in his diary, it must have arrived quite a bit later. News of an accident could have come with the messenger, but considering how inaccurately the Swiss papers reported it for some days, not knowing all the names, misspelling some and attributing the fall to Lord Douglas, it seems most unlikely that Martin learnt all the details much before dining at six, if indeed by then. The fact that he wrote in his diary 'Cette horrible nouvelle nous poursuit *toute la journée*' suggests therefore that he wrote it a day or two later, particularly as the entry for Saturday ends with 'Dîner à 6h. Belle soirée'.

But regardless of when Martin learnt his accurate details, Augusta Gautier wrote her letter to the *Journal de Genève* on the Sunday morning. She does not seem to have learnt anything new from Seiler or anyone else at the Monte Rosa hotel where she had stayed on the Friday night and where she probably remained most of the Sunday morning. She gives only a general account that must have mostly come from the Taugwalders, as she reveals less detail than Martin recorded in his diary. Claire Engel was therefore not strictly accurate when she said that Gautier got the party in the right order on the descent. She said that Michel Cropt [sic] was the first, followed by three Englishmen, but nowhere did she even mention the names of Hadow, Hudson and Lord Douglas. She said the accident happened when one of them, who had never done a major climb and was making his first attempt, lost his footing:

> 'He falls and is held by the safety rope. Whether it was this shock or their own fatigue, the other two Englishmen did not prevent themselves being hurled into empty space and the sudden weight broke the rope, doubtless frayed by the rock friction. The rope that broke dragged the unfortunate four into a 4000 foot abyss. The others owe their lives to their presence of mind; they had time to fasten the remainder of the rope to a projecting rock and continuing their terrible descent they carried on until 10 o'clock and then spent the night leaning against a rock. Mr.Whymper, the surviving Englishman, it is said, did not utter a word throughout this frightful night...'

Gautier completed her letter on the Sunday morning and did not subsequently amend it to report the outcome of Whymper's search party. She no doubt posted it to the *Journal de Genève* from Visp around midday on the Monday. Extracts from it and another letter appeared in the paper on Thursday 20th July, the other letter having apparently been written on the Monday. It refers to the survivors continuing their descent by fixing ropes and to the English search party finding three bodies but not that of Lord Francis Douglas. 'They have been provisionally buried in the snow, until it is known how they can be brought down.'

Gautier's account concluded with the thought that some adventurous member of the Alpine Club would probably attempt to repeat the climb no later than next year, and she was quite right, as although Birkbeck got no further than the shoulder with his seven guides, it was on 14th July 1866, the anniversary of the first ascent, that he chanced to attempt to repeat the climb.

2.37
OBER, PETER (1812 – 1869)

Ober was the proprietor of the Pension Schlössli in Interlaken, where Whymper seems to have stayed on 24th and 25th July 1865 on his way home from Zermatt. Formerly a teacher, Ober played a leading role in the development of Interlaken as a tourist resort, and his books on Interlaken and on the Bernese Oberland appeared in several editions.

He translated Whymper's long letter to von Fellenberg into French and German at the request of Hawker, when the latter discovered that von Fellenberg was in Grindelwald and decided to get the letter ready for insertion in the *Journal de Genève* and *Der Bund*. Heinrich Dübi believed Ober to have been the author of the strong criticism in the *Anzeiger von Interlaken* of Alfred Meissner's article in the Vienna *Neue freie Presse* of 4th August 1865. This gives rise to the possibility that Meissner stayed at the Pension Schlössli at the end of July and maybe learnt from Ober himself certain details of the accident that were not otherwise available at that time, or that in some other way he breached Ober's confidence.

2.38
PARKER, CHARLES STUART (1829 – 1910)
PARKER, ALFRED TRAILL (1837 – 1909)
PARKER, SAMUEL SANDBACH (1837 – 1905)

The Parker brothers' link with the first ascent of the Matterhorn and its aftermath stems not only from their pioneering guideless attempts on the Hörnli in 1860 and 1861 reaching a height of c.11,700 feet, but also from their arrival in Zermatt via the Triftjoch on the 29th July 1865. It seems quite probable that they had intended to make a further attempt on the Matterhorn until they heard of the accident. Instead, they had to content themselves with a bold guideless attempt on Monte Rosa on 4th August, only eight days after the avalanche that killed a porter.

Whymper gives some details in *Scrambles* of their 1860 and 1861 attempts and refers to there being no published account of them. It was not until 1916 and 1918 that Farrar published some of their letters and also photographs of them, in *AJ30 & 32*. However it is Dangar's article 'The Parkers and the Matterhorn' which is of greatest interest, as it publishes a letter which Charles Parker wrote, but seems not to have actually sent, to his father on 3rd October 1865, which gives details of a conversation he had with Old Peter Taugwalder, most probably on about 28th August 1865. But a letter that Sandbach Parker sent to J.D.Forbes on 5th August has also survived, and it suggests that Sandbach had by then already spoken to Old Peter, as it states: 'At present Peter Taugwald would on no account attempt the ascent, as he says the snow renders the rocks quite impracticable'.

Charles was some eight years older than his two brothers and it seems that by 1865 he had moved to University College Oxford, whilst the rest of the family still lived in Liverpool. This would explain how he was out of touch with Sandbach and his father and also his writing to the latter in October 1865. Margaret was a sister of the three brothers, judging from Charles Parker's letters. It seems as though father Parker had written to Charles towards the end of September 1865, mentioning that Margaret and Sandbach had recently met Whymper, which caused Charles to reply to his father that had he known they were going to meet he would have 'asked Sandbach to try to make out the truth about Peter Taugwalder'. This suggests that Whymper may have met them in Liverpool, or even in Birmingham on about 9th September when he was there for the British Association meeting.

It would seem as though Charles saw Taugwalder on his own as otherwise Sandbach would already have appreciated the need 'to make out the truth'. The likely explanation for Sandbach's ignorance is that Charles did not speak to Taugwalder at the beginning of August, when all three brothers were in Zermatt, but on about 28th when he seems to have returned to Zermatt with W.H.Gladstone and they climbed Monte Rosa; Taugwalder may even have been their guide. Mumm records that Sandbach was educated at Eton and Bonn University and the probability is that Charles was also a fluent German speaker, bearing in mind that Taugwalder spoke no English or French. Alfred's letter of 30th July to his father describes their reaching Zermatt the previous day and attending the Monte Rosa avalanche victim's funeral that morning. He also refers to 'a first-rate sermon from McCormick' and to his intention to have a talk to him. His next letter is from Belalp on 5th August, but it gives no indication as to how long they stayed in Zermatt nor what they did there. They seem, however, to have stayed at the Monte Rosa until 3rd August, when they moved up to the Riffelhaus for the night before heading for the Eggishorn, according to their entries in the hotel guestbooks. But Sandbach's letter to Forbes shows that bad weather forced them to retreat from the saddle on Monte Rosa and to take the valley route to Belalp instead of crossing the Adler to Saas.

Charles' letter of 3rd October 1865 is of considerable importance in that it refers to a number of matters troubling Taugwalder, whereas there is hardly any other post-accident record of anything relating to him, apart from his evidence at the Enquiry, Whymper's footnote in *Scrambles* and brief mention by Güssfeldt, Jordan and others. The question may be asked as to how and why Charles Parker came to talk to him, as from his limited acquaintance with the Zermatt area and the guideless nature of the brothers' expeditions there is no reason to suppose that he had ever climbed with him or even met him previously. The probability is that, whether or not Charles Parker employed Taugwalder on Monte Rosa, having been on the Hörnli ridge on two occasions he simply wanted to learn more about it and the accident, and had no idea that he would be met with such a tale of woes. Taugwalder was dissatisfied with his pay, with the absence of the money reward for the first ascent of the Matterhorn and with Whymper's behaviour 'especially in the colouring he gave to his evidence at Zermatt which has damaged Taugwalder'.

It should be borne in mind that Charles Parker wrote his letter at least one month after talking to Taugwalder. Nevertheless he had promised to write to Taugwalder after making enquiries and there is no reason to doubt that the letter he drafted to his father was an accurate record of what Taugwalder had said to him. If Taugwalder's Führerbuch has been preserved and not destroyed, it is possible that a letter Charles Parker may have written to him in about October 1865 will also still be in existence.

So far as Taugwalder's pay is concerned, there is an inconsistency between the details in Whymper's diary and what Parker recorded: 'Taugwalder says that he was promised a much larger sum, that he wd. never have run so much risk for the payment he rec'd. (120 francs and his son 80).' Whymper recorded that he paid Taugwalder 100 francs and the son 80 with a bonnemain of 20. Whether or not the bonnemain was supposed to be all for Young Peter or to be shared between the two of them, Old Peter seems to have helped himself to all of it and to have still been unsatisfied. Whymper sent 100frs to Croz' representatives via Adams Reilly and judging from the guides fees subsequently laid down both in Zermatt and in Breuil there is no reason to doubt Parker's comment on the payments Whymper made; 'It is very possible that the payment was just right under the circumstances'. Perhaps Douglas had promised something higher, and if regard is to be had to Taugwalder's refusal to accompany Whymper on the Italian ridge in 1861 for less than 200frs whether they succeeded or not, Taugwalder may well have charged Douglas more than the normal rate for his several attempts to find and climb the Gabelhorn. It should be borne in mind that Carrel's fees in 1861 for the Matterhorn were, according to Whymper, 'Twenty francs a day, whatever the result'.

But Taugwalder's comment to Parker that he would never have run so much risk for the payment he received, reflects against him not so much as to expose his greed but his unsuitability for such an ascent. It probably also explains why he never attempted the Hörnli again. The official tariff published by Ruden in his book in 1869 provided 40frs as far as the shoulder and 100frs for the summit, and it may well be that this was to some extent influenced by the opinions of the Taugwalders, as in the same list the Weisshorn and the Dent Blanche each commanded only 60frs. As for the money reward for the first ascent of the

Matterhorn – the universal belief in Zermatt according to Parker – there is nothing to suggest that one was ever offered, the inaccurate reports in the contemporary newspapers being consistent with the numerous inaccuracies relating to other aspects of the climb.

As for Taugwalder and Whymper each saying that the other behaved ill, Dangar questioned Taugwalder's reference to the colouring that Whymper gave to his evidence, and pointed out that nothing in Whymper's evidence quoted in the Official Report could be regarded as detrimental to Taugwalder. It is most unlikely that Taugwalder would have been told precisely what Whymper had said, although his cousins Johannes Julen the bailiff to the Enquiry and Alois Julen the Zermatt judge would have known and may well have told him something. It may well be that Taugwalder had in mind the tenor of the questions that Whymper drafted for him and that he did not realise that it was his cousin Alois Julen, and not Whymper, who probably acted to his detriment, by preventing him from giving the full and forthright answers which could have exonerated him altogether. There can therefore be no question of Whymper's evidence having damaged Taugwalder, but if Clemenz had recommended Taugwalder to Lord Francis Douglas, and if he should after the Enquiry have ceased recommending him to his guests, it is conceivable that Taugwalder might have mistakenly thought that Whymper was to blame rather than Clemenz himself.

Parker also wrote of Whymper saying that Taugwalder was greedy about pay, but by October 1865 Whymper had not published any reference to Taugwalder's pay. Likewise the reference to Taugwalder imperilling Whymper's life suggests rather more than the phrase in Whymper's letter to *The Times* that they 'were in such a state that a slip might have been expected from one or other at any moment'. It seems therefore as though Parker must, when writing to his father, have been relying in part on what others had told him, which may or may not have been accurate.

2.39
PAYOT, FRÉDÉRIC (1839 – 1927)

Payot, a Chamonix guide, was one of those who volunteered to go with Whymper on the second search party leaving early on the Sunday morning. He became a friend of Whymper.

2.40
PERREN, JOHANN PETER (1834 – ?)

'Peter Perren', as he was known, was undoubtedly the leading guide of his day in Zermatt. The SAC review of Gletscherführer in 1865 shows that there were then three active guides by the name of Perren, the other two being Peter Perren and Joseph Maria Perren, who seem mainly to have confined their activities to Monte Rosa and to passes in the Zermatt area. It is probable that most if not all references to Peter Perren in climbing literature refer to J.P.Perren rather than to P.Perren.

Peter Perren's record by 1864 was already an impressive one including first ascents of Alphubel, Lyskamm, Dent d'Herens and Grivola, ten ascents of Mont Blanc, and such varied peaks as the Dom, Weisshorn, Grand Paradis, Monte Viso, Wetterhorn, Galenstock, Tödi and Jungfrau (three times), as well as 20 ascents of Monte Rosa and 15 of the Breithorn. In 1864 he added the Ecrins and in 1865 the Aiguille Verte.

The 1863 edition of Ball's *Western Alps* states 'Peter Perren (of Zermatt) First rate. The best guide at Zermatt. Well acquainted with the Pennine and Graian Alps.' However in the 1873 edition of his *Introduction* Ball wrote 'Peter Perren of Zermatt. Has been the best guide at Zermatt, but not first rate. Well acquainted with the Pennine and Graian Alps.' In 1873 Perren was still only 39 years old and his down grading by Ball may perhaps be attributable not to any loss of mountaineering skill but to his 'clumsy attempt to shield his fellow villagers and fellow guides from the blame which he found had come to be attached to them' for the fatal accident to Mr.Chester on the Lyskamm in 1869.

Perren was chosen by Kennedy to accompany him on his winter attempt on the Matterhorn by the Hörnli ridge in 1862, and there is a record made by Morshead in the Monte Rosa guestbook in 1863 of Perren agreeing with him 'that an ascent was quite practicable by the Hörnli arête as far as the last sattel about 150 feet from the summit but [they] could see no way beyond that'. He was with Kennedy and Hudson on the Aiguille Verte and Mont Blanc during the first week of July 1865 and it seems probable that if Kennedy and Birkbeck had not had to return to England but had been able to join Hudson in the planned attempt on the Matterhorn, Perren and Croz would have been the leading guides. Perren almost certainly accompanied Hudson, Hadow and Croz to Zermatt but in the absence of McCormick, due to meet them on the 11th July in Visp but delayed by bad weather on his journey from Grindelwald, Hudson seems to have decided that he only needed Michel Croz for his Matterhorn venture with Hadow.

Perren was in Zermatt on the 15th and 16th July. He took part in the Hohlicht search party on the Saturday and would have accompanied Whymper's search party on the Sunday, but for the threat of excommunication; 'nothing else would have prevented him from joining in the search for his old comrades', Whymper wrote in *Scrambles*. On the 19th and 20th July Perren was a member of the party that recovered the bodies.

The next record of Perren attempting the Matterhorn is on 30th July 1869, when with Heathcote, Joseph Maquignaz and Young Peter Taugwalder he got beyond the Col Felicité on the Italian ridge and close to the summit when thunder and lightning forced them to retreat, all four sustaining injury from the lightning. Although in July 1871, in an exceptionally strong party including Lucy Walker and her father, Perren was to be the first Zermatt guide to reach the summit since the 1865 accident, he had become a victim of the Taugwalders' exaggerated and distorted views of the difficulties and by then it was almost too late to challenge the St.Niklaus guides' near monopoly of the Hörnli ridge. According to Whymper's table of ascents, Perren's only other ascent in the 15 years following the accident was in 1876.

Peter Perren occupies a prominent place in Whymper's drawing in *Scrambles*, 'The Clubroom of Zermatt in 1864'.

2.41
PHILLPOTTS, JAMES SURTEES (1839 – 1930)

J.S.Phillpotts (not to be confused with T.H.Philpott, who climbed with J.J.Hornby, and apart from meeting Whymper in Interlaken on about 25th July 1865 had no connection with the Matterhorn accident) arrived in Zermatt on 15th July with James Robertson and others. He volunteered to go on the search party with Whymper, setting off in the early hours of the Sunday morning, but there is no record of whatever else he did to help in the aftermath of the accident. He clearly played a lesser role than Whymper's principal advisers Robertson, Adams Reilly and McCormick and he may have done less than Vecqueray. He left Zermatt with Robertson on the morning of Saturday 22nd July.

Phillpotts, like Robertson, was a master at Rugby School (1862–1874), and subsequently became Headmaster of Bedford Grammar School (1874–1903). He never joined the Alpine Club. He climbed the Jungfrau and Mont Blanc and did the High Level route with Robertson, as well as several routes with Peter Knubel in 1872, but nothing else appears to be known of his climbing. Further confirmation that he and not T.H.Philpott was climbing with Robertson in 1863, comes from an entry in the Riffelhaus guestbook, four days after their Jungfrau ascent, in which J.Robertson, H.Chaytor and J.S.Phillpotts all appear together in the same handwriting.

2.42
PRIOR, REV WILLIAM PHELPS

Prior, the English chaplain at Vevey, seems to have made his way to Zermatt via the Val d'Herens and the Val d'Anniviers with a large family party, arriving at the Monte Rosa hotel on 18th July 1865 and moving up to the Riffelhaus the following day. Ronald Clark quotes from a letter he sent to his friend Mackenzie the Consul in Geneva, referring to his disgust with the Taugwalders' conduct an hour after the accident, and also to Whymper: He 'suffers awful mental anguish', and, 'The poor fellow will go beside himself if he does not leave the place'.

2.43
PULLER, ARTHUR GILES (1833 – 1885)

Giles Puller had apparently arrived in Zermatt by about midday on Saturday 15th July 1865, as the two Lochmatters took part in the Hohlicht search that afternoon and he was the one Whymper referred to in *Scrambles* as 'another Englishman lent us Joseph Marie and Alexander Lochmatter'. Clark records how 'During the day Arthur Giles-Puller had come into the Monte Rosa with the Lochmatter brothers and he now willingly agreed that they should join the search party'. The Lochmatters did not go on the recovery party on 19th/20th July and Puller may have laid them off on the Monday, as there is no record of his having made any further ascent that season. He had climbed the Aletschhorn with J.H.Kitson, descending to Belalp on 13th July. There is no record of their guides, but it seems likely they were the Lochmatters, as when Kitson then stayed on in the Oberland he joined H.D. Evans and Christian Almer. Puller had climbed Monte Rosa in 1864 with Old Peter Taugwalder and his son Joseph, a couple of days before making a high glacier tour round Monte Rosa with Old Peter and Alexander Lochmatter, in the course of which they also climbed the Lyskamm.

Although Puller practised at the Bar for no more than three years, he may have been able to give Whymper some legal advice following the accident in the absence of the many practising barristers in the Alpine Club, who would not arrive until the Long Vacation in August. It would be remarkable if Whymper's strict adherence to the facts and his abstention from offering observations or casting blame in his evidence at the Enquiry and also in his letter to von Fellenberg were entirely his own idea, in view of his lack of any legal training, and any legal advice he received in Zermatt could have come from Puller.

Puller climbed the Matterhorn from Breuil in July 1873 with J-A Carrel and J-J Maquignaz, a few days after climbing the Dent d'Herens.

2.44
QUEENSBERRY, 9TH MARQUESS OF; JOHN SHOLTO DOUGLAS (1844 – 1900)

Born on 20th July 1844, his 21st birthday celebrations planned for the 20th July 1865 have a bearing on the participation of his younger brother Lord Francis Douglas in the Matterhorn ascent and on his plans for the Matterhorn prior to his meeting Whymper at Breuil on 12th July. Had there been no accident Lord Francis should have just been able to reach the family home in Glen Stuart by

Wednesday 19th July after leaving Zermatt on the Saturday. As it was the news of the disaster reached Glen Stuart on the 19th July and within hours the Marquess was on his way to Zermatt, where he arrived on Monday 24th July, accompanied by a Mr.Stephenson. They stayed at the Monte Rosa. The same day his mother had sent a telegram to the Rev Joseph McCormick.

Ronald Clark quotes from material in the Coolidge archives regarding the Marquess staying in the same room and bed his brother had occupied. Adams Reilly's diary also refers to his stay in Zermatt, where on Wednesday 26th July they all seem to have dined at the Riffel. Queensberry and Hadow's uncle got lost on the way down, not getting back to the hotel until 1 a.m. But only 24 hours later Queensberry set off alone for the Matterhorn, leaving a letter explaining his purpose. When Stephenson found this he alerted Reilly, and Stephenson and McCormick collected a party of guides and started after him. Reilly followed with Hadow and met the others on the Hörnli arête, where they had found Queensberry. 'He had found his way to the Hörnli in the dark, clambered up the E face, had several narrow escapes and slipped down an ice slope. He was completely done.' Further details of these incidents appear in a letter Adams Reilly wrote to J.D.Forbes. The following day Saturday 29th July Queensberry and Stephenson left Zermatt, Reilly and Hadow walking part of the way down the valley with them.

On 28th July *The Times* published an extract from the *Dumfries Courier* stating inter alia that Lord Queensberry had hurried off to Switzerland being expected to arrive there on the Sunday. 'It is to be hoped that he will not expose himself to needless danger in an effort to recover the remains of his unfortunate brother.'

The Enquiry Report lists the belongings of the victims and, with the exception of Lord Francis Douglas, records the name of the person such as Seiler, J-B Croz or McCormick who signed for them. The explanation may be that Douglas's possessions were already in the custody of the Enquiry President Clemenz, in his other capacity as owner of the Hotel Mont Cervin, and that he handed them direct to Queensberry.

Whymper had in fact paid Douglas's debts in Zermatt, including his bill at the Cervin and reimbursement of an advance to him to pay his guide. Whymper presumably did not know that Douglas had deposited £15 with Clemenz or whoever was managing the hotel during his stay. On his return from Zermatt, Queensberry contacted Whymper and called to see him on Saturday 5th August. He wrote again on the 7th saying that he had quite forgotten to ask if Whymper had paid anything for his brother at Zermatt, and it seems that they corresponded further from time to time. In mid-August there seems to have been a rumour about the body being found and Whymper offered to do anything he could to help.

In December 1865 Lady Caroline Queensberry was corresponding with Whymper. At her request he sent a large photograph of the Matterhorn marking the spot from which they fell, and she sent him some lines that Horner had written about the Matterhorn. Queensberry seems to have followed up his brother's Matterhorn verses by writing some of his own at Zermatt in July 1865. There is a typewritten copy in the Alpine Club Archives, but the Queensberry family no longer has any archive material relating to the Matterhorn accident. Queensberry contributed £50 to the Zermatt Church subscription launched by McCormick, according to McCormick's letter of 14.8.65 to *The Times*.

Lord Francis's younger sister appears to have sought publicity in 1905, under the name of Florence Dixie, by writing to *The Times* asking readers going to Zermatt to keep a sharp lookout for the long-lost body of her brother, as 40 years had elapsed and she expected it to be delivered up by the Zmutt glacier. The same idea appeared in an article in the *Tatler*, but her letter to the Editor of the *Daily Graphic* the same year described a mysterious incident that occurred on the night of the 14th July 1865, which may well account for such things as the telegram, which her mother Lady Queensberry sent to McCormick on 24th July 1865. The telegram stated 'Is it not possible to seek in the rocks above or to let down food'. The editor of the *Alpine Journal* commented, when publishing the contents of the telegram in 1965, that Lord Francis Douglas's mother seems not to have realised the true nature of the catastrophe despite McCormick's letter to *The Times* appearing on 22nd July. But even as late as December 1865 she commented in a letter to Whymper, thanking him for the photograph of the Matterhorn on which he had marked the spot from which they fell, 'I can imagine how very possible it was for my precious one to have remained somewhere here above in the rocks which I had *always* believed to be the case most firmly'.

Florence Dixie's letter to the *Daily Graphic* referred to spending the night of 14th July 1865 in London to break the journey on the way home. She and her mother were sharing a room and went to bed early, but at about 10.30p.m. her mother's maid, Emily Whiting, appeared asking if she had been called. She retired after a negative reply, but reappeared at about 11 p.m. saying that her name had been distinctly called, only to be sent away again. It was nearly 12 o'clock when she reappeared once more assuring Lady Queensberry that a voice had called her by the name of Whiting (a name used by Lord Francis, but not by Florence or her mother). She was then told to go back to bed and not to come again, but later on she appeared once more, the fourth time, in a very agitated state, declaring that she had had a dream or vision in which she saw Francis 'lying on a rocky ledge on a great precipice, terribly wounded. He was dragging himself along.' Florence Dixie concluded her letter by saying that the incident was an indelible reminiscence of her childhood.

It seems probable that John Tyndall's fruitless endeavours to recover the body were inspired by the information that Lord Francis Douglas's mother suffered much from the idea of her son not having been found. Newman Hall, who met Tyndall on the way to St.Niklaus recorded that 'the mother of Lord Douglas had a morbid idea that her son was still alive on the rocks. [Tyndall] knew this to be impossible, but to calm her mind he had gone to Geneva and purchased 3000 feet of rope, by which to be suspended so that he could with his eye sweep the precipice.'

Clark refers to a cousin of Douglas asking the British Mission in Bern for a copy of the evidence Whymper had given at the Enquiry, and says 'He was duly provided with the information a few days later'. There appears to be a copy of the document on which it was based in the bundle of papers relating to the Enquiry.

Queensberry returned to Zermatt in September 1871 with Hon.E.Ellis, and they employed Young Peter Taugwalder for a week as guide, making 'several excursions'. The entry in Young Peter's Führerbuch includes 'he also went with his father with us over the Theodule pass to Breuil & back by the Furggen pass to Zermatt. I found him most willing & obliging, always cheerful and I should consider him to be a first rate guide in all respects & can recommend him accordingly.' It seems that this was not an isolated visit to the mountains, as a four or five page account Queensberry wrote of an ascent of Piz Linard on 17.7.1873 was published in the German/Austrian Alpine Club Yearbook and also mentioned by Zsigmondy in his book.

de Beer records that Queensberry went to Zermatt again in 1876, but there does not seem to be any record of his doing any mountaineering and it is no doubt based on the date 'Jun 10, 1876', which appears at the end of his lengthy poem, *The spirit of the Matterhorn*, published in London in 1881. It does not seem to have any historical or mountaineering interest.

In 1879 Queensberry with his sister Florence Dixie and her husband visited Patagonia, and, as Edward Peck has said in his article 'Pioneers of the Paine', their expedition was the first tourist foray into the Paine. The illustrations in Dixie's book were engraved by Whymper's firm.

2.45
REILLY, ANTHONY MILES WILLIAM ADAMS (1836 – 1885)

Adams Reilly, as he is generally referred to, was very active in the Alps in the 1860's largely in connection with the surveys he carried out for his maps of 'The chain of Mont Blanc' and of 'Monte Rosa'. He had been going to try the Hörnli ridge of the Matterhorn in 1864 with Whymper, had the latter not had to return home suddenly to attend to his business. He appears to have been a close friend of Whymper and, when in early June 1865 he heard from Birkbeck that he, Hudson, and Kennedy intended to try the Aiguille Verte at the end of June and then the Matterhorn, he immediately wrote to Whymper on the off chance that the letter might reach him, if he should have had to delay his departure for the Alps. Adams Reilly was in the Alps from 27th June until the beginning of August, including a fortnight on the Italian side of Monte Rosa followed by some fifteen days in Zermatt, and after calling at Chamonix he returned to London via Paris. When Whymper was in the vicinity of Breuil prior to meeting Lord Francis Douglas on

Adams Reilly

11th July Adams Reilly was in the Macugnaga area, but as they never met and as Whymper had left London for Switzerland on the very day that Reilly had written to him, Whymper seems never to have received advance warning of Hudson's plans even though they corresponded further in the Alps.

Adams Reilly learnt of the Matterhorn accident at Breuil on 17th July and the next day he went to Zermatt, slipping and cutting open his left knee cap on the way as he jumped a glacier stream. The entries in his diary over the next twelve days or so contain a lot of details of post-accident events in Zermatt, some of which are not mentioned elsewhere. He records, amongst others, the arrival of J-B Croz, Lord Queensberry, Hadow's uncle and the Parker brothers, as well as the departure of the first two and of Robertson, Phillpotts and Vecqueray. He also records Whymper's departure after his own guide Charlet and a porter had returned to Zermatt on the Saturday morning with the remainder of Whymper's luggage from Breuil. This would seem to explain why Whymper had to delay his departure on the Saturday morning, instead of accompanying Robertson to Visp, where he himself arrived not far short of midnight and too late to call on Robertson. The alternative explanation for Whymper's late departure could be that Clemenz did not release him until he had received Taugwalder's replies to the questions he had prepared for him, which may well not have been until midday on the Saturday.

It is doubtful whether Robertson was more than an acquaintance of Whymper's in July 1865, although they subsequently became friends, and Adams Reilly appears therefore to have been the only established friend of Whymper's at Zermatt during most of the week he was detained there. Reilly acted on Whymper's behalf in dealing with J-B Croz, giving him 100 francs for his brother's fees on the Matterhorn and arranging to see him again in Chamonix two weeks later to collect his brother's hat and take it home for Whymper. J-B Croz arrived in Zermatt during the evening of Saturday 22nd July and set off home again the following morning. It seems probable that Croz and Whymper passed each other on the Saturday afternoon somewhere in the vicinity of St.Niklaus, but that they did not see or recognise each other, having never climbed together nor even spoken to one another in the past.

Reilly's diary also refers to the Riffelhorn search for Wilson, to the funerals conducted by McCormick and Downton and to the extraordinary events when Lord Queensberry and Hadow got lost after dining at the Riffel and did not get back to Zermatt until 1 a.m., and when, exactly 24 hours later, Queensberry set off on his own for the Matterhorn, leaving a letter explaining his purpose. This incident is mentioned by Clark in *The Day the Rope Broke*, but seems in fact to have been considerably more serious than Coolidge or Miss Brevoort recorded. Reilly refers to McCormick setting off after Queensberry with a party of guides who eventually found him on the end of the Hörnli arête. 'He had found his way to the Hörnli in the dark, clambered up the E face, had several narrow escapes & slipped down an ice slope.' Some further details of these two incidents appear in Reilly's letter of 1st August to J.D.Forbes.

There is also a letter that Reilly wrote to Forbes on 19th July, which refers to the Matterhorn accident and must be one of the earliest accounts to have survived. Although one would expect Reilly to be a particularly reliable historian, the value of the information he was passing to Forbes is unfortunately undermined by his apparent failure to distinguish between facts that he probably learnt direct from the likes of Whymper or McCormick and hearsay or even rumour that he probably picked up at Breuil. The letter must have been written only 24 hours after Reilly reached Zermatt, as he lay on a sofa with his knee in an ice-water bandage, and therefore before he had the opportunity of hearing all the details from Whymper himself. The letter includes:

> 'I arrived at Breuil on the 17th, (having entirely completed my survey, from the Matterhorn to Mte Moro, with the exception of my base line) when I was met by the sad news of the accident on the Matterhorn, of which you have probably by this time heard. I felt much for poor Whymper, and immediately crossed the Theodule for Zermatt, to see whether I could be of any comfort to him. He is terribly cut up poor fellow.
>
> The authentic account of the accident went off to *The Times* yesterday, but I believe that the blame (which rests on the dead) was softened down as much as possible. Mr Hudson, with a young friend of his, Mr Hadow and Michel Croz of Chamounix came here to try the Matterhorn, with wire rope to tie to the rocks, & all sorts of quackery, and found here Lord Fr Douglas, a fine young fellow, quite a boy, who had after several plucky attempts ascended the Gabelhorn, and who appears to have been anxious to try something else still more difficult. Whymper was at Breuil, where he had gone to meet me, and Douglas went over the St Theodule to find him, and borrow his tent.
>
> They brought the tent over, and the whole party, Hudson, Hadow, Whymper, Douglas, Michel Croz, & Peter Taugwalder and his son, slept above the Hörnli, and tried the Riffelberg face of the Matterhorn. Steep as it looks, they found it perfectly practicable, almost easy, owing to the stratification of the rock, – the reverse of what it is on the Breuil side, which though apparently the easiest, has been so often tried in vain. *[Reilly then gives a sketch of the stratification dipping from the Riffel side towards the Breuil side]*
>
> You will see how on one side the footing is on rock sloping *towards* the precipice, and on the other, sloping from the precipice, and of course much safer. There was however one difficult spot near the top, where they had to cross the face diagonally, but they got well over it, and reached the summit.
>
> But in coming down, at this spot, Mr Hadow slipped. Croz was first, he second, then Mr Hudson, Lord F Douglas, Peter Taugwald, Whymper, and the other Taugwald last, all roped. In his fall, Mr Hadow carried off first Croz, then the two behind him. Peter Taugwald kept his footing, but the rope broke, and the first 4 were dashed to pieces. How the rope broke, without carrying Peter Taugwald off his legs, does not appear: there is some suspicion that he had given it a turn round a projecting rock, which may have cut it. This will however be investigated.
>
> Mr Hadow was quite a novice, he had only been up three mountains before, but though Mr Hudson knew this, he never told any of the party, and this was, at least in its consequences,

> an unhappy error; for Whymper would have strongly remonstrated had he known it, as he well knew that the Matterhorn is no work for a novice. Poor Mr Hudson was responsible for his friend, and it was the want of practice of the latter that caused this sad business.
> Some fragments of the bodies have been found, but not an atom of poor Douglas can be traced.'

It is interesting to note Reilly's belief that in the authentic account (McCormick's letter to *The Times* despatched the previous day) 'the blame was softened down', as this was confirmed in Whymper's letter of about 4th August to the *Times* editor. It suggests that Reilly was relying on what he had learnt from McCormick, as does the later reference to Hadow having only been up three mountains. But the details Reilly gives about Hudson finding Douglas at Zermatt and about Douglas going to Breuil to meet Whymper and borrow his tent are wholly inconsistent with what we know from the writings of McCormick and of Girdlestone, never mind what Whymper himself later wrote. It seems, therefore, that the possibility of Reilly being correct on these details can be dismissed. It is nevertheless desirable to take a more detailed look here at some of the obvious objections to such a novel version of events in order to justify not considering it elsewhere.

Much depends on the date that Hudson reached Zermatt. We know from *A sad holiday* that McCormick was due to meet him at Visp on Tuesday 11th but was prevented from doing so by bad weather. We do not know Hudson's movements after driving with Kennedy from Chamonix to Les Ouches on the latter's unexpected departure on Saturday 8th July but, after revising his plans, it would have taken him some time to reach Visp and there is no reason to suppose that he would have let McCormick down by passing through Visp on the Monday, particularly when there could be no advantage in reaching Zermatt early in such bad weather. But McCormick would have learnt later from Campbell of any such change in Hudson's plans. The fact that Hudson and Hadow were late going into dinner at the Monte Rosa on the Wednesday evening after 'inspecting' the Matterhorn – and doing so without Croz – is consistent with their having reached Zermatt that afternoon after perhaps spending the Tuesday night at St.Niklaus, but the strongest evidence of Hudson not having reached Zermatt until Wednesday 12th appears in McCormick's letter to *The Times*. As Campbell was with Hudson until his departure on the 13th and was with McCormick following his arrival at about midday on the 14th, there is no scope whatever for any misunderstanding on McCormick's part and we therefore know beyond doubt that Hudson reached Zermatt 24 hours after Douglas reached Breuil. Furthermore, as Douglas spent the Monday night at the Riffel prior to crossing the Theodule, he is hardly likely to have encountered Hudson in Zermatt even if contrary to all the evidence he should have arrived there on the Monday afternoon. Hudson cannot therefore have 'found' Douglas at Zermatt before he left for Breuil.

As for Douglas going to Breuil to meet Whymper and borrow his tent, there is no evidence that the two had ever met previously and no reason why Douglas should have known of Whymper's movements, even if Reilly did. But it would not make sense for anyone to contemplate borrowing the tent when Whymper was also at Breuil and likely to want to use it himself, and we know for a fact that he would have been using it had not Carrel been engaged by Giordano. The probable explanation for this error on Reilly's part is that he was merely quoting what he had heard in Breuil, which no doubt had its origin in a rumour that Douglas and a porter had been seen to arrive from Zermatt on the Tuesday and to depart again early on the Wednesday with Whymper's tent.

Reilly's account of the accident rings true and the point about the stratification of the rock (which might have been of particular interest to Forbes) could only have come from Whymper, but the matter of Hadow having only been on three mountains seems more likely to have originated with McCormick. As for the suspicion that Old Peter had given the rope 'a turn around a projecting rock, which may have cut it', this was expressly denied by Whymper in his letter to von Fellenberg, and it seems to have been some general comment that Reilly picked up in Zermatt, based no doubt on the account that seems to have originated with Young Peter and which also appeared in the *Journal de Genève* on Tuesday 18th July.

Reilly's diary also provides confirmation of the rather extraordinary fact that Clemenz did not hold the Official Enquiry until 2 p.m. on the Friday, the other evidence of this being the summons Whymper received the same day requiring him to attend at 2 p.m. After leaving Zermatt on 3rd August, Reilly called at Chamonix and Paris where he collected various French newspapers for Whymper, which probably included *L'Abeille de Chamonix* of 23rd July as well as a cutting from a Paris newspaper describing how everyone was stopping to admire the two drawings by Gustave Doré, showing the arrival at the summit of the Matterhorn as well as the fall. Reilly arrived back in London on 12th August.

Reilly's obituary in the *Alpine Journal* by C.E.Mathews refers to his having been present at Mathews' house when the British Association met in Birmingham in 1865 and when Whymper related to Principal Forbes the story of the tragedy on the Matterhorn. This was probably on Monday 11th September, judging from a letter Forbes wrote to his wife the following evening, referring to the meetings of the Association and including: 'The little time I had to spare I spent not in Section A but in the Geographical with the Alpine Clubbists. I had a great deal of interesting conversation with Whymper last evening. He was considered an immense Lion at the Association, but conducted himself with the greatest discretion.'

Reilly's notebooks and some diaries were presented to the Alpine Club in about 1917 but, apart from Farrar quoting from an 1864 notebook the same year, there is no sign of anyone like Dangar or Blakeney ever having come across them and their present whereabouts are unknown. Fortunately Graham Brown saw the 1865 diary, amongst others, perhaps in the early 1930's, and the copies he made of many of the entries are in the Graham Brown archives at the National Library of Scotland.

2.46
ROBERTSON, REV JAMES (1836 – 1903)

James Robertson was an assistant master at Rugby School in 1865, moving to Harrow in 1872 and to Haileybury in 1884, where he was Headmaster until 1890. He then became Vicar of Whittlesford, where he remained until his death. It has been said that he declined Hudson's invitation to join in his proposed attempt on the Matterhorn, but this is open to doubt. They certainly did not meet in Zermatt on 12th July, as Gos has stated, nor does there appear to be any basis for Clark's embroidered account of Hudson discussing his programme with Robertson at Chamonix on the evening of 7th July and then inviting him to try the Matterhorn. Mumm recorded Robertson as having climbed Mont Blanc on 4th July and he was probably still at Chamonix, but it hardly seems right for Clark to state that 'Yeats Brown was there [on the 7th] with his friend the Rev James Robertson', when Yeats Brown wrote of first meeting Robertson and his party [on 10th July], 'The eldest of them, who, as leader of the party, had hesitated about admitting me to walk with them was, I think, called Robertson'.

Robertson took the High Level route to Zermatt with Brown, Phillpotts and Wilson, arriving on the afternoon of Saturday 15th after meeting some of the first search party on the way. He and Phillpotts joined Whymper on the second search, leaving Zermatt at 1 a.m. the following morning, after the Zermatt guides had been 'threatened with excommunication by their priests if they failed to attend the early mass' and, so, were unable to accompany Whymper.

Robertson, whom Whymper included in his drawing 'The Clubroom of Zermatt in 1864', had stayed at the Riffelhaus in August 1862, climbing Monte Rosa, and again in July 1863, recording a visit with J.S.Phillpotts and H.Chaytor. He stayed at the Monte Rosa in 1864 with C.G.Heathcote, whose article on the Laquin Joch suggests that his climbing was far more extensive than recorded by Mumm. 1865 seems to have been the first occasion when he was accompanied by Knyvet Wilson, another master at Rugby, who was killed on 18th July when he fell alone on the Riffelhorn. Robertson and Phillpotts subsequently took control of his possessions and signed for them, according to a document inexplicably forming part of the Matterhorn accident Enquiry Report headed 'Inventory of Edouard Wilson'.

'I am glad to see your handwriting', were the opening words of Whymper's letter of 27th August 1865 to Robertson, acknowledging his contribution to the Croz fund. This appears to have been the first contact between the two men since parting company in Zermatt on 22nd July. Although some four years older than Whymper, Robertson had not joined the Alpine Club until the previous year and there is nothing to suggest that they were close friends rather than mere acquaintances, prior to their meeting in Zermatt on 15th July. It may well be therefore that Whymper's familiarity with Robertson's handwriting arose out of the help that he gave Whymper during the week following the accident. This may well have included help with the drafting of his factual answers to Clemenz' questions and also perhaps with the drafting of the questions to be put to Taugwalder. He may have been particularly interested in the matter of the ropes, as the Alpine Club has a letter he received from Whymper in March 1869, which includes 'the white rope is made as thick as ever. I don't know if the Committee are doing anything about a lighter one'.

Robertson never published anything about the Matterhorn accident but it seems as though he did keep a diary in which he recorded details, as in 1957 Dangar & Blakeney wrote in the *Alpine Journal* of his son Ainslie J.Robertson telling them that Croz' crucifix was found embedded in his jaw and James Robertson had dug it out with a penknife. Presumably this was recorded in his father's diary which, if it is still in existence, is likely also to record the two incidents of which Whymper wrote in his article in the *Graphic* in 1894, as having recently come to his knowledge. Firstly, in relation to the Zermatt guides being threatened with excommunication, Whymper wrote of Franz Andenmatten being the first to volunteer to attempt to recover the remains of the victims. 'Next Sunday Franz Andenmatten went to Mass, and this was his reward. "I saw him", said my informant (who is now Head Master of one of our public schools), "turned out, *ejected* from the church at Zermatt!" ' The fact that Robertson left Zermatt on the day before the 'next Sunday' need not invalidate the substance of the incident, as Andenmatten probably left Zermatt himself soon after giving evidence before the Enquiry on the Friday and there would have been additional opportunities for Robertson to witness such bitter behaviour during the intervening week. The actual day of the week is therefore of little consequence.

> 'The other incident' – as Whymper wrote – 'relates to Peter Taugwalder, the father. No sooner had the survivors of the ill-fated expedition returned to Zermatt, than the baseless, monstrous rumour was circulated that the old man had *cut* the rope which broke. It passed from lip to lip, spreading like wildfire, and emanated in his own village amongst his neighbours. The calumniated man, walking about shunned like a murderer, met the returning volunteers. "Mr. R–" he said to one of them, "they say I *cut* the rope. Look at my fingers!" and, opening his hands, showed how they had been lacerated by the jerk which all but tore him from his grasp.'

It seems that Whymper was not aware in 1894 that Robertson was no longer at Haileybury, so he probably learnt of the two incidents sometime between 1884 and 1890. Ronald Clark wrote of the latter incident, 'the fact that he should speak thus at all shows that even by that time, only 24 hours after the survivors had returned to the village, the ugly rumours were beginning to sprout'.

On 29th September 1866 Whymper sent Robertson a proposed inscription for

Croz' tomb, seeking his advice on it and asking if he could get Vecqueray to translate it. Robertson suggested an improvement to the last two lines, which Whymper accepted. Whymper and Robertson seem to have corresponded spasmodically for some 30 years on various topics. In 1895 Whymper sent him a photograph of Calkin's portrait of Croz and in return Robertson sent Whymper a sonnet in memory of Croz. Charles Gos gave a few more facts about Robertson's climbing career in his book *Le Cervin*, relying on the *AJ* obituary, but some of them are so obviously inaccurate that there is little purpose in considering them here.

2.47
SEILER, ALEXANDER (1819 – 1891)

Alexander Seiler

Seiler was an outstanding hotelier and his achievements appear all the more remarkable when one bears in mind what Theodore Wundt described as 'his lifelong fight with the Zermatters who continually looked upon him as a stranger, indeed as an enemy of the whole valley'. He recognised immediately the potential of the Matterhorn, both for the development of Zermatt as a resort, and as a magnet for mountaineers once the first ascent had been accomplished. In direct contrast to Old Peter Taugwalder, who was overwhelmed by the jealousy, envy and cunning of those who did everything they could to make his life as unbearable as possible (see section 4.62, Rudolf Taugwalder letter to Montagnier), Seiler refused to give in despite being 'constantly harassed by the short-sighted and petty persecutions of this benighted community' (Gardiner). While the Zermatt guides were boycotting the Matterhorn, Seiler was planning to build a hut on the Hörnli, relying no doubt on the judgment and encouragement of his guests, such as Whymper and Jordan. He arranged for his guests to be able to climb the Matterhorn with guides from St.Niklaus in the absence of any local initiative, and to all intents and purposes he performed the same role in Zermatt as did Canon Carrel in Breuil in opening up the mountain and helping climbers to avoid being exploited.

Born and brought up in the tiny village of Blitzingen in the upper Rhone valley, it was not apparently until 1851 that Seiler first went to look at Zermatt following the recommendation of his elder brother Joseph some four years previously, when he was appointed chaplain of Zermatt. Joseph's intention of building a hotel on the Riffelberg with the priest Ruden fell through when he was appointed to a post in Brig, but Ruden and two other local clerics went ahead and the Riffelhaus was opened in 1854. Seiler meanwhile had begun by leasing the Lauber Inn for the 1853 and 1854 summer seasons, after Clemenz had built and opened his Hotel Mont Cervin in 1852, and it seems that he also took a lease of the Riffelhaus in 1854. The same year he bought the Lauber Inn, improved it and renamed it the Hotel du Mont Rose.

The success of the Riffelhaus gave rise to the earliest recorded display of envy by the Zermatters. It is mentioned by Ruden, who seems to have owned three quarters of the hotel by the time it opened, and again by Kronig. Coolidge in his 'History of Zermatt' wrote how

> 'the Zermatt people were jealous at the success of the inn, and created such disturbances that in 1862 the house was sold to the commune, which gave a fresh lease for fifteen years to M.Seiler, after and on condition of paying the debt on the house (20,000 francs) and of enlarging it and improving it within and without, the Zermatt men delivering the building materials on the spot.'

By 1867 Clemenz seems to have had enough of the life of a hotelier and he sold the Mont Cervin to Seiler. Apart from Ignaz Biner, who in 1865 opened his Hotel des Alpes about which very little is known, the Zermatters seem to have had no interest in running hotels and the most extraordinary thing of all is that when the Commune finally got round to deciding in about 1873 to build a hotel, there was so much infighting that it was not until 1879 that the Hotel Zermatterhof actually got built and it was immediately leased to Seiler! But in the meantime the Zermatters had been doing some very nasty things to Seiler, to which reference will be made below.

Whymper's drawing 'The Clubroom of Zermatt' illustrates the importance of the Monte Rosa hotel to the development of Zermatt as a mountaineering resort, and the hotel owed everything to Alexander Seiler and his wife. There are many instances recorded of his kindness to guests and of the welcome they received whenever they returned. Things would probably have gone far less smoothly in the aftermath of the Matterhorn accident without his assistance, but there is little recorded. When Whymper finally left Zermatt on 22nd July, he seems to have left his tent and ropes at Seiler's disposal, as when Seiler came to open the tent so that Tyndall could use it on his mad escapade to try and recover the body of Lord Francis Douglas the ropes were not there. He wrote to Whymper asking what he should do as his enquiries revealed that Peter Taugwalder had taken and not returned them. Unfortunately Whymper's reply seems no longer to be in existence, as although in 1942 Werner Kämpfen cited a private collection of Seiler's correspondence in the possession of one of his grandsons in Zürich, recent enquiries suggest that only letters of a business nature have survived. Seiler seems to have helped Whymper resolve a number of problems relating to the proposed Croz monument after he had received an almost indecipherable letter from the Curé Welschen. Whymper appears to have consulted someone on the letter, which accounts for a note he wrote: 'No doubt a place will be granted for it *if* you pay considerably (or handsomely) for it. Communicate the offer that you will make to me direct and avoid the intervention of a third party and I will see about it.' The Consul Mackenzie wrote to *The Times* on the related subject of an exorbitant demand in respect of land for the Hudson/Hadow monument, but two further letters from Seiler suggest that he ultimately managed to negotiate with the Curé a reasonable figure for the Croz land.

In 1866 Seiler was already vice-president of the Monte Rosa section of the Swiss Alpine Club, which had been founded on 4th October 1865, although he had to resign at the end of the year due to too many other commitments. But in 1867 when there was talk of building a hut at the foot of the Matterhorn he offered to build it and give 500 francs towards it. He considered it indispensable to have the moral support of the Monte Rosa section in seeking the necesary authority from the Zermatt commune. In the event the hut was built at a height of 3818 metres in 1868 by guides from St.Niklaus, thanks to Seiler's generosity. It seems likely that Seiler was encouraged by the entry made in his Monte Rosa guestbook by Jordan in October 1867, after being the first to tread the whole of both the Swiss and Italian routes, although the first complete traverse was not made until 1868 by John Tyndall. Jordan's long account included, 'As far as my experience of mountaineering in Switzerland goes, this ascent of the Matterhorn is the most glorious and enjoyable trip a mountaineer can make'.

In 1860 when the French took possesssion of Savoy, Lieutenant Seiler spent several weeks with a Valais battalion in Geneva, where he met a group of mountain walkers including the dentist Thioly who made an annual excursion to the Alps. As a result of Seiler's encouragement the Thioly group decided to be a little more adventurous and went to Zermatt that summer, climbing Monte Rosa and staying at Seiler's hotel. For Thioly himself this was the start of a highly successful climbing career which finished in 1868, almost as suddenly as it had begun, with the first traverse from Zermatt to Breuil of the Matterhorn. There is an amusing letter Seiler sent Thioly in 1866, the day after Birkbeck's seven guide attempt had failed, which shows his sense of humour as he tried to dissuade Thioly from coming to Zermatt little knowing that he was already on his way. It seems likely that Seiler was responsible for introducing Birkbeck to the St.Niklaus guides, as well as Jordan and others, and it is interesting to note the number of ascents made by the men of St.Niklaus before any Zermatt guide dared to venture on the Hörnli ridge again after the 1865 ascent. The guides of St.Niklaus acquired a virtual monopoly in the valley for ascents of the Matterhorn and it seems that when the Zermatters ultimately recognised their own stupidity in having boycotted the Hörnli for six years, whether on account of the Taugwalders exaggeration of the difficulties and dangers or some unjustified local fear from which other guides did not suffer, their envy led them to seek their revenge against foreign guides and also in part against Seiler. Not only had the Zermatters lost a lot of Matterhorn business, but they had helped to create such a good reputation for the Knubels, Lochmatters and others that they were losing out on their other peaks as well.

In 1876 Frederick Gardiner spent about a month in the Zermatt area and he published an article 'Expeditions round Zermatt and the Riffel in 1876' some eighteen months later. After referring to a deplorable incident in which his guide Peter Knubel had been taken seriously ill at the Stockje and two Zermatt guides had secretly commandeered the wine that their German tourist had generously left with some food for Knubel, Gardiner wrote:

> 'After an incident like this I can understand the difficulties M.Seiler must suffer under when dealing with such a body of men. He told me that early in the season he had been waited upon by a deputation of guides, who suggested that he should refuse accomodation to all foreign guides, and recommend only guides connected with the commune, excluding even the guides of St.Niklaus. Of course it is needless to say M.Seiler at once repudiated so atrocious an idea, and he has since been constantly harassed by the shortsighted and petty persecutions of this benighted commune; they endeavour to refuse him the right of citizenship, and are combined not to supply him with wood, eggs or other produce, and he is compelled to obtain his supplies from below St.Niklaus. While I was staying at Zermatt his cows were seized and driven from the mountains, the wiseacres of the neighbourhood having decided to refuse him the right of pasturage. Telegraphic orders from Bern forced them to send the cows back to their pasturage, and indemnify M.Seiler for his inconvenience. As I feel rather strongly and feel also rather inclined to make unpleasant remarks about those in authority at the village, I think it better to say no more than offer M.Seiler the testimony of my highest admiration for withstanding the communistic tendencies of Zermatt.'

The cow seizure incident was probably the same as that recorded by Kämpfen as occurring on Sunday 23rd July 1876. Kämpfen wrote of:

> '37 Zermatt burgers armed with sickles, forks and scythes going to the Augstkummen alp led, according to some reports, by the burger and commune presidents. They drove Seiler's cattle from the meadow and led them down to Zermatt. Here there was almost a serious fight between the burgers on the one side and some guests and hotel staff on the other. Spontaneously Seiler's supporters were ready to meet force with force. Only by Seiler's cool intervention was a serious confrontation avoided.'

Brief mention has already been made of Theodor Wundt, who wrote in his first book within five years of Seiler's death, of

> 'his life long fight with the Zermatters who continually looked upon him as a stranger, indeed as an enemy of the whole valley. Initially it was a question of timber for building, which was free for the long established families, but Seiler could not even secure it with payment. This was followed by the battle for citizenship rights lasting many years, which the Zermatters would under no circumstances let him have.'

Wundt continues with an extract from the *Neue Zürcher Zeitung* to the effect that although all the Courts found in his favour the Gemeinde stubbornly refused to accept him until the authorities sought to enforce their decision with a garrison of gendarmes. 'But Seiler, magnanimous and peace loving as he was, himself bore the costs of the garrison for which the Gemeinde were liable.' Wundt says that running the hotels was a much more difficult undertaking than the regular visitors ever imagined in view of the poverty in the valley and the generally bad means of communication. ' "Are you saying that the English really eat so many potatoes that Seiler has to buy them all as far down the valley as Visp and even beyond?" asked one worthy farmer.'

Seiler made his application to become a Burger in June 1871 and he had to wait 17 years for it to be granted, but he was taken ill in 1888 and he never really recovered. It has been said that he died the very hour the first train entered Zermatt. Two years later one of his sons, Andreas, was killed on the Italian ridge of the Matterhorn. His widow died in 1895 and Whymper attended her funeral.

2.48
STEPHEN, LESLIE (1832 – 1904)

Leslie Stephen

One of the leading pioneers, whose record of first ascents must be second to none including in the Valais the Alphubel, Rimpfischhorn and Rothorn, he seems also to have been interested in second ascents. He made the second ascent of the Weisshorn and of the Dom and in 1866 he made the second ascent from Zermatt of the Obergabelhorn, which raises the question as to whether he also intended to make the second ascent of the Matterhorn from Zermatt the same year. There is a letter Stephen wrote to America in February 1866, which suggests that he was not going to attempt the Matterhorn or any other mountain for a while, but his activities in July including the Obergabelhorn and the Fletschhorn indicate a change of mind, and he may well have contemplated an ascent of the Matterhorn in 1866. His letter included:

> 'I have nearly exhausted the Alps for the present. The last inaccessible mountain (the Matterhorn) has been climbed and the accident that took place on that occasion will prevent my attacking it for the present – not that it is particularly dangerous but that the guides would probably be particularly nervous. So I shall leave the mountains to themselves for a little and come over to see America in peace.'

There is no record of his ever climbing the Matterhorn, but there are signs of his having taken a particular interest in it prior to the first ascent. Mumm records his visiting the Hörnli in 1858 and he seems to have been there again in 1862 with Melchior Anderegg. His comments on the prospects of a successful ascent from Zermatt, made in *Macmillan's Magazine* in the course of his review of Whymper's *Scrambles*, are a salutary reminder of the peak's reputed inaccessibility.

> 'Thousands of visitors to Zermatt have looked at it, and assumed, without hesitation, that it

> was totally inaccessible. Many of them were experienced mountaineers, but were hopelessly deceived by the boldness of the imposition. Even when the veil was lifted for a moment, it always returned after a brief interval. Some years before the final assault, old Peter Taugwald, one of Mr. Whymper's guides, remarked to me that it would be tolerably easy to climb it to the point called the "shoulder", and his assertion turned out to be strictly true; but at the time neither he nor I fully realized the possibility. If we believed, it was with that faint and unsteady belief which only apes conviction. Three years before the ascent, Melchior Anderegg made the same remark to me on the Hörnli; and though for the instant the truth flashed upon us, it disappeared again under the influence of a short stroll to another point of view. Thus a comparatively easy and certain route to a point close below the summit had been staring mountaineers in the face for years before it was actually tried. The story reminds me of the ordinary anecdotes about apparently impregnable fortresses. All the proper methods of siege are carried on energetically and unsuccessfully, till somebody remembers an easy mode of reaching a neglected postern, and calmly walks in without any particular trouble. Though it is clearly foolish, I cannot remember without a sense of shame that I and others must have contemplated this convenient staircase some hundreds of times, and every now and then thought vaguely of trying it, and yet that we never had the necesary resolution or clearheadedness to make the assault.'

Stephen probably arrived in Zermatt in 1866 on 14th July, the day Birkbeck made his seven guided attempt on the Hörnli. Even if the snow conditions were not immediately ideal, he had some ten days or so when he might have had a go at the Matterhorn and the probability is that he was unable to find a guide willing to go with him. Knowing Old Peter (he had climbed the Allalinhorn with him in 1860), and being fluent in German (he had translated Berlepsch's *The Alps* into English in 1861), he would surely have spoken to him and would have wanted him to accompany his party on the climb. But it was on 26th July 1866 that the *Journal de Genève* stated 'since last year's accident the Zermatt guides have a real fear of engaging in an enterprise of this nature'.

Stephen had been ordained priest in 1859 but by 1862 he ceased to regard himself as a clergyman and resigned his Fellowship at Trinity Hall, Cambridge. By 1865 he had settled in London and become a journalist, contributing regularly to such publications as *Saturday Review* and *Pall Mall Gazette.* He married in 1867 and although he still went to the Alps, his expeditions thereafter were more modest. Mumm has pointed out how Stephen took a very serious view of the dangers of mountaineering and he listed his utterances on the subject in the *Alpine Journal.* Stephen was vice-president of the Alpine Club in 1864–5 and President from 1866 to 1868. He wrote a six page review of *Scrambles* in the *Journal*, but it is his review in *Macmillan's* of August 1871 which was later 'rediscovered' by Arnold Lunn which merits more attention to-day.

Arnold Lunn prided himself in his criticism of Whymper. He welcomed Egger's supposed vindication of Taugwalder in his book *Pioniere der Alpen*, turning a blind eye to some of his distortions, such as the 'incomprehensible chessmove' which is nothing less than an Egger own goal, whilst adopting others like the Cowell memorandum despite neither writer knowing anything of the circumstances in which it came to be made. Lunn seems to have regarded Stephen as the original Whymper critic and quotes a passage from *Macmillan's* after describing Stephen as 'one great contemporary of Whymper's who realised that attacks such as Whymper's should not be made without tangible evidence, and that it was impossible to acquit Taugwalder without condemning Whymper'. Before looking at what Stephen actually wrote and how it falls far short of Lunn's purpose, it is interesting to note something else Stephen wrote in the same review, which is wholly inconsistent with Lunn's exaggerated and distorted assessment of the capabilities of Old Peter as a guide. Writing some 80 years after the event with all his usual skill and bluster, Lunn refers to Old Peter as one of the three men (with Whymper and Carrel) 'who from the first believed that the mountain could be climbed' and also as 'this outstanding Zermatt guide of the period'. Again in the same seven page article he states that 'Taugwalder was, by common consent, one of the leading guides of his generation'. Stephen, on the other hand, who clearly knew what he was talking about, wrote in relation to the accident: 'Four amateurs, one of whom was inexperienced, with three guides, of whom two were comparatively incompetent, should never have thought of attacking the most difficult mountain in the Alps.'

'Comparatively incompetent' is not a condemnation of the real Taugwalder but a reminder of the truth that fashion has so often chosen to exaggerate and distort in the last half century. The true situation also shows in Old Peter's climbing record; he was a good Monte Rosa guide but he certainly was not one of the leading guides of his generation such as Michel Croz, Christian Almer and Melchior Anderegg, to name but three. As Dangar & Blakeney put it 'Looking to his past record, one is inclined to think that it was unfortunate that Old Peter was engaged by Douglas in 1865, for it took him out of his class'.

The passage in Stephen's review that so excited Lunn reads:

> 'I will only make one remark in passing. Mr. Whymper very properly denounces the absurd fable that the elder Taugwalder cut the rope...But I rather regret that he should not reject decidedly another grave, though less serious accusation, which comes in fact to this, that Taugwald intentionally used a weak rope in fastening himself to Lord F. Douglas, in order to have a chance of being separated from him in case of accident [Lunn omits the last fifteen words]. Knowing the carelessness too often displayed on such occasions, the confidence which guides will show in weak ropes, and the probable state of excitement of the whole party, which would easily account for such an oversight, I think that the hypothesis of deliberate intention on Taugwald's part is in the highest degree improbable; and there is not a particle of direct evidence in its favour. The presumption would be that Croz was almost equally responsible; and, at any rate, such accusations should have some more tangible ground than a vague possibility. A discussion of the point would be out of place here, and I venture upon this digression merely for the sake of an old guide, who has always had a high character, and, to the best of my knowledge, has well deserved it.'

It should be noted that Stephen was expressing regret that Whymper should not have rejected 'decidedly another grave, though less serious accusation' that Old Peter intentionally used a weak rope. He was not suggesting that the accusation had originated with Whymper or that Whymper had made an 'attack' on Old Peter in his book, as Lunn would have us believe. Much of the criticism that has been levelled against Whymper on this aspect is based on what he wrote in *Scrambles*, but as it was not published until 1871 there can obviously be no question of it having adversely affected Old Peter between 1867 and 1871, which is when his career as a guide seems to have come to an end. The matter is considered in greater detail in section 2.57.10 (Whymper), but the answer to Stephen's regret is that to Whymper there was a clear distinction between the breaking of the rope, which he had actually seen and which enabled him to exclude Old Peter cutting it, and the use of the weakest rope, which was something for which only Old Peter could answer. It seems that Whymper referred to the issue in *Scrambles* because it had not yet been resolved and because it had been raised originally by friends of the victims. Whymper himself had no reason to suspect even that Old Peter used the rope intentionally.

As for Stephen's observations on guides' carelessness and the confidence they show in weak ropes, Dangar & Blakeney summed them up by saying, 'Stephen's defence consists of saying that guides are always careless about ropes'. It is interesting to note that in May 1870 Stephen had tried to defuse the controversy surrounding the Lyskamm accident to Chester (Clemenz second case in Alpine literature) with somewhat similar wording in relation to the guides' use of the rope, as that which he applied later to Old Peter; 'Carelessness in fastening rope is unfortunately so common that it is quite unnecessary to impute any deliberate intention to men who may be guilty of it'. But it was precisely one week before the Matterhorn accident that Old Peter had had his miraculous escape on the Obergabelhorn, when he fell more than 20ft with the cornice and the rope held, and it is hardly likely that he would have been equally careless on the Matterhorn. The probability is that he honestly (albeit wrongly) believed that the plaited rope was as strong as the others, but was prevented from explaining this at the Enquiry and thereby from dispelling the suspicions created by the accident.

Leslie Stephen's familiarity with the mountaineering scene in Zermatt is readily apparent from his obituary of Alexander Seiler in the *Alpine Journal.*

2.49
TAIRRAZ, JEAN (18?? – 1876)

A Chamonix guide, he volunteered to go with Whymper's search party setting off early on the Sunday morning. He, like the Lochmatter brothers, had also taken part in the first search party on the Saturday afternoon.

2.50 TAUGWALDER, FRIEDRICH (1850 – ?1877)

Friedrich, or Friederik, the third and youngest son of Old Peter Taugwalder was the 'sharp-eyed lad' who actually saw the accident from Zermatt. Downton and McCormick wrote of him in 1865, without identifying him, but Long and Whymper did not publish their accounts until 1867 and 1871 respectively. Very little is known of Friedrich, but it seems probable that his life in Zermatt was closely affected by the fundamental change in his father's career and outlook following the accident in July 1865. His future may also have been influenced by the death of his brother Joseph in 1867, at the age of 22. Whereas Ruden's book, published in 1869, simply records the birth of 'Friederik', the 1925 enlarged and revised edition by Kronig records '1850 Friedrich [sic], nach Amerika ausgewandert', meaning that he emigrated to America.

It might be expected that as Old Peter's two eldest sons became guides the youngest would have become one as well, having particular regard to the way Young Peter seems to have served an apprenticeship with his father, who seems almost to have insisted that he should be taken on a climb as second guide. Joseph's apprenticeship must have been badly affected by the interruption of his father's career, although we know nothing of the effect it had on him. But if Old Peter ever intended that Friedrich should also become a guide, the latter's hopes must have been dashed when in 1866, for no clear reason, his father chose to switch his own role from that of the family's leading guide to acting as second guide to Young Peter on climbs away from Zermatt which he himself had never previously attempted.

But even if Friedrich had little prospect of becoming a great guide if he stayed in Zermatt, why did he go to America? Despite the unreliable writings of Arnold Lunn on the subject of emigration, there is no evidence to suggest that any native of Zermatt ever emigrated to North America before Friedrich, although this is not to exclude the possibility that anyone who did intend to emigrate subsequently changed his mind and returned to Zermatt. But Ruden records no one emigrating prior to the publication of his book in 1869, apart from Peter Moser, who went to South America. So, when did Friedrich go, and why?

Hannes Taugwalder has written of him going after his father's death, but this seems most unlikely. A possible clue may come from the fact that Old Peter went to live in America in 1874 and returned in 1878. But did they both go together, or did Old Peter go to visit his son Friedrich? Walter Schmid has written of Old Peter emigrating with his youngest son and other Wallisers, but without quoting his source. There is some evidence, which is not strong enough to merit quoting, that Friedrich may have died in America in his 20's, that is, in the 1870's. If there were found to be any substance in this, it would have a bearing on Old Peter's visit and dispose once and for all of the false allegations that have been made about Old Peter's misfortunes since 1865 being attributable to a book Whymper published in 1871! It could also explain Schmid's reference to Old Peter returning home from

America as a mentally broken man. One other aspect of 'Taugwalder' emigration is that Young Peter's son Kamil, born in 1871, is also recorded by Kronig as emigrating to America. If in fact Friedrich was then still living in America, perhaps his nephew went to live somewhere near and there may well be descendants living there to-day who can clarify the history, even if Zermatt maintains its silence.

Ronald Clark quotes a report of 20th July 1865 by Downton the English chaplain at Geneva to the British Consul, which includes:

> 'The Master of this Hotel, M.Seiler, told me last night that a boy of the village with a small telescope had seen two or three persons on the mountain about 3 o'clock. That half an hour afterwards he had observed what he described as an avalanche. M.Seiler had said that that was impossible as there was no snow to form one. He has no doubt since that what he saw was the party who fell, who rolling over and over, habited chiefly in white and light-coloured clothing, might give the boy this idea! They fell 4,000 ft.'

McCormick wrote towards the end of 1865 in *A sad holiday*:

> 'It is said that, about three quarters of an hour afterwards, a boy, who was examining the mountain with a telescope, saw, what he thought was an avalanche. Alas! we know too well what that falling mass was which he beheld!'

Charles Long wrote in the *Echo des Alpes* in 1867:

> ' "Oh!" shouts one of Taugwald's sons after a few minutes search, as ardent as any to follow the course of his father and his brother, "an avalanche"! I look at Seiler who has grown pale. Taugwald speaks in his ear. "Nonsense! an avalanche! that's often seen on a hot summer's day." '

Whymper wrote in *Scrambles*:

> 'A few minutes later a sharp-eyed lad ran into the Monte Rosa, to Seiler, saying that he had seen an avalanche fall from the summit of the Matterhorn on to the Matterhorngletscher. The boy was reproved for telling idle stories; he was right, nevertheless, and this is what he saw...'

Dangar & Blakeney commented critically in 1966 on Lunn's oft repeated hint that Whymper himself had invented the sharp-eyed lad, and this finally led Lunn to admit that he had been wrong.

2.51
TAUGWALDER, JOSEPH (1845 – 1867)

The second son of Old Peter Taugwalder, Joseph was by 1865 older than his brother Peter had been in 1862, when he accompanied his father and Kennedy on the Dent Blanche fiasco. It is therefore probable that Joseph had already considerable experience of Monte Rosa and of the Breithorn as well as many of the passes in the Zermatt district, although there does not appear to be any record of his climbs, apart from an ascent of Monte Rosa with his father and Giles Puller, his two excursions on the Matterhorn, his crossing of the Theodule pass with Lord Francis Douglas and his participation in the search party which recovered the bodies on 20th July. If his Führerbuch is still in existence, it would be interesting to see what else it records.

Joseph led Douglas to Breuil on Tuesday 11th July, returning to Zermatt on the 12th, when he transported some of Whymper's baggage. Joseph and his brother Peter were taken as porters on 13th July, and Whymper wrote of Joseph: 'To ensure steady motion, one tourist and one native walked together. The younger Taugwalder fell to my share, and the lad marched well, proud to be on the expedition, and happy to show his powers'. On 14th July after camping for the night at 11,000 ft, Young Peter went on as guide, whilst Joseph returned to Zermatt on his own.

The next mention of Joseph is in the Official Report of the Enquiry, where he appears in the list of 21 men who recovered the bodies on 20th July, as 'Joseph Taugwalder fils de Pre.', immediately after his brother 'Pre. Taugwalder fils de Pre'. Joseph received 20frs from Clemenz for going on the recovery party and Whymper paid him 20frs, via his father, for the Matterhorn and 15frs for the Theodule.

In September 1865 Paul Güssfeldt arrived at Zermatt wanting to climb the Hörnli, but Old Peter refused to accompany him on it. They did however arrange 'in great secrecy' to make the ascent from the Italian side, and for the second guide to join them en route so as to avoid creating a stir in Zermatt. But, contrary to general belief, it was Joseph and not Young Peter who accompanied his father and Güssfeldt on this Matterhorn attempt on 18th September 1865. Güssfeldt refers to him as 'the younger son of Old Taugwalder' and Young Peter's Führerbuch seems to confirm that Peter was busy elsewhere with an entry dated 25th September covering Monte Rosa, Theodule pass, Col du Géant, Grand Mulets, Mont Blanc and Tête noir, signed by Paul Müller of Berlin, an engagement that must have lasted at least a week.

Ruden records that Joseph drowned in the Schwarzsee in 1867, but reveals nothing of the circumstances. As one would not expect drowning to result from an accidental fall into the Schwarzsee, as opposed to a fall into a swollen river or into a deep lake, the question arises as to how Joseph came to drown and as to whether the event or the circumstances surrounding it caused or contributed to Old Peter's decline. Apart from one ascent of Mont Blanc in 1870 there is no record of Old Peter climbing anything between 1867 and 1870 inclusive, nor of the reason for his giving up guiding apart from Whymper's footnote in Scrambles: 'I am told that he is now nearly incapable for work – not absolutely mad, but with intellect gone and almost crazy...' So did Old Peter's virtual abandonment of guiding at Zermatt adversely affect Joseph's apprenticeship and did Joseph's death in 1867 have an adverse effect on Old Peter and perhaps cause the condition recorded by Whymper?

2.52
TAUGWALDER, OLD PETER (1820 – 1888)

Very little was written about Old Peter in his lifetime and this has led to the likes of Arnold Lunn and Carl Egger making a number of assumptions that simply are not true. Other critics have relied upon them, repeated them and thereby created further distortion and it is time to take a fresh look at the facts and to try and distinguish them from the distortions, inventions and contradictions. The following list shows some of the main events in Old Peter's life and career as a guide.

Old Peter Taugwalder

1820 Born.
1841 Married Anna Maria Zumtaugwald.
1843 Son Peter born.
1845 Son Joseph born.
1848 Daughter Maria born.
1850 Son Friedrich born.
1851 First record of guiding (*AJ70*, 27).
1861 Wanted 200frs for Matterhorn from Breuil.
1862 Attempted Matterhorn in January, as Kennedy's second guide.
Attempted Dent Blanche with Kennedy. His nerve failed.
1864 By now he had climbed Monte Rosa some 85 times.
1865 Obergabelhorn, second ascent with Douglas. Fell with summit cornice.
First ascent of Matterhorn.
Attempted Matterhorn from Breuil with Güssfeldt and son Joseph.
1866 Some climbs recorded (*AJ70*, 37).
1867 No climbs recorded.
Son Peter married.
Son Joseph drowned in Schwarzsee.
1868 Old Weissthor. Lost way with Güssfeldt.
1869 No climbs recorded.
1870 Climbed Mont Blanc.
1871 Theodule and Furggen passes with Lord Queensberry and Young Peter.
First publication of Whymper's *Scrambles*.
1872 No climbs recorded this year or subsequently.
1873 Daughter Maria married.
1874 Went to America.
1878 Returned to Zermatt.
1888 Died 11th July at Schwarzsee.

2.52.1 His family

Whereas the Taugwalder and the Zumtaugwald families may have been one and the same in the distant past, they were already quite distinct at the start of the two centuries covered by the records compiled by Ruden and by Kronig. The Taugwalder family can in fact be split in two from the beginning of the nineteenth century, between Old Peter's father and his uncle, both sides featuring many members with the name of Peter. Ruden and Kronig do not record any Zumtaugwald's with the name Peter, which does on at least one occasion enable us to identify Old Peter under a wrong name. He married Anna Maria Zumtaugwald in 1842 and they had four children Peter, Joseph, Maria and Friedrich. Peter, the eldest, otherwise known in mountaineering literature as Young Peter, married twice and his third child Kamil born in 1871 emigrated to America. Old Peter had many cousins in Zermatt, and two of them, Johannes and Alois Julen, seem to have played an influential role in the aftermath of the Matterhorn accident.

Old Peter's second son Joseph, who in 1865 went as porter with Lord Francis Douglas to Breuil and back and the following day accompanied the Matterhorn party as far as the bivouac, actually attempted the Matterhorn with his father from Breuil in September that year, when Güssfeldt had really wanted to climb the Hörnli. But in 1867 Joseph somehow came to drown in the Schwarzsee. This must surely have had a demoralising effect on Old Peter and may possibly have aggravated his adverse reaction to the accident and its aftermath. It may even perhaps account for there being no record of any guiding activity by him in 1867. The same year his eldest son Peter got married.

In September 1869 Whymper was in Zermatt and it seems probable that he then learnt from someone like Alexander Seiler certain facts about the Taugwalders, which he subsequently incorporated in a long footnote published in *Scrambles* in 1871. These included, in relation to Old Peter, 'I am told that he is now nearly incapable for work – not absolutely mad, but with intellect gone and almost crazy'. Unfortunately nothing is known about Old Peter's Führerbuch, which should have recorded most of his climbs and which had probably been issued to him in 1858, and without it we know of only three more expeditions he made, one in each of the years 1868, 1870 & 1871. In 1965 Dangar & Blakeney enquired in the course of an article in the *Alpine Journal*, reviewing Old Peter's climbing career, 'Are there no members of the Taugwalder family in Zermatt who could institute a house search for the missing volume?' There appears to have been no response and a recent enquiry directed by a Zermatt resident to one member of the family produced the response that even if there was a Führerbuch still in existence nobody was going to see it.

In 1873 Old Peter's daughter Maria got married and the following year he himself left Zermatt to go to America. Hannes Taugwalder, the son of Rudolf the first custodian of the Zermatt Museum, whose relation to Old Peter must be traced through the latter's uncle, Peter Martin Taugwalder, the founder of the other side of the family, has written a few lines about Old Peter going to America. He makes it appear as though he may secretively have brooded over the idea for some time and then suddenly made up his mind and went, leaving his wife behind him. Old Peter returned to Zermatt in 1878 and according to Hannes Taugwalder he had become even more taciturn and nobody knows to-day how he got on in America. This may well be so, but it gives rise to a number of other questions. But first there is the consideration that Old Peter's youngest son Friedrich, the 'sharp-eyed lad' who actually witnessed the four victims falling off the Matterhorn, is recorded by Kronig as having emigrated to America, although no date is given. Hannes Taugwalder has stated that this was after Old Peter's death, which would mean that he was some forty years old and still unmarried, as Kronig would otherwise have recorded his wife's name. But there is also some evidence, which is not strong enough to warrant detailing, that suggests that Friedrich may have died in America in his 20's.

Whereas it may not have been all that unusual for young men in some of the remoter parts of Switzerland to leave their home village and seek their fortune in some other country, Old Peter was in a very different situation at the age of 54. Young Peter later wrote in his 'Narrative' of the 1865 accident 'my father spoke nothing else but the Zermatt dialect of the German language' and there is little reason to suppose that he had learnt English or even French by 1874. He could scarcely have gone, or even have made the arrangements to go, on his own and the explanation may be that he was accompanied by his son Friedrich or by some other Wallisers. He must have known where he was going and he presumably intended to make a living as a carpenter, or in whatever other trade he had engaged when he was not guiding. His grandson Kamil, born in 1871, also emigrated to America and it is likely that there was some family link in place even if there was none in time. Old Peter would have told his teenage grandson about America, even if the boy's uncle Friedrich had died there some ten years previously and this had accounted for his own return to Zermatt. But there may be further generations of Taugwalders in America to-day who will know about their family's first foray there, even if no one in Zermatt really knows precisely why and how Old Peter came to go.

Whereas the likes of Egger and Lunn have sought to attribute all Old Peter's problems to Whymper, without a shred of evidence in support, there is one interesting document that purports to state the reason for his going to America. This is a letter from Rudolf Taugwalder to Henry Montagnier, the American Alpine historian and mountaineer, of 8th May 1917. Montagnier spoke fluent French but no German and he corresponded with Rudolf Taugwalder in English in his attempts to trace some of the old Zermatt and St.Niklaus guides' Führerbücher. He had sent Rudolf eight questions which he wanted him to put to Young Peter Taugwalder and Rudolf's reply in English duly set out what Young Peter had to say on various matters relating to the 1865 accident and in particular his father's involvement in it. The last two answers read as follows:

> 'VII. The father went to America – anno 1874 and remained there till 1878.
> VIII. His father (old Peter) day of death was July 11 – 1888.'

Inexplicably the next eight lines are written by Rudolf in German in the old fashioned script, which is almost indecipherable to anyone familiar only with the modern style in which Rudolf wrote virtually all the rest of his letter. The eight lines translate as follows:

> 'The ninth question would be: why did old Peter Taugwalder go to America? Answer: After this accident and this success on the Matterhorn, all the guides of Chamonix and St.Niklaus were so envious and cunning that they did everything they could to make the lives of the Taugwalders as unbearable as possible. All sorts of jealousy and slander were used to weaken their good reputation in every respect. Both the guides of St.Niklaus and those of Chamonix caused thousands of francs loss by their shameful slanders. Peter Taugwalder eventually wanted to escape from these envious people and these slanders and so he went to America.'

The reason for Rudolf suddenly switching into German may be that Young Peter wanted Montagnier to be told this additional information, but Rudolf was not prepared to go to the lengths of translating such a long and complicated answer into English. This does not however explain why Rudolf should have made it doubly difficult for Montagnier to understand by resorting to the old-fashioned script. The collapse of Old Peter's career as a guide is referred to below, as is also the evidence of his post-accident problems with fellow guides and neighbours in Zermatt, but it is interesting to note that the ninth answer does not include the Zermatt guides. There certainly was ill feeling between Chamonix and the German speaking guides generally even before the Matterhorn accident, as Whymper wrote in a letter to Wigram, and the St.Niklaus guides' virtual monopoly in the valley of ascents of the Matterhorn from Zermatt for the next five or more years seems to have caused great bitterness amongst the Zermatt guides when they eventually woke up to what they were missing, but it may have been nothing more than diplomacy that led Young Peter to exclude the Zermatt guides from the ninth answer. Arnold Lunn has quoted Bernard Biner, the great Zermatt guide, philosopher and friend of impecunious post-war British climbers, as saying of Old Peter,

> 'Taugwalder had an unhappy time after the accident. Many guides were jealous of his success in making the first ascent of the Matterhorn and some of them were really unpleasant about him. There were one or two disagreeable incidents. And then he drank a little too much and was criticised on that account by serious people.'

2.52.2 His career as guide

There are two principal sources for listing Old Peter's climbs, the article in the 1865 *SAC Jahrbuch* on glacier guides and Dangar & Blakeney's article in the 1965

Alpine Journal 'Old Peter Taugwalder'. A third potential source, which would never be exhaustive but might contain some additional climbs particularly in 1864, would be his Führerbuch, but as already stated, it is not available. Old Peter's career is best divided into two at 1864, the date when particulars seem to have been recorded for the SAC article.

Pre-1864
Allalinhorn.
Breithorn frequently.
Cima di Jazzi.
Lyskamm 3 times.
Monte Rosa some 85 times.

Various passes including Adler, Allalin, Schwarzberggletscher, Alphubel (6 times), Weissthor (frequently), Lysspass (8), Schwarzthor (2), Trift and Evolena passes repeatedly, Col d'Herens, Col de Colon, Col delle Loggie etc.

1864
1.8. Pollux (first ascent).

1865
28.6. Unter Gabelhorn (first ascent).
1.7. Wellenkuppe (first ascent).
6.7. Triftjoch.
7.7. Obergabelhorn (second ascent, first from Zinal).
14.7. Matterhorn (first ascent).
18.9. Attempted Matterhorn from Breuil. With Güssfeldt and Peter's son Joseph.

1866
7.8. Mont Blanc. With Young Peter.
1.9. Attempted Monte Rosa.
2.9. Klein Matterhorn. With Young Peter.
4.9. Dom. With Young Peter.
14.9. Mont Blanc. With Young Peter.

1867 (Nothing recorded)

1868
1?.8. Old Weissthor. With Güssfeldt.

1869 (Nothing recorded)

1870
26.8. Mont Blanc. With Stogdon and Moritz Andenmatten.

1871
15.9. Theodule and Furggen passes. With Lord Queensberry and Young Peter.

2.52.3 His reputation as guide

As a result of an ill-considered remark by Farrar in 1919 in the course of a lengthy article in the *Alpine Journal*, there has been much misunderstanding about Old Peter's abilities as a guide, particularly in view of the alacrity with which Swiss writers have adopted and quoted it. 'Peter Taugwalder, père, ...was certainly at the time one of the boldest guides in the Alps, and probably much the best of the Zermatt men'. The reasons why the first part is so patently a false assessment will be considered below, but as far as Zermatt is concerned, Peter Perren was way ahead of him in experience and ability, the Zumtaugwald brothers were probably better guides and by 1865 Franz Biner had also overtaken him. It is unfortunate that when Old Peter undoubtedly had many good qualities these should have been so exaggerated as to place him where he did not belong at the top of his profession, as it then becomes necessary to dwell on his faults and weaknesses in order to try and restore the proper perspective. His abilities and his downfall can be summed up briefly by stating that he was a good Monte Rosa guide with more than twice as much experience of that mountain as anyone else but, as Dangar & Blakeney wrote in the article already referred to, 'Looking to his past record, one is inclined to think that it was unfortunate that Old Peter was engaged by Douglas in 1865, for it took him out of his class'.

John Ball referred to him in the first edition of his *Guide to the Western Alps* in 1863 as 'Peter zum Taugwald (of Zermatt). Although older than his namesakes above mentioned, he is a better guide, a first rate cragsman, strong and willing. Rather eccentric in his ways.' The 1870 edition gave him his correct name and retained much of the previous wording with 'a steady climber, strong and willing, though no longer young. Rather eccentric in his ways'. But by 1873 his name had been omitted from the list of guides in Ball's *Introduction*. There are several references to his eccentricities including that of Leslie Stephen in an article on the Allalinhorn:

> 'Old Peter Taugwald...is a solid, steady going old fellow, as broad as he is long, and as firm as a rock. The stolid calmness, from which he never wavers, becomes occasionally tiresome. He annoyed me now by the extreme deliberation with which he halted every few minutes to munch a great lump of sugar, whose good qualities he delights to expatiate upon, as being an excellent thing on the snow.'

Lunn quoted Stogden as saying: 'I had a good many expeditions with Old Peter Taugwalder including Mont Blanc and Monte Rosa and I had rather a tender spot for the somewhat coarse, dirty old beggar', and Thioly, the Geneva dentist, who climbed Monte Rosa with Old Peter as head guide, wrote how:

> 'the cold had become so intense that we were shivering in all our limbs, but the head guide in order to protect himself from the cold had taken the precaution of having a few swigs of rum from time to time whilst we were reduced to drinking some cold tea that an Englishman had recommended us to put in our flasks as we left the Riffel. Having heeded this advice punctiliously we were freezing with cold whilst Peter Taugwalder was secretly gulping the liquor. All he needed to do was to bend his head beneath his jacket, slightly raise the pocket in which he had the bottle and the trick was done; we were well aware of this little wile and it was only later when it came to paying the bill that we saw that we had been tricked by Peter Taugwalder; M.Seiler had handed him the bottle with the provisions, but Master Peter had simply appropriated it himself.
> Our teeth were chattering, we were almost frozen stiff and only then did Peter Taugwalder bring out his cherished bottle and give us a few mouthfuls; it was high time! as F.S. could no longer speak, his hands from which icicles hung had completely lost all feeling and his face was as white as the snow that was falling.'

Old Peter's greatest recorded failure was with Kennedy on the Dent Blanche in 1862, and he was also the first to say he could go no further on Kennedy's extraordinary winter attempt on the Matterhorn in January the same year. In an article on the Dent Blanche Kennedy wrote:

> 'After paying out fifty or sixty feet, I heard him clattering down, and was surprised to see the weatherbeaten old fellow with a face as white as that of a frightened girl. He seized eagerly upon some spirits of wine we chanced to have, and then told me he had thought himself done for. His nerve being entirely destroyed by the fright, I fixed the rope round my waist, and led the way upwards. But presently his courage failed again – he declared that he could not follow, and the son sided with his father; so it being useless to think of ascending alone, I was obliged to yield.'

It is this account, which Farrar must have read in the *Alpine Journal*, which completely undermines his comment about Old Peter being certainly one of the boldest guides in the Alps. But there is another comment on the same incident, made by Woolmore Wigram in a letter to Whymper in August 1865. He had made the first ascent of the Dent Blanche with Kennedy and different guides a few days after the Taugwalder fiasco, and he wrote to Whymper:

> 'We know that Taugwalder's acquaintance with the pass from Zermatt to Gressonay was acquired by smuggling and if he has done much business of that kind he has probably drank hard so that his nerve is now failing or failed. He broke down altogether at the first attempt on la D.B. He returned to Kennedy from an attempt to surmount the last difficulties...pale, trembling and refusing to do anything but return immediately.'

Dangar & Blakeney referred in *AJ61* & *AJ70* to other climbers like Hinchliff and Tuckett, who may have made favourable comments about Old Peter but who subsequently seem to have dropped him like Kennedy. A guide who can lose his nerve so readily and is dependent on his drink cannot be relied upon in a crisis, when he is most likely to be needed. It may be wondered what state Old Peter was in after his free fall of more than 20 feet on the Obergabelhorn after his luncheon cornice collapsed, and whether he had really recovered from this completely before ascending the Matterhorn exactly a week later. It is hard to judge someone like Old Peter merely from recorded events such as his difficulty in finding a way up the Gabelhorn and his failure to appreciate the presence of the cornice, and the opinions of the leading climbers of his day must be the best possible indicators. It is therefore particularly interesting to find that Leslie Stephen made a pertinent comment about Old Peter in his review of Whymper's *Scrambles* in *Macmillan's Magazine*, the one that Arnold Lunn was always so proud of having rediscovered. Stephen knew Old Peter from his ascent of the Allalinhorn and he would have been able to converse freely with him as he was sufficiently fluent in German to be able to translate Berlepsch's book *Die Alpen* into English; he may well have spoken to him about the Matterhorn in July 1866. He himself was one of the leading amateurs of the golden age having made numerous first ascents amongst the great peaks. He usually had the benefit of the very best guides and he knew that a strong team was necessary in order to tackle a reputedly difficult mountain. His comment on the Matterhorn party is therefore as reliable an expression of contemporary opinion as can be found on the calibre of the guides, and it can hardly be concluded that Old Peter was a first rate guide when Leslie Stephen wrote, 'Four amateurs, one of whom was inexperienced, with three guides, of whom two were comparatively incompetent, should never have thought of attacking the most difficult mountain in the Alps'. 'Comparatively incompetent' may not have been a very complimentary remark to make about Old Peter, but by all accounts it does appear to have been apt. Another contemporary but more broadly based exclusion of Old Peter from the ranks of 'undoubtedly great guides' amongst the pioneers, is his omission from Cunningham & Abney's book, in which the authors detailed their selection process in the Preface.

2.52.4 His competence as guide

Leslie Stephen's assessment of comparatively incompetent seems to be borne out by what we know of Old Peter's faults from other sources. The incident related by Thioly on Monte Rosa may have seemed amusing in retrospect and it was certainly the normal practice to drink wine and spirits on the mountains, but to commandeer his employers' bottle of rum, when they did not even know it belonged to them, and consume it surreptitiously only offering them a little as a last resort, shows either a selfish dependence on alcohol or a confused understanding of a guide's priorities and duties to his clients. Old Peter's inability to cope with the difficulties on the Dent Blanche, which Kennedy and Wigram overcame with comparative ease a few days later led by J-B Croz, shows either a technical inability on rocks or as Wigram suggested a failing nerve, consequent on too much hard drinking. His climbing record up to 1865 was confined to Monte

Rosa and other snow peaks in Zermatt's south eastern sector such as the Breithorn and Lyskamm, as well as passes in the same region and to the west of Zermatt, such as the Trift and Evolena passes. He seems never to have ventured as far as the Dom, let alone Mont Blanc, until his son Peter led him there in 1866, despite the normal routes being little more than long snow plods like his favourite Monte Rosa.

The Zumtaugwalds were greater pioneers than he was, but he did succeed in making the first ascent of Pollux in 1864. He seems however to have taken many days and to have had great difficulty in finding the way to lead Lord Francis Douglas up the Obergabelhorn, inadvertently acquiring in the process the first ascents of the Untergabelhorn, the as yet unnamed Wellenkuppe and, if the SAC guidebook is to be believed, the Trifthorn as well; but see section 2.14.2 (Douglas). Maclean, who was staying at the time at the Monte Rosa hotel and visited Douglas at the Mont Cervin and learnt of his Obergabelhorn attempts, recorded how they had 'proved unsuccessful, owing to his Zermatt guide, Taugwald, having led them by a circuitous route'. By contrast Jakob Anderegg led A.W.Moore and Horace Walker straight to the top of the Obergabelhorn at their first attempt, without the Douglas party even realising, when they saw them on the summit from the Triftjoch, that they had made the ascent from Zermatt. Douglas was full of praise for Old Peter's performance the next day, when they climbed the Obergabelhorn from Zinal, despite the folly of going onto the summit cornice, particularly when the footsteps left by the Anderegg party the day before had stopped short of it. The question of Douglas's misjudgment of the cornice accident is a complex one and is considered in detail in sections 2.14.5 (Douglas) and 3.16 (The special rope). It does however raise the possibility of an excusable reason for Old Peter choosing to use the weakest rope on the descent of the Matterhorn exactly one week later. Had Old Peter been allowed to answer Whymper's questions to the Enquiry, including the one as to why a different kind of rope was used between him and Lord Douglas, and had Clemenz or the responsible authorities made known to the Swiss press the evidence that he and Whymper had given to the Enquiry, instead of cloaking the whole affair in secrecy, he might have recovered from the shock of the accident and been able to resume his former relatively modest but successful career as a Monte Rosa guide. His would-be helpers misguidedly seem to have left him in the impossible position of having to try and maintain a posture of professional skill that he never possessed in the past and could never aspire to in the future, having already begun to lose his nerve.

2.52.5 His Matterhorn ambition

It was said by Egger that Old Peter was the only one who maintained right from the very beginning that the Matterhorn could be climbed, but, as with so many other claims made by Egger and by Lunn on behalf of Old Peter, there does not appear to be any evidence to support it. The earliest occasion linking his name with the Matterhorn seems to be in 1861, which Whymper later recorded in *Scrambles*. Old Peter was in Breuil and Whymper with an Oberland guide whom he does not name wanted to attempt the ascent (his first attempt), but needed another guide,

> 'We endeavoured to induce another man to accompany us, but without success. Matthias zum Taugwald and other well-known guides were there at the time, but they declined to go on any account. A sturdy old fellow – Peter Taugwalder by name – said he would go! His price? "Two hundred francs." "What, whether we ascend or not?" "Yes – nothing less." The end of the matter was, that all the men who were more or less capable showed a strong disinclination, or positively refused to go (their disinclination being very much in proportion to their capacity), or else asked a prohibitive price. This, it may be said once and for all, was the reason why so many futile attempts were made upon the Matterhorn. One first rate guide after another was brought up to the mountain, and patted on the back, but all declined the business. The men who went had no heart in the matter, and took the first opportunity to turn back. For they were, with the exception of one man, to whom reference will be made presently, universally impressed with the belief that the summit was entirely inaccessible.'

The 'one man' Whymper had in mind was J-A Carrel, and not Old Peter, whose exorbitant demand for 200 francs was tantamount to a refusal, bearing in mind what Whymper wrote of Carrel's own fees that year, 'Twenty francs a day, whatever was the result, was his price'. This suggests that Old Peter had no interest in climbing the Matterhorn, whether or not he thought it possible.

There is however a record of the view he expressed of the Hörnli ridge at about the same time. Leslie Stephen wrote in his review of *Scrambles* published in *Macmillan's Magazine*:

> 'Some years before the final assault, old Peter Taugwald, one of Mr. Whymper's guides, remarked to me that it would be tolerably easy to climb it to the point called the "shoulder," and his assertion turned out to be strictly true; but at the time neither he nor I fully realized the possibility. If we believed, it was with that faint and unsteady belief that only apes conviction.'

It is interesting to compare Old Peter's remark to Stephen with what was recorded by F. Morshead in the Monte Rosa guestbook in 1863 on the first passage of the Matterjoch: '[Peter] Perren and I examined the Mont Cervin carefully from the top of the col and agreed that an ascent was quite practicable by the Hörnli arête as far as the last sattel about 150 feet from the summit but could see no way beyond that.'

Old Peter's next association with the Matterhorn seems to have been in January 1862, when Kennedy engaged Peter Perren for a winter attempt on the Hörnli and fairly soon after starting back for Zermatt on the first day after having difficulty making steps in the deep snow, 'old Peter Taugwalder met us, evidently wishing for work, and I engaged him, for two men would be necessary for the next day's expedition'. The next day they got as far as the Schwarzsee chapel where they spent the night. They then set off at 6 a.m. in an increasingly fierce north wind and despite having to wade through knee-deep snow they slowly toiled upwards.

> 'The work was laborious: steps had to be hewn, loose gravelly couloirs to be carefully crossed, and unsafe rocks to be avoided. Presently old Peter halted, announcing that he could not go farther; Perren looked upwards, and thought he could climb up again to the arête.'

They all continued a little longer,

> 'Still no one seemed to like to be the first to give in, till a gust fiercer than usual forced us to shelter for a time behind a rock. Immediately it was tacitly understood that our expedition must now end; but we determined to leave some memento of our visit, and after descending a considerable distance, we found a suitable place with loose stones of which to build a cairn. In half an hour a tower 6 feet high was erected.'

Whymper calculated that as the cairn was at 10,820 feet their highest point was little more than 11,000 feet, the same height as his own bivouac on 13th July 1865.

The only other sign of Old Peter having any special interest in the Matterhorn comes from his employment by Lord Francis Douglas from 27th June until 7th July 1865. It is not known how Douglas came to engage him, whether he had arranged to do so in advance by letter or whether he asked Clemenz to recommend a guide when he reached Zermatt. Although Douglas had climbed from Zermatt the three previous years, there is no known record of his having employed Old Peter before. Young Peter said in his 'Narrative' in 1917 that Douglas 'did a number of climbs in the company of my late father, among them the first ascent of the Ober Gabelhorn. He also intended to attempt the ascent of the Matterhorn.' Whereas there is no reason to doubt the report in the *Dumfries Courier*, later quoted in *The Times*, that 'the ascent of the Matterhorn was the last adventure which he had planned previous to his return to Glen Stuart', in the sense that he had planned it before leaving home, any such plan had been frustrated by the unexpectedly long time wasted in finding a way up the Gabelhorn. There is little doubt, therefore, for the reasons set out in section 2.14.3 (Douglas) that when Douglas paid Old Peter off on Saturday 8th July he no longer had any intention of trying the Matterhorn in 1865. Whether he had intended to make an attempt from Zermatt rather than from Breuil and would have engaged Old Peter for it had he been able to stick to his original plan is uncertain, but there is some evidence that Old Peter did at least indulge in a little salesmanship at some stage to account for Whymper writing of Douglas's arrival at Breuil: 'He brought good news. Old Peter had lately been beyond the Hörnli, and had reported that he thought an ascent of the Matterhorn was possible upon that side.'

It has been suggested that Old Peter had made a reconnaisance on his own not long before, with the express purpose of making an attempt with Douglas, but this can hardly have been the case. It would have been too early on account of the snow to have made a reconaissance in June before Douglas arrived and there was no opportunity after returning from the Gabelhorn at 10.30p.m. on the Friday. It would in any event have taken Old Peter a few days to recover from the shock of his fall of more than 20 feet with the cornice, he would have had to attend Mass on Sunday 9th, and it snowed on the Matterhorn on the Monday. It may also be asked why he did not take Douglas with him and what he would have expected to achieve? Without going to the shoulder or at least far beyond the height of 11,000 feet he reached with Kennedy three years earlier, he would have been wasting his time. There is no sign of his having learnt anything subsequent to what he had learnt in 1862, as, when Whymper's party reached a suitable site for a tent platform slightly higher than Kennedy's cairn, Croz and Young Peter 'went on to see what was above, in order to save time on the following morning'. Their report of 'not a difficulty, not a single difficulty' would have revealed nothing new had Old Peter been there before, and the simple explanation for having 'lately been beyond the Hörnli' (and not 'a few days before' as appears in *Escalades dans les Alpes*) must be that it was hardly an inappropriate term for an event three years earlier for a salesman who had been in the business for at least 15 years.

There seems therefore to be no reason to suppose that Old Peter had any realistic ambition to climb the Matterhorn. The prospect of further expeditions with an exceptionally wealthy employer would have appealed to him greatly, and it may well be that his dissatisfaction with the sum of 120frs that he took for the ascent of the Matterhorn, 'the highest price ever given for mountain ascents' according to Whymper, was the result of Douglas having offered him substantially more on his own account. The subject of guides fees is considered in section 3.6.1, but if Charles Parker recorded correctly in a letter to his father, what Old Peter had told him in August 1865, 'that he was promised a much larger sum, that he wd. never have run so much risk for the payment he rec'd. (120 francs and his son 80)', this can only mean that Old Peter was not competent to participate in such a climb.

2.52.6 His ascent of the Matterhorn

Whymper wrote of his tent, blankets and ropes etc having been left at the Schwarzsee chapel when he returned from Breuil, and on the 13th July the party stopped there to collect them on its way up from Zermatt. Old Peter's answer to Question 29 (Q29) at the Enquiry implies that he inspected the ropes at the Schwarzsee, as he said in relation to the strength of the rope between him and Douglas, 'If I had found that the rope was too weak, I would have recognised it as such before the ascent of the Matterhorn and rejected it'. He must therefore have noticed that the rope in question was at least different from the two other types of rope that they took, and there is confirmation of this in A24 when he said 'and I tied myself to Lord Douglas with a special rope'. Unfortunately he was not asked in what way it was special, but the probability is that he had in mind that it was not a brand-new rope like the one extending between Douglas and Croz (A26) and that it was of plaited rather than twisted construction. We know that he had in mind the likely need to leave fixed ropes on the mountain (A53) and bearing in mind that the ascent turned out to be very much easier than everyone had expected, they had all no doubt anticipated fixing ropes on the ascent at or above the shoulder, particularly in view of the various ropes already fixed on the Italian ridge, which virtually everyone had reckoned to offer an easier route to the summit. There is therefore little reason for concluding, as some critics have, that Old Peter was unaware of the purpose for which the plaited rope was being taken. 'It was not brought, and should not have been employed, for the purpose for which it was used', Whymper wrote later in *Scrambles*. 'It was old rope, and, compared with the others, was feeble. It was intended as a reserve, in case we had to leave much rope behind, attached to rocks.' It is likely that Old Peter carried all of it ('more than 200 feet'), on the ascent as well as on the descent, and that it was in several separate pieces. But the fact that he knew the purpose for which it was intended, does not exclude the possibility that he honestly believed that it was nevertheless not too weak for use as a climbing rope.

The party pitched camp at the approximate height of Kennedy's highest point in January 1862 and it seems improbable, as already noted, that Old Peter had been any higher previously. He helped make a platform for the tent whilst Croz and his son reconnoitred higher up. The three Taugwalders spent the night in the tent with Whymper and Douglas, the others preferring to remain outside, where they probably also found, as Whymper wrote in his letter to von Fellenberg but not apparently elsewhere, that 'the sleep which we might otherwise have enjoyed was driven away by the snoring of the Taugwalder family'! The following day they had an uneventful climb to the top, not using the rope much prior to 'the solitary difficult part', as Whymper termed the final hour and a half of the climb, when Croz was in the lead and Old Peter was the last man.

It seems clear from what Whymper wrote that they intended all along to descend as one long roped party of seven, a course similar to that adopted by Hudson, Kennedy and Croz on the Aiguille Verte the week before. With the order of descent as Croz, Hadow, Hudson, Douglas, Old Peter, Whymper and finally Young Peter, it is likely (subject to the point mentioned in section 5.4.2 at the end of the Notes on Q28) that two ropes would have been used, meeting in the middle at Douglas. In this event Croz would have tied the far end of his rope to Douglas either initially or after measuring off the necessary lengths and tying on Hadow and Hudson, the point being that whatever the length of his rope it is unlikely that any excess would have been carried by Douglas rather than by Croz himself. Old Peter was unable to tell the Enquiry which of the three Croz tied first (A25), but he did say in effect (A28) that there was not enough rope at the Douglas end to attach himself to the Croz rope. Whymper wrote in *Scrambles* how 'The party was being arranged in the above order whilst I was sketching the summit, and they had finished, and were waiting for me to be tied in line, when some one remembered that our names had not been left in a bottle. They requested me to write them down, and moved off while it was being done.'

Taken literally that could mean that Old Peter had already tied himself to Douglas with his special rope, that Young Peter was tied to the other end of the same rope and that they were all waiting for Whymper to tie himself on between the Taugwalders. But this seems unlikely for a number of reasons, unless the same rope had been used on the ascent, which would make complete nonsense of everything that has ever been written on the subject of the ropes, and not least of the questions that Clemenz seems to have invited Whymper to draft for Old Peter. The most feasible explanation for what Whymper wrote is that Young Peter had the strong rope with which the last three intended to tie on to Douglas and that until Whymper finished sketching there was no point in Young Peter doing anything but wait. However when Whymper was asked to put their names in a bottle after finishing his sketch it seems to have been decided that the leading five should start and that Old Peter should therefore attach himself to Douglas right away. Not carrying one of the twisted ropes himself and with no spare rope available at the Douglas end of the Croz rope, Old Peter decided to use the plaited rope, which he had ready for use as fixed rope (see A53), and tied himself to Douglas with it. Had he any doubt about its strength being adequate, he would surely have used it double. The first five then set off and when they reached the difficult part only one man moved at a time.

Whymper and Young Peter tied up, soon caught the others up and followed behind 'detached from them, and should have continued so had not Lord Francis Douglas asked me, about 3 p.m., to tie on to old Peter, as he feared, he said, that Taugwalder would not be able to hold his ground if a slip occurred'. It has been suggested by Egger that when Whymper 'tied on' to Old Peter he must have noticed the weak rope already tied round his waist, but that assumes not only that Whymper had to tie the knot for his guide but that he was also on the same stance where he would have been unable to give Old Peter any real support with the rope until such time as all four ahead of him had descended the next pitch. It is much more likely that Young Peter and Whymper would have maintained their intervals above Old Peter and that Whymper would have thrown the end of the rope down to him. Another consideration arising at this stage is that if Old Peter had had any doubt about the strength of the special rope he would surely have taken enough strong rope from Whymper to replace or strengthen the weak link between him and Douglas, bearing in mind that any exhilaration that might have made him over confident on the summit would have soon evaporated as he stood watching Hadow having to be helped down by Croz.

2.52.7 The accident

Whymper's earliest known account of the accident, with the possible exception of what Girdlestone recorded, appeared in McCormick's letter of 17th July to *The Times*: 'The two Taugevalds and Whymper, having a warning of a second or two from the time that Croz called out, planted themselves as firmly as possible, to hold the others up. The pressure upon the rope was too much. It broke...' Whymper said in evidence to the Enquiry (A11) after describing the sequence of the victims fall, 'The few instants that this lasted afforded sufficient time for the three at the rear to plant themselves firmly, so firmly indeed that the rope broke between Lord Douglas and Taugwalder father'. In his letter to von Fellenberg he wrote 'immediately I heard the exclamation from Croz, I planted myself as firmly as the ground would permit, Taugwalder did the same, the rope was tight between us and the shock came upon us both as on one man. We held, but the rope broke.' His wording to *The Times* was almost identical, using italics for 'the rope was tight' until the end of that sentence. The same wording appears in *Scrambles* without the italics, but there are also two footnotes, one of which reads 'Or, more correctly, we held on as tightly as possible. There was no time to change our position.' The other footnote is a lengthy one referring in considerable detail to the exact position of each man and to how well he was placed, stating that the rope was not taut between Hudson and Hadow, with the result that Hadow and Croz fell 10 or 12 feet before the jerk came upon Hudson. 'Old Peter was firmly planted, and stood just beneath a large rock, which he hugged with both arms.'

Old Peter's evidence, such as it is, is detailed in the next section and its main difference from that of Whymper comes in his final answer to the Enquiry (A64) stating 'to be more secure I turned towards the rocks and as the rope which was between Whymper and myself was not taut I was fortunately able to wind it round a projecting rock, which then gave me the necessary and life saving anchorage; the rope that connected me with Douglas and those ahead gave me such a pull from their fall that I am still suffering a lot at the place where my body was tied with the rope'.

It is hardly surprising that Old Peter was paralysed by terror after the accident, having regard to his performance on the Dent Blanche three years earlier. There is no reason to doubt what Whymper wrote about how 'the Taugwalders, utterly unnerved, were not only incapable of giving assistance, but were in such a state that a slip might have been expected at any moment'. Whereas Young Peter seems to have been the ringleader in asking not to be paid and also perhaps in their threatening behaviour, Old Peter must bear equal responsibility for not dissociating himself from such blatant breach of a guide's duty to his client. It is interesting to note the reaction of Alfred Wills after reading Whymper's memorandum of 17th August, and contrast it with the remarkable restraint exercised by Whymper in what he actually published about the Taugwalders.

'Now as to the statement you have so kindly forwarded to me. I take a little different view from you as to the desirability of saving the Taugwalders from the natural & proper consequences of their scandalous conduct. So much do *I* feel this that I was intending to write to you & say that your narrative left on my mind the strong impression that in this respect there was something behind wh. I intended to urge you when you wrote for the Journal to set forth. I think a great deal of mischief is done by shielding fellows like this. They get quite enough of that at Zermatt & amongst their own people, and it is greatly for the *public* benefit that people of this sort shd. be *exposed*. I crossed the Trift last yr. with a mixture of brag, bullying, selfishness & cowardice named Kronig; I have never hesitated to say what I thought of him, not I assure you from any revengeful feeling but because I felt it to be quite shocking that such a fellow should fall to the lot of others as he did to mine in consequence of a heap of laudatory writings concerning him wh. I am quite convinced he never *can* have deserved. These Taugwalders are not fit to be trusted – & the world ought to know it: & I think myself, if you will pardon me for saying so, that you will make a great mistake if you hesitate to speak of them as they should be spoken of.'

2.52.8 His evidence and accounts of the accident

Old Peter's earliest account seems to have formed the basis of the article published in the Bern newspaper, *Der Bund*, on Wednesday 19th July, the report in the *Journal de Genève* the previous day being almost certainly taken from an interview with Young Peter; see section 3.9 (Newspapers). *Der Bund*'s report was based on a despatch from Zermatt on Saturday 15th July, and it got the names just about right apart from Hadow to whom it referred as 'another gentleman whose name it has not been possible to establish'. It got the order on the rope right and stated that 'the least experienced climber in the whole party slipped'. The *Journal de Genève* on the other hand did mention 'Haddo', but said that Lord Francis Douglas slipped. It also got the order wrong. Such errors were quite inconsistent with the facts coming from Old Peter who knew Douglas well after climbing with him for ten days or so. The *Bund* report included:

'About 200 feet below the summit, the Englishman immediately behind the leading guide, the least experienced climber in the whole party, slipped, dragging the next behind him down with him, and he the third, behind him. Even Croz could not go on holding such a weight...Fortunately, the elder Taugwalder managed to throw his weight upon a rock and, before his strength had entirely ebbed, the rope broke below him, a circumstance to which he and Mr. Whimper and his own son at the back owe their survival.'

This involves two fresh matters not in Whymper's initial account, Old Peter throwing his weight upon a rock and Croz holding on to the falling climbers as long as he could, rather than being knocked over by Hadow. But Girdlestone in fact recorded a few days later what Whymper had told him on 16th July including: 'Taugwald caught hold of a rock but the jerk passed through him to Whymper who had placed his axe in front of him'; and in *Scrambles* Whymper wrote in the footnote how: 'Old Peter was firmly planted and, and stood just beneath a large rock, which he hugged with both arms'.

The further matter of Old Peter winding the rope round the rock (A64) is not so free from doubt. Montandon in his 1929 article with Heinrich Dübi looked at this in detail and suggested that either Taugwalder or the Court must have made an error in referring to the upper stronger rope between him and Whymper rather than to the lower thinner rope. It is indeed hard to see how he would have gained any purchase with the upper rope, unless he had left so much slack in it, by not descending its full length on the last pitch, that there was enough to wrap round the rock twice. But even then he would have had to rely on Whymper to secure him by tightening the rope once he had it in place. Not only would he have had insufficient time to make such an elaborate belay, but he would have been competing with Whymper whose instinct would be to tighten the rope instantly, if it was not already tight as he said. Belaying was then in its infancy, but if Taugwalder did have such a possibility already in mind, and if the rock was of the right shape, the further question arises as to why he did not pass the Douglas rope round the rock even before Douglas descended his last pitch, particularly when Taugwalder had already suggested to Croz that they ought to fix a rope (A53). Bearing in mind that the first mention that 'he had the good fortune to be able to pass his rope over a rock rib' came in the *Journal de Genève* report of 18th July, which seems to have been based on what Young Peter had said, it is probable that he in fact did no such thing; see final paragraph of section 3.12.4 (The rope in 1865). Other doubts include whether, and if so how, he sustained injury to his wrist from the lower rope being twined round it, as Güssfeldt was told by him in September, if his attention was in fact concentrated on handling the upper rope, and whether the injury caused to his body by the Douglas rope (A64) is more consistent with the lower or with the upper rope having been round the rock, when the rope broke in mid air. But the main objection to Old Peter having wound the rope round the rock he hugged is that it is wholly inconsistent with Whymper's account in *Scrambles*:

> 'So perished our comrades! For the space of half an hour we remained on the spot without moving a single step. The two men, paralyzed by terror, cried like infants, and trembled in such a manner as to threaten us with the fate of the others...Fixed between the two, I could neither move up nor down. I begged young Peter to descend, but he dared not. Unless he did, we could not advance. At last Old Peter summoned up courage, and changed his position to a rock to which he could fix the rope; the young man descended and we all stood together.'

As for Croz holding the others, and not being knocked off by Hadow in his initial slip, Old Peter conceded to the Enquiry (A63) that 'as Mr. Whymper was above me where he could see the unfortunate course of events better than I could, his deposition may be more correct, so much so that I could not insist that Croz only fell after the three tourists'. This is translated from the original German, the official French translation lacking the positive statement that, from above, Whymper could see better than he could.

Although Old Peter spoke to Charles Parker in August 1865, to Tuckett in 1867 and probably to Leslie Stephen in 1866, the only record of his account of the accident is his evidence to the Enquiry. This is analysed in detail in section 5.4.2 & 5.4.3 (The Enquiry) and will be summarised here. He was lucky to have a friend at Court, his cousin the ad hoc bailiff, Johannes Julen and to have another cousin hovering around the Court. Even if he did not formally represent Old Peter before the Tribunal, Alois Julen, the Zermatt judge who was also a glacier guide seems to have helped him to draft his answers. In fact it seems more than likely that Alois Julen translated from French into German the questions Whymper drafted for Old Peter to answer, probably at Clemenz' request, and that in so doing he altered the sense and whole purpose of some of them. For example, in Q26 Old Peter was asked about the rope that did not break between Douglas and Croz and replied that it was a strong and brand-new rope, but he was not asked a similar question about the rope that did break. He seems to have been given the opportunity of considering the questions at his ease and giving his answers in writing, as Whymper did, and some of his answers, like A29, look as though they were drafted by a lawyer rather than by a peasant. Having been steered clear of a question that might have revealed why he chose to tie on to Douglas with the weakest rope, when there were stronger ropes remaining out of use, he nevertheless volunteered that it was a special rope (A24). But he was not asked to elaborate on this and thereby lost another opportunity of justifying the use as a climbing rope of the rope that had been intended for use as fixed rope. But the gravest defect relating to his evidence is that it never was disclosed, to Whymper as promised by Clemenz, or to the public as demanded by the press. Clemenz was certainly in an invidious position by the time he had digested Old Peter's answers and realised that they did not answer the questions Whymper had actually drafted. Had he put the original questions to Old Peter on his second examination or even on a third one, he would have offended Alois Julen who must have known exactly what was involved in the accident, having gone to the Matterhorn glacier with Young Peter and other members of the recovery party, even if he was not the one responsible for distorting Whymper's questions for his cousin. Had Clemenz disclosed the distorted questions and answers to Whymper, he would have been exposed to criticism from whoever read what Whymper might have written, comparing the questions he handed in with those actually put to Old Peter and drawing attention to the resulting nonsense with no attempt by Clemenz to resolve it with further questions of his own.

But the one that suffered from Clemenz neglect was not Whymper, who is likely to have raised the points in the first place primarily for the benefit of Old Peter and of the victims' friends and relations rather than to satisfy his own curiosity; it was Old Peter Taugwalder. There were two or three reported instances in the second half of the last century of the authorities seeking to cover up the fault of guides that had resulted in the death of a tourist. What seems to have happened here is that someone assumed that there was fault where there was none and the resulting cover up aggravated the suspicions that could so easily have been dispelled. Having mentioned in his letter to *The Times* when the matter was still fresh, that he had handed in a number of questions which he desired to be put to Old Peter, because that which he had found out respecting the ropes was by no means satisfactory to him, and that the answers although promised had not yet reached him, Whymper was obliged to follow it up in *Scrambles* when it was published six years later.

'For the sake of the old guide (who bore a good reputation), and upon all other accounts, it was desirable that this matter should be cleared up; and after my examination...was over I handed in a number of questions which were framed so as to afford old Peter an opportunity of exculpating himself from the grave suspicions which at once fell upon him.'

Whymper added in a footnote,

'This was not the only occasion upon which M.Clemenz (who presided over the inquiry) failed to give up answers that he promised. It is greatly to be regretted that he did not feel that the suppression of the truth was equally against the interests of travellers and of the guides. If the men were untrustworthy, the public should have been warned of the fact; but if they were blameless, why allow them to remain under unmerited suspicion?'

2.52.9 His reaction

Apart from the possibility that he gave an interview on Saturday 15th July to the correspondent of *Der Bund*, who had seen the party on the summit the previous day and may have been staying at the Hotel Mont Cervin, the earliest reference to Old Peter after the accident is of his meeting Whymper's search party of volunteers returning from finding the three bodies on the Matterhorn glacier on the Sunday afternoon. Whymper wrote in the *Graphic* in 1894 of an incident that had recently come to his knowledge:

'No sooner had the survivors of the ill-fated expedition returned to Zermatt, than the baseless, monstrous rumour was circulated that the old man had *cut* the rope which broke. It passed from lip to lip, spreading like wildfire, and emanated from his own village amongst his neighbours. The calumniated man, walking about shunned like a murderer, met the returning volunteers. "Mr. R–," he said to one of them, "they say I *cut* the rope. Look at my fingers!" and, opening his hands, showed how they had been lacerated by the jerk which all but tore him from his grasp.'

It seems probable that Whymper's informant was the Rev James Robertson, who was one of the eight men that accompanied Whymper, and that the information had been recorded in his diary.

On the Wednesday afternoon the recovery party set off, returning with the bodies the following morning. Old Peter was not one of the 21 men, who included his sons Peter and Joseph and his cousin Alois Julen the judge, and it can only be assumed that he was not in a fit state to go. It will be recalled that Whymper organised his search party, when the Zermatt guides refused to go because it would be Sunday, and set off with it less than 16 hours after he had returned to Zermatt from the climb. Had Old Peter been able and willing to participate in the recovery, he might have been able to avoid some of his subsequent troubles, particularly in view of the presence of two Chamonix guides Henri Charlet and Michel Devouassoud, who would almost certainly have spoken with J-B Croz, Michel's brother, when he arrived in Zermatt the following Saturday evening.

Whymper referred in his memorandum of 17th August to hardly seeing Old Peter after the accident. After reciting his conversation with Young Peter on the evening of the accident, he continued:

> 'I was so disgusted with this heartless talk that for the whole distance down to Zermatt I did not speak, – excepting when I was obliged, and this probably gave rise to the rumour that I had not uttered a single word during the whole of that fearful night. And when the Taugwalders suggested that we should continue the descent by moonlight, and again that I should lay down and endeavour to sleep when we stopped, I objected, feeling that men who could view the loss of their fellow creatures with such commercial feelings as these, might not, possibly, be ill pleased if I also slipped. They seemed to understand that what they had said was displeasing to me, for during the whole of the time (8 days) that I remained at Zermatt after the accident, I did not even see either of them until the last two days. The son indeed left Zermatt for Chamonix soon after the accident and I did not see him at all excepting for half a minute. It is unnecessary to say that they *were* paid, and paid the highest price ever given for mountain ascents.'

Whymper probably saw Young Peter returning with the recovery party before he set off for Chamonix on the Thursday afternoon. He paid Old Peter for both of them, probably on the Friday morning, and he presumaby paid him for Joseph at the same time, the entry in his diary being set out as follows:

'Paid Peter Taugwald for self and son for Matterhorn & Theodule

Peter	100	bonnemain	20	
son	80			
son	20	Theodule	15	235 – '

The word bonnemain starts about midway between the figures 100 & 80 and slopes downwards so that 20 ends at the 80 level. This may perhaps mean that the tip was to be shared between the two Peters, rather than that it was given wholly to one or the other and it is interesting to deduce from a letter Whymper wrote to Hadow's uncle, that although he divided such things as guides' fees for the Matterhorn and bills for provisions into four, being reimbursed for Hudson's, Hadow's and Douglas's shares, he bore the whole of the tip himself. A little over a week after Whymper paid Taugwalder, the Parker brothers arrived in Zermatt having probably intended to make a further guideless attempt on the Matterhorn until they heard of the accident. They stayed at the Monte Rosa from 29th July until 3rd August and at some stage Charles Parker talked to Taugwalder. But this could well have been on about 28th August, when he climbed Monte Rosa from the Riffelhaus with W.H.Gladstone and it may even be that Old Peter was one of their guides. But all Parker seems to have got was a tale of woe, according to a letter he addressed to his father in October, one of Old Peter's chief complaints being the amount he had been paid by Whymper.

> 'Taugwalder says that he was promised a much larger sum, that he wd. never have run so much risk for the payment he rec'd. (120 francs and his son 80), and that he has had no opportunity of being heard on this matter by anyone but Whymper, who had quarrelled with him.'

It seems from this that Old Peter pocketed the whole of the tip, but was still not satisfied, yet Parker's comment was 'It is very possible that the payment was just right under the circumstances'. The sum of 100frs had been passed to Croz' representatives and Whymper recorded in his memorandum how the Taugwalders were paid 'the highest price ever given for mountain ascents'. The subject of guides fees is dealt with in section 3.6.1, but the official tariff, published by Ruden in 1869 in his book provided for 40frs as far as the shoulder and 100frs for the summit. Even so, it may well be that these sums were to some extent influenced by the opinions of the Taugwalders, as in the same list the Weisshorn and the Dent Blanche each commanded only 60frs.

Whether he had been promised a much larger sum no one will ever know, as it was Lord Francis Douglas who engaged him. Whereas it is possible that Douglas had been overcharged as Old Peter tried to find a way up the Obergabelhorn, it should be borne in mind that the 1869 tariff for Monte Rosa, Old Peter's speciality until Douglas 'took him out of his class', was only 40frs. But the key to Old Peter's dissatisfaction may be that he would never have run so much risk for the sum of 120frs. This raises the question as to what risk he was referring to, bearing in mind in particular that the ascent proved far easier than anyone had expected. He may have been referring to the basic climb, in which case this only goes to prove that he was out of his class, as any higher figure he might have been promised by Douglas would have taken account of the considerably greater difficulties and risks that were expected but never materialised. If he had in mind the terrifying experience of seeing four men fall to their death, he could not have been talking of any agreement made in advance and it is hardly likely that Douglas would have paid him an extra fee for the equally if not more terrifying experience of falling more than 20 feet with the cornice from the top of the Obergabelhorn, particularly when Old Peter's negligence on that occasion forced Douglas to share the experience. A more likely cause of his dissatisfaction over the shortfall in the fees he was expecting might be that, after falling off the

Obergabelhorn less than a week before, only the promise of an exorbitant sum would induce him to risk his life again so soon.

There is something else that may have aggravated the envy and the jealousy of other guides that inevitably accompanied the ascent by a Monte Rosa guide of the peak that had previously been considered inaccessible by the leading guides and amateurs of the day, and it may also have aggravated Old Peter's frustration at having had to make what he thought was such a risky ascent for a mere 120frs. The non-existent 'reward' for making the first ascent of the Matterhorn seems to have been widely reported in the press in the first week or so of August and reports of it were still rife in Zermatt at the time Parker saw Old Peter: 'Of course nothing is easier than to tell him in writing, what he was not content to be told when I saw him, that there is no sort of truth in the belief (wh. at Zermatt is universal) that a money-reward was to be given for the first ascent of the Matterhorn.' The subject is considered in greater detail in section 3.11 and it is sufficient to mention here that one report referred to the three guides being promised 5,000frs.

But another aspect of Old Peter's discontent, recorded by Parker, is less easy to explain; 'Taugwalder says that Whymper behaved ill, especially in the colouring he gave to his evidence at Zermatt, wh. has damaged Taugwalder.' It looks as though Old Peter was referring to Whymper's evidence at the Enquiry, but although both of his cousins, the bailiff and the judge, may have had access to what Whymper said, there is in fact nothing in his answers that could reasonably have offended him. It is however possible that Old Peter was referring to the wording of the questions Whymper handed in for him to answer and that whoever mistakenly thought there was a need to alter some of them in the course of translating them into German told Old Peter that Whymper was at fault. But did Old Peter realise or did anyone tell him that Clemenz had washed his hands of actually questioning him about the accident on the Friday (apart from the ambiguous Q36) and that he had relied on Whymper to do it for him? In any event the word 'damaged' seems inappropriate, unless it relates to Clemenz no longer recommending Old Peter to his hotel guests. But that would not be the fault of Whymper. It would involve something far more serious, such as gross negligence or incompetence on Clemenz' part in not asking Old Peter the proper questions, or it might even perhaps have been Clemenz' reaction to not having been able to question Old Peter in the way he would have wished. Clemenz was no less a foreigner than Alexander Seiler in the eyes of the Zermatt Burgers and we know that when the highest Courts in the land all ruled in Seiler's favour on his application to become a Burger, the Zermatters took no notice of them until they finally sent a garrison of gendarmes. So perhaps Clemenz' conflicting interests as a hotelier undermined his position and prevented him from acting as judicially as the Cantonal Government in Sion would have expected.

It seems as though Old Peter was already by August 1865 excluding the possibility of his ever repeating the ascent, as without the benefit of a first class guide like Michel Croz to lead him, he would presumably have wanted an even higher fee and one so far in excess of what he actually took on the first ascent that he would have had great difficulty in finding anyone who was prepared to pay it. The fact that Young Peter and Moser wanted Thioly to pay them 150frs each for an ascent in 1867 may throw some light on what Old Peter would have wanted in 1865. The official tariff of 100frs, which probably came into force in 1868, must therefore have excluded him from even contemplating another ascent, having priced himself out of the market. In September 1865 Güssfeldt had arrived in Zermatt determined to make the ascent. He immediately sent for Old Peter, who, it seems, was determined to avoid the scene of the accident but having failed to dissuade Güssfeldt, 'he implored [him] to refrain from that which could not come to good'. But although they agreed to attempt a secret ascent from Breuil, which proved unsuccessful, Güssfeldt does not quote Old Peter's fees.

But before Güssfeldt or even Parker met Old Peter the rumour that he had cut the rope had spread far and wide. J-B Croz seems to have taken it with him when he left Zermatt on Sunday 23rd July, judging from the writings of Wigram and E.N.Buxton, if it had not already reached Chamonix via some of the six Chamonix guides involved in the three search parties. On 8th August Wigram wrote to Whymper,

> 'I have not the honour of your acquaintance and I have no wish to intrude upon you; still I think that you ought to hear what has come to my knowledge.
> I have received a letter from Jean Baptiste Croz (Michel's brother, & my tried companion during 3 campaigns), in which he speaks of a suspicion prevalent in the Valley of Chamonix, and I fear shared by himself that Taugwald *cut* the rope on the Matterhorn. The grounds for this dreadful charge are the improbability of such a rope breaking and the fact that young Taugwald had just come to Chamonix whence it was assumed that he was escaping justice.'

Buxton wrote in an article in the *Alpine Journal* on the Glacier du Dôme of a strike by his party's guides early in August 1865;

> 'We had one day found young Taugwald lounging outside the hotel, having been just paid off by his employer, and looking out for a return job. As he is a strong lad we engaged him as a porter. Just at this time Jean Baptiste Croz had come back from Zermatt, looking emaciated and almost crazed at the loss of his brother. His grief found vent in wild tales and half-formed accusations against the men who had been with him at the time of his death. The garrulous Frenchmen who listened, sympathized, and believed, and spread these reports, and the morning after engaging Taugwald our guides came to us, and made an abominable accusation, first against him and then against his father, and announced that they dare not and would not go with him.'

Charles Gos quotes Stéphen d'Arve's account of confronting Old Peter at Chamonix a fortnight after the accident, when a Swiss cabinet maker introduced him to Old Peter as a journalist, saying that he was writing about him and asking if he would furnish some more details; 'You cut the rope didn't you? The axe worked well didn't it? Yes! yes! echoed the voices of fifteen guides sitting at the same table.' He goes on to describe Old Peter's reaction and the look he gave his son without saying a word. It seems that d'Arve was not the most reliable writer and there is no reason whatever to suppose that Old Peter went to Chamonix in July 1865, but there could have been some such incident in 1866 when he went there on at least two occasions. d'Arve's account may well have been published elsewhere prior to 1876.

But there is a reliable first hand account, published by Canon Carrel in 1868, which whilst not expressly implicating Old Peter shows that the question of cutting a rope was still a subject for discussion a year after the accident. 'In 1866 I was in the Hotel du Mont-Cervin at Giomein in the company of several tourists, whom I did not know. Someone propounded the question: Can a tourist or a guide cut the rope attaching himself to his climbing companion in the event of the latter falling when he is unable to hold him?' Further reference to the subject is found in the notorious article written by the Austrian writer Meissner, in which he even went so far as to suggest that Whymper might have cut the rope. It was published in *Die neue freie Presse* of 4th August 1865, the last paragraph of which read, 'The Swiss press, which answers for the guides tries to deny the cutting of the rope and sticks to its chance parting'. Whymper ignored Meissner's article, although he seems to have had it in mind in a letter to Robertson at the end of August, but he dealt with the accusation against Old Peter in the long footnote in *Scrambles*, which he probably wrote after visiting Zermatt in September 1869 on the basis of what he had learnt from Seiler.

> 'Old Peter Taugwalder is a man who is labouring under an unjust accusation. Notwithstanding repeated denials, even his comrades and neighbours at Zermatt persist in asserting or insinuating that he *cut* the rope which led from him to Lord F. Douglas. In regard to this infamous charge, I say that he *could* not do so at the moment of the slip, and that the end of the rope in my possession shows that he did not do so beforehand.'

Leslie Stephen remarked on this in his *Macmillan's* review of *Scrambles*:

> 'Mr. Whymper very properly denounced the absurd fable that the elder Taugwald cut the rope. It was a simple impossibility for him to do so; and if the rope had not instantaneously snapped, the whole party must have been killed. In fact, the three survivors probably owe their lives to Taugwald's presence of mind, to which Mr. Whymper does justice. But I rather regret that he should not reject decidedly another grave though less serious accusation, which comes in fact to this, that Taugwald intentionally used a weak rope in fastening himself to Lord F. Douglas, in order to have a chance of being separated from him in case of accident. Knowing the carelessness too often displayed on such occasions, the confidence which guides will show in weak ropes, and the probable state of excitement of the whole party, which would easily account for such an oversight, I think that the hypothesis of deliberate intention on Taugwald's part is in the highest degree improbable; and there is not a particle of direct evidence in its favour. The presumption would be that Croz was almost equally responsible; and, at any rate, such accusations should have some more tangible

> ground than a vague possibility. A discussion of the point would be out of place here, and I venture upon this digression merely for the sake of an old guide, who has always had a high character, and, to the best of my knowledge, has well deserved it.'

It should be noted that Stephen did not seek to attribute these 'accusations' to Whymper, unlike some twentieth century critics. So far as the other 'grave though less serious accusation' is concerned, Whymper had written in the same footnote, after referring to the fact that Clemenz had failed to give up the answers that he had promised,

> 'There remains however the suspicious fact that the rope which broke was the thinnest and weakest one that we had. It is suspicious, because it is unlikely that any of the four men in front would have selected an old and weak rope when there was abundance of new, and much stronger, rope to spare; and, on the other hand, because if Taugwalder thought that an accident was likely to happen, it was to his interest to have the weaker rope where it was placed.'

So far as Whymper was concerned there was a clear distinction between the two issues. The breaking of the rope was something he had actually seen with his own eyes and he could speak of it as a matter of fact. But the use of the weak rope was something that only Taugwalder could account for, and he was not going to express his own opinion in public, when it was the friends and relatives of the victims that were primarily affected. Indeed it is common to his whole attitude towards the accident that whilst he was prepared to answer questions of fact, and even wanted the Alpine Club to conduct an Enquiry into the death of Hudson, he did not want to be both the principal witness and the judge of what matters should be given in evidence, any more than he wanted to express an opinion on matters of fact unknown to him, which Clemenz had failed to elucidate from Old Peter or even perhaps from Young Peter. 'I scrupulously abstain from offering observations and casting blame on anyone', he wrote to Sir T.F.Buxton on 8th August referring to the letter to *The Times*, which he had been so reluctant to write.

It seems that the only reason he ever raised the question for Taugwalder 'Why was a *different kind of* rope used between Lord Douglas and yourself?' was because Clemenz wanted him to draft appropriate questions and this was the one question that all his fellow guests at the Monte Rosa, such as McCormick, Robertson, Campbell and other friends of the victims, had probably been asking him. He did not know the answer and referred the question to Clemenz, little realising that Clemenz had allowed the question to become distorted during translation into German (Q28), so as to produce the facile answer that *another* rope was used because the first rope was not long enough. The question had never been an accusation, but when the answer was not forthcoming Whymper was hardly likely to neglect his duty to the relatives and friends, by condoning Clemenz' breach of promise. It is furthermore probable that the likes of Alexander Seiler and others in

Zermatt also wanted to know the answer, that the lack of such a simple answer was causing continuing damage to Old Peter and that Whymper possibly thought the publication of *Scrambles* might lead to Clemenz finally providing the answers. Whymper had expressed his own personal view privately to Wigram in his letter of 9th August 1865: 'How it came to pass that the weakest rope was used between Taugwalder and Lord Douglas I have no idea, that is I have no idea why he did not use the stronger ropes. Still I have no reason to suspect even that this was done *intentionally*'. Old Peter's possible explanation and answer to the question he was never asked are considered more fully in section 3.16 (The special rope) and it is sufficient to state here that it may well be in the light of his experience on the Obergabelhorn only a week before, that he honestly, albeit wrongly, believed that the plaited rope was as strong as the others.

2.52.10 1866

Some critics have sought to explain the marked drop in Old Peter's employment as a guide after the Matterhorn accident (judged without reference to his Führerbuch, should it still exist) by blaming Whymper, as though Old Peter had no control over his own destiny. But there are a number of different factors involved and they must be kept separate, if any judgment is to be made as to cause and effect. There is Old Peter's pre-Douglas career as a Monte Rosa guide and as a guide for glacier passes, which could hardly have been adversely affected to any material degree by anything that any outsider said or did, whether an English climber, a Chamonix guide or even a guide from St.Niklaus. Old Peter's local trade would be in part dependent on local goodwill from hoteliers such as Seiler and Clemenz and, subject to what has been said above about Parker's record of Old Peter being damaged, there is no reason to suppose that the ascent of the Matterhorn caused him to lose or forfeit it. Contrary to what Egger and Lunn have suggested Whymper did not display any illwill towards Old Peter and he even allowed him to use his climbing ropes, judging from a letter written by Seiler to Whymper towards the end of September 1865 referring to 'Peter Taugwald' not having returned the ropes that Whymper had left at Seiler's disposal. The odd thing about Old Peter's pre-Douglas career is that he seems to have abandoned it by 1866 and to have reversed the relationship with his son, so that instead of insisting that Young Peter be taken as second guide it seems to have been Young Peter that arranged for his father to be taken as second guide.

There are two ascents of Mont Blanc and one of the Dom recorded for 1866, all with Young Peter, peaks that Old Peter seems never to have climbed before, and it looks as though he may already have lost the capacity or nerve to lead a party himself. It would have been easier for him to escape attention as second guide away from Zermatt, and judging from Güssfeldt's experience two years later when Old Peter would only go with him as long as no one else came as well, it looks as though he may have been avoiding the company of other Zermatt guides.

Nevertheless Chamonix was an extraordinary place for him to go to in view of the hostile attitude there, as recorded by Buxton and by Wigram, quite apart from what his own son Peter was to tell Montagnier in 1917 via Rudolf Taugwalder. Instead of abandoning Monte Rosa and glacier passes, one would expect him to have taken advantage of so many new tourists visiting Zermatt and to have climbed Monte Rosa even more often. He might also be expected to have repeated all his recent first ascents, unless he was already in decline before he achieved them.

As for the Matterhorn there is not the slightest doubt that if he had been capable and willing to lead another ascent he would have been in such great demand that he would never have looked back, as long as his fees were reasonable. Birkbeck could not find a Zermatt guide willing to accompany him on the Matterhorn in July 1866. He had climbed the Weisshorn with Young Peter in 1863 and it is inconceivable that he did not offer Old Peter the opportunity of climbing the Matterhorn. A few days later Thioly could not find a single guide willing to try the Matterhorn and on Seiler's advice climbed the Dom instead, with Young Peter. The opportunities were there but Old Peter seems to have declined them. Leslie Stephen, who had previously made the second ascents of the Weisshorn and of the Dom, was also in Zermatt in 1866. That year he made the second ascent from Zermatt of the Obergabelhorn and as he knew Old Peter it is almost certain that he would have spoken to him and that if he had been keen, willing and able, Stephen would have taken Old Peter along with his other guide and made the second ascent of the Matterhorn from Zermatt in 1866. One cannot avoid the conclusion, that apart from his inflated idea as to what his services were worth, Old Peter had no intention of ever attempting the Hörnli ridge again. This was entirely his own fault, if someone has to be blamed, but it is understandable, when one bears in mind the Dent Blanche fiasco, his miraculous escape on the Obergabelhorn and his further good fortune on the Matterhorn, that he may well have decided that the time had come when he was no longer prepared to climb at the sharp end of the rope or incur the risks attendant on difficult ascents. There is no evidence to suggest that he himself sought to blame anyone else for not taking advantage of the opportunities that opened up for him after the Matterhorn ascent. But his pre-accident reputation and character seem to have left him very vulnerable to the taunts that were bound to come sooner or later, as the Zermatt guides reacted to the way his exaggeration of the difficulties and dangers caused them to boycott the mountain and give the guides of St.Niklaus a virtual monopoly in the valley for five or more years.

2.52.11 1867

This was the year of Joseph's death in the Schwarzsee and there does not appear to be any record of Old Peter making any climbs. Although many of the pioneers wrote about their climbs and published accounts in the journals, they were clearly a small minority and for every would be climber of the Matterhorn in the late 1860's of whom we know there must have been many others who kept quiet about being unable to realise their ambition because they could not get a guide. We know that Thioly failed once more to find a guide in 1867 and that he expressly referred to being unable to induce Old Peter to accompany him, and it may be assumed that Jordan would have approached him in August when he wanted to climb the Hörnli, unless he had already learnt from Seiler that he would be wasting his time even asking him. Instead he employed Peter Knubel and Tobie Couttet on his first attempt, with J-M Lochmatter replacing Couttet on the second. Having been able to get no further than the scene of the accident before snowfall forced a retreat, Jordan then switched his attention to Breuil:

> 'When I found that Zermatt had decided the season to be too late for any further attempt, I went over the Théodule to Breil. The Taugwalders, father and son, were there and wanted immediately to go for the ascent with me from Zermatt; but the Maquignaz party were then in sight descending the mountain...and I arranged with Joseph Maquignaz to wait for the Indian summer and then repeat the ascent he had just made. I wanted to cross the mountain, and could not do that without guides for the Italian side.'

Jordan was fortunate in making the decision he did, as there is no reason to suppose that Old Peter would ever have led him to the summit via the Hörnli and it was not until 1872 that even Young Peter was to make his second ascent from Zermatt. As it was, Jordan not only repeated the Maquignaz ascent, but did more than anyone else to open up both the Breuil and the Zermatt routes. After stopping for eighty five minutes on the summit Jordan and the Maquignaz brothers descended the Hörnli as far as the scene of the accident, where they explored an alternative route. After spending three hours on the ridge they returned to the summit and the next day to Breuil, from where Jordan crossed to Zermatt a few days later and made an entry in the Monte Rosa guestbook. There could hardly be a greater contrast between Old Peter's repeated refusal to accompany anyone up the Hörnli, his complete lack of initiative towards making a second ascent from Zermatt and the fearful account that he must have given to the other Zermatt guides of the difficulties and dangers, sufficient to deter them from making any attempt whatever before 1871, and the enthusiasm of Jordan about the rocks in the vicinity of the scene of the accident, as recorded by him in Seiler's hotel book on 7th October 1867.

> 'After thus making certain of a route by which, in confidence of fine weather, we intended to descend to Zermatt on the following day, we spent some time in endeavouring to make out a better though a more giddy route down the rocky face which looks towards the Riffel and Monte Rosa.
> Having lingered about these glorious slopes as long as we considered prudent at this season of the year, we returned to the summit.'

Tuckett, who had climbed with F.A.Y.Brown the previous year and would have heard from him all about the Matterhorn accident, was in Zermatt towards the end of June 1867 and he went to see Old Peter as well as seeing the victims' graves.

2.52.12 1868 – 1871

The year 1868 brought to Zermatt J.M.Elliott, who wrote to a friend a few days after making the second ascent of the Hörnli, 'I was alone and all Zermatt against me; not a Zermatt guide would go'. Being greatly encouraged by Jordan's account he seems to have been intent on trying it alone, until he encountered Knubel and Lochmatter at the hut they were building for Seiler and persuaded them to accompany him. There is no point in referring to any of the further opportunities that might have presented themselves to Old Peter this year, when six separate ascents were made from Zermatt, except to say that Thioly found all the guides of Zermatt trembling at the temerity of Elliott, so that it was useless asking any of them. But there is one incident that reveals something of Old Peter's mental state. Güssfeldt made the ascent of the Matterhorn with St.Niklaus guides and thereafter 'found old Taugwalder ready to be my guide if other company was excluded'. They crossed to Macugnaga over the old Weissthor, but Old Peter lost the way on the descent and they had to spend the night out. This is his only known expedition in 1868 and with none at all recorded for 1869 it is time to look further at Whymper's long footnote in *Scrambles*, which was probably written after visiting Zermatt in September 1869.

'I am told that he is now nearly incapable for work – not absolutely mad, but with intellect gone and almost crazy...' This must have been based on what Whymper learnt from Seiler or some equally reliable source, as it is stated as a matter of fact. Bearing in mind the shock of the Obergabelhorn and Matterhorn accidents, the death of his son Joseph in the Schwarzsee and the persistent assertions or insinuations that he cut the rope on the Matterhorn, it is understandable that Old Peter's mental state should have undermined his ability to work, and with only one ascent of Mont Blanc recorded for 1870, plus the possibility of Monte Rosa and the Tête Blanche, and only one engagement for 1871 and nothing at all therafter he seems never to have recovered. Indeed it is probable that his mental condition was further aggravated by the gradual realisation of his neighbours and fellow guides in Zermatt that he had by his exaggeration of the difficulties and dangers of the Hörnli, however unwittingly, deprived the Zermatt guides of a great deal of business by giving the guides of St.Niklaus uninterrupted use of the Matterhorn for over five years.

The publication of *Scrambles* in 1871 probably did little if anything at all to cause him further harm, by making known some of the facts that might otherwise have remained unknown or forgotten. The burst of Matterhorn activity produced by *Scrambles* is obvious from the appendix in later editions, which records only 20 successful expeditions prior to 1871 compared with seven that year, 12 in 1872 and another 21 in 1873. Old Peter would have felt more and more left out of things, even if none of his comrades or neighbours at Zermatt ever tried to taunt him over his inability to show that he was capable of climbing the Matterhorn without Croz. Young Peter by contrast took advantage of the publicity afforded to him by the first ascent and soon built up a reputation as a good guide on other peaks, even if his recollections of the nightmare descent or his father's influence prevented him from taking an objective view and returning to the Hörnli for many years.

2.52.13 Misleading criticism?

Egger has written of the Taugwalders sitting on the bench in front of the Giomein waiting for the work that the Matterhorn should have brought but never did, but it would surely have been more to the point for Old Peter to have sought work in Zermatt. Egger asserts that for at least five years after the catastrophe Old Peter was an active participant in expeditions 'quite contrary to Whymper's frivolous verdict about his physical and mental constitution'. As usual Egger provides no evidence to support his contradiction of facts recorded by Whymper, which is hardly surprising when he dismisses Whymper's statement 'I am told that he is by now nearly incapable of work – not absolutely mad, but with intellect gone and almost crazy' as 'Whymper's frivolous verdict'. He cites merely the two Güssfeldt accounts, the Jordan encounter and Stogdon's letter to Lunn mentioning three expeditions including the one when Old Peter took the rope off when descending the Tête Blanche with two inexperienced men. He says they bear witness to Old Peter's activity, but five climbs in a period of six years, including turning back on one and getting lost on another is more consistent with the facts recorded by Whymper. It is an odd feature of Egger's book *Pioniere der Alpen* that it relies almost entirely on English sources, particularly in the case of Old Peter, and does not reveal anything true that was not known already. Egger might have found the Führerbuch or discovered what had happened to it, or enquired as to when and why Old Peter went to America or have told us something more about his character and about his climbs with other nationalities, but he did not.

Soon after the publication of Egger's book, Lunn wrote an article in the *Alpine Journal* praising Egger and full of misleading statements such as: 'Taugwalder was, by common consent, one of the leading guides of his generation' and 'For some years, old Taugwalder might have been seen waiting in vain for the employment which never came. His reputation had suffered from Whymper's attack. In the end this outstanding Zermatt guide of the period left Zermatt and lived for some years in retirement in the United States.'

Charles Gos was also influenced by Egger's book and wrote shortly afterwards in a strangely uncharacteristic and inaccurate chapter, 'La Corde Maudite', in his book *Le Cervin*, of Old Peter's post-accident adversity, including: 'meanwhile famous alpinists engaged him (Güssfeldt, Kennedy etc)'. But he quotes no more details and there is no reason to suppose that Kennedy did engage him or would ever have contemplated doing so again after the Dent Blanche fiasco.

> 'The blow dealt to his reputation and to his honour by Whymper's suspicions finally destroys him. A few years after the drama he goes to the United States, but returns to his homeland in a pitiful state of physical and mental health. He takes up his ice axe again, but the tourists keep clear of him. He dies in 1888.'

Needless to say there is no evidence quoted by Gos, nor apparently elsewhere, to suggest that Old Peter even tried to resume guiding when he returned home from America. All that is known is that he took a share in the building of the Schwarzsee hotel, which seems to have been completed in the year he died.

2.52.14 Conclusion

There is therefore nothing to suggest that the publication of *Scrambles* affected Old Peter adversely, except perhaps indirectly by increasing his frustration as a result of the book attracting even more tourists to Zermatt and increasing the demand for guides for the Matterhorn and other peaks, at a time when he was already no longer capable of leading a climb. The 'accusations' in *Scrambles*, as certain critics label the facts stated by Whymper, were published six years after the first signs of Old Peter's post-accident decline, and they can have no relevance. Despite Whymper's reluctance to condone the Taugwalders' heartless and threatening behaviour during the descent, he did not after writing to *The Times* publish anything more about either of them until 1871, despite being advised to do so, and even then he only included the first part of his own memorandum in *Scrambles*. He never published the contents of the Cowell memorandum, preferring the advice of Browne to that of Wills and Cowell. As for anything he may have said in Zermatt after the accident, he appears to have acted with discretion, refusing to speak to the press, and not even referring to the question of the weak rope in his evidence to the Enquiry, apart from saying that the Taugwalder – Douglas rope was less thick than the others. Even the questions Clemenz seems to have relied upon him to draft for Old Peter were very fair ones in the circumstances, and had Clemenz made sure that they were answered and the answers published, it is quite possible that Old Peter would have been able to adjust to his new role as second guide and gradually improve upon the promising start he made in 1866. But something went wrong in 1867 and having initially perhaps just lost his nerve for difficult climbs, he seems thereafter to have declined steadily. Nor can Young Peter be right to blame everything on the jealousy and envy of the Chamonix and St.Niklaus guides. It is much more likely that the envy and jealousy of his comrades and neighbours in Zermatt drove him to want to escape to America, as suggested by the comments of

Bernard Biner already quoted above. The tragedy of Peter Taugwalder may not have been entirely of his own making, but there is no need to try and hold Whymper responsible, through a book published six years after the event, for the faults of those who misguidedly prevented him from dispelling the suspicions created by the accident or of those who out of jealousy contributed by their unpleasantness to the further decline of someone whose vulnerability had been revealed even before the accident and before tragedy struck his family.

Little else has been been published about Old Peter Taugwalder, but in 1927 Stanislaus Kronig wrote of the old Zermatt legend, which continued until the new church was built early this century, that on the eve of St. Hilarius when the clock struck 12 the ghosts of those who were going to die that year went in procession to the church in the order in which they were going to die. In 1888 Old Peter is said to have been watching the procession from his house near the church when he suddenly saw a man run past. He could not recognise him but suspected it was his neighbour, as he subsequently told his family. But oddly enough, wrote Kronig, it was his own ghost, for he died that year and his neighbour did not. His other predictions were all correct.

The final word on Old Peter's involvement in the accident on the first ascent of the Matterhorn should come from Whymper; 'I should rejoice to learn that his answers to the questions which were put to him were satisfactory. Not only was his act at the critical moment wonderful as a feat of strength, but it was admirable in its performance at the right time.'

2.53
TAUGWALDER, YOUNG PETER (1843 – 1923)

Young Peter Taugwalder

By 1865 Young Peter was almost certainly a better climber than his father, although with only about 30 ascents of Monte Rosa compared with about 85 for his father he had not yet accumulated anything like his father's experience as a guide. But he was prepared to venture further afield and had already climbed the Weisshorn and had an engagement arranged in Chamonix for the last week in July 1865. This led to another visit there in the third week of September when he made a number of climbs including his first ascent of Mont Blanc. Many of his early climbs had been made as porter with his father, who is said to have insisted sometimes on his son being taken as well. There is little doubt that he would have been able to accompany T.S.Kennedy to make the first ascent of the Dent Blanche in 1862, had his father not been in the party and lost his nerve. The following list shows some of the main events in Young Peter's life and career as a guide.

1843 Born.
1859 Führerbuch issued.
1862 Dent Blanche attempt with Kennedy.
1863 Ascended Weisshorn.
1864 By now he had climbed Monte Rosa 26 times, and the Breithorn 'often'.
1865 First ascent of Matterhorn.
1867 Married Barbara Salzgeber. Brother Joseph drowned in Schwarzsee.
1868 Son Joseph born.
1870 Daughter Leonie born.
1871 Son Kamil born.
1872 Made his second ascent of Matterhorn.
1874 Daughter Bertha born. Father went to America.
1878 Married Maria Lerjen. Father returned from America.
1888 Father died.
1894 Daughter Balbina born, the sixth child of his second marriage.
1900? Knee injury from falling stone put an end to his career as guide.
1917 Recorded for Montagnier his 'Narrative' of the Matterhorn first ascent.
1923 Died 10th March.

Significant climbs 1865-1872. (Dates from Führerbuch entries)
1865
14.7. First ascent of Matterhorn.
7.8. Glacier du Dôme. (Pages missing from 26.6 until 13.8)
28.8. Trift pass.
4.9. Monte Rosa and Weissthor.
11.9. Dom.
13.9. Dom.
25.9. Entry records Monte Rosa, Theodule pass, Col du Géant, Grands Mulets, Mont Blanc, Tête noir.

1866
20.7. Dom. (Thioly)
8.8. Mont Blanc. With Old Peter.
26.8. Cima di Jazzi, Alphubel.
1.9. Monte Rosa attempt. With Old Peter.
4.9. Dom. With Old Peter.
15.9. Mont Blanc. With Old Peter.

1867
27.7. Lyskamm.

29.7. Weisshorn. (Thioly)
12.8. Monte Rosa. Klein Matterhorn.
28.8. Breithorn, Eggishorn, Strahleck.

1868
27.7. Alphubel pass. (Ulrich)
1.8. Lyskamm.
3.9. Tyrol and Salzkammergut. Gross Glockner, Ortler and Bernina.

1869
30.7. Attempted Matterhorn from Breuil, retreating in storm. (Heathcote) Aiguille Verte, Grandes Jorasses, Aiguille du midi, Jungfrau, Täschhorn, Hohberghorn.

1870
(?) Mont Blanc (twice). Finsteraarhorn.

1871
10.7. Castor. (Frank Walker)
16.9. Several expeditions with Lord Queensberry, including Theodule pass to Breuil and back by Furggen pass with Old Peter.

1872
Two ascents of Mont Blanc and of the Weisshorn, as well as one ascent of the Jungfrau and of the Finsteraarhorn. But these must have been of considerably less importance to his career than his second ascent of the Matterhorn, which he traversed from Zermatt to Breuil.

2.53.1 His career as guide

The first ascent of the Matterhorn was a turning point in Young Peter's career and he was able to take full advantage of it. His name became widely known and he managed to avoid following his father's somewhat parochial outlook and record. Their positions soon became reversed and Young Peter was leading his father on climbs that he seems not even to have attempted previously, like the Dom and Mont Blanc. Instead of acquiring a reputation as a good if somewhat eccentric Monte Rosa guide, Young Peter followed the example of Peter Perren and Franz Biner and climbed in other parts of the Alps with clients. But there was one climb in which he like his father seems surprisingly to have had little or no interest – the ascent of the Matterhorn from Zermatt. His father's psychological reaction to the accident and to its aftermath seems not only to have prevented himself from ever daring to attempt the route again, but also to have cast a blight on it, sufficient not only to deter Young Peter but every single guide of Zermatt. As the *Journal de Genève* stated in its report of Birkbeck's attempt in July 1866, 'since last year's accident the Zermatt guides have a real fear of engaging in an enterprise of this nature'. This presented the guides of St.Niklaus with the opportunity of securing a virtual monopoly of the Zermatt side of the Matterhorn amongst local guides, which they proceeded to enjoy for more than five years. But even after Peter Perren and Young Peter finally made their ascents in 1871 and 1872 respectively, re-opening the mountain to the guides of Zermatt, the jealousy engendered by the success of the St.Niklaus guides was to cause much further bitterness in which Young Peter is known to have played some part.

There is no record of Young Peter being asked to attempt a second ascent of the Matterhorn in 1865, although his father was approached by Güssfeldt in September. He did his utmost to dissuade Güssfeldt who was in no mood to be dissuaded and Old Peter eventually agreed to make a secret trip to Breuil and attempt the ascent from there. It has been supposed that Young Peter went with them, but in fact it was his younger brother Joseph, the one who had accompanied Lord Francis Douglas to Breuil and back and had acted as porter on 13th July. This is clear from what Güssfeldt wrote, but any doubt about it can be excluded by the entry in Young Peter's Führerbuch for 25th September which includes so many expeditions that he could not possibly have been climbing the Italian ridge with the others on 18th September 1865.

In July 1866 Birkbeck, who had climbed the Weisshorn with Young Peter in 1863, almost certainly tried to engage Young Peter and his father for the Hörnli and ended up with seven guides from St.Niklaus instead. Thioly the Geneva dentist then arrived in Zermatt a few days later set on making the climb, but he could not find a single guide willing to accompany him. Young Peter was clearly one of those who refused as Thioly then decided to climb the Dom instead, and he did this with him and Moser. The following winter Young Peter and Moser visited Thioly in Geneva, assuring him they would not be afraid of tackling the Matterhorn with someone of his calibre and although they wanted 150frs each plus 75frs for each of two porters Thioly 'so wanted to make this climb that [he] accepted the onerous propositions'. But when July 1867 came it seems that the two guides were afraid of tackling the Matterhorn and took him up the Weisshorn instead, although Thioly had to take over the lead for a while and cut some steps himself in order to get them to persevere. Thioly had no better luck in 1868 with the Zermatt guides, who 'were still trembling at Elliott's temerity' after he had made the second Zermatt ascent only the day before. Elliott had had the same difficulty in trying to find a guide and had resolved to try it alone as 'not a Zermatt guide would go', when he found Knubel and Lochmatter of St.Niklaus at the hut they were building for Seiler and they agreed to accompany him.

It is likely that Jordan encountered the same reluctance on the part of the Taugwalders in August 1867 when he arrived in Zermatt determined to climb the Hörnli. This was followed in September by the extraordinary situation when after a second attempt on the Hörnli with St.Niklaus guides, Jordan crossed to Breuil; 'The Taugwalders, father and son, were there and wanted immediately to go for the ascent with me from Zermatt'. When one bears in mind that Güssfeldt had found the previous year in Zermatt that Old Peter would only try from Breuil, it looks rather as though, when it came to engaging either of them to attempt the Matterhorn, the Taugwalders had a problem for every solution.

In all probability there were other climbers as well, who did not publish anything about being unable to find a guide for the Matterhorn, who approached Young Peter as well as his father but without success, and it is not until 30th July 1969 that there is any record of Young Peter actually setting foot again on the mountain. Along with Joseph Maquignaz and Peter Perren, Young Peter attempted the Italian route with Heathcote and they got beyond the Col Felicité and close to the summit when thunder and lightning forced them to retreat, all four suffering injury from the lightning. As Maquignaz had already made two complete descents of the Hörnli ridge in addition to the three hour exploration he had made of its upper part with Jordan in 1867, it seems probable that the Heathcote party intended to traverse to Zermatt and, had bad weather not intervened, Young Peter's career as a Matterhorn guide would have started three years sooner than it did. Heathcote in fact made the ascent from Breuil and back again with the Maquignaz brothers a month later, but Young Peter was not with them.

He does not appear to have tried again in 1870 nor in 1871, although he had been with Frank Walker on Pollux some ten days before he and his daughter Lucy made the ascent from Zermatt on 22nd July 1871 with an exceptionally strong team of guides that included Peter Perren. This ascent seems finally to have convinced Young Peter that he could safely make it from Zermatt and on 24th July 1872 he was employed as leading guide by Pendlebury and Taylor traversing the Matterhorn from Zermatt to Breuil.

2.53.2 His character

Several critics, notably Arnold Lunn and Carl Egger, have sought to contradict some of Whymper's statements about Young Peter for no apparent reason other than that they themselves were allergic to Whymper and trying to disparage him. These worthless attempts to distort history are dealt with in detail elsewhere, but in order to set the record straight it is necessary to refer to some other incidents which show an insight into Young Peter's character. Whymper confined himself to facts and, unlike Lunn and Egger, did not express his opinion, although, having climbed the Matterhorn with Young Peter and having spoken with him, and having discussed the situation with and having received advice from the likes of Alexander Seiler, the Rev Joseph McCormick, the Rev James Robertson, the Rev G.F.Browne, Adams Reilly, Alfred Wills and the Cowells father and son, he was not merely in a better position than Lunn and Egger to judge Young Peter from his actions and his words; they were in no position at all to do so having probably never even met him and certainly never having heard him in 1865. Egger even went so far as to accuse Whymper of an incomprehensible chessmove to denigrate Young Peter, whereas it was Egger himself who chose to take a typographical error out of the 1872 German translation of *Scrambles*, alter it slightly but without reinstating the vital six words 'he has endeavoured to trade upon', that were the crux of Whymper's original sentence but had never been translated into German, and then blame Whymper for what was in fact Egger's own resulting nonsense.

There were three incidents, in about 1869, in 1876 and in 1886, which tend to support Whymper's conclusion with regard to Young Peter, 'Whatever may be his abilities as a guide, he is not one to whom I would ever trust my life, or afford any countenance'. The trouble began on the descent and can be summed up in the words Whymper used in a letter to W.Wigram on 9th August 1865:

> 'I can however express to you privately...my extreme dissatifaction with both the Taugwalders, but particularly with the younger man. They not only showed a most unmanly fear for their own lives, but directly we got to the easy part of the descent showed a heartlessness that was perfectly revolting.'

The first published record of anything untoward happening after the accident comes in McCormick's letter of 17th July to *The Times*, when after describing the accident he continued:

> 'Mr.Whymper's feelings at this time may be imagined. The two remaining guides were so completely unnerved by the calamity which had befallen their companions that he found it difficult to descend with them. He and they spent a miserable night on the mountain at a great height.'

Rather more is disclosed by the Rev W.P.Prior, the English chaplain at Vevey, who arrived with family and friends at the Monte Rosa hotel on 18th July and wrote to Mackenzie, the British Consul in Geneva,

> 'I am much disgusted with the conduct of the Taugwalders père & fils. An hour after the accident they bothered Whymper to know who was to pay them, and asked him to send an account to the Newspapers mentioning their names, in order that among travellers they might have next year a "succès de curiosité".'

A week later Whymper included in his letter to von Fellenberg,

> 'I need not trouble you with the details of our descent, it is enough to say that for more than two hours afterwards, I thought every moment would be my last; the two Taugwalders, utterly unnerved, cried like infants, and trembled in such a manner as to threaten us with the fate of the others.'

There is no reason whatever to doubt the truth of Whymper's account, but it is as well to bear in mind Old Peter's reaction three years before on the Dent Blanche after his foot slipped, when Kennedy wrote how he

> 'was surprised to see the weatherbeaten old fellow with a face as white as that of a frightened girl. He seized eagerly upon some spirits of wine we chanced to have, and then told me that when on the top of the rock his foot had slipped, and that for a moment he had thought himself done for. His nerve being utterly destroyed by the fright, I fixed the rope round my waist, and led the way upwards. But presently his courage failed again – he declared that he could not go on.'

Another material factor is that precisely a week before, Old Peter had actually fallen more than 20 feet off the Obergabelhorn when the cornice broke and he would clearly have 'thought himself done for'. It is also interesting to read the contemporary comment of Woolmore Wigram, who made the first ascent of the Dent Blanche with Kennedy a few days after the Taugwalder débacle and learnt exactly what had happened on that occasion, in his letter to Whymper of 10th August 1865,

> 'We know that Taugwalder's acquaintance with the pass from Zermatt to Gressonay was acquired by smuggling: and if he has done much business of that kind he has probably drank hard so that his nerve is now failing or failed. He broke down altogether at the first attempt on la D.B. He returned to Kennedy from an attempt to surmount the last difficulties...pale, trembling and refusing to do anything but return immediately.'

Whymper's letter to *The Times*, written on 7th August 1865, by which time he had received further independent advice including almost certainly that of G.F.Browne, expanded on what he had said to von Fellenberg:

> 'For more than an hour afterwards I thought every moment would be my last; for the Taugwalders utterly unnerved, were not only incapable of giving assistance, but were in such a state that a slip might have been expected at any moment. I do the younger man, moreover, no injustice when I say that immediately we got to the easy part of the descent he was able to laugh, smoke and eat as if nothing had happened. There is no occasion to say more of the descent.'

But the reaction of Alfred Wills and J.W.Cowell to the *Times* letter was that there was occasion to say more of the descent and they separately advised Whymper that he should immediately record in writing what he had withheld from *The Times*. Cowell wrote to him observing how he had passed over in his narrative

> 'some points in the demeanour of the Taugwalds which I venture to think it is due to yourself that you should consign to writing exactly in the manner in which you related them to my son and myself at this house on Wednesday the 2nd of August.
> You do not know what relations these men may endeavour to propagate; their answers to the questions which you proposed should be put to them have been withheld from you;

there will be a strong *local* feeling to support any pretensions of these men to your detriment, you know what sort of men they are, and that their first thoughts after the dreadful disaster – and when, alone and unprotected you appeared almost at their mercy – were to urge you to shape your account of it in such a manner as should turn to their pecuniary advantage.
You have yet to learn what they have said, and what impression it may make.
I submit to you that it would be prudent, not only as regards yourself, but also as regards the memory of those who are gone, to consign to writing exactly what you communicated to my son and myself on the 2nd of August, so that we might, if the necessity for your making it public should arise hereafter, be in a condition to certify that what you may say regarding these men is no afterthought.'

So Whymper created his memorandum of 17th August 1865, the last sentence of which reads, 'It is unnecessary to say that they were paid and paid the highest price ever for mountain ascents'. Wills wrote to Whymper on 20th August after seeing the memorandum,

'These Taugwalders are not fit to be trusted – and the world ought to know it; and I think myself, if you will pardon me for saying so, that you will make a great mistake if you hesitate to speak of them as they should be spoken of...Life is a very uncertain thing with the best of us and you may be glad (though it is not likely that what you say will ever be called in question) to have it in writing that so and so knows it is what you told him at the first.'

When the Cowells saw Whymper's memorandum they drew up their own memorandum or certificate dated 1st September, which includes the following:

'Edward Whymper informed us that upon the occurrence of the Catastrophe the Taugwalders displayed the most abject cowardice, entire want of resource – utter and helpless bewilderment – that after he had succeeded in rallying them and enabled them to reach a place of comparative safety, the young one broke out into frightful levity, displaying the most brutal insensibility – eating – drinking – smoking – laughing – vociferating – that then the two, after consulting together apart for some time, made to him the horrid proposal that he should enable them to make a more lucrative market of the Catastrophe by leaving them unpaid and publicly announcing that they would take no payment: so that he would save his money and they wd. profit by public esteem and sympathy – that their demeanour gradually became, and continued to be, suggestive of personal danger to himself – that at night they, as it were, hustled him to induce him to attempt the further descent *by Moonlight* – that thereafter they urged him to lie down in a manner so importunate and minatory as to induce him to place himself with his back to a rock, and with his axe in his hand to order them to keep at a greater distance from him – and that he passed the night standing in that manner and prepared to defend himself.
The inferences which arose in our minds from what E.Whymper described were that the Taugwalders saw that the additional loss of E.Whymper would afford them an opening to a future notoriety of a very lucrative nature, and that they were prepared to avail themselves of any opportunity that might offer during the descent of bringing about that loss – and Edward Whymper did not deny to us that similar inferences suggested themselves to him during the whole of that dreadful night.'

Six years later when *Scrambles* was published, Whymper revealed his conversation with Young Peter as recorded in his memorandum of 17th August:

> 'I was ready to leave, and waiting for the others. They had recovered their appetites and the use of their tongues. They spoke in patois, which I did not understand. At length the son said in French, "Monsieur." "Yes." "We are poor men; we have lost our Herr; we shall not get paid; we can ill afford this." "Stop!" I said, interrupting him, "That is nonsense. I shall pay you, of course, just as if your Herr was here." They talked together in their patois for a short time, and then the son spoke again. "We don't wish you to pay us. We wish you to write in the hotel-book at Zermatt, and to your journals, that we have not been paid." "What nonsense are you talking? I don't understand you. What do you mean?" He proceeded, "Why, next year there will be many tavellers at Zermatt, and we shall get more *voyageurs*." '

Whymper did not disclose the main paragraph of his memorandum, nor the Taugwalders' behaviour as recorded in the Cowell memorandum. But after referring in a footnote to Old Peter's problems following the accident, with his comrades and neighbours asserting or insinuating that he cut the rope, and after paying tribute to him, 'Not only was his act at the critical moment wonderful as a feat of strength, but it was admirable in its performance at the right time'; he then referred to Young Peter:

> 'In respect to young Peter, it is not possible to speak in the same manner. The odious idea that he propounded (which I believe emanated from *him*) he has endeavoured to trade upon, in spite of the fact that his father was paid (for both) in the presence of witnesses. Whatever may be his abilities as a guide, he is not one to whom I would ever trust my life, or afford any countenance.'

This reference to Young Peter endeavouring to trade upon the idea of not being paid has been ignored by the critics, no doubt because it undermines their groundless contention that Whymper misunderstood Young Peter's proposition that he should not pay them. It is likely to have been based on what Whymper learnt from Seiler when he was in Zermatt in September 1869. There is not the slightest reason to doubt that it was true, as contrary to what some critics have suggested there is no sign of Whymper ever exhibiting any malice towards the Taugwalders. There are in fact several signs of Whymper's generosity to the Taugwalders after the accident, notwithstanding their conduct, such as the 20frs tip and the inclusion of Young Peter in the Clubroom of Zermatt drawing, and there is nothing to suggest that he met either of them a year or two later and that this brought about any change in his matter of fact attitude towards them. The 1876 and 1886 incidents point to the same mean streak in Young Peter's character involving firstly Peter Knubel, when he was extremely ill at the Stockje hut, and secondly the death on the Matterhorn from exposure of F.C.Borckhardt.

The Knubel incident related by Frederick Gardiner in the *Alpine Journal* may have arisen indirectly out of the Zermatt guides' jealousy of the St.Niklaus guides supremacy on the Matterhorn over a period of years, but it is the inhumanity shown to a fellow being that is so appalling. Gardiner wrote how Knubel 'was evidently suffering horribly from cramp in the stomach...I was really very much alarmed and scarcely knew what to do'. He went on to describe how two other climbers at the hut,

> 'The Baron and his cousin were most kind, and did all they could to assist, and as they were returning to Zermatt and did not require all the provisions, and above all the wine, they had brought with them, they most generously offered it for my acceptance. I need scarcely say how gratefully I accepted their kind offer, for I scarcely knew how long we might be detained at the hut.'

Gardiner then goes on to explain how the Baron ordered the guides to unpack, after which

> 'three bottles of wine, half a bottle of brandy, and sundry eatables were made over to me by him. I then went out of the hut to say adieu to my kind friends, and saw them fairly off. Returning to the hut I immediately missed the wine and brandy which the Baron had left, and then found to my disgust that his guides had actually, after having been ordered to leave us the wine for the benefit of a sick fellow-guide, when our backs were turned repacked it in their knapsacks and made off with it! The Baron himself discovered it in Weisshorn Biener's knapsack, who professed the utmost amazement at finding it there.'

The Baron's two guides were Franz Biner and Young Peter and it seems most unlikely that the real culprit was Biner rather than Young Peter. Biner was a completely different sort of character, of whom Elliott had written in 1868: 'But most of all I like to mention his genuineness, his extreme simplicity, his diffidence, his perfect straightforwardness, his candour, his trustworthiness and his kindness of heart'.

The death of Borckhardt, in which Young Peter was not directly involved, has a complicated history and the incomplete story filled some 23 pages of volume 13 of the *Alpine Journal* in four separate articles. Like the 1865 accident Enquiry conducted by Clemenz, the 1886 official enquiry into the circumstances of this fatality seems to have obscured as much as it revealed and although an administrative investigation was subsequently ordered in response to newspaper accusations and a report was later published, the evidence actually given by the witnesses was once again withheld. The three main issues were the conduct of Borckhardt's own guides, the repositioning in the storm by Young Peter and Moser of a fixed rope resulting in a long search for it by the following party, and questions relating to the conduct of actual or potential rescuers. Suffice it to say here that the full truth seems never to have been revealed, but that the investigation report concluded that although Young Peter deserved praise for bringing his own party down safely, he deserved blame for having done nothing to help either Borckhardt's party or another party that also had to spend the night on the mountain. There have been other instances of unsatisfactory explanations for the conduct of guides involved in cases of storm and death on mountains, notably after the Lyskamm accident in 1869 and the death on the Mer de glâce in 1873. All they go to show is that the authorities were sometimes quite prepared to cover up fault and omission, and they certainly do not establish that the standards of integrity and dedication that one might expect from the guides of to-day were attained by more than a few really first class guides in the nineteenth century.

2.53.3 His accounts of the accident

Montagnier is the key figure in looking at what Young Peter recorded about the 1865 accident, as until 1917 there does not seem to be any sign of anything he may have said about it, apart from the account in the *Journal de Genève* of 18th July 1865 which is likely to have been based on an interview with him on Saturday 15th July. The reasons for this conclusion are set out in section 3.9 (Newspapers), and it is only necessary to mention here that a lot of the details were incorrect and in particular that the slip was wrongly attributed to Lord Francis Douglas. Young Peter was not called as a witness by Clemenz, but was allowed to leave Zermatt before the Enquiry began, although Clemenz subsequently took the precaution of justifying this by asking Old Peter (Q54) if his son had seen how the accident occurred. 'I do not think so', was the reply, 'for he asked me at once "are you still there father?".'

Montagnier spoke fluent French but no German. He was friendly with Whymper and corresponded with Farrar regarding matters of Alpine history that he managed to unearth. In April 1917, in a letter to Farrar, he made reference to Young Peter,

> 'My recollection of young Taugwalder is that he was exceedingly reticent in speaking of the accident. In 1900 when I tried the Zinal Rothorn with him I tried my best to make him talk but even with the aid of a few glasses of schnapps I found it almost impossible to pump him. It may be pure imagination on my part but that that time I really fancied that there were details of the accident which he was determined not to divulge.'

In May 1917 Montagnier was corresponding in English with Rudolf Taugwalder, the keeper of the Zermatt museum, in his quest for some of the old guides' Führerbücher. There does not apppear to be any surviving record of his seeking the Taugwalders' books, apart from Rudolf stating that Young Peter would sell him his new book for 125frs, if he wanted it. The Alpine Club does however have Young Peter's book covering the period from 1859 until 1883 which was presented to it by Richard Kay in about 1928. Montagnier sent Rudolf Taugwalder eight questions for Peter to answer, presumably because Rudolf had a fairly good command of English and it would be easier for Peter to relay his answers through him in German rather than have to try and correspond with Montagnier in French.

Young Peter's answers do not throw any fresh light on the accident or the events surrounding it, but two of them do reveal something of his own attitude 50 years later. Question 3 sought 'His recollections of Mr.Hadow', to which he replied, 'Mr.Hadow whose slip caused the accident was a very bad climber, those who followed him always were compelled to place his feet into the right foothold'. This will be referred to below in connection with his 'Narrative'. The other interesting answer is that to Question 5, 'Did Old Peter choose the rope used to attach himself, his son and Mr.Whymper to the rest of the party?' Rudolf gives Young Peter's reply as, 'Old Peter also said the rope would not be strong enough but, Michel Croz wanted to have it so – and attached Mr.Whymper between the two Taugwalders, father and son – for Michel Croz acted as commander of the caravan'. Too much should not be read into this reply, particularly as the question itself is somewhat confused and ought not to have included the words 'his son and Mr.Whymper', but it does suggest a bit of a guilty conscience in the way it seeks to implicate Croz.

The last two questions related to the dates Old Peter went to America (1874), returned (1878) and died (11.7.1888). The answers as well as the opening and closing paragraphs of the letter are all in English in reasonably clear and legible handwriting, but after Answer 8 Rudolf Taugwalder inexplicably writes eight lines in German in the old fashioned script which is practically indecipherable to those not familiar with it. There is no reason to suppose that Montagnier had ever posed the ninth question, but did it originate with Rudolf or with Young Peter and did the answer come from Young Peter? A possible explanation is that Question 7 led Young Peter to want to state the reason why his father went to America, but that this was too long and complicated for Rudolf to translate into English, so he left it to Montagnier to get it translated for himself should he so wish. The eight lines translate as follows,

> 'The ninth question would be: why did old Peter Taugwalder go to America? Answer: After this accident and this success on the Matterhorn, all the guides of Chamonix and St.Niklaus were so envious and cunning that they did everything they could to make the lives of the Taugwalders as unbearable as possible. All sorts of jealousy and slander were used to weaken their good reputation in every respect. Both the guides of St.Niklaus and those of Chamonix caused thousands of francs loss by their shameful slanders. Peter Taugwalder eventually wanted to escape from these envious people and these slanders and so he went to America!'

The interesting thing about this answer is the way it fixes the blame on the guides of Chamonix and St.Niklaus rather than those of Zermatt. Bearing in mind that Old Peter had apparently never climbed from Chamonix prior to 1866, it hardly seems consistent with this explanation that he should have climbed Mont Blanc twice in that year. Quite a few Chamonix guides climbed in the Zermatt area, as the composition of the three search parties shows, but this could hardly have undermined Old Peter's status as a guide on his own home ground if he had the support of his fellow Zermatt guides. As for blaming the St.Niklaus guides as well, this seems to be closely linked with the question of the post-accident history of the Matterhorn and its domination for more than five years by the guides of St.Niklaus, a subject considered in section 3.6.3. It is interesting that Young Peter does not seek to attribute his father's departure for America to any jealousy on the part of the Zermatt guides despite what Bernard Biner told Lunn, or indeed to any fault on the part of Whymper, notwithstanding what Rudolf Taugwalder's son Hannes was to allege about Whymper 75 years later.

Young Peter's principal legacy of the accident is his 'Narrative', which was published in the *Alpine Journal* in 1957, with notes and comment by Dangar & Blakeney. The original document in the Alpine Club Archives comprises eight handwritten sheets of the account in German on paper with tiny rectangles all over it and a ninth much smaller sheet, written sideways on a single lined page from a notebook. The handwriting is the same on each page, but is not that of Young Peter judging from the shaky hand that has signed the ninth page 'Peter Taugwalder'. It is not dated. Dangar & Blakeney referred to a note being sent to Taugwalder asking him to agree to any necessary deletions when it was published in the *Alpine Journal* and said they knew nothing of the result, but there is in fact with the 'Narrative' a short typewritten form, undated but signed 'Peter Taugwalder former mountain guide', agreeing to this. The signature is in the same hand as before, but not quite so shaky. A letter of 27.11.1917, thanking Montagnier for sending him 50frs, is written in the same hand as the 'Narrative' but is not actually signed by Taugwalder – perhaps because there was not much room at the bottom of the last page. The writer of the letter has simply written: 'Peter Taugwalder, alt Bärgführer' without trying to make it look like his signature.

It has been suggested that the 'Narrative' was obtained by Montagnier's 'man', who interviewed Taugwalder and wrote it out and in so doing introduced his own efforts at fine writing. It is beyond doubt that Rudolf Taugwalder was not involved in the making of the 'Narrative', and because it is in the same handwriting as the later November letter, Montagnier's 'man' can also be excluded. That letter also includes a hint of fine writing with reference to fate not having made life a bed of roses for him and the most likely correspondent would seem to have been one of Young Peter's daughters, either 37 year old Salomena or 23 year old Balbina, who probably gave him some help in composing the 'Narrative', although she herself would have known little of the facts surrounding the accident. It would have taken a very long time for someone to have written it out, following which a number of minor amendments were made, and it hardly seems likely that anyone other than a member of the family would have had the time, patience or sufficient interest to get so involved with it. This conclusion is supported by a letter Montagnier wrote to Farrar in December 1917 which includes: 'I enclose the document you wished him to sign. His narrative is obviously not in his writing but I feel pretty certain that the old man dictated it in good faith.'

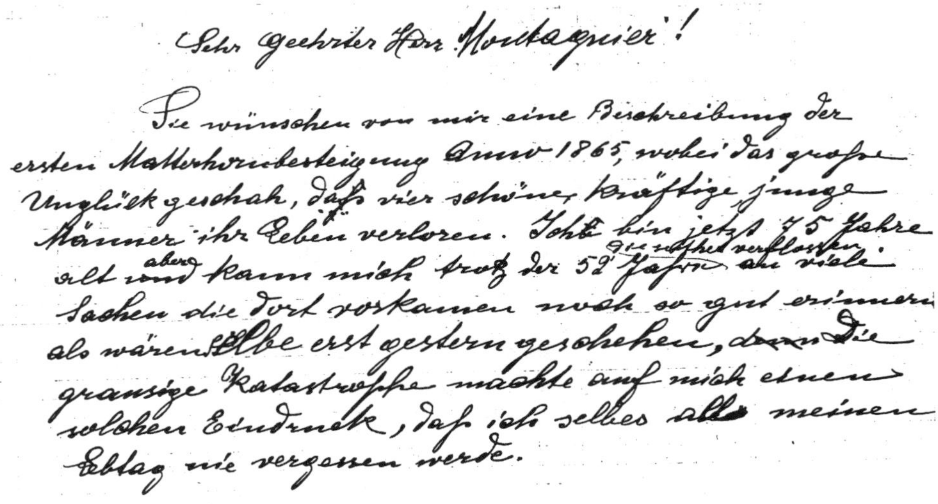

Sehr geehrter Herr Montagnier!

Sie wünschen von mir eine Beschreibung der ersten Matterhornbesteigung Anno 1865, wobei das große Unglück geschah, daß vier schöne, kräftige junge Männer ihr Leben verloren. Ich bin jetzt 75 Jahre alt ~~und~~ aber kann mich trotz der 52 Jahre die seither verflossen an viele Sachen die dort vorkamen noch so gut erinnern als wären selbe erst gestern geschehen, ~~denn~~ die grausige Katastrophe machte auf mich einen solchen Eindruck, daß ich selbes ~~alle~~ meinen Lebtag nie vergessen werde.

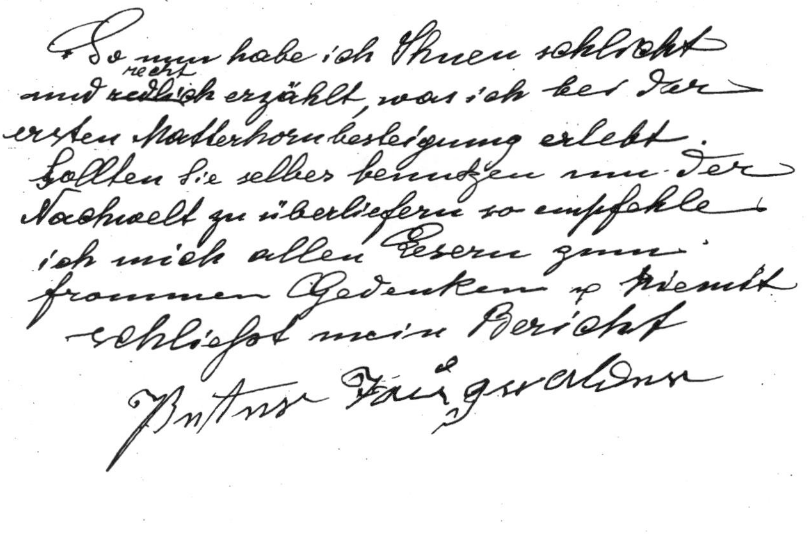

So nun habe ich Ihnen schlicht und recht ~~redlich~~ erzählt, was ich bei der ersten Matterhornbesteigung erlebt. Sollten Sie selbes benutzen um der Nachwelt zu überliefern so empfehle ich mich allen Lesern zum frommen Gedenken & hiemit schließt mein Bericht

Peter Taugwalder

Young Peter's 'Narrative' (beginning and end)

In 1918 Montagnier wrote again direct to Taugwalder, asking him this time if he knew anything about Birkbeck's Matterhorn attempt in July 1866 and if he himself made any attempts in 1866 or 1867. There seems to be only a typewritten copy of Taugwalder's reply, which is not very intelligible but does say he has no recollection of Birkbeck. Brief mention should be made of the Geneva writer Johannes Jegerlehner, who apparently interviewed Taugwalder within a year or so of his giving his 'Narrative' to Montagnier. He published in 1928 a Matterhorn novel of which the *Alpine Journal* wrote, 'Herr J.F.Jegerlehner has incorporated a degenerate idea into a remarkably foolish work: Michel Croz in the rôle of passionate lover and rival to the Younger Taugwalder. When will this kind of vulgarity and bad taste cease to be published?' Whereas the book might reflect an odd comment of Taugwalder, it seems to rely heavily on *Scrambles* for such accurate details as it does contain about the first ascent and the accident, and the rest is nothing more than fantasy.

Taugwalder's 'Narrative' seems to have been written in November 1917, judging from a note at the top of the first page probably written by Farrar. Although it gives a long, fairly detailed and lucid account, it is remarkable that it makes no mention of the quality, length, strength or condition of the ropes, apart from stating 'the rope broke as if it were a piece of string', and that it makes no mention of Hadow's slip, of his ability as a climber or of anyone having to give him the slightest assistance throughout the climb. It will be recalled that Young Peter's answer to Montagnier's Question 3, as recorded by Rudolf Taugwalder, referred to Hadow's slip causing the accident, to his being a very bad climber and to those following having to place his feet into the right foothold. In the 'Narrative' Young Peter seems to go out of his way to emphasise that Lord Douglas 'was not a good climber' saying that he had to plant his feet for him, when only the page before he had said that 'Douglas in front of me had great difficulty in putting his feet down in the steps and several times he slipped'. It seems therefore highly likely that he was confused by the presence of two Douglases in the party, and that without the guidance of Rudolf Taugwalder, who would have been familiar with what Whymper wrote, he got Hadow and Lord Francis mixed from time to time. He does say a little later that 'if only that good Mr.Douglas had not changed places, he and not Whymper would have been safe', and he cannot then have been referring to Hadow, but this inconsistency cannot justify a conclusion that his father was willing to take on the Matterhorn such a poor climber as he describes, after having spent spent almost a fortnight placing his feet in thousands of steps on the Untergabelhorn, Wellenkuppe and Obergabelhorn!

No new facts are disclosed in the 'Narrative' except those that are clearly incorrect. These range over a wide area and include such matters as the mountain being entirely snow-free, the party roping up at once when they set off from their bivouac, not staying long on the top, seeing from the shoulder that the victims were lying on the glacier and how 'the search party' did not set out on the Saturday but waited for dawn to break with neither Whymper nor the Taugwalders going on it. As Ronald Clark has said in relation to the equally erratic recollections of a bishop (G.F.Browne) as to what he was doing on about 14th July 1865, 'The trouble, of course, is not that old men forget but that they are apt to remember, with the best will in the world, slightly out of focus.'

2.54
THIOLY, FRANÇOIS (1831 – 1911)

Described by Louis Seylaz in *Die Alpen* in 1949 as a forgotten pioneer of Swiss mountaineering, Thioly was an original member of the SAC, the first president of his local Geneva section and the promoter of the Club's French language journal *Echo des Alpes*. His articles, including one in each of the first six volumes of the *SAC Jahrbuch*, and his brochures on climbs like Monte Rosa, the Weisshorn and the Matterhorn, whilst virtually unknown to English Alpine literature, still make entertaining reading as well as throwing light on such things as the impossibility of getting a Zermatt guide to climb the Matterhorn in the late 1860's and the eccentricities of Old Peter Taugwalder.

François Thioly, a Geneva dentist, appears to have been the first Swiss amateur to have made up his mind to climb the Matterhorn soon after hearing of the first ascent and accident in 1865. He was one of a group of five keen walkers with no experience of big mountains when in 1860 Lieutenant Alexander Seiler was a member of a battalion billetted in Geneva to keep an eye on the French after their seizure of Savoy. During his stay of several weeks Seiler got to know the Thioly group and encouraged them to visit Zermatt and climb Monte Rosa. Thioly's private narrative of the expedition *Voyage en Suisse et ascension du Mont Rose 1860* includes an amusing account of Old Peter Taugwalder nicking a bottle of rum and taking surreptitious swigs to keep himself warm in freezing conditions on the summit, whilst the remainder of the party had to content themselves with cold tea recommended to them at the Riffel by an Englishman, unaware until they came to pay their hotel bill that the bottle did not even belong to Taugwalder but had been provided for them by Seiler along with the other provisions for the climb.

In Spring 1866 Thioly wrote to Seiler about the Matterhorn, but the latter's reply of 15th July (the day after Birkbeck's attempt) reveals that there was still far too much snow on the mountain, and Seiler did his best to persuade Thioly to stay in Geneva if he was still intent on climbing it. But Thioly was already on his way, soon arriving in Zermatt via the Trift pass. He could not find a single guide willing to try the Matterhorn and on Seiler's advice he made do with the Dom, climbing it on 20th July with Young Peter Taugwalder and Josef Moser.

Next winter Taugwalder and Moser visited Thioly in Geneva, Taugwalder assuring him that he would not be afraid of tackling the Matterhorn with someone of his calibre. They wanted 150frs each plus 75frs for each of two porters. 'That was a lot of money, but I so wanted to make this climb that I accepted these onerous propositions.' The magnitude of these fees may be judged by comparison with Whymper's payment of 100frs to Old Peter Taugwalder for the first ascent, 'the highest price ever paid for mountain ascents', and with the official tariff published in 1869 in Ruden's book, of 100frs for a guide and 50frs for a porter. But when Thioly arrived in Zermatt at the end of July 1867,

Taugwalder and Moser refused to accompany him on the Matterhorn, declaring that the ascent was at present impracticable. They therefore climbed the Weisshorn instead, but noting that the guides' courage was failing after step cutting became necessary, Thioly had to take over the lead for a while and cut some steps himself in order to get them to persevere.

By 1868 he was absolutely determined to succeed at his third attempt and took with him to Zermatt an eccentric by the name of Hoiler with the idea that they would perhaps climb the mountain on their own if the guides really were scared by it. They therefore left Geneva 'with all the tackle (axes, ropes and crampons)' and on their arrival in Zermatt found that everyone was talking about the Matterhorn, as Elliott had made the second ascent from Zermatt only the day before. But the Zermatt guides 'were still trembling at Elliott's temerity' and Thioly realised that it was useless reiterating his previous proposal. He therefore engaged Elliott's St.Niklaus guides J-M Lochmatter and Peter Knubel, but only after a thousand difficulties had been resolved. And then, some hours later, under the pretext that Elliott had left without paying them, the guides disappeared in pursuit of him and Thioly did not see them again for five days. None of the guides passing through Zermatt inspired him, but then Ritz with whom he had previously climbed the Finsteraarhorn arrived and they agreed to set off the next day. But when Ritz also defaulted the same evening, it began to dawn on Thioly that neither Lochmatter, Knubel nor Ritz had refused to climb the peak with him, and that it was only when Hoiler came on the scene that objections started. One of them had actually said to him 'As for you Sir, we will go wherever you wish, but as for your friend – that needs some thought'.

Thioly then goes on to reveal that Hoiler was adorned with a frightful hat, half a metre wide, and that having vowed to the Vieux Grenadiers at home that he would climb the formidable giant in this ludicrous headdress, nothing in the world was going to make him change his mind. By now Thioly was resigned to implementing his original plan, and if all the guides allowed themselves to be dominated by fear, then they would climb the Matterhorn without any, and with all the more merit. The following day, the 29th, it was snowing on the mountains. 'What does on do in an Alpine village in bad weather? Smoke, drink, chat. But chat with whom? Nearly all the guests in both hotels are English and consequently not very communicative.'

So Thioly goes to the guides' room, where he learns from a Valtournanche porter that the Maquignaz brothers arrived in Zermatt from Breuil the previous day after traversing the Matterhorn with John Tyndall. With his hopes raised at the prospect of making the first north to south traverse of the mountain, he immediately seeks out J-Joseph and Pierre Maquignaz and finds them happy to agree to such an original way of getting back home. But this time Thioly had taken the precaution of not mentioning Hoiler to the guides, realising that all the trouble arose from the unfortunate hat, which was hardly capable of inspiring confidence in its wearer. He also engaged Elie Pession of Valtournanche, so that the guides would outnumber the tourists. It was necessary to wait a few days for the new snow to melt and on the afternoon of 1st August, when Thioly returned from a walk, Joseph Maquignaz was waiting to tell him they could set off the following day. Thioly was now poised to see one of his dreams realised at last, but he was taking no further chances; Hoiler was supposed to be accompanying him only as far as the new hut in order to make a sketch.

The expedition got underway after Zermatt had given it a good send-off and Thioly describes the remains they found of the bivouac used by Whymper's party prior to the first ascent. An hour or two after arriving at the new hut where they spend the night, they are surprised to hear voices outside and the door opens to reveal an Englishman, named Forster, and his two guides. Forster, (whom Thioly says was not G.E.Foster, who made the ascent on 4th August) whom Thioly had seen the evening before in Zermatt, produces a note from Seiler asking for him to be allowed to join in the ascent. But Joseph Maquignaz refuses to join up with the guides (who are not named) as he does not believe they are capable of making the climb. How to take Forster without his guides and without compromising Joseph's standing in the eyes of his colleagues is altogether too delicate a question and much to his regret Thioly has to refuse Forster, whom Seiler had recommended as a good climber. In the event Forster, who was spending his honeymoon in Zermatt, dined off such a profusion of food which made him so ill in the night that he would have been unable to accompany them. It was arranged that Hoiler could continue with them as long as he gave the guides a tip.

The following morning they were much inconvenienced by the cold and could only advance with difficulty. Thioly's hands were so cold he could scarcely hold his axe, whilst Hoiler in less warm clothing complained particularly of his feet and hands till he became incapable of taking another step upwards and leaned his head against a rock. However, the guides restored his circulation by rubbing his hands with snow and giving him a few mouthfuls of rum. Thioly takes a keen interest in the views, recording how a caravan of tourists on the Theodule who stop to acknowledge their shouts are so far away that they look like microscopic insects. He gives a detailed two page description of the view from the summit, comparing Monte Viso to the canine tooth of some antediluvian monster. After they have been on the summit for about an hour and Hoiler's fingers have thawed somewhat, he produces from his haversack a clarinet and, not without difficulty, plays the first few notes of the Swiss and Italian national anthems.

The descent of the Italian ridge is slow and Thioly is struck by the grandeur of the situation even more than on the summit. Although he describes the climb in some detail he makes no specific mention of whatever incident gave rise to the naming of 'Le Pas Thioly', which Guido Rey described as 'the last corner on the [Italian] ridge to the south-east before the summit is reached, at about 20 metres from the latter'. They do not reach the Cravate hut until 6 o'clock. After a rough night they resume the descent and at the foot of the great tower they come across the tent used by Whymper during his numerous attempts, now in tatters. They reach Breuil safe and sound and Thioly is back in Zermatt on 5th August. He pays great tribute to the skill of Joseph Maquignaz.

The Matterhorn was Thioly's last major climb and by the age of 40 his climbing career had finished. He seems to have fallen out with his colleagues on the editorial committee of the *Echo des Alpes* and although he transferred to the Monte Rosa section for three years he resigned from the SAC altogether in 1872. By the time he died in 1911 everyone seems to have forgotten the prominent part that he had played in the development of Swiss mountaineering.

2.55
TYNDALL, JOHN (1820 – 1893)

John Tyndall

One of the great pioneers in the Alps, John Tyndall's links with the Matterhorn began in 1860 when he and Hawkins made the first attempt by tourists to climb the peak from Breuil. This was followed by his further attempt in 1862, with Bennen and J-A Carrel, when he succeeded in reaching the Pic Tyndall, as it is now called. In the meantime, in 1861, he had merely inspected the Matterhorn but had made the first ascent of the Weisshorn. He was in Switzerland in July 1865, when the Matterhorn accident occurred, and he subsequently wrote:

> 'On quitting Gadmen next morning I was accosted by a guide, who asked me whether I knew Professor Tyndall. "He is killed, sir," said the man – "killed upon the Matterhorn." I then listened to a somewhat detailed account of my own destruction, and soon gathered that, though the details were erroneous, something serious if not shocking had occurred. At Imhof the rumour became more consistent, and immediately afterwards the Matterhorn catastrophe was in every mouth, and in all the newspapers. My friend and myself wandered on to Mürren, whence, after an ineffectual attempt to cross the Petersgrat, we went by Kandersteg and the Gemmi to Zermatt.'

Tyndall reached Visp on 30th July, according to Ronald Clark, going on to St.Niklaus where they spent the night. The previous day Lord Queensberry had left Zermatt on his way home and the probability is that he had stopped for the night at the Hotel Monte Rosa in St.Niklaus, where his brother had stayed a month before and also in previous years. There is no suggestion that Tyndall had met Queensberry in Visp earlier in the day, but it is probable that Tyndall learnt at the St.Niklaus hotel of his recent passage and heard something of Lady Queensberry's concern and even perhaps that she had sent a telegram to McCormick, which must have been based on the subject of her daughter

Florence Dixie's letter to the *Daily Graphic* in 1905. This would account for Tyndall writing in relation to only three of the bodies being recovered, 'I had heard, however, of other griefs and sufferings consequent on the accident, and this prompted a desire on my part to find the remaining one and bring him down'. Tyndall then goes on to describe his extraordinary scheme for searching for the body of Douglas.

> 'None of the Zermatt guides would second me, but I found one of the Lochmatters of St.Nicholas willing to do so. Him I sent to Geneva to buy 3000 feet of rope, which duly came on heavily laden mules to Zermatt. Hammers and steel punches were prepared; a tent was put in order, and the whole was carried up to the chapel by the Schwarz See...My notion was to climb to the point where the men slipped, and to fix there suitable irons in the rocks. By means of ropes attached to these I proposed to scour the mountain along the line of the glissade. There were peculiarities in the notion which need not now be dwelt upon, inasmuch as the weather rendered them all futile.'

Tyndall planned to climb the Matterhorn in 1867, by traversing it from Zermatt to Breuil. He had corresponded with Carrel for some time 'and from his letters an enthusiastic desire to be my guide might be inferred'. He then crossed from Zermatt to Breuil by the Theodule on 21st July, but when he saw Carrel, 'His demands were excessive, and he also objected to the excellent company of Christian Michel. In fact my good friend Carrel was no longer a reasonable man. I believe he afterwards felt ashamed of himself and sent his friends Bich and Meynet to speak to me while he kept aloof.'

Somewhat inconsistent with this and with the fact that Tyndall subsequently switched allegiance to the Maquignaz' brothers for his ascent of the Matterhorn, he goes on to relate how he and Michel together with Grove, 'who had engaged Carrel as his guide', then crossed to Zinal via the Trift pass, and the next day went on to Evolène. He writes that 'This excursion had been made with the view of allowing the Matterhorn a little time to arrange its temper; but the temper continued sulky, and at length wearied me out'. They returned to Zermatt by the Rhone valley, but the weather there was even worse, and he and Grove descended to Visp, intending to leave Switzerland altogether. But Grove changed his mind, returned to Zermatt and, in fine weather which lasted a fortnight, he subsequently made with Carrel from Breuil on the 14th August the third successful ascent of the mountain.

On 18th September 1867, only a matter of days after the Maquignaz brothers had made their ascent from Breuil, Canon G.Carrel wrote to Tyndall expressing his regret at the way he had been treated, despite his having helped to make the route as far as the Pic Tyndall and having contributed to the cost of constructing the hut. He described the new route made by the Maquignaz, saying that they were equally good and intrepid, not to say better, and that it would be a pleasure for them to accompany him, without asking him to make a great financial sacrifice. 'A "pourboire" would suffice.' Tyndall replied a month later, thanking him very much for having written to him and saying that he had vehemently refused the extravagant proposition that he take four guides and pay them each 150frs, a total of 600frs. He was most interested to hear of the new ascent and said that he would probably return to Switzerland next year with the aim of climbing the Matterhorn from Zermatt and descending to Breuil. Canon Carrel also referred to Tyndall's problems in his book *La vallée de Valtornenche en 1867*, saying that the demands of Carrel, Bic and Meynet were too high. He pointed out that Tyndall had pioneered the route, placed rope on it and been the first on the shoulder, subsequently called the Pic Tyndall, as well as contributing 50frs to the hut. 'The only way of avoiding similar inconvenience in the future was to find some other guides. There are now several.'

It seems likely that Tyndall corresponded further with the Canon the following year, as on 21st July 1868 he met him in Aosta and they travelled to Breuil together. Tyndall mentions having seen Felicité, the Canon's niece who had accompanied the Maquignaz the previous year as far as the Col which now bears her name. 'Her wrist was like a weaver's beam, and her frame seemed a mass of potential energy.' Before reaching Breuil he saw Joseph Maquignaz, 'who seemed to divine by instinct my name and my aim...My desire was to finish for ever my contest with the Matterhorn by making a pass over its summit from Breuil to Zermatt. In this attempt my guide expressed his willingness to join me, his interest in the project being apparently equal to my own.'

It seems as though Tyndall was unaware of Jordan's ascent, or at least the extent of his explorations with the Maquignaz the previous October, when they descended from the summit as far as the scene of the accident, found a better route that avoided it and then returned to the hut on the Cravate; for Tyndall wrote of Joseph 'he only knew the Zermatt side of the mountain through inspection from below; and he acknowledged that a dread of it had filled him the previous year. He now reasoned, however, that as Mr.Whymper and the Taugwalds had managed to descend, we ought to be able to do the same.' The problem of starting on a Sunday was resolved by Maquignaz arranging to have a Mass at 2 a.m., and Tyndall readily accepted the tariff published by the Canon.

There seems to have been some contact between Zermatt and Breuil a day or two before they set off, as Elliott who made the second ascent from Zermatt on the Saturday wrote in a letter to his friend Wood: 'Almost our first act on reaching the arête was to look down on the Italian side to see if we could see any traces of a party with which Tyndall was said to be attacking the mountain that day from the S. side. Nothing in the shape of a human being appeared.' Although Tyndall's party accomplished the traverse slowly and steadily without any major problems, he did not seek to make light of the difficulties, his account of the route in the vicinity of the scene of the accident contrasting with that of Jordan. 'I wish to stamp this slope of the Matterhorn with the character that really belonged to it when I descended it, and I do not hesitate to say that the giving way of any one of our party would have carried the whole of us to ruin.'

Tyndall was easily offended and, following publication of *Scrambles* in 1871, he added two pages to the second edition of *Hours of exercise in the Alps*, in which he referred to his attempt in 1862 and took issue with Whymper over some matters of detail. They are of little consequence to-day, but are useful in showing the lengths to which Whymper went to ensure accuracy in what he wrote. Whymper wrote to the Editor of the *Alpine Journal* rebutting what Tyndall had said and the Editor published his letter of almost six pages, and commented on the issues. The letter not only shows that Whymper had much more information available to support what he had written, but includes: 'In 1869 I read over to [Carrel] that portion of my relation of Dr. Tyndall's expedition precisely as it appears in *Scrambles amongst the Alps*, and he expressed himself perfectly satisfied with its accuracy...I hope these explanations will assure Dr. Tyndall that I took pains to give an accurate account of his expedition...'

2.56
VECQUERAY, JOHN WILLIAM JOSEPH (c.1830 – 1901)

'Old Vec', as he was affectionately known at Rugby School where he taught German and French from 1859 until his death in 1901, was of Belgian origin, educated at Namur and Master of a preparatory school in Bruges prior to moving to Rugby. His Christian names, which hardly seem consistent with Belgian birth, may well have been anglicised at Rugby, as one of his sons was named Edward Guillaume and another Arthur Hermann and he appears to have written his name elsewhere as though it was F.W.J. Vecqueray.

He was one of at least four Rugby School masters staying in Zermatt during the week following the Matterhorn accident. There are many references in publications to Robertson and Phillpotts and also to Wilson, who reached Zermatt from Chamonix on 15th July 1865, but there is no record of Vecqueray arriving or even staying in Zermatt at the same time. There is however little doubt that he was there and that he had previously stayed at the Riffelhaus on his way from Vevey to the Grimsel in July 1863.

In September 1866 Whymper was planning a memorial stone to put on Croz' tomb and he wrote a letter to the Rev James Robertson, which seems to imply that Vecqueray played an important role in the post-accident events at Zermatt even though this is not mentioned in *Scrambles*. Whymper sought advice on his proposed inscription and also assistance in turning it into French.

> 'I want it as well, and as elegantly (to use a word I detest) rendered as I can get it, and it has occurred to me that it might be accomplished by your intervention. I have a lively recollection of the kindness of M. Vecqueray, and I do not call to mind anyone who would be likely to do it so well as he, or who would take the pains that I think he would be likely to exercise.
>
> What I wish then, and I ask it with hesitation, is, that you will endeavour to obtain the

> translation of this epitaph by M.Vecqueray. It should be scarcely becoming for myself, almost a stranger, to prefer the request, or I should not trouble you in the matter, and it will be doing me a genuine favour if you will make it.'

Robertson's reply of 14th October suggested one or two slight modifications including a new last line, and enclosed a French translation of both the original and modified versions in what must be Vecqueray's handwriting.

The kindness of M.Vecqueray, of which Whymper wrote, might have related to his giving Whymper some help in Zermatt in connection with the evidence he gave in French at the Enquiry, acting as interpreter perhaps or translating his description of the actual happening of the accident (see Answer 11), but in fact it went very much further. There is amongst Whymper's papers a four page document, which sets out in French the sixteen questions and answers which, with only a few minor alterations, became Questions & Answers 2-17 inclusive in the Official Enquiry Report. The exact nature of the document and some of the more significant details, including alterations, are referred to more fully in section 5.4.1 (Enquiry) and it is sufficient here to stress that Whymper must have been given a list of questions in advance of the hearing. If they were not already in French, Vecqueray must have translated them from German into English. Whymper then wrote out his answers in English and Vecqueray translated everything into French. When the Enquiry started Whymper must have handed in his own fair copy of the Questions and Answers as translated by Vecqueray to enable Clemenz then to recite the Questions one by one whilst he interposed his Answers. Vecqueray definitely did not act as interpreter.

Express confirmation of Vecqueray's presence in Zermatt can be found indirectly in the diary of Adams Reilly. Having heard on 17th July 1865 of the accident, Adams Reilly reached Zermatt the following day. The daily entries in his diary over the next fortnight record various events and comings and goings, including for Saturday 22nd July: 'Mr.Vicary [sic] went. Charlet arrived. Phillpotts and Robertson went. Whymper went...Jean Baptiste Croz came in the evening'.

Thus we can be sure of the presence of Vecqueray in Zermatt during the week that ended with the Enquiry. We do not know the date of his arrival, but there is an alteration in his translation of Answer 13, which is too complicated to detail here, which suggests that prior to the Enquiry he knew the identity of Franz Andenmatten better than Whymper did. As Andenmatten accompanied the other three Rugby masters on the Haute Route from Chamonix to Zermatt, Vecqueray may also have been with them then and may have reached Zermatt on Saturday 15th July. Alternatively, he may merely have climbed with them at Zermatt, travelling there independently as he had done in 1863.

It only remains to be said that although the handwriting of the Croz inscription and of the Questions and Answers do not at first sight look identical, the former slopes to the right and the latter is more nearly vertical, they are not dissimilar and certain letters of the alphabet are identical in both documents (M, C, d and z).

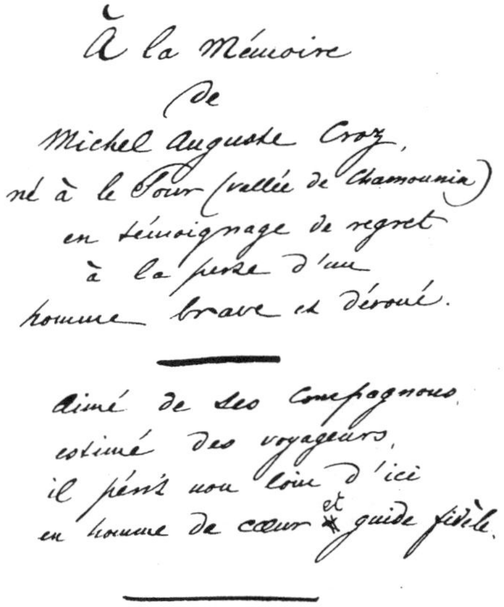
À la Mémoire
de
Michel Auguste Croz,
né à le Tour (vallée de Chamounix)
en témoignage de regret
à la perte d'un
homme brave et dévoué.

Aimé de ses compagnons,
estimé des voyageurs,
il périt non loin d'ici
en homme de cœur et guide fidèle.

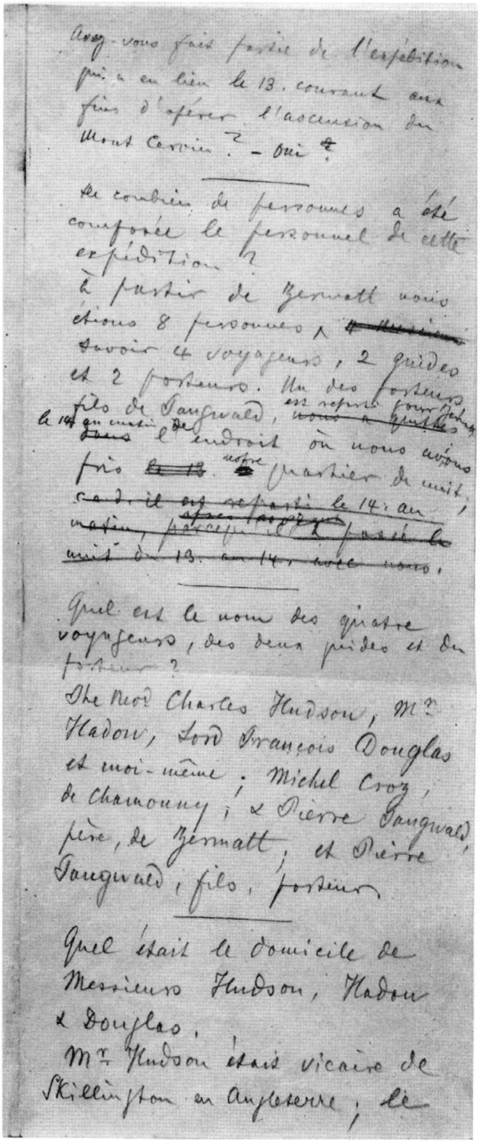
Avez-vous fait partie de l'expédition qui a eu lieu le 13. courant aux fins d'opérer l'ascension du Mont Cervin? – Oui.

De combien de personnes a été composé le personnel de cette expédition?
À partir de Zermatt nous étions 8 personnes, [illegible] savoir 4 voyageurs, 2 guides et 2 porteurs. Un des porteurs fils de Taugwald, est reparti pour Zermatt le 14 au matin de l'endroit où nous avions pris notre quartier de nuit, [illegible]

Quel est le nom des quatre voyageurs, des deux guides et du porteur?
The Revd Charles Hudson, Mr Hadow, Lord François Douglas et moi-même; Michel Croz, de Chamouny; & Pierre Taugwald père, de Zermatt, et Pierre Taugwald, fils, porteur.

Quel était le domicile de Messieurs Hudson, Hadow & Douglas.
Mr Hudson était vicaire de Skillington en Angleterre; le

Vecqueray's translations of the Croz inscription and of Whymper's evidence

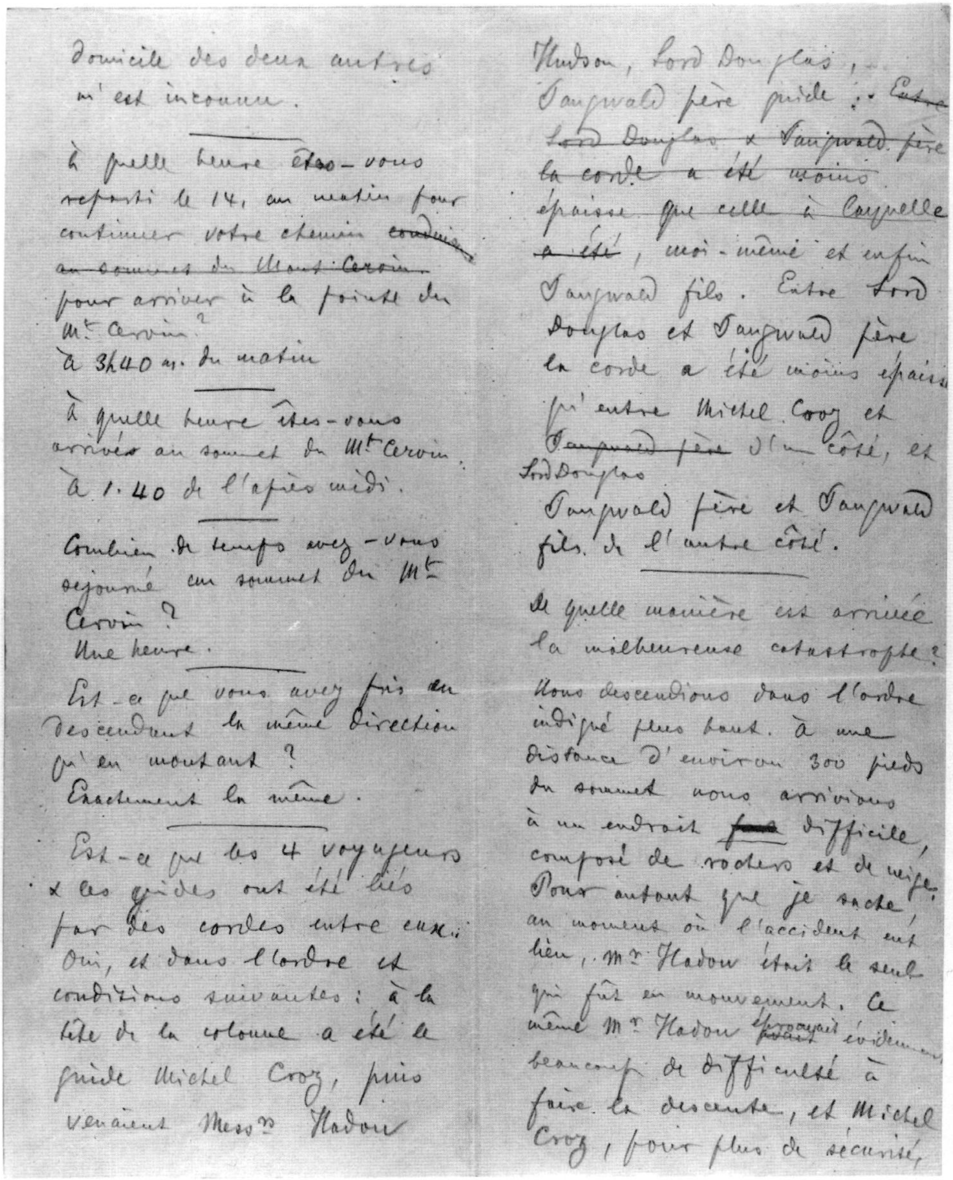

domicile des deux autres
m'est inconnu.

À quelle heure êtes-vous
repartis le 14, au matin pour
continuer votre chemin ~~conduisant~~
~~au sommet du Mont Cervin~~
pour arriver à la pointe du
Mt Cervin?
À 3h40 m. du matin

À quelle heure êtes-vous
arrivés au sommet du Mt Cervin.
À 1.40 de l'après midi.

Combien de temps avez-vous
séjourné au sommet du Mt
Cervin?
Une heure.

Est-ce que vous avez pris en
descendant la même direction
qu'en montant?
Exactement la même.

Est-ce que les 4 voyageurs
& les guides ont été liés
par des cordes entre eux?
Oui, et dans l'ordre et
conditions suivantes: à la
tête de la colonne a été le
guide Michel Croz, puis
venaient Messrs Hadow

Hudson, Lord Douglas,
Taugwald père guide; ~~Entre
Lord Douglas & Taugwald père
la corde a été moins
épaisse que celle à laquelle
a été~~, moi-même et enfin
Taugwald fils. Entre Lord
Douglas et Taugwald père
la corde a été moins épaisse
qu'entre Michel Croz et
~~Taugwald père~~ Lord Douglas d'un côté, et
Taugwald père et Taugwald
fils de l'autre côté.

De quelle manière est arrivée
la malheureuse catastrophe?
Nous descendions dans l'ordre
indiqué plus haut. À une
distance d'environ 300 pieds
du sommet nous arrivions
à un endroit ~~[illegible]~~ difficile,
composé de rochers et de neige.
Pour autant que je sache,
au moment où l'accident eut
lieu, Mr Hadow était le seul
qui fût en mouvement. Ce
même Mr Hadow ~~paraît~~ éprouvait évidemment
beaucoup de difficulté à
faire la descente, et Michel
Croz, pour plus de sécurité,

Q6 – A10 A10 – A11

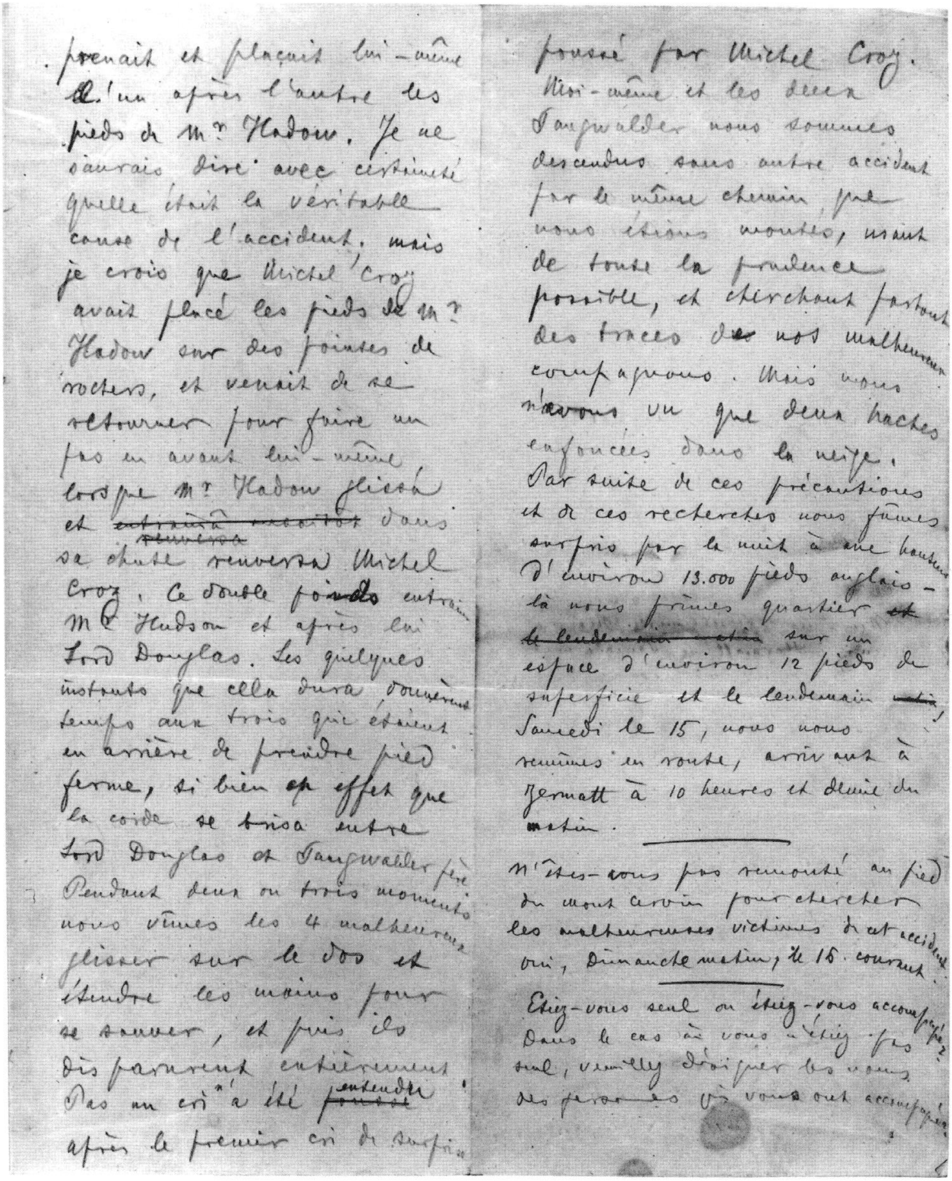

prenait et plaçait lui-même
l'un après l'autre les
pieds de Mr Hadow. Je ne
saurais dire avec certitude
quelle était la véritable
cause de l'accident, mais
je crois que Michel Croz
avait placé les pieds de Mr
Hadow sur des pointes de
rochers, et venait de se
retourner pour faire un
pas en avant lui-même
lorsque Mr Hadow glissa
et ~~entraina Michel~~ ~~renversa~~ dans
sa chute renversa Michel
Croz. Ce double poids entraina
Mr Hudson et après lui
Lord Douglas. Les quelques
instants que cela dura donnèrent
temps aux trois qui étaient
en arrière de prendre pied
ferme, si bien en effet que
la corde se brisa entre
Lord Douglas et Taugwalder père.
Pendant deux ou trois moments
nous vîmes les 4 malheureux
glisser sur le dos et
étendre les mains pour
se sauver, et puis ils
disparurent entièrement.
Pas un cri n'a été ~~poussé~~ entendu
après le premier cri de surprise

poussé par Michel Croz.
Moi-même et les deux
Taugwalder nous sommes
descendus sans autre accident
par le même chemin que
nous étions montés, usant
de toute la prudence
possible, et cherchant partout
des traces de nos malheureux
compagnons. Mais nous
n'avons vu que deux haches
enfoncées dans la neige.
Par suite de ces précautions
et de ces recherches nous fûmes
surpris par la nuit à une hauteur
d'environ 13.000 pieds anglais.
là nous prîmes quartier ~~et le lendemain matin~~ sur un
espace d'environ 12 pieds de
superficie et le lendemain ~~matin~~,
Samedi le 15, nous nous
remîmes en route, arrivant à
Zermatt à 10 heures et demie du
matin.

N'êtes-vous pas remonté au pied
du mont Cervin pour chercher
les malheureuses victimes de cet accident?
oui, Dimanche matin, le 16 courant.

Étiez-vous seul ou étiez-vous accompagné?
Dans le cas où vous n'étiez pas
seul, veuillez désigner les noms
des personnes qui vous ont accompagné.

A11 A11 – Q13

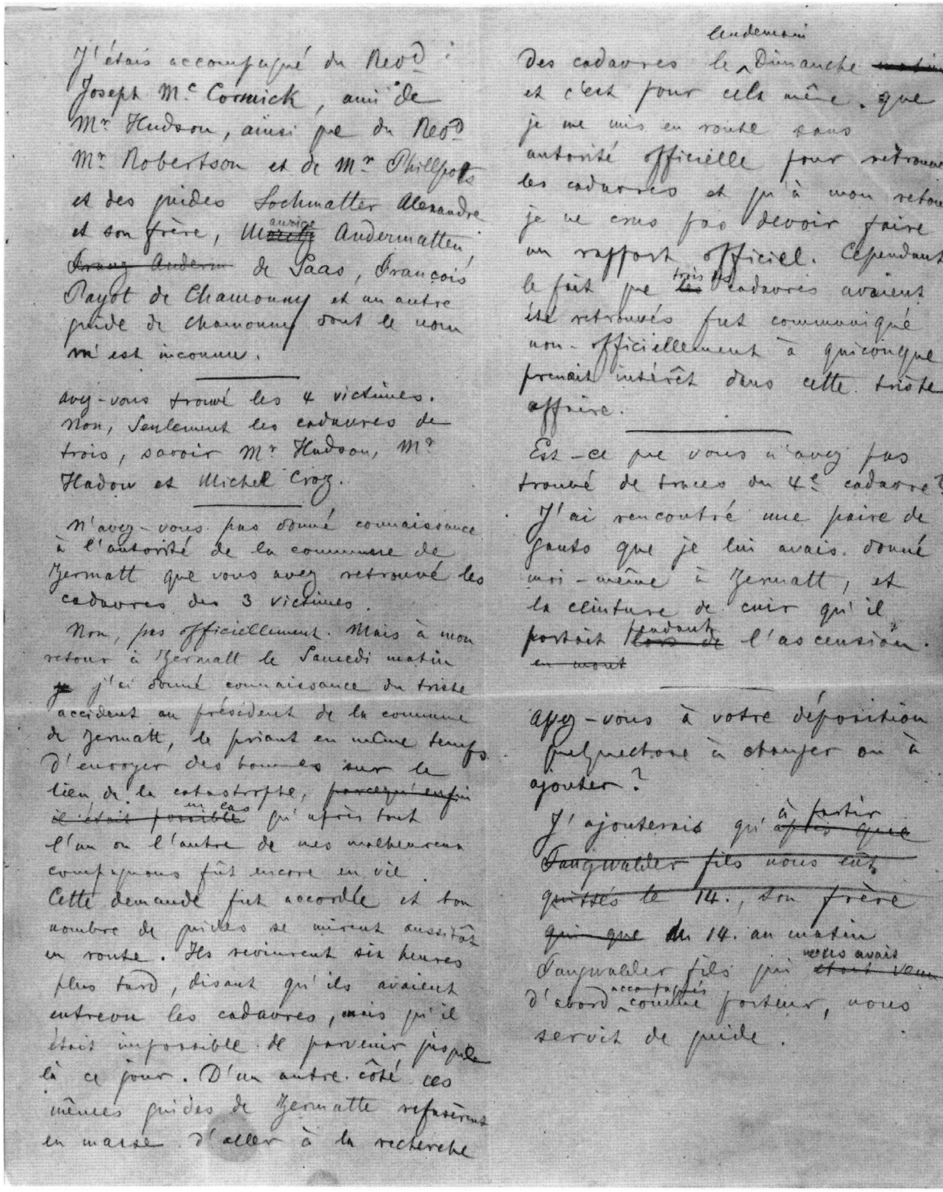

J'étais accompagné du Revd. Joseph McCormick, ami de Mr Hudson, ainsi que du Revd. Mr Robertson et de Mr Phillpotts et des guides Lochmatter Alexandre et son frère, ~~Moritz~~ auxiliaire Andermatten ~~Franz Anderm~~ de Saas, François Payot de Chamouny et un autre guide de Chamouny dont le nom m'est inconnu.

Avez-vous trouvé les 4 victimes.
Non, seulement les cadavres de trois, savoir Mr Hudson, Mr Hadow et Michel Croz.

N'avez-vous pas donné connaissance à l'autorité de la commune de Zermatt que vous avez retrouvé les cadavres des 3 victimes.

Non, pas officiellement. Mais à mon retour à Zermatt le Samedi matin j'ai donné connaissance du triste accident au président de la commune de Zermatt, le priant en même temps d'envoyer des hommes sur le lieu de la catastrophe, ~~parce qu'enfin il était possible~~ en cas qu'après tout l'un ou l'autre de nos malheureux compagnons fût encore en vie. Cette demande fut accordée et bon nombre de guides se mirent aussitôt en route. Ils revinrent six heures plus tard, disant qu'ils avaient entrevu les cadavres, mais qu'il était impossible de parvenir jusque là ce jour. D'un autre côté ces mêmes guides de Zermatt refusèrent en masse d'aller à la recherche

des cadavres le lendemain Dimanche ~~matin~~ et c'est pour cela même que je me mis en route sans autorité officielle pour retrouver les cadavres et qu'à mon retour je ne crus pas devoir faire un rapport officiel. Cependant le fait que trois ~~3~~ cadavres avaient été retrouvés fut communiqué non-officiellement à quiconque prenait intérêt dans cette triste affaire.

Est-ce que vous n'avez pas trouvé de traces du 4e cadavre?
J'ai rencontré une paire de gants que je lui avais donné moi-même à Zermatt, et la ceinture de cuir qu'il portait ~~Hadow~~ durant ~~de~~ l'ascension. ~~en mont~~

Avez-vous à votre déposition quelque chose à changer ou à ajouter?

J'ajouterais qu'à partir ~~après que~~ ~~Taugwalder fils nous eut quittés le 14.~~, son frère ~~qui que~~ du 14. au matin Taugwalder fils qui nous avait ~~était venu~~ d'abord accompagnés ~~comme~~ porteur, nous servit de guide.

A13 – A15 A15 – A17

There can be no doubt that Vecqueray performed a very valuable service not only to Whymper, but also to Clemenz and the other members of the Enquiry as well, in that he enabled Whymper to recite his evidence in fluent French without wasting any time, whilst the German speaking Clerk was spared the ordeal of having to note it all down as French dictation and was able to copy it out at his leisure.

Nothing seems to have been published about Vecqueray's mountaineering activities, but the name F.W.J. Vecqueray appears with that of Mrs. Vecqueray in a list of contributors to an appeal fund following the destruction by fire of Jakob Anderegg's house in August 1873.

2.57
WHYMPER, EDWARD (1840 – 1911)

Whymper is undoubtedly the key figure in the exploration of the Matterhorn and in its first ascent, as, apart from his own contribution towards climbing it, it was his determination and in particular his five unsuccessful attempts from Breuil in 1862 that inspired the founders of the Italian Alpine Club including Giordano to decide that they should make the first ascent from Italy. It was Giordano who was directing J-A Carrel's attempt in July 1865 when Whymper suddenly discovered what was going on and how he had been 'bamboozled and humbugged' and as a result decided to cross to Zermatt and try and make the ascent from there ahead of the Italians. It was Giordano who on 11th July in a letter to his co-founder Quintino Sella, describing the situation in Breuil and alerting him to come at once on receipt of a telegram he would send when they could then make the ascent together, wrote

> '...please send me a few lines in reply, with some advice, because I am head over ears in difficulty here, what with the weather, the expense, and Whymper.
> I have tried to keep everything secret, but that fellow, whose life seems to depend on the Matterhorn, is here, suspiciously prying into everything. I have taken all the competent men away from him, and yet he is so enamoured of this mountain that he may go up with others and make a scene. He is here, in this hotel, and I try to avoid him.'

The following list shows the main events in Whymper's life in relation to the Matterhorn.

1840 Born 27th April.
1860 First visit to the Alps.
1861 First attempt at the Matterhorn from Breuil.
1862 Second, third, fourth, fifth and sixth attempts from Breuil.
1863 Seventh attempt from Breuil.
1864 Intended to try the Hörnli from Zermatt, but had to return home.

1865 Attempted south-east face. Wanted to attempt Hörnli with Croz and Biner and later with Carrel.
First ascent of the Matterhorn from Zermatt via Hörnli ridge.
1871 *Scrambles amongst the Alps* published. 1st and 2nd editions.
1874 His second ascent of the Matterhorn from Zermatt.
1880 3rd edition of *Scrambles* published as *The Ascent of the Matterhorn*.
1893 4th edition of *Scrambles* (Zaehnsdorf).
1894 Article in the *Graphic*, 'The Alps revisited'.
1895 *Journal de Zermatt* article by Monod, based on interview with him.
Revisited Matterhorn from Breuil till weather forced a retreat.
1897 Publication of guidebook *The valley of Zermatt and the Matterhorn*, a new edition appearing each year up to 1911.
1900 5th edition of *Scrambles*.
1906 Married Edith Mary Lewin.
1908 Daughter Ethel born.
1911 Died 16th September at Chamonix.

2.57.1 His family

Edward was the second of eleven children of Josiah Wood Whymper, who as a wood-engraver built up a good business for the production of book illustrations. He attained the age of ninety, not dying until 1903, his first wife having died in 1859 and his second in 1886. Edward's elder brother Frederick travelled in Alaska and in 1868 John Murray published his book about his adventures there.

Edward's marriage was short-lived, but his daughter Ethel was brought up by an aunt and she was the guest of honour at Zermatt in 1965 during the celebrations to mark the centenary of the first ascent of the Matterhorn. She is recorded as having first visited Zermatt in 1929 and having made a number of climbs in the next few years including the Dom, the Zinal Rothorn by the Rothorngrat, the Breithorn by the Younggrat, Mont Blanc by the Brenva ridge and a traverse of the Matterhorn from Zermatt to Breuil. She married in 1937 Edward Blandy, a member of the Alpine Club, and died in 1969.

2.57.2 His Alpine climbing career

Whymper's first season in the Alps in 1860 was for the most part confined to a wide range of walking, but the following year he climbed Mont Pelvoux and made his first attempt on the Matterhorn. In 1862 he concentrated on the Matterhorn making a further five attempts, apart from climbing Monte Rosa. In 1863 he made another attempt and also attempted the Dent d'Herens, the ascent of the Grand Tournalin being his only success. It was in 1864 that his career really took off and he wrote subsequently in chapter 13 of *Scrambles* how it

Edward Whymper in about June 1865

'had been one of unbroken success, but the great ascent upon which I had set my heart was not attempted, and until it was accomplished, I was unsatisfied. Other things, too, influenced me to visit the Alps once more. I wished to travel elsewhere, in places where the responsibility of direction would rest with myself alone. It was well to know how far my judgment in the choice of routes could be relied upon.'

He went on to refer to the journey of 1865 being chiefly undertaken to find out to what extent he was capable to select a way over mountainous country.

'The programme, which was drawn up for this journey was rather ambitious, since it included almost all of the great peaks which had not then been ascended; but it was neither lightly undertaken nor hastily executed. All pains were taken to secure success. Information was sought from those that could give it, and the defeats of others were studied, that their errors might be avoided. The results which followed came not so much, perhaps, from luck, as from forethought and careful calculation...Up to a certain point the programme was completely and happily carried out. Nothing but success attended our efforts so long as the excursions were executed as they had been planned. Most of them were made upon the very days which had been fixed for them months beforehand.'

His climbs during these two seasons were almost all made with Michel Croz, amongst others, and included the following; apart from the Dent Blanche they were all first ascents or first crossings of a pass.

1864
Brèche de la Meije, Mont Dolent, Barre des Ecrins, Aiguilles d'Argentière and de Trelâtre, Moming pass, Col de Triolet.

1865
Grand Cornier, Dent Blanche, Grandes Jorasses (west peak), Col Dolent, Aiguille verte, Col de Talèfre, Ruinette, Matterhorn.

Although Whymper went to Zermatt in 1866 and made the first ascent of the Tête de Valpelline, this was in the course of some research into the veined structure of glaciers, inspired by Principal J.D.Forbes, whom he had met the previous September and again in the spring. The following year he went to Greenland and in 1868 he visited Grindelwald. In 1869, the last of the years covered by the full title of *Scrambles amongst the Alps*, he spent eight days with Carrel in the Dauphiné at the end of July and beginning of August. He then returned to London for a few days, when he sent the first instalment of *Scrambles* to John Murray, and on 10th August he set off for Turin. Although his further movements are not recorded he was in Zermatt on 1st September. In 1874 he made his second ascent of the Matterhorn from Zermatt, and in 1893 he made a camping tour starting from Randa and finishing with Mont Blanc. The following year he spent two nights on the summit of Mont Blanc and in 1895 he returned to Breuil and revisited the Italian ridge of the Matterhorn for the first time in 30 years, but had to retreat from the hut after bad weather. He made some other visits to the Alps as well but without any notable ascents, and in connection with his Chamonix and Zermatt guidebooks he visited the Alps virtually every year from 1896 until his death.

2.57.3 His Matterhorn ambition

There is no doubt that Whymper wanted to be the first to climb the Matterhorn, but he was not so obsessed with the idea that he could not contemplate anyone else getting there first. In 1864 he had been intending to try the Hörnli with Adams Reilly and, when he received a letter which forced him to abandon the idea and return home immediately to attend to his business, he suggested that Reilly and Croz should make the attempt without him but Reilly declined. It should also be borne in mind that his eight unsuccessful attempts do not compare unfavourably with Clinton Dent's nineteen attempts on the Dru!

His first seven attempts from Breuil are fully detailed in *Scrambles*, but there is a letter that he wrote to his father, describing the accident on his fourth attempt (or, more accurately, on his lone excursion – judging from his 1865 article on 'Camping out'), which has survived and which provides an interesting comparison with what he later wrote of the incident in *Scrambles*. On 8th August 1862 his father wrote to John Murray, with whom he obviously had a very close business connection, sending him the original pencil written letter he had received from his son dated 1st August.

> 'The inclosed, just received, relieves me. He had not previously given me the faintest idea that his accident was of so serious a nature and I can but feel deeply grateful for God's merciful providence in saving him. You need not trouble yourself to return the letter as I have a copy.'

> La Tour
> Valley of the Vaudois
> Piedmont.
> 1|8|62.
>
> My dear Father,
>
> Failure. I have been obliged to leave the Matterhorn and am now coming home as fast as possible.
>
> I had one more try with 3 men on the 23 and 24th and had bad snow storms on the second day. I renewed my attempts on the 25th and on the 26th got to my highest point where I found perpendicular cliffs which needed a ladder. We were obliged to return as we could not possibly get beyond them without. When I got to Breuil I found Professor Tyndall about to start and put my tent provisions and bags etc at his service (they were then about 12000 feet). This was of course an immense advantage to him, and he tried it on Sunday & Monday got higher than I did (as he took a ladder) and failed. I was just leaving Breuil as he came in disheartened and somewhat broken hearted. He abandoned it forthwith and has gone elsewhere.

"IN ATTEMPTING TO PASS THE CORNER I SLIPPED AND FELL"

Whymper's 1862 fall, as he portrayed it in *Scrambles*

My cuts are going on well. I purposely wrote to you a mild account of the fall which was one of the most wonderful escapes from a smash that has ever happened. I fell – as I have since measured the place more than 200 feet down which I went literally flying head over heels, struck my head four times against the rocks and finally by the goodness of God pitched into some jagged rocks on one side of the gully down which I was going in which I stuck. Had I gone 10 feet further I should have shot over a precipice of 800 feet and must have been smashed to atoms. The slope over which I fell was 52°. The cuts on my hands and back of head have healed in a wonderfully quick manner but one on the top of my forehead is likely to be the reverse of ornamental for a long time. It is not easy to say when I shall be home to a day but unless wet weather obliges me to stop for my drawings it will be on Friday evening next 8th Aug.

Yours very truly
Edward Whymper.

It has been wrongly suggested that it was Whymper's fault that all the serious attempts to climb the Matterhorn were made from Breuil instead of from Zermatt and that it needed Hudson to show him the easiest way. The best contemporary comment on the former is that of Leslie Stephen in his review of *Scrambles* in *Macmillan's Magazine*, which includes:

'Thousands of visitors to Zermatt have looked at it, and assumed, without hesitation, that it was totally inaccessible. Many of them were experienced mountaineers, but were hopelessly deceived by the boldness of the imposition. Even when the veil was lifted for a moment, it always returned after a brief interval. Some years before the final assault, old Peter Taugwald, one of Mr. Whymper's guides, remarked to me that it would be tolerably easy to climb it to the point called the "shoulder", and his assertion turned out to be strictly true; but at the time neither he nor I fully realized the possibility...Three years before the ascent, Melchior Anderegg made the same remark to me on the Hörnli; and though for the instant the truth flashed upon us, it disappeared again under the influence of a short stroll to another point of view. Thus a comparatively easy and certain route had been staring mountaineers in the face for years before it was actually tried...Though it is clearly foolish, I cannot remember without a sense of shame that I and others must have contemplated this convenient staircase some hundreds of times, and every now and then thought vaguely of trying it, and yet that we never had the necessary resolution or clearheadedness to make the assault.'

As for Whymper's intention to try the Hörnli in 1864 there is confirmation in his letter of 18th August 1865 to the Rev Richard Glover in which he wrote: 'Last year I was at Zermatt intending to go by the same route as we followed this year. I was however obliged by business to return without trying. If it had not been for that I should doubtless have done it then, and we should not most likely have had to deplore this frightful calamity.' There is also his reference in *Scrambles* to proposing the new route to Carrel in 1865, that they should cross the Theodule on 9th July and on the 10th pitch the tent as high as possible on the east face (Hörnli ridge), and this is confirmed by Gorret in his account of the Italian ascent, first published in October 1865.

2.57.4 His encounters with Girdlestone and with Douglas

Whymper had met Girdlestone and his pupil Hargreaves in Chamonix and on 3rd July they had crossed to Courmayeur by different passes. In *Scrambles* he referred to Girdlestone by name in relation to these ventures, but he did not otherwise mention him although he wrote of being in Breuil on 8th July when, 'Towards evening a young man came from Val Tournanche, and reported that an Englishman was lying there extremely ill'. Whymper would have recognised Hargreaves, who was on his way to meet his father at the Riffelhaus, and he would have known that the invalid was Girdlestone when he went down the valley to look after him, having vowed three years earlier that 'if an Englishman should at any time fall sick in the Val Tournanche, he should not feel so solitary' as he himself had when waiting for his cuts to heal. The explanation for the fact that he does not identify Girdlestone nor disclose that he accompanied him and Douglas across the Theodule to Zermatt is unlikely to be that he had been offended by what Girdlestone had written in his book about the cause of the Matterhorn accident, but simply that, as Graham Brown put it, 'the suppression of the name in the present instance might perhaps have been made in rather unnecessary deference to the proprieties, for which Whymper was a stickler'.

By Tuesday 11th Girdlestone was well on the way to recovery and was with Whymper in Breuil waiting for the weather to improve to allow them to cross the Theodule pass, when Lord Francis Douglas appeared from Zermatt. It has been suggested by Graham Brown that Douglas was already intent on making an attempt on the Matterhorn with Old Peter and that he may have dashed over to Breuil 'on the chance that he might find Jean-Antoine Carrel and engage that great guide's services for his own attempt in addition to those of old Peter'. Graham Brown goes on to say that 'there is therefore something rather magnificent in Whymper's words about Douglas: "before long it was determined that he should take part in the expedition" '. But there is a great deal of evidence to suggest that Douglas no longer had any intention of attempting the Matterhorn in 1865, that he was about to set off home and that he was probably therefore simply making plans for the following year. It must certainly be wrong to think of Carrel as the 'great guide' prior to his actually making the first ascent from Breuil a week later, and there would be no reason whatever for Douglas to contemplate taking him away from his native valley.

There is therefore no reason to doubt the accuracy of what Whymper recorded in *Scrambles* and it is interesting to note how Girdlestone recorded in his letter journal a great deal of consistent detail, his account of the ascent and of the accident being based on what he learnt from Whymper on 16th July. Graham Brown commented on this; 'But what in general is remarkable about this, Whymper's immediate story, is its almost exact correspondence with all which Whymper subsequently wrote, most consistently, about the incidents at the very time of the accident itself'.

It seems that Douglas had spent the Monday night and possibly the Sunday night as well at the Riffelhaus, the rest of his luggage being already packed at the Hotel Mont Cervin, and that he and Whymper spent the night of Wednesday 12th July at the Monte Rosa, where they also dined. Girdlestone recorded how the Whymper and Hudson 'parties joined and set off on Thursday morning, I having sat with them all on the previous evening whilst they arranged their plans'. It is not clear where Girdlestone stayed that night, but after climbing Monte Rosa on Saturday 15th and spending a second night at the Riffelhaus he descended to Zermatt on the Sunday morning and stayed the night at the Mont Cervin. Unfortunately Girdlestone's journal does not record any fresh details of the plans made by Whymper and Hudson on the Wednesday evening, nor throw any further light on the question as to why Hudson took Hadow on the climb.

2.57.5 His ascent of the Matterhorn

Whymper had left his tent, blankets and ropes etc at the Schwarzsee chapel and they stopped there on the Thursday morning to collect them. He did not at that time know anything about Hudson having brought a wire-rope to Zermatt but he had himself brought more than 200 feet of stout sashline, intended as a reserve, in case they had to leave much rope behind attached to rocks. The question of the different ropes is dealt with in detail in sections 3.12 (The rope in 1865) and 3.16 (The special rope), but it seems reasonable to conclude that the 1864 report of the Alpine Club's Special Committee on ropes etc had by 1865 led Whymper and other leading climbers to discard for use as a climbing rope, the stout sashline or plaited ropes which they had used formerly, which had generally been supposed to be so strong and which had all failed to pass the Committee's preliminary test and bear the strain of twelve stone falling five feet. In its place Whymper had brought 200 feet of Alpine Club manilla rope, as well as 150 feet of a stouter and probably stronger rope. Despite what some critics have suggested there is no reason to suppose that any member of the party was unaware that the sashline was intended for use only as fixed rope, simply because Whymper never subsequently said so in writing. Old Peter carried the sashline, he had in mind stretching a rope, as he called fixing a rope in his evidence at the Enquiry (A53), and he referred to it in evidence as 'a special rope' (A24).

Whymper wrote how he and Croz raced each other to the top, his exact words in *Scrambles* being: 'The slope eased off, at length we could be detached, and Croz and I, dashing away, ran a neck-and-neck race, which ended in a dead heat'. Girdlestone's record of Whymper's account includes 'Whymper & Croz & Hudson had raced up the last part to the top unroped it was so easy'. Whereas it is of little consequence whether or not Hudson took part in the race, even though Graham Brown sought to rely upon it as evidence of Whymper suppressing the part played by Hudson in the ascent, the event has given rise to the somewhat ludicrous issue involving A.E.W.Mason. He is said to have been told by Whymper after some dinner that 'Thinking it over, I believe that I did cut the rope behind me so that I could more easily race Croz to the top'. But even in the unlikely event that there should be any truth in the story, any minor shortening of one rope would no more have caused Old Peter to have to use the sashline to tie himself on to Douglas (which seems to have been Lunn's hope), than it would have prevented him from using the sashline double or from postponing their start of the descent for a few more minutes until Whymper had finished putting their names in a bottle.

2.57.6 The accident

Whymper's account of the accident, repeated with such consistency in his various publications and letters, was given to McCormick on 15th and 16th July and partly incorporated by him in his letter of 17th to *The Times*. Whymper gave it to Girdlestone on Sunday 16th July, when the latter called to see him at about 2 p.m. when he had returned from finding the bodies, and the same evening when he went to see Girdlestone at the Mont Cervin. Girdlestone recorded it sometime between the 16th and the 20th, having left Zermatt on the morning of Monday 17th after offering to stay with Whymper but agreeing with him that there was nothing he could do to help. At about the same time Whymper must have made his own earliest written record of the accident, apart from any letter he may have sent home on the Sunday or Monday which has not survived, this being his answers to the written questions passed to him by Clemenz in advance of the Enquiry that started on the afternoon of Friday 21st. It is significant that some of his answers like A11 appear almost word for word in his subsequent letter to von Fellenberg and later accounts, due no doubt to his retaining the original English version of his answers, which Vecqueray had translated into French alongside the questions in French. Whymper's subsequent published accounts include his letter to *The Times*, the chapter in *Scrambles* and articles in the *Graphic*, the *Journal de Zermatt* and the *Strand Magazine,* as well as a chapter in his *Guide to Zermatt and the Matterhorn*.

The only other account of the accident is that of Old Peter, such as it appears from his evidence given to the Enquiry. But it seems that he was not allowed to say what he wanted in evidence and that his written answers to the questions drafted by Whymper were probably set out by his cousin the Zermatt judge. Young Peter was excluded altogether by being allowed to depart for Chamonix before the Enquiry even started and the 'Narrative' that he gave to Montagnier in 1917 contains nothing new, apart from inaccuracies. There is therefore no reason to doubt what Whymper wrote about the accident, despite the unsuccessful attempts made to discredit him by the likes of Egger and Lunn, and it is interesting to read Frank Smythe's comments to a correspondent shortly before publication of his biography of Whymper. 'Having read all Whymper's diary through his life it is not possible to come to any conclusion other than that he was an absolutely honest and scrupulous man of a hard and unsympathetic type.'

So far as the immediate cause of the accident is concerned, there is no reason to doubt that Hadow slipped and that he did so at the wrong moment, that is, when he should have stood still so as to enable Croz to descend a few steps, after Croz had helped him by putting his feet into their proper positions. The secondary cause seems to have been that Hudson was not paying attention, so that 'The rope was not taut from him to Hadow, and the two men fell ten or twelve feet before the jerk came upon him', as Whymper wrote in a footnote in *Scrambles*. A further cause of the catastrophe and of it not being possible to arrest the initial fall was that the rope broke. Whereas rumours began to circulate soon after the accident that Old Peter had cut the rope, Whymper was able to contradict them and he did so, having himself seen the rope break. But he was not able to state why Old Peter had used the weakest rope, or as he put it in a letter to Woolmore Wigram: 'How it came to pass that the weakest rope was used between Taugwald and Lord Douglas I have no idea, that is, I have no idea why he did not use the stronger ropes. Still I have no reason to suspect even that this was done *intentionally*.'

Twentieth century critics have tended to criticise Whymper for omitting certain details from his initial accounts and they have failed to appreciate that just as he was not prepared to identify Girdlestone as 'The sick man [who] declared that he was better, though the exertion of saying as much tumbled him over onto the floor in a fainting fit', so he was not prepared to volunteer anything that might offend the relatives of the victims. Nor was he prepared to reveal voluntarily the full truth about the behaviour of the Taugwalders following the accident, nor speculate as to why the weakest rope was used. These aspects and the influences bearing on him after the accident are considered more fully below.

2.57.7 His actions following the accident

According to the *Journal de Zermatt* article Whymper left the Taugwalders when they got down as far as the Hörnli and he ran down to Zermatt. He immediately went to see Seiler, who set to work to arouse the village, and it seems from Whymper's evidence at the Enquiry (A15) that he then 'informed the President of the Zermatt Commune of the sad accident and at the same time asked him to send some men to the scene of the catastrophe, in case after all one or other of my unfortunate companions was still alive. This request was granted and a good number of guides set off immediately.' He then sent a message to McCormick, who had gone to the Gornergrat, stating that a party of guides had gone off in search and asking him to return by 4.30p.m. so that they could follow after them. McCormick's reaction to receiving the news is of interest:

> 'Upon reading this note, I thought it very strange that an accident should have happened to Hudson, the most prudent and expert of mountaineers, and not to others. I could not conceive how it was possible; but when, on my arrival in Zermatt, the appalling truth was made known that he was but one of four who had fallen, I saw that Mr. Whymper had not told the whole disaster, lest the news might be too distressing.'

McCormick ran down from the Riffel but it was too late to do anything that day as it would have been night by the time they reached the glacier. The search party returned after six hours, having apparently failed to reach the glacier via the Stöckli and having then ascended the Hohlicht heights above Kalbermatten and Zmutt, from where they were able to see the bodies lying motionless on the snow. The first search party had been led by Joseph Welschen, the President of the Commune, and it was proposed to set out again on the Sunday evening, but Whymper and McCormick unwilling to lose the slightest chance resolved to start on Sunday morning and they seem to have organized a party of Zermatt guides including Peter Perren to go with them. The accounts in the *Graphic* and in the *Journal de Zermatt* imply that everything was arranged and that they were going to start at midnight until the plan became known, when the guides were then threatened with excommunication if they did not attend Mass at 5.30a.m.

Whether or not political considerations came into play, whether the President wanted to lead any search party himself but did not want to set out again so soon or whether the authorities resented the initiative being taken by foreigners may never be known for certain unless access is given to the local council meeting minutes, but there are indications that the local leaders subsequently resented the way in which Whymper was nevertheless able to organize an alternative party and proceed with the original plan. Firstly, the wording of Q15 and Whymper's reference in A15 to setting out 'without official authority' and to not making an official report suggest that he may have been ticked off for doing what he did and, secondly, there is the incident reported by Whymper in the *Graphic* of Franz Andenmatten being subsequently 'turned out, *ejected*, from the church at Zermatt'.

It was Franz Andenmatten who had been the first to volunteer in response to the call made by Seiler on Whymper's behalf and it was he who led the party to the glacier in conditions very different from those prevailing to-day when there is no longer any danger from séracs. Whymper wrote how it was a severe trial to several of the Zermatt guides not being allowed to take part in the search and how 'Peter Perren declared with tears that nothing else would have prevented him from joining in the search for his old comrades'. Perren was able to take part in the third search party that recovered the bodies on the Thursday morning, as did Old Peter Taugwalder's sons Peter and Joseph, but it is significant that Old Peter himself was not there.

Whymper and McCormick were accompanied by James Robertson and J.S.Phillpotts, as well as the guides Franz Andenmatten, J-M and A.Lochmatter, Frédéric Payot and Jean Tairraz. Whymper wrote nothing in his letters to von Fellenberg or to *The Times* or even in *Scrambles* of the carnage they found on the Matterhorn glacier, but details appeared in a letter written by Gabriel Loppé to *L'Abeille de Chamonix* and extracts were quoted in *The Times* on 2nd August. The account which must have originated with Payot and Tairraz includes reference to enormous stones ceaselessly bombarding the searchers 'who had to move smartly out of the way on several occasions in order to avoid them. Mr.Whymper alone was unperturbed and ignored all entreaties to take cover; in the presence of this horrible scene he solemnly swore that he would never set foot on a mountain again.'

Another account is quoted by Clark in a letter written at Zermatt by Downton, the English Chaplain at Geneva at the request of the Consul, Mackenzie, including 'It was a matter of extreme peril to remain on the spot as rocks & stones were falling continually, and as the guides could not be got to render any assistance, but lay down and *howled*, it was hastily resolved to cover up the mangled remains in the snow'. James Robertson, who took a lock of hair off Hudson and subsequently sent it to his widow, seems to have recorded details in his diary, as in 1957 Dangar & Blakeney quoted his son Ainslie J.Robertson as informing them that Croz' crucifix had been found embedded in his jaw and that he had dug it out with a penknife.

Whymper did refer to the state of the bodies in the *Journal de Zermatt* and to their having found all eight boots.

> 'It was as if a giant had taken the bodies by their feet and struck them violently against the rocks. I saw no sign of Douglas apart from his boots, which I recognised at once because they were too small and he had cut and rectified them before setting off. I looked everywhere...As it was not possible to suppose that he being lighter than the others had sunk into the snow one can only think that he must have been completely torn to shreds or else that he remained caught by a bit of rope on a spike of rock. At all events nothing has ever been found of him.'

He wrote in somewhat similar terms in an article in the *Strand Magazine* in 1909:

> 'The spectacle that their remains presented when they were recovered was revolting. I have seen nothing like it before or since, and do not wish to see such a sight again...Lord Francis Douglas was not below, and until now no one knows what became of him – whether he was literally knocked and torn to pieces, or whether his descent was arrested and he was suspended on the cliff.'

In Zermatt, Whymper seems to have had to do a considerable amount of Clemenz' work for him in connection with the Enquiry. This may sound a bit far-fetched when a twenty five year old foreigner was to be summoned to give evidence before a tribunal headed by a fifty five year old lawyer/local hotelier, but a close look at some of the facts does suggest a somewhat extraordinary state of affairs. It has generally been assumed that on the first day (Friday) Whymper was questioned by Clemenz in French and Taugwalder was questioned by Clemenz in German, and that as a result of Whymper handing in some questions he wanted to be put to Taugwalder the latter was recalled on the Sunday when the Whymper questions were included. But as the Enquiry did not start until 2 p.m. there would not normally have been enough time even for Whymper's evidence to be given that day, when account is taken of the need for the Englishman first to understand the French question, and thereafter compose and give his answer in French, bearing in mind in particular that many of his sentences exceeded 20 words and two of them exceeded 50 words. A witness has to pause from time to time to allow the Court clerk to write down his answers, and a German speaking clerk recording the French evidence of an English speaking witness would have problems even if the witness spoke fluent French. The possibility that the Enquiry used an interpreter can be excluded on several grounds which need not be detailed here.

Clemenz solved the problem, not by taking a detailed statement from Whymper in advance of the hearing, but by giving him the list of questions earlier in the week. It is not known whether Clemenz was in residence at his Hotel Mont Cervin on Sunday 16th July, but he probably was. He might not then have known that he was to be instructed to hold the Enquiry, although he may have guessed as much, but he would naturally have been interested in learning about the accident from his guest Girdlestone, who had heard it direct from Whymper. He may also have spoken to Whymper that evening when he called to see Girdlestone. In any event Clemenz was soon in touch with Whymper, who was quoted in the *Journal de Zermatt* as saying:

> 'I gave judge Clemenz who was in charge of the enquiry all the information and details he asked me for, including amongst other things a questionnaire drafted by me, signed by me and intended to clear up the accident completely, dealing inter alia with the fact that the weakest rope had been used to tie Douglas to father Taugwalder. The questionnaire should have been returned to me by Mr.Clemenz, but I have never seen it since.'

The conduct of the Enquiry is considered in section 3.4 and in section 5 but there is little doubt that Clemenz asked Whymper to answer the questions in writing in French and that he did this with the assistance of the Rugby School French and German master Vecqueray, who was almost certainly staying at the Hotel Monte Rosa. Whether Vecqueray translated the questions from German into English or into French (or whether Clemenz drafted them in French) is not clear, but there is no doubt that he translated Whymper's English answers into French and that when the Enquiry opened Clemenz must have recited the questions one by one to which Whymper then read out his answers, handing in a copy of the Vecqueray document which the clerk was able to write up at his leisure. Whymper wrote out his own report of the hearing and it is significant that, apart from two trivial questions that do not appear in the Official Report (Q8½ & Q16½), Clemenz seems to have paid no heed to the answers and never to have sought any clarification or amplification. This is particularly significant in the case of Taugwalder.

But Clemenz' prime use of Whymper was in the questioning of Taugwalder on the Friday, as apart from the formalities at the start of his evidence (Q18-Q21) and the ambiguous final question (Q36) every single question that Clemenz put to Taugwalder came from Whymper's list. Some of the questions seem to have been deliberately distorted in the process of being translated from Whymper's French into German, and it seems likely that this was done by Taugwalder's cousin the Zermatt judge. It is almost certain that Taugwalder, like Whymper, was given time to compose his answers in writing, but the most remarkable aspect of Clemenz' sheltering behind Whymper in the questioning of Taugwalder is the fact that he took no notice of Old Peter's answers. He condoned the evasive answer and he disregarded the ambiguous answer. He showed not the slightest interest in getting the witness to provide the answers to Whymper's original questions about the use of the weak rope and it is difficult to avoid the conclusion that his whole questioning of Taugwalder, or at least that recorded for the Friday, was a sham. Clemenz seems to have virtually opted out of questioning Taugwalder himself and to have washed his hands of any issue that might have reflected against him. It also looks very much as though Clemenz must have provided Whymper with some of the questions that were ultimately included in his list (see Q22, 23, 30, 31, 32 & 35). The possibility that Clemenz was influenced by the conflict of interests confronting him as hotelier is considered in section 2.9 (Clemenz).

It is therefore hardly surprising that Clemenz never kept his promise to send Whymper Taugwalder's answers. But it was Taugwalder and not Whymper or the relatives of the victims who suffered as a result of Clemenz' weakness or incompetence. It seems probable that Old Peter could have provided an excusable explanation for using the plaited rope and that had he been given the opportunity to do so and had his evidence been released to the press, the suspicions that attached to him would soon have been forgotten. He went so far as to say that he tied himself to Douglas with a special rope (A24), but Clemenz seems not to have taken the slightest notice as he never sought any elaboration or amplification. In addition to the Vecqueray document Whymper retained his original English draft of the questions to be put to Taugwalder. He handed in to Clemenz a French copy dated 21st July, but it is not clear whether he had translated it himself or whether Vecqueray did this for him, although the former seems more likely in view of certain inconsistencies.

Apart from the Enquiry, Whymper busied himself with a number of other matters during the week that followed the accident. On the Tuesday he set off for the Gorner but soon came back, according to Adams Reilly's diary. On the Wednesday when rumour reached Zermatt that someone was missing from the Riffel he set off up with McCormick, but on the way they met someone who told them that the body of Knyvet Wilson had been found. On the Friday morning he received the summons to attend the Enquiry at 2 p.m. The funerals also took place that morning, with the interment of Michel Croz at 8.30a.m. followed by Hudson, Hadow and Wilson at 10 o'clock. Whymper paid 20frs for Croz' interment and via Adams Reilly he paid his representatives 100frs in respect of his fees for the Matterhorn, having no means of knowing if anything else was

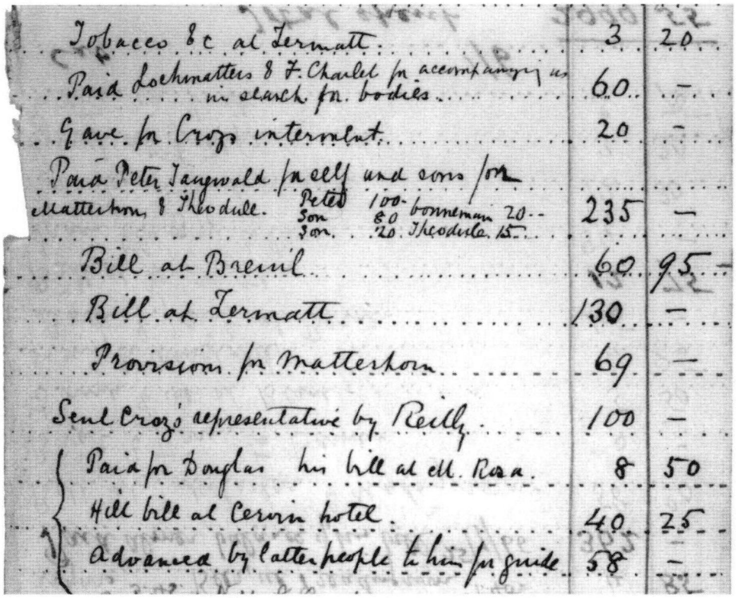

Tobacco &c at Zermatt	3	20
Paid Lochmatters & F. Charlet for accompanying us in search for bodies	60	–
Gave for Croz's interment	20	–
Paid Peter Taugwald for self and sons for Matterhorn & Theodule. Peter 100 Son 80 Son 20 bonnemain 20 Theodule 15	235	–
Bill at Breuil	60	95
Bill at Zermatt	130	–
Provisions for Matterhorn	69	–
Sent Croz's representative by Reilly	100	–
Paid for Douglas his bill at the M. Rosa	8	50
Hill bill at Cervin hotel	40	25
advanced by latter people to him for guide	58	–

Some of Whymper's expenses at Zermatt in July 1865

outstanding. He paid for the provisions they had taken on the climb as well as the fees of the Taugwalders, and McCormick reimbursed him for Hudson's and Hadow's shares. He also paid Douglas's 'debts' including 8.50frs at the Monte Rosa and 40.25frs at the Mont Cervin, as well as reimbursing an advance of 58frs made by the latter to Douglas for a guide.

A letter he wrote to McCormick from Interlaken on 25th July expressed his disapproval at having been detained at Zermatt so long, 'merely, as it seems to me, to suit M.Clemenz' pleasure'. This seems to suggest that he had answered Clemenz' questions some time before he was summoned to attend the Enquiry, and although one might expect the authorities to have wanted the bodies brought down before any Enquiry was held, it is remarkable to find that there was no evidence given by anyone about the recovery of the bodies (Andenmatten was only questioned about his first search) despite the party including Welschen, the President of the Commune, and Alois Julen, the Zermatt district judge who was also a glacier guide.

Whymper's detention in Zermatt was no doubt made somewhat more bearable by the arrival on 18th July of his friend Adams Reilly, who had heard of the accident the day before at Breuil. On Friday 21st Reilly sent his guide Charlet over the Theodule to Breuil with a porter to collect his 'things and Whymper's'. They returned on the Saturday and it may well be that this was the reason why Whymper left Zermatt so much later than Robertson, the alternative explanation being that Clemenz did not release him until he had received Taugwalder's replies to his questions. Whymper must have met or passed Jean-Baptiste Croz on the way down the valley in the vicinity of St.Niklaus, but they obviously did not recognise each other, having never spoken before. Adams Reilly stayed on in Zermatt until 3rd August and on his way home he collected Michel Croz' hat in Chamonix and various French newspapers in Paris, which he subsequently delivered to Whymper.

Whymper spent nights at Visp and Kandersteg before reaching Interlaken on 24th July. There he completed his letter to von Fellenberg, which for the most part he must already have written in Zermatt, arranged for it to be translated into French and German by Peter Ober and to be forwarded by W.H.Hawker, with whom he had climbed some six weeks before. He also despatched a similar letter to the Secretary of the Italian Alpine Club, read the newspapers and met Christian Almer in order to pay him the balance of his fees. He continued his journey home on 26th July via Bern, Neuchâtel and Paris.

2.57.8 Overwhelmed by letters

On his return to London Whymper wrote almost immediately to J.J.Cowell, the former Secretary of the Alpine Club, in the absence of the then Secretary Crauford Grove. The initial exchange of letters has not survived but Cowell's reply to a second letter pasted in a scrapbook kept by Whymper, suggests that he had asked if the Club would hold an enquiry into Hudson's death and then make known its findings so as to avoid the need for him to have to decide what to tell the public and what not to tell them, in view of the desirability of not saying anything that might cause unnecessary distress to the relatives of the victims. Cowell suggested that an Extraordinary General Meeting might be called and he set out a timetable involving nineteen days. The letter concluded by inviting Whymper to a quiet dinner with Cowell and his father on Wednesday 2nd August.

The scrapbook contains various contemporary newspaper cuttings and dozens of incoming letters. Some letters like that from Leslie Stephen are merely expressions of sympathy whereas the majority relate to problems of one sort or another, like those from the Editor of *The Times* pressing for a detailed account of 'the lamentable catastrophe' or Woolmore Wigram writing on 8th August of a letter he had received from J-B Croz 'in which he speaks of a suspicion prevalent in the Valley of Chamonix, and I fear shared by himself that Taugwald *cut the rope* on the Matterhorn'. The letters that have survived must be only a small proportion of the whole and there are even fewer copies of Whymper's replies. But those that are in the book reveal not only certain facts and matters not recorded elsewhere, but also Whymper's conscientiousness, his prompt attention to even the most delicate and difficult situation and his remarkable skill as a letter writer. Some of the correspondence is reproduced in section 4 and extracts from other letters are quoted in the sections dealing with the particular individuals or subjects to which they relate. Thus the Cowell correspondence culminating in the creation of the Cowell memorandum is referred to not only in section 2.11 (Cowell) but also in section 3.2 (The Cowell memorandum).

The correspondents included Lord Queensberry and his mother, Hudson's widow and Hadow's father. The latter had been not at all pleased to be informed by Gustave Doré's publishers that it was 'their intention to publish a print of the catastrophe of the "Matterhorn" and that you [Whymper] are going to supply the drawing for it, while I am actually asked to supply a likeness of my dear son for the picture'. Hadow went on to suggest that Whymper should exert his influence with the publishers and the artist to omit from the design any attempted likeness of his son or of Hudson. Whymper replied the same day, 23rd August, telling Hadow what he knew, explaining the situation at some length and stating: 'I have endeavoured in all that I have done since this much lamentable accident, to avoid giving pain to yourself and to the relatives of Lord Douglas and Mr.Hudson'. Hadow's reply indicated that he was now satisfied, and he continued:

> 'With regard to your letter in the *Times* after Mr McCormick's account, there were indeed some portions which caused us pain, as they appeared to enter into unnecessary details; I have however no desire to criticise these for I can well believe you had a difficult and painful task; I would much rather take the opportunity of sincerely thanking you for your gallant and successful exertions in recovering the remains of our dear boy and his companions, which at first seemed so improbable.'

Emily Hudson had written to Whymper on 11th August:

> 'Having obtained your address from a friend, I feel I can no longer delay writing to you. I am at a loss to find words to express all the gratitude I feel towards you, who would have saved the life of my dear husband if he could.
> When I think of how you started off again, after all the horror & fatigue of the previous days, to look for those whom you *knew* no human help could avail, – I can only say, God bless you for it! – and I am sure you will understand me when I say, that these are the only words I can find...
> It would be a sad pleasure for me to see you some day; as one of the last persons who saw my beloved husband in life.'

Lord Queensberry called to see Whymper on 5th August on his return from Zermatt and they corresponded further in August and September. There seems to have been some rumour of Douglas's body being found, which prompted Whymper to offer his services. Douglas's mother wrote in December 1865, asking for a photograph of the Matterhorn, which Whymper later sent having marked the spot from which they fell. Some of the Queensberry and Hadow letters are reproduced in section 4, as is Whymper's correspondence with Sir T.Fowell Buxton about the harmful wording of Buxton's letter in *The Times* of 31st July. A letter from Elijah Walton, written in Piedmont on 21st December 1865 states, 'Enclosed is the portrait of your guide Carrel. He came to see me and wished me to say he could not write to you knowing not your address.' In 1866 after returning home from Zermatt Whymper corresponded about the land and the inscription for Croz' tomb. He received a rather extraordinary letter from the Curé Mathias Welschen, a cousin of the President Joseph who had led the search parties the previous year. A similar problem over the land for the Hudson/Hadow monument resulted in the Geneva Consul Mackenzie writing to *The Times* referring to an exorbitant demand and saying they would pay no more than a local would pay for the same land. The wording of the Croz inscription, which Whymper had drafted, was translated into French by Vecqueray the Rugby schoolmaster who had been in Zermatt with Robertson during the week after the accident. Robertson and Vecqueray suggested an alteration in the wording, which Whymper adopted.

The month of August 1865 seems to have brought the majority of the correspondence, but Whymper was still able to fit in a number of appointments as well, and it is probable that he went to see G.F.Browne in Cambridge on 3rd August after seeing the Cowells the previous evening, in addition to seeing Lord Queensberry on the 5th, Adams Reilly on the 14th and Gustave Doré's publisher's agent on the 19th.

2.57.9 Influences on Whymper

Whymper had the benefit of advice and guidance from McCormick, Robertson, Adams Reilly and Giles Puller amongst others in Zermatt and on his return home from G.F.Browne, the Cowells, and Alfred Wills. Yet such beneficial influence is in itself unlikely to account for the extraordinary composure and maturity that he displayed not only in his actions with the search party and other arrangements that had to be made in Zermatt after the accident, but also in his letter to *The Times* and in his private correspondence, revealing a standard of letter writing that must be rare to-day. It is however probable that in McCormick he chanced to find the ideal adviser and friend.

After first meeting McCormick on the Saturday afternoon, Whymper walked with him in the early hours of Sunday morning from Zermatt to the Matterhorn glacier, a distance of more than six hours, during which it is likely that Whymper recounted everything he could recall about the ascent and the subsequent accident on the descent. After finding the three mutilated bodies and burying them, McCormick would have had a further opportunity of questioning Whymper on their descent to Zermatt. There would be no cause for Whymper to withhold anything and it is highly likely that they would have discussed the question as to how the weakest rope came to be used between Taugwalder and Douglas, particularly after Whymper had found to his astonishment 'that all of the three [bodies on the glacier] had been tied with the Club, or with the second and equally strong, rope, and consequently there was only one link – that between Taugwalder and Lord F. Douglas – in which the weaker rope had been used.' Although Whymper told Wigram in his letter of 9th August, that he had 'no reason to suspect even that this was done *intentionally*', and in his letter to *The Times* said that if the rope had not broken the Editor would not have received his letter, there was room for a different opinion and construction of the events. It is therefore probable that McCormick as a friend of Hudson's would have wanted to know how the rope came to be used or, as Whymper put it subsequently in the Wigram letter, why Taugwalder did not use one of the stronger ropes.

In his letter of 17th July to *The Times* McCormick referred to Hudson's ladder, and he would have known also of his wire-rope, of which Whymper wrote in his letter to *The Times*, 'It has been repeatedly asked, "Why was not the wire-rope taken which Mr.Hudson brought to Zermatt?" ' It seems inconceivable that the more immediate question about using the stronger rope was not also asked 'repeatedly', and asked by the likes of McCormick and Robertson and Seiler. McCormick's own attitude to the accident and to the possibility of someone having been at fault appears in his pamphlet *A sad holiday*, but there is a difference between criticising and laying blame on the one hand and, on the other hand, determining the facts that led to the accident. McCormick would when he returned home at the end of the month have had to explain things in private to Hudson's widow and to Hadow's parents and to be in a position to answer any questions they might ask. He would therefore have wanted to know about the rope that broke and it is probable that he was one of those who advised Whymper to take advantage of the opportunity Clemenz gave him to question Taugwalder about the circumstances in which it came to be used.

McCormick wrote of Hudson and his former pupil Hadow,

> 'Say not they were rash or inconsiderate, inexperienced or careless, fools or tempters of Providence; for they would not thus have spoken of others who might have met with their fate. By unjust judgment do not thrust a sword into hearts already tender and wounded by their loss. It matters little who or what led to their destruction. The fact of their death preaches all the lessons which need to be learned. As to what those lessons are, there will, of course, be great difference of opinion. Climbers will specify many, which non-climbers will reject, and vice versa. There are plenty for both of us, only let us learn them.'

McCormick wrote to Hadow's father on Sunday 16th July and presumably wrote to Hudson's widow as well at the same time. The following day he wrote his first letter to *The Times*, giving the background to the climb and describing the accident as well as the finding of the bodies. The letter is not very long and does not go into much detail, and it is therefore of some significance that it should briefly mention Whymper's problems with the Taugwalders after the accident. 'Mr.Whymper's feelings at this time may be imagined. The two remaining guides were so completely unnerved by the calamity which had befallen their companions that he found it difficult to descend with them.' The letter, clearly written by arrangement with Whymper, seems to have had two aims, firstly, to give the public a reliable account of the accident and, secondly, to avoid upsetting the relatives in the process. When Whymper was subsequently being pressed by the *Times* editor for a more detailed account, he explained to him:

> 'I had hoped that the letters of the Revd. J.McCormick would have been sufficient for the information of the public, although they were intentionally silent on certain points, including the exact cause of the accident, in order to spare the families of Messrs Hadow and Hudson the additional pain they must feel if it is published.'

This wish to spare the relatives, whether it was initiated by McCormick or merely appeared first in his letter, seems to have governed all that Whymper said or wrote in public about the accident for the next 25 years. Moreover, despite the advice he received from Wills and from the Cowells, he did not publicly criticise the Taugwalders, apart from what he wrote in a footnote in *Scrambles* about Young Peter (in about 1869) after learning that he had endeavoured to trade upon the idea that Whymper had not paid them. It may therefore well be that McCormick, even if he did not initiate the idea, supported Whymper's own view that he should abstain from offering observations and casting blame on anyone. The advice that Whymper did receive from McCormick and Browne, apart from one minor exception in the case of Browne, seems to have prevailed when it conflicted with that of the Cowells or Wills.

Whymper accepted the Cowells' advice and took the precaution of recording the Taugwalders' heartless behaviour in his memorandum of 17th August 1865, but did so in only general and moderate terms, which led to the Cowells producing the supplementary memorandum recording the full details which Whymper had told them before his meeting with Browne. He stopped short of heeding Wills advice; 'These Taugwalders are not fit to be trusted – and the world ought to know it: and I think myself, if you will pardon me for saying so, that you will make a great mistake if you hesitate to speak of them as they should be spoken of.'

Those critics who have shown themselves to be allergic to Whymper obviously had no appreciation of the difficulties facing him after the accident, or of his decision not to reveal the contents of the Cowell memorandum. To contend therefore that Whymper did reveal Cowell and accused the Taugwalders of attempting to murder him would be inexcusable if it were not so obviously an 'uninformed verdict' based on ignorance. The precise nature of the advice given to Whymper is considered in the various sections relating to the individuals involved.

2.57.10 His attitude to the Taugwalders

Whymper's attitude towards Old Peter and his son must be looked at in stages, as it necessarily changed as time passed and healed the wounds caused by their heartless behaviour shortly after the accident. Lunn and Egger in their attempts to denigrate Whymper with their 'uninformed verdicts', as Lunn would surely have called their groundless criticisms had he taken the trouble to acquaint himself with the true facts, seem to have had no regard for any time factor. They treat what they see as a specific fault on the part of Whymper as though it had existed perhaps 40 years before the event upon which they rely or alternatively as though it still existed 40 years later, just as they attribute events in the late 1860's to a book not published until 1871. But the passage of time affected both Whymper and the Taugwalders and it is necessary to look much more closely at some of the controversial issues than has been the case in the last 60 years.

(a) *Young Peter, pre-accident conduct*

Whymper seems never to have said or written anything that could be regarded as adverse criticism of Young Peter's conduct prior to the accident. By 1865 he was already a competent and ambitious guide with greater all round experience than his father, although he could not yet have acquired the particular skills that develop only from long familiarity with his profession. Nevertheless his 30 ascents of Monte Rosa already compared well with his father's 85 and his standing as a guide was recognised by Whymper in *Scrambles* as one of only two Zermatt guides included in the full page illustration 'The Clubroom of Zermatt in 1864'. As for his conduct on the Matterhorn up to the happening of the accident, Whymper said nothing in particular about it but Young Peter would be covered by the comment in his letter to von Fellenberg, 'No blame can be attached to any of the guides; they all did their duty manfully'. There is however one other aspect that seems to reflect Whymper's regard for Young Peter's climbing skill as a guide, which is the tip of 20frs. Although Old Peter kept it for himself and still complained he had not been paid enough, it seems more likely – but not altogether free from doubt – that it was intended in part if not in whole for Young Peter as a recognition of his contribution as a guide being worth no less than that of his father.

(b) *Young Peter, post-accident conduct*

Whymper's disgust at the Taugwalders' heartless behaviour once they got down to the easy part was omitted from *Scrambles*, although he did quote the conversation with Young Peter asking him not to pay them, but there is plenty of evidence of it elsewhere in addition to what Whymper wrote to von Fellenberg about how they were 'utterly unnerved, cried like infants, and trembled in such a manner as to threaten us with the fate of the others'. McCormick's first letter to *The Times* of 17th July referred to the Taugwalders being completely unnerved by the calamity and to Whymper finding it difficult to descend with them, and the following day Prior wrote to the Consul Mackenzie:

> 'I am much disgusted with the conduct of the Taugwalders père et fils. An hour after the accident they bothered Whymper to know who was to pay them, and asked him to send an account to the Newspapers mentioning their names, in order that among travellers they might have next year a "succès de curiosité".'

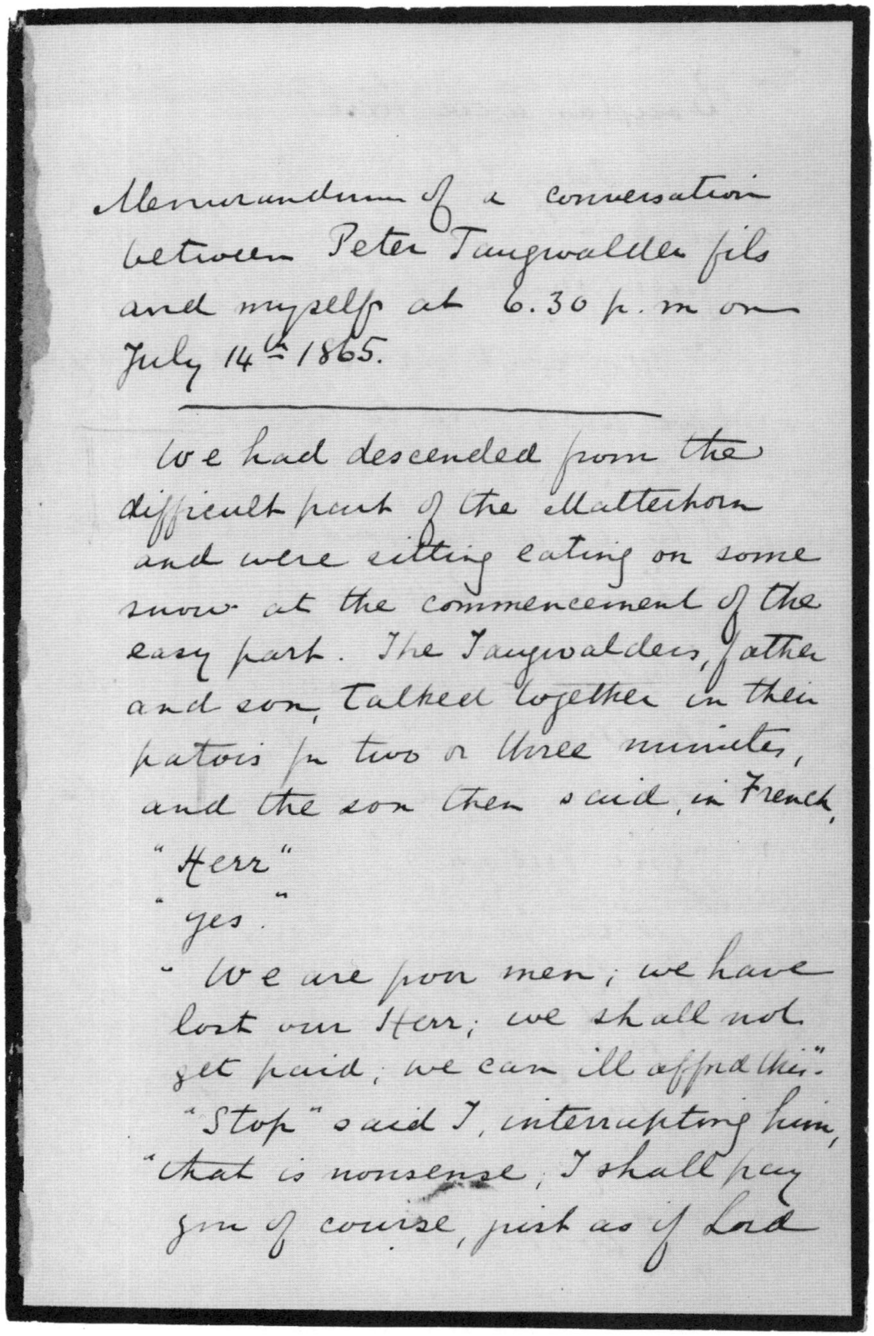

Memorandum of a conversation between Peter Taugwalder fils and myself at 6.30 p.m on July 14th 1865.

We had descended from the difficult part of the Matterhorn and were sitting eating on some snow at the commencement of the easy part. The Taugwalders, father and son, talked together in their patois for two or three minutes, and the son then said, in French,

"Herr"

"yes."

"We are poor men; we have lost our Herr; we shall not get paid; we can ill afford this."

"Stop" said I, interrupting him, "that is nonsense, I shall pay you of course, just as if Lord

Whymper's memorandum of 17th August 1865

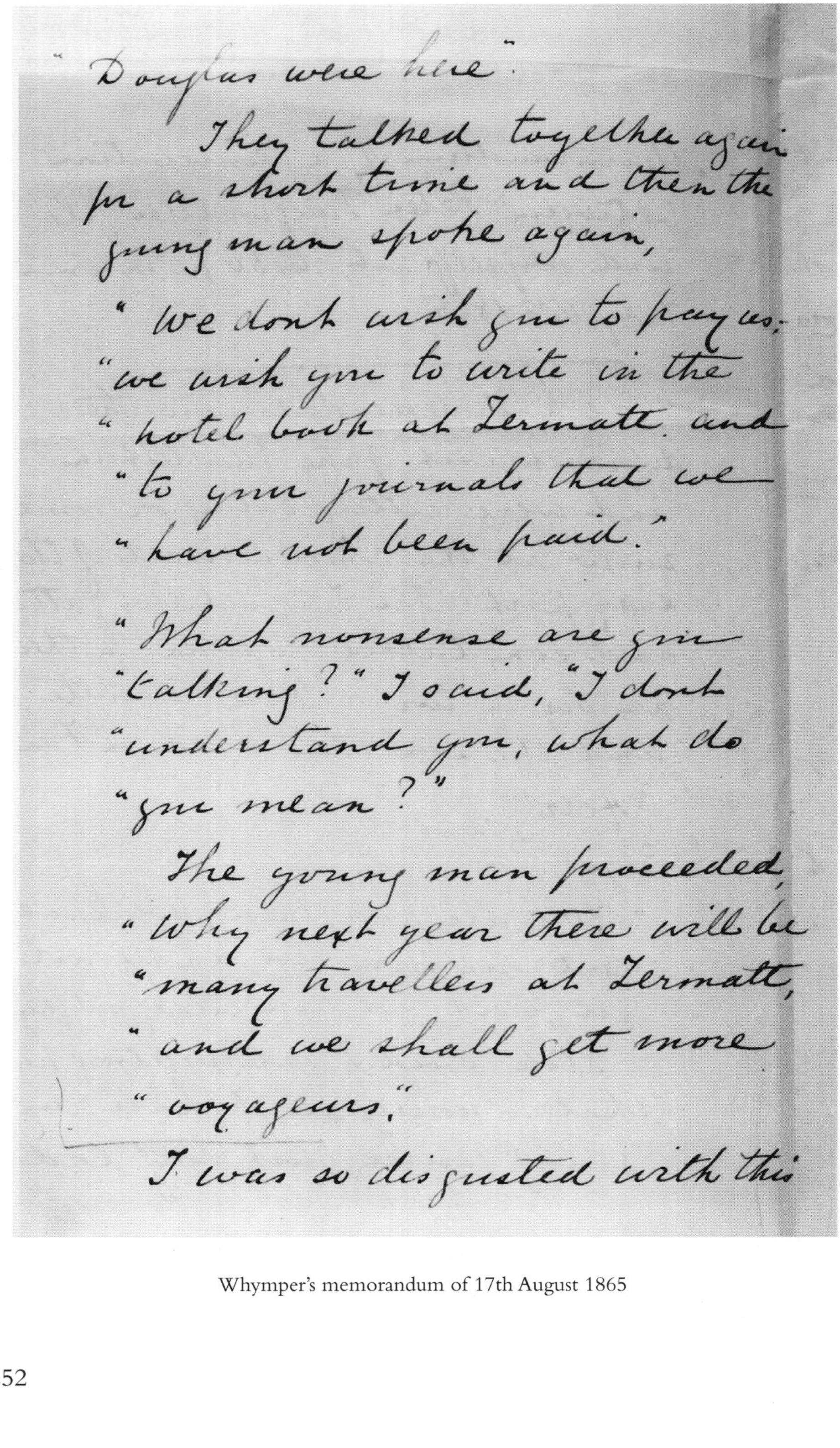

"Douglas were here".
They talked together again
for a short time and then the
young man spoke again,
"We dont wish you to pay us;
"we wish you to write in the
"hotel book at Zermatt. and
"to your journals that we
"have not been paid."

"What nonsense are you
"talking?" I said, "I dont
"understand you, what do
"you mean?"
The young man proceeded,
"Why next year there will be
"many travellers at Zermatt,
"and we shall get more
"voyageurs."
I was so disgusted with this

Whymper's memorandum of 17th August 1865

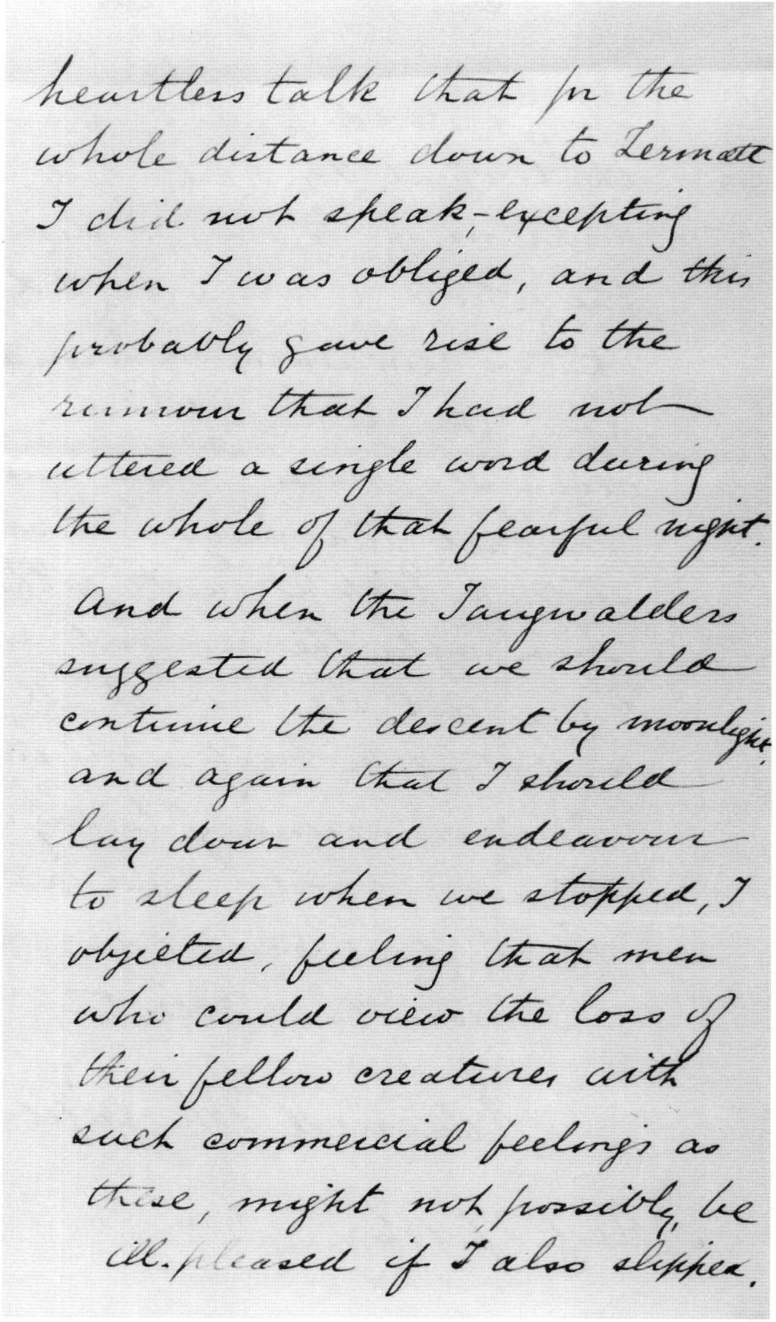

heartless talk that for the
whole distance down to Zermatt
I did not speak—excepting
when I was obliged, and this
probably gave rise to the
rumour that I had not
uttered a single word during
the whole of that fearful night.
And when the Taugwalders
suggested that we should
continue the descent by moonlight
and again that I should
lay down and endeavour
to sleep when we stopped, I
objected, feeling that men
who could view the loss of
their fellow creatures with
such commercial feelings as
these, might not possibly be
ill-pleased if I also slipped.

Whymper's memorandum of 17th August 1865

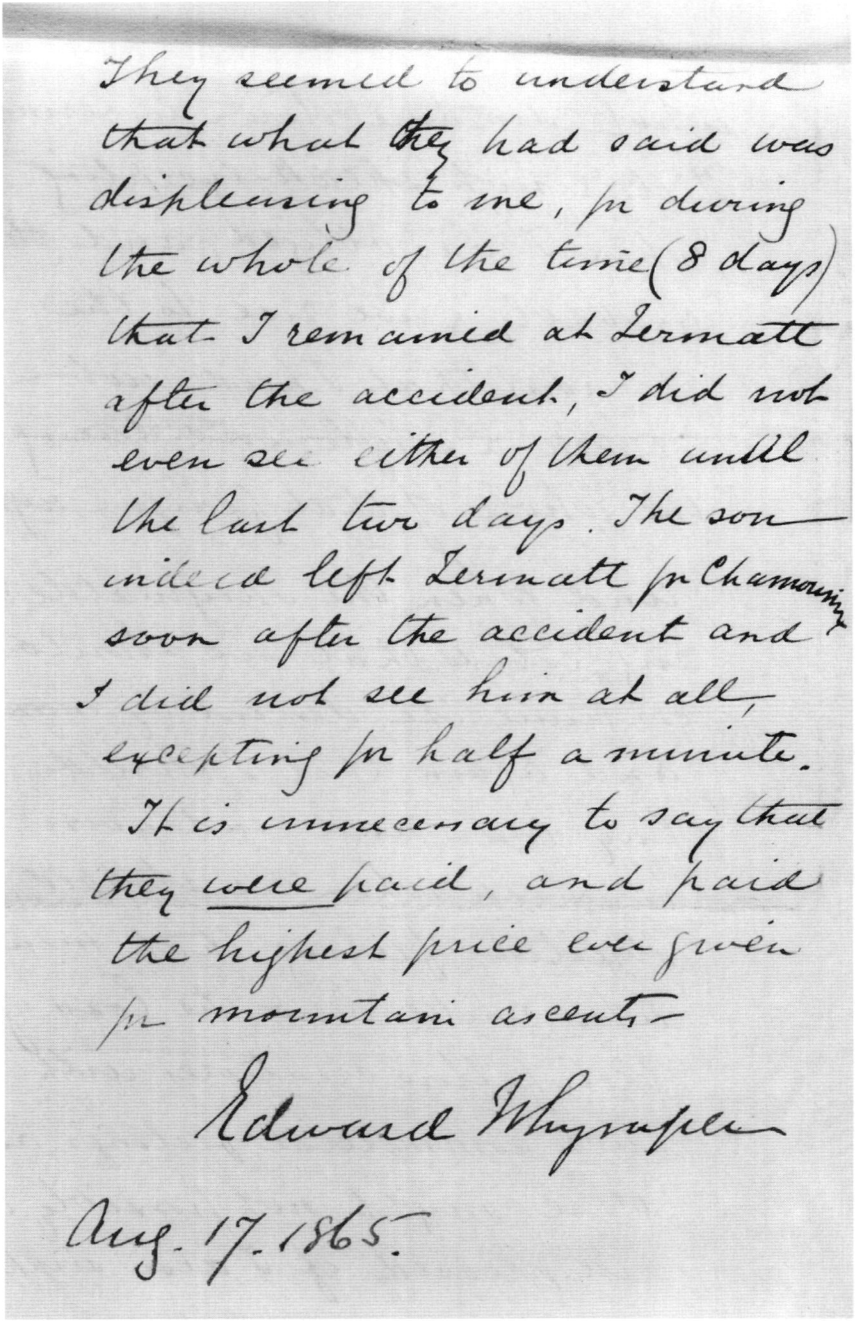

They seemed to understand that what they had said was displeasing to me, for during the whole of the time (8 days) that I remained at Zermatt after the accident, I did not even see either of them until the last two days. The son indeed left Zermatt for Chamounix soon after the accident and I did not see him at all, excepting for half a minute.

It is unnecessary to say that they were paid, and paid the highest price ever given for mountain ascents –

Edward Whymper

Aug. 17. 1865.

Whymper's memorandum of 17th August 1865

In his letter to *The Times* Whymper wrote how,

'For more than an hour afterwards I thought every moment would be my last; for the Taugwalders utterly unnerved, were not only incapable of giving assistance, but were in such a state that a slip might have been expected at any moment. I do the younger man, moreover, no injustice when I say that immediately we got to the easy part of the descent he was able to laugh, smoke and eat as if nothing had happened. There is no occasion to say more of the descent.'

The day after *The Times* published this, he wrote in a letter to Wigram:

'I can however express to you privately, but it ought not to go to Croz, as it could do no possible good and would only add to the ill feeling of which I have spoken, my extreme dissatisfaction with both the Taugwalders, but particularly with the younger man. They not only showed a most unmanly fear for their own lives, but directly we got to the easy part of the descent showed a heartlessness that was perfectly revolting.'

There is further evidence of their misconduct in Whymper's memorandum of 17th August 1865, of which he published only the first part in *Scrambles*. This includes their reference to losing their employer [Douglas], not getting paid and being unable to afford that. Whymper interrupted Young Peter assuring him that he would pay them. They spoke together in patois and the son said:

' "We don't wish you to pay us. We wish you to write in the hotel-book at Zermatt, and to your journals, that we have not been paid." "What nonsense are you talking? I don't understand you. What do you mean?" He proceeded, "Why, next year there will be many travellers at Zermatt, and we shall get more voyageurs." '

Whymper omitted from *Scrambles* the remainder of the memorandum:

'I was so disgusted with this heartless talk that for the whole distance down to Zermatt I did not speak – excepting when I was obliged, and this probably gave rise to the rumour that I had not uttered a single word during the whole of that fearful night. And when the Taugwalders suggested that we should continue the descent by moonlight, and again that I should lay down and endeavour to sleep when we stopped, I objected, feeling that men who could view the loss of their fellow creatures with such commercial feelings as these, might not, possibly, be ill pleased if I also slipped. They seemed to understand that what they had said was displeasing to me, for during the whole of the time (8 days) that I remained at Zermatt after the accident, I did not even see either of them until the last two days. The son indeed left Zermatt for Chamonix soon after the accident and I did not see him at all excepting for half a minute. It is unnecessary to say that they *were* paid, and paid the highest price ever given for mountain ascents.' *[The rumour of not speaking a word all night appears in Mme. Gautier's letter in the Journal de Genève of 20.7.65 – see section 2.36 (Martin).]*

Yet further evidence in somewhat blunter terms appears in the Cowell memorandum, which Whymper himself did not write, did not publish and did not in fact acknowledge as true or accurate, although it might be said that it differs only in detail from his own memorandum and that there is no reason to suppose that it misrepresented what the Cowells had recorded when they questioned him on 2nd August. He was advised by the Cowells and by Alfred Wills to publish all he knew about the Taugwalders, but he did not do so and this suggests that as the months and the years went by he was prepared to forgive their heartless conduct, viewing it perhaps as a peculiar psychological reaction to an utterly appalling experience, by means of which they had tried to relieve their tension and anxiety by pretending to make light of the incident and by conspiring against the foreigner in their midst.

But then something happened, and although Whymper had no reason to alter his opinion of Young Peter's climbing ability and may not have bothered to redraw the Clubroom of Zermatt without him, he had second thoughts and added further comment in a footnote in *Scrambles*. As mentioned below it seems probable that the footnote in question, which relates primarily to Old Peter, was based on information Whymper learnt in 1869 from someone like Seiler. It refers sympathetically to Old Peter being incapable of work and pays tribute to his reaction on the happening of the accident – 'Not only was his act at the critical moment wonderful as a feat of strength, but it was admirable in its performance at the right time' – and then the footnote changes key:

> 'In respect to Young Peter, it is not possible to speak in the same manner. The odious idea that he propounded (which I believe emanated from him) he has endeavoured to trade upon, in spite of the fact that his father was paid (for both) in the presence of witnesses. Whatever may be his abilities as a guide, he is not one to whom I would ever trust my life, or afford any countenance.'

No critic has ever sought to contradict the fact that Young Peter endeavoured to trade upon the idea of non-payment, although Egger reacted strangely to it as is mentioned below, and there is not the slightest reason to doubt that it is true. It is understandable that Whymper should have reacted to it in the way he seems to have done, as if he had previously been inclined to give Young Peter the benefit of any slight doubt, he would suddenly have realised his error and that Young Peter had not been so overcome by the shock of the accident that he did not know what he was saying. Furthermore if Whymper had intended that the 20frs tip, which he himself bore in full and did not share with the relatives of the victims, should go to Young Peter in whole or in part, he would have been particularly dismayed or incensed at his ingratitude, not knowing as we do to-day that Old Peter had kept it all. There are some other incidents that suggest that Young Peter was not the same straightforward sort of character as his father (see section 2.53.2), and with more than one entry in his Führerbuch describing him as 'very intelligent' it seems as though he may from time to time have used his wits to act with complete disregard for the welfare or feelings of others for his own selfish ends. But his endeavour to trade upon the idea of not being paid does at least dispose once and for all of the claim by some critics that Whymper misunderstood his conversation with Young Peter after the accident.

(c) *Old Peter, pre-accident conduct*

There is an incident in 1861 which Whymper recorded in *Scrambles*, which Egger sought to make a lot of but which hardly reflected adversely against Old Peter until undue attention was drawn to it. It was when Whymper and an Oberland guide were looking for another guide at Breuil to accompany them on the Matterhorn and various well-known guides all refused to go. 'A sturdy old fellow – Peter Taugwalder by name – said he would go! His price? "Two hundred francs." "What, whether we ascend or not?" "Yes – nothing less." ' Whymper had written of Carrel's fees just before, 'Twenty francs a day, whatever the result, was his price'. He also wrote how 'The end of the matter was, that all the men who were more or less capable showed a strong disinclination, or positively refused to go (their disinclination being very much in proportion to their capacity), or else asked a prohibitive price'. It seems that Old Peter was in the latter category and that Whymper only mentioned him by name as he was to feature later in the story. But Egger attacks Whymper for treating 'the old fellow's offer as ridiculous' and says that it was his intention to make him look ridiculous. He refers sarcastically to Whymper using the royal 'we', when in fact Whymper wrote 'My guide and I arrived at Breuil...' and then a few lines later 'We endeavoured to induce another man to accompany us, but without success'. But Egger's most misleading comment to his German readers, who would not have Whymper's original text before them, comes next when he states: 'Nowhere is it stated that Taugwalder mentioned this high price at all'.

Whereas it seems fair to treat Old Peter's demand as just one example of those who asked a prohibitive price, a closer look at his attitude to fees suggests that he may well have expected or demanded to be paid well above the normal rates for any climb likely to present anything well above the normal difficulties to which he was accustomed as a good Monte Rosa guide; see section 3.6.1 (Guides fees) and section 2.38 (Parkers). Old Peter's adverse reaction to Whymper's payment for the first ascent of the Matterhorn of 'the highest price ever given for mountain ascents' reflects against him and his ability to cope with the difficulties, and this (quite apart from other factors) must have excluded him from ever attempting the mountain again once the official tariff was fixed at the same sum of 100 francs; but Whymper would not have known what Old Peter had said to Charles Parker and so he made no comment on the wider implications. This is a typical example of a critic taking a bad point and trying to hold it against Whymper, when further enquiry reveals only further vulnerability on the part of Taugwalder. It would not have been necessary to relate the 200frs incident cited by Whymper to Old Peter's actual Matterhorn fees or to the Parker conversation, had Egger not distorted the situation. His intention may have been to defend Old Peter, but the effect is to draw attention to faults that Whymper never mentioned.

There is one other pre-accident issue that has been wrongly regarded by some critics as an attack on Old Peter or as an accusation against him by Whymper. It is far more complex than Egger's 200frs issue, and its distortion since Whymper's death and particularly in the last 60 years has been accompanied by misquotation, confusion of context and loss of perspective. It is the question as to how Old Peter came to use the weakest rope to tie himself to Douglas. It is referred to in other sections including 3.4 and 5.4.2 (The Enquiry), 3.16 (The special rope), 2.14.5 (Douglas) and 2.52.6 (Old Peter Taugwalder), and specific errors by the critics are for the most part dealt with under the name of the critic concerned. Here it is necessary to look first at what Whymper actually wrote on the subject.

(c) i *The rope that broke*

In the written answers Whymper prepared in response to the questions given to him in advance of the Enquiry by Clemenz, which he subsequently handed in and read out in reply to Clemenz' recital of the same questions, he said nothing of the rope that broke, apart from A10 which included 'Between Lord Douglas and Taugwalder father the rope was less thick than between Michel Croz and Lord Douglas on the one side and Taugwalder father and Taugwalder son on the other side'. Only six weeks later Old Peter complained to Charles Parker, and Parker subsequently recorded: 'Taugwalder says that Whymper behaved ill, especially in the colouring he gave to his evidence at Zermatt, wh. has damaged Taugwalder'. Whatever this may have been referring to it can hardly have related to what he said about the rope that broke, which was a straightforward matter of fact; and if it was accurately communicated to Taugwalder, he could hardly have been upset to hear it, nor could he possibly have reckoned to be damaged by it. It is however possible that he was referring to the questions that Whymper handed in for him to answer, but it is unlikely that Taugwalder would have been told more than his cousin judge Julen disclosed to him and if he misrepresented the situation, that would be nothing to do with Whymper. The Whymper questions that related to the rope that broke, before someone distorted them, were Q26, 27, 28, 29 & 34. They were not leading questions, not even Q28 – coming as it did after A24 – and the fact that Whymper handed them in may have been more Clemenz' idea than his own, as already stated. The only way it would seem Old Peter could have been damaged following anything Whymper said or did in relation to the Enquiry, would be if Clemenz had subsequently stopped recommending him to his hotel guests as a guide. But as Clemenz did nothing to ensure that the questions were answered, and even allowed some of them to become so distorted in the course of translation into German that they became futile, he can hardly have reacted against Old Peter on account of Whymper. It is much more likely that if Clemenz did stop giving Old Peter business, of which there is no direct evidence, it would have been because Old Peter's cousin Julen the Zermatt judge put such pressure on Clemenz to avoid enquiring as to the adequacy of or the reason for using the rope that broke, that Clemenz became exasperated and later reacted against Taugwalder; but again that could not be Whymper's fault. Alternatively the conflict of interests confronting hotelier/judge Clemenz may have led to any such reaction.

In his letter to von Fellenberg Whymper may have complained of the snoring of the Taugwalder family the night before they made the ascent, but he made no mention of there being more than one sort of rope and said only that the rope broke in mid-air, mid-way between Taugwalder and Lord F. Douglas. The subsequent letter which Whymper 'was forced – most unwillingly, to write to *The Times*' is the only other public account he gave prior to the publication of *Scrambles* in 1871, so that if, as some critics have suggested without quoting any evidence in support, Old Peter's career as a guide was destroyed by the suspicion or 'accusation' of Whymper that he used the weak rope intentionally, the *Times* letter would have to be to blame, as his career seems almost to have come to an end by 1869.

The *Times* letter referred to the different types of rope, the Alpine Club rope, secondly a kind Whymper believed to be stronger and thirdly 'more than 200ft. of a lighter and weaker rope than the first, of a kind used by myself until the Club rope was produced'. After detailing events up to the happening of the accident the letter continued:

> 'Immediately we had descended to a safe place I asked for the rope that had broken, and to my surprise – indeed, to my horror – found that it was the weakest of the three ropes. As the first five men had been tied while I was sketching, I had not noticed the rope they employed, and now I could only conclude that they had seen fit to use this in preference to the others.'

After referring to the search party reaching the glacier and finding three bodies, Whymper continued:

> 'To my astonishment, I saw that all of the three had been tied with the Club, or with the second and equally strong, rope, and consequently there was only one link – that between Taugwalder and Lord F. Douglas – in which the weaker rope had been used...
> I was detained in Zermatt until the 22nd of July, to await the inquiry instituted by the Government. I was examined first, and at the close I handed into the Court a number of questions which I desired should be put to the elder Taugwalder; doing so because that which I had found out respecting the ropes was by no means satisfactory to me. The questions, I was told, were put and answered before I left Zermatt; but I was not allowed to be present at the inquiry, and the answers although promised, have not yet reached me.'

The *Times* letter therefore made no 'accusation' against Old Peter, nor did it express any 'suspicion', but merely stated the facts and that Whymper was not satisfied about the ropes and had handed in some questions, which had been put to Taugwalder although the answers had not yet reached him. No doubt if Whymper's actual questions had been put and Taugwalder had been allowed to answer them and Clemenz had kept his promise, Whymper would have told the Editor of *The Times* and everyone would have been satisfied. No one would have thought the worse of Old Peter for what they had read, and his former career as a good Monte Rosa guide could not possibly have been affected. As for any prospect of extending his career by taking advantage of the publicity and gaining a reputation as a Matterhorn guide, it seems that this was always beyond his capabilities and that Dangar & Blakeney summed up the situation correctly when they wrote: 'Looking to his past record, one is inclined to think that it was unfortunate that Old Peter was engaged by Douglas in 1865, for it took him out of his class'.

(c) ii *The ugly look*

In *Scrambles* Whymper slightly altered the two passages quoted above referring to his discovery that the weakest rope had been used, so that the first reads:

> 'I asked for the rope which had given way, and found, to my surprise – indeed, to my horror – that it was the weakest of the three ropes. It was not brought, and should not have been employed, for the purpose for which it was used. It was old rope, and, compared with the others, was feeble. It was intended as a reserve, in case we had to leave much rope behind, attached to rocks. I saw at once that a serious question was involved, and made him give me the end. It had broken in mid-air, and it did not appear to have sustained previous injury.'

The second passage reads:

> 'All those who had fallen had been tied with the Manilla, or with the second and equally strong rope, and, consequently, there had been only one link – that between old Peter and Lord Francis Douglas – where the weaker rope had been used. This had a very ugly look for Taugwalder, for it was not possible to suppose that the others would have sanctioned the employment of a rope so greatly inferior in strength when there were more than two hundred and fifty feet of the better qualities still remaining out of use. For the sake of the old guide (who bore a good reputation), and upon all other accounts, it was desirable that this matter should be cleared up; and after my examination before the court of inquiry which was instituted by the Government was over, I handed in a number of questions which were framed so as to afford Old Peter an opportunity of exculpating himself from the grave suspicions which at once fell upon him. The questions, I was told, were put and answered; but the answers, although promised, have never reached me.'

Dangar & Blakeney wrote in 1957 how Whymper's remarks about the very ugly look for Taugwalder had always seemed to them uncalled for. They referred to his mention in the Taugwalder footnote in *Scrambles*

> 'of the suspicious fact that this rope between Old Peter and Douglas "was the thinnest and weakest one that we had". By making these comments, Whymper inevitably accentuated a

suggestion of foul play, though it is only fair to him to say that the Zermatt guides also are said to have accused Taugwalder...Farrar opined that there was "some justification" for Whymper's words.'

This is a reference to Farrar having written in 1920 how 'Whymper alludes to "the suspicious fact" that this weaker rope was used by Taugwalder, and there is some justification for the words, since it was *only between old Peter and Douglas* that it was used'. In 1966 Dangar & Blakeney commented further:

'Whymper's use of the phrase "ugly look" in connexion with the use of the weak rope (when there was ample good rope available) may be regretted, since it has occasioned so much heart burning. Yet in fact the term was not inaccurate; there is a sense in which it did have an ugly look, but this is not to say that Whymper was saying in effect that there had been dirty work done. He was stating how the matter *looked*.'

The point about Whymper's use of words like 'suspicious' is not that he was expressing his own opinion, in the way that someone might comment a century later 'it is very suspicious that Taugwalder should have used the weakest rope when there were strong ropes available'. He was stating the fact that the existence of only one link where the weaker rope had been used *had caused suspicion*. He referred expressly to 'the grave suspicions which at once fell upon [Taugwalder]'. It has even been suggested that, as Whymper was the only one who noticed that the weak rope had been used, he should have kept it to himself (and, presumably, should also have destroyed the evidence!) so that no one else would have suspected that it might have been used intentionally. Not only would such dishonesty have been completely out of character for Whymper but it is naïve to suppose that no one else knew or that anyone could have anticipated that the authorities would not have carried out any investigation into the circumstances of the accident or even that they would have turned a blind eye to the fact that the rope that broke was greatly inferior in quality to the other ropes used. There was also a real possibility that Douglas's body might be found with the weak rope attached to it. In *Scrambles* Whymper was reiterating the account he gave to *The Times* with some additional paragraphs and a few corrections. There was therefore no question of his deleting reference to the unexplained use of the weak rope, and he was updating his readers with the news that Clemenz had still not provided any answers from Taugwalder 'exculpating himself from the grave suspicions which at once fell on him'. He appears to have updated his readers again a year or so before *Scrambles* was published by adding the footnote (quoted below) implying that Taugwalder's near incapacity for work was attributable to Clemenz' allowing him to remain under unwarranted suspicion.

There is nothing to suggest that Whymper ever met Old Peter again, although when he left Zermatt in 1865 he seems to have left his tent and ropes with Seiler at the disposal of anyone who wanted to use them, and on 22nd September Seiler wrote saying that when the tent had been opened for Tyndall at the time he was going to look for Douglas the ropes were not there. Seiler's enquiries revealed that 'Pierre Taugwald' had taken them and not returned them and he asked what he should do. It seems likely that when Whymper was in Zermatt in August/September 1869 he learnt of Old Peter's misfortunes from Seiler, and that this must account for the long footnote in *Scrambles*. This is Whymper's most important comment on the Taugwalders, and it seems that his critics have been relying primarily on it when trying to blame Whymper for the misfortunes that had caught up with Old Peter two or three years before *Scrambles* was even published. It has been misquoted and parts have also been taken out of their context. The footnote has also been wrongly blamed for causing Old Peter to have to go to America.

(c) iii *The Taugwalder footnote*

The original wording appears in *Scrambles* 1st & 2nd edns. p404, 3rd edn. p294.

> 'This is not the only occasion upon which M.Clemenz (who presided over the inquiry) has failed to give up answers that he has promised. It is greatly to be regretted that he does not feel that the suppression of the truth is equally against the interests of travellers and of the guides. If the men are untrustworthy, the public should be warned of the fact; but if they are blameless, why allow them to remain under unwarranted suspicion?
>
> Old Peter Taugwalder is a man who is labouring under an unjust accusation. Notwithstanding repeated denials, even his comrades and neighbours at Zermatt persist in asserting or insinuating that he *cut* the rope which led from him to Lord F. Douglas. In regard to this infamous charge, I say that he *could* not do so at the moment of the slip, and that the end of the rope in my possession shows that he did not do so beforehand. There remains, however, the suspicious fact that the rope which broke was the thinnest and weakest one that we had. It is suspicious, because it is unlikely that any of the four men in front would have selected an old and weak rope when there was abundance of new, and much stronger, rope to spare; and, on the other hand, because if Taugwalder thought that an accident was likely to happen, it was to his interest to have the weaker rope where it was placed.
>
> I should rejoice to learn that his answers to the questions which were put to him were satisfactory. Not only was his act at the critical moment wonderful as a feat of strength, but it was admirable in its performance at the right time. I am told that he is now nearly incapable for work – not absolutely mad, but with intellect gone and almost crazy; which is not to be wondered at, whether we regard him as a man who contemplated a scoundrelly meanness, or as an injured man suffering under an unjust accusation.
>
> In respect to young Peter, it is not possible to speak in the same manner. The odious idea that he propounded (which I believe emanated from *him*) he has endeavoured to trade upon, in spite of the fact that his father was paid (for both) in the presence of witnesses. Whatever may be his abilities as a guide, he is not one to whom I would ever trust my life, or afford any countenance.'

Apart from the reference to Young Peter, already considered above, it is a sad note expressing regret at Clemenz' suppression of the truth, with the result that in two quite separate cases guides remained under unwarranted suspicion. It seems likely that the note was written long after Whymper wrote the chapter in which it appears, and probably in mid 1870. The Lyskamm accident had happened in September 1869 only a fortnight after Whymper had made his second 'Matterhorn' entry inside the back cover of the Monte Rosa hotel guestbook, which was probably the occasion when he was told of Old Peter's condition and of Young Peter endeavouring to trade upon the idea of not having been paid. The Lyskamm article in the *Alpine Journal*, reviewing the evidence and referring to Clemenz' failure once more to keep a promise, was published in May 1870, based on a paper read to the Club in March, and Whymper would at that time have been particularly aware of the harm that Clemenz had caused. He would have realised that there was no longer the remotest prospect of Old Peter's replies being revealed and with the damage already done to Old Peter he was sympathising with him and setting out the facts of the matter. W.E.Hall's comments on Clemenz must have been reassuring to Whymper, coming as they did from a lawyer:

> 'For a long time expectation that M.Clemenz would fulfil his promise naturally and necessarily closed our mouths. But when more than six months have gone by...it becomes necessary...that the dilatory courtesy of M.Clemenz should no longer be waited for. I have no wish to express any opinion as to the conduct of M.Clemenz. I am content that my action should be sufficiently justified by the fact that like promises were made after the accident on the Matterhorn, and that they were never fulfilled...I cannot help uttering a protest, however useless it may be, against the secrecy which the character of M.Clemenz or that of Swiss law has imparted to the judicial inquiry.'

As the rope broke between Old Peter and the four who fell to their deaths, it was inevitable that everyone should have wanted to know how or why it broke, particularly as mountaineering was still in its infancy and very few people would know anything at all about the use of a rope. As *The Times* put it in its leader of 27th July, 'Above all things, their ropes must not break'. Arnold Lunn once wrote that 'The Matterhorn accident first popularised the theory that Alpine ropes existed to be cut' and it is easy to see how ignorance, envy or mischief could have led to the rumour that Old Peter cut the rope. There is evidence of it as early as Sunday 16th July, as Whymper wrote in the *Graphic* in 1894,

> 'No sooner had the survivors of the ill-fated expedition returned to Zermatt, than the baseless, monstrous rumour was circulated that the old man had cut the rope which broke. It passed from lip to lip, spreading like wildfire, and emanated from his own village amongst his neighbours. The calumniated man, walking about shunned like a murderer, met the returning volunteers. "Mr. R–," he said to one of them, "they say I *cut* the rope. Look at my fingers!" and, opening his hands, showed how they had been lacerated by the jerk which all but tore him from his grasp.'

It is probable that Whymper's informant was James Robertson, but there is plenty of other evidence of the rumour circulating soon after the accident. It had reached Croz' brother in Chamonix by August if not before, it formed the basis for the scurrilous article by Meissner in a Vienna newspaper at about the same time, and even Canon Carrel saw fit to mention in his book a discussion in 1866 about the circumstances in which cutting a rope could be justified. Whymper did his utmost to dismiss the absurdity, but the secrecy of the Clemenz Enquiry and its disregard of at least one plea from a Swiss newspaper to publish the evidence in order to dispel the rumour, allowed it to flourish.

Leslie Stephen in his review of *Scrambles* in *Macmillan's Magazine* provides contemporary comment on Whymper's denunciation of the cutting of the rope and goes on to refer to Old Peter's second problem:

> 'Mr.Whymper very properly denounces the absurd fable that the elder Taugwald cut the rope...But I rather regret that he should not reject decidedly another grave, though less serious accusation, which comes in fact to this, that Taugwald intentionally used a weak rope in fastening himself to Lord F. Douglas, in order to have a chance of being separated from him in case of accident. Knowing the carelessness too often displayed on such occasions, the confidence which guides will show in weak ropes, and the probable state of excitement of the whole party, which would easily account for such an oversight, I think that the hypothesis of deliberate intention on Taugwald's part is in the highest degree improbable; and there is not a particle of direct evidence in its favour. The presumption would be that Croz was almost equally responsible; and, at any rate, such accusations should have some more tangible ground than a vague possibility. A discussion of the point would be out of place here, and I venture upon this digression merely for the sake of an old guide, who has always had a high character, and, to the best of my knowledge, has well deserved it.'

Whymper no doubt shared Stephen's regret, in so far as he could not reject the idea that Old Peter intentionally used a weak rope, and we know from his letter of 9th August to Wigram that he had 'no reason to suspect even that this was done *intentionally*'. But there was a distinction between the two issues which Whymper could not blur. He knew for a fact that Old Peter did not cut the rope, having seen it break with his own eyes, but he did not know why he had used the weak rope. 'How it came to pass that the weakest rope was used between Taugwald and Lord Douglas I have no idea, that is, I have no idea why he did not use the stronger ropes.' It has been suggested by some critics that it was Whymper who raised the question of using the weak rope, but this ignores altogether the interest shown immediately after the accident by the friends and acquaintances of the victims and others in Zermatt and elsewhere, in how they came to use a rope that could break. 'It has been repeatedly asked, "Why was not the wire-rope taken which Mr.Hudson brought to Zermatt?" ', Whymper wrote in his letter to *The Times*; but the far more obvious question as to why one of the brand-new thicker ropes that were taken was not used in place of the old sashline that broke, must have been asked even more frequently. Whymper's answer to both was that he did not know.

The questions that he handed in to Clemenz for Old Peter to answer were primarily directed at the unexplained use of the weak rope and, as already suggested above, they cannot have been just his own idea. Whether Clemenz actually asked for them we may never know, but it does seem as though he delegated to Whymper the task of drafting questions relating to the controversial issues affecting the rope. Clemenz would know of the rumours that it was cut and he may have thought that it was better not to get himself involved in the question as to why it was ever used, little knowing perhaps at the time he promised to give Whymper the answers that someone was going to distort the questions to such an extent as to render them futile, and make it impossible for him ever to reveal the answers. Looking at Old Peter's evidence there is no reason to suppose that Clemenz ever became any the wiser as to why he had used the weak rope than he was when Whymper handed him the questions, apart from Old Peter volunteering in A24 that it was a special rope. Clemenz therefore knew no more than Whymper!

The *Sonntagspost*, a Bernese Sunday newspaper edited by Abraham Roth, a prominent Swiss mountaineer, commented on 20th August 1865 on Whymper's letter to *The Times* and on the use of the weak rope: 'Mr. Whymper himself states that the information he received respecting the ropes was by no means satisfactory to him and he therefore handed in to the Examining Magistrate in Zermatt a list of questions that should be put to Taugwalder, but he was still in ignorance of the answers, although their communication to him had been promised.' The newspaper went on to emphasise the need for the authorities in the Valais to publish the evidence in view of the malicious nonsense doing the rounds of the European press, but its plea was disregarded.

Whymper's reference to Old Peter's two problems was relevant to the cause of his being 'now nearly incapable for work – not absolutely mad, but with intellect gone and almost crazy'. His further comment 'which is not to be wondered at, whether we regard him as a man who contemplated a scoundrelly meanness, or as an injured man suffering under an unjust accusation' may seem superfluous and yet it serves the purpose of emphasising the link between Old Peter's incapacity and Clemenz' failure to disclose his answers. But there is another matter which may have contributed to Old Peter's mental state in about 1869, which is the death by drowning in the Schwarzsee in 1867 of his second son Joseph, as regardless of the circumstances it must surely have added to his depression, following so soon after the shock of his own two narrow escapes from death in July 1865.

The publication of *Scrambles* in 1871 could therefore hardly have aggravated Old Peter's condition or caused him to lose any business. On the contrary by bringing more tourists to Zermatt it provided him with yet further guiding opportunities of which he was unable to take advantage, although he did manage to accompany Lord Queensberry and Young Peter over the Theodule and Furggen passes in September that year. But indirectly, by encouraging more climbers to tackle the Matterhorn and helping the Zermatt guides to end their boycott of it, with Peter Perren climbing it in 1871 and Young Peter in 1872, it no doubt increased the local animosity towards Old Peter. For the Zermatt guides must have begun to realise too late to do anything very much about it, that they had quite unnecessarily given the guides of St.Niklaus a monopoly of the Matterhorn in the valley, as a result of Old Peter's exaggeration of the difficulties and his inability to repeat the climb.

In the 4th edition of *Scrambles* published in 1893 Whymper changed the tenses in paragraph 2 of the Taugwalder footnote to read that Old Peter 'laboured for a long time under an unjust suspicion' and that his comrades and neighbours 'persisted' in asserting etc. The third sentence of paragraph 3 and the whole of paragraph 4 were deleted and replaced by: 'He left Zermatt, and lived for several years in retirement in the United States; but ultimately returned to his native valley and died suddenly on July 11, 1888, at the Lac Noir (Schwarzsee).' If Old Peter had been offended or adversely affected by anything Whymper had written in the original footnote, one might have expected some alteration to have been made in the 3rd edition, but in fact there is no sign whatever of his having taken the slightest notice of the book. Furthermore the German and French editions which incorporated the footnote in full so far as it affected Old Peter, and would have been more likely to come to Old Peter's attention than the English edition, seem never to have revised the original wording.

Some errors in the French and German translations appear to have led the critics astray at times. The French edition, for example, when referring to the rope and to Whymper finding to his surprise and indeed to his horror that '*it* was the weakest of the three ropes', states that he found 'avec horreur, que cette corde *maudite* était la plus faible'. Charles Gos adopted this as a chapter heading, 'La corde maudite', saying that 'The accursed rope' was Whymper's own expression, not realising that it was a mistake or invention of the translator. It was furthermore retained by Claire Engel in her new translation in 1944. Such errors are dealt with elsewhere under the name of the critic concerned, but there is one that should be mentioned here as it relates to Young Peter, and Carl Egger made use of it to try and denigrate Whymper. It is the error in the official German translation of *Scrambles*, first published in 1872 and apparently never corrected, which comes in the fourth paragraph of the Taugwalder footnote set out above. Ignoring the precise German wording for the sake of simplicity and translating it back into English using Whymper's original English words, the error involves the complete omission of Whymper's words – 'he has endeavoured to trade upon' – so that the second sentence effectively reads:

> 'The odious idea that he propounded (which I believe emanated from him), ⋆ in spite of the fact that his father was paid (for both) in the presence of witnesses.'

It does not make sense without the missing words at the point marked ⋆, as those words were the whole purpose of Whymper's sentence. In his book *Pioniere der Alpen*, Carl Egger relied very heavily on English sources for his chapters on Swiss guides, including the Taugwalders. The book is full of quotations which he has translated from the original English into German and there is no doubt that Egger was thoroughly familiar with Alpine literature including Whymper's *Scrambles*. In fact Egger made his own fresh German translation of some parts of the original Taugwalder footnote and referred to Whymper deleting certain things in the later editions. But as he approached the final paragraph referring to Young Peter and containing the sentence just quoted above, Egger resorted to the official (and defective) German translation. Although he did improve it slightly, he still quoted the sentence without the vital words 'he has endeavoured to trade upon'. He then commented on the resulting nonsense by stating that 'To set the proposition and the payment together in time as cause and effect is an incomprehensible chessmove by Whymper'.

But it seems inconceivable that Egger should have been unaware of the truth or that he innocently made a gross error in misquoting and condemning Whymper, particularly when in the very next sentence he resumed his own new German translation of Whymper's original English wording. His German readers would never have gone to the lengths of checking what Whymper actually wrote in English, and, judging by some of the other adverse things he wrote about Whymper without the slightest justification, it is hard to avoid the conclusion that he thought he would be able to get away with it. Rather than an incomprehensible chessmove by Whymper it seems to have been an own goal by Egger, revealing such malice that even Arnold Lunn, his most ardent anti-Whymper ally, seems to have turned a blind eye to it.

(d) *Old Peter, post-accident conduct*

Whymper wrote of Old Peter's instant reaction after Hadow's slip, in the long footnote in *Scrambles*: 'Not only was his act at the critical moment wonderful as a feat of strength, but it was admirable in its performance at the right time'. As for Old Peter being utterly unnerved after the accident, there is little to add to what has already been said about Young Peter except that Old Peter was far more badly affected than his son, due in part no doubt to the fact that he saw it happen. But his son seems to have been responsible for the heartless behaviour, Old Peter's fault perhaps being that he was prepared to go along with it, as he was in no fit state to dissociate himself or exert any influence for good. It seems as though Whymper was prepared to forgive Old Peter, despite the advice of the Cowells and Wills, and that he went out of his way to try and scotch the rumour that Old Peter had cut the rope. When Wigram wrote to him on 8th August stating that he had received a letter from J-B Croz 'in which he speaks of a suspicion prevalent in the Valley of Chamonix, and I fear shared by himself that Taugwald *cut the rope* on the Matterhorn', he not only replied by return 'the rumour is absolutely without foundation', but wrote to Croz himself, saying to Wigram, 'I think it would be desirable for you to write to Croz as well as myself, and pray give him my most positive assurance that there is not the slightest reason for suspecting that there was any foul play with the rope'.

2.57.11 Advice not to shield the Taugwalders

Several of Whymper's friends and acquaintances seem to have reacted in the same sort of way to what he wrote about the Taugwalders in his letter to *The Times*. Wm. Longman the publisher wrote to him on 9th August, his opening sentences being:

> 'I read your letter in the *Times* with very great interest, and I think it was written with great discretion and good feeling. You were quite right to say no more about those wretched Taugwalders, but their conduct ought to be made known somehow. Of course it will be expected that some account should appear in the *Alpine Journal*, but, for the next number, I fear it is too late to do more than print your letter.'

Alfred Wills also wrote to Whymper on 9th August thanking him for his prompt and effectual reply to his request. His letter of 20th August acknowledging Whymper's memorandum of 17th August (and a letter which has not survived) included:

> 'I take a little different view from you as to the desirability of saving the Taugwalders from the natural & proper consequence of their scandalous conduct. So much do *I* feel this that I was intending to write to you and say that your narrative left on my mind the strong impression that in this respect there was something behind wh. I intended to urge you when you wrote for the Journal to set forth. I think a great deal of mischief is done by shielding fellows like this. They get quite enough of that at Zermatt & amongst their own people, and it is greatly for the *public* benefit that people of this sort shd. be *exposed*... These Taugwalders are not fit to be trusted – & the world ought to know it: & I think myself, if you will pardon me for saying so, that you will make a great mistake if you hesitate to speak of them as they should be spoken of.'

J.W.Cowell expressed a similar view in the course of correspondence leading to the creation of his own memorandum. His letter to Whymper of 11th August included:

> 'I might have repressed my desire to signify my sentiments on what to you must be so very painful a subject had I not observed that you had passed over in your narrative, some points in the demeanour of the Taugwalds which I venture to think it is due to yourself that you should consign to writing exactly in the manner in which you related them to my son and myself at this house on Wednesday 2nd of August.'

In a further letter of 4th September Cowell wrote:

> 'I sympathize with the feeling which leads us as Englishmen, on every occasion of service to

> us in disaster, to be over generous in reward or compensation but on this occasion I think it was – if I may take the liberty of saying so – a duty devolving on you in the odious circumstances of the conduct of the Taugwalders, to have repressed every emotion of generosity...
> But I...hope that you will be called upon to publish all you know about the Taugwalders, and I trust that the Club will, upon consideration of the matter, invite you to do so.'

It would be interesting to know how the hostile critics would have reacted had Whymper heeded this advice, having regard to the way they have overreacted to what little he did publish about the Taugwalders' conduct. Attitudes and conventions change from one generation to the next and the fundamental flaw in the critics' approach to the Cowell memorandum and to Whymper's own memorandum of 17th August, quite apart from their ignorance as to the circumstances in which they came to be made, is that they seek to judge by the standards of 1940 or later, as though Whymper himself was still alive and had just decided to publish them. It may well be that Wills was right and that Whymper made 'a great mistake' in not speaking of the Taugwalders in the way that the majority of his generation might have thought 'they should be spoken of'. But he certainly did not deserve to get the worst of both worlds by exercising restraint and showing, perhaps, greater humanity than those whom history may have treated with more respect, only to be accused a century later by some ignorant critics of having 'attacked' the Taugwalders. It may not be a bad thing that critics should find fault in the standards of an earlier generation, when such standards have subsequently been raised, but they serve no purpose but their own if they temporarily distort the perspective by using a metric yardstick.

2.57.12 His accounts of the accident

(a) *The von Fellenberg and Rimini letters*

Whymper intended that his letter to von Fellenberg should be published in the *Journal de Genève* and in *Der Bund*, stating in a covering letter, 'I cannot bring myself to write to the newspapers respecting this sad affair, but it seems to me, there is no impropriety in addressing this letter to you, and its being published by you. It is, I am sure you will feel with me, highly desirable, that a correct account of it should be made known to the public.'

He arranged for French and German translations to be made by Peter Ober of the Pension Schlössli in Interlaken, but owing to von Fellenberg's absence in the mountains there was some delay in his receiving the letter and the original plan was never carried out. The letter was passed to Abraham Roth and quoted extensively in the Bern newspaper he edited, the *Sonntagspost* of 13th August 1865. Roth's article relating the account given in the letter was already in the press when Whymper's letter to *The Times* was published on 8th August, so that it had less impact than might otherwise have been the case. Whymper asked that his letter of 26th July to G.B.Rimini the secretary of the Italian Alpine Club, in the same terms, be communicated to members of the Club, and this was done in the first number of the Club's *Bolletino*. The date of publication is not clear, but it cannot have been prior to September 1865, as the same *Bolletino* contains reference to a Geneva newspaper of 30th August.

It seems that Whymper had decided in Zermatt to make no other communication to the press and he certainly did not give any interview while he was there, judging from the inaccuracies in almost every early account. His letter of 27th August to Robertson says in relation to his letter to *The Times* being a difficult one to write, 'I would have stuck to the resolution I made at Zermatt had it been possible, but it was not'.

(b) *Letter to The Times*

Whymper was in communication with the Editor of *The Times* for more than a week before his letter was published. On 2nd August it published a short note at his request:

> 'THE ACCIDENT ON THE MATTERHORN. We are requested to state, upon the best authority, that Lord Francis Douglas did not make the fatal slip which caused the lamentable accident on the Matterhorn.'

The same day the Editor wrote to Whymper:

> 'The Editor of *The Times* presents his compliments to Mr.Whymper and begs to suggest that the public will expect from him a much more detailed account of the lamentable catastrophe on the Matterhorn than the bare contradiction of one unimportant statement which at Mr.Whymper's request he has published to-day.
> As the only English survivor, the only one capable of explaining what really occurred, the Editor trusts he will not appeal in vain to Mr.Whymper for the full explanation which is so anxiously expected.'

Whymper replied on about 4th August:

> 'I regret that my absence from Haslemere has prevented an earlier reply to your note of 2nd inst.
> I had hoped that the letters of the Revd. J.McCormick would have been sufficient for the information of the public, although they were intentionally silent on certain points, including the exact cause of the accident, in order to spare the families of Messrs Hadow & Hudson the additional pain they must feel if it is published.
> It appears however that the cause of this silence is misunderstood and I have, in consequence, requested an enquiry on the part of the Alpine Club into the causes of the accident. I cannot say if my request will be granted, but if it is the report cannot be presented in less time than three weeks.
> As a matter of taste I should have preferred any information from myself coming before the public as the result of an enquiry on the part of the Alpine Club, but should you consider it undesirable to delay it for so long a time, I will at once forward a plain statement of the facts.'

The Editor replied that he had no hesitation in advising him to make a plain statement of the facts without waiting for the intervention of the Alpine Club. It seems that Whymper had by now decided that he would have to give way and write to *The Times* and although no other letters pressing him to write seem to have survived there is one from Longman dated 7th August, which starts:

> 'On all sides I hear the opinion expressed that you should write an account of the sad expedition. I can quite understand how unwilling you must be to write about so distressing an occurrence, but it seems to me a duty to yourself to tell your own story. People wonder why you do not, & you are more likely to have blame cast upon you, most unjustly, if you are silent than if you relate what really occurred. In the latter case, it appears to me that the only ground on which you can possibly be open to blame is, for not more strongly opposing poor Hudson's wish to take Hadow on the expedition. But, would not almost everyone have yielded in like manner?'

Alfred Wills, the President of the Alpine Club in 1865, seems to have been put in the picture by Cowell junior before writing privately to Whymper for the first time on 6th August, enclosing another letter dated 7th and advising him to write an account of the accident in reply, so that he could then send both letters to *The Times*. Such an arrangement in fact coincided with what Whymper himself had suggested previously to von Fellenberg, when he could 'not bring [himself] to write to the newspapers', but having corresponded with the Editor he no doubt felt it was better to address his letter to him rather than to Wills. Nevertheless Wills' formal letter to Whymper of 7th was published alongside Whymper's in *The Times* on 8th August. Wills letter of 6th included:

> 'I would have liked to write to you before but I felt sure that would happen which Cowell tells me has happened and that you would be exposed to positive torture from the inquisitive and the rude and the thoughtless, and I almost feared to take up my pen and write to you.
>
> There is, however, in my judgment only one way to put an end to all this – Give your own account; let it be truthful, manly and unflinching – wherever blame is due / if blame there be / let it rest – but don't let people go on conjecturing the worst and talking and writing in the feeblest and most ignorant and most uncharitable manner when you could silence the greater part of it all by your utterance. To some extent the Club is on trial. People are daily writing to abuse us and our doings. I don't care greatly about it myself, but still it does not do for a body of men associated for any purpose to let needless aspersions fall thick and threefold upon them. It is a great deal better for us – as it always is for everybody under all circumstances as I venture to think – to have the whole truth known and *then* let people make what they will of it.
>
> I think the same observations apply with tenfold force to yourself – you will be open to all sorts of misconstruction if you *don't* give an account. After all you have gone through, you will perhaps think this a very small matter, but let us, your friends, whose judgment is not disturbed, as yours can hardly fail to be, by the mental suffering you have gone through, judge a little for you in this matter.
>
> The A.C. Journal is published on the 1st September. What I would ask you to do, would be

THE TIMES, TUESDAY, AUGUST 8, 1865.

THE MATTERHORN ACCIDENT.

TO THE EDITOR OF THE TIMES.

Sir,—After the direct appeals which I have received from the President of the Alpine Club and from yourself to write an account of the accident on the Matterhorn, I feel it is impossible to remain silent any longer, and I therefore forward to you for publication a plain statement of the accident itself and of the events that preceded and followed it.

On Wednesday morning, the 12th of July, Lord Francis Douglas and myself crossed the Col Theodule to seek guides at Zermatt. After quitting the snow on the northern side we rounded the foot of the glacier, crossed the Furgge glacier, and left my tent, ropes, and other matters in the little chapel at the Lac Noir. We then descended to Zermatt, engaged Peter Taugwalder, and gave him permission to choose another guide. In the course of the evening the Rev. Charles Hudson came into our hotel with a friend, Mr. Hadow, and they, in answer to some inquiries, announced their intention of starting to attack the Matterhorn on the following morning. Lord Francis Douglas agreed with me it was undesirable that two independent parties should be on the mountain at the same time, with the same object. Mr. Hudson was therefore invited to join us, and he accepted our proposal. Before admitting Mr. Hadow I took the precaution to inquire what he had done in the Alps, and, as well as I remember, Mr. Hudson's reply was, "Mr. Hadow has done Mont Blanc in less time than most men." He then mentioned several other excursions that were unknown to me, and added, in answer to a further question, "I consider he is a sufficiently good man to go with us." This was an excellent certificate given us, as it was by a first-rate mountaineer, and Mr. Hadow was admitted without any further question. We then went into the matter of guides. Michael Croz was with Messrs. Hadow and Hudson, and the latter thought if Peter Taugwalder went as well that there would not be occasion for any one else. The question was referred to the men themselves, and they made no objection.

We left Zermatt at 5 35 on Thursday morning, taking the two young Taugwalders as porters, by the desire of their father. They carried provisions ment of the party. We agreed that it would be best for Croz to go first, as he was the most powerful, and Hadow second; Hudson, who was equal to a guide in sureness of foot, wished to be third; Lord F. Douglas was placed next, and old Taugwalder, the strongest of the remainder, behind him. I suggested to Hudson that we should attach a rope to the rocks on our arrival at the difficult bit, and hold it as we descended, as an additional protection. He approved the idea, but it was not definitely settled that it should be done. The party was being arranged in the above order while I was making a sketch of the summit, and they were waiting for me to be tied in my place, when some one remembered that we had not left our names in a bottle; they requested me to write them, and moved off while it was being done. A few minutes afterwards I tied myself to young Taugwalder and followed, catching them just as they were commencing the descent of the difficult part described above. The greatest care was being taken. Only one man was moving at a time; when he was firmly planted the next advanced, and so on. The average distance between each was probably 20 feet. They had not, however, attached the additional rope to rocks, and nothing was said about it. The suggestion was made entirely on account of Mr. Hadow, and I am not sure it even occurred to me again.

I was, as I have explained, detached from the others, and following them; but after about a quarter of an hour Lord F. Douglas asked me to tie on to old Taugwalder, as he feared, he said, that if there was a slip Taugwalder would not be able to hold him. This was done hardly ten minutes before the accident, and undoubtedly saved Taugwalder's life.

As far as I know, at the moment of the accident no one was actually moving. I cannot speak with certainty, neither can the Taugwalders, because the two leading men were partially hidden from our sight by an intervening mass of rock. Poor Croz had laid aside his axe, and in order to give Mr. Hadow greater security was absolutely taking hold of his legs and putting his feet, one by one, into their proper positions. From the movements of their shoulders it is my belief that Croz, having done as I have said, was in the act of turning round to go down a step or two himself; at this moment Mr. Hadow slipped, fell on him, and knocked him over. I heard one startled exclamation from Croz, then saw him and Mr. Hadow flying downwards; in another moment Hudson was dragged from his steps and Lord F. Douglas immediately after him. All this was the work of a moment; but immediately we heard Croz's exclamation Taugwalder and myself planted ourselves as firmly as the rocks would permit; *the rope was tight* down one man after another and bring destruction on all; but if the rope is tight this is all but impossible. I am, Sir, your obedient servant,

Haslemere, Aug. 7. EDWARD WHYMPER.

The following letter has been addressed to Mr. Whymper by the President of the Alpine Club:—

"Dear Whymper,—I cannot refrain from asking you to accept the assurance of my deep and heartfelt sympathy with you in the terrible and afflicting circumstances in which you have so lately been placed; and I advisedly name yourself first, for there are few men who would not feel that in many respects it were more tolerable to be of the lost than of the survivors. If the sympathy and confidence of your friends can be of any avail, I think I may assure you you will have it freely; for I think it will not be suspected by any one who knows you that with two such mountaineers as yourself and Hudson of the party any reasonable precaution was likely to be neglected, so far as you and he, at all events, were concerned. I speak only of you and him, because I did not know the others. Hudson I did know, and therefore know that there never was a man who had a more active frame, a more steady hand, or head, or foot, a firmer mind in danger, or a more keen and scrupulous sense of right and wrong. A man more unlikely rashly or inconsiderately to put in jeopardy his own life and that of others I never knew, and this not because he feared danger when it came in a proper way, but because he appreciated too highly the ties that bound him for the sake of himself and others to life and to duty.

"But may I make an appeal to you to relieve those who take an interest in this sad matter from the state of anxiety and suspense in which your own silence—a silence which I at once understand and respect—has kept us? It is impossible now to get together the committee, and therefore I hope I am not taking too much on myself, as President of the Alpine Club, to make the request which I know the committee would make—namely, that you should give us a full and detailed account of the accident, and the causes which led to it. You will remember that once before, when a fatal accident happened to one of a party, of which a member of the Club was also one, the committee took all the means in their power to investigate the affair, in the hope that from so lamentable an experience warning and instruction for the future, if nothing more, might be gathered. I am sure you will feel that it is only right and proper that the Club should exercise this kind of friendly jurisdiction over its members, and will do justice to yourself and to your companions in misfortune by giving us a faithful and fearless narrative of this deplorable disaster.

"Pray take this into your consideration, and if you can sufficiently command your feelings to face the painful task of narration, I hope you will accede to my request.

"Believe me, dear Whymper, yours most truly,

"ALFRED WILLS.

"E. Whymper, Esq., Inner Temple, Aug. 7."

Whymper's letter in *The Times* (extract)

to give an account both of the ascent and the accident in that number – but meanwhile to write a somewhat more considered account of the accident itself in answer to my letter and let me send both my letter and your answer to the *Times*.'

Other correspondence retained by Whymper throws further light on his letter to *The Times*. The following extracts are from letters written by him:

Letter 8.8.65. to Sir T.F.Buxton.

'I now beg to refer you to my letter in the *Times* of this day.
In my letter I scrupulously abstain from offering observations and casting blame on anyone, and also from taking notice of the remarks that have been made on my personal capability for the expedition we undertook...
Mr.Hadow was the sole cause of the accident. If any fault can be found with us it can only be for allowing him to go. If after what I have stated in the *Times* it is considered that I am to blame in the matter, I must bear the blame; but few men would have acted differently if they had been in the same position.'

Letter 23.8.65. to P.D.Hadow.

'I have endeavoured in all that I have done since this much lamentable accident, to avoid giving pain to yourself and to the relatives of Lord Douglas and Mr.Hudson.
I came home with a firm intention to print nothing and to say nothing. I found this was impossible. Most injurious rumours were circulated and I was forced – most unwillingly, to write to the *Times*; a more difficult and more painful task it is impossible to imagine.'

Letter 27.8.65. to the Rev James Robertson.

'You are right in supposing that letter was a difficult one to write. It appears to have given satisfaction to most people, but not to all, as I will show you one day. I would have stuck to the resolution I made at Zermatt had it been possible, but it was not, all kinds of pleasant * rumours were propagated and among them it was said that *I* cut the rope from fear of being pulled over. The amount of silly nonsense that was being written rendered it also desirable that I should write. Therefore after having received two letters from Wills pressing me to write, two from the Ed. of *Times* and a score of others from friends whose opinion I value more or less, I gave way.'
* *Note: 'pleasant' is not an error! See also Smythe pp218 & 236.*

(c) *Scrambles amongst the Alps*

The various editions of *Scrambles*, including the 3rd abridged edition with the title *The ascent of the Matterhorn*, are referred to in section 3.14.

(d) *The Graphic 1894 (25th September and 6th October)*

In an article called 'The Alps revisited' published in four parts, Whymper made some brief comments on the 1865 accident in the course of describing a month long expedition starting at Randa and finishing on Mont Blanc. He mentioned two incidents that had recently come to his knowledge and it is almost certain that James Robertson was his informant. The first related to Franz Andenmatten, who had been the first to volunteer to recover the bodies, 'a first rate mountaineer, who lived at Saas, beyond the jurisdiction of the priests of Zermatt...Next Sunday Franz Andermatten went to Mass, and this was his reward. "I saw him," said my informant (who is now Head Master of one of our public schools), "turned out, *ejected*, from the church at Zermatt!"' The second incident relates to the rumour Old Peter had cut the rope spreading like wildfire and to his meeting the party of volunteers on their return. '"Mr. R–," he said to one of them, "they say I *cut* the rope. Look at my fingers!" and, opening his hands, showed how they had been lacerated by the jerk which all but tore him from his grasp.'

The article also refers to Hadow by name, but not to Hudson, and emphasises how it is presupposed that everyone on a rope has acquired some proficiency in balancing, will move only one at a time in difficult places and that the rest will be on the look out to render assistance.

> 'There were two great faults committed on this occasion. The first was in allowing a very young and inexperienced man to go with us, who had not acquired the art of keeping on his legs. The second was the neglect of an ordinary measure of precaution.
> It is the habit of mountaineers now, and it was customary with them long before 1865, besides being tied together, to fix ropes and to hold them, as an additional protection against the consequences of a slip, when descending difficult places. The accident took place on a spot where rope ought to have been fixed, and if it had been fixed no accident would have happened...I have always regarded this accident as arising from divided responsibility, through no *one* person being in command of the party.'

(e) *Journal de Zermatt 1895 (25th August)*

It is not known exactly how this article came to be written, despite several references to it in Whymper's diary. But it seems probable that the idea of an interview came from Monod judging by the entry for Friday August 16th, which records seeing Monod in the evening and agreeing to visit him the next day. On the Saturday morning Whymper took Monod a letter, stating the conditions on which he would allow him to have him photographed, and after Monod had signed it they went to the right bank of the Mattervisp where the local photographer performed the task. Whymper then went with Monod to his office '& stopped until lunchtime dictating "the first ascent of the Matterhorn" while he wrote it down'. On the Monday he went back to Monod and spent the whole morning dictating – presumably in English. The article heading refers to the distinguished author passing through Zermatt and to having had the good fortune to interview him. The last sentence of the opening paragraph states 'We will let

JOURNAL DE ZERMATT 25 Aug 1895

Chronique de Zermatt

La première ascension du Cervin.

INTERVIEW DE M. ED. WHYMPER. — RÉCIT COMPLET DE LA GATASTROPHE DE 1865. — DÉTAILS INÉDITS.

M. Ed. Whymper, le premier ascensionniste du Cervin et l'auteur distingué des livres connus de tous les Alpinistes, se trouvant de passage à Zermatt, nous avons eu la bonne fortune de l'interviewer, et nous publions ci-dessous le récit complet et détaillé de la terrible catastrophe du 14 juillet 1865, ainsi que le portrait de M. Whymper.

M. Ed. Whymper est un homme de cinquante-six ans, imberbe, à figure énergique; blond, avec une physionomie d'un grand caractère personnel, il a le regard d'un homme qui sait ce qu'il veut et comment il le veut. Enthousiaste de la montagne, savant dans toute l'expression du terme, M. Whymper, en tout et partout est quelqu'un. Nous lui laissons la parole :

« Vous savez que c'est par hasard que je me rencontrai à Zermatt le 14 juillet 1865, avec M. le Révérend Ch. Hudson et son élève M. Hadow. J'étais accompagné du jeune lord Francis Douglas, frère cadet du marquis de Queensberry. Nous avions engagé les deux guides Taugwalder père et fils, et nous avions déjà pris toutes nos dispositions pour tenter l'ascension du Cervin, que j'essayais pour la huitième fois, quand ces Messieurs, qui m'étaient inconnus, arrivèrent, avec le guide Michel Croz, de Chamonix, pour faire, eux aussi, une tentative d'ascension du Cervin par le côté nord. Michel Croz avait déjà été avec moi, au commencement de la saison, comme guide-chef, mais il m'avait quitté vers la fin de juin, à Chamonix, pour attendre l'arrivée d'un M. Birkbeck, qui l'avait retenu. Croz connaissait mes idées; j'avais discuté souvent avec lui la possibilité de l'ascension du Cervin par le versant du nord, et il pensait, lui aussi, qu'elle était praticable, bien que l'opinion générale était qu'il fallait la tenter par le côté italien. Après avoir attendu plusieurs jours à Chamonix, il reçut une lettre de M. Birkbeck, lui disant que, pour cause de maladie, il ne pouvait venir. A ce moment, M. Hudson et son ami arrivèrent à Chamonix et, trouvant Croz libre, l'engagèrent immédiatement. Coïncidence curieuse, Croz leur communiqua mes projets sur le Cervin et ils décidèrent de suite de tenter l'ascension avec moi. Bien qu'au premier abord, je fusse un peu vexé de voir la conquête du

Mr ED. WHYMPER, à ZERMATT

dômes énormes, blancs fantômes dressés à l'horizon, avec leurs innombrables contreforts. Au loin, le groupe imposant de l'Oberland, avec le Finsteraarhorn, dressé en sentinelle; puis les massifs du St-Gothard et du Simplon; la Disgrazia et l'Orteler. Au sud, ce sont le mont Viso, la plaine du Piémont et, à quelque cent kilomètres, les contreforts des Alpes Maritimes. A l'ouest, derrière le Pelvoux et les Ecrins, flanqué des sommets des Alpes Graïes, le royal mont Blanc, dont l'armure d'argent scintille sous les rayons du soleil. A nos pieds, à plus de 3000 mètres, Zermatt, ses champs en damier et ses chalets minuscules; de l'autre côté, les pâturages du Breuil. Ce sont partout d'épaisses forêts, de claires prairies, des cascades qui bondis-

sans jeter un seûl cri. Arrivés au bord de l'abime effroyable, ils culbutèrent l'un après l'autre et disparurent dans le vide, au milieu d'un grand tourbillon de pierres.

Nous restâmes plusieurs instants dans l'horreur et la stupéfaction, sans pouvoir prononcer une parole, inertes, anéantis. Puis, je demandai à Taugwalder père de me faire passer le bout de corde qui l'attachait à nos amis. J'avais, en effet, apporté trois espèces de cordes, celle du Club alpin Anglais, faite exprès pour les ascensions, très résistante et capable de supporter un poids de 2000 kilos, une seconde d'égale grosseur, mais moins forte, et enfin une troisième, plus faible, d'un centimètre de diamètre, destinée à être coupée et abandonnée, après la descente, dans les endroits trop à pic, et qui n'était pas fait pour supporter un homme.

Il me la donna sans hésitation, et je vis que c'était justement la plus faible avec laquelle avaient été attachés nos amis, sans savoir par qui, comme je l'ai expliqué plus haut.

Que devions-nous faire? Il était inutile de chercher à descendre à la recherche des malheureux, parce qu'il était évident qu'ils étaient tombés dans le grand précipice de 1200 mètres, qui aboutit au glacier du Cervin. Néanmoins, pendant quelques minutes, nous poussâmes des cris d'appel, mais personne ne nous répondit; seul, le silence effrayant et profond! Alors nous continuâmes la descente, pas à pas, suivant le chemin que nous avions pris en montant, et dont les traces étaient encore visibles. De temps en temps nous fixions la corde aux rochers, pour nous soutenir, et en coupions les extrémités que nous laissions en arrière. Les fragments en sont restés une douzaine d'années, parce que personne ne voulut plus

Whymper's interview in the *Journal de Zermatt* (extract)

him do the talking', and this is followed by the account written in the first person. The article concludes 'Certified true copy. Jules Monod'.

The article contains much precise detail and it is probable that Monod made a French translation of Whymper's dictation, yet there is one particularly blatant error in the very last sentence, which is difficult to account for: 'Since that day I have often come back to Zermatt, which I like very much, but I have never wanted to climb the Matterhorn again, so deeply engraved in my mind is the memory of the death of my companions.' It is not just that Whymper had repeated his ascent via the Hörnli in 1874, but that on the very day the article was published bad weather forced him to retreat from the hut at the foot of the great tower on the Italian ridge after having left Zermatt three days earlier with three Italian guides and a son of Franz Biner on what may have been intended primarily as a photographic expedition on the Matterhorn. It cannot be that Whymper was dictating from an account he had written many years before, as it would have been much easier to hand such an acccount to Monod and only four paragraphs earlier he had referred to 'J.Robertson of Cambridge' which suggests that after his *Graphic* article the previous September he had learnt that Robertson had become a vicar near Cambridge and was no longer Headmaster of Haileybury. It is most unlikely and scarcely possible in view of his impending expedition from Breuil, that Whymper could have forgotten his 1874 ascent and the most likely explanation would seem to be that Monod phrased the last sentence after misunderstanding something Whymper had said. He may have learnt that Whymper was off to Breuil with Biner and asked him why he was not going to make another ascent from Zermatt. If his reply had been that he did not want to climb the Matterhorn again from Zermatt in view of the memories it had for him, Monod could well have added the last sentence himself if he knew nothing of the 1874 ascent, particularly as the inverted commas, which open at the start of Whymper's narrative, appear never to have closed.

The article includes a number of details that Whymper had not given before, such as those of the injuries and the finding of eight boots inluding those of Douglas which he had cut before the climb because they were too small. He identifies 'M. le curé de Zermatt' as the culprit threatening the guides with excommunication, rather than the 'priests', and says that 'It was an incredible imprudence on the part of Hudson to have let [Hadow] come with us'. This appears to be the first occasion on which he publicly blamed Hudson. He refers to leaving the two Taugwalders at the Hörnli and running down to Zermatt and, more dubiously, to the weak rope not being made to support a man. He did not notice whether the rope was tied by Taugwalder or by Croz. Its ends recoiled violently like a whip when it broke suddenly some eight feet from Taugwalder. Douglas had been worried about Hadow's unsteady gait; the bodies somersaulted and then disappeared amidst a great swirl of stones. He says that Croz told Hudson and Hadow of his plans to try the Matterhorn from the north and that they immediately decided to do the same, which is hardly consistent with what is said in his earlier accounts. He pays a further tribute to Old Peter, whilst regretting that he never learnt his answers to the questions put to him by Clemenz, and states that he himself gave Clemenz 'all the information and details he asked me for, including amongst other things a questionnaire drafted by me and intended to clear up the accident completely, dealing inter alia with the fact that the weakest rope had been used to tie Douglas to father Taugwalder'.

(f) *A Guide to Zermatt and the Matterhorn (1897–1911)*

This guide book, published the year after a similar guide to Chamonix and Mont

Blanc, was revised, kept up to date and reprinted each year with sixteen editions in all, including the one and only French edition published in 1911. It is by far the most comprehensive guide to Zermatt and its mountaineering history, the chapters on the first ascent of the Matterhorn and on the accident coming from the fourth edition of *Scrambles* and including the Taugwalder footnote in its revised form. The twelfth edition is not fundamentally different from the others, and it seems as though Charles Gos must have confused himself when he made some inaccurate criticism in his book *Le Cervin*, in the chapter 'La corde maudite'.

(g) *The Strand Magazine 1909*

In an article on 'Mountaineering Tragedies', Whymper referred to the accident in 1865, as well as to the occasion in 1861 when John Birkbeck junior had been with Hudson and fell one third of a mile. Some of the facts are clearly wrong so far as Hudson's responsibility for Birkbeck is concerned and Whymper's criticism is unfair and inconsistent with Montagnier's recollection to Farrar of what Whymper had said to him about Hudson. The article also mentions having spoken at some time to Gustave Doré, who had earlier published his dramatic lithographs of the 1865 ascent and accident.

(h) *L'Auto 1911 (18th September)*

Whymper did not write this article, nor may he even have known that it would be written by the French climber Georges Casella, whom Charles Gos described as 'a charming man, an excellent mountaineer and a first class author and experienced journalist'. Casella described it elsewhere as an interview with Whymper, whom he chanced to meet on the terrace of the Hôtel de Paris in Chamonix only three days before his death. Casella had climbed the Aiguille Verte the previous day and after returning from the hut he was chatting with two friends, one of whom was praising the courage and energy of the pioneers who had had to bivouac in contrast to comfortable huts.

> 'That's true, that's true, said a voice close to us.
> Someone was listening to us...The accent disclosed an Englishman.
> Yes, said the man, it was very difficult and since you have climbed the Verte you should understand the problems I had at that time in reaching the virgin summit before the others. Yes. indeed, a lot of problems, even more than with the Matterhorn.
> Whymper! I cried...'

It was Charles Gos who unearthed the article and republished it in his book *Le Cervin*. He had no hesitation in stating that he regarded it as apocryphal or rather, 'knowingly arranged and presented'. Gos referred to it being 'so live and interesting, despite its errors' but it is hard to find any real errors in what

Whymper is quoted as saying and it contains details that Casella could only have learnt from him. Whymper's age may be one year too many, just as it was in the *Journal de Zermatt* article, but it is true that he attended the funeral of Mme Seiler, who had died on 12th September 1895, and that his own father died at the age of ninety. The narrative is accompanied by a sketch on the back of a menu, to which Whymper added (not quite in the right place) a line showing how the victims fell. He refers to Taugwalder being 'a miserable old man' and to Hadow being a fool but emphatically contradicts the suggestion that Taugwalder cut the rope, repeating this twice. He refers correctly to the accident happening forty six years ago and says he recalls seeing 'Peter Taugwald turn and pass both arms round a gigantic rock'. He also says that every night he sees his companions sliding on their backs with their arms outstretched.

In the circumstances it seems probable that Casella recorded the conversation accurately and that Gos was wrong to conclude that it would be out of character for Whymper to talk in that manner to strangers, even if he were under the influence of alcohol. It is an interesting article, which throws some new light on Whymper, and there is also one matter which, although it remains obscure as Whymper never finished the sentence, could throw a little faint light on the question as to why Hudson took Hadow.

> 'Besides I explained all that to the *Times* on the orders of the Alpine Club. But what I can tell you, is that the Matterhorn was very easy and that we only took Hadow – a fool, I can tell you – because the guide...no, I am not going to tell you that...let's drink!'

(i) *Other accounts*

On about 21st July 1865 Whymper made an entry covering several pages in the Monte Rosa guestbook, including an account of the accident, but the pages were later torn out, as he recorded in a further short entry on 1st September 1869, which gave no details of the accident. Some thirty years later he also gave accounts of the accident in lectures, but little record seems to have survived, apart from mention in the *Echo des Alpes* and some diary notes quoted by Smythe, although in 1894 *The Times* reported on 'Mr. Whymper's lecture on mountaineering' and the Alpine Club has a leaflet referring to it. He lectured extensively at home and abroad, including a lecture tour in the United States. As Smythe wrote, 'His lectures at Grindelwald had proved a success and in 1896 he left England for Switzerland under the aegis of Lunns, the tourists agents, complete with slides, magic lantern, lantern operator and gas-cylinders. At Davos he gave a new lecture entitled *Scrambles Amongst the Alps*.

An illustration of the accident in Manning's book, *Swiss pictures drawn with pen and pencil*, has been wrongly attributed to Whymper, in particular by Charles Gos. The many reasons why it had nothing to do with Whymper are given in section 3.8 (Illustrations), and it is sufficient to state here that it shows only five climbers and includes an unknown range of mountains immediately to the west. But it is almost certain that the precise detail in the foreground of Gustave Doré's famous lithograph of the accident, published on 1st October 1865, came from a sketch that Whymper supplied to him via his publishers Goupil et Cie. Whymper retained several letters relating to Doré's request for information about the scene of the accident and for photographs of the victims and it is probable that only a month after writing to *The Times* he recorded his own pictorial impression of the actual accident, which Doré then incorporated into the original drawing which his publishers had been displaying in their Montmartre premises since early August.

2.57.13 Biographies of Whymper

Remarkably little has been written about Whymper himself despite the many references made to him in books and articles relating to the Matterhorn accident. Apart from Walter Unsworth's children's book *Matterhorn man* and Max Chamson's *Whymper. Le fou du Cervin*, the only full length work seems to be Frank Smythe's *Edward Whymper* published in 1940 and subsequently translated into French, German and Japanese. The English edition begins with some seventy

Edward Whymper (November 1908)

pages on his youth quoting from his diaries and then deals in successive chapters with his first six seasons in the Alps, followed by three chapters devoted to the ascent of the Matterhorn, the disaster and the repercussions. The remaining five chapters cover his subsequent expeditions to Greenland, the Andes and the Rockies as well as his further activity in the Alps.

It seems as though in the 1930's Graham Brown may perhaps have had in mind writing some substantial work on Whymper as a mountaineer, or even that he may perhaps have been going to produce a joint work with Frank Smythe, his close climbing companion until they fell out. The basis for saying this is the very extensive research he carried out and the copious notes and lists that he prepared, including such things as a line by line comparison of Whymper's accounts to von Fellenberg and *The Times* with what he later wrote in *Scrambles*, as well as a close analysis of the contents of *Scrambles*. But apart from his most informative article in the *Alpine Journal*, 'Girdlestone and the Matterhorn accident, 1865', which relates primarily to what Whymper told Girdlestone on 16th July, and one of less than a page in *The Field* in 1932, headed 'The great Matterhorn disaster of 1865' dealing with why Hadow was taken, he seems to have published nothing of any substance about Whymper or the accident.

Whymper's obituary in the *Alpine Journal* was fairly short, supplemented by an account of his scientific work by T.G.Bonney. But G.W.Young devoted more than three pages to Whymper in his article 'Mountain prophets' and there is also a review of Smythe's biography, believed to have been written by Claud Schuster, of which E.H.Stevens wrote, 'surely one of the best things ever written about Whymper'. The *Alpine Journal* also contains 'An interesting sidelight' relating to his concern about Cooper the tourist who disappeared at Zermatt in 1897. The *SAC Jahrbuch* of 1911 has an article 'Zur Erinnerung an Edward Whymper' (In memory of Edward Whymper), which is a most comprehensive thirty page review of his mountaineering achievements by his friend Dr.Heinrich Dübi, devoting ten pages to the Matterhorn accident with several extracts from contemporary Swiss newspapers.

The only other work meriting special mention is a small book by Coulson Kernahan, *In Good Company*, which includes forty pages on Whymper amongst some other short biographies. As Dangar & Blakeney wrote, 'Kernahan had no mountaineering axes to grind, but he knew Whymper well, having lived quite near him at Southend for about a dozen years'. Kernahan himself wrote: 'Of all the men I have ever known none so habitually refrained from talking shop as Whymper. Hence of Whymper the mountaineer...I have nothing of interest to say.'

2.57.14 The growth of criticism

Soon after the first news of the happening of the accident, reported by the papers with even more errors and omissions of material fact than might be expected to-day, people seem to have begun to criticise, the most common fault being their ignorance of the subject matter. This applies as much to the comrades and neighbours of Old Peter Taugwalder in Zermatt asserting or insinuating that he cut the rope as to the Editor of *The Times* writing of the ascent, 'But is it life? Is it duty? Is it common sense? Is it allowable? Is it not wrong?' When Whymper wrote to James Robertson on 27th August 1865, after leaving Zermatt on 22nd July too late to be able to call on him at Visp, he reported how 'The manner in which I was persecuted by impertinent people on my way home passes all belief'.

William Mathews wrote in a letter of 4th August to Whymper: 'The bosh that is being written to the *Times* by a lot of silly people is perfectly sickening, but I don't think it much matters'. It seems likely that Whymper thought much the same, judging from some further comments in his letter to Robertson:

> 'I have not seen the paragraph which you mention in *Punch*, but I will look for it. There was a tolerably strong and intolerably stupid article in *All the Year Round* of the week before last which irritated me somewhat. But really after all, abuse or condemnation by these kinds of people does not amount to much. Slander is another matter.'

Whereas Whymper wrote to Charles Dickens about his article in *All the Year Round* of 19th August, to which Dickens responded with a second article on 2nd September, James Robertson's complaint to *Punch* (which may have related primarily to McCormick) produced their letter to him of 28th August, which included: 'Nothing [was] further from the intention of the writers of *Punch* than to give pain to anyone specially to a gentleman of such esteemed character as your friend.'

Although the majority of the publications that criticised are not readily available to-day, two examples of constructive criticism have survived, written by the Swiss mountaineers Eugène Rambert and Abraham Roth. Apart from reviews of books like *Scrambles* there does not seem to have been much further criticism of Whymper or of matters relating to the accident, once the initial furore died down, until after Whymper's death. But within a week of his death, a Freiburg newspaper *La Liberté* had revived the rumour about the missing body, which had circulated soon after the accident alongside the rumour of cutting the rope; the idea being that Whymper, as his private tutor, had taken Lord Francis Douglas to Switzerland to climb, and had borrowed 30,000frs from him. When Douglas's father (sic) had asked for the money back, Whymper was supposed to have replied that he had repaid him and that Douglas would have had the receipt in his pocket at the time of the accident!

Gradually as the years went by and the circumstances surrounding the accident became more and more blurred in the general recollection of succeeding mountaineers, who were the only ones likely to take any interest in the accident, a new class of critic began to emerge. The contemporaries of the survivors were long since dead and the mature historians of the next generation were also out of the way, so that there was no one in a position to prevent or correct the successive distortions which gradually fed on each other. Frank Smythe in his biography written in the late 1930's had been as honest as his subject, but he made one bad mistake which not only encouraged Arnold Lunn and his friend Carl Egger to demonstrate their allergy to Whymper by seeking to denigrate him in every possible way, but it ultimately caused Smythe to mislead himself as well. He published, without any regard for the circumstances in which it came to be made, part of the Cowell memorandum and Lunn leapt at the opportunity of publicising what he regarded as an accusation by Whymper that the Taugwalders had wanted to murder him!

> 'Mr.Smythe has done a disservice to Whymper's memory by publishing this document,' – Lunn wrote – 'but a real service to truth and justice. The fact that Whymper could, in all seriousness, make this charge against the Taugwalders wholly discredits him as a witness against them.'

Egger was soon echoing the cry of murder and even Charles Gos caught the allergy and wrote a strangely uncharacteristic chapter of errors in his book *Le Cervin*, under the heading 'La corde maudite'. Lunn was also soon priding himself on having converted Smythe, after Smythe had written an extraordinary essay on Whymper as the Introduction to a new edition in 1949 of Whymper's *Andes* book. And so it went on, with the new history straying further and further from the truth until 1957, when Dangar & Blakeney wrote the first of a number of joint articles defending Whymper and challenging the extravagant distortions and contradictions of Arnold Lunn. In relation to the Cowell memorandum, they wrote in 1966: 'We think that too little is known on the latter subject for it to be wise for anyone to pronounce upon it'.

Lunn boasted repeatedly of having been told by a Zermatter that he had been 'the first to say a good word for the Taugwalders', although by 1965 in *Matterhorn Centenary* he had changed it to 'the first to defend the Taugwalders against an unfair attack'. But as Dangar & Blakeney have pointed out, there had been 'no lack of distinguished Swiss writers who might have spoken up for Taugwalder years before Lunn went into action. Yet they did not'. Lunn's continuing campaign against Whymper was supposed to be defending Taugwalder, but through making so many bad points it may in the long run have done his reputation more harm than good by repeatedly drawing attention to his faults. Smythe's foolish essay in the style of Lunn is hidden away in an obscure edition of a book that is probably of greater scientific than mountaineering interest and it will do little harm to Whymper or to Smythe. But Lunn kept on repeating his pronouncements of the Lunadorned truth, as it has been called, so that there is plenty of it around, where it will continue to mislead people and undermine Lunn's reputation as a historian for many years to come.

It is particularly unfortunate that Othmar Gurtner should have allowed himself to be misled by Lunn after selecting him to be the author of *A Century of Mountaineering*, the centenary tribute to the Alpine Club from the Swiss

Foundation for Alpine Research. Gurtner should have vetted the first ten pages of chapter six and realised how inconsistent they were with his stated object, as he revealed it in his preface to the book:

> 'Had our first consideration in selecting an author been to choose a learned historian we might have run the risk of finding ourselves at the mercy of a bore. If, on the other hand, we gave preference to an essayist, he might open too many windows onto his favourite foregrounds and the resultant draught might sweep away too many essential facts. It was therefore with relief that our search ended when we decided on a writer who could combine the factual approach of the historian with the personal interpretation of the essayist, Arnold Lunn.'

It is surprising to find so much taken word for word from Lunn's book *Zermatt and the Valais*, which had been published only two years before, as well as other paragraphs from other books in which he had also expressed and sometimes already repeated his 'uninformed verdicts' about Whymper. The book seems otherwise well written and ought to be regarded as an authoritative account of the first century of serious mountaineering, were it not so badly flawed. Gurtner should have made sure that he kept the Whymper window shut and should not have allowed a draught of vintage Lunn to sweep away the essential facts of the Matterhorn accident and its aftermath.

A far more significant assessment of the way Whymper coped with the aftermath of the Matterhorn accident is to be found in the spontaneous comments of Professor J.D.Forbes, who had met Whymper in Birmingham on about 11th September 1865 at the annual meeting of the British Association. The following month Forbes wrote in a letter to Professor Studer in Berne of having learnt from Whymper privately every detail of the accident; 'Whymper's letter to the *Times* was in excellent taste and he has most prudently abstained from the temptation of being made a hero of.'

On 2nd January 1866 Forbes included in a letter he wrote to Alfred Wills:

> 'I met your brother at Birmingham at the house of Mr.C.E.Mathews. There was a large Alpine party, and I had the melancholy pleasure of hearing from Mr.Whymper's own lips the details of that awful accident. For a long time it quite haunted me. Mr.Whymper's letter to the *Times*, so perfect in taste and tone as well as in narration, raised him immensely in my estimation, and the impression was confirmed by his bearing and behaviour at Birmingham, which was everything that could be wished, though he was subject to the temptation of being violently lionized.'

2.58
WIGRAM, REV WOOLMORE (1831 – 1907)

Wigram gave up climbing two years before the Matterhorn accident, having climbed Mont Blanc with Michel Croz and had two or three seasons with his brother Jean-Baptiste, including making the first ascent of the Dent Blanche. Following the Matterhorn accident J-B Croz wrote to Wigram, a week or so after returning from Zermatt with his brother's belongings, about the suspicion prevalent in the Chamonix valley that Taugwalder had cut the rope. Wigram informed Whymper and they both wrote to Croz reassuring him to the effect that there was not the slightest reason for suspecting that there had been any foul play. Subsequently Wigram seems to have learnt of Croz' deteriorating condition and he provided the information about the Croz family that appeared in the appeal fund leaflet.

2.59
WILLS, ALFRED (1828 – 1912)

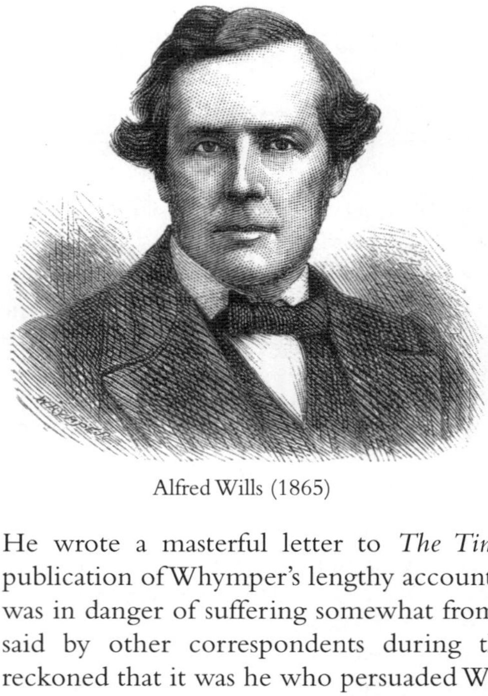
Alfred Wills (1865)

Wills ascent of the Wetterhorn in 1854 has given rise to considerable controversy, being often regarded as the start of mountaineering as a sport, but he seems never to have contemplated an ascent of the Matterhorn and his only connection with it stems from his role as President of the Alpine Club in 1864–5. He was an original member of the Club. He was a High Court judge from 1884 until 1905, but already by 1865 he had some fourteen years experience as a barrister and was particularly well qualified to cope with the adverse publicity resulting from the accident. He wrote a masterful letter to *The Times* on 11th August, following on the publication of Whymper's lengthy account of the accident, as he thought the Club was in danger of suffering somewhat from the many hard things which had been said by other correspondents during the previous fortnight. It is generally reckoned that it was he who persuaded Whymper to write to *The Times*, although Whymper had conceded to the Editor on about 4th August that he would send a plain statement of the facts if the Editor considered it undesirable to delay this pending an enquiry by the Alpine Club. Wills wrote to Whymper privately on 6th August sending him his more formal letter dated 7th August, which was subsequently printed in *The Times* on 8th August 1865 alongside Whymper's narrative. Wills also corresponded with Whymper on other aspects of the aftermath of the accident, and it was the advice he gave to Whymper that led to the creation of the Cowell memorandum, which has been so distorted and misunderstood in the 50 years or so since its discovery. Wills also suggested setting up the Croz fund.

It is well known that Whymper received advice from G.F.Browne, later Bishop of Bristol, on how much he should reveal about the behaviour of the Taugwalders during the descent after the accident, but he also received advice from the Cowells, father and son, and from Wills. From what Browne subsequently wrote there would seem to have been a fundamental difference between his advice and that of Cowell senior and of Wills, who both appear to have reacted in the same way after reading Whymper's letter to *The Times*. After receiving from Whymper a copy of his memorandum of August 17th, 1865, Wills reply of 20th August included:

> 'Now as to the statement you have so kindly forwarded to me. I take a little different view from you as to the desirability of saving the Taugwalders from the natural & proper consequences of their scandalous conduct. So much do *I* feel this that I was intending to write to you & say that your narrative left on my mind the strong impression that in this respect there was something behind, wh. I intended to urge you when you wrote for the Journal to set forth. I think a great deal of mischief is done by shielding fellows like this. They get quite enough of that at Zermatt & amongst their own people, and it is greatly for the *public* benefit that people of this sort shd be *exposed*...These Taugwalders are not fit to be trusted – & the world ought to know it; & I think myself, if you will pardon me for saying so, that you will make a great mistake if you hesitate to speak of them as they should be spoken of.
>
> As Mr.Cowell senr. has written you so kind & so judicious a letter, if you are disposed to consult him on the matter again, I should be very glad if you would show him what I have said about it & see how it strikes him. I would suggest to you also to let him and his son write under your narrative that it is in substance – or in any way they like to put it – what you told them on the 2nd Aug. and let me write also that I read it on the 20th. Life is a very uncertain thing with the best of us & you may be glad (though it is not likely that what you say will ever be called in question) to have it in writing that so & so knows it is what you told him at first.'

Whereas Wills has been proved right by certain critics who called in question what Whymper recorded about the Taugwalders, they only did this long after Whymper's death, and it is unfortunate that Smythe should have taken both memoranda out of their context and should have published the whole of one and only part of the other in such a way as to afford a sword for the critics in place of a shield for Whymper, as both Wills and the Cowells had intended.

2.60
WILSON, WILLIAM KNYVET (1838 – 1865)

Wilson seems to have arrived in Zermatt with Robertson and Phillpotts, all three being masters at Rugby School. They were staying at the Riffelhaus on Tuesday

18th July and after dinner Wilson wandered out on his own with a book never to return, his body being found the following morning at the bottom of the Riffelhorn. His funeral took place on the Friday at the same time as that of Hudson and Hadow, and an inventory of his possessions was inadvertently included amongst the documents relating to the Matterhorn Enquiry. The fact that the names of the same Tribunal members appear on his inventory suggests that Clemenz may have held a formal enquiry into his death as well, probably on the Friday morning.

The graves of Hudson, Hadow and Wilson

3
A VARIETY OF SUBJECTS

3.1
THE ALPINE JOURNAL (articles and notes)

	Vol 1. 1863–4.
77–82	Kennedy's article, Zermatt and the Matterhorn in winter.
321–331	Report of the special committee on ropes, axes and alpenstocks.
	Vol 2. 1865–6.
148–153	Whymper's letter in *The Times* of 8.8.65.
154	Note of Italian ascent.
237–245	Gorret's account of Italian ascent, extracted from *Feuille d'Aoste*.
	Vol 4. 1868–9.
56	Note of Grove, Maquignaz and Jordan ascents.
158	Note about Seiler hut.
158	Note of Elliott, Tyndall, Thioly and Foster ascents.
158–159	Account of ascent by G.E.Foster.
185–193	Grove article. The northern and southern ascents of the Matterhorn.
	Vol 5. 1870–2.
234–240	Whymper's *Scrambles* reviewed by Leslie Stephen.
	Vol 14. 1888–9.
169	Note of death of Old Peter Taugwalder.
	Vol 25. 1910–1.
757	Note of Whymper's death and funeral at Chamonix.
	Vol 26. 1912.
54–61	In Memoriam. Edward Whymper.
	Vol 28. 1914.
281–296	Elliott's accounts of the second ascent of the Matterhorn from Zermatt, taken from his *Memoir* and from his letter of 25.7.65 published in *The Field* in 1910.
	Vol 30. 1916.
316–323	Farrar article and accounts by Jordan of his attempts and ascent in 1867.

	Vol 31. 1917.
87–94	[Montagnier] Early ascents of the Matterhorn. (Extracts from the Hotel Monte Rosa guest book including Whymper, Grove, Jordan, Girdlestone, Marke and Giordano)
338	Family tree of Taugwalders and Zum Taugwalds.
	Vol 32. 1918–19.
2–36	Farrar. Days of long ago. (An article based primarily on Charles Hudson and on the first ascent of the Matterhorn)
	Vol 33. 1920–1.
234–247	Report of the Official Enquiry into the 1865 accident. (in French)
247–250	Farrar's comments on the above.
	Vol 35. 1923.
115	Note of death of Young Peter Taugwalder.
	Vol 37. 1925.
338	Note of unveiling of Zermatt memorial to Edward Whymper.
	Vol 45. 1933.
319–327	Edwards. The ropes in the Matterhorn accident.
	Vol 46. 1934.
164–165	Edward Whymper: an interesting sidelight. (The outcome of Whymper's interest in the disappearance at Zermatt of J.R.Cooper, an elderly Englishman; see also *AJ18*, 479 & 567–8 and his letter in *The Times* 24.7.97)
	Vol 52. 1940.
138	Note about Long's *Echo des Alpes* account of 'sharp-eyed lad'.
147–151	Review of Smythe's *Edward Whymper.* (?by C.Schuster)
	Vol 53. 1941–2.
156–158	E.H.Stevens. Portraits of Whymper. (Mainly about the well known photograph taken in 1865; see also *AJ91*, 294-5)
362–367	H.E.Cooke. Whymper again. (Three short pieces dealing with Dickens criticism of the accident, a modern journalist and G.F.Browne)
	Vol 54. 1943–4.
82	C.Schuster commenting on Cooke's note on G.F.Browne in *AJ53*.
102–106	G.W.Young. Mountain prophets. (Whymper)
	Vol 55. 1945–6.
290–296	Lunn. Taugwalder and the Matterhorn. (This was Lunn's first anti-Whymper article in the Journal, seemingly inspired by similar criticism in Egger's book, *Pioniere der Alpen*, which Lunn praised)
	Vol 57. 1949–50.
108	Note by Graham Brown about what Conway heard from Bishop Browne.

339–340	Whymper and Mummery. By T.S.Blakeney. (A red herring, which Blakeney probably regretted publishing once Lunn caught hold of it, as Whymper's state of mind two years before his death throws no light on his earlier years)
369–384	Graham Brown. Girdlestone and the Matterhorn accident. (Based on Girdlestone's letter journal, this article throws fresh light on events surrounding the accident)
	Vol 59. 1953–4.
344	'Whymper's engravings'. (Contribution from Lunn trying to contradict Graham Brown in order to belittle Whymper)
436–441	Dangar. The Führerbuch of young Peter Taugwalder. 1860-1883. (An article quoting extracts)
	Vol 60. 1955.
381	Relic of the Matterhorn. (Photograph of piece of rope given by Seiler to tourist in 1871, plus comment)
	Vol 61. 1956–7.
484–506	Dangar & Blakeney. The first ascent of the Matterhorn. (An article presenting the 'Narrative' of Young Peter Taugwalder, obtained by Montagnier in 1917, including copious notes and an appendix)
	Vol 63. 1958.
124	Hadow's boots. (Note by Blakeney)
255	Note, quoting Taugwalders' fees from Whymper's diary.
	Vol 65. 1960.
94–95	Whymper and the Taugwalders. Note by Blakeney correcting some Lunn mistakes about the Parkers in another publication. (Whilst Blakeney was no doubt correct, C.S.Parker in fact climbed Monte Rosa with W.H.Gladstone on 28.8.65)
	Vol 68. 1963.
285–290	Dangar. The Parkers and the Matterhorn.
	Vol 70. 1965.
8–15	Some dates in the history of the Matterhorn, 1865-1965.
15–26	Some documents relating to the first ascent of the Matterhorn.
26–37	'Old' Peter Taugwalder, 1820-88. By D.F.O.Dangar and T.S.Blakeney.
38–43	Random thoughts on the Matterhorn. By H-F. von Tscharner.
43–47	The Matterhorn: an impression from Italy. By Gaetano de Luca.
135–136	Note by Blakeney. Whymper and Southend.
159–161	Review by Dangar & Blakeney of R.Clark's *The Day the Rope Broke.*
191–196	The Matterhorn Centenary. By B.R.Goodfellow.
199–204	The Matterhorn. A diary of events after the disaster of 1865. By Dangar & Blakeney. (Plus some biographical notes)
323	'Some corrections and additions'. (to the above)

	Vol 71. 1966.
111–132	A word for Whymper: a reply to Sir Arnold Lunn. By D.F.O.Dangar and T.S.Blakeney. (A critical review of Lunn's book, *Matterhorn Centenary*)
228–233	Whymper again. By Arnold Lunn. (Lunn's reply)
233–235	Dangar & Blakeney's comments on Lunn's reply.
308–309	Whymper and the Royal Society. (Note by Blakeney)
334–335	Review by Blakeney of *The Mountain World 1964/65*, which included an article on the Matterhorn first ascent.
	Vol 97. 1992–3.
311–312	Review of Taugwalder and Jaggi's book *Der Wahrheit näher.*
	Vol 100. 1995.
215–221	The Matterhorn Lithographs of 1865. By A.Lyall. (Gustave Doré's links with Whymper)

3.2 THE COWELL MEMORANDUM

Whymper's first words to Seiler after the accident, 'The Taugwalders and I have returned', should not be taken too literally, as it seems from Whymper's interview in the *Journal de Zermatt* that once they were off the mountain and had reached the Hörnli, Whymper had parted company with the Taugwalders and had run down to Zermatt. This is hardly surprising when one considers what he recounted about their behaviour after the accident and in particular during the night that followed. Some critics have sought to say that Whymper imagined things or misunderstood the Taugwalders' conversation or actions, but the evidence is all the other way. The Cowell memorandum, which Smythe discovered some 70 years or so after it was written, and distorted by taking it out of its context, not fully realising apparently that it was written by Cowell senior and not by Whymper, is only one of several documents critical of the Taugwalders, but it is the one that has given rise to the greatest misunderstanding and groundless criticism of Whymper.

The earliest document recording anything untoward about the guides' behaviour is McCormick's letter of 17th July to *The Times* in which he stated that, 'The two remaining guides were so completely unnerved by the calamity which had befallen their companions that [Mr.Whymper] found it difficult to descend with them. He and they spent a miserable night on the mountain at a great height.' The next document seems to be a letter from the English chaplain in Vevey, the Rev William Prior, to the British Consul in Geneva. Prior seems to have arrived at the Monte Rosa hotel in Zermatt on Tuesday 18th July with a large party of friends and relations and according to Clark his letter included:

'I am much disgusted with the conduct of the Taugwalders père & fils...An hour after the

> acccident they bothered Whymper to know who was to pay them, and asked him to send an account to the Newspapers mentioning their names, in order that among travellers they might have next year a "succès de curiosité".'

We know from *Scrambles* that after such a proposition Whymper 'made no reply in words, but they knew very well the indignation that I felt. Nor did I speak to them afterwards, unless it was absolutely necessary, so long as we were together'. The 17th August memorandum stated 'this probably gave rise to the rumour that I had uttered not a word during the whole of that fearful night' and there is evidence of that rumour in Mme Gautier's letter in the *Journal de Genève* of 20.7.65.

The next document seems to be Whymper's letter of 25th July to von Fellenberg, which he despatched from Interlaken. After describing the accident he continued: 'I need not trouble you with details of the descent, it is enough to say that for more than two hours afterwards, I thought every moment would be my last; the two Taugwalders, utterly unnerved, cried like infants, and trembled in such a manner as to threaten us with the fate of the others'. Whymper left Interlaken for home the following day and seems to have been much troubled over the question as to how much he should say on several topics relating to the accident and its aftermath. He seems to have made almost immediate contact with the former secretary of the Alpine Club, J.J.Cowell, with a view to the Club holding an enquiry into the death of Hudson. The details of his correspondence with Cowell and his father are considered in section 2.11 (The Cowells). It need only be mentioned here that Whymper dined with them on Wednesday 2nd August, when the young barrister and his father questioned him about the accident. It is almost certain that they recorded Whymper's answers, which they subsequently transcribed on about the 1st September when creating their certificate or memorandum.

It is probable that Whymper visited G.F.Browne in Cambridge the day after he met the Cowells, seeking Browne's advice on how much he should disclose. The probable nature of his discussion with Browne is considered in section 2.5 (Browne), but it seems to be generally accepted that it included the conduct of the Taugwalders and that Browne probably told him it was better to say nothing. Only a few days later Whymper despatched his lengthy account to *The Times*. It followed the general lines of the evidence he gave to the Enquiry in Zermatt and of his letter to von Fellenberg, but there are some differences. The sentence quoted above from the von Fellenberg letter was expanded to read:

> '...for the Taugwalders, utterly unnerved, were not only incapable of giving assistance, but were in such a state that a slip might have been expected from one or the other at any moment. I do the younger man, moreover, no injustice when I say that immediately we got to the easy part of the descent he was able to laugh, smoke, and eat as if nothing had happened. There is no occasion to say more of the descent.'

By now the scene was set for the creation of the Cowell memorandum. It was the result of advice from both Alfred Wills, the President of the Alpine Club, who was one of those who persuaded Whymper to write his letter to *The Times*, and from Cowell senior. Wills got the strong impression from reading Whymper's letter in *The Times* that he had withheld something about the Taugwalders. But Cowell knew this to be the case and he wrote to Whymper a few days later:

> 'I submit to you that it would be prudent, not only as regards yourself, but also as regards the memory of those who are gone, to consign to writing exactly what you communicated to my son and myself on the 2nd of August, so that we might, if the necessity for your making it public should arise hereafter, be in a condition to certify that what you may say regarding these men is no afterthought'.

Whymper heeded Cowell's advice and drew up his memorandum of 17th August 1865. He sent it to Wills with Cowell's letter, no doubt seeking his advice. Wills reply of 20th August included:

> 'I take a little different view from you as to the desirability of saving the Taugwalders from the natural & proper consequences of their scandalous conduct. So much do *I* feel this that I was intending to write to you & say that your narrative left on my mind the strong impression that in this respect there was something behind wh. I intended to urge you when you wrote for the Journal to set forth. I think a great deal of mischief is done by shielding fellows like this. They get quite enough of that at Zermatt & amongst their own people – and it is greatly for the *public* benefit that people of this sort shd. be *exposed*...These Taugwalders are not fit to be trusted – & the world ought to know it; & I think myself, if you will pardon me for saying so, that you will make a great mistake if you hesitate to speak of them as they should be spoken of.
> As Mr.Cowell senr. has written you so kind & so judicious a letter, if you are disposed to consult him on the matter again, I should be very glad if you would show him what I have said about it & see how it strikes him. I would suggest to you also to let him and his son write under your narrative that it is in substance – or in any way they like to put it – what you told them on the 2nd Aug. & let me write also that I read it on the 20th. Life is a very uncertain thing with the best of us & you may be glad (though it is not likely that what you say will ever be called in question) to have it in writing that so & so knows it is what you told him at first.'

Alfred Wills therefore went a little further than Cowell senior by advising Whymper to get the Cowells to endorse his memorandum of 17th August. At that stage Wills knew nothing of the Taugwalders' threatening behaviour of which the Cowells subsequently wrote, and there is no evidence to show that he ever learnt of it, although J.W.Cowell did ask Whymper to communicate to Wills his letter of 4th September. Whymper never did write anything for the *Alpine Journal* about the Matterhorn accident, but he did publish the first part of his 17th August memorandum in *Scrambles*, setting out what Young Peter had said about their not wanting to be paid. He also added a footnote, which stems directly from the advice he had received, stating: 'Transcribed from the original memorandum'.

This footnote must have baffled readers of *Scrambles* until Smythe published the full memorandum in 1940 together with an extract from the Cowell memorandum, although Smythe did not reveal how either memorandum came to be made.

Sometime in the last ten days of August, probably at the end of the month, Whymper sent his memorandum and Wills' letter to J.W.Cowell. It seems as though the memorandum surprised the Cowells and that they did not consider it adequate to achieve the object of the advice they had given Whymper nor that of Wills. Whymper had been given very clear and firm advice about the need to protect himself by creating a written and certified record, yet unknown to Wills one of the most serious aspects had not even been mentioned in Whymper's own memorandum. The Cowells therefore wrote how the memorandum recorded 'the substance of a communication made to [them] on Wednesday August 2. 1865 by Edward Whymper in answer to questions which they put to him. But it was fuller, more comprehensive and more significant than this Mem: exhibits it.' They went on to refer in slightly greater detail to some aspects Whymper had covered and then wrote of the Taugwalders threatening behaviour:

> 'that their demeanour gradually became, and continued to be, suggestive of personal danger to himself – that at night they, as it were, hustled him to induce him to attempt the further descent *by Moonlight* – that thereafter they urged him to lie down in a manner so importunate and minatory as to induce him to place himself with his back to a rock, and with his axe in his hand to order them to keep at a greater distance from him – and that he passed the night standing in that manner and prepared to defend himself.
> The inferences which arose in our minds from what E.Whymper described were that the Taugwalders saw that the additional loss of E.Whymper would afford them an opening to a future notoriety of a very lucrative nature, and that they were prepared to avail themselves of any opportunity that might offer during the descent of bringing about that loss – and Edward Whymper did not deny to us that similar inferences suggested themselves to him during the whole of that dreadful night.'

The somewhat strange wording of the last two lines seems to be attributable to Whymper's answers to the Cowells' questions being confined to the actual questions and to statements of fact. It is a remarkable feature of all his early accounts of the accident that they match what he wrote in a letter to Sir T.F.Buxton on 8th August about his letter published in *The Times* that day: 'In my letter I scrupulously abstain from offering observations and casting blame on anyone'. His evidence to the Zermatt Enquiry simply answered the questions and he did not volunteer anything he was not asked, which accounts for his saying nothing more of the rope that broke than that it was less thick than the rope between Croz and Douglas. Nor were the questions he handed in for Taugwalder leading questions. It seems that he was willing to let others judge for themselves and preferred that any potentially controversial issues should be dealt with by others.

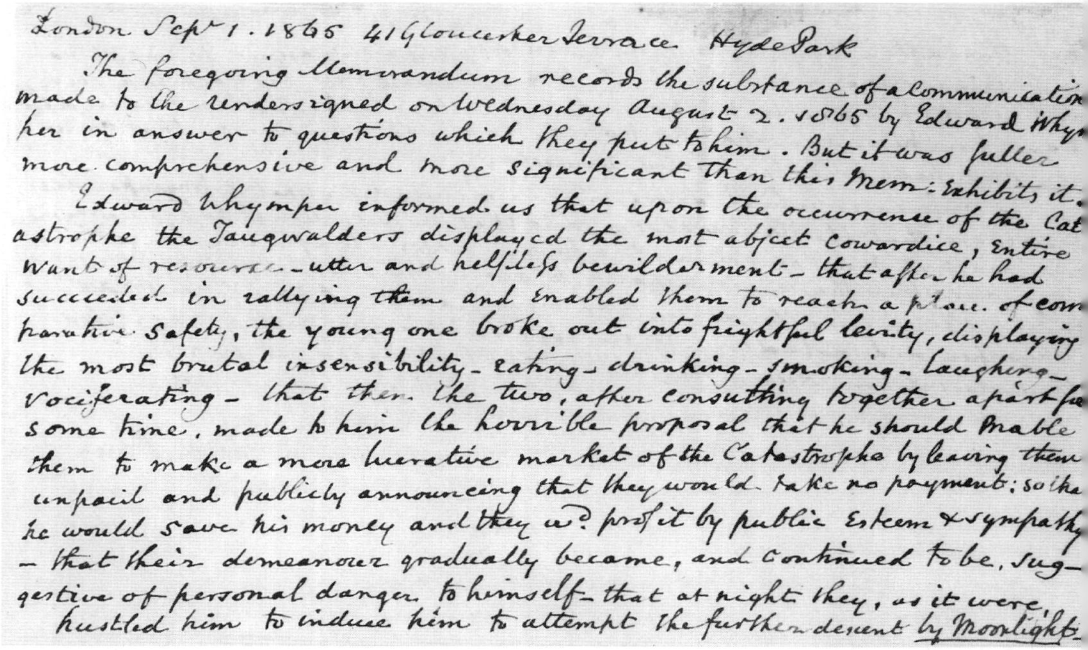

London Sept 1. 1865 41 Gloucester Terrace Hyde Park

The foregoing Memorandum records the substance of a communication made to the undersigned on Wednesday August 2. 1865 by Edward Whymper in answer to questions which they put to him. But it was fuller more comprehensive and more significant than this Mem: exhibits it.

Edward Whymper informed us that upon the occurrence of the Catastrophe the Taugwalders displayed the most abject cowardice, entire want of resource – utter and helpless bewilderment – that after he had succeeded in rallying them and enabled them to reach a place of comparative safety, the young one broke out into frightful levity, displaying the most brutal insensibility – eating – drinking – smoking – laughing – vociferating – that then the two, after consulting together apart for some time, made to him the horrible proposal that he should enable them to make a more lucrative market of the Catastrophe by leaving them unpaid and publicly announcing that they would take no payment: so that he would save his money and they wd profit by public Esteem & sympathy – that their demeanour gradually became, and continued to be, suggestive of personal danger to himself – that at night they, as it were, hustled him to induce him to attempt the further descent by Moonlight –

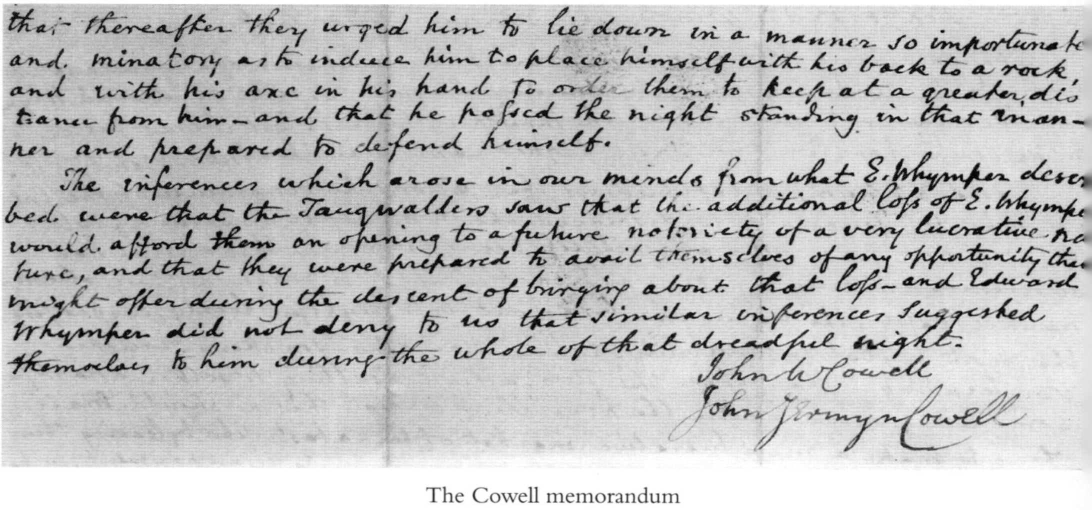

that thereafter they urged him to lie down in a manner so importunate and minatory as to induce him to place himself with his back to a rock, and with his axe in his hand to order them to keep at a greater distance from him – and that he passed the night standing in that manner and prepared to defend himself.

The inferences which arose in our minds from what E. Whymper described were that the Taugwalders saw that the additional loss of E. Whymper would afford them an opening to a future notoriety of a very lucrative nature, and that they were prepared to avail themselves of any opportunity that might offer during the descent of bringing about that loss – and Edward Whymper did not deny to us that similar inferences suggested themselves to him during the whole of that dreadful night.

John W Cowell

John Jermyn Cowell

The Cowell memorandum

It seems to follow from this that those like Wills and the Cowells who knew more of the full facts than the general public, but were particularly impressed by Whymper's letter to *The Times*, were in the best position anyone ever will be to judge Whymper's credibility as a witness. Some of the comments of Wills and Cowell about guides may strike us to-day as somewhat severe, but there is no reason to doubt their wisdom and their sincerity, nor their ability to judge to what extent Whymper was still affected by the shock of his frightful experience. They knew Whymper before the accident and the Cowells, if not Wills also, met him, talked to him and questioned him in August 1865. They could judge for themselves far better than some 20th century critic whether he was telling the truth or whether he was so confused and upset as to be unable to distinguish between what actually happened and something he merely imagined or dreamt. They were sympathetic towards him and would have advised him to dismiss from his mind any such absurdities, had they not believed that he told the truth and considered it desirable that he should record in writing the events covered by his own memorandum of 17th August and that of the Cowells. Wills in particular, as a barrister of some fourteen years experience, would have seen through anything that did not ring true.

From subsequent events we know that Whymper seems to have heeded the advice of G.F.Browne more than that of Wills and the Cowells, so far as publishing all he knew about the Taugwalders was concerned. Perhaps it was the publication of the first part of the 17th August memorandum in *Scrambles* that Browne was referring to, when he made known many years later that 'on at least one [question] he did not take my advice'. But there seems to have been a special reason for quoting the conversation with Young Peter Taugwalder, namely, that he had subsequently endeavoured to trade upon the idea of not being paid. The evidence of this, probably learnt and recorded by Whymper in about September 1869, comes in the long footnote about the Taugwalders in the 1st, 2nd & 3rd editions of *Scrambles*. After paying tribute to Old Peter, Whymper continues:

> 'In respect to young Peter, it is not possible to speak in the same manner. The odious idea that he propounded (which I believe emanated from *him*) he has endeavoured to trade upon, in spite of the fact that his father was paid (for both) in the presence of witnesses. Whatever may be his abilities as a guide, he is not one to whom I would ever trust my life, or afford any countenance.'

Whymper did not subsequently publish anything from the Cowell or 17th August memoranda, nor is there any sign of his having borne any grudge against his guides. On the contrary there are several signs of his having been able to take a remarkably objective view and of having shown generosity towards them, despite their deplorable behaviour induced by the shock of the accident. It may have been no fault of the Taugwalders that they should have been more severely affected by the trauma of the accident than Whymper, but that seems to have been the case, in the same way that the guides who accompanied Whymper to the

Matterhorn glacier to find the bodies were incapable of giving any assistance. This was mentioned by Downton the English chaplain in Geneva in his report of 20th July to the Consul Mackenzie, stating 'the guides could not be got to render any assistance, but lay down and *howled*'.

Smythe seems carelessly to have interpreted Cowell's reference to 'a communication made to the Undersigned' as though Whymper had written the Cowell memorandum. He says very little in his book about it, and his misunderstanding is more apparent in a letter he wrote in October 1939 to H.E.Cooke, who had written to him about Whymper.

> 'You have not seen Whymper's memorandum to Cowell Hon. Sec. of the A.C. at that time. He was obviously greatly exercised in his mind over the conduct of the Taugwalders after the accident...He accuses the Taugwalders of trying to encompass his death after the accident and states that he *stood* all night when bivouacking with his back to a wall prepared to defend himself as by their callous behaviour he suspected that they would prefer to be the sole survivors on account of the publicity it would give them.'

But the clearest evidence of Smythe's misunderstanding of the nature of the Cowell memorandum, which was in turn to mislead Arnold Lunn, Carl Egger and Charles Gos and others who relied on Smythe, comes in a fifteen page essay on Whymper's life which he wrote as an Introduction to the 1949 edition of Whymper's *Travels in the Andes*. Smythe described the Matterhorn accident and how the descent of the survivors was a nightmare, and then said: 'Later, Whymper wrote an extraordinary letter to the Secretary of the Alpine Club in which he accused the Taugwalders of wanting to murder him'.

Arnold Lunn's reaction to Cowell was to quote Smythe's extract in the *Alpine Journal* in 1946 and to comment: 'Mr.Smythe has done a disservice to Whymper's memory by publishing this document, but a real service to truth and justice. The fact that Whymper could, in all seriousness, make this charge against the Taugwalders wholly discredits him as a witness against them.'

Carl Egger, in his book *Pioniere der Alpen* published in 1946, referred to the memorandum being written by the secretary of the Alpine Club, but it is apparent that he had no understanding of the circumstances in which it came to be made, nor did he make clear that it was never published by Whymper. After quoting some extracts he told his readers:

> 'This monstrous accusation of Whymper's that the guides had the idea of murdering him in order to remove him and thereby clear the way to profitable fame must be regarded as the fantastic invention of a youthful brain and at all events can only be explained by the nerve shattered state in which he found himself on the night that followed the accident. But even so one shakes one's head in disbelief and asks how a man of Whymper's education and ability was in a position to let it be raised at all and furthermore assume the responsibility of making it known to third parties as a fact.'

Charles Gos referred to Cowell in his book *Le Cervin* in a chapter headed 'The accursed rope', which is so uncharacteristic of him and contains so many inaccuracies on other aspects as well that it may be in part attributable to the advanced state of his long-standing illness. The particular section is headed 'A frightful misunderstanding' and it refers to 'the mental disarray under which young Whymper struggled after the accident'. He even referred to two copies of the Cowell memorandum being found by Smythe amongst Whymper's papers. 'It demonstrates decisively the frightful misunderstanding existing between Whymper and his guides (since when do guides plot to encompass the death of their tourist?).' Gos referred in a footnote to the writings of Egger and Lunn already cited, and, clearly influenced by Egger, he also went on about Whymper's completely different social background and his psychological state. He referred to Whymper's tendency towards solitude and like Lunn and Egger he clearly had no inkling of the context out of which Smythe had taken the memorandum.

Only Dangar & Blakeney had the good sense to tread warily, when they wrote in 1966, 'We think that too little is known on the latter subject [of Whymper's conversations with the Cowells] for it to be wise for anyone to pronounce upon it'.

3.3
EMIGRATION TO AMERICA BY ZERMATTERS

Arnold Lunn seems to have been responsible for distorting this subject like so many others relating to the aftermath of the Matterhorn accident with the repeated publication of one of his 'uninformed verdicts', so as to make it appear as though Old Peter Taugwalder's emigration in 1874 was a perfectly normal if not common event at that time. Fortunately there is some reliable evidence available and it merits consideration. But first two examples of Lunn, from 1947 and from 1955: (1) 'It is also, I am told, false to imply that Taugwalder emigrated for any other reason than that emigration to America was, at that time, very frequent among Zermatters.' (2) 'Taugwalder was persuaded to emigrate by the example of many Zermatters at a time when emigration suddenly seemed attractive, and like many of those who did emigrate, he returned to Zermatt.'

Ruden's *Familien-Statistik* published in 1869, together with the 1927 edition revised and brought up to date by Kronig, records the family circumstances of the various Burger families of Zermatt. Details include the year of birth and of marriage, and if the latter is not recorded the reason is usually given, such as early death or emigration. Thus in the case of emigration to America the words 'nach Amerika ausgewandert' may appear after someone's name. No such entry appears against Old Peter's name (because he went after publication of Ruden and returned before publication of Kronig), but there is one against his son Friedrich, born in 1850, and another against his grandson Kamil, born in 1871. Excluding two instances of emigration to South America, one of which is recorded by

Ruden, and disregarding for the moment Alphons Zumtaugwald, there are only ten instances of an individual emigrating to America recorded by Kronig and none by Ruden. This means that no one emigrated to America prior to about 1868, even allowing for a change of mind thereafter. Old Peter went in 1874, according to his son Peter, when he was already 54 years of age. There is no record of the dates when the others emigrated, but if they were all at least 14 years of age, then, with the possible exception of Old Peter's youngest son Friedrich, none of them could have emigrated before Old Peter. If one assumes each emigrant was 20 years old, the first one did not leave Zermatt until 1881, three years after Old Peter had returned. It is nevertheless possible that other Zermatters went to America between 1868 and 1874 with the intention of emigrating, changed their minds and returned home unmarried, but this seems most unlikely. The ten who did in fact emigrate were all unmarried, whenever they actually went, and if there was indeed 'a time when emigration suddenly seemed attractive' the attraction must have been for the young unmarried and not for 54 year olds leaving their wives and children at home. Alphons Zumtaugwald, President of the Zermatt Gemeinde from 1885 until 1891, was married but childless when he emigrated in 1892 at the age of 34.

It seems probable that the emigration of Old Peter's son Friedrich holds the key to his own journey to America. Unfortunately very little is known of the Taugwalders' family circumstances, but it is said that Old Peter could speak only the Zermatt German dialect so that going abroad would hardly have 'suddenly seemed attractive' to him! After the Matterhorn accident the roles of the two Peters seem to have been reversed with the son taking over the role of leading guide and the father that of second. Yet by 1865 the second son Joseph was about the same age as Young Peter had been when he first climbed the Weisshorn and when he took part in Kennedy's attempt on the Dent Blanche. It would furthermore have required considerable skill and experience for him to have been able to descend alone with the tent from the place where they had camped at 11,000 ft on the Matterhorn on 13th July. It was in fact Joseph who accompanied his father and Güssfeldt on the Italian ridge in September 1865 and he had also been a member of the party that recovered the bodies on 20th July. But in 1867 Joseph suddenly drowned in the Schwarzsee.

Nothing has ever been revealed about Joseph's death, but whatever the circumstances it must have had a devastating effect on Old Peter. Did he then concentrate on training Friedrich to become a mountain guide or had he so lost hope and ambition that Friedrich had little opportunity to learn and therefore decided to try his luck in America? Unfortunately we do not know the year that Friedrich emigrated or even whether it was before or after Old Peter went in 1874. But it is quite possible that they both went together; that Friedrich made up his mind to go and Old Peter decided that he might as well go as well and escape the torment at home. He may not necessarily have intended to stay there indefinitely, but the presence of Friedrich could certainly have solved his otherwise almost insuperable language problem.

As Friedrich did not marry in Zermatt before emigrating nor apparently ever feature in Alpine literature as a guide or even as a porter, but only as the sharp-eyed lad who actually witnessed the Matterhorn accident, the probability is that he went to America in the 1870's. He did not return to Zermatt and there is a distinct possibility that he died in America in his twenties, which would almost certainly mean that if Old Peter had gone there with him he must have died by 1878, the year Old Peter returned to Zermatt. Although Hannes Taugwalder has written of Friedrich going to America after his father's death, which would mean some time after 1888, a more reliable historian, Walter Schmid, referred in his book *Menschen am Matterhorn* to Old Peter going there 'accompanied by his youngest son and other Wallisers'. But even if no reliable information is available from Zermatt, it should be possible for someone to check in America on the extent of the Taugwalders' stay there.

Old Peter's grandson Kamil, son of Young Peter and nephew of Friedrich, also emigrated to America but as he was only born in 1871 the probability is that he did not go before his grandfather died in Zermatt in 1888. Nevertheless it may well be that he got his inspiration from Old Peter and that there is some further as yet undiscovered link between the three generations of American immigrants named Taugwalder.

The references in Kronig to Zermatters emigrating to N.America are as follows:

Name	*Kronig No.*	*Page No.*	*Date of birth*
Albert Biner	71	32	1877
Johann Biner	538	39	1866
Peter Julen	581	71	1879
Johannes Julen	183	72	1861
Magdalena Perren	264	102	1868
Johannes Perren	300	120	1862
Joseph Schuler	695	130	1879
Friedrich Taugwalder	354	135	1850
Kamil Taugwalder	701	135	1871
Adolf Zumtaugwald	419	151	1866
Alphons Zumtaugwald	418	151	1858 (He emigrated in 1892)

Although Walter Schmid stated in relation to Old Peter that emigration to America was nothing unusual at that time, he did not provide any further evidence and he may well have been misled by Lunn. The above list does not include any who may have intended to emigrate but later had a change of mind and returned home. The list does however suggest that it was not Old Peter's generation nor even the next one that was attracted by the idea of emigration, but the generation of his grandchildren. It seems therefore that the time scale has once more become distorted and that it is wrong to associate Old Peter's emigration at the age of 54 with the several youngsters who were seeking new horizons in the last fifteen or twenty years of the 19th century. There is plenty of evidence linking Old Peter's departure from Zermatt with the aftermath of the accident, not least that of his son Peter, but if it is true that he went to America with his youngest son Friedrich his situation may well not have been as desperate as some critics have suggested, nor as might appear from the picture of a Swiss-German speaker with no other language and with virtually no ambition prior to the Matterhorn accident to travel more than about ten miles from his remote Alpine village, suddenly deciding to escape to America on his own.

3.4
THE ENQUIRY. INTRODUCTION

'Was there any difficulty in remaining on the top?' 'No', Whymper replied to Clemenz, having just given evidence of his party arriving at the summit of the Matterhorn at 1.40p.m. on 14th July and remaining there for one hour. Whymper had been handed a summons on the morning of Friday 21st July to attend the Tribunal at the Hotel Mont Cervin to reply to questions at 2 p.m. that afternoon, precisely one week after his 'stop on top' as he referred to it in his own notes of the Enquiry. Hadow's fatal error of falling off at the wrong moment must have occurred at 3.45pm judging from the hands of Hudson's broken watch. At the very same hour one week later, the Tribunal had probably already completed 'taking' Whymper's lengthy evidence, had sent Taugwalder away to write out his answers to the list of questions Whymper had provided for him and would probably have been questioning Franz Andenmatten prior to adjourning until the following day, when they were due to hear Alexander Lochmatter and draw up inventories of the victims' possessions with the help of the Randa (not Zermatt) district judge.

It might be wrong to describe the conduct of the Enquiry as unconventional, particularly when we know something about the way a similar sort of Enquiry was conducted into the Lyskamm accident in 1869, and a more appropriate word would be 'extraordinary'. For a start the presiding judge, J.A.Clemenz from Visp, was the owner of the Hotel Mont Cervin in Zermatt, where the Enquiry took place. He had opened the hotel in 1852 and seems to have been a regular resident landlord during the summer season until he sold it to Alexander Seiler in 1867. He seems to have taken a keen interest in the activities of his guests, such as the first ascent of the Dom by J.Llewelyn Davies in 1858. Davies had been planning to make what would have been the first ascent of the Weisshorn but, as he later wrote, 'happening to talk about it to Mr.Clemenz, the landlord of the Mont Cervin hotel,

I found that he strongly recommended us to substitute the Dom for the Weisshorn. The worthy landlord was also President of the Council of his canton.'

Clemenz must by 1865 have been a man of considerable experience and influence and may have had no compunction in presiding over an official enquiry into the circumstances surrounding a fatal accident to four foreigners, despite the fact that one of the victims had been staying at his hotel since the end of June; and yet there are some signs suggesting that the conflict between his judicial and his hotel interests may have so undermined his standing that he was prevented from conducting an impartial Enquiry and within two years had to sell his hotel. For Clemenz was no less a foreigner than his infinitely more successful rival hotelier Seiler, who had to endure 'a life long fight with the Zermatters who continually looked upon him as a stranger, indeed as an enemy of the whole valley' (Theodor Wundt). As Lord Francis Douglas climbed from Zermatt for four consecutive years, it seems probable that he had stayed with Clemenz before and that Clemenz would have known him and would have taken an interest in his mountaineering activities, even perhaps to the extent of recommending guides.

The prime difficulty facing the German speaking Tribunal was that the principal witness was to be an Englishman, who spoke no German although he could converse in French. There was no Court interpreter and although Clemenz might have acquired a smattering of English from his hotel guests, this would probably not have been adequate either to express precise questions or to understand detailed answers, quite apart from the problems that English evidence would present to the Clerk charged with the duty of recording it in writing, a high speed exercise in foreign language dictation. Another difficulty facing the Tribunal must have been to understand the circumstances surrounding the accident and appreciate the finer points and relevant factors without the benefit of witness statements and expert evidence such as are provided to a modern Court of Enquiry by the police or by some form of expert witness.

Whymper in fact gave his evidence in French, without the need for the Clerk to record it nor even for Clemenz to understand it, and there are grounds for supposing that advantage was taken of both. The main clue is to be found in Whymper's answer to Question 11 (Q11), but there are others elsewhere in his evidence. His answer A11 is a very detailed description of the happening of the accident, taking it step by step, and it would be surprising if a German speaking Clerk had been able to record it correctly even at dictation speed, particularly when account is taken of the punctuation and the very long sentences. However much Whymper might have anticipated the questions that would be put to him and have prepared in advance some general description of the accident, his A15 in particular reveals quite unexpected fluency, as do his other answers to a lesser extent. There has been argument amongst the critics about the extent of Whymper's knowledge of French, and, although it seems that he was able to converse reasonably well, no one has probably ever believed that he was as fluent as the record of his evidence might suggest.

In September 1866 Whymper wrote to James Robertson about having a proposed inscription for Croz' tomb translated into French,

> 'I want to have it turned into French, and correct French. Of course I could do it myself, or get a translator in London to do it but this won't do. I want it as well and as elegantly...rendered as I can get it and it has occurred to me that it might be accomplished by your intervention. I have a lively recollection of the kindness of M.Vecqueray, and I do not call to mind anyone who would be likely to do it so well as he, or who would take the pains that I think he would be likely to exercise.'

This suggests that Vecqueray, a man of Belgian origin who taught German and French at Rugby School, must have been staying at the Monte Rosa with Robertson, Phillpotts and Wilson, also masters at Rugby, during the week following the accident and that it was he who gave Whymper help with the translation. In fact he seems to have translated all Whymper's evidence into French prior to the opening of the Enquiry and Clemenz' questions as well. It is probable that the questions were originally in German and Vecqueray may have translated them into English as well as into French.

The identity ofVecqueray as translator is confirmed in two ways. Firstly there is a record in Adams Reilly's journal of his leaving Zermatt on Saturday 22nd July, although no earlier record of his arrival or presence there seems to have survived. Secondly there are amongst Whymper's surviving papers four pages of Questions & Answers corresponding to Q&A 2-17 in the Official Report and the handwriting is the same as that in Vecqueray's translation of the Croz inscription sent to Whymper by Robertson. The question arises however as to how Whymper came to possess a record in Vecqueray's hand of not only the questions which Clemenz asked him on the afternoon of Friday 21st July but also of the answers he gave as not even an official interpreter would be able to make such a record.

The Answers in the Vecqueray document include a number of alterations. Sometimes a word is crossed out and a replacement is written in above it, but on other occasions an alteration follows a deletion, appears on the next line or even several lines lower down, showing that it was made as he went along or when he paused to find a better word. Vecqueray even made an alteration in Q6 to improve the fluency of the French, which, if it were not already his own French translation of Clemenz original German, might suggest that Whymper and not Clemenz drafted the questions as well as the answers, but there are a number of reasons for rejecting this possibility. Firstly Whymper would not have been familiar with the general form of questions that lawyers put to witnesses on such occasions. Although he clearly received much helpful guidance and advice from his fellow guests in the hotel including McCormick, Robertson, Adams Reilly and perhaps the qualified barrister Giles Puller, there is no reason to suppose that any of the many practising British lawyer mountaineers had yet started their summer holidays. Secondly, no 25 year old in Whymper's position, even allowing for his remarkable composure during the days following the accident, would draft for himself questions such as Q12, 13 or 17, let alone the potentially controversial Q15.

It is therefore necessary to conclude that Clemenz made contact with Whymper some days prior to his being served with the summons on the morning of Friday 21st July inviting him to appear at 2 p.m. to answer questions that would be addressed to him. Although the Court copy of the summons omits the starting time, Adams Reilly's journal confirms that the Enquiry opened at 2 p.m. Clemenz must have drafted the questions in German (or French) earlier in the week and asked Whymper to answer them in French and bring both the questions and the answers to the hearing. Whymper must have handed in a fair copy and Clemenz then recited each question in turn, whilst Whymper in turn recited each answer. It is significant that apart from two minor questions recorded by Whymper but not by the Clerk, his actual questioning was an automatic and seemingly thoughtless process with the Tribunal apparently taking no notice of the answers and never seeking any clarification. They never, for example, asked Whymper to amplify his reference in A10 to the rope between Lord Douglas and Old Peter being 'less thick'. It appears as though the Clerk took no notes and merely incorporated the fair copy of the Vecqueray document into the Court record. Whymper may have made some notes during the hearing, but more likely did this immediately afterwards. His own rough four page report almost entirely in English and based on the Vecqueray document, refers to Clemenz 'opening with an oration to explain the motives which prompted the Government to make the Enquiry'. It proves that Clemenz and he recited the Questions and Answers aloud, as it contains two extras that might be called 8½ & 16½. Q8 asked how long they stopped on the top, to which Whymper replied 'one hour', and Clemenz then asked 'Was there any difficulty in remaining on the top, to which the answer was 'No'. Q16½ is recorded by Whymper as 'What was my opinion about Douglas body. Gave it'. By contrast the evidence of Lochmatter and to a lesser extent that of Andenmatten must have been given orally and not in writing, judging from the way a question often relates to the previous answer.

These details are only a few of those in the various documents which go to show that the Tribunal in effect took Whymper's evidence in writing, by means of a series of questions which he had the opportunity of answering at his leisure. For reasons that are not apparent the Tribunal did not question him in detail, nor did it make reference to anything M. le juge Julen (the Zermatt judge) might have noticed or asked himself when he went with the party that recovered the bodies the day before. It seems deliberately to have avoided probing into anything that could possibly raise any issue of culpable fault. Any conclusion drawn from the manner in which Whymper was questioned should also take account of the Tribunal's attitude to the next witness Old Peter Taugwalder. Apart from the procedural and formal matters covered by Q18-21, it seems on his first examination to have asked Taugwalder only one question of its own, Q36, an ambiguous, hypothetical question which the answer did little to clarify. All the

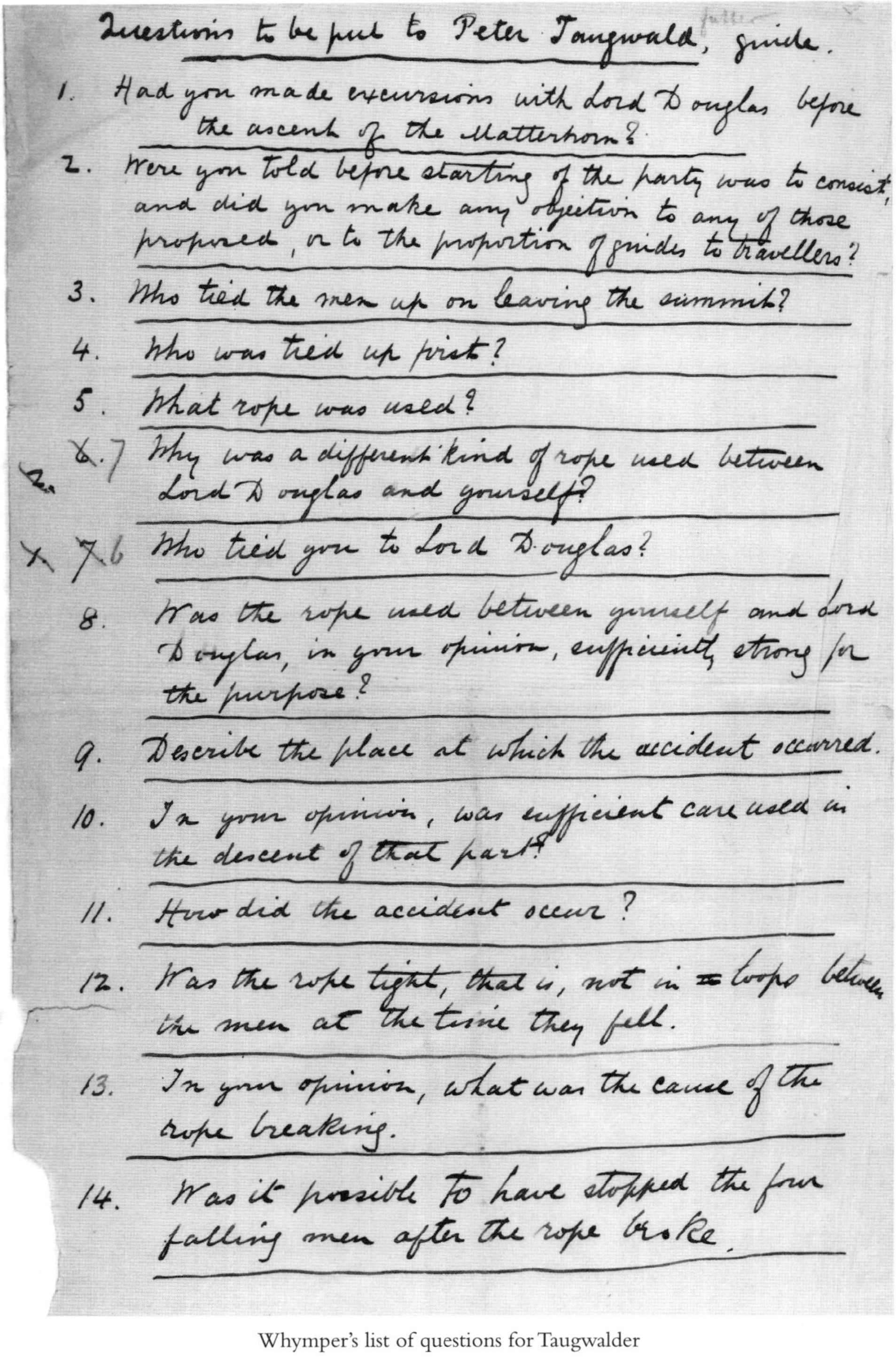

Questions to be put to Peter Taugwald, guide. [father]

1. Had you made excursions with Lord Douglas before the ascent of the Matterhorn?
2. Were you told before starting of the party was to consist, and did you make any objection to any of those proposed, or to the proportion of guides to travellers?
3. Who tied the men up on leaving the summit?
4. Who was tied up first?
5. What rope was used?

6.7 Why was a different kind of rope used between Lord Douglas and yourself?

7.6 Who tied you to Lord Douglas?

8. Was the rope used between yourself and Lord Douglas, in your opinion, sufficiently strong for the purpose?
9. Describe the place at which the accident occurred.
10. In your opinion, was sufficient care used in the descent of that part?
11. How did the accident occur?
12. Was the rope tight, that is, not in loops between the men at the time they fell.
13. In your opinion, what was the cause of the rope breaking.
14. Was it possible to have stopped the four falling men after the rope broke.

Whymper's list of questions for Taugwalder

other questions (Q22-35) that Taugwalder was asked about the accident appear in the list drafted by Whymper, subject to some minor but crucial alterations, and one can but wonder what the Tribunal would have done without him. Although there is nothing anywhere to prove that Clemenz had asked Whymper to draft some relevant questions, this is the inescapable conclusion from consideration of the matter, which is dealt with in greater detail in section 5.4.2 (Notes on the evidence). It is sufficient to mention here that Clemenz seems to have given Whymper a short list of questions for Taugwalder, including Q22, 23, 30, 31, 32 & 35, and to have asked him to supplement it with some questions relating to the rope.

The questioning of Taugwalder appears to have been conducted in writing, like the questioning of Whymper, and it would have been unfair to him had he not been given the same opportunity to compose written answers. Apart from asking no questions of substance of its own, the Tribunal persevered with Q32 'How did the accident occur?', only to be reminded by Taugwalder 'I have already described it'. Further signs of his answers having been submitted in writing – along with a German translation of the questions that sometimes distorts in such a way as to miss the whole point Whymper had in mind – come from the Tribunal's failure to appreciate until later the inconsistency between A30 and Whymper's A11, and the fact that it never once sought immediate amplification or clarification of an inadequate answer.

It is necessary to point out that when H.E.G.Tyndale drew attention to some of the Whymper questions in the 6th edition of Scrambles he caused confusion by quoting words from Whymper's English list, despite the occasional fundamental change introduced in the course of the subsequent French and German translations. The questions Whymper handed in for Taugwalder were in French, but by the time they reached Taugwalder they were in German and it seems probable that they were translated by his lawyer or adviser. In all probability Taugwalder handed in his written answers on the Saturday morning, as Whymper's departure from Zermatt seems to have been delayed long beyond that of Robertson and Phillpotts, despite their not signing for Wilson's possessions until the Saturday. The Tribunal seems to have decided that there was no need to question Whymper further and that he could go, but that they would need to question Taugwalder further on the Sunday. Whether they gave him some more questions to answer in writing or only asked further oral ones is not clear. Three or four of the questions related to the timing of events and others to the composition of the party. Another dealt with the inconsistency they had noticed between A11 and A30 and they also asked who supplied the rope that broke (Q57). But once again they steered clear of seeking any amplification of Taugwalder's reference to it being a special rope (A24) or of Whymper's reference to it being less thick than the other ropes. They sought no description or specification of the rope, nor evidence as to its condition and they failed to realise, unless it was intentional, that Whymper's general question Q26 had been rendered completely worthless and irrelevant by being related to A25. It is incredible that they should have concerned themselves with the quality and age of the rope that did not break between Douglas and Croz, and that they should not have asked a similar question about the rope that actually did break! Old Peter's A28, that he had used another rope because the first one was not long enough for him to tie on to it as well, was not a skilful evasion of the most important question that anyone could have asked him, but a straightforward answer to a distorted and irrelevant question. He had nothing to hide and had already volunteered some crucial information, but it had gone unheeded instead of eliciting a request for elaboration. 'I tied myself on to Lord Douglas', said Old Peter in A24, 'with a special rope'. Clemenz ignored it.

Clemenz may have thought that he was being kind to Old Peter by avoiding questions about the rope that broke (apart from Q29 & Q34) in view of the rumours circulating in Zermatt; but if so he made a bad mistake and deprived Old Peter of the opportunity of justifying his action, at the same time frustrating Whymper's purpose in giving him the chance 'to exculpate himself from the grave suspicions which at once fell on him'. Whymper's attitude to Old Peter after the accident seems to have confused the critics, although it is clear that he said nothing in his evidence to the Enquiry that either accused or even raised suspicion against Old Peter in connection with the rope. Despite ample opportunity to consider what he should say in his answers before committing anything to writing, the furthest he went was to mention that the rope between Lord Douglas and Taugwalder was less thick than the others. But this alone would not necessarily reduce its strength.

The wording of Whymper's questions for Taugwalder is hardly consistent with his critics' contention that he tried to shift responsibility away from himself. The questions were fairly worded and they were not leading questions. Even Q28 in its original form could be said to relate to the special rope in A24 and it would have seemed inconceivable to Whymper that Taugwalder could have been able to avoid answering Q26 in its original form and be allowed to treat it as though it related solely to the Croz rope that did not break. In their undistorted form the questions could well have enabled Taugwalder to justify his use of the weak rope.

It would have been so easy for Whymper in his answer to Q17 to have drawn attention to Taugwalder's use of the weak rope despite plenty of strong rope being available. Critics have taken no account of the influence on Whymper of those Englishmen staying at the Monte Rosa during the week following the accident, such as McCormick, Robertson and Adams Reilly. They no doubt helped him to take an objective view and the explanation in his letter to *The Times* for handing in the questions for Taugwalder, 'because that which I had found out respecting the ropes was by no means satisfactory to me', may partly have reflected McCormick's concern over the death of his friend Hudson. But Whymper was clearly not the only one asking questions about the ropes, as is shown by his letter to *The Times*: 'It has been repeatedly asked, "Why was not the wire-rope taken which Mr.Hudson brought to Zermatt?" I do not know'. Robertson seems to have been particularly interested in the qualities of ropes as he was still corresponding with Whymper on the subject in 1869, and there can be no doubt that the many climbers in Zermatt who saw the broken rope or merely talked about it after the accident would have wanted to know, as much as Whymper did, why Taugwalder chose to use the weakest rope.

It is inconceivable that Clemenz and other members of the Tribunal, (whose ad hoc bailiff was a cousin of Taugwalder and a brother of judge Julen) as well as judge Julen himself should not have known prior to the start of the weekend Enquiry that the rope that broke was of inferior quality. It may even be that Clemenz or someone acting on his behalf saw the broken end when he made contact with Whymper earlier in the week and gave him the list of questions to answer. In the 1895 article in the *Journal de Zermatt* Whymper is quoted as saying that he gave Clemenz all the information and details he asked for 'including amongst other things a questionnaire I drew up and signed intended to clear up the accident altogether, based amongst other things on the fact that the weakest rope had been used between Douglas and Old Taugwalder'. This tends to imply that Clemenz asked for the questionnaire and it is hard to imagine what he would have done without it, had Whymper not produced it. Analysis of the questions and the witnesses' answers reveals that only A10, 24, 29, 34 & 57 have any relevance to why the rope was used or why it broke. But even so there was no evidence before the Court that the rope was in any way inferior, whether by specification or by condition, to the other ropes used on the descent or to any other ropes used by mountaineers in 1865. Whymper said that the rope was less thick, but this would not in itself determine strength, and Hudson's wire-rope was no doubt less thick again. Calling it a special rope revealed nothing in terms of its construction, quality, condition or age, and there is no ground for concluding that the Court made any findings as to its adequacy or as to the justification for using it.

It is hard to avoid the conclusion that Clemenz deliberately avoided these issues and condoned the distortion of Whymper's questions during translation into German. It is not therefore surprising that he never kept his promise to send Whymper a copy of Taugwalder's answers, as Whymper would never have been satisfied with them and he would no doubt have drawn public attention to the way the most important questions had been distorted and rendered futile. One can sympathise with the view expressed by a London barrister in the *Alpine Journal* in relation to an Enquiry that Clemenz conducted four years later into the 1869 fatal accident on the Lyskamm. 'I cannot help uttering a protest, however useless it may be, against the secrecy which the character of M.Clemenz or that of Swiss Law has imparted to the judicial enquiry.'

The Enquiry Report is further considered, and extracts are quoted, in sections 4 and 5, under the following headings:

1. The Enquiry documents (5.1).
2. Evidence of the witnesses in English (5.2).
3. Notes on the evidence of Whymper and Taugwalder (5.4).
4. Whymper's questions for Taugwalder. Comparison of the three versions (5.5).
5. The verdict in English and German (5.3 and 4.74.6).
6. The original German wording of the evidence (4.74). (Whymper's in French)
7. The inventories in German (4.75). (see *AJ33*, 244-7 for French version).

See also section 3.15 (search parties) and the list of illustrations for facsimiles of Whymper's note of the hearing, his list of questions for Taugwalder and the Vecqueray document.

3.5
THE EXCOMMUNICATION THREAT

> 'They returned after six hours, and reported that they had seen the bodies lying motionless on the snow. This was on Saturday; and they proposed that we should leave on Sunday evening, so as to arrive upon the plateau at daybreak on Monday. Unwilling to lose the slightest chance, the Rev J.M'Cormick and I resolved to start on Sunday morning. The Zermatt men, threatened with excommunication by their priests if they failed to attend the early mass, were unable to accompany us. To several of them, at least, this was a severe trial. Peter Perrn declared with tears that nothing else would have prevented him from joining in the search for his old comrades.'

Arnold Lunn persistently sought to distort history by vainly contradicting the above statement by Whymper in *Scrambles*. One of his earliest pronouncements on the subject is the most revealing and seems to be based on the false principle that no one is ever threatened with injury, loss or damage, if, unknown to the victim, an armed robber has already run out of ammunition or, as in this case, a priest does not in fact possess the 'threatened' power of excommunication. '...it *may* be true that some ignorant priest insisted that the guides should attend Mass, and thus prevented them from joining the other guides who took part in the search for the victims. It is certainly untrue that they were "threatened with excommunication".'

Lunn may have had no sympathy with the Zermatt guides' ignorance of the powers of their priests, which he himself seems to have shared until he was 'informed by a learned theologian and a priest that priests do not possess the power of excommunication...that in this particular case the guides ought to have joined the search party and that if a priest advised them to the contrary, the priest in question blundered badly'. But saying that does not alter the fact that they were 'threatened with excommunication' and that the threat achieved its object. Like so many of Lunn's 'uninformed verdicts' he seems to have lost no opportunity of repeating it in the hope of discrediting Whymper; he also persisted in saying that there were guides of Täsch in Whymper's search party, but that again was not true.

The earliest record of the Zermatt guides' refusal to join the search party is in McCormick's letter of 17th July to *The Times*, where he wrote:

> 'After consulting together, Mr.Whymper and I agreed to start in search of our friends on the following morning at 1 o'clock...The Zermatt guides refused to go with us, as it would be Sunday, and urged us, as there was no hope of saving any lives, to defer our expedition until they had made preparations for overcoming the difficulties on the way. Mr.Whymper, though exhausted by upwards of 60 hours' work, gallantly refused to accede to their request.'

In his evidence to the Enquiry (A15) Whymper said how '...these same Zermatt guides refused en masse to go in search of the bodies the following morning Sunday, and it was on this account that I set out without official authority to recover the bodies'. In his letter to *The Times*, he stated: 'The guides of Zermatt, being threatened with excommunication if they did not attend the early mass, were unable to accompany us. To several, at least, I am sure this was a severe trial; for they assured me with tears that nothing but that which I have stated would have prevented them from going.'

Disregarding for the moment any possible political motive, the priests' lack of humanity may best be judged by Tyndall's almost contemporary account of the solution to the problem confronting him when in 1868 he wanted to take advantage of the fine weather and set off in the early hours of a Sunday morning for what turned out to be the first traverse of the Matterhorn from Breuil to Zermatt.

> 'I enquired of my companion whether, in the event of the day being fine, he would be ready to start on Sunday. His answer was a prompt negative. In Val Tournanche, he said, they always "sanctified the Sunday." I mentioned Bennen, my pious Catholic guide, whom I permitted and encouraged to attend his mass on all possible occasions, but who, nevertheless, always yielded without a murmur to the demands of the weather. The reasoning had its effect. On Saturday Maquignaz saw his confessor, and arranged with him to have a mass at 2 a.m. on Sunday; after which, unshaded by the sense of duties unperformed, he would commence the ascent.'

In marked contrast to the anti-Whymper extravagances of Lunn, Charles Gos referred objectively to the subject in his book *Le Cervin*, commenting that a less intransigent priest would have understood the tragedy of the situation and would not have said no. He also commented on how strange it was that L.G.Mylne should have revived the excommunication issue by adding to the note that Whymper made in the Hotel Monte Rosa guestbook on 1st September 1869. Whymper had in 1869 written a short note about the accident inside the back cover of the 1865 guestbook after discovering that his original account had been torn out. He made little reference to the actual accident and was principally protesting about the misappropriation of the several pages on which he had written his original account:

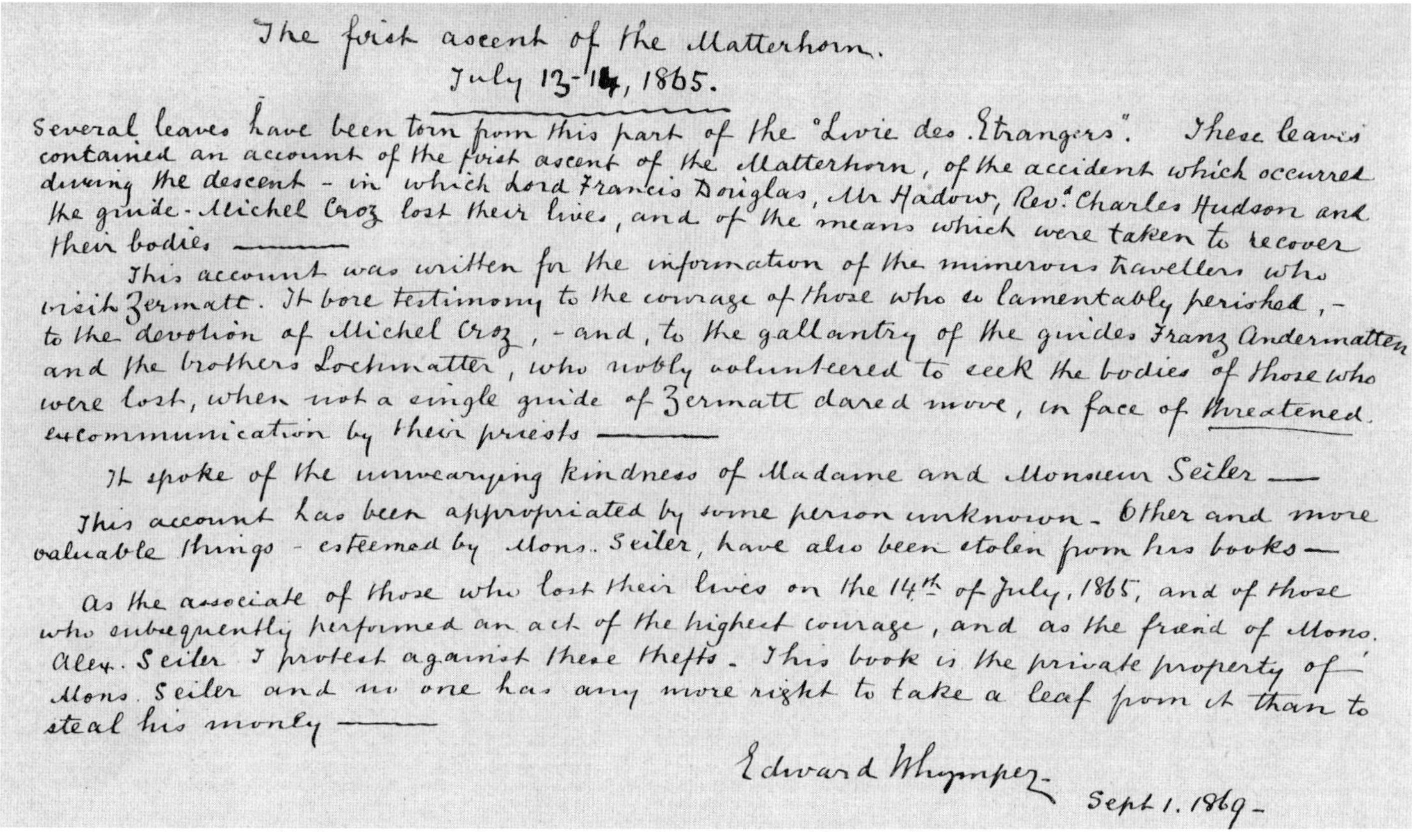

The first ascent of the Matterhorn.
July 13-14, 1865.

Several leaves have been torn from this part of the "Livre des Etrangers". These leaves contained an account of the first ascent of the Matterhorn, of the accident which occurred during the descent - in which Lord Francis Douglas, Mr Hadow, Revd. Charles Hudson and the guide - Michel Croz lost their lives, and of the means which were taken to recover their bodies ——

This account was written for the information of the numerous travellers who visit Zermatt. It bore testimony to the courage of those who so lamentably perished, - to the devotion of Michel Croz, - and, to the gallantry of the guides Franz Andermatten and the brothers Lochmatter, who nobly volunteered to seek the bodies of those who were lost, when not a single guide of Zermatt dared move, in face of threatened excommunication by their priests ——

It spoke of the unwearying kindness of Madame and Monsieur Seiler ——

This account has been appropriated by some person unknown. Other and more valuable things - esteemed by Mons. Seiler, have also been stolen from his books ——

As the associate of those who lost their lives on the 14th of July, 1865, and of those who subsequently performed an act of the highest courage, and as the friend of Mons. Alex. Seiler I protest against these thefts. This book is the private property of Mons. Seiler and no one has any more right to take a leaf from it than to steal his money ——

Edward Whymper
Sept 1. 1869 -

Whymper's entry in the Monte Rosa hotel guestbook (1869)

> 'It bore testimony to the courage of those who so lamentably perished, to the devotion of Michel Croz, and to the gallantry of the guides Franz Andermatten and the brothers Lochmatter, who so nobly volunteered to seek the bodies of those who were lost, when not a single guide in Zermatt would move, in face of threatened excommunication by their priests.'

Unfortunately Whymper left room for someone to deface the page by adding some seven lines. It is not known when this further 'crime' was committed, but it must have been within the next 25 years, as Wundt reproduced it in facsimile. The reference to one passage having been frequently misunderstood suggests that it cannot have been soon after Whymper made his entry. The addition reads

> 'Owing to the brevity of the above statement one passage in it has been frequently misunderstood. As one of the nearest relatives of Mr.Hudson, I am anxious to state for the benefit of those who may hereafter read it that the threat of excommunication launched against the Zermatt guides was not intended to prohibit their —— in the search, but to prevent their missing the Sunday morning m—— purpose. The fact that Michel Croz was a Roman catholic should of itself remove the idea ——ject was to prevent their doing a service to those of another creed. Louis George W—— [?Mylne].'

The bottom right hand corner of the page is missing, which accounts for the gaps in the text and the absence of a surname, but when the above was reproduced by Montagnier in the *Alpine Journal* in 1917 the editor added a footnote about the incomplete name. 'This, we are informed by Mrs.Charles Hudson, was Bishop Mylne, formerly Bishop of Bombay.' Mumm records that Mrs.Hudson was the daughter of Major Mylne of H.M.'s Bombay Army, so the Bishop was presumably her brother.

In September 1895 Jules Monod, the Editor of the *Journal de Zermatt*, published a letter he had received from the Zermatt Curé Zurbriggen, referring to the interview with Whymper that had been published on the 25th August. Zurbriggen sought to refute the reference to the guides being threatened with excommunication, on the ground that a priest could never carry out such a threat, and he added that Ruden himself had gone to the glacier the following day (Monday) with some leading Zermatt guides to recover the bodies. But this is inconsistent with the evidence in the Official Enquiry documents and elsewhere of the bodies being recovered on the Thursday, and it is hard to believe that Ruden would have made a special visit to the scene, when he could have learnt everything he wished to know from either McCormick or Whymper.

Ronald Clark made some odd comments on the threat of excommunication issue in his book *The Day the Rope Broke*, implying that there was just a misunderstanding and that the idea that 'the guides of Zermatt, being "threatened with excommunication by their priests if they did not attend the early Mass, were unable to accompany us"' became rooted in Whymper's head. 'Now this was an ignorant observation...More surprising is the fact that he believed this in such company. Neither M'Cormick nor Robertson, neither Philpott nor Girdlestone can have believed the tale; all must have known that the words did not mean what they appeared to mean.'

But in seeking to attribute the whole idea of the Zermatt men being prevented from going on the rescue party, as a result of their priests threatening them with excommunication, to a misunderstanding, Clark has ignored the other evidence and completely overlooked the reaction of the Zermatt guides, as recorded by Whymper; 'To several of them, at least, this was a severe trial. Peter Perrn declared with tears that nothing else would have prevented him from joining in the search for his old comrades.'

Clark reckoned that 'in the communication from guides via Seiler to Whymper the story became garbled', but that cannot possibly account for Perren's near despair at not being allowed to go and search for Michel Croz, Charles Hudson and Douglas Hadow with whom he had climbed Mont Blanc and subsequently travelled to Zermatt only a few days before. Clark seems also to have misled himself by omitting the start of the sentence which he quotes from McCormick's *Times* letter on p159. 'The Zermatt guides refused to go with us, as it would be Sunday'. *Refused* is the important word. McCormick also referred in his pamphlet *A sad holiday* to the difficulty they had in getting a party together without any Zermatt guides. 'Mr. Whymper, the Rev J. Robertson, Mr. Phillpotts, and I, accordingly arranged to leave at one o'clock in the morning (Sunday). With some trouble we secured the services of five guides, none of whom were Zermatt men. The Revs. Messrs. Warr and Sanders kindly undertook my duty.'

Very little is known about Phillpotts, but Girdlestone's involvement in these events is certainly incorrect as he remained at the Riffel on the Saturday night and did not meet Whymper until he returned on the Sunday afternoon. As for Robertson, Clark has overlooked the strongest evidence in support of the theory that in those days Zermatt was ruled by its priests who resented any outside interference by foreigners. But before looking further at Robertson, it is necessary to draw attention to some other factors that may have been at work.

The Curé Ruden left Zermatt and was succeeded there in 1865 by Mathias Welschen. The two men were contemporaries, both born in Zermatt in 1817, and they were both original partners in the plan to build the Riffel hotel. Welschen was a cousin of Joseph Welschen, who was the President of the Zermatt Gemeinde from 1863 until 1867. It may be that Ruden was still in office in July 1865. Joseph Welschen the President was not a mountain guide, but he led the first search party on the Hohlicht on the Saturday. They were out for six hours and Welschen may not have been very keen to set out again after only a few hours rest, although this is exactly what Jean Tairraz and the Lochmatter brothers did. Up to now nothing has ever been revealed of the minutes of the Council meetings held in Zermatt relating to the accident and its aftermath nor of such things as the report which Welschen would almost certainly have made out after the search. It was Joseph Welschen who also led the third search party that recovered the three bodies the following Thursday and it is most probable that he would have led the second party had it not left Zermatt until the Sunday evening. Regardless of the wishes of the priesthood he should have been capable of exercising leadership as President and it must be assumed that he approved of the Zermatt men not being allowed to accompany Whymper, even if he did not instigate it. There is however a hint in one of the questions Clemenz put to Whymper at the Enquiry (Q15) and in particular in Whymper's answer that he may have been reprimanded for taking the initiative:

> (A15) '...They returned six hours later, saying that they had caught sight of the bodies but that it was impossible to reach them that day. On the other hand these same Zermatt guides refused en masse to go in search of the bodies the following morning, Sunday, and it was on this account that I set out without official authority to recover the bodies and that on my return I did not think I had to make an official report.'

It looks very much as though Whymper had probably already taken the initiative on the Saturday evening and had organized a private party of Zermatt guides led by Perren to accompany him and McCormick and to set off in the early hours of Sunday morning, as this is consistent with what he wrote in his article in the *Graphic* in 1894:

> 'To minimise the peril, it was arranged to start at midnight so as to pass through the séracs before they were struck by the sun. When this became known, the Zermatt guides were threatened with excommunication if they failed to attend the early Mass, and were thus debarred from coming. Volunteers were then called for, and a sufficient number of men came forward. First to offer himself was Franz Andermatten, a first-rate mountaineer, who lived at Saas, beyond the jurisdiction of the priests of Zermatt; and under his leading the bodies were recovered and buried. Next Sunday Franz Andermatten went to Mass, and this was his reward. "I saw him," said my informant (who is now Head Master of one of our public schools), "turned out, *ejected*, from the church at Zermatt!"'

Whymper prefaced the above by stating that two incidents in connection with the catastrophe had recently come to his knowledge and it seems almost certain that his informant was James Robertson, who was Headmaster of Haileybury from 1884 until 1890. The fact that he was no longer Headmaster by 1894 is of no great significance, particularly as the second incident related to a Mr. R– who must have been Robertson, but there is also another inconsistency at first sight in that Robertson in fact left Zermatt on Saturday 22nd July. It is likely that his guide Andenmatten also left that day, if not the previous evening, as there would be no reason for staying on after giving evidence to the Enquiry. But it is quite possible that Andenmatten tried to attend Mass on the Monday, Tuesday, Wednesday or Friday of the week following the accident and that the incident took place then. Theodor Wundt seems to be the only writer to have referred to Whymper quoting this incident, which may well have been recorded in Robertson's diary.

It therefore looks very much as though the intention had been to frustrate Whymper's private search party and that after this had proved impossible Andenmatten became the target for spite. And surely no ordinary search or rescue party organised in an atmosphere of goodwill and cooperation would have caused McCormick to pay such a forthright tribute as he did in his letter of 17th July to *The Times*: 'Franz Andermatten of Saas; the brothers Lochmatter of Macugnaga; and Frederic Payot and Jean Tairraz, of Chamounix, generously offered their services for the expedition. We hope their names will not be forgotten.'

3.6 GUIDES

3.6.1 Fees

Although the pound was worth twenty five francs in the 1860's, not all the tourists who went to the Alps to climb could afford to employ a guide every day as the following extract from Girdlestone's book published in 1870 shows. 'There are a number of travellers who can by no means afford the luxury of carrying a guide about with them: for the ordinary charge of one is from six to ten francs a day and twenty francs for glacier days: often it is much higher!'

The fixing of fees for mountain ascents seems to have been a natural progression from the tariffs fixed for travellers employing porters and mules between one place and another. When in 1858 the authorities in Sion fixed the tariff for guides and porters starting from Zermatt, the excursions specified were mostly passes to such places as Tournanche, Macugnaga and Saas and only three peaks were included, Monte Rosa, Cima di Jazzi and Mettelhorn. It seems as though the fees for any special ascent or long engagement were a matter for negotiation and that the wealthier employers could afford to pay more for the better guides, which would explain a passage in a letter Whymper wrote to Adams Reilly in 1865 after finding that Croz had been engaged by Birkbeck for six weeks from the end of June.

> 'I have been very much annoyed by Croz throwing me up. I s*uppose* he is tempted by more £. s. d., otherwise I cannot account for it, as it was a distinct understanding when we parted that he was engaged by me for the early part of the season; but when I wrote a few weeks ago, he informed me that he was already engaged.'

In 1861 Whymper arrived in Breuil with an Oberland guide he did not name, and he endeavoured to induce another guide to accompany them on the Matterhorn.

> 'A sturdy old fellow – Peter Taugwalder by name – said he would go! His price? "Two hundred francs." "What whether we ascend or not?" "Yes – nothing less." The end of the

> matter was, that all the men who were more or less capable showed a strong disinclination, or positively refused to go (their disinclination being very much in proportion to their capacity), or else asked a prohibitive price.'

Old Peter's demand of 200 francs contrasts strangely with that of J-A Carrel the same year, although he did insist that Whymper should take a third guide as well. 'Twenty francs a day, whatever was the result, was his price.' Old Peter's exorbitant demand probably has some relevance to his dissatisfaction in receiving only 100 francs from Whymper after the first ascent from Zermatt, even though Whymper was to describe it as 'the highest price ever paid for mountain ascents'. There is no means of knowing what Kennedy paid Old Peter in 1862 for the abortive attempts to climb the Hörnli in January and the Dent Blanche in July, but it seems probable that he was generously rewarded by Lord Francis Douglas for the numerous excursions they carried out in June and July 1865 whilst trying to find the way up the Obergabelhorn. Indeed, one of the reasons why Douglas can no longer have intended to attempt the Matterhorn in 1865 until Whymper invited him to join him must be that he had spent almost all the money he had with him in Zermatt, whatever arrangements he may have had for drawing more in a town. Taking account of the fact that Old Peter had dropped vertically some 24 feet with the cornice that collapsed under their luncheon party on the top of the Obergabelhorn, a far more alarming experience for him than the incident with Kennedy on the Dent Blanche when he had insisted on retreating, he may well have been reluctant to attempt any more new mountains without the expectation of receiving a very high reward. His expectations would in any event be related to whatever Douglas had paid him for finding the Obergabelhorn, of which Whymper would have known nothing. It seems as though it was Douglas who persuaded Old Peter to accompany them and when the time came for Whymper to pay the guides on behalf of all the employers he chose to pay 100 francs for Croz and for Old Peter and 80 francs for Young Peter. He also gave a tip of 20 francs, which he bore himself and did not share with the victims' families like the fees, and it seems that Old Peter kept it all for himself but was still not satisfied. Even the tip of 20 francs compares very favourably with the tip Whymper gave Croz in 1864, which was only 25 francs for a whole month's employment.

Charles Parker spoke to Old Peter within six weeks of the accident and later expressed the opinion 'It is very possible that the payment was just right in the circumstances'. Old Peter had told Parker 'that he would never have run so much risk for the payment he received', which is perhaps consistent with his wanting 200 francs as leading guide on the Italian ridge, even though Croz was the leading guide on the Hörnli. But having regard to the fact that the Hörnli proved very much easier than anyone had anticipated he would presumably have been even more dissatisfied with 120 francs had they had to overcome some real difficulties. The substance of his complaint may therefore have been that he expected to be compensated for the shock he suffered after the accident.

Although the Matterhorn featured in a new tariff included in Ruden's book, published in 1869, there had clearly been differences of opinion both at Zermatt and at Breuil as to what it was worth in the years that followed the first ascent. There is no knowing what it cost Birkbeck to take his seven St.Niklaus guides as far as the shoulder in 1866, but Thioly wrote of Young Peter Taugwalder and Moser visiting him in Geneva the following winter with a view to making the ascent the next summer: 'the two guides asked me for 150 francs each in addition to two porters at 75 francs. This was a lot of money, but I so wanted to make the climb that I accepted these onerous propositions.' But when the summer came the guides opted out!

In July 1867 Tyndall encountered similar greed at Breuil when he met Carrel, after having corresponded with him for some time with a view to climbing the Matterhorn. 'He had naturally and deservedly grown in his own estimation. But I was discomfited by the form his self-consciousness assumed. His demands were exorbitant, and he also objected to the excellent company of Christian Michel. In fact my friend Carrel was no longer a reasonable man.'

In a letter to Canon Carrel, Tyndall disclosed that Carrel had required him to take four guides and pay them 150 francs each, a total of 600 francs just for guides! But some good came out of this extortion and the Canon encouraged the Maquignaz brothers to make the ascent so as to avoid Carrel getting a monopoly. He told Tyndall that it would be a pleasure for them to accompany him on the climb, without demanding a large financial sacrifice. 'A tip would suffice!' Jordan found the same constructive attitude when he employed the Maquignaz brothers, writing in the guestbook of the Hotel Mont Cervin at Breuil in 1867,

> 'My companions on this trip have, in a great measure, acted as volunteers: but those intending to make the ascent cannot as a rule, I think, expect to obtain guides and porters at less than 40frs a day for the former and 25frs a day for the latter: paying half price for any idle days which may be spent on the mountain.'

But Jordan was also very helpful to the Italians and he must have done more than anyone else to open up both the Zermatt and the Breuil routes. Canon Carrel wrote on the subject of fees in his book *La Vallée de Valtornenche en 1867*,

> 'There is still no tariff for ascents of the Matterhorn. I thought initially one could base it on Mont Blanc and Monte Rosa but having spoken at length on the subject with Messrs Leighton Jordan and F. Giordano, the engineer, and after having consulted several Valtornenche guides one can it seems to me adopt the following tariff:– 100frs for each guide and 50frs for each porter. If travellers want to descend to Zermatt the guides fee is 150 each. I should make the observation that two guides are necessary for one traveller and at least two porters, as the ascent is steep and long. I say nothing about tipping which is at the traveller's discretion.'

It is interesting to note how the tariff published by Ruden is consistent with the comments of the Canon. But the fees for the Matterhorn were altogether out of line with those for the Dent Blanche and the Weisshorn. The fee of 100frs for the Matterhorn remained the same for 50 years and although the Dent Blanche and Weisshorn gradually crept up from 60frs, it was not till much later that they drew ahead to command the premium that they still do to-day. The following details are extracted from the list published by Ruden.

Ascent	Distance in hours	Guide francs	Porter francs
Monte Rosa	10	40	25
Weisshorn	18	60	35
Täschhorn	11	40	25
Matterhorn	12	100	50
As far as shoulder	10	40	25
As far as the hut	8	20	15
Lyskamm	11	40	25
Dent Blanche	15	60	30
Rothorn	15	50	25
Gabelhorn	10	30	20
Rimpfischhorn	10	20	15
Breithorn	8	20	12

3.6.2 Rivalry between Zermatt and Chamonix

Even before Croz' death on the Matterhorn relations between the Chamonix guides and the German guides, as those of Zermatt and Grindelwald seem to have been known, were not good and they had already been aggravated in 1865 by Whymper's first ascent of the Aiguille Verte in the company of Christian Almer and Franz Biner. Chamonix had for many years with its petty regulations and bureaucratic interference sought to impose its inferior guides on tourists, with the inevitable result that there were few good guides there and the better climbers brought their German guides with them. Kennedy wrote of the first ascent of the Aiguille Verte in July 1865:

> 'On the very day I entered Chamouni, Mr. Whymper succeeded in making the first ascent of our mountain, with two German guides, but, from various circumstances, of which not the least one was the ill-temper shown by the Chamouni guides as a body to their more fortunate German brethren, a groundless doubt was cast by them upon his success...I may here state that the Chamouni guides have made at least twenty attempts to scale this peak, of which some were really hard tussles with the mountain, whilst others were merely sham expeditions organized to extort money from their employers, it being well understood amongst the guides that the first difficulty should stop them.'

Whymper commented in *Scrambles* on how the ascent might have been expected to please the locals, and the prospect of more francs flowing as a result might have stifled any jealousy consequent on the success of foreigners, but

> 'It was not so. Chamounix stood on its rights. A stranger had ignored their regulations – had imported two foreign guides; and, furthermore, he had added injury to that insult – he had not taken a single Chamounix guide. Chamounix would be revenged! It would bully the foreign guides; it would tell them they had lied – that they had not made the ascent! Where were their proofs? Where was the flag upon the summit?
> Poor Almer and Biener were accordingly chivied from pillar to post, from one inn to another, and at length complained to me. Peter Perrn, the Zermatt guide, said on the night that we returned that this was to happen, but the story seemed too absurd to be true. I now bade my men go out again, and followed them myself to see the sport. Chamounix was greatly excited. The bureau of the 'guide chef' was thronged with clamouring men. Their ringleader – one Zacharie Cachat – a well-known guide, of no particular merit, though not a bad fellow, was haranging the multitude. He met with more than his match. My friend Kennedy, who was on the spot, heard of the disturbance, and rushed into the fray, confronted the burly guide, and thrust back his absurdities into his teeth.
> There were the materials for a very pretty riot; but they manage these things in France better than we do, and the gendarmes – three strong – came down and dispersed the crowd.'

Whymper goes on to state that Cachat was put into confinement, so it is not altogether surprising in view of the death of Croz at Zermatt a fortnight later, that there should have been more trouble when Young Peter Taugwalder arrived in Chamonix some ten days after the accident, as Buxton described in the *Alpine Journal*:

> '...we were much troubled by a strike of our guides – a strike not for rise of wages, but against the employment of non-union men. We had one day found young Taugwald lounging outside the hotel, having been just paid off by his employer, and looking out for a return job. As he is a strong lad we engaged him as our porter. Just at this time Jean Baptiste Croz had come back from Zermatt, looking emaciated and almost crazed at the loss of his brother. His grief found vent in wild tales and half-informed accusations against the men who had been with him at the time of his death. The garrulous Frenchmen who listened, sympathized, and believed, and spread these reports, and the morning after engaging Taugwald our guides came to us, and made an abominable accusation, first against him and then against his father, and announced that they dare not and would not go with him.'

J-B Croz was not the only Chamonix guide to get involved in the aftermath of the accident at Zermatt, as the following list of dates in July shows.
15th. Michel Balmat & Jean Tairraz went on the search party to the Stockje and the Hohlicht.
16th. Jean Tairraz & Frédéric Payot went on Whymper's search party, which found the body of Michel Croz.
19/20th. Henri Charlet & Michel Devouassoud went on the recovery party.
22nd. Jean-Baptiste Croz arrived at Zermatt in the evening. The following morning he collected and signed for his brother's possessions and then left.

On 8th August Wigram wrote to Whymper, telling him of a letter he had received from J-B Croz in which he 'speaks of a suspicion prevalent in the Valley of Chamonix, and I fear shared by himself that Taugwald *cut* the rope on the Matterhorn. The grounds of this dreadful charge are the improbability of such a rope breaking and the fact that young Taugwald had just come to Chamonix whence it was assumed that he was escaping justice.' Whymper's reply by return of post included: 'I cannot say that I am altogether surprised at the rumour to which you refer, as there is not amiable feeling (this year particularly) between the guides of Chamounix and the German guides, but the rumour is absolutely without foundation.'

Whereas it was unfortunate for Young Peter that he had to go to Chamonix little more than a week after the accident, presumably as a result of a long standing arrangement, it is remarkable to find him in effect taking his father there in 1866 to climb Mont Blanc on at least two occasions, if there was hostility towards them there. Young Peter was capable of looking after himself and his visits to Chamonix clearly helped to open up his career, but for Old Peter to fill the role of second guide behind his son on a mountain he had not climbed before, when previously his son had been second guide to him, represents a fundamental change that is hard to understand, particularly if the Chamonix guides had not changed their attitude.

When Montagnier was corresponding with Rudolf Taugwalder in 1917 he sent him eight questions about the accident that he wished Young Peter to answer, and Rudolf duly replied setting out the eight answers in English, but after Answer 8 Rudolf suddenly switched from English to German (which Montagnier did not understand), adding:

> 'The ninth question would be: why did old Peter Taugwalder go to America?
> Answer: After this accident and this success on the Matterhorn, all the guides of Chamonix and St.Niklaus were so envious and cunning that they did everything they could to make the lives of the Taugwalders as unbearable as possible. All sorts of jealousy and slander were used to weaken their good reputation in every respect. Both the guides of St.Niklaus and those of Chamonix caused thousands of francs loss by their shameful slanders. Peter Taugwalder eventually wanted to escape from these envious people and these slanders and so he went to America!'

This is a most remarkable (and unlikely) explanation for Old Peter going to America as, apart from the separate issue of the guides of St.Niklaus of whom the Zermatt guides had become extremely envious by the 1870's, it hardly seems likely that Old Peter would have gone to Chamonix even once, let alone on two or more occasions, if the Chamonix guides were ruining his business and reputation whenever they went to Zermatt. It seems most unlikely that a Chamonix guide in Zermatt could damage Old Peter and there is no evidence to suggest that this ever happened. Nor can there surely be any question of whatever a Chamonix guide might choose to say or do in Chamonix damaging the career that Old Peter had until 1865 confined to the Zermatt area. If the guides of Chamonix resented the interest in Mont Blanc that the Taugwalders seem to have developed after Croz' death and conducted themselves in such a manner as to be offensive to Old Peter, he would surely have been able stay in Zermatt and continue his old career there.

The most likely explanation for the attempt to blame the guides of Chamonix would seem to be the wish to divert attention from the real culprits, the guides of Zermatt. They, unlike the guides of Chamonix, must have had the opportunity of making Old Peter's life unbearable, whether or not they took advantage of it. It seems therefore that despite the ill feeling that did exist between the guides of Chamonix and the German guides, aggravated in the case of the Taugwalders by the death of Croz, this cannot have played any significant role in the virtual collapse of Old Peter's pre-accident career as a good Monte Rosa guide.

There seems to be a distinct possibility that the reason why Old Peter broke new ground in Chamonix after the accident was to escape from his Zermatt comrades, a very easy option compared with his later alternative of escaping to America. Stéphen d'Arve, a French journalist who does not seem to have been a very reliable writer and who certainly did not as he said meet the two Taugwalders in Chamonix a fortnight after the accident although he may perhaps have met them there in 1866, wrote of a German Swiss cabinet maker living in Chamonix introducing him to Old Peter in the Hotel d'Angleterre, where he was eating with about twenty other guides: 'This is the journalist who has written your story; do you want to give him some more details?...You cut the rope didn't you? The axe worked well didn't it?' –Yes! yes! echoed the voices of fifteen guides sitting at the same table.' But the odd thing about this reported encounter in Chamonix is that d'Arve expressly stated that the group of twenty guides were from the Valais. The story does not therefore reflect against the guides of Chamonix, and even if it is consistent with the idea that Old Peter was trying to escape from his comrades at Zermatt it suggests that he did not always succeed.

3.6.3 Rivalry between Zermatt and St.Niklaus

In 1865 when the Swiss Alpine Club published in its yearbook details of the leading glacier guides in the various resorts, it devoted some three pages to the guides of Zermatt and a mere eleven lines to those of St.Niklaus. Only two men of St.Niklaus got a full entry, J-M Lochmatter and J.M.Ritz, with a note that the latter was in Zermatt in the summer, whereas eleven Zermatters had entries ranging from a mere three lines to as many as twenty one in the case of Peter Perren. Peter Knubel, Alexander Lochmatter and P.J. and J.Imboden of St.Niklaus were also named as deserving recommendation for the Zermatt mountains. Disregarding Ritz, who seems to have been based at the Riffel, the Zermatters seem therefore to have had relatively little competition from St.Niklaus. The experience of the Lochmatters and Knubels appears to have been somewhat limited and J.M.Elliott may well have been justified in his criticism of the technique of J-M Lochmatter and Peter Knubel on the Matterhorn in 1868, simply because they had not at that time had much experience of climbing steep rock.

There does not appear to be any record of any Zermatt guide attempting the Hörnli ridge of the Matterhorn between the first ascent on 14th July 1865 and Peter Perren's ascent on 22nd July 1871. For six years they kept away from it no doubt as a result of the Taugwalders' exaggerated accounts of the dangers and difficulties. They seem to have turned a blind eye to what was going on round about them; the building of the hut at 3818 metres, the various attempts and ascents by guides from St.Niklaus, Breuil and elsewhere including six successful expeditions up the Hörnli in 1868 alone, and even Jordan's account of the Hörnli in 1867, which he recorded in the guestbook of the hotel Monte Rosa. Jordan had climbed the Hörnli as far as the scene of the accident before having to retreat on account of snowfall, and after reaching the summit from Breuil a few weeks later he then descended the Hörnli as far as his previous highest point. He returned to the summit, descended to Breuil and called at Zermatt on his way home. In the guestbook he referred to the upper part of the Hörnli as 'these glorious slopes' and included in his long account for the benefit of tourists 'As far as my experience of mountaineering in Switzerland goes, this ascent of the Matterhorn is the most glorious and enjoyable trip a mountaineer can make'. The guides of Zermatt no doubt thought they knew best but by boycotting the mountain they gave the guides of St.Niklaus a virtual monopoly of the Matterhorn in the valley and this was to last for more than five years.

On 26th July 1866 the *Journal de Genève* reported how John Birkbeck with seven guides had failed even to reach the shoulder of the Matterhorn; 'we should add that since last year's accident the Zermatt guides have a real fear of engaging in an enterprise of this nature'. Birkbeck had in fact made the attempt on 14th July 1866 and all seven of his guides came not from Zermatt, as the *Journal de Genève* implied, but from St.Niklaus. It is not known who they all were, but they certainly included Peter Knubel and the two Lochmatters and the other four were probably those whose names feature in the early ascents of the Hörnli, as the occasion was the ideal opportunity for the guides of St.Niklaus to discover what the Matterhorn was really like. The guides were so nervous that they made Birkbeck agree 'not to mention afterwards which of them went with me to the top so that any one of them might have no hesitation in remaining behind if he found himself at all afraid'. But the fact is that they had a go and the following year J-M Lochmatter made another two attempts with Jordan, Knubel joining him in the second.

In 1868 Lochmatter made three ascents, Peter Knubel made four and his brother Niklaus three. By the end of the 1872 season when Peter Perren, Young Peter Taugwalder and Franz Biner had each made one post-accident ascent of the Matterhorn, the guides of St.Niklaus had more than thirty ascents to their credit.

Even though in 1873 there were four ascents by Zermatt guides, compared with fourteen by St.Niklaus, and the number gradually increased thereafter, the St.Niklaus figures increased far more quickly so that by the end of 1875 when there had according to the tables published by Whymper been less than twenty ascents by Zermatt guides, there had already been more than ninety by the guides of St.Niklaus. This seems to have had several far-reaching effects. It is probable that it aggravated the difficulties that Old Peter Taugwalder had been experiencing with 'his comrades and neighbours at Zermatt', particularly when each succeeding ascent would make it more and more obvious that the Zermatt guides need never have let the guides of St.Niklaus dominate their mountain. If the other Zermatt guides had been jealous of Old Peter having made the first ascent, their jealousy would have turned to resentment when they realised that it was his inability to cope with such relatively minor difficulties as there were above the shoulder that caused him so to exaggerate the dangers as to deter them from even attempting the ascent, whilst the guides of St.Niklaus prospered. It is, therefore, hardly surprising that by 1874 Old Peter should have decided he could stand no more and that he went to America.

In 1876 the Zermatt guides gave vent to their jealousy of their St.Niklaus rivals by trying to prevent Seiler giving them any employment or accomodation. They were no doubt losing out on other peaks as well and not just on the Matterhorn, and it is probable that when they found they could not get their way with Seiler they decided to make life as difficult as they could for him as well. This may account to some extent for Seiler's application to become a burger being resisted for 17 years. Frederick Gardiner was in Zermatt in 1876 and he wrote subsequently of Seiler:

> 'He told me that early in the season he had been waited upon by a deputation of guides, who suggested that he should refuse accomodation to all foreign guides, and recommend only guides connected with the commune, excluding even the guides of St.Niklaus. Of course it is needless to say that M.Seiler at once repudiated so atrocious an idea, and he has since been constantly harrassed by the shortsighted and petty persecutions of this benighted commune; they endeavour to refuse him the right of citizenship, and are combined not to supply him with wood, eggs or other produce, and he is compelled to obtain his supplies from below St.Niklaus. While I was staying at Zermatt his cows were seized and driven from the mountains, the wiseacres of the neighbourhood having decided to refuse him the right of pasturage. Telegraphic orders from Bern forced them to send the cows back to their pasturage, and indemnify M.Seiler for his inconvenience.'

As for the guides of St.Niklaus, they were no doubt also victims of the Zermatters' envy and spite, whenever the opportunity presented itself. In the same article Gardiner wrote of one such incident relating to Peter Knubel. They were at the Stockje hut when Peter Knubel's brother Hans told Gardiner that Peter was 'extremely ill'.

> 'He was indeed very ill, and evidently suffering horribly from cramp in the stomach; his face was black, his lips blue, his hands clenched, and his limbs almost rigid. I was really very much alarmed and scarcely knew what to do; we applied heated stones, warm brandy, &c., and he shortly got a little better. The Baron and his cousin were most kind, and did all they could to assist, and as they were returning to Zermatt and did not require all the provisions, and above all the wine, they had brought with them, they most generously offered it for my acceptance. I need scarcely say how gratefully I accepted their kind offer, for I scarcely knew how long we might be detained at the hut. In order to make myself clearly understood I may state that when the offer was made to me, their guides had already packed up all the provisions and wine and were ordered by the Baron to unlade, which being done, three bottles of wine, half a bottle of brandy, and sundry eatables were made over to me by him. I then went out of the hut to say adieu to my kind friends, and saw them fairly off. Returning to the hut I immediately missed the wine and brandy which the Baron had left, and then found to my disgust that his guides had actually, after having been ordered to leave us the wine for the benefit of a sick fellow-guide, when our backs were turned repacked it in their knapsacks and made off with it! The Baron himself discovered it in Weisshorn Biener's knapsack, who professed the utmost amazement at finding it there.'

It seems probable that the culprit was in fact Young Peter Taugwalder, the Baron's other guide, as such an act would have been completely out of character for a man like Biner, of whom Elliott had written some years earlier; 'But most of all I like to mention his genuineness, his extreme simplicity, his diffidence, his perfect straightforwardness, his candour, his trustworthiness and his kindness of heart.'

It seems therefore that by discouraging the other Zermatt guides from climbing the Matterhorn, whether by word or by his own example, and indeed by failing to encourage them to try it – even by going on their own without any tourist, as the Maquignaz brothers had done from Breuil in 1867 – Old Peter Taugwalder must have lost his fellow Zermatt guides a great deal of business and he must have been largely responsible for creating the antagonism that developed between Zermatt and St.Niklaus. There is no reason why in 1865 the few good guides of St.Niklaus should have been envious of the Taugwalders for having made the first ascent and should have gone out of their way to cause them harm. On the contrary, as the years went by, the guides of St.Niklaus grew in experience and in number, and by their willingness to accompany tourists up the Matterhorn they came to dominate the climbing scene in Zermatt to such an extent that Seiler became the focal point of the Zermatters' envy. It is, therefore, remarkable to find that in 1917 when Montagnier was asking Young Peter some questions about his father in relation to the 1865 accident, using Rudolf Taugwalder as correspondent, he should have been given the answers to the eight questions he had asked and that Taugwalder should then have posed and answered a ninth question and in the course of so doing blamed the guides of St.Niklaus (and those of Chamonix) for making life so unbearable for Old Peter that by 1874 he was forced to escape to America!

> 'The ninth question would be: why did old Peter Taugwalder go to America?
> Answer: After this accident and this success on the Matterhorn, all the guides of Chamonix and St.Niklaus were so envious and cunning that they did everything they could to make the lives of the Taugwalders as unbearable as possible. All sorts of jealousy and slander were used to weaken their good reputation in every respect. Both the guides of St.Niklaus and those of Chamonix caused thousands of francs loss by their shameful slanders. Peter Taugwalder eventually wanted to escape from these envious people and these slanders and so he went to America!'

3.7
HADOW'S BOOTS

'Hadow's heels' was the title of a three page article in *Die Alpen* in 1950, in which Frédéric Montandon sought to attribute the Matterhorn accident not to Hadow's inexperience but to the nailing of his boots, said to be such that he was shod like a mule. However it was not Montandon, but Charles Gos in his book *Alpinisme anecdotique* in 1934, who first raised the idea after examining the boots in the Zermatt Museum. But after boots belonging to the two Douglases were exhibited in London as part of the Alpine Club's Centenary celebrations in 1957, some confusion seems to have arisen over the identity of the owner of the boot with the horseshoe metal plate round the heel.

Whymper is quoted in the *Journal de Zermatt* as stating that although they only found three of the four bodies on the Matterhorn glacier after the accident, they found all eight boots. He referred expressly to recognising Lord Francis Douglas's boots because they were too small for him and he had remedied this by cutting them before setting off. The Enquiry Report Inventory also records a broken boot belonging to Lord Douglas. It seems therefore that there was a clear distinguishing feature on Lord Douglas's boots, which was also recorded in somewhat different terms in the *Echo des Alpes* of 1872. A climber named Bruel wrote of his party having asked Seiler to show them his relics of the 1865 accident. One object they were shown was a boot with the sole peeled away but still attached to the heel. Bruel states that the boot had been recognised as that of Douglas as on the side of the heel a piece some two inches in diameter had been removed to accomodate an injury he had sustained at that point three weeks earlier. The boot described by Bruel is further identified as that of Douglas by a photograph in Theodor Wundt's 1896 book, *Das Matterhorn und seine Geschichte*, which shows the peeled sole and some sort of cut in the

Boot worn by Lord Douglas

leather on the side of the heel. Fry, a tourist, also saw Lord Douglas's boot in 1871.

Blakeney wrote in 1958 of the two boots exhibited in the Zermatt Museum having the names written on the soles and of Hadow's boot having no iron plate but some hob nails round the heel. He said it was not known who had identified the boots in the first place. It seems however that the boots must have been labelled wrongly at some time in the last fifty years and that whatever doubts there may or may not be about the boot illustrating Montandon's article having belonged to Hadow, rather than to Hudson or even to the victim of some other climbing accident, it certainly did not belong to Lord Francis Douglas. As for the relevance to Hadow's slip of any semi-circular metal plate on the heel of his boot, it is not uncommon nowadays for the death of a mountaineer, who falls in unknown circumstances, to be attributed to his boots if it is found that they are worn or not the most suitable for the conditions, as though someone armed with such a pair of boots will be never be guilty of any carelessness or bad judgment that could cause or result in loss of balance. But when the facts are known, there is no need for such a scapegoat.

There is no evidence whatever that Hadow was deliberately descending when he slipped, when the inability to gain a secure foothold could conceivably have been due to a lack of friction at his heel. Montandon misquoted Taugwalder's evidence at the Enquiry by attributing to him Whymper's precise words in A11 'As far as I know at the moment the accident occurred Mr.Hadow was the only one moving'; but Whymper did not mean by this that Hadow was moving intentionally. For Hadow's fault was not that he slipped but that he slipped at the wrong moment. Hudson was clearly not paying attention at the vital moment as he should have been, and the reason may well be that after Hadow had taken some steps down it was then Croz' turn to descend. In *Scrambles* Whymper clarified his belief as to what had happened:

> 'So far as I know, no one was actually descending. I cannot speak with certainty...but it is my belief, from the movements of their shoulders, that Croz, [having taken hold of Hadow's legs and put his feet, one by one, into their proper positions], was in the act of turning round, to go down a step or two himself; at this moment Mr.Hadow slipped, fell against him, and knocked him over.'

For Hadow to have slipped in such circumstances would require that he must first have lost his balance and been unable to regain it, and as Croz would hardly have stood him with only half an inch or so of his heels in contact with the mountain, rather than in bucket sized steps if he was standing on snow, it does not seem possible that the narrow metal plates at the back of Hadow's heels should have caused him to slip.

Montandon likened the manner of Hadow's fall with the 'bizarre' metal plates on his heels, to the role played by some unsuspected orange peel on which a pedestrian slips, but even if Hadow had unwittingly been standing with his heel on a banana skin there would have been no risk of his slipping on it, had he stood still and upright. He lost his balance and could not regain it without moving, at a time when it was Croz' turn to move and when even Hudson did not expect him to move, or else he would never have allowed the rope to go slack between them. Had the rope been taut Hudson would surely have been able to hold Hadow and prevent him knocking Croz over. Whymper wrote how 'The rope was not taut from [Hudson] to Hadow, and the two men fell ten or twelve feet before the jerk came upon him'. There is therefore no evidence to suggest that anyone expected Hadow to move, nor reason why the nailing of his boots should have initiated the loss of balance against which a more competent and experienced mountaineer could have been expected to guard in such a relatively exposed situation.

3.8
ILLUSTRATIONS OF THE ACCIDENT

The most dramatic pictures of bodies flying off the Matterhorn relate not to the 1865 accident but to that on 7th August 1893, when Alexander Seiler's son Andreas and Johann Biner were killed on the Italian ridge. They are mentioned here merely to distinguish them from the 1865 catastrophe as some illustrations of the latter hardly depict the scene any more accurately and show only five climbers. Whereas two of the Seiler pictures appeared in Italian periodicals a fortnight after the accident, another even more spectacular one was included as a full page illustration in Whymper's 1894 article in the *Graphic*. The origin of the latter is not clear, although the name 'O.Angerer & Göschl' appears in the bottom left hand corner. It shares a number of features with one of the others, such as the taut rope between the two falling climbers and an ice axe in mid-air.

A number of illustrations of no great merit, and of which little trace now remains, were probably published in newspapers and periodicals in the months that followed the 1865 accident. Whymper retained a couple of them including one from *A New Year's tract*, which shows the now conventional view of the Matterhorn from Zermatt with four gigantic figures falling from it. A more realistic but nevertheless inaccurate drawing appeared in *Le Monde Illustré* of 5th August, accompanied by an extract from the article in the *Journal de Genève* of 18th July. The drawing relied on a sketch by M.Pajot, who, it is said, happened to be in the valley at the time and based it on the account of an eye witness. The illustrations mentioned below are listed according to the date of publication and each is given an initial letter,which is also used as a reference in section 7.3.8 (sources).

3.8.1 1st October 1865 [D]

The best known 1865 drawing was probably the lithograph of Gustave Doré

ASCENSION DU MONT CERVIN _ 14 JUILLET 1865.
La Chute
THE ASCENT OF THE MATTERHORN, ON JULY 14TH 1865
The Fall
BESTEIGUNG DES MATTERHORNS, 14 JULI 1865

Gustave Doré's lithograph 'The Fall'

published on 1st October 1865. Charles Gos pointed out in his book *Le Cervin* the similarity between Whymper's description of the accident in the *Journal de Zermatt* article in 1895 and Doré's representation of it and there seems little doubt from correspondence retained by Whymper in a scrapbook that he must have provided Doré with a sketch of the scene. Doré's original drawings of the accident and of the arrival at the summit were displayed at the Montmartre premises of his publishers Messrs Goupil et Cie early in August 1865 and it is probable that the prints, which were slightly smaller in size, incorporated a number of alterations and improvements after Goupil had approached Whymper and the relatives of the victims with a view to adding every possible true detail. Doré's lithographs have been reproduced in many books and their importance has been increased considerably by the attention paid to them by the popular Swiss artist Ferdinand Hodler in about 1894. But, as Gos pointed out, it is their attention to precise detail that distinguishes them from the fantastic and ridiculous prints that other artists produced of the Matterhorn drama. Whymper and Young Peter Taugwalder in the background are probably pure Doré, whereas Old Peter may to some extent be Whymper's impression, although he is not hugging a large rock with both arms. But the four victims, the rope and the cascade of stones fit in with Whymper's account. Originally Doré cannot have had much more than Whymper's *Times* letter to go by, and it is unlikely that he would have appreciated for himself how the rope would probably have been slack between Hadow and Croz, as Croz fell headlong. Even Whymper seems to have overlooked this initially, referring as he did at the Enquiry (A11) to the 'double weight' dragging down Hudson, as had McCormick's letter to *The Times*. But he seems subsequently to have realised his error as it does not recur in his later accounts, apart from brief reference in the *Strand Magazine* in 1909.

3.8.2 26th October 1865 [L]

The *Leipziger Illustrierte Zeitung* included a drawing of little merit entitled 'Katastrophe bei Besteigung des Matterhorns am 13.Juli', which shows four falling bodies close together. Quirinus Reichen reproduced it in an article in *Bergsteiger* in 1990.

3.8.3 1869 [G]

In Zurcher and Margollé's book *Les Ascensions Célèbres* there is a small drawing bearing the names A. de Bar and J. Gauchard, entitled 'Catastrophe du Mont Cervin'. It shows only three victims and two survivors.

3.8.4 1873 [F]

Appearing first in *Die Schweizerische Alpenwelt* by August Feierabend, this drawing, 'Das Unglück am Matterhorn' attributed to E.Heyn and F.Specht, again shows only five climbers omitting a victim as well as a survivor. It has been wrongly attributed to Whymper as a result of its appearance in the 1891 'New edition' of *Swiss Pictures drawn with Pen and Pencil*, by Samuel Manning. Charles Gos referred to it in *Le Cervin* as a very little known drawing by Whymper himself, having presumably been misled by the Preface in Manning. This refers to the first edition in 1866 being illustrated by Whymper and to the present edition being partly re-arranged and re-written, taking the opportunity 'to introduce a considerable number of entirely new engravings by Mr.Whymper'. The title page states 'With several additional illustrations by Edward Whymper', whereas in earlier editions it stated 'With illustrations by Mr.Whymper, and others'. Although Whymper is well represented in all editions, the majority of the illustrations clearly come from other sources. It is indeed inconceivable that the drawing in question should have been done by Whymper as, quite apart from the missing figures, the orientation is wrong with an unknown range of mountains immediately to the west.

3.8.5 Date unknown [C]

An engraving of unknown origin appears in the Italian edition of Ronald Clark's book *The Day the Rope Broke*. It is said to be in the Emile Gos collection. Whilst taking almost everything from Doré, it cleverly manages to combine his scene of the accident with his view of the summit, by removing the ascending climbers, extending the mountain downwards to show more of the foreground and placing the survivors in the vicinity of the last man on the ascent. The falling four, in attitudes very similar to those in Whymper's probable sketch, appear in the new foreground to the left of the summit. There is more snow than Doré provided and the accident may be much too close to the summit and above the east instead of the north face, but it all looks much more feasible. It is far too inaccurate to be the work of Whymper, but it would be interesting to know its origin.

3.8.6 1894 [H]

Ferdinand Hodler was commissioned by a Geneva businessman to paint something with a Swiss content for the 1894 World Exhibition in Antwerp and he produced two 25ft canvasses, called 'Ascent' and 'Fall'. Both paintings were clearly based on Doré's Matterhorn lithographs, particularly the one of the accident, but Hodler introduced numerous variations of his own. Although the canvasses were subsequently cut into several sections the surviving pieces which include the four victims are now displayed in the Alpine Museum in Bern. Hodler's painting of the accident has received much attention. In an article in *Die Alpen* in 1934 Werner Müller wrote of the two Hodler's: 'They are not pictures, they are not mere painted canvasses: they are monuments! Monuments to the many unknown heroes and conquerors of the mountains! Gravestones and rolls of honour for every victim of the mountains.'

3.9
NEWSPAPER REPORTS AND LETTERS

In 1865 the fastest means of communication was the telegram and it seems to have taken about twenty four hours for a report to get from Zermatt or Randa to Geneva or Bern; thus the earliest reports of the first ascent of the Matterhorn on Friday 14th July did not appear in the *Journal de Genève* and *Der Bund* until Sunday 16th. Both reports were very brief, *Der Bund* stating merely that 'On the 14th inst. the summit of the Matterhorn was reached by an unnamed climber'. The *Journal de Genève* made rather more of the news but the actual report was only the brief message from its correspondent in Randa, which it described as 'received yesterday from the Monte Rosa Hotel Zermatt. "The expedition that set off on the 13th July reached the summit of the Matterhorn on the 14th." ' The paper said it hoped soon to have more details to give its readers, but believed that it was to Professor Tyndall that the ascent should be attributed.

It may well be that the Randa correspondent heard the news from the Long party that had arrived late on the Friday afternoon. The presence of the Rev R.Wood might account for the correspondent getting the climbers' names right in his next report, apart from misspelling 'Haddo', something that seems to have defeated everyone else including the Clerk to the Enquiry, who also recorded names such as 'Wimper' and 'Cropt'. The reference to the Monte Rosa hotel suggests the Long party as they had stayed and lunched there that day, and it is a feature of all the other early reports that they do not appear to come from anyone in the hotel. It seems that not only Whymper, but Seiler as well, must have refused to say anything to 'reporters' with the result that the much fuller reports published on the 18th and 19th July, dealing with the accident, were almost certainly based on interviews with the Taugwalders. It seems probable that for the most part the *Journal de Genève* interviewed Young Peter and that *Der Bund* interviewed Old Peter.

The *Journal de Genève* report on Tuesday 18th refers to a letter of 15th from Randa, which begins: 'When I sent a telegram yesterday informing you of the ascent of the Matterhorn I did not expect to have to report to you the terrible accident that followed it. Here is the information I have been able to obtain about the catastrophe.' The wording suggests that both reports came from the same person and that they both came from Randa. Even to-day Randa is still sufficiently remote that no ordinary native there would be likely to send news to Geneva, and it is doubtful whether in 1865 anyone living there would even know of the name or the existence of its principal newspaper, let alone have any interest in providing it with news. It seems therefore probable that the paper's correspondent was a French speaking tourist from the Geneva area, who happened to be staying in Randa and that he or she decided to report the news to their home newspaper in the same way that another Geneva tourist, Mme.Gautier, wrote to the same paper from Zermatt on the Sunday. The correspondent must have gone to Zermatt on the Saturday, remained there until late afternoon to account for the report mentioning that the search party had seen the bodies, and then returned to Randa to despatch the letter to Geneva. The main account includes:

> 'Messrs Edward Whymper and Charles Hudson, members of the Committee of the alpine club in London, and Mr.Haddo and Lord Francis Douglas, members of the same club, met in Zermatt, each one of them wanting to conquer the giant Matterhorn, until now inaccessible. Mr.Hudson had brought from London some wire ropes to facilitate his ascent; but finding Mr.Whymper ready to start, he left his devices at the hotel and set off with his improvised comrades whose only object was to study the route. They took with them as guides Michel Croz of Chamonix and Zum Taugwald and his sons of Zermatt. It was July 13th; no member of the expedition expected to succeed that day; they only had in mind finding the way that would lead them to their wished for goal. They had indeed left their gear in Zermatt and were equipped only with seven bottles of wine. One of the Zum Taugwald sons even left them and descended to Zermatt.
>
> Our tourists spent the night of July 13th/14th on the snow at the foot of the Matterhorn. Only Lord Fr.Douglas slept, due to fatigue (he was only 19), the others stayed awake. At daybreak they started off again and finding the climb easier than they had hoped they pushed ahead and reached the summit at about 2 p.m. This was when they were distinctly visible from Zermatt with the help of telescopes. They remained on the summit until about 3 o'clock, when they started their descent. Michel Croz was in the lead; after him came the four tourists, Messrs Douglas, Haddo, Hudson and Whymper. Young Zum Taugwald and his father brought up the rear. They were all tied to the same rope and were climbing down happy with their success, when Lord Fr.Douglas chanced to slip, and imparting a violent jerk to the rope he dislodged in turn Messrs Haddo and Hudson and the whole party was swept down the wall of rocks at frightening speed.
>
> Yet father Zum Taugwald, the last in the chain, did not lose his presence of mind; he had the good fortune to be able to pass his rope over a rib of rock, and believed for a moment that he had stopped this appalling fall; but the rope broke between Messrs Whymper and Hudson and the unfortunate four, Michel Croz, Lord Fr.Douglas, Haddo and Hudson bounded from rock to rock from a height of about 4000 feet. The three survivors returned to Zermatt this morning at ten; I leave you to imagine their condition. About twenty men set off immediately to find the bodies, which are believed to have been sighted with the help of a telescope, separated in pairs, the rope that held them having consequently broken again.
>
> The whole village and the many tourists there are dismayed...'

This account seems almost certainly to be based primarily on an interview with Young Peter. It gives fairly precise details even though some of them are wrong and it could not be based on mere gossip. The reason for suspecting Young Peter rather than his father is because Lord Douglas is said to be the one who slipped, a mistake that Old Peter would never have made, having been roped to

Douglas and having spent a week with him trying to find the way up the Gabelhorn. Young Peter on the other hand could be forgiven for confusing Lord Douglas with Douglas Hadow, particularly if, as is likely, Hudson called his former pupil Hadow by his Christian name, as he had never met either of them before. There is further evidence to support such a misunderstanding on the part of Young Peter in the 'Narrative' he provided in 1917 at the instigation of Montagnier. In it he seems deliberately to avoid reference to the one that slipped or even to the order on the rope beyond his father. He does however criticise Lord Douglas's climbing ability on the ascent, saying, 'But Douglas in front of me had great difficulty in putting his feet down in the steps and several times he slipped. However, I held his legs firm in the steps with my hands almost all the time.' It would be remarkable if Young Peter had made no comment about the real Hadow's rock climbing ability, when his father described him at the Enquiry (A31) as 'a very bad climber'. Another reason for attributing the *Journal de Genève* account to Young Peter is that he unlike his father would have been able to converse in French with a tourist from Geneva. Furthermore the reference to passing the rope over a rib of rock is likely to have come from Young Peter as, not having been able to see his father until half an hour after the accident, he did not know that by then he had changed his position to a rock to which he could fix the rope, and he must have mistakenly assumed that he had fixed the rope before or immediately after Hadow slipped.

The detailed report in *Der Bund* of Wednesday 19th July is based on a despatch of the 15th from Zermatt and shows several signs of coming from an interview with Old Peter rather than his son. Hadow is referred to as 'the Englishman immediately behind the leading guide, the least experienced climber in the whole party', which fits in with Old Peter's references to him at the Enquiry (other than in A55) as 'the first tourist after the guide Croz' (see A30 & A31). The tourists are referred to as:

> 'Messrs Hudson, president of the English Alpine Club, Whimper, Douglas (an eighteen year old son of Lord Douglas), and another gentleman whose name it has so far been impossible to establish...
> Your correspondent saw the tourists up there himself and has himself heard the descriptions of the subsequent disaster from the lips of the survivors themselves. On the descent they were all roped together on one rope: the guide Croz was leading, followed by three Englishmen, then Taugwalder, then Mr. Whimper between him and his son, who was last. About 200 feet below the summit, the Englishman immediately behind the leading guide, the least experienced climber in the whole party, slipped, dragging the next behind him down with him, and he the third behind him. Even Croz could not go on holding such a weight, and the four men were in thin air over the abyss. Fortunately, the elder Taugwalder managed to throw his weight upon a rock and, before his strength had entirely ebbed, the rope broke below him, a circumstance to which he and Mr. Whimper and his own son at the back owe their survival.'

The reference to Croz holding such a weight is consistent with Old Peter's reply A30, even though he subsequently retracted (A63) the idea that Croz had been the last to fall. Old Peter throwing his weight upon a rock is consistent with Whymper's subsequent account of his hugging a rock with both arms and also with his sustaining injury to his fingers but not with Old Peter's later evidence at the Enquiry (A64), although there are doubts about this; see section 2.52.8. What must be certain is that Young Peter could not have given first hand evidence that his father threw his weight upon a rock, as he could not even see him after the accident (A54). The report includes a postscript stating that 'At this very moment a large expedition is leaving for the foot of the Matterhorn to look for traces of the victims'. But the final paragraph is somewhat baffling when it says, 'In Zermatt anxiety rose to a pitch when, on the 15th, nobody had returned from the mountain. Guides were sent out and not recalled till, at about 10 o'clock, two guns were fired to signal the return of the remnants of the unfortunate party'.

The report suggests that the writer had been in Zermatt on the Friday and also on the Saturday, possibly at the Mont Cervin, but it is hard to reconcile the high pitch of anxiety and the sending out of guides with McCormick writing

> 'I rather expected to see [Hudson] in Zermatt that night [the 14th]; but as he did not arrive, I concluded he would be there before nine in the morning. Though he did not then come, I was not in the least alarmed, and never expected that any harm had befallen him. Before ten, Campbell and I set off with a party for the Gorner Grat. How often we turned, as we toiled up to the Riffel, to look at that strange, awful mountain on our right! Many were our thoughts concerning those who had robbed it of its glory.'

It seems probable that McCormick was correct rather than the *Bund* correspondent as it could hardly have been necessary to fire guns to recall guides who would surely have already met the survivors, even if the Taugwalders were some distance behind Whymper. Such a level of anxiety would inevitably have disturbed McCormick to some extent regardless of his own confidence in his friend Hudson, and it seems inconceivable that he would have gone off to enjoy himself on the Gornergrat if a search party had already been sent out. Even more incongruous would be the fact that he ignored the guns, even if they were fired half an hour later than reported, as being still so close to Zermatt he would surely have turned back to join in the celebrations over the first ascent.

On 20th July the *Journal de Genève* published extracts from two letters from Zermatt the first of which has been identified as that of Mme.Augusta Gautier. Claire Engel drew attention to it in 1949, when she published extracts from the diary of A-J Martin, professor of law at Geneva University. Gautier, who had spent the night of Friday 14th at the Monte Rosa with her family along with Martin and his son Ernest, stayed in Zermatt on the Sunday morning looking after Ernest, while the others walked up to the Schwarzsee. They had all spent the Saturday night at the Riffel, where they heard of the accident, and it seems from Martin's diary that Gautier amused herself during their absence by writing a report to send to the *Journal de Genève*. But unlike Martin, who recorded the names and the rope order correctly, Gautier named only Whymper and 'Cropt' and despite what Claire Engel has written she did not state the rope order but only that Croz was in the lead. But she did record the rumour, mentioned by Whymper in his memorandum of 17.8.65, that he 'had not uttered a single word during the whole of that fearful night'. The other letter, also despatched from Zermatt on 16th July, mentioned that 'The last two guides and Whymper stood fast, winding the rope round a rock' and also that the three bodies had been provisionally buried in the snow, not yet knowing how they could be recovered.

McCormick's first letter to *The Times* published on 22nd July appeared in translation in the *Journal de Genève* on 27th and in *Der Bund* on 29th July. Whymper's long letter of 25th to von Fellenberg was not forwarded to the two papers as he had hoped, due to von Fellenberg's absence in the mountains, and it was subsequently overtaken by his letter to *The Times*. Had it been published in the *Journal de Genève* and *Der Bund* on about 29th July the later history of Whymper's accounts might have been somewhat different from what it is, as it would almost certainly have been translated back into English and published by *The Times* at the beginning of August. It would no doubt have satisfied the British public, Whymper would have been spared the ordeal of writing the further letter which appeared in *The Times* on 8th August and the correspondence columns in *The Times* would have taken a somewhat different course. There was further mention of the accident in the *Journal de Genève*, which published on 28th July an article by Rambert and on 1st August a report from Zermatt referring to the recovery of the bodies and to the Enquiry. The von Fellenberg letter was reported in full detail in the *Sonntagspost* on 13th August, but by then Whymper's *Times* letter had been published. Three numbers of the *Sonntagspost* contain worthwhile articles, a report of the accident on the 30th July, the von Fellenberg letter on 13th August and comments on Whymper's *Times* letter on 20th August, the editor being the well known Swiss mountaineer Abraham Roth. Whymper's letter to *The Times* appeared in a French translation in the *Journal de Genève* on 12th August.

Whereas there must be many other contemporary Swiss newspaper reports of the accident, some of which may contain additional facts of interest or significance, the only other paper apart from *Die Neue Freie Presse* (of Vienna) of 4th August that is known to be of particular interest and has been quoted by Charles Gos, is *L'Abeille de Chamonix* of Sunday 23rd July 1865. It contains a number of articles that have a bearing on the accident and the circumstances surrounding it, including details of the latest ascents of Mont Blanc:

> 'Cinquième ascension au Mont-Blanc
> Le 7 juillet 1865.
> M. Frédéric G. Brown, Anglais.
> Guide: Devouassoux Michel

Sixième ascension.
Le 7 juillet 1865.
Sir Thomas Kennedy, lord Douglas, Rd.J.Cormik et C.Hudson, Anglais.
Guide: Cros Michel-Auguste.'

The above details are of interest in that they provide further evidence of the confusion between the two Douglases, which features particularly in the various accounts by Young Peter Taugwalder, and was responsible for *The Times* stating on 21st July on the authority of the report in the *Journal de Genève* of 18th that it was Lord Francis Douglas who slipped. It is not that the Chamonix authorities made an incorrect record on about 7th July, when Lord Douglas was in fact in Zermatt, but that subsequently someone, who knew that the one who slipped on the Matterhorn had climbed Mont Blanc only the week before, must have seen fit to amend some Chamonix record of Douglas Hadow climbing Mont Blanc, 'knowing' from the report in the *Journal de Genève* that the name of the one who slipped on the Matterhorn was Lord Douglas.

An article by the Editor, Stéphen d'Arve, in the same issue gives an account of the Matterhorn accident and refers to two of the party as 'Lord Douglas, son of the Marquess of Huntley aged 19, [and] Mr.Haddo aged 25'.

> 'They reached the summit without needing to use the devices and implements which they had left in Zermatt for the actual ascent which they had not reckoned on achieving that day...
> The guide Croz assessing from the summit the very considerable difficulties of the descent exclaimed with simple frankness: "We have got here, but I would give thousands of francs to be back down again!" '

The article goes on to give a fanciful account of the accident after 'Lord Douglas makes a slip' and concludes by stating that Hudson leaves a widow and three children and that Lord Douglas came first out of 156 candidates for army commissions. It is remarkable that d'Arve should have stated this last fact in an article apparently written as early as 19th July, as it was not until 28th July that *The Times* quoted something similar (first out of 119) from an article in the *Dumfries Courier*. The only explanation can be that d'Arve learnt it from an English tourist, possibly from J.W.Charlton who wrote his letter of 21st July to *The Times* whilst staying in Chamonix.

Another article in the same number of *L'Abeille* is a letter to the Editor from Gabriel Loppé, describing the search for the bodies and said to be based on the account of an eye witness, presumably either Frédéric Payot or Jean Tairraz. It mentions that none of the Zermatt guides was willing to go on this further search, but does not state why. It describes the mutilated remains and says that the searchers were ceaselessly bombarded by enormous stones and had to move smartly out of the way on several occasions; 'Mr.Whymper alone was unperturbed and ignored all entreaties to take cover; in the presence of this horrible scene he solemnly swore that he would never set foot on a mountain again.'

3.9.1 *The Times*

Only brief mention will be made here of the various reports, the leading articles and the dozens of letters written to the editor in July and August 1865. Some of them are reproduced in section 4 and extracts from others appear elsewhere. They should all be found in the copies of *The Times* available on microfilm in most major British reference libraries. Many cuttings are also available in the archives of the Alpine Club and elsewhere.

19.7. Brief report. Berne July 18.
20.7. Brief report. Geneva July 19.
21.7. *Journal de Genève* of 18.7. quoting 15.7. letter from Randa.
21.7. J.A.Hudson letter.
22.7. J.McCormick letter of 17.7. (Whymper account)
24.7. J.McCormick letter about Riffelhorn accident to Wilson.
26.7. J.W.Charlton letter.
27.7. Leading article.
27.7. R.Glover letter.
28.7. *Dumfries Courier* quote about Douglas.
28.7. J.McCormick letter about bodies brought down.
28.7. T.S.Kennedy letter.
29.7. J.J.Cowell letter.
31.7. [J.Barrow] letter from 'Late private 38th Artists' etc.
31.7. T.Fowell Buxton letter.
1.8. R.Glover letter.
1.8. Prof.P.Chaix letter.
1.8. 'R.S.' letter.
2.8. 'J.A.' letter enclosing Whymper & Hudson Aig. Verte hotel book accounts.
2.8. Editor's note. 'Douglas did not make the fatal slip.'
2.8. (Reuters express) Anneçy report on bodies, based on Loppé letter.
3.8. J.W.Tyas letter.
3.8. F.Trench letter.
4.8 A.Rivington letter.
4.8. A.W.Moore letter.
5.8. 'A friend of one of the victims' letter.
5.8. 'H.' letter.
5.8. J.McCormick letter about Monte Rosa avalanche accident.
5.8. Leading article inspired by above letter.
8.8. E.Whymper letter.
8.8. A.Wills letter of 7.8. to E.Whymper.
8.8. J.R.Bailey letter with extracts from letters re Monte Rosa accident.
9.8. Leading article.
14.8. A.Wills letter as President of the Alpine Club.
14.8. J.McCormick letter re Zermatt church appeal.

15.8. 'F.R.G.S.' letter.
16.8. 'Oxford M.A.' letter.
16.8. 'A Swiss.' letter.
17.8. 'M.R.C.S.' letter.
19.8. W.Mathews letter about Croz fund.
19.8. E.Whymper letter about Croz fund.
22.8. J.McCormick letter about Monte Rosa accident.
25.8. *Journal de Genève* article of 12.8. (Italian ascent)
21.11. Croz fund.

30.8.66. [A.G.Butler] verse 'Zermatt churchyard'.
7.9.66. Mackenzie letter about land for monument.

3.10
POEMS

There only seems to be a record of one poem published in London in the aftermath of the accident, although another one of uncertain origin must also have appeared in a newspaper or periodical. The former consists of 62 lines by 'B' [A.G.Butler], called 'Zermatt Churchyard'. It appeared in *The Times* on 30th August 1866 and was reprinted privately in Cambridge in 1909, so that it features in the lists of privately printed mountaineering books in volumes 57 and 96 of the *Alpine Journal*. Extracts have appeared in anthologies by R.L.G. Irving and Hugh Merrick. The other poem consists of four verses by S.S.Horner headed 'The Matterhorn' and dated Paris, August 1865. In the course of correspondence with Whymper in December 1865 Lady Queensberry wrote 'I dare say you saw those lines sent from Paris', but it seems that he had not seen them and she therefore sent them to him a fortnight later. He returned the original to her after making his own copy:

THE MATTERHORN

Where ether dims the Alpine steeps,
  Beyond the verge where mortals stray;
Calm on the berg young Douglas sleeps,
  Whence none may bear his corse away.

For monarch ne'er had tomb so grand,
  However potent was his sway;
No conqueror led a nobler band
  Than perished on that fatal day.

His grave shall mark the meteor's trail,
  Its beacon flame the lightning flash;
His requiem be the tempest's wail
  As whirlwinds with the thunder clash.

There stars will ever shed their light,
  The sun will guild each rising morn;
His winding sheet – the glacier bright;
  His monument – the Matterhorn.

Paris, August, 1865. S.S.Horner.

The Horner poem seems to have appealed to Lady Queensberry, the last verse giving her the idea that she should have tinted, with the rising sun, the large photograph of the Matterhorn which she asked Whymper to order for her. Whymper also possessed another poem, which he probably did not obtain from her. It is of much greater historical interest, as appears from the heading on his copy: 'Lines written by Lord F. Douglas four days before his death'

At Zermatt when the sun is low,
How brightly shines the untrodden snow
Where no one yet has dared to go,
  On Monte Cervin's head.

But yet, I say, a day will come,
When aloud the noise of gun
Shall proclaim the deed as done
  On Monte Cervin's head.

It is true and you may rave,
But you'll not be in your grave
When the English flag shall wave
  On Monte Cervin's head.

The circumstances in which Douglas came to write the poem are not known but it seems probable that he wrote it on the Sunday or Monday and left it at the Mont Cervin before going to the Riffel on his way to Breuil. The following week Clemenz must have shown it to Whymper who then copied it onto the back of a note that Clemenz had sent him asking for the address of Mme.Douglas. Alternatively Douglas may have left it at the Monte Rosa. There is a typewritten copy of the poem in the Alpine Club Archives with no record of its origin nor indication that it is not an exact copy of the original, although it refers to Mont instead of Monte Cervin and to the British instead of to the English flag.

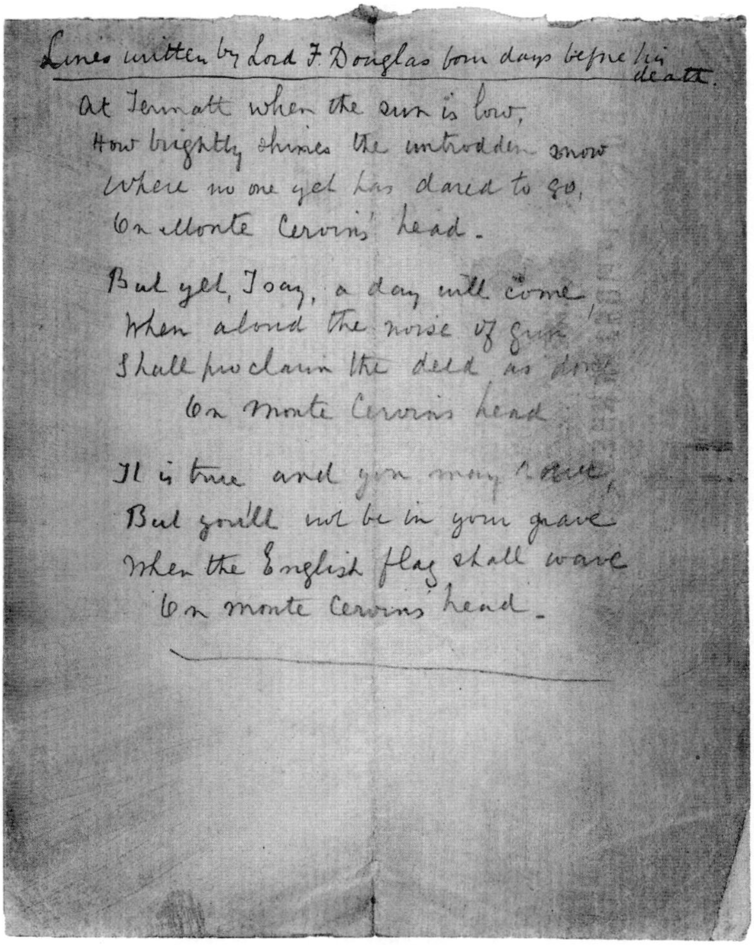
Lines written by Lord F. Douglas four days before his death.

At Zermatt when the sun is low,
How brightly shines the untrodden snow
Where no one yet has dared to go,
On Monte Cervin's head.

But yet, I say, a day will come,
When aloud the noise of gun
Shall proclaim the deed as done
On Monte Cervin's head.

It is true and you may rave,
But you'll not be in your grave
When the English flag shall wave
On Monte Cervin's head.

Whymper's copy of the poem by Lord Douglas

Attached to the Alpine Club copy is a typewritten copy of another poem, which must have been written by Lord Queensberry when he was staying in Zermatt between the 24th and 29th July 1865. As it is obviously based on his brother's poem it can be assumed that it also referred originally to the 'English' flag and to 'Monte Cervin's head', which some unknown person subsequently chose to alter. The original wording has therefore been restored:

It is true the English flag has waved
On Monte Cervin's head
Yet ah! the cost is dearly paid
By those who now are dead.

They came to where no mortal man
Before had set his foot,
And stood in pride all side by side
Upon that awful brink.

For one short hour they thought and gazed
From off that fearful height
Ah! who can tell their thoughts? Not we
To God belongs the right.

They now descend – alas – that slip
From off their feet they fly
Oh one faint hope – the rope it holds –
T'is gone – before their God they reach.

He in his mercy spared the three
To tell this awful tale
Two mothers mourn their darling sons
A wife her husband wails.

A father for a son must weep
And think of days gone by
When by his side his dear loved child
Would sport and run and play.

One was my brother – he alone
Of all those gone not found
Will one day rise in glory
To that dreadful trumpet's sound.

Ah! ye who read these verses
My simple warning take
Ye may not have that one short hour
On Monte Cervin's head.

July 1865 Queensberry.

Lord Queensberry visited Zermatt on subsequent occasions as well. He was there in September 1871, making several excursions with the Taugwalders, and he was there in June 1876. 'Zermatt June 10th 1876' appears at the end of his lengthy poem *The spirit of the Matterhorn*, which he published in London in 1881. But, although it does refer briefly to the accident including 'The brother that I loved, his earthly frame / Lies bleaching on the rocks, oh, Matterhorn', it does not appear to have any great historical interest from a mountaineering point of view.

The only other poem relevant to the 1865 accident seems to be the sonnet that the Rev James Robertson wrote in 1895 in memory of Michel Croz. He wrote and sent it to Whymper after receiving from him a photograph of the portrait which Lance Calkin had painted of Michel Croz based on a photograph. Robertson's copy of the portrait is now in the Alpine Club Archives. The sonnet was first published by Frank Smythe in his biography of Whymper.

My heart, to which in less sustainëd flight,
  Dear also were the mountains and the men,
  Welcomes this kindly gift from thee again;–
Yea welcomes, though of many a haunted night
Too shrewd memorial, the limner's might
  With Rembrandt-brush the shattered shrine to mend;
  Each feature of thy true Savoyard friend
Flashing in darkness o'er the empanelled white;–
The knotted brows that guard the daring eye,
The trusty smile just held in grim reserve;–
  Quenched, where on yonder Sabbath snows we stood
Awe stricken; for beyond the eagle's cry
  Had soared the kindred soul that could not swerve,
  And reft thy triumph of its plenitude.

3.11
REWARD FOR THE FIRST ASCENT

Graham Brown and Gavin de Beer wrote in their authoritative book, *The first ascent of Mont Blanc* of how, in 1760 and again in 1761 during his visits to Chamonix, de Saussure had offered a prize to the guides of Chamonix for the discovery of a practicable route to the summit. They referred to it as 'a substantial reward', to which they added a footnote 'This prize was said to have been one of two guineas'. It is therefore not altogether surprising that when over a century later the far more spectacular Matterhorn received its first ascent it was widely believed in Zermatt that there was a money reward waiting for Taugwalder. How prevalent the belief was before the ascent was actually accomplished cannot be determined and it may well be that the rumour only really took off after the ascent and then spread rapidly, but there is at least one reliable record, dating back to 1862, of the idea that such an award should be made, even though the idea was immediately dismissed.

Canon Carrel wrote in his book *La Vallée de Valtornenche en 1867*:

> 'In 1760 M. De Saussure had offered a reward to those who could find the way to the top of Mont Blanc. I thought the same could be done for the Matterhorn. Consequently on

> 9th January 1862 I had written to Mr. F. F. Tuckett of Bristol, with whom I was well acquainted, and I had asked him to speak to the President of the Alpine Club about it. He replied that he did not believe it was right to tempt with a pecuniary promise some poor people who might perhaps risk their lives in an enterprise that had no scientific purpose. The matter rested there.'

A fortnight, or more likely six weeks, after the accident Charles Parker learnt from Old Peter Taugwalder that he was unhappy about the pay he had received and also about the absence of a reward. Parker subsequently wrote in a letter to his father; 'Of course nothing is easier than to tell him in writing, what he was not content to be told when I saw him, that there is no sort of truth in the belief (wh. at Zermatt is universal) that a money-reward was to be given for the first ascent of the Matterhorn.' Numerous newspaper reports about the reward were published some three weeks after the accident. Several of them have been quoted by Charles Gos and others appear in *Mountain World 1964/65*. One reported that: 'The Englishman Whymper, who nearly lost his life on the Matterhorn, has won the bounty of £1,000 which the London [Alpine] Club earmarked for this purpose some years ago', the *Mond Illustré* stating that 'in the event of their succeeding, the three guides had been promised £200 (5,000 francs), half the sum voted by the English Alpine Club'. Another report even referred to the promised 5,000 francs having being paid out on Friday 21st July in the presence of members of the Enquiry Tribunal!

It is therefore hardly surprising that Old Peter should have been a bit fed up when Parker saw him, if he had been led to believe that he was entitled to a reward of 5,000 francs or even to one third of that sum, when his fees for the ascent, 'the highest price ever given for mountain ascents', had amounted to only 100 francs. The magnitude of the supposed reward would inevitably have aggravated the jealousy of his 'comrades and neighbours' at Zermatt, the consequences of which he had to endure even though he did not receive any money to compensate for it. The ludicrous nature of the sums involved in the false rumours, with £1,000 for Whymper and £200 for the guides, is apparent from a comparison with de Saussure's Mont Blanc reward of two guineas or with Girdlestone's 108 day holiday in 1865 costing him less than £61!

3.12
THE ROPE IN 1865

The technique of roped climbing was still in its infancy in 1865 and it is difficult to appreciate to-day just how rudimentary things still were. The Matterhorn accident helped to focus attention on the subject and no doubt accelerated the development of better safeguards and better discipline in the use of a rope, but a major step forward had been taken only the year before when the Alpine Club appointed a Committee to test and to report upon the most suitable ropes for mountaineering purposes. The fact that in 1936 the Editor of the 6th edition of Whymper's *Scrambles* saw fit to delete Whymper's reference to this report and to its approval of ropes made of Manilla and of Italian hemp manufactured by Mr.J.Buckingham, which would sustain 168 lbs. falling 10 feet or 196 lbs. falling 8 feet, only goes to show how distorted the modern understanding had become. It is not therefore altogether surprising to find someone like Carl Egger misjudging the 1865 scene to such an extent as to suggest without the slightest justification that Whymper exaggerated the difference in quality between the ropes. It may be helpful to look first at some contemporary references to the provision and use of ropes.

3.12.1 Contemporary practice

In 1859 in the first series of *Peaks, Passes and Glaciers* we find that the editor John Ball concluded with a chapter 'Suggestions for Alpine travellers', stating in relation to snow covered glaciers: 'A strange notion seems to prevail with some travellers, and occasionally among the guides, that the constant use of the rope is a sign of timidity and over-caution'. He followed this on the next page with 'It may be hoped that before long the rope will be considered as essential a part of an Alpine traveller's equipment as reins are in a horse's harness'. In 1863 Ball wrote in the Introduction to his *Guide to the Western Alps*:

> 'Still more essential than the alpenstock to those who wish to explore the higher regions of the Alps is the rope. The uses of this are noticed in the next Article. It is better to procure this in England, though a tolerable article may be had in most foreign towns. Some mountaineers use a fine sashline. However good the material this is too slight, both because it is too quickly worn by pressure at a single point, and because it cuts the hands when used to draw up a heavy weight. Others carry ropes much too heavy which become a positive incumbrance, and are sometimes left behind when they are wanted. The best rope that the writer has seen is made of Manilla hemp, strong enough to bear the weight of several men, yet not heavy. A length of 40ft. is quite enough for three men. There is some convenience in having each member of a party provided with a separate short piece of rope fastened round his waist...A leather belt, with swivel spring-hook attached, is preferred by some.'

Ball also stated that

> 'The duty of a guide is not merely to point out the way but further to make himself generally useful to his employers. He is expected to carry a knapsack of 20 or 25 lbs. weight, and to find himself in the articles requisite for his profession such as rope and ice-axe.'

As for the quality of rope used, we find a few pages later:

> 'It would seem scarcely necessary to add that the rope should be sound and strong, if it did not often happen that untrustworthy articles are taken by guides; and it is not less important

to note that it should be fastened round the body of each member of the party, *guides included*, leaving both hands free to use the alpenstock in case of a slip. A neglect of this obvious rule led in 1860 to the loss of three English travellers, and one of their guides, in the descent from the Col du Géant to Courmayeur.'

There are several other instances of guides not being attached to a rope, such as the von Grote crevasse fatality, and in 1863 William Longman wrote of the extraordinary practice of a guide leading his son on the Aletsch glacier by their each holding one end of a knotted handkerchief, until his son disappeared 50 feet down a crevasse! Lunn quoted Stogden as saying that Old Peter took the rope off coming down a long steep slope of bare rock from the top of the Tête Blanche; 'I had a couple of men with me who were inexperienced; and I fancy he must have thought that, if one of them let go, which was not unlikely, he would be able to choose whether to hold on or let go. I happened to look up and see what was going on, and I made him tie up at once.'

Both Jordan, in 1867, and Elliott, in 1868, had problems on the Matterhorn with Knubel holding the rope instead of tying on to it, because he considered this to be safer. Whymper commented on the use of the rope in chapter 20 of *Scrambles* and also in his article in the *Graphic* in 1894. It is also interesting to read the comments of Canon Carrel on the use of ropes. He took a very keen interest in all aspects of climbing as his book *La Vallée de Valtornenche en 1867* shows, and the views he expressed would be not just his own theories but based on discussions with climbers and guides. He clearly had the Matterhorn accident in mind when he wrote

'The use of ropes. – Using ropes for crossing glaciers offers foolproof security. The party should be tied at 4 to 5 metre intervals, and the rope should be almost taut. It is quite a different matter when it is a case of climbing or descending very steep slopes. Alpine history has proved to us that the practice of everyone being tied together has caused many deaths.
So much has been written on this subject already, that I do not know what to say. I think it must be left to the judgment and ability of the travellers, and above all to the prudence and wisdom of the first class guides who should organise and direct difficult climbs.
It is absolutely vital to proceed one at a time in the most difficult places: the fall of one produces a violent shock that will cause the others to fall as well, if they are not paying attention and not well placed. For greater safety it is adviseable to have two ropes, using one to secure the party together by means of a hook attached to the belt with the other free and held in the hand. The best ropes available are those of Manilla hemp from Buckingham brothers in London, 33, Broad Street, Bloomsbury. Their belts are strong and comfortable.'

As for the number of climbers on one rope, this was well summed up by Claud Schuster in his 1940 review of Smythe's biography of Whymper. 'The technique of roped climbing was still in its infancy. What are to-day elementary rules, namely, not to climb more than 3 or 4 on a rope and to let the weakest climber go first on the descent were not yet fully realised.' Kennedy's letter of 28.7.65 to *The Times* might suggest that he already appreciated both these points, but there is little reason to believe that he was ahead of his contemporaries as he certainly did not practise what he preached, when with Hudson and Croz and others he descended the Aiguille Verte the week before the Matterhorn accident, 'all 6 tied to one long rope' and with Croz again in the lead. Even as late as 1876 the Abbé Gorret advised in his *Guide de la vallée d'Aoste* against having too many on one rope 'three, or five, at the very most six'.

3.12.2 Report of the Committee on Ropes, Axes etc

The Special Committee was made up of six members, including a chairman E.S.Kennedy (the 'other' Kennedy), a secretary F.C.Grove and J.J.Cowell amongst others. They presented their report to the Club on 5th July 1864, it was circulated privately to members and it was also published in the September issue of the *Journal*. The report included reference to knots, which need not concern us here except in as much as the Editor of the *Journal* H.B.George who had also been on the Committee gave some further advice on knots in the subsequent June 1865 issue, commenting on the report

> 'As this report was not published till late in the season, it is probable that its contents were never made known to the very persons who ought to know them best, the guides, who in practice arrange the rope for a party. It will be a great advantage if mountaineers during the coming season will impress on their guides the main facts.'

George then went on to deal specifically with knots, but his exhortation to make the contents of the report known to the guides applied equally to other aspects of the report and confirms the probability that most of the second rate guides and even perhaps the majority of the first class guides would not have heard anything of the report's findings prior to the start of the 1865 season.

In 1864 Whymper was in the Alps in June and July and he could not have known of the Committee's findings before he went, nor is it likely that he would even have heard rumour of the outcome of any of the tests on ropes, as it was only in May that the Club had initiated the exercise by inviting members to send noteworthy ropes and axes to the Club. He would therefore have used for his 1864 climbs, in as much as his ropes were used rather than the ropes of one of his companions of which we know nothing, the 'stout sashline' as he called it, of a kind which he had used for some years. This was the rope that broke in the Matterhorn accident, to which he referred in chapter 20 of *Scrambles* when he was detailing the three kinds of rope that made up the total of about 600 feet they took with them: 'and third, more than 200 feet of a lighter and weaker rope than the first, of a kind that I had used formerly (stout sashline)'. In *The Times* he had described it as 'of a kind used by myself until the Club rope was produced'.

There is no reason to suppose that this was the 'fine sashline' condemned in Ball's *Guide* and already mentioned above, despite the specimen in the Zermatt Museum looking somewhat less than stout to-day. Indeed the view seems to have been widely shared before the Committee carried out its tests that stout sashline was one of the most reliable ropes to use. The Committee carried out nearly a hundred experiments based on twelve stone as the average weight of a light man.

> 'In the preliminary experiments, therefore, all ropes were rejected which did not support the strain produced by twelve stone falling five feet. Under this trial, all those plaited ropes which are generally supposed to be so strong, and many most carefully-made twisted ropes, gave way in such a manner as was very startling to some of our number, who had been in the habit of using these treacherous cords with perfect and most unfounded confidence.'

This must be the reason why Whymper, and others no doubt as well, rejected so suddenly and so absolutely for use as a climbing rope, the plaited (sashline) ropes with which he was so familiar. He seems to confirm in the same paragraph as he refers to the 1864 Committee, that it was only in 1865 that he stopped using stout sashline as a climbing rope when he writes, 'In 1865 we carried two 100 feet lengths of the Manilla rope, and the inconvenience arising from its weight was more than made up for by the security which it afforded.' It is virtually certain that Michel Croz, Christian Almer and other first class guides would have learnt of the report's findings by 1865 if not the year before, but in the normal way it might have taken much longer for the message to percolate through to the likes of Old Peter Taugwalder, a good Monte Rosa guide with no ambition to travel beyond his home territory. If such a guide had a plaited rope of his own and shared the view that such ropes were stronger than twisted ropes, he would no doubt have continued to use it, except when an employer produced a rope of his own.

The 1864 report found that none of the ropes tested, reckoned to be the heaviest which can be conveniently carried about in the Alps, would withstand a weight of 14 stone falling 10 feet. The three which were recommended would all bear 12 stone falling 10 feet and 14 stone falling 8 feet, which means that the 'Manilla rope' which Whymper carried in 1865 would withstand a sudden jerk at least twice as great as the sashline. He described his third rope as '150 feet of a stouter and probably stronger rope'.

Having heeded the findings of the Committee and replaced his ropes by the start of the 1865 season, it may be asked why Whymper still took the sashline to the Alps instead of scrapping it altogether. The answer is that just as Hudson thought the difficulties on the Hörnli ridge would be so great as to require a special ladder and a wire-rope to overcome them, so Whymper thought that it might be necessary to secure the route by leaving a lot of fixed ropes. The sashline would be perfectly adequate for this, much lighter to carry and more obviously expendable so that they need have no hesitation about wasting it as they might with a brand-new twisted rope. Whymper actually wrote of the rope that broke, on discovering that it was the weakest of the three ropes, 'It was not brought, and should not have been employed, for the purpose for which it was used. It was old rope, and, compared with the others was feeble. It was intended as a reserve, in case we had to leave much rope behind, attached to rocks.'

Some critics have expressed the opinion, as though they were stating a fact, that no one had explained to Old Peter that the old rope which he seems to have carried both up and down the mountain was only intended for use as a spare. Egger even went so far as to declare that only Whymper knew the qualities of the different ropes, but there does not seem to be any justification for him imputing his own ignorance to Old Peter Taugwalder (as well as to Croz, Hudson and Douglas) just because Whymper did not spell out the obvious in his book. Whether or not laziness was the cause of Old Peter using the weak rope is an entirely separate question, but to infer that he could not tell the difference between a new rope and an old one, between a thick rope and a thin one or between a strong one and a weak one, seems to be not only an insult to his intelligence and skills as a guide but is also contrary to the evidence given by Old Peter himself at the Enquiry.

The question as to why Old Peter used the weak rope is considered fully elsewhere; see sections 3.16 (The special rope), 2.14.5 (Lord Francis Douglas) and 2.52.6 (Old Peter Taugwalder). It is sufficient just to mention here some of the considerations:

Old Peter described it as 'a special rope'. (A24)
He distinguished it from a strong rope. (A34)
He had in mind fixing ropes. (A53)
He seems to have inspected the ropes before setting off. (A29)
A rope had saved his life the week before when he fell 24 feet.
Douglas would also have been well aware of the contrast in the appearance of the two ropes tied to him.

There has been a great deal of speculation about the length of the various ropes and about where they were at the time Old Peter tied himself on to Douglas. In an article in the *Alpine Journal* in 1933 Edwards even suggested that some of Whymper's drawings in *Scrambles* might throw some light on who was carrying what. But such considerations seem to be somewhat irrelevant and remote from the question as to why Old Peter did not use one of the stronger ropes, like the dubious story of A.E.W.Mason being told by Whymper after some dinner that 'Thinking it over, I believe that I did cut the rope behind me so that I could more easily race Croz to the top'. Any minor shortening of one rope would no more have caused Old Peter to have to use the sashline to tie himself on to Douglas than it would have prevented him from using the sashline double or from postponing their start of the descent for a few more minutes until Whymper had finished putting their names in a bottle.

There are many recorded instances of guides using poor quality ropes, but the essential difference on the Matterhorn was that 'brand-new rope', as Old Peter described it, was available. In August 1865 Wigram, who had not in fact climbed since 1862, wrote in a letter to Whymper,

> 'I am not surprised at their using any rope you had with you: that you had brought it would be sufficient warrant in their eyes; and the best guides are too apt to think of a rope as a rope, even if it be an old rotten clothes line. I have absolutely known a man propose to take the line from the laundry ground at the Riffelberg.'

In 1870 Girdlestone referred in his book to what he called 'average guides':

> 'Indeed, so reckless are men of this class that, constantly on snow covered crevasses, they either dispense with the use of the rope altogether or employ such poor cord as would be of no use in case of need; though this last charge cannot be brought against the first class guides, who usually now have English club rope.'

In 1893 Claud Wilson wrote of an encounter with a guide, which shows just how wrong a guide could be in his judgment of a good rope:

> 'Two years ago I saw a guide with a shocking bit of frayed and worn-out rope on board a Lucerne steamer. I asked where he lived and how it was he had not got a better one. He said he came from Engelberg, and that it was the best that could be got – a piece of Alpine Club rope, which had been given, some twelve years before, to his father who, on becoming too old for active guiding, had handed it on to him: he had used it that morning in crossing a pass in the Tödi district, and was on his way home.'

But on the occasion of the first ascent of the Matterhorn the situation was very different. The employer had provided the ropes, there was an abundance of good rope and it was known that the old rope had been brought for use as fixed rope. There must have been a specific reason for preferring the sashline. Laziness cannot be the explanation, any more than the intention to introduce a weak link into the chain, as neither takes any account of the reaction of the highly intelligent Douglas, who seems to have been content to accept the situation. Yet with a brand-new twisted rope already attached to him by Croz (or by Hudson), it is hard to understand how he could have consented to Old Peter securing him with the less thick old plaited rope, particularly when he would almost certainly have read and studied the Committee's report as a new member of the Alpine Club. Furthermore his life had been saved only the week before by a remarkable rope that did not break, even when his own 12 foot fall was followed immediately by the shock of Old Peter falling a total of at least 24 feet, quite inconsistent with the Committee's finding that no rope tested would withstand a weight of 14 stone falling even 10 feet.

So far as the 1864 tests are concerned, attention must be drawn to an article by R.P.Mears in the *Alpine Journal* in 1950, 'The climbing rope defined', which reviewed various technical references to ropes in the *Journal* and commented on the 1864 tests: 'One is...led to believe that weights of cast iron or other such rigid material were used. These would not be representative of the weight of a human body, being much more severe on the rope.' There seems to be another factor as well, to which Mears referred in a further article the following year, which suggests that the performance of ropes on a mountain in 1864 would have been better than the tests had indicated, which might go some way towards explaining the Obergabelhorn escape, of which Douglas wrote 'The weight on the rope must have been about 23 stone, and it is wonderful that, falling straight down without anything to break one's fall, it did not break too'. Mears wrote how:

> 'Natural fibre ropes are made from fibres of limited length not exceeding ten feet...Therefore when natural fibre ropes break slip of fibres accompanies fracture of fibres. Consequently it is not surprising that, under impact loading, natural fibre ropes reveal strengths considerably in excess of their strengths as registered in ordinary machine testing...for under shock loads there would be little time for slipping to take place.'

The subject is clearly a technical and complicated one, and without going into such matters as stretch and recoverable elasticity, it would seem as though the first attempted investigation into mountaineering ropes was of real value and that it was correct in its finding that twisted ropes were by no means inferior to plaited ones. The 1864 report does not seem to have contemplated leaders falling off rock, so much as 'a man falling suddenly into a crevasse, or down an ice-slope', and the same idea seems to underlie the contemporary comments of Girdlestone, writing in his book published in 1870:

> 'I obtain and use with perfect satisfaction, Buckingham's lightest club rope. Much that is said about the necessity of very strong rope is founded on error. I use the same rope for several years in succession, although it certainly becomes weaker: because a place must be very bad where the rope cannot be kept so far taut as to prevent the chance of a sudden and tremendous strain upon it, and on such a place everyone would infallibly be pulled over by the shock of the strain before an ordinary window cord would reach its point of rupture. On this ground I think that club rope might be made a size smaller than it is. The apparent exception to this statement presented by the fatal accident on the first ascent of the Matterhorn vanishes before the fact that, owing to the inexperience of one of the mountaineers, the rope could not be kept taut between him and his guide, and thus the rope was subjected to a sudden strain where the holding of some of the party was good. Bad mountaineering – not a bad rope – appears to have been the cause of that lamentable catastrophe.'

3.12.3 A taut rope

Dangar & Blakeney in their review of Ronald Clark's book, *The Day the Rope Broke*, referred to his covering all points of discussion very fairly and sensibly, but said that he did not deal with 'Whymper's assertion, that had the rope been taut between those who fell the whole accident might have been averted'. Clark was indeed guilty of this omission, but so, it would seem, have been virtually all the other critics who have ever tackled the subject of the accident. Eugène Rambert, however, seems to have rejected Whymper's assertion and perhaps there is something else hidden away somewhere but, if there is, it cannot have made much of an impression and it is time to take another look at what Whymper wrote.

His earliest – indirect – reference to the subject comes in one of the questions he drafted for Old Peter to answer at the Enquiry. 'Was the rope tight, that is not in loops, between the men at the time they fell?' It seems to have been Whymper's own fault, judging from his French version, that the question actually put to Old Peter omitted the reference to 'between the men', as well as that to 'loops', so that it seemed to be asking whether the rope between Old Peter and Douglas (instead of that between Hudson and Hadow) was tight or not, at the time the men fell. The answer (A33) was yes (which is consistent with Whymper writing in *Scrambles* 'Between Hudson and Lord F. Douglas the rope was all but taut, and the same between all the others who were *above*'). But even if the answer had been no, it seems most unlikely that Clemenz would have asked a further question. The next question (Q34) might also in theory have led to Old Peter supporting Whymper's subsequent assertion that had the rope been taut between Hadow and Hudson, Hadow and Croz would never have fallen ten or twelve feet before the jerk came upon Hudson. Had Old Peter said that the slack rope between Hadow and Hudson gave rise to far too great a momentum for Hudson to be able to withstand it, he might have avoided the false impression given by his evidence that little more than the static weight of the three tourists was enough to break the rope with which he chose to tie himself on to Douglas. In contrast to this the ropes recommended by the Committee required a deadweight of two tons to break them.

Whymper's next reference to the rope not being tight was in his letter to von Fellenberg, in which he wrote:

> 'I cannot but think that had the rope been tight between those who fell as it was between myself and Taugwalder, that the whole of this frightful calamity might have been averted...The rope when used properly is a great safeguard; but...if two men approach each other so that the rope falls in a loop, the whole party is involved in danger; for should one slip, or fall, he may acquire before he is arrested, a momentum that may drag down one man after another, and bring destruction on all; but, if the rope is tight, this is all but impossible.'

A fortnight later in his letter to *The Times* he wrote: 'But, at the same time, it is my belief no accident would have happened had the rope between those who fell been as tight, or nearly as tight, as it was between Taugwalder and myself'. The paragraph then continues with much the same wording as in the von Fellenberg letter. A few days later Alfred Wills referred in his letter of 11th August to *The Times* to 'the slackened rope – the best friend of the climber converted only too easily into his most insidious and dangerous foe', having commented in a letter of 9th August to Whymper on 'it being impossible not to see that...the slackened rope effectually did its deadly work'.

In *Scrambles* Whymper expressly stated in a footnote, as already mentioned above, that the rope was not taut between Hadow and Hudson so that there was ten or twelve feet of slack to be taken up before the jerk came upon Hudson. But he made no mention of his belief that there would have been no accident had the rope been tight etc. It seems as though the reason for this omission may have been his wish to avoid giving pain to Hudson's widow. He had not previously made any mention of the slack between Hadow and Hudson, although it was to be inferred that it existed. The footnote appears to have been something of an afterthought, adding details which he had previously withheld and it is not possible to determine whether he had already deleted the earlier reference to the accident resulting from the rope not being taut or whether the footnote brought about its deletion. It was however one of only a few items in the Fellenberg and *Times* letters which did not also feature in *Scrambles*. All he wrote in *Scrambles* on the subject was in chapter 20, where it is said 'It is of the first importance to keep the rope taut from man to man. If this is not done, the rope affords no real security, and your risks *may* be considerably magnified...On rocks and on slopes it is used for a different purpose (namely, to guard against slips), and in these cases it is equally important to keep it taut.'

In these circumstances it does seem as though a principal cause of the catastrophe, after recognising that Hadow's error was not so much that he slipped but that he slipped at the wrong moment, was Hudson's inattention which caused the rope between him and Hadow not to be taut, to such an extent that the momentum of Hadow's fall had increased by a factor of ten or twelve feet by the time the jerk came upon him. This not only prevented him from checking the slip, but increased his own momentum to such an extent that Douglas was unable to hold him even though his section of rope was 'all but taut'. The actual strength of the sashline may therefore have had little bearing on the inevitability of a catastrophe once Hudson had been dislodged so violently. Either the entire party would be dragged off or, if someone had a secure stance, the rope would be likely to break.

If only Old Peter had been allowed to answer the questions frankly and his answers had been published, the truth might have been obvious and he might have been exonerated, instead of being made to look as though he had a guilty conscience. It has been suggested that Whymper made an 'accusation' that Old Peter intentionally used a weak rope in fastening himself to Douglas in order to have a chance of being separated from him in case of accident. But this ignores the fact that Whymper did not believe he used the weak rope intentionally and it also assumes that no one else was in the least bit interested in learning why he did not use one of the stronger ropes. This can hardly have been the case. Not only friends and relatives of the victims would have wanted to know the answer, about which Whymper himself could say nothing unlike the accusation from Old Peter's comrades and neighbours at Zermatt that he cut the rope, but all those who had taken an interest in the reason as to why the chain of events set in motion by Hadow's slip could only be broken by the rope. Even the *Times* leader on 27th July emphasised 'Above all their ropes must not break'.

'It has been repeatedly asked', wrote Whymper in his letter to *The Times*, '"Why was not the wire-rope taken which Mr.Hudson brought to Zermatt?"'

It is surely naïve to suggest in these circumstances that it was only Whymper who ever asked the far more obvious question, as to why Old Peter chose to attach himself to Douglas with the weakest rope when there were other stronger ropes available? This must have been 'repeatedly asked', and Whymper therefore did what he could to discover the answer by incorporating it in what should have become Question 28, 'Why was *a different kind of rope* used between Lord Douglas and yourself?' Little did he know or could he ever have imagined that Clemenz would allow someone to distort the question before it reached Old Peter and that he would then turn a blind eye to the resulting irrelevance.

Q 28. Why was *another rope* used between Lord Douglas and you?

A 28. Because the first rope was not long enough...

3.12.4 Use of the rope

There is an inconsistency between Whymper's and Old Peter's evidence about the state of the rope between them at the time of the accident, as to whether or not it was tight. Whereas it is difficult to try and resolve such an issue, it seems to be so closely linked to the actual use of the rope that a close study of this may provide a likely answer. Although Whymper devoted several pages in *Scrambles* to the use of the rope, he does not mention using it for a belay and it seems as though the relatively easy rock climbing of the day had not yet led to any recognised system or procedure.

Whymper wrote in his letter to von Fellenberg, '...immediately I heard the exclamation from Croz, I planted myself as firmly as the ground would permit, Taugwalder did the same, the rope was tight between us and the shock came upon us both as on one man.' In his letter to *The Times* the wording was almost the same, the last seventeen words being identical but in italics. In *Scrambles* there were only minor word changes such as 'taut' instead of 'tight' and 'jerk' instead of 'shock'. Old Peter on the other hand said in evidence to the Enquiry (A64), almost as an afterthought, prompted by the final question whether he had anything to add:

> 'I have to add that to be more secure I turned towards the rocks and as the rope which was between Whymper and myself was not taut I was fortunately able to wind it round a projecting rock, which then gave me the necessary and life saving anchorage; the rope that connected me with Douglas and those ahead gave me such a pull from their fall that I am still suffering a lot at the place where my body was tied with the rope.'

Whymper would never have known that Old Peter had given such conflicting evidence, but it is interesting to note that in *Scrambles*, in the footnote in which he gives more precise details of everyone's position at the moment of the accident, he added, 'Old Peter was firmly planted, and stood just beneath a large rock, which he hugged with both arms'. There is also another version of what Old Peter did, which is worth considering even though its uncertain origin and many inaccuracies undermine its reliability. It is considered in greater detail in section 3.9 (Newspapers), but comes in a report in the *Journal de Genève* of 18th July 1865, which seems likely to have been based on an interview with Young Peter. The report includes: 'Zum Taugwald, father, the last in the chain did not lose his presence of mind; he had the good fortune to be able to pass his rope over a rock rib and for a moment believed he had arrested this appalling fall; but the rope broke between Messrs Whymper and Hudson...' The following day a report appeared in *Der Bund*, which for reasons too complex to detail here seems likely to have been based on an interview with Old Peter. It contains fewer inaccuracies and includes: 'Fortunately, the elder Taugwalder managed to throw his weight upon a rock and before his strength had entirely ebbed, the rope broke below him, a circumstance to which he and Mr.Whimper and his own son at the back owe their survival.'

In an article in 1929 Dübi & Montandon, more particularly the latter, suggested that there might have been an error by Taugwalder or the Court and that it must really have been the Douglas rope that was not taut, as it would have been an unusual procedure to secure the upper, Whymper, rope round a rock. Montandon also suggested that there might have been some confusion with the precautions taken during the further descent after the accident. It is therefore interesting to note that in 1917 Young Peter was guilty of such a confusion in his 'Narrative' when he stated, just prior to describing the accident, 'From time to time my father belayed the rope round a spike of rock to safeguard them as they went down'.

But the most important question about Old Peter's Answer 64 is why he had to wait until an accident had happened before seeking such security and why he did not run the Douglas rope round the rock when Douglas was descending the pitch below the rock some time before and then leave the rope round the rock for the greater security of all. The most likely explanation seems to be that Old Peter did not in fact wrap the rope round the rock the moment after the accident occurred, or even before, but that he had the presence of mind to grasp the rock with both arms, as recorded by Whymper and inferred by *Der Bund*'s reference to his throwing his weight upon a rock. His inconsistent evidence at the Enquiry did not come in a direct or spontaneous reply to a specific question and whether it originated with Old Peter or with his lawyer it may simply have been seeking to take advantage of the inaccuracy in the *Journal de Genève*. For the idea of Old Peter wrapping a rope round a rock before the rope broke is wholly inconsistent with what Whymper wrote in *Scrambles* about the two men being paralysed by terror after the accident:

> 'For the space of half an hour we remained on the spot without moving a single step...Old Peter rent the air with exclamations...The young man did nothing but scream or sob, "We are lost! we are lost!" Fixed between the two, I could neither move up nor down. I begged

> young Peter to descend, but he dared not. Unless he did we could not advance. Old Peter became alive to the danger, and swelled the cry, "We are lost! we are lost!"...At last Old Peter summoned up courage, and changed his position to a rock to which he could fix the rope; the young man then descended and we all stood together.'

This passage by Whymper indirectly provides the explanation for Young Peter wrongly telling the *Journal de Genève* that his father 'had the good fortune to be able to pass his rope over a rib of rock'. For, as long as Young Peter dared not descend, Old Peter could not secure the taut rope between him and Whymper to the rock he was hugging, and there was nothing Whymper could do to provide any slack, fixed as he was between the two and unable to move up or down, except beg the son to descend. Ultimately Old Peter must have climbed up a few feet to create some slack and 'changed his position to a rock to which he *could* fix the rope'. He presumably then shouted up to Young Peter, that it was safe to descend, and he did so. The important factor is that the two Taugwalders were out of each others sight when the accident occurred (A54 'are you still there father?'). Young Peter would not therefore have seen his father change his position to the rock to which he fixed the rope, so that when his father had recovered sufficiently from the shock to be able to summon him to descend, Young Peter would have seen him with the rope passed over the rib of rock and he would not have known that he had not been standing like that ever since the moment Hadow slipped.

3.13
ROPES, CHAINS AND LADDERS

Siege tactics seem to have been employed almost immediately on the Italian ridge of the Matterhorn, with the way being secured by ropes at the difficult places. Both Tyndall and Whymper took ladders, the latter describing in *Scrambles* (ch.6) the problems he faced at the customs and at hotels in travelling across France and Italy with two twelve foot ladders in his luggage. After eight or nine years' siege most of the route was therefore already well established, even before Giordano despatched to Châtillon early in July 1865 '300 metres of rope, and some iron hoops and rings', for the ascent he had planned to make with Quintino Sella. It is nevertheless somewhat surprising to note that when Giordano had been in Zermatt the previous year he had, according to Guido Rey, drawn a sketch of the Matterhorn from the Riffel, noting against the Shoulder, 'This is the highest point which has hitherto been reached on the other side', and observing further on:

> 'From information received, we gather that the western face has been ascended to within about five hundred feet of the summit. In order to complete the ascent it would be necessary to cut steps and do other work in the rock for a height of about a hundred feet; eight or ten days, and three or four stone cutters at twenty francs a day would be required.'

Yet when the first attempt was made to climb above the shoulder on 14th July 1865, no great difficulties were encountered and they saw no need even to fix any of the special rope they had taken for the purpose. Prior to the descent Whymper suggested to Hudson (*Times* letter) that they should fix rope at the difficult bit, but, whereas he approved the idea, 'it was not definitely settled that it should be done'. Taugwalder also said at the Enquiry (A53), 'I said to the guide Croz, before we reached the dangerous place that one ought for greater safety to stretch a rope. Croz replied that it was not necessary.' It was therefore only after the accident that the survivors did 'that which should have been done at first, and fixed rope to firm rocks, in addition to being tied together. These ropes were cut from time to time, and were left behind.' Whymper's footnote to this in the 1st edition of *Scrambles* reads: 'These ends, I believe, are still attached to the rocks, and mark our line of ascent and descent'. In the 3rd edition (1880) he added: 'I saw one of them in 1873 [sic]', but in the 4th edition (1893) the footnote changed into the past tense, beginning 'These ends, until recently, were still attached...'

In 1887 Cunningham & Abney wrote in *The Pioneers of the Alps*, of an Englishman taking possession of the rope that had remained there for 20 years and distributing it at the table d'hôte, until Josef Seiler rescued it. So it is interesting to read in the 1955 *Alpine Journal* of the small piece of rope found wrapped up inside a vase that someone bought in 1951, with a label stating: 'Rope broken on the Matterhorn in the accident on July 14th 1865 when Lord F. Douglas perished. Given me by M.Seiler at the request of our courier Tanner on Septr 15th 1871 as a special favour & on condition that I would not tell people whom I met. I saw Lord D's boot also. Frederick M.Fry.'

The ropes left on the first descent are not to be confused with others which subsequent parties seem to have fixed and left on the route they followed, and which slowly rotted as time passed. Whereas Tyndall found in 1868 on his ascent from Breuil 'chains placed at all difficult places', a note that year in the *Alpine Journal* referring to the hut Seiler had built on the Hörnli arête included, 'On this side no chains have been fixed, and they are, indeed, quite unnecessary'. But gradually opinion seems to have changed and the Monte Rosa section of the SAC replaced some ropes on the Hörnli in 1870 and by 1872 it had accepted the suggestion made by two guides of getting some chains. But after the chains had been specially made in London and taken up to the hut the two guides – who must have been Knubels or Lochmatter – seem to have changed their minds, an article in the *Echo des Alpes* suggesting that having become familiar with the dangers they now preferred to exploit their monopoly rather than facilitate the ascent for other guides. But ultimately in 1874, the chains were fixed by Moser of Täsch and two or three friends, a paper by Wethered reproduced in the *Alpine Journal* in 1875 referring to them:

> '...rotten ropes, as formerly on the Zermatt side of the Matterhorn, and still on the Rothorn and elsewhere, might lead to lamentable accidents, and thus what was intended for one's

> welfare be converted into a means of bitter falling. I was, therefore, glad to find that the chains which in 1874 I had seen hanging idly on the outside of the Matterhorn hut had supplemented the ropes above the "shoulder".'

But in the discussion which followed the reading of the paper A.W.Moore 'expressed his regret that the great peaks should be vulgarised by means of mechanical appliances, and the multitude of resting places. He should like to see all huts destroyed and all ropes and chains cut down.' A note in the *Alpine Journal* in 1923 reported that

> 'the younger Zermatt guides are much inclined to remove all the ropes on the Swiss side of the Matterhorn – these are provided and maintained by the Corps of Guides. It is argued that the ropes enable guideless climbers to make the ascent to which their unaided powers are not equal. It would seem that the guides are within their rights in taking in the matter such steps as their interests dictate. From the climbing point of view, the Matterhorn is, of course, spoiled, as it is inconceivable that anyone will exert himself to *climb* the mountain when for long distances a rope dangles down alongside of him.'

But whatever wisdom there might or might not be in removing the ropes and chains on the Hörnli to-day, where recent fatalities have averaged over seven a year, such features as the Corde Tyndall and the Echelle Jordan on the Italian route are virtually indispensable. It was initially intended to secure a cable rather than the ladder but it also would have been named after Jordan, not just because he provided Canon Carrel with the money to buy it but because he did so much in 1867 to help the Maquignaz brothers reposition the original rope. It was not until 27th August 1869 that the ladder was actually fixed. The wide range of modern fixed ropes on the Italian ridge is shown in Bernardi's book, *Il Gran Cervino.*

3.14
SCRAMBLES AMONGST THE ALPS IN THE YEARS 1860–69

1st edition (July-September) 1871. John Murray, London.
2nd edition (November) 1871.
3rd abridged edition *The ascent of the Matterhorn* 1880. 10s. 6d.
4th edition de luxe 1893. 2½ guineas. (Remaining copies in 1900 3 guineas)
5th edition 1900. 15s.
Nelson Shilling series. (1908)
6th edition 1936. John Murray, London. Reprinted 1948.

USA

1st edition 1871. Burrows, Cleveland.
2nd edition 1873. Lippincott, Philadelphia.
3rd edition 1899. Burrows, Cleveland.

Germany
Berg- und Gletscherfaharten in den Alpen in den Jahren 1860 bis 1869.
1st edition 1872. Westermann, Brunswick. (Trans. F. Steger)
2nd edition 1892.
3rd edition 1909. (With introduction by Theodor Wundt)
4th edition 1922. Hamburg.
5th edition [1931]

France and Switzerland
Escalades dans les Alpes de 1860 à 1869. (Trans. Adolphe Joanne)
1st edition 1873. Hachette, Paris.
2nd edition 1875.
New edition 1912. Jullien, Geneva (also 1922 and 1931)
Escalades (Abridged edition including Andes) 1944. Neuchatel. (Trans. C.Engel)

Whymper took infinite care over the preparation of this his first book and it is said that he began writing it soon after climbing the Matterhorn. He had kept diaries of his climbs, although he recorded nothing in his 1865 diary after 2nd July, apart from details of his expenses. In March 1866 the *Alpine Journal* published an article by him on the first ascent of the Ecrins in 1864, which he also later described in *Scrambles*. A footnote in chapter 10 of *Scrambles* refers to a particular passage having been written in 1864 and the probability is that Whymper had decided at an earlier stage to write a full book, and that as far as the ascent of the Matterhorn was concerned he soon began to develop further the account which he first committed to paper in the form of the answers he would later give to the Enquiry at Zermatt. His first continuous narrative was his letter of 25th July 1865 to von Fellenberg, which formed the basis for his subsequent letter to *The Times*, published on 8th August. This in turn was developed further for *Scrambles*, and Graham Brown who carried out a very considerable amount of research on Whymper and the Matterhorn accident, but published little more on the subject than his valuable article based on the Girdlestone letter journal and a short article in *The Field* in 1932, undertook a comprehensive comparison of the three versions. His 40 pages of notes look at the text line by line, with a further 50 pages devoted to an analysis of *Scrambles*.

The long time it took to produce the first edition seems to have been attributable to the illustrations, as Whymper wrote in the preface of their preparation having occupied a large part of his time during the last six years. Sadly the wood blocks which he assigned to his publishers in 1905 seem no longer to have been available, when in 1936 Tyndale produced his new (6th) edited version of *Scrambles*, which led Graham Brown to write that 'The very bad reproduction of the original illustrations in the sixth edition (1936) was a crime against art, and it is only in one of the earlier editions that their delicacy can be appreciated'. Although the six years between the accident and the appearance of *Scrambles* is

A cannonade on the Matterhorn (1862)

therefore accounted for, it is much more difficult to understand the long delay in the appearance of the abridged 3rd edition. In November 1873 it was stated in the *Alpine Journal* that the principal portion of *Scrambles* would reappear 'next season' under the title of *Ascent of the Matterhorn* with numerous fresh illustrations and a new frontispiece by Gustave Doré, and that the work would not be reprinted in its original form, but it was not until six years later that the new edition was ready for publication with its frontispiece by Doré, which adds nothing to the book. Whereas this contribution from Doré might appear to be the only link between the two artists, there are probably at least two others, relating to the engraving of Whymper's spectacular illustration 'The crags of the Matterhorn, during the storm...' and to Doré's large lithographed prints of the Matterhorn showing the arrival at the summit on 14th Jult 1865 and the accident on the descent, and it is possible that they in fact helped each other in a number of different ways.

Whymper seems to have assumed responsibility for the production of *Scrambles*, having special paper expressly made by Dickinson's for the extremely fine engraving and again for the text. He commented in the preface on it being the most perfectly manufactured paper that had come under his notice. His firm undertook the printing of the full page illustrations, some of which like the Cannonade and the Col Dolent have a slightly tinted sky in some of the first editions, which Graham Brown has pointed out was probably applied with a second block. The printing of the text was entrusted to Mr.Clark in Edinburgh and the only fault in the production of the book, if it can be called such rather than evidence of the exceptional demand to read the first edition, is that many copies found to-day seem to have had to be rebacked, by laying down the old spine on top of new cloth.

Graham Brown quotes Montagnier as saying that a few 'proof' copies were prepared and one example, given by Mr.Clark to a friend, is in the Graham Brown collection in the National Library of Scotland. The care that Whymper also took over the preparation of the text is apparent from such things as his dispute with John Tyndall and the lengthy letter he wrote to the Editor of the *Alpine Journal*, revealing many additional facts in support of what he had written and how in 1869 he had actually checked with Carrel the accuracy of what he had written of certain matters in which Carrel had been involved with Tyndall. There appear to be two different types of footnote in the book. Firstly there are those deliberately kept out of the text like bibliographical references or matters not strictly relevant to the subject matter and secondly those which make good previous omissions or which update the narrative with information recently acquired. A good example of the former is the reference to his memorandum of 17th August 1865, where the footnote states merely 'Transcribed from the original memorandum'. This must have baffled everyone until Smythe published the complete text in 1940, but even then Smythe failed to appreciate and could not therefore pass on to his readers that Whymper had drawn up the memorandum and referred to it in the footnote, only as a consequence of the advice he had received from J.W.Cowell and from Alfred Wills.

The best example of the updating footnote, which has given rise to much uninformed criticism of Whymper, is the long one referring to Clemenz failing to give up answers that he had promised and to the two Taugwalders, with Old Peter labouring under an unjust accusation and nearly incapable of work and Young Peter endeavouring to trade upon his odious idea of not being paid for the ascent of the Matterhorn despite his father having been paid for both of them in the presence of witnesses. It must have been written late in 1869 or early the following year, based on the Enquiry Clemenz conducted into the Lyskamm accident in the autumn of 1869 and on what Whymper must have learnt from Seiler or others about the Taugwalders when he had been in Zermatt in August/September the same year. This footnote, which Whymper amended in the 1893 edition to take account of Old Peter's death etc but which seems to have remained the same in the foreign editions, is considered in detail in section 2.57.10.(c) iii (Whymper).

Some foreign translation errors have given rise to unnecessary and unjustified criticism of Whymper and to misunderstanding, as though he himself had deliberately given a false account. These are referred to under the individual critics, but two must be mentioned here. Charles Gos, the most enterprising and diligent researcher of everything remotely connected with the early history of the Matterhorn, unwittingly allowed himself to be misled by the incorrect addition of the word 'maudite' to what Whymper actually wrote about his surprise and horror when he discovered that the rope which had given way was the weakest of the three ropes. Whymper's words were 'found, to my surprise – indeed to my horror – that *it* was the weakest of the three ropes', which the first French edition translated as 'je m'aperçu avec une profonde surprise, que dis-je, avec horreur, que *cette corde maudite* était la plus faible'. In his otherwise almost unexceptionably excellent book *Le Cervin*, Charles Gos has a fifteen page chapter with the title 'La corde maudite', the accursed rope, which he incorrectly states is Whymper's own expression. With uncharacteristic bitterness and inaccuracy he allows himself to get completely carried away in his false criticisms of Whymper, no doubt influenced at the time by some recently published writings of Carl Egger and Arnold Lunn in a similar vein, to which he refers in a footnote. The 'accursed rope' also crops up as 'dieses verfluchte Seil' in the German edition of Ceresole's *Zermatt Guide*, which quotes Whymper extensively and must have originally been based on the French edition of *Scrambles*.

The other more blatant error occurs in the 1872 official German translation and involves the omission of six of Whymper's words, without which the rest of the sentence is nonsense. In his book *Pioniere der Alpen*, Egger who clearly had a very good command of English and must have been relying primarily on the 1st English edition as well as on the 4th, 5th or 6th, quoted the defective sentence in the German edition in such a way as to make it appear as though Whymper had expressly written the resulting nonsense. He then had the nerve to call it 'an incomprehensible chessmove on the part of Whymper', whereas it seems to be nothing less than an Egger own goal, based presumably on the near certainty that none of his Swiss readers would ever have been likely to check what Whymper had actually written. Any doubt about Egger's motive or about his knowing exactly what Whymper had written and why, can be excluded by the fact that he seems to have made his own completely new German translation of every sentence of Whymper's footnote, apart from the sentences immediately preceding the defective one. He even went so far as to improve other parts of the defective sentence, whilst retaining the nonsense.

The changes in the successive English editions were relatively minor until the 6th edition in 1936, when apart from quoting interesting extracts from Whymper's diaries and adding in an appendix some of Whymper's correspondence as well as his questions for Taugwalder to answer at the Enquiry, Tyndale chose to delete the tenth paragraph of chapter 20 in previous editions. This referred to the Alpine Club Special Committee's 1864 report on ropes and it could be said that it is even more relevant to-day than it was during Whymper's lifetime, and that had he known what some future critics were to suggest about his exaggerating the difference between the sashline and the other ropes or about not making it clear that the former was only to be used for fixed ropes, he would probably have quoted much more from the Committee's report.

In 1905 Whymper told his publisher, Mr.Hallam Murray, in a letter:

> 'It may perhaps be interesting to the Public at some future date to hear what the Illustrations of the books cost. As I paid the bills I have the best means of knowing. The Illustrations to "Scrambles" (including the copper plate maps) cost more than £1250 irrespective of my own work upon them; and the Illustrations to "Great Andes" cost more than £1650, irrespective of my own work upon them. Should anything of this kind be said, it may be added that the outlay was repaid, and that the author was satisfied.'

3.15
THE SEARCH AND RECOVERY PARTIES

Three separate parties were involved in searching for and ultimately recovering the bodies of the victims. They consisted of guides and others from Zermatt, as well as guides from Täsch, St.Niklaus, Saas and Chamonix and even one from the Oberland. Four English climbers including Whymper also took part. Although several men took part in more than one expedition, none of them went on all three. The details that follow treat the three parties **A B** and **C** separately, identify most of the Zermatt men by their Ruden or Kronig (*Familien-Statistik*) birth numbers, and indicate those who took part in more than one. Party **A** consisted of 20 men on Saturday 15th July, party **B** of 9 men on Sunday 16th July and party **C** of 21 men on Wednesday/Thursday 19th & 20th July. The sources are

Whymper's *Scrambles* and the documents accompanying the Official Enquiry Report.

3.15.1 Search party **A**

364. 'M. le Président Joseph Welschen' [**C**]
70. Franz Biner [**C**] (Not Weisshorn Biner 96 who was with Girdlestone)
75. Johann Biner 'der Kurze'
75. Joseph Biner 'der Kurze' [**C**]
179. Moritz Julen
268. Franz Perren
258. Peter Joseph Moser [**C**]
Joseph Brantschen (? Ruden 116)
268. Moritz Perren
266. Joseph Marie Perren [**C**]
263. Johann Peter Perren [**C**] (The well known Peter Perren)
Peter Perren [**C**] (? Ruden 266 or 285)
Ignaz Biner (? Ruden 67)
Ignaz Sarbach (St.Niklaus)
Johann Imboden (St.Niklaus)
Joseph Marie Lochmatter (St.Niklaus) [**B**]
Alexander Lochmatter (St.Niklaus) [**B**]
Peter Moor (Bernese Oberland)
Michel Balmat (Chamonix)
Jean Tairraz (Chamonix) [**B**]

Each member of this search party was paid six francs and also enjoyed a share in the thirteen bottles of wine provided by Ignaz Biner at a franc a bottle. It is not certain exactly when they set off. It may have been at about 2 p.m., as Loppé recorded in *L'Abeille de Chamonix*, although Whymper told the Enquiry (A15):

> 'on my return to Zermatt on the Saturday morning I informed the President of the Commune of Zermatt of the sad accident and at the same time asked him to send some men to the scene of the catastrophe, in case after all one of my unfortunate companions was still alive. This request was granted and a good number of men set off immediately. They returned six hours later.'

It would have taken some time to organise a search party particularly if they had been going to go to the Matterhorn glacier as Whymper requested and not just to the Hohlicht heights from where they were able to see the bodies lying on the glacier. It seems probable that the party all went initially to the Stöckli, as reported in *The Times* on 2nd August, but found it impossible to gain access to the glacier from there (see final paragraph of 3.15.2 below). McCormick's letter to *The Times* also referred to the width of the crevasses preventing them from reaching the bodies.

Joseph Welschen, the 56 year old President of the Commune, appears to have gone in his official capacity, although there is nothing to suggest that he was a guide. The only other Zermatter of particular interest is Peter Perren, who had been with Hudson and Croz on the Aiguille Verte and Mont Blanc only the week before and had probably accompanied them back to Zermatt. The two Lochmatters and Tairraz accompanied Whymper the following morning, but Perren was unable to go for fear of excommunication. As Whymper wrote in *Scrambles*, 'Peter Perren declared with tears that nothing else would have prevented him from joining in the search for his old comrades'.

3.15.2 Search party **B**

Edward Whymper
Rev Joseph McCormick
Rev James Robertson
J.S.Phillpotts
Franz Andenmatten (Saas) [**C**]
Joseph-Marie Lochmatter (St.Niklaus) [**A**]
Alexander Lochmatter (St.Niklaus) [**A**]
Frédéric Payot (Chamonix)
Jean Tairraz (Chamonix) [**A**]

The party left Zermatt at 2 a.m. on the Sunday and as far as the Hörnli took the same route that Whymper had taken the previous Thursday. They then went down to the right of the ridge and mounted through the seracs of the Matterhorn glacier. The Lochmatters and Tairraz would have known roughly where the bodies lay. Whymper described the scene in general terms, but there is a detailed description of the carnage in a letter from Gabriel Loppé to the editor of *L'Abeille de Chamonix* (23.7.65), which he presumably got from either Payot or Tairraz. The letter also included:

> 'Whilst these searches were going on, enormous stones were ceaselessly bombarding the searchers who had to move smartly out of the way on several occasions in order to avoid them. Mr.Whymper alone was unperturbed and ignored all entreaties to take cover; in the presence of this horrible scene, he solemnly swore that he would never set foot on a mountain again.'

Whymper himself gave more details to the *Journal de Zermatt* in 1895 and in the *Strand Magazine* in 1909. The search and the scene were also described by McCormick in his pamphlet, *A sad holiday*. He referred to an incident when a guide shouted a warning and they had to run down the slope to avoid a shower of stones of various sizes; but he did not mention Whymper. The party returned to Zermatt at 2 p.m. according to Girdlestone's letter journal. As they returned Old

Peter Taugwalder met them and showed Robertson his injuries; 'Mr. R–, they say I *cut* the rope. Look at my fingers'. (*Graphic*).

Whymper said in evidence to the Enquiry (A15),

> '...these same Zermatt guides refused en masse [sic!] to go in search of the bodies the following morning, Sunday, and it was on this account that I set out without official authority to recover the bodies and that on my return I did not think I had to make an official report. Nevertheless the fact that three bodies had been discovered was unofficially communicated to anyone who took an interest in this sad affair.'

This reference to not making an official report suggests that the authorities took exception to Whymper's action. As only Whymper, McCormick or Robertson could have identified any of the bodies and as the Enquiry Report includes in the inventories the possessions found on the bodies, it seems clear that the authorities must have woken up on about Monday 17th July, must have impounded the possessions found on the bodies and must have told Whymper to stay in Zermatt until the Enquiry had taken place. Handing over the possessions and noting exactly whom they belonged to must have been a lengthy procedure. Although no minutes, reports or other documents required or drawn up by the Zermatt Commune have ever been published, there must have been a good deal of communication between Whymper and McCormick on the one hand and Welschen and Clemenz on the other, during which Clemenz must have hatched the idea of handing Whymper a list of questions to answer. Something may well have been said at the same time about Whymper preparing a list of questions to be put to Old Peter, as it is most unlikely that he would ever otherwise have realised in advance of the hearing that such an option was even available to him. It would also perhaps explain why Clemenz did not apparently prepare any questions of his own to put to Taugwalder about the accident.

It may well be that the guides were so appalled at the scene of the tragedy that they stayed away from the bodies, and in particular did not look exhaustively for Douglas's body. Two records seem to confirm this, Andenmatten's answer to the Enquiry (A41) that he was on his own some distance from the victims, and Downton's letter to Mackenzie referring to how 'the guides could not be got to render any assistance, but lay down and *howled*'. There was no cause, however, for criticism of the guides, whom McCormick identified in his first letter to *The Times*, saying how they had generously offered their services; 'We hope their names will not be forgotten'.

Whymper's article in the *Graphic* in 1894 rather implies that he had organized the Zermatt guides for a search on the Sunday and that all was well until the authorities got to hear of it. There could well have been some rivalry between Welschen and Whymper, in view of Welschen's **A** party not even reaching the scene of the accident on the glacier. The following account published in *The Times* on 2nd August is based on Loppé's letter in *L'Abeille de Chamonix*.

> 'Mr. Whymper and his guide, Taugwald, arrived at Zermatt at 11am on Friday the 14th. A caravan of 21 persons, consisting of guides and peasants, was immediately organised, and left at 2 in the afternoon to search for the bodies. They repaired to the Zermatt glacier in the hope of thence rejoining the base of the great escarpment of Mount Cervin, where they expected the remains of the sufferers would be found. Upon reaching the Stöckli an enormous rocky mass lost in the midst of these deserts of snow, the party perceived that the glacier which ought to conduct them to the objects of their search was utterly impossible. By the aid of telescopes they thought they perceived the bodies hanging upon points of the rocks and retraced their steps, convinced of the uselessness of further effort.'

3.15.3 Search party **C**

364. 'M. le Président Welschen' [**A**]
186. 'M. le juge Louis Julen' (Alois Julen, Zermatt judge aged 42)
70. Franz Biner [**A**]
263. Johann Peter Perren [**A**]
417. Johann Zumtaugwald
266. Joseph M.Perren [**A**]
Peter Perren [**A**] (? Ruden 266 or 285)
Joseph Biner 'Tomele'
356. Peter Taugwalder, son of Peter Joseph
354. Peter Taugwalder, son of Peter (Young Peter)
354. Joseph Taugwalder, son of Peter (Old Peter's second son)
258. Peter Joseph Moser 'maréchal' [**A**]
157. Peter Inderbinen
Domestic of J.P.Perren
Franz Andenmatten (Saas) [**B**]
Joseph Moser (Täsch)
Etienne Willisch
75. Joseph Biner 'der Kurze' [**A**]
417. Mathias Zumtaugwald
Henri Charlet (Chamonix)
Michel Devouassoud (Chamonix)

Each member of this recovery party was paid 20 francs and those who acted as porters of the victims also enjoyed a share in 11 litres of wine provided by Mathias Zumtaugwald at 80 cents a bottle. The party appears to have left Zermatt on the Wednesday evening spending the night at the last chalets. It was led again by Joseph Welschen the President, one of only seven who had been on the Hohlicht search. Once again Old Peter Taugwalder did not take part, but Young Peter did, as well as the next son Joseph, who had acted as porter on 13th July. Amongst the newcomers were two of Zermatt's best guides Johann and Mathias Zumtaugwald. The party was also reinforced by the glacier guide Alois Julen, who seems to have been there in his official capacity as the Zermatt district judge, although he is not otherwise mentioned in connection with the Enquiry or other post-accident events. It seems inconceivable that he should not have reported to Clemenz, who conducted the Enquiry, whatever he observed at the scene of the accident and it is likely that his official involvement with these events is recorded in the Zermatt Council meeting minutes or other such records. Looking at it the other way round it is inconceivable that the part-time hotelier Clemenz faced with the prospect of holding such an Enquiry in his other capacity as judge, would have failed to discuss the situation with his fellow judge Julen, a native of Zermatt, particularly as the judge doubled up as a mountain guide and therefore had some practical experience of how to avoid accidents on mountains. Nevertheless the absence of Julen's name from the records of the victims' inventories attached to the Enquiry Report, such work having been carried out by the Randa judge Alois Biner, raises the probability that his real involvement with the Enquiry was to safeguard the interests of his fellow guide and cousin Old Peter Taugwalder, by acting as his lawyer.

3.16
THE SPECIAL ROPE

(This section incorporates the evidence and comments that feature in several other sections of the book in relation to the crucial question that Old Peter was never asked at the Enquiry, namely, why did he use the sashline to attach himself to Douglas rather than one of the stronger ropes?)

The 'special rope', as Old Peter Taugwalder called the rope with which he tied himself on to Lord Francis Douglas before they began their descent of the Matterhorn on 14th July 1865 (A24), was described by Whymper after the accident in various ways. In his letter to *The Times* he called it 'a lighter and weaker rope than the [Alpine Club rope], of a kind used by myself until the Club rope was produced'. In *Scrambles* he wrote 'It was old rope, and, compared with the others, was feeble'. He also described it as 'stout sashline'. Writing to Woolmore Wigram on 9th August 1865 Whymper said 'How it came to pass that the weakest rope was used between Taugwald and Lord Douglas I have no idea, that is, I have no idea why he did not use the stronger ropes. Still, I have no reason to suspect even that this was done *intentionally*.' Whymper would have expected to find the answer in the Report of the Official Enquiry but when this was ultimately published in 1920 the answer was not there. The question therefore remains unanswered. Certain critics who seem to be more interested in finding fault than truth have furthermore distorted the evidence since Whymper's death. It is the object of this section to take a closer look at the facts that are known and to try and put them back into their proper perspective and see whether there is in fact a perfectly straightforward and understandable reason why Taugwalder chose to tie on with the special rope.

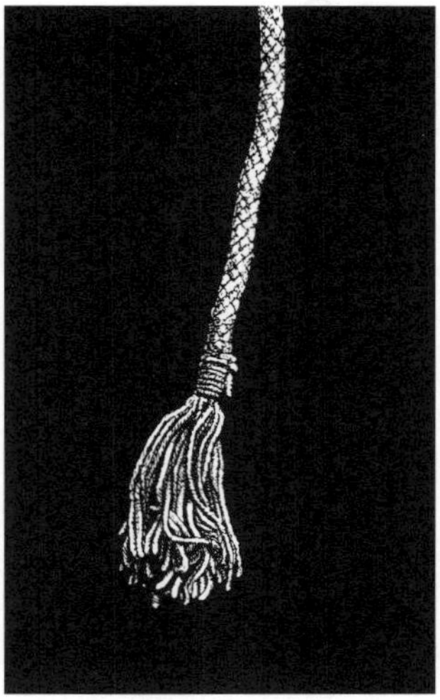

"Rope broken
on the Matterhorn"

The special rope was of plaited rather than twisted construction, a distinction that was of considerable significance in the 1860's. Although John Ball wrote critically in his 1863 *Guide to the Western Alps* of some mountaineers using a fine sashline and advocated a rope of Manilla hemp of which 'a length of 40 ft. is quite enough for three men' it seems as though 'stout sashline' was very popular and that many believed it to be superior to twisted ropes until the publication in July/September 1864 of the Report of the Alpine Club's Special Committee on Ropes etc. Whymper referred in chapter 20 of *Scrambles* to the Committee being appointed to test and to report upon the most suitable ropes for mountaineering purposes and he mentioned that the Manilla and Italian hemp ropes approved would sustain a weight of 168lbs falling 10 feet or 196lbs falling 8 feet. Unfortunately the Editor of the 6th edition of *Scrambles* in 1936 saw fit to delete Whymper's reference to the report, as a result of which those unfamiliar with its findings have sought to say wrongly that Whymper exaggerated the difference between the two types of rope. The significance of the report lies in the Committee's preliminary test in which they rejected any rope which would not bear 168lbs (12 stone) falling 5 feet.

> 'Under this trial, all those plaited ropes which are generally supposed to be so strong, and many most carefully made twisted ropes, gave way in such a manner as was very startling to some of our number, who had been in the habit of using these treacherous cords with perfect and most unfounded confidence.'

The Report was not published in the *Alpine Journal* until September 1864, and the June 1865 *Journal* commented: 'As this report was not published till late in the season it is probable that its contents were never made known to the very persons who ought to know them best, the guides, who in practice arrange the rope for a party...' It seems therefore highly probable that at the start of the 1865 season most guides were still unaware of the relative weakness of plaited ropes.

After giving his evidence at the Enquiry, Whymper handed in a list of fourteen questions to be put to Taugwalder in order to elicit further information about the use of the rope and its breakage. Although, as we shall see, there is doubt as to how some of these questions came to be altered before they were put to Taugwalder, it can be said with certainty that Questions 22 to 35 inclusive were all submitted by Whymper and that the majority were put to Taugwalder in German in precisely the same terms as Whymper's original list in English. But the situation is complicated by the existence of three or even four different versions, in English,

French (two) and German. The English list is in Whymper's handwriting and is obviously the first version. The second version, involving some minor alterations in wording (of no great significance), is in French and appears on pages 22 & 23 of the documents released from the Court file in 1920. It is headed 'Questions à faire à Pierre Taugwald père, au nom de Mr.Whymper' and after No.14 it concludes with the words 'Le juge d'instruction est prié d'addresser les questions ci-contre au guide Taugwald, père. Zermatt, ce 21 juillet 65. Edouard Whymper.'

What is not absolutely clear is whether the original document handed to the Court by Whymper was in French or whether it was in English and subsequently translated, but the former seems probable. There would have been no purpose in the Tribunal in Zermatt translating any English into French rather than straight into German and the Cantonal authorities in Sion would not have needed a separate French translation made when there was already an official French translation of the questions actually put to Taugwalder. Furthermore the document forms part of the first batch obtained by Jullien, the remainder (pages 24-33) obtained on his second trip to Visp and typed out on a different machine being translations made (presumably in July 1865) by the State translator Oggier.

The third version of Whymper's questions is the record of questions actually put to Taugwalder in German, i.e. Questions 22-35. The fourth version, the original French translation of the third, published by Farrar in 1920, could be disregarded altogether were it not necessary to draw attention to the fact that it can be misleading, as it contains several errors. For example, in A34, Taugwalder did not say that the weight of the three tourists with the force of their fall 'could have broken a *really* strong rope' but 'could *even* have broken a strong rope'.

It is hardly practicable for such a Tribunal to conduct an Enquiry into such a fatal accident and hear evidence from witnesses without some reliable advance information or documentary evidence of some sort. A modern British Coroner in such circumstances would have the benefit of statements taken on his behalf from witnesses as well as a report from a police officer or some other sort of expert, in the same way as he is given technical help and guidance when a death results from an industrial accident or disease. Such an expert could be expected to inspect any equipment that might have a bearing on the cause of the accident and might well also visit the scene of the fatality.

It goes without saying that unless Clemenz based the Enquiry on gossip and rumour, he must have made some preliminary enquiries into the accident and its possible cause, even though nothing that has ever been published supports this. He could not have postponed the formal opening of the Enquiry until 2 p.m. on Friday 21st July without knowing in advance roughly how long it was going to take to hear and record the evidence of the two main witnesses and one other witness, having particular regard to the complications likely to result from a German speaking Tribunal questioning an English witness in the French language, of which neither appears to have had a perfect command. Whymper's lengthy Answer 11, with several sentences of more than 30 words and one of over 50, would tax the most fluent speaker of a foreign language, having to pause every eight or nine words to enable the Clerk to record what was also for him a foreign language. There must therefore have been a good deal more to the Enquiry than meets the eye on a perusal of the documents published in *AJ33*.

Whymper may well have first spoken to Clemenz about the accident on the evening of Sunday 16th July, when he called at the Mont Cervin to talk to Girdlestone. Clemenz, the hotelier, would not yet then have been asked to conduct the Enquiry in his judicial capacity, but he would already have had a keen interest in the Matterhorn accident in which one of his recent guests, Lord Francis Douglas, had lost his life. Although in a letter to McCormick Whymper subsequently expressed his displeasure at having been detained in Zermatt so long to suit Clemenz' pleasure, it is likely that Whymper and Clemenz had met and communicated on a number of occasions during that week. Whymper certainly paid Lord Francis Douglas's hotel bill and somehow acquired from Clemenz a list of questions which became Q2-17 in the Official Report. Whereas it is possible that Whymper was asked by Clemenz in the course of a detailed discussion to frame his own questions, this can almost certainly be excluded by the wording of some of the questions put to him, such as the somewhat official nature of Q15. The fact that Q4 appears to have arisen out of A3 and could hardly have been drafted by Clemenz in advance, can be explained by Whymper or Vecqueray having amended Q4 in the same way that Vecqueray improved the wording of Q6.

The advance list of questions enabled Whymper to prepare his answers and to have them translated into French by the Rugby schoolmaster J.W.J.Vecqueray. When the Enquiry opened it seems that Whymper handed in the list of questions together with his answers and that Clemenz then read out the questions one by one and Whymper duly recited the answers. This may perhaps have been the normal Swiss practice in 1865, even though it was not followed in the case of the witnesses Andenmatten and Lochmatter, but it is not what one would have expected. It is significant that none of the questions put to Whymper (except Q4 mentioned above) nor of those put to Taugwalder on Friday 21st July is based on, or seeks clarification or further details of, any previous answer, although Clemenz did raise two minor matters with Whymper, which the Clerk did not bother to record. It is probably fair to say that, despite the Tribunal's further questions to Taugwalder on Sunday 23rd July showing some signs of attention and of the need to avoid any major inconsistency in the evidence, there is no sign of it having wanted to obtain any evidence whatever on those matters relating to the use of the special rope which have so occupied the minds of some critics in the last 75 years. Nor is there any record or sign of Clemenz or any one else having examined the end of the rope that broke.

The search party on 15th July appears to have been organized and led by the President of the Zermatt commune Joseph Welschen and it seems likely that he helped to coordinate events once the Cantonal Government had appointed

Clemenz to conduct the Enquiry. It seems probable that the Zermatt Gemeinde archives will contain reports by Welschen as well as other documents relating to the accident and the events of the following week. Welschen also led the third search party, which on the 19th & 20th July went and recovered the bodies. The only evidence Clemenz heard about this was brief mention by Franz Andenmatten, and it seems inconceivable that there should have been no official interest taken in the scene of the tragedy on the Matterhorn glacier. Clemenz cannot have been unaware that Young Peter Taugwalder accompanied the third search party, yet Clemenz' only interest in him seems to have been to ask Old Peter on 23rd July (Q54) whether his son saw how the accident occurred – by which time Young Peter had already left Zermatt! In similar circumstances to-day a police officer would no doubt have accompanied the recovery party and the probability is that one or more members of the 21 strong party in fact made observations of an official nature on behalf of the Commune or on behalf of Clemenz or the Government of the Canton. Joseph Welschen might be the obvious choice were there not someone else far better qualified to act as adviser and go-between for the Zermatt guides and the Cantonal judge.

Alois Julen, a native of Zermatt, was not only recognised as a good glacier guide for the lower routes but he was a lawyer. His name appears immediately after that of 'M. le président Welschen' in the list of the third search party, under the title 'M. le juge Louis Julen'. His identity is confirmed by *Ruden*, where he appears as 'Alois Julen, Richter' (judge) and it seems probable that he was the Zermatt equivalent of the Bezirksrichter Alois Biner von Randa (district judge of Randa). Biner appears to have been coopted by Clemenz to deal with the inventories of the victims' belongings, whereas the Zermatt judge Alois Julen would surely have been the obvious candidate had he not been otherwise engaged with the Enquiry. Another reason for anticipating the involvement of Alois Julen is that his elder brother Johannes Julen was the ad hoc bailiff for the Enquiry.

Like some of Whymper's answers to Clemenz' questions, so also some of Taugwalder's answers to the Whymper questions put to him by Clemenz, seem too good to be true, but in a different way. The unreality of Whymper's replies under oral examination stems from the language problem and the great length of some of his sentences. With Taugwalder's answers the mystery is as to how he could give such concise, logical, yet sometimes ambiguous and subtly evasive replies on his first examination on the Friday without inviting a single request for clarification of his evidence. But there is also a mystery about some of the questions put to him, quite apart from his answers.

The oddest thing about the questions put to Taugwalder on the Friday is that apart from Q18-21, which were little more than introductory formalities, and Q36, which was ambiguous and of no real import, all the others, Q22-35, originated with Whymper, suggesting that if he had not handed in his list of fourteen questions Clemenz would not have asked Taugwalder anything of substance. It may be therefore that Clemenz not only knew in advance that

Whymper was going to hand in a list of questions for Taugwalder but that he actually asked Whymper to prepare such a list. Q22 looks as though it may indeed have been drafted by Clemenz, relying on his knowledge as landlord of the repeated attempts by his guest to climb the Gabelhorn with Taugwalder. It can hardly be said in Clemenz' defence that he recognised the value of Whymper's questions and did not need to ask any more of his own, as there is no sign of his having taken the slightest notice of any of Taugwalder's answers as he recited or otherwise gave them on the Friday or Saturday. Why else did he not realise, but have to be reminded by Taugwalder, that he had already answered Q32 in A30. He should also have realised that Q27 had already been answered by A24 and he should surely have sought clarification or amplification of such answers as A24, 26 & 34. It now seems fairly certain that Clemenz paid no heed to most of Whymper's answers at the time he recited them, e.g. A10, 'between Lord Douglas and Taugwalder father the rope was less thick', or A11, 'Hadow slipped and in his fall knocked Michel Croz over'. Had he been alert and had he wanted to establish the truth, he would surely have questioned Taugwalder about the 'less thick' and also the 'special' rope, and he would have responded immediately to A30 (when Taugwalder said that Croz was only dragged off *after* the rope broke) by putting to Taugwalder what eventually became Q63 on the Sunday. The most feasible explanation for the apparent lack of interest in the evidence recorded as having been given by both Whymper and Taugwalder on the Friday, is that both handed in their answers in writing, which the Clerk only wrote up at a later stage.

Apart from the rewording of some of Whymper's questions for Taugwalder (referred to below) there are other grounds for supposing that Taugwalder answered his Friday questions in writing, such as the inclusion of the word 'above' in A32 (first line) and the inflexibility in persevering with Q27 & Q32, notwithstanding A24 & A30. The fact that Whymper said nothing of having handed in the Taugwalder questions *prior* to giving his own evidence on the Friday afternoon does not necessarily exclude such a possibility, as he said nothing about his own evidence effectively being given in writing. And there is another possibility; that he passed a copy of the list to Taugwalder a day or two before, via the Bailiff Johannes Julen, so that Taugwalder would have had an equal opportunity of considering and preparing his answers in advance of the hearing. It should furthermore be noted that Whymper's questions 22, 23, 30, 31, 32 & 35 do not relate to the use or breakage of the special rope and there is a possibility that he merely supplemented some questions in a list already prepared by Clemenz. In the *Journal de Zermatt* article, Whymper said that he gave Clemenz 'all the information and details he requested including, amongst other things, a questionnaire'.

The two obvious questions that needed to be put to Taugwalder were for him to describe the special rope and to explain how it came to be used. The Tribunal only learnt one detail about the rope from Whymper, namely that the Taugwalder – Douglas rope was less thick than the Croz – Douglas rope or the Taugwalder –

Taugwalder rope. There is nothing to indicate that Clemenz heeded or even noticed this reference by Whymper to the Taugwalder – Douglas rope being potentially inferior to the other ropes, although thickness is not the sole criterion of a strong rope. Of the questions actually put to Taugwalder and of his answers, only eleven made any reference at all to the rope that broke and of these, six can be dismissed at once as having no bearing on the rope's quality or use – A30, A32, Q35, Q36, Q&A57 and A64. Q33 can also be disregarded in the present context, leaving only A24, Q&A 28, Q&A 29 and Q34.

There is nothing to suggest that Clemenz had seen the broken rope end in Whymper's possession. Taugwalder said that it was a 'special' rope but he was not asked to amplify this. Otherwise both the questions put to him and his answers were in neutral and general terms and there was no distinction drawn between the construction, quality or strength of the different ropes. Another rope was used between Taugwalder and Douglas because the Croz – Douglas rope was not long enough (A28). If he had found the rope too weak Taugwalder would have rejected it (A29). He did not know how the rope came to break although the weight and the force of the fall could even have broken a strong rope (A34). This was the nearest he came to saying that it was a weak or weaker rope and as in the case of A24 he could and would no doubt have clarified and amplified his answer, if only he had been asked to do so.

Whymper seems to have taken considerable care to avoid as far as possible asking a leading question of Taugwalder, in the same way that he did not in his own evidence volunteer any adverse comment on the quality or use of the sashline. But his Question 7, on which Q28 was based, did ask why a different kind of rope was used between Taugwalder and Douglas and it is necessary to look at how this question and others came to get distorted to such an extent as to become irrelevant. Q25 & Q26 for instance were asked in such a way as to make Taugwalder concentrate on the Croz rope that did not break to the total exclusion of the rope that did break between him and Douglas.

Although Clemenz may well have been faced with a conflict between his interests as hotelier and as judge and this may have undermined his authority in Zermatt, it is hardly likely that he was incompetent, lazy or merely going through the motions of holding an Enquiry with no intention other than to reach a verdict that the cause was a slip by Hadow and that there had been no culpable negligence on anyone's part. The cause of the distortions and inadequacies in the questioning of Taugwalder may therefore lie elsewhere, if one disregards the limitations resulting from Clemenz decision to base the evidence of Whymper and Taugwalder on their written answers.

The distortion in the German version of Whymper's questions comes in Q26 and Q28. Q25 had been a general question about who was roped up first and it followed on the previous question on the same topic. However in A25 Taugwalder confined his answer to the Croz – Douglas rope, 'I do not recall for certain which of the three tourists was tied up first by Croz'. Q26 was then altered in the course of its translation into German and instead of a general question on a new topic, 'What kind of rope was used?', Taugwalder was asked in effect what kind of rope Croz had used. This was the result of the additional word 'dazu' (for that), which related the question to his last answer. His answer highlighted the irrelevance of the question by stating that 'the rope to which Croz and the three tourists were tied was a strong and brand-new rope'. Did someone deliberately confine the question to the irrelevant Croz – Douglas rope to protect Taugwalder from having to give details of the special rope? Clemenz himself is unlikely to have needed to misdirect Whymper's question if he did not like it, as Whymper would never have been satisfied by such distortion and it would have made life easier for Clemenz to abandon the question altogether. If on the other hand he trotted it out thoughtlessly during oral questioning he ought certainly to have been alerted by Taugwalder's emphatic reply and to have followed it up with a similar question relating to the relevant rope. Q26 & A26 therefore add weight to the probability that Taugwalder was given the list of questions in French in advance so as to have the opportunity of preparing his answers.

Q28 is the most blatant distortion, because the mistranslation into German involves the same words 'espèce de corde' as in Q26, where they had been translated correctly as 'what kind of rope'. But in Q28 he was asked not why was a *different kind of rope* used but 'Why was *another rope* used between Lord Douglas and you?' Taugwalder had already acknowledged in A24 that the rope between him and Douglas was in some way of a different kind when he described it as a special rope, but he gave the literal reply to Q28 conveying nothing more than that if one rope is not long enough two ropes are necessary. It is difficult to avoid the conclusion that in the course of translation from French into German Q28 was altered by someone who misguidedly thought that he was doing Taugwalder a favour, by helping him to avoid having to answer the most important question on Whymper's list. But Taugwalder should have been allowed to say why he used the special rope.

There has been comment on the harm that Clemenz caused by not publishing the evidence. He had promised to supply Whymper with the answers to the questions for Taugwalder, but he never did this, nor did he apparently offer any explanation. It must however have been obvious to him that having drawn the attention of the public to the outstanding answers in his letter to *The Times*, Whymper would have commented adversely on the way his questions had been distorted and so remained unanswered. Whymper would no doubt also have drawn attention to the Enquiry's senseless feat in getting Taugwalder to describe the rope that did *not* break instead of the one that did!

It looks as though Taugwalder was allowed or even encouraged to receive assistance in drafting his answers, at least on the first day, in advance of the questions being put to him by Clemenz. It would hardly be fair if it were otherwise, when Whymper was given time to prepare his answers. Not only does A32 suggest that the answers were written out for Taugwalder, by use of the word 'above' which would be quite inappropriate in a purely oral examination, but the wording of many of his answers is far too clever, precise, lengthy, logical and formal, instead of the somewhat hesitant answers that might be expected from a simple peasant, bewildered by the ordeal of having to give evidence before the Enquiry. His elaborate answer to Q29, for which the single word 'yes' might have sufficed, looks more like the pleading of a lawyer than of a peasant, with its long elaborate sentences setting out three separate grounds for not using a weak rope. Although A29 is undermined somewhat by the subsequent A34, implying that the Taugwalder – Douglas rope was not a strong rope, both A29 and A34 suggest considerable skill in avoiding a direct answer. Answer 55 also displays unexpected sophistication with its two stage logic and the formal deferential reference to the Examining Magistrate, which could only come from someone well versed in legal procedures. Although the Clerk could conceivably have introduced the reference to the Examining Magistrate as he recorded Taugwalder's reply, it would seem as though he would already have had more than enough to record if the questioning had been entirely oral, without adding in such niceties. Further instances of well polished phraseology, more to be expected from a professional lawyer than a simple layman, come in the last six words or so of A23, in the literally true but irrelevant A28 and in the methodical progression of the two long sentences that make up A30. It therefore looks very much as though Taugwalder was allowed to have the assistance of his cousin judge Alois Julen in drafting his answers to the majority, if not all, of the questions and that in the mistaken belief that Taugwalder could not justify the use of the special rope Alois Julen modified some of the questions in the course of translating them into German and so avoided any specific reference to the qualities of, or to the reasons for using, the special rope that broke.

As already noted, only three of Taugwalder's answers have any real relevance to the rope that broke. In two of them, A29 and A34, he was giving his opinion and it looks as if his indirect replies may have been drafted by Alois Julen. They are hardly consistent, as A34 implies that the rope was not a strong one (unlike the Croz rope described in A26). This is the furthest Taugwalder went in any of his answers towards saying that the rope that broke was in any way inferior to the other ropes. But A24 was altogether different; he stated that he tied himself to Lord Douglas and then volunteered the additional fact that he did so with a special rope.

It has often been suggested that the reason he used the weak rope was simply laziness. Laziness may have been a contributory factor but was certainly not the principal one. There must have been a special reason for using the special rope and it is necessary to try and look at the matter from Taugwalder's point of view. He was in 1865 a guide of considerable experience, but not a guide of the top class. One could call him a good Monte Rosa guide, having ascended that mountain some eighty five times, more than twice as often any other Zermatt guide. Leslie Stephen in fact referred to him and his son as 'comparatively incompetent'.

Unlike Peter Perren the leading Zermatt guide of the day, who had climbed from Chamonix, Grindelwald, Randa and elsewhere, Taugwalder's only peaks the Breithorn, Pollux, Lyskamm and Monte Rosa had all been to the south or east of his own doorstep, until he was engaged by Lord Francis Douglas at the end of June 1865. As Dangar & Blakeney wrote a century later, 'Looking to his past record, one is inclined to think that it was unfortunate that old Peter was engaged by Douglas in 1865, for it took him out of his class.'

Douglas was a keen and ambitious mountaineer, but at the age of 18 with only three previous Alpine seasons he had not yet acquired as much experience as his rivals, as is shown by the comparative ease with which Moore and Walker beat him to the first ascent of the Gabelhorn. He joined the Alpine Club in December 1864 and would almost certainly have read the September 1864 number of the *Alpine Journal* from cover to cover. It started with the Report of the Special Committee on Ropes, Axes and Alpenstocks and it seems inconceivable that he would not have studied it carefully and heeded it in so far as he could. In addition to the extracts quoted above, the Committee found that none of the ropes tested, 'the heaviest which can be conveniently carried about in the Alps', would bear 14 stone falling 10 feet.

Ball pointed out in his 1863 *Guide to the Western Alps* that a guide was expected 'to find himself in the articles requisite for his profession such as rope', and when Douglas engaged Taugwalder at the end of June 1865 the latter would almost certainly have provided the rope. There is no evidence as to whether the rope was a plaited one or not, but let us for the present assume that it was, as if Taugwalder had possessed any such rope he is unlikely to have discarded it by June 1865. Douglas would no doubt have suggested that it was inadequate, recalling the AC Committee's report, but if the 45 year old guide had replied to the effect that there might be some weak plaited ropes but his was a really strong one and his own practical experience was to be preferred to the secondhand reports of those whose recommendations were only based on theory and contrived tests, the keen and ambitious 18 year old would have had little alternative but to accept the plaited rope.

Amongst Douglas's belongings was found the account he had written for the *Alpine Journal* describing his ascent of the Gabelhorn with Taugwalder and Viannin on 7th July, exactly a week before the Matterhorn accident. This refers to their finding a cairn at a point very little below the summit, indicating that the party that had made the first ascent the day before

> 'had not gone to the actual summit, as it was a peak of snow and there were no marks of footsteps. On this peak we sat down to dine, when, all of a sudden, I felt myself go, and the whole top fell with a crash thousands of feet below, and I with it as far as the rope allowed (some 12 feet). Here, like a flash of lightning, Taugwald came right by me some 12 feet more; but the other guide who had only the minute before walked a few feet from the summit to pick up something, did not go down with the mass, and thus held us both. The

> weight on the rope must have been about 23 stone, and it is wonderful that, falling straight down without anything to break one's fall, it did not break too.'

Douglas's reference to the distance they fell and to the weight on the rope seems to confirm his familiarity with the Committee's Report, particularly when he expresses wonder that the rope did not break. So if the rope involved on the Gabelhorn had indeed been a plaited one, Douglas would thereafter have had perfect confidence in such a rope. And so would Taugwalder. Douglas's tribute to Taugwalder in the same article reveals a certain lack of mountaineering judgment or experience, when he states 'Peter Taugwald acted admirably, and really showed himself a first rate guide'. This fails to take account of the folly of lunching on the cornice but could in fact be based, at least in part, on Taugwalder's assurance that the plaited rope was a good rope, if indeed such a rope was involved.

Extrapolating from the AC test results, it would seem as though no rope either twisted or plaited would sustain 12 stone falling 12 feet. This may almost have been the force of Douglas's own fall, which was followed immediately by the further shock on the same stretch of rope of some 12 stone of Taugwalder falling a total of 24 feet. Even if the Douglas – Viannin rope absorbed some of the shock by cutting into the snow slope away from the cornice and if Douglas only fell about 8 feet vertically, the force of his fall would still equal if not exceed the theoretical capacity of all the plaited and many of the twisted ropes tested by the Committee. But Taugwalder's 12 stone free fall of 20–24 feet seems to be beyond doubt and his half of the rope therefore sustained twice the maximum load calculated in the tests on twisted ropes and without any regard for the shock load Douglas had imparted to the other half only a moment before.

It would be wrong to impute to Taugwalder too great an understanding of the qualities of ropes of different construction. He would however no doubt recognise a rope of the type with which he was familiar and conversely might reject the unfamiliar in favour of that of which he had experience, particularly in the case of a rope that had saved his life. The balance of probabilities seems therefore to favour his familiarity with plaited rope as if a twisted rope had saved his life on his last climb exactly a week before the ascent of the Matterhorn, he would surely have insisted on using one of the almost new twisted ropes that was readily available, rather than an elderly looking and obviously thinner plaited rope. The Gabelhorn accident should have served to remind Taugwalder that danger can present itself unexpectedly and there would be no reason for him to assume that he was immune from risks such as stonefall, so that if he had been hit and had fallen (before Douglas asked Whymper to tie on to Taugwalder) any deliberate use of a weak rope could have endangered himself. It therefore looks as though he may well have chosen to use the plaited rope on the Matterhorn because he had been carrying it ready to use as fixed rope and because he honestly believed in the light of a similar looking rope saving his life on the Gabelhorn that it was the equal of, if not superior to, the brand-new twisted ropes.

Disregarding whatever went through Taugwalder's mind as he attached the special rope to Douglas, what would the situation be as far as Douglas was concerned? Croz would already have tied the end of the twisted Manilla or the stouter and probably stronger rope round his waist, when Taugwalder decided to attach the end of the special rope. The superficial contrast between the two ropes must have been blatantly obvious to Douglas. He could not have forgotten his miraculous escape on the Gabelhorn and if it had been attributable to the use of a thicker, twisted rope then no matter how great his exhilaration at having just made the first ascent of the Matterhorn he would surely have objected to Taugwalder using the obviously inferior, old and thinner plaited rope, which he would know had been taken on the climb for use as fixed rope. The *Dumfries Courier* reported that he had in April 1865 come first out of 119 seeking direct commissions in the Army, gaining some 8% more marks than any other candidate, and it seems reasonable to conclude that he would both have recognised and objected to a situation that involved unnecessary danger. But if it had been a plaited rope that had saved his life on the Gabelhorn, it is understandable that he should have been prepared to allow Taugwalder to use a similar rope on the Matterhorn, as in such a large and for the most part competent party it would have seemed inconceivable that the rope would ever have had to sustain a load anywhere near that of a 12 stone man falling 20 feet or more.

Whereas one should be able to exclude the possibility that Douglas encouraged Taugwalder to use the plaited rope, he did in fact lose two separate opportunities of insisting on a twisted rope. His exhilaration must have worn off by the time he asked Whymper to tie on to Old Peter saying that 'he feared...Taugwalder would not be able to hold his ground if a slip occurred'. It would have been so easy to ask Whymper to lower enough strong rope for him to attach himself to it as well, if he had any doubt about the security of the 'special' rope. It seems therefore that both Taugwalder and Douglas may have had good reason to suppose (albeit wrongly) that the plaited rope was as strong as the others; an instance of how good fortune can deceive.

3.17
ZERMATT AND THE MATTERHORN

3.17.1 Some important events

1789. de Saussure was the first visitor to publish a detailed account of his visit; see *Voyages dans les Alpes*. Vol 4, (1796) 382-3.

1792. de Saussure spent three days on Theodule pass, studying the Matterhorn and making the first ascent of Klein Matterhorn; ibid 408-37.

1795. Abraham Thomas visit; see Murith. *Le Guide du Botaniste* 15-16.

1800. George Cade, first English visitor; see *AJ*7, 436.

1803. Murith visit; see *Le Guide du Botaniste* 30.

1806. Escher visit. Earliest(?) drawing (coloured) of Matterhorn, taken from Winkelmatten. See Hans Conrad Escher von der Linth. *Views and panoramas of Switzerland 1780–1822*. Atlantis, Zürich. 1975. plate 126. Also in Gattlen. *Das Matterhorn im Bild*. Brig. 1979. p14.
1839. Lauber's guesthouse acquired a monopoly as the only lodging for visitors.
1852. Clemenz opened Hotel Mont Cervin.
1853. Seiler arrived and took lease of Lauber Inn.
1854. Seiler bought Lauber Inn, renaming it Hotel du Mont Rose.
1854. Riffelhaus opened and leased to Seiler.
1855. Earthquake, centred on St.Niklaus.
1855. First ascent of Monte Rosa.
1865. First ascent of the Matterhorn.
1867. Seiler bought Hotel Mont Cervin.
1879. Hotel Zermatterhof finally built by Commune and leased to Seiler.
1884. Hotel Riffelalp opened by Seiler.
1891. Alexander Seiler died. First train service to Zermatt.
1898. Gornergrat railway opened.
1927. First winter season at Seiler's Hotel Victoria.
1929. Railway electrified and first operated in winter.
1980. Klein Matterhorn cablecar opened.

3.17.2 Twenty literary milestones

The following list is aimed at the English reader, but the selection is not restricted to English language books as this would exclude some of the most important ones and leave gaps which no English book could ever fill. Novels have been disregarded, even though one or two are quite readable. Many of the English titles are available in French (5, 8, 10, 11, 12 & 16) or German (5, 8, 11, 12, 15 & 16). 5, 11 & 18 are also available in Italian. 17 is now available in French and also in English.

(1) de Saussure, H.B. *Voyages dans les Alpes.* Vol 4. Neuchatel. 1796.
The four volumes of his Alpine travels published between 1779 and 1796 deal primarily with his scientific and geological research, but the 2300 pages also cover his mountaineering and they helped to draw attention to Zermatt.

(2) Murith, L.J. *Le guide du botaniste qui voyage dans le Valais*. Lausanne. 1810.
The book consists of a series of letters passing between Murith and Thomas, the first Zermatt one being in 1795, which may in fact pre-date de Saussure as a communication but not as a publication. It describes Thomas's walks and records the flowers in the vicinity. Murith's letter of 1803 covers similar ground. (see *AJ23*, 301-3 & 351-2.)

LE GUIDE
DU
BOTANISTE
QUI VOYAGE DANS LE VALAIS,
AVEC UN

CATALOGUE des plantes de ce pays et de ses environs ; auquel on a joint les lieux de naissance et l'époque de la fleuraison pour chaque espèce.

PAR

M. MURITH, Chanoine Régulier du St. Bernard, Prieur de Martigni, Membre de l'Académie Celtique de Paris, et de la Société d'Emulation de Lausanne.

Non omnia novimus omnes. Linn. Fundamenta Botanicos.

LAUSANNE,
Chez HENRI VINCENT, Imprimeur-Libraire.

1810.

The title page of Murith's book

(3) Engelhardt, C.M. *Naturschilderungen, Sittenzüge und wissenschaftliche Bemerkungen...* Basel. 1840.
Known as the father of Zermatt, Engelhardt was the first visitor to explore and describe the Zermatt valley in detail, staying there on ten occasions between 1835 and 1855, when he made his last visit at the age of 80.

(4) Ruden, J. *Familien-Statistik der löblichen Pfarrei von Zermatt...* 1869.
An invaluable record of the Zermatt families compiled by the local priest, with much additional information about the history of the village, its people and such things as its hotels. A new edition by S.Kronig in 1927 is even more comprehensive, and it brings the family statistics into the 20th century. It was reissued in 1982 in facsimile, apart from amending two paragraphs.

(5) Whymper, E. *Scrambles amongst the Alps in the years 1860-69*. 1871.
Although the 1865 accident attracted many people to Zermatt, Whymper's book helped to bring even more mountaineers, as is apparent from the considerable increase in the number of ascents of the Matterhorn during the years that followed its publication.

(6) Conway, W.M. *Zermatt pocket book*. 1881.
The first ever climbing guide, the second English edition of which appeared ten years later as two volumes, Central and Eastern Pennine Alps.

(7) Coolidge, W.A.B. *Swiss travel and Swiss guide-books*. 1889.
Includes 72 pages on the history of Zermatt and how it became a mountaineering centre.

(8) Yung, E. *Zermatt and the Valley of the Viège*. 1894.
Contains in the text many interesting photographs of Zermatt, its people and mountains.

(9) Wundt, T. *Das Matterhorn und seine Geschichte*. [1896].
Profusely illustrated, it includes much that is hard to find elsewhere, with high quality reproduction of such things as Whymper's 1869 Monte Rosa hotel guestbook entry.

(10) Whymper, E. *The valley of Zermatt and the Matterhorn. A guide*. 1897-1911.
The most comprehensive guidebook ever likely to be published on the subject, re-issued and up-dated each year. Contains the Matterhorn first ascent and descent chapters out of *Scrambles*. There was also a French edition in 1911.

(11) Rey, G. *The Matterhorn*. 1907.
An Italian look at the mountain's history based on the author's own close

association with it, both as a nephew of Quintino Sella, who had hoped to make the ascent in July 1865, and as a climber intent on finding a way up the Furggen ridge. An inspiring book.

(12) Gos, F. *Zermatt and its valley.* 1926.
A well illustrated guide to the area and its mountains.

(13) Gos, C. *Le Cervin.* 1948. 2 vols.
The most comprehensive book relating to the Matterhorn's history, revealing all sorts of things previously forgotten or overlooked. Unfortunately it has no index and one fifteen page chapter 'La corde maudite' is riddled with uncharacteristic error, suggesting that Gos suffered a temporary bout of the Lunn/Egger anti-Whymper allergy that broke out in the 1940's.

(14) Bernardi, A. *Il Gran Cervino.* 1963.
A comprehensive anthology with an Italian text, containing many interesting illustrations and facsimile documents not available elsewhere.

(15) Williams, C. *Zermatt saga.* 1964.
A personal account of the author's long association with Zermatt and some of its people, including the history and development of the resort, local customs and even Zermatt in the 1939-45 war.

(16) Rébuffat, G. *Men and the Matterhorn.* 1967.
A fine picture book including some of Bradford Washburn's best photographs, with archive material, much magnified enlargements of portraits and of some of Whymper's drawings, and a text that not only recounts in great detail the first ascent and comments critically upon it, but also gives the history of the other principal routes.

(17) Taugwalder, H. *Das verlorene Tal.* Aarau. 1979. *The Lost Valley.* [c.1996]
A most entertaining autobiographical account of the life and adventures of a boy in a typical Zermatt family after the first world war. It is hard to believe that so much has changed in such a short time and that Zermatt was then just about to embark on its development as a winter resort, but it helps us to imagine what life must have been like there in 1865.

(18) Gattlen, A. *Das Matterhorn im Bild.* Brig. 1979.
A well produced and authoritative guide to virtually all the non-photographic Matterhorn illustrations of the 19th century.

(19) Gindraux, P. *La folle histoire du Cervin.* Editions Slatkine. Genève. 1990.
An amusing and irreverent look at the history, by a Geneva journalist.

(20) Perren, B.H. *Matterhorn*. 1990.
Splendid fair weather photographs of the mountain taken from his helicopter.

3.18
IS THERE ANYTHING NEW TO BE FOUND?

Lost, stolen and strayed may cover such things as the body of Lord Francis Douglas, Whymper's original account in the Hotel Monte Rosa guestbook and Adams Reilly's diaries, but there are at least two other categories of Matterhorn matter remaining to be discovered before everything eventually progresses to the final category 'destroyed', including the Matterhorn itself! These categories are 'undisclosed' and 'unknown'. The Enquiry Report was an example of the 'undisclosed' until its release in 1920, and the records of the Zermatt authorities remain another example. The diary of A.J.Martin was in the 'unknown' category until its surprise existence and survival were revealed to Claire Engel in about 1949.

3.18.1 Lost

(a) The body of Lord Francis Douglas was not with the other three on the Matterhorn glacier and it is doubtful whether any trace of it has ever been seen, although Jordan may have seen something in 1867. Florence Dixie, the sister of Lord Francis, wrote to *The Times* in 1905 stating that her brother's body was due to be delivered up by the Zmutt glacier and asking any reader going to Zermatt to keep a sharp lookout for it. But it has never been established that the body even reached the glacier, the alternative being that it got caught up in the rocks. This was Whymper's own view and it gains support from Jordan's accounts to his sister and to Canon Carrel. The more obvious explanation, that it fell into a bergschrund or crevasse, would almost certainly have been excluded by Whymper during his search, and there is no reason to suppose that the body was completely covered by snow when the others were not. Some further items of clothing may yet be found and if in fact the body reached the glacier, there may be a remote possibility that it lodged in some backwater as meteorites have done in Antarctic glaciers and that it may reappear one day, as Oetzi did on the Tisenjoch in September 1991 having apparently withstood far less favourable firnification conditions and weather cycles for several thousand years after he died. But the most probable explanation seems to be that the body got caught up in the rocks, where it was later discovered by one or more of the eight eagles seen by the Parker brothers at the end of August, leaving only bones and fragments of clothing thereafter; see section 4.20 (Parker's letter to Forbes).
(b) Other items in the 'lost' category, if not already 'destroyed', include the bottle Whymper left on top with their names inside, and certain correspondence. Solid

snow and ice prevented Jordan searching for the bottle in 1867 and it does not appear to have been mentioned since. The letter written by McCormick to Hadow's father on 16th July and another almost certainly written by him to Mrs.Hudson the same day, would be the earliest written accounts of the accident, together with any letter Whymper may have written to his father at about the same time.

(c) Pages missing from Young Peter Taugwalder's Führerbuch between 26th June and 13th August 1865, whilst obviously containing no account of the Matterhorn ascent, could have thrown light on other aspects. It seems likely that they were torn out prior to the book being given to Richard Kay, if not long before, and that they were probably destroyed at the same time.

(d) Various hotel guestbooks including the Mont Cervin in Zermatt and the Monte Rosa in St.Niklaus.

3.18.2 Stolen

Whymper's entry in the Monte Rosa guestbook on 1st September 1869 refers to several pages being torn from the book including an account of the first ascent of the Matterhorn, of the accident on the descent, and of the means which were taken to recover the bodies. The gap extends from the 18th to the 28th July. The pages may have been taken to keep as a souvenir or more likely to destroy them on account of their content, as Whymper wrote in 1869 of his original entry: 'It bore testimony...to the gallantry of the guides Franz Andermatten and the brothers Lochmatter, who nobly volunteered to seek the bodies of those who were lost, when not a guide of Zermatt dared move, in face of threatened excommunication by their priests.' If Andenmatten was rewarded for his humanity by being ejected from the church at Zermatt, as recorded in the *Graphic*, it would at least be consistent that testimony to his gallantry should have been extracted from the book.

3.18.3 Strayed

'The notebooks and some diaries of the late Adams Reilly', covering inter alia his stay in Zermatt from 18th July until 3rd August 1865, were given to the Alpine Club in about 1918, but apart from Graham Brown making a copy of certain entries (perhaps in the 1930's) there appears to be no further record or trace of them. They can hardly have been deliberately destroyed, so perhaps they will turn up one day. Smythe seems to have been unaware of their existence in the late 1930's, likewise Dangar & Blakeney in the 1950's and 1960's.

3.18.4 Undisclosed

(a) The records of the Zermatt authorities could be wide ranging and extensive and only a few examples can be given of what they might have contained and may still contain. The President Joseph Welschen appears to have organized and accompanied the first and third search parties and he must have liaised with Clemenz once he was appointed to conduct the Enquiry, as the men were all paid by Clemenz for searching and for recovering the bodies, including Welschen himself. The 'administration sent strict instructions to recover the bodies' after Whymper's party had buried them on the glacier and, according to Reilly, immediately prior to the burial in Zermatt 'The official came down and said that the government wished everything to be done according to the wishes of the English'. The Zermatt judge Alois Julen had also gone on the recovery party, presumably in his official capacity, and he or Welschen must have written out some form of report. There was probably a Gemeinde dossier on the accident and there must surely be something in the Sitzungsprotokollbuch or in whatever other minutes or records they kept, referring to the accident and to its aftermath.

(b) The Enquiry documents released in 1920 are considerably more extensive than Farrar published in the *Alpine Journal*, but there must have been even more and they may still be in existence. For instance, it is most unlikely that Whymper signed a deposition prepared by Clemenz in the short time available on the Friday, rather than his own list of questions and answers, which he must have handed in. Likewise Whymper's original questions for Taugwalder, in French, were translated into German and it would be interesting to see a photocopy of Taugwalder's evidence in its original form, as it may well have been written out by someone other than the Clerk to the Enquiry. The inadvertent inclusion of the inventory relating to Knyvet Wilson, killed on the Riffelhorn, is indicative of the existence of other documents in the file and an examination of the originals might throw further light on the circumstances in which the Enquiry failed to achieve the stated object and unintentionally caused so much harm to Old Peter Taugwalder.

(c) Old Peter Taugwalder's Führerbuch has never been accounted for, despite Dangar & Blakeney asking in 1965 (*AJ70*, 37), whether some member of the Taugwalder family in Zermattt could institute a house search for it. It may well not yet have been destroyed and it could throw light on a wide variety of subjects, ranging from such things as Lord Francis Douglas's entry after the cornice collapsed on the Obergabelhorn to the decline and ultimate extinction of Old Peter's career as a guide.

(d) Charles Parker's letter to Taugwalder, presumably written in about October 1865; see *AJ68*, 289.

(e) Newspaper reports, or records in Zermatt, relating to the circumstances surrounding the death of Joseph Taugwalder in the Schwarzsee in 1867.

(f) Documents in Zermatt or America relating to Old Peter's emigration and to that of his son Friedrich, including the circumstances of the latter's death.

3.18.5 Unknown

One can only hazard a guess as to what other documents may once have existed and may still exist, such as the diaries, notebooks and correspondence of those who were in Zermatt the week after the accident. They include Hudson's pupil A.J.Campbell and the likes of Robertson, Phillpotts, Vecqueray and Yeats Brown. Others, taken from the more legible names in the Monte Rosa and Riffelhaus guestbooks, include:

C.A.Elliott, Bengal Civil Service.
Rev J.M.Elliott.
J.J.Ennery, Cincinatti. USA.
A.Fytche (?), Colonel H.M.B.Staff...
J.H.Friedrichs, Amsterdam.
Mr & Mrs Geo.T.Hawley.
Mr & Mrs J.W.Morris of Bath
Rev W.P.Prior and F.G.Prior.
Arthur Giles Puller.
Rev & Mrs George Spottiswood, Westminster.
William Townsend.
M.Marc Triunod(?), Amsterdam.
John Venn and Henry Venn of Caius College, Cambridge.
Thos. Wyles, (?)Ilford.

3.18.6 Destroyed

It cannot be said with certainty that anything relating to the accident and its aftermath has been destroyed, although the odds against Whymper's original account in the hotel guestbook and the missing pages from Young Peter's Führerbuch still being in existence must be high. Even some of the mementos which Lady Queensberry collected of her son Francis could conceivably still exist, although the family no longer has any such material. They would have included any past climbing diaries, showing the full extent of his climbing career and the extent of any previous acquaintance with Old Peter Taugwalder and with Clemenz, as well as his letters home in 1865, amongst which would almost certainly have been one written on about Sunday 9th July reporting his ascent of the Obergabelhorn and how he would be making his way home after a brief visit to Breuil. Dangar & Blakeney wrote in 1966 how 'we cannot say that nothing new is to be found about the Matterhorn catstrophe' and that is still true to-day. Much that had remained undiscovered or unknown will by now have been destroyed by accident or in the belief that it was of no real interest or value, but hopefully there will still be some documents that may have been overlooked and others that have been treasured for a different reason, which may one day help to fill in some of the remaining gaps in our knowledge of the mountaineering accident that must have caused more discussion and, indirectly, have done far more good than all the others put together.

The Clubroom of Zermatt, in 1864

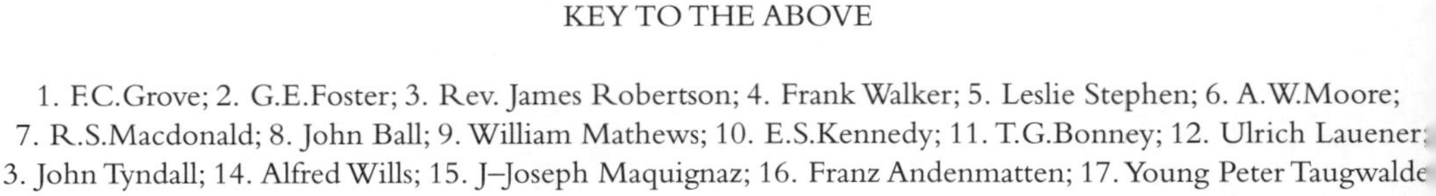

KEY TO THE ABOVE

1. F.C.Grove; 2. G.E.Foster; 3. Rev. James Robertson; 4. Frank Walker; 5. Leslie Stephen; 6. A.W.Moore; 7. R.S.Macdonald; 8. John Ball; 9. William Mathews; 10. E.S.Kennedy; 11. T.G.Bonney; 12. Ulrich Lauener; 13. John Tyndall; 14. Alfred Wills; 15. J–Joseph Maquignaz; 16. Franz Andenmatten; 17. Young Peter Taugwalde 18. Peter Perren.

Notes to the above

(3.18.1) Lost

(a) For Florence Dixie details, see section 2.44 (Queensberry).
Oetzi, found in the Oetztal Alps, has had many books written about him.

(b) McCormick letter of 16.7.65, see Hadow's reply of 22.7.65. ACA. *AJ70*, 60.

(c) Young Peter Taugwalder's Führerbuch. ACA. *AJ59*,436-41 (article by Dangar). For Richard Kay, see *AJ40*, 408.

(3.18.3) Strayed

Adams Reilly notebooks and diaries, see *AJ32*, 24n. & 109. For 1865 diary copy extracts, see Graham Brown papers. NLS.

(3.18.4) Undisclosed

(a) Search parties members, see section 3.15 (Search and recovery parties). Reilly quote, see 1865 diary entry for 21st July.

(b) Enquiry documents, see section 5.1 (List of Enquiry documents).

(3.18.5) Unknown

Monte Rosa guestbook, Seiler Hotels, Zermatt.
Riffelhaus guestbook, Zermatt Museum.

(3.18.6) Destroyed

Mementos, see section 4.23 (Queensberry – Whymper letter of 7.8.65).
Dangar & Blakeney 1966 quote, see *AJ71*, 111.

4
A VARIETY OF DOCUMENTS

4.0
INDEX OF CORRESPONDENCE AND OTHER DOCUMENTS

13.7.65.	1.	Hudson – McCormick
15.7.65.	2.	Whymper – McCormick
19.7.65.	3.	Reilly – Forbes
22.7.65.	4.	P.D.Hadow – McCormick
22.7.65.	5.	McCormick – *The Times*
25.7.65.	6.	Whymper – von Fellenberg
27.7.65.	7.	Glover – *The Times*
27.7.65.	8.	Leader in *The Times*
28.7.65.	9.	Kennedy – *The Times*
31.7.65.	10.	J.J.Cowell – Whymper
31.7.65.	11.	Glover – Whymper
31.7.65.	12.	Buxton – *The Times*
1.8.65.	13.	Glover – *The Times*
1.8.65.	14.	Reilly – Forbes
2.8.65.	15.	*Times* Editor – Whymper
[4.8.65]	16.	Whymper – *Times* Editor
5.8.65.	17.	*Times* Editor – Whymper
5.8.65.	18.	Leader in *The Times*
5.8.65.	19.	Queensberry – Whymper
5.8.65.	20.	S.Parker – Forbes
6.8.65.	21.	Wills – Whymper
7.8.65.	22.	Wills – Whymper
7.8.65.	23.	Queensberry – Whymper
7.8.65.	24.	*Times* Editor – Whymper
8.8.65.	25.	Whymper – Buxton
8.8.65.	26.	Whymper – *The Times*
8.8.65.	27.	Wigram – Whymper
9.8.65.	28.	Leader in *The Times*
9.8.65.	29.	Wigram – Whymper
9.8.65.	30.	Whymper – Wigram
9.8.65.	31.	Buxton – Whymper

9.8.65.	32.	Wills – Whymper
10.8.65.	33.	Wigram – Whymper
10.8.65.	34.	P.D.Hadow – McCormick
11.8.65.	35.	J.W.Cowell – Whymper
11.8.65.	36.	Mrs. Hudson – Whymper
12.8.65.	37.	Whymper – Buxton
14.8.65.	38.	Wills – *The Times*
17.8.65.	51.	Whymper's memorandum (see 50 below)
17.8.65.	39.	Queensberry – Whymper
18.8.65.	40.	Whymper – Glover
19.8.65.	41.	H.Hadow – Whymper
20.8.65.	42.	Wills – Whymper
21.8.65.	43.	Whymper – H.Hadow
23.8.65.	44.	Glover – Whymper
23.8.65.	45.	P.D.Hadow – Whymper
23.8.65.	46.	Whymper – P.D.Hadow
26.8.65.	47.	P.D.Hadow – Whymper
[26.8.65]	48.	Robertson – McCormick
27.8.65.	49.	Whymper – Robertson
1.9.65.	52.	Cowell memorandum (see 50 below)
4.9.65.	50.	J.W.Cowell – Whymper
10.9.65.	53.	Queensberry – Whymper
3.10.65.	54.	C.Parker – his father
16.12.65.	55.	Whymper – Lady Queensberry
Friday	56.	Lady Queensberry – Whymper
1?. 9.66.	57.	Mackenzie – *The Times*
29. 9.66.	58.	Whymper – Robertson
14.10.66.	59.	Robertson – Whymper
4. 9.71.	60.	Pennell – Tyndall
[1905]	61.	Dixie – *Daily Graphic*
8. 5.17.	62.	R.Taugwalder – Montagnier
undated	63.	Montagnier's Questions & Answers
[Nov. 17]	64.	P.Taugwalder – Montagnier (Young Peter's Narrative)
undated	65.	P.Taugwalder's consent (to shortening Narrative)
27.11.17.	66.	P.Taugwalder – Montagnier
9.10.39.	67.	Smythe – Cooke
		Other documents
	68.	Birkbeck's lecture extract
	69.	Douglas's Gabelhorn account
	70.	Jordan's timetable
	71.	Adams Reilly diary extracts

72. Whymper *Graphic* article extracts
73. Whymper interview in *Journal de Zermatt*
74. Enquiry Report in German (Whymper's evidence in French)
75. Enquiry Report inventories in German
76. Questions à faire à Pierre Taugwalder

4.1
HUDSON – McCORMICK

Monte Rosa Hotel, Thursday, 5 A.M.
[13.7.65]

My dear M'C,

We and Whymper are just off to try the Cervin. You can hear about our movements from the landlord of the Monte Rosa Hotel. Follow us, if you like. We expect to sleep out to-night, and to make the attempt to-morrow. Please give an eye to Campbell as long as you are with him, and take him to the Riffel, in case you go there. We expect to be back to-morrow. It is possible we might be out a second night, but not likely.

Ever yours affectionately,
C.HUDSON.

4.2
WHYMPER – McCORMICK

Hotel du Mont Rose. Zermatt.
July. 15 [1865].

My dear Sir,

I am told that you are a friend of the Revd. C.Hudson who was with me yesterday on the Matterhorn; I regret most deeply to say that an accident has occurred to him. I am afraid a fatal one. A party of guides have been sent immediately from here to search for him, and I follow them, but I wish particularly to have an Englishman with me and I therefore beg, if you can possibly return here by 4.30 p.m, to do so, in order to go with me.

I am, my dear Sir,
Yours very truly
EDWARD WHYMPER.

Revd. J.McCormack.

4.3
ADAMS REILLY – J.D.FORBES

Zermatt. July 19 [1865].

My dear Mr.Forbes,

I arrived at Breuil on the 17th, (having entirely completed my survey, from the Matterhorn to Mte Moro, with the exception of my base line) when I was met by the sad news of the accident on the Matterhorn, of which you have probably by this time heard. I felt much for poor Whymper, and immediately crossed the Theodule for Zermatt, to see whether I could be of any comfort to him. He is terribly cut up poor fellow.

The authentic account of the accident went off to *The Times* yesterday, but I believe that the blame (which rests on the dead) was softened down as much as possible. Mr Hudson, with a young friend of his, Mr Hadow and Michel Croz of Chamounix came here to try the Matterhorn, with wire rope to tie to the rocks, & all sorts of quackery, and found here Lord Fr Douglas, a fine young fellow, quite a boy, who had after several plucky attempts ascended the Gabelhorn, and who appears to have been anxious to try something else still more difficult. Whymper was at Breuil, where he had gone to meet me, and Douglas went over the St Theodule to find him, and borrow his tent.

They brought the tent over, and the whole party, Hudson, Hadow, Whymper, Douglas, Michel Croz, & Peter Taugwalder and his son, slept above the Hörnli, and tried the Riffelberg face of the Matterhorn. Steep as it looks, they found it perfectly practicable, almost easy, owing to the stratification of the rock, the reverse of what it is on the Breuil side, which though apparently the easiest, has been so often tried in vain.

[There follows a sketch of the Matterhorn, as seen from the east, illustrating the stratification dipping from the Riffel side towards the Breuil side]

You will see how on one side the footing is on rock sloping *towards* the precipice, and on the other, sloping from the precipice, and of course much safer. There was however one difficult spot near the top, where they had to cross the face diagonally, but they got well over it, and reached the summit.

But in coming down, at this spot, Mr Hadow slipped. Croz was first, he second, then Mr Hudson, Lord F Douglas, Peter Taugwald, Whymper, and the other Taugwald last, all roped. In his fall, Mr Hadow carried off first Croz, then the two behind him. Peter Taugwald kept his footing, but the rope broke, and the first 4 were dashed to pieces. How the rope broke, without carrying Peter Taugwald off his legs, does not appear: there is some suspicion that he had given it a turn round a projecting rock, which may have cut it. This will however be investigated.

Mr Hadow was quite a novice, he had only been up three mountains before, but though Mr Hudson knew this, he never told any of the party, and this was, at least in its consequences, an unhappy error; for Whymper would have strongly remonstrated had he known it, as he well knew that the Matterhorn is no work for a novice. Poor Mr Hudson was responsible for his friend, and it was the want of practice of the latter that caused this sad business.

Some fragments of the bodies have been found, but not an atom of poor Douglas can be traced.

There appears to be [a] curse on this place. Yesterday evening three men strolled out, after dinnner, from the Riffel Hotel, and spent some time reading and smoking on the hillside. When they were going back, one of them lingered behind, and instead of following them, attempted to get up the Riffelhorn on the wrong side, (you know there is only one spot at which it is accessible). He never returned, they searched for him all night, and he has just been found this morning, dashed to pieces at the bottom of the peak. His name is Wilson.

The day I arrived at Breuil, 4 guides of Val Tournanche in the pay of a Signor Giordano, affected the ascent of the Matterhorn by the old Breuil arrete route, and their drapeau now floats beside Whymper's. As it has been now ascended by both routes, I hope no more lives will ever be hazarded on this unfortunate peak.

I write from a sofa. Coming down from the St Theodule yesterday I slipped in jumping a glacier stream and cut open the cap of my left knee against a rock, or possibly the spike of my axe. It is of course impossible to say how this will turn out, but I am at all events laid up in ordinary for several days. My work is as I said before finished, and even should I be unable to visit the points I had intended on the boundary line, I can still work *backwards* to them instead of starting from them. I have however given up all idea of attempting to survey the Valpelline this year. I have not the spirits to begin to break a lot of new and difficult ground, and I hate the sight of these bloodstained mountains. So I shall (if possible) spend a couple of days next week on the St Theodule, and then return to England by Chamounix & Geneva. Hotel Suisse, Geneva is the safest address after this.

With kindest remembrances, believe me, affectionately yours,

A.ADAMS REILLY

4.4
P.D.HADOW – McCORMICK (see also 4.34)

Sudbury Priory, Middlesex.
July 22, 1865.

My dear Sir,

Your letter of 16th inst. reached me last evening, having been delayed by going to Sudbury, Suffolk; I can hardly tell you how grateful we feel to you for your kind exertions about my dear son, and for your truly Christian attempts to give us some consolation, in alluding to his attractive and religious character...We had indulged the hope that his remains, with those of poor Mr.Hudson, might have been conveyed to Zermatt, and there deposited where we might perhaps have visited them, and placed a tombstone over them; you have however no doubt acted wisely, and much do we thank you; still, if this could even now be done, *without endangering life*, I should willingly incur the expense of accomplishing it, for I know it would be a consolation for his dear mother, and I doubt not for Mrs.Hudson also. As regards poor Mr.Hudson, I will gladly bear any expenses that may have been incurred on his account, and shall feel a pleasure in paying even so trifling a tribute to his memory.

My brother left London last evening for Zermatt, and will be at the Mont Cervin hotel about the time you receive this; he will of course meet you, and do all that is necessary in recompensing the guides and those who accompanied you, and will receive my dear boy's effects &c.

Yours very truly,
P.D.HADOW.

4.5
McCORMICK – *THE TIMES*

TO THE EDITOR OF THE TIMES (published 22.7.65)

Sir,– As the news of the fatal accident on the Matterhorn must by this time have reached England, I think it is right for the sake of the friends of those who have been killed, and to prevent mistakes, to give a correct account of it, and of what has taken place with reference to it.

Some months ago the Rev. Charles Hudson determined to ascend the Matterhorn this season. Before leaving England he invented and had made a kind of ladder for scaling precipices.

Mr.Birkbeck and I agreed to accompany him on his expedition. On arriving in Zermatt on Wednesday the 12th. instant, he met with Mr.Whymper, who for some years past has been anxious to conquer the Matterhorn, and has made several attempts to do so. They agreed to work together. Mr.Birkbeck and I were both prevented from joining them. Lord Francis Douglas, who had made several successful ascents this season, and had been with Mr.Whymper for a few days previously, and Mr.Hadow, who had been up some high mountains with Mr.Hudson, were allowed to go with them. Having secured the services of Michel Croz, one of the best of the Chamounix guides, and of Peter Taugevald and his son, they started on their expedition on Thursday morning. That night they slept on the Hörnli *arrête*, and at 3.40a.m. on Friday they began the ascent of the rocks on the left of it. They met with no great difficulty, and reached the top about 2 o'clock. There they were in the greatest delight at the accomplishment of their purpose. We saw them distinctly from Zermatt. About 3 o'clock they began the descent. Soon after they were all roped together, Croz was first, Hadow next; then came Hudson, Lord Francis Douglas, Peter Taugevald, Whymper and Peter

Taugevald's son. Not far from the summit they had to pass over a difficult and rather dangerous place. It was a decline composed of snow and rock, with very indifferent holding for the feet. They were descending with very great care, when Whymper was startled by an exclamation from Croz, and the next moment he saw Hadow and Croz flying downwards. The weight of the two falling men jerked Hudson and Lord Francis Douglas from their feet. The two Taugevalds and Whymper, having a warning of a second or two from the time that Croz called out, planted themselves as firmly as possible, to hold the others up. The pressure upon the rope was too much. It broke, and Croz, Hadow, Hudson, and Lord Francis Douglas fell headlong down the slope and shot out of sight over a fearful precipice.

Mr.Whymper's feelings at this time may be imagined. The two remaining guides were so completely unnerved by the calamity which had befallen their companions that he found it difficult to descend with them. He and they spent a miserable night on the mountain at a great height. As they came down they looked in all directions for some trace of their companions, but from the shape of the mountain they could not catch even a glimpse of them. At 10.30a.m. on Saturday they reached Zermatt.

Though he had no hope that any of his companions were alive, Mr.Whymper immediately sent guides to search for them. In the evening they returned to tell us that they had been able with the aid of their telescopes to see where they lay, but had been prevented by the width of the crevasses from reaching them. Being a friend of Mr.Hudson, Mr.Whymper sent for me. I had gone to the Gorner Grat. On my return it was too late to do anything that day. After consulting together Mr.Whymper and I agreed to start in search of our friends on the following morning at 1 o'clock. The Rev. J. Robertson and Mr. Phillpotts most kindly volunteered to accompany us. The Zermatt guides refused to go with us, as it would be Sunday, and urged us, as there was no hope of saving any lives, to defer our expedition until they had made preparations for overcoming the difficulties of the way. Mr.Whymper, though exhausted by upwards of 60 hours' work, gallantly refused to accede to their request. Franz Andermatten, of Saas; the brothers Lochmatter of Macugnaga; and Frederic Payot and Jean Tairras, of Chamounix, generously offered their services for the expedition. We hope their names will not be forgotten.

After an arduous walk, in which we were exposed to much danger, we reached the snowfield on to which our friends had fallen. When we looked up at the 4,000 feet above us, and observed how they must have bumped from rock to rock before they reached the bottom, we knew they could not be alive, and we feared that they would be so awfully mangled that we should not be able to recognise them. Our worst fears were realised. We found no trace of Lord Francis Douglas, with the exception of some trifling articles of dress. His body must either have remained on some of the rocks above or been buried deeply in the snow. Croz lay near to Hadow. Hudson was some 50 yards from them.

From the state of their remains, the danger of the place (for it is exposed to showers of stones), and the very great difficulty of the way to it, we came to the conclusion that the best thing we could do would be to bury them in the snow. We drew them all to one spot, covered them with snow, read over them the 90th psalm from a Prayer-book taken from poor Hudson's pocket, repeated some prayers and a few words from the Burial Service, and left them.

They are mourned here with heartfelt grief, and the greatest sympathy is expressed for the bereaved.

Mr.Seiler, the landlord of this hotel, and his wife have assisted us in every way in their power. They are deeply distressed at what has happened.

Your obedient servant,

JOSEPH M'CORMICK.

Hôtel Mont Rose, July 17. Chaplain at Zermatt.

4.6
WHYMPER – VON FELLENBERG

Interlachen.
July 25, 1865.

Sir,

The great interest taken in the recent lamentable accident that occurred during the descent of the Matterhorn, renders one anxious for the sake of truth, that an account of it should be made known to the Swiss public, free from errors, in order to correct the numerous versions already published all of which contain statements more or less inaccurate. I therefore send you a simple statement of facts, and beg as a favour, that you will take the earliest opportunity of submitting it to the members of the Swiss Alpine Club; and that you will, should you see fit, forward the enclosed copy of it to the Editor of the *Journal de Genève* (Editor of *Der Bund*).

On Wednesday the 12th inst. I crossed the Col Théodule with Lord Francis Douglas, from Breuil to Zermatt with the intention of endeavouring to ascend the Matterhorn from the northern side. On arriving at Zermatt we engaged Pierre Taugwalder as guide, giving him the liberty to select another guide, and porters. In the course of the evening, we learnt however that the Revd. Charles Hudson with a friend – Mr.Hadow, was in the same hotel, and intending to start at nearly the same hour as ourselves, with the guide Michel Croz of Chamounix. He was invited to join us; but as we had not the acquaintance of Mr.Hadow (who was not a member of the English Alpine Club), we took the precaution to enquire what expeditions he had made in the Alps. Mr.Hudson's reply was that he had made the ascent of Mont Blanc in less time than most men, and also named a few other excursions that he had made; adding, in answer to a further question, that he considered he was a sufficiently good man to accompany us on the present expedition. We then discussed the matter of guides. Mr.Hudson thought that

Croz and Taugwalder were sufficient and they made no objection on being told of the proposed arrangements: the latter by his own desire, took his two sons as porters.

We started with these at 5.35 on Thursday morning, not intending to go to any great height on that day, but to stop when we found a good position for placing my tent. We took provisions amply sufficient for three days, in case the ascent should prove longer than we anticipated. At 11.50a.m. we found an eligible situation for the tent, and halted, at a height of about 11,000 English feet, sending Croz and the elder of Taugwalder's sons on in advance, in order to save time on the next morning; the remainder built the platform on which we passed the night, and by the time it was finished the two men returned, reported they had seen nothing but that which was good, and triumphantly asserted that had we gone on with them that day, we could have ascended the mountain and returned to the tent with facility. Well pleased with the intelligence we retired to our blankets, Lord F. Douglas, myself and the Taugwalders occupying the tent, the others remaining by preference outside; but the sleep which we might otherwise have enjoyed was driven away by the snoring of the Taugwalder family, and long before daybreak we had risen, breakfasted, and were ready to start again.

We started on Friday morning at 3.50, leaving the youngest of Taugwalder's sons below, and mounted easily and rapidly; at 6.20 we had attained a height of 12,800 feet – halted for half an hour and then ascended again without a break until 9.55, when we stopped for 50 minutes. By this time we had arrived at the foot of that part which from Zermatt appears perpendicular or overhanging; it is in reality neither one nor the other, although extremely precipitous. Thus far we had ascended by the north-eastern face and had not met a single difficulty, but here we could no longer continue on the same side and therefore went over to the north-western face. For two or three hundred feet the ascent was difficult, and required caution, but as we approached the summit it became easier, and at last it was so gentle that Croz and myself detached ourselves from the others and ran on to the top; we arrived there at 1.40p.m. and the others about 10 minutes after us.

We remained an hour on the summit and then commenced the descent. Michel Croz, the most powerful of our party, led the way and by arrangement between Mr.Hudson and myself, Mr.Hadow was placed next to Croz in order that he might receive every assistance. Mr.Hudson, who in surefootedness was equal to a guide, was third, Lord F. Douglas fourth, Pierre Taugwalder fifth. I remained on the summit with Taugwalder fils a few minutes after the others, to write our names on a card, but we caught them before they had descended any great distance, and I then tied myself in line behind old Taugwalder.

On arriving at the difficult part of which I have already spoken, the greatest care was taken: only one man moved at a time; when he was firmly planted the next advanced, and so on. The difficulty arose, not from the inclination of the mountain – for, probably, it was at this part in angle of not more than 35°, but from the nature of the footing. The rocks were mixed with snow and occasionally with ice; they were firm, it is true, but they afforded little hold in some places. Still it was a part over which any good mountaineer might pass in safety. Michel Croz, however, in order to give Mr.Hadow greater security, did not trust to his descending by himself, but absolutely took hold of his feet and placed them in their proper positions. As far as I know, at the moment of the accident, no one was actually moving. I cannot speak with certainty, neither can Taugwalder, because the two leading men were partially hidden from our sight by an intervening mass of rock, but it is my belief that Croz had just placed the feet of Mr.Hadow in the manner I have described and was turning to go down a step or two himself, when Mr.Hadow slipped, fell upon him, and knocked him over. I heard one startled exclamation from Croz, then saw him and Mr.Hadow flying downwards; in another moment Mr.Hudson was dragged from his steps and Lord F. Douglas immediately after him. All this was the work of a moment, but immediately I heard the exclamation from Croz, I planted myself as firmly as the ground would permit, Taugwalder did the same, the rope was tight between us and the shock came upon us both as on one man. We held, but the rope broke mid-way between Taugwalder and Lord F. Douglas. It has been stated that it broke in consequence of its fraying over a rock; this is not the case, it broke in mid-air, and the end does not shew any traces of its having been previously injured. For two or three seconds we saw our unfortunate companions sliding downwards on their backs and spreading out their hands endeavouring to save themselves; they then disappeared from our sight and fell from precipice to precipice on to the Matterhorn glacier below, a distance of nearly 4,000 feet in height.

I need not trouble you with details of our descent, it is enough to say that for more than two hours afterwards, I thought every moment would be my last; the two Taugwalders, utterly unnerved, cried like infants, and trembled in such a manner as to threaten us with the fate of the others. We looked in every direction during the descent for some traces of our companions, but saw none, save two of their axes arrested in the snow. We thus lost much time, and spent another night on the mountain at a height of more than 13,000 feet, arriving at Zermatt at 10.30 on Saturday morning.

Mr.Hudson, Mr.Hadow and Michel Croz, the first of all the Chamounix guides, now lie buried in the church-yard at Zermatt: to bring their bodies down was a work of some difficulty and of great danger, and the thanks of all Englishmen are due to the brave men who performed this duty. The body of Lord Francis Douglas is – God alone knows where – probably arrested in the rocks above.

This, Sir, is the end of this sad narrative; a single slip, or a single false step, has been the cause of all this misery. No blame can be attached to any of the guides; they all did their duty manfully, but, I cannot but think, that had the rope been tight between those who fell as it was between myself and Taugwalder, that the whole of this frightful calamity might have been averted, and that I should have been spared the pain of writing this letter. The rope when used properly is a great safeguard; but, whether on rocks, or whether on snow, or glacier, if two men approach each other so that the rope falls in a loop, the whole party is involved in danger; for should one slip, or fall, he may acquire before he is arrested, a momentum that may drag down one man after another, and bring destruction on all; but, if the rope is tight, this is all but impossible.

I am, Sir,
Your very obedient servant,
EDWARD WHYMPER.

4.7
GLOVER – *THE TIMES* (see also 4.13)

TO THE EDITOR OF THE TIMES (published 27.7.65)

Sir,– The late lamented fatalities on the Matterhorn have a very painful interest to me from the fact that I was Mr. Whymper's companion on a similar occasion (that is, on a tour of inspection and survey of that mountain with a view to an ascent on Mr. Whymper's part on the morrow) a few days previous to the accident, and from the fact that the very rope that broke was recently round my own body. Our chief guide, too, on that occasion was poor Michel Croz himself, together with Christian Almer of Grindelwald, and Franz Biener. And it has occurred to me that I may be able, with your kind permission, to say something that may administer a little consolation to the friends of the unfortunate gentlemen who have so sadly perished, and that may lead them to exonerate my friend Mr. Whymper from all blame.

It would appear from the accounts already published that Mr. Whymper was the proposer and leader of the fatal expedition. Mr. Hudson, it seems, had intended an ascent, and he seems to have found Mr. Whymper ready to start on an independent one, and then, with the others of the party, resolved to join him. There seems to have been no previous intention of attempting the actual ascent to the summit on that occasion; but, as on the occasion when I started with Mr. Whymper from Zermatt, it seems to have been an expedition of survey with a view to ascertain a possible route. But the difficulties appearing less than they anticipated they were induced to push on to the top at once. Thus, I have no doubt the expedition was Mr. Whymper's, the guides of his employ, and the ropes his own; and thus I fear that much of the responsibility will be thought to rest with him. And it is with a desire to do simple justice to my distressed and absent friend, as well as with a desire to administer some comfort to the relatives of the departed, that I venture to trouble you with a few remarks.

And first let me say that (whatever may be thought of the wisdom or prudence of attempting such a terrible climb as that of the Matterhorn, where not undertaken for the advancement of science or some other noble end), from my knowledge of the parties, as such an expedition was resolved upon by the deceased, they could hardly have had a more prudent and cautious leader than Mr. Whymper or a better guide than Michel Croz. The latter was regarded as one of the best Chamounix guides; and Mr. Whymper, though a young man, is no novice in Alpine work (as his companions well knew), but has had as much experience as perhaps any living Alpine adventurer. He is no mere honorary member of the Alpine Club, but has done at least as much hard Alpine work as any man on its roll, besides having made several first ascents of some mountains hitherto deemed inaccessible. When I was at Chamounix a few weeks ago, he made the first ascent of the Grandes Jurasses, and also of the Aiguille Verte, alone with his guides.

In addition to this, perhaps no man, save Professor Tyndall, is better acquainted with the Matterhorn itself. Two or three years ago he succeeded in getting up very far towards the summit, when he fell down a precipice and by almost a miracle escaped the fate which has now befallen his friends, though not without sustaining serious injury. And the day after I lately [left] him at Breuil he made a second attempt, which, after having got still higher than before, he was compelled to abandon from the refusal of his guides (among whom was poor Michel Croz) to accompany him any higher. That attempt was made from the Italian side. This last and successful ascent was made from the Zermatt side, which he had previously surveyed from the glacier bed 11,000ft. high, on the occasion when I accompanied him.

But not only did he proceed thus cautiously, but I am in a position to testify that for so bold and intrepid an adventurer, he carries his precautions to the extremest length of prudence, so much so that he will always insist upon the use of the ropes, even when the guides (who are often too anxious to save themselves trouble) declare them to be unnecessary. Thus, on the occasion I refer to, he insisted on our being tied together over the St. Theodule pass. (It must be borne in mind that this was in the middle of June.) The guides, and foremost among them was Michel Croz, wished to dispense with them, but Mr. Whymper was firm and decided, and we were accordingly harnessed. And as the pass was not open, and the snow proved to be in a very rotten state, and as I myself fell into one or two crevasses (out of which I was helped by Michel Croz, who was next to me), I felt very thankful that I was led by so prudent a man.

Then, as to the ropes themselves. Mr. Whymper told me that he never trusts himself to the ropes provided by the guides, but always carries his own with him. And as I have no doubt that the same coil was used on the occasion of the accident as was used by ourselves, I can answer for it being an unusually strong one – much stronger than those used by the guides, as I myself compared it with them.

I may mention another proof of Mr. Whymper's extreme caution. When we rested occasionally on the ascent I took a drink of the glacier streams, but Mr. Whymper refused, lest his example should send the guides to their flasks. When we rested on the Col Theodule I had a full flask of brandy with me, and I asked him if I should offer the guides some. "Not for the world," said he, almost in alarm; "don't let them see it. I am obliged to deny myself often in these expeditions for the sake of example, for these fellows cannot resist drink, and a trifle too much might be very serious." But as wine must be taken he takes the lightest, and sets the example using that very sparingly. His coolness and watchful preparedness for danger is, I think, sufficiently apparent from his firm stand with the Taugwalds against the fearful tug of the rope on such a slippery declivity. Had the rest of the party displayed his caution I have no doubt the accident would never have happened. It seems to me that the unfortunate slip was most likely made (as one account stated) by the youngest of the party, poor Lord Francis Douglas. Mr. M'Cormick tells us that Mr. Whymper's first knowledge of danger was from hearing an exclamation by Croz. If I knew Croz aright, he was a much more likely man to utter such a cry at another's peril than at his own; and probably in trying to rescue Lord Francis the poor fellow slipped himself, and being a heavy, powerful man, he dragged the other down. A similar accident, though happily not a fatal one, happened to a young Cambridge man with whom I once ascended the Schilthorn in the Bernese Oberland. Elated with our achievement of the summit, my friend was not as cautious as he ought to have been in descending, and slipped and rolled over. The guide in front tried to save him, and both went bowling down a snow slope together. A dense fog being on the mountain they were out of my sight in a moment, and I was left alone. But happily they fell on snow, and so were saved, and in great alarm I soon reached them.

But I hope we shall shortly have a full account from Mr. Whymper himself.

I would merely add, by way of caution to those who may be induced from Mr. Whymper's statement of the few difficulties encountered, rashly to attempt another ascent of the Matterhorn, that his account must so far be received with great caution; for, from a characteristic modesty in such matters, Mr. Whymper, so far from exaggerating the difficulties of an ascent in order to magnify his achievement is exceedingly prone to underrate them. Thus, when lately the guns were firing at Chamounix in honour of his successful ascent of the Aiguille Verte, and (as recorded in your paper), the guides were full of excitement and wonder at the apparently impossible achievement, he quietly told me over his late and solitary dinner that evening that "it was really quite easy." One had only to glance up at that needle-like peak above the clouds (13,600ft. high) to see what his modest estimate of his difficulties was worth.

My advice may be little regarded – and I claim no sort of authority in this matter – but yet, having been round three sides of the Matterhorn on different occasions, and having stood aghast at my friend's determination to scale its almost perpendicular precipices, I feel constrained as a prudent man to say to all tourists, "Leave Mr. Whymper and the Taugwalds alone in their sad glory of being the only living climbers who have stood on the ear-tips of what Ruskin justly calls 'that rearing horse of rock.' "

If this letter shall prove to the relatives of the deceased gentlemen that (such a perilous expedition having been undertaken) every precaution was used that could have been looked for under the circumstances, and that it was, perhaps, an advantage, rather than the contrary, that they met with my friend Mr. Whymper, you, Sir, I am sure, will be glad to have been the channel of its communication to them.

I am, Sir, very faithfully yours,

RICHARD GLOVER.

Christ Church Parsonage, Dover, July 25.

4.8

LEADER IN *THE TIMES* (see also 4.18 and 4.28)

LONDON, THURSDAY, JULY 27, 1865.

There are occasions on which a journal must brave certain unpopularity and ridicule, even in quarters where it may most wish to stand well. We desire the sympathies of the young, the courageous, and the enterprising, and we can feel their taunts. But we have our Matterhorn to ascend as well as they – not without a cause. Why is the best blood of England to waste itself in scaling hitherto inaccessible peaks, in staining the eternal snow, and reaching the unfathomable abyss never to return? We believe it was the heir presumptive to one of our noblest titles, but, far more than that, one of the best young fellows in the world, who fell, with three others and a guide, down a precipice of 4,000 feet. A hundred feet, indeed, would have been enough, but this was forty times as much. The two English gentlemen who shared his fate, and now another who has perished in the attempt to do in the afternoon without ropes and ladders what he had done with them in the morning, were all just the men that England is proud of, and that would be the salt of any age, even more corrupt, more self-indulgent, than our own. They were scholars and gentlemen. They were men who had distinguished themselves at school and at college, and in the path of honourable employment. They were admired and loved. The touching notices of the obituary show what fond eyes are now resting on that fatal spot. So many of our readers have "done" Zermatt that it is almost needless to describe the well-known scene. As you stand in that deep valley and look to the southern sky, you see across it, and almost overhead, a vast shelf of rock and snow – a very pathway in the heavens, along which the Olympian deities might be imagined to drive their cars. Upon this shelf stands a mass, in shape between an obelisk and a pyramid, for all the world like an immense ornament of alabaster and frosted silver upon a gigantic marble mantelpiece. A giant might take it up in his hand and place it right or left, as the fancy took him, and they who were heaved to and fro in their beds in that valley nine years ago might think this not so inconceivable. But this charming ornament, this Pelion upon Ossa, is itself loftier than Snowdon. To the humble beholders in the valley below it looks about as accessible as the dome of St. Paul's. If compelled to make the choice, we might reasonably prefer to scale with fingers and toes the front of a well-built London house, with good stone window-sills, cornices, and water-courses. If anybody wants to know what 200 feet sheer is, let him go the top of the Monument. This is 4,000 feet, and looks very sheer. As the successful ascent is utterly incomprehensible, of course we do not wonder at the disastrous descent. Indeed, throughout these many hours of continual and painful effort there must have been few places where the climbers could rest their limbs and close their eyes with the momentary feeling of safety. Well, this is magnificent. But is it life? Is it duty? Is it common sense? Is it allowable? Is it not wrong?

There certainly are limits to audacity. We may go even further, and dispute that a wanton exposure to peril is the best school of courage. It is not the best and coolest rider who takes the most headlong leaps. English common sense leaves to young Irish gentlemen the steeplechases in which a certain average loss of man and horse is found necessary to keep up interest. In this island ladies do not like to see a noble horse staked or broken-backed, or a fine young man carried writhing or lifeless from the field. There is a point of danger which, if gratuitous, becomes ridiculous, if not disgusting. Five hundred years ago the young Romans of noble or Papal families thought to revive the glories of the Amphitheatre with bullfighting. "Every champion," says GIBBON, "successfully encountered a wild bull; and the victory may be ascribed to the quadrupeds, since no more than eleven were left on the field, with the loss of nine wounded and eighteen killed on the side of their adversaries." No one can read this without a smile at the utter folly of staking the life of a COLONNA against that of a wild bull; but a time may come when a historian will tell us irreverently how English noblemen, scholars, and divines passed in endless succession to the loftiest peaks of the Alps, accepting the equal alternative of an idle boast and a horrible death. Surely courage, to be respectable, ought to be reasonable, and ought also to have some regard to the end? What is the use of scaling precipitous rocks, and being for half an hour at the top of the terrestrial globe? There is use in the feats of sailors, of steeple-climbers, vane-cleaners, chimney sweepers, lovers, and other adventurous professions. A man may be content to die in such a cause, for it is his life's battle. But in the few short moments a member of the Alpine Club has to survey his life when he finds himself slipping, he has but a sorry account to give of himself. What is he doing there, and what right has he to throw away the gift of life and ten thousand golden opportunities in an emulation which he only shares with skylarks, apes, cats, and squirrels? Life requires a great deal of courage, moral as well as physical, whatever the meaning of the distinction. Every gentleman with a sphere of duties and a station in society requires courage and presence of mind, otherwise he is sure to be scorned and to become an object of civil contempt. A man cannot hold his own in a parish vestry, or in the committee of a coal fund, without knowing what he is about, and standing to his colours, and defending his rights. If he has not this courage he had better purchase a lathe, or write metaphysics, for he is good for nothing out of doors. But this courage is not acquired in a succession of desperate adventures. The Age of Chivalry is over. A man does not now learn temperance by a toilsome journey through a desert. By these processes a man only makes himself the slave of a necessity, and reduces himself to the helpless and pitiable condition of being obliged to do something disagreeable, whether he likes it or not. His whole existence centres for the time in that one act or that one suffering, and he can no longer be called a responsible being.

All this, we shall be told, is utilitarian, matter of fact, calculating, coldblooded, and so forth. But there is no harm in considering the end and counting the cost. The wisdom of all ages points to the very great advantage of combining discretion with valour, and the immense improvement which valour itself gains by the connexion. Discretion compels a man to contemplate and realize his danger, and to face it, instead of rushing at it with a wild, unthinking impulse, and perhaps closed eyes. In these days there is a great waste of energy, that often ends in bringing the impulsive and adventurous into disagreeable collision with their mother earth or a stone wall. When a man of middle age turns to look about him, he sees the path of life behind him strewn with as many sufferers as the half-burnt moths that cover our carpets these summer nights. These are the martyrs of passion. They are the men whose first notion of life was a grand adventure, in which they were to rush at some object or other of which they were enamoured, and win it with a blow. That is the theory of human life which is shadowed in these Alpine expeditions. But, of course, our young men will go to Switzerland, and they will ascend mountains, and they will feel a very natural and irresistible desire to do what everybody has done before, and, still more, what nobody has done. This is the great prize which caps and leads on the lesser attempts. It was the blue riband of the Alps that poor Lord FRANCIS DOUGLAS was trying for the other day. If it must be so, at all events the Alpine Club, that has proclaimed this crusade, must manage the thing rather better, or it will soon be voted a nuisance. If the work is to be done, it must be done well. They must advise youngsters to practise, and make sure of their strength and their endurance. "They must take heed to their paths that their footsteps do not slip." They must devise implements of a practical character, unless they are above such weaknesses. They must instil a habit of caution, and calculation as to rests, and such particulars. Above all things, their ropes must not break. If a people chose to despise the aid of improved weapons and defences as unworthy of a true military genius, it would soon find itself under the heel of its more scientific and mechanical neighbour. We do not see why the Matterhorn must be conquered with sinew alone. With every aid that can be applied it will still be a work of great labour and peril; and we entertain no doubt that the man who submits to be assisted, and incurs no more danger than is necessary, will be a more useful member of society than the other who thought only of the glory of a desperate enterprise. We trust we have not said a word to increase the grief of surviving friends. Our argument shows the value we set on the lives that have been lost. They fell into a fashionable rivalry, as was but natural to their time of life and to a forward age. They will not have died in vain if this warning is taken as it is meant.

4.9
KENNEDY – *THE TIMES*

TO THE EDITOR OF THE TIMES (published 28.7.65)

Sir,– Permit me to make a few remarks on Alpine mountaineering, which the two recent accidents in Switzerland seem to warrant. I speak not, of course, to those who are better mountaineers than myself, but to the numerous tribe of climbers who, without experience, and without the necessary powers of mountaineering, induce guides to conduct them up the most difficult summits.

The conditions of safety against all Alpine dangers, excepting that of thunderstorm, are easily insured. Three men, when the traveller is an ordinary one, are sufficient to ascend any mountain; two, when the traveller and guide are such magnificent fellows as my lamented friend Charles Hudson and his guide Michel Croz; but such men are not plentiful. A large party should always be divided into threes, or, at the most, fours, and this for many reasons. It does not stop the whole party when one man calls for a halt; it is the safest method, for if one division should slip the other is not dragged after it, it being impossible to arrest three men on a steep slope whatever be the force behind, for one man after another is dragged off his feet and shares the fate of those in front. This system also usually admits of a greater length of cord for each man. I am now speaking for difficult summits; for these a length of 30 or 35 feet between each pair is not too great. The first man descends an awkward place, while his companions behind anchor themselves upon a firm rock or some secure place and pay out his rope; the process is repeated for the second man; the two then unite their forces below to receive the third, who, having no rope from above to trust to, should usually be the best cragsman of the three.

It is probably to the neglect of this obvious rule that the terrible accident at Zermatt is to be assigned; men who have succeeded in a difficult task usually become indifferent to danger, and their thoughts are wholly directed to the quickest mode of getting down again.

By this slow but sure method long and dangerous slopes of softened snow lying on smooth rocks may be safely traversed in the late afternoon; in extreme cases the central man may be detached from the rope in order to give number one a chance of attaining a more secure position, which the increased length of rope will allow him to reach.

Further, a long steep *couloir* of softened snow or of ice should always be descended backwards, a mode of descent which is also fully twice as fast as the ordinary one.

The ice axe is grasped in one hand, close beneath and touching the head; its broad flattened end is pressed with the weight of the body into the snow; if on ice its sharp spike is used, the greater the strain upon it the deeper it anchors itself; the left hand and arm are thrust into the snow even to the shoulder, or the hand rests in the icy step above, and the toes – not the heels – bear the weight of the body, the climber looking for his footing between his legs. In this manner, about three weeks ago, I twice brought up a man who slipped beneath me while descending from the Aiguille Verte. Many guides foolishly think it undignified to descend thus. Any one can descend face foremost, but he cannot possibly arrest a slip below; the pull of the rope brings him off balance, his heels slip from under him, and away he goes.

I may also call attention to the great use of crampons on an icy slope, more especially for the man who is engaged in cutting steps; with their aid it is scarcely possible to slip.

Finally, it is necessary to protest against the practice of inexperienced men ascending difficult peaks. A man who has spent only three or four years on the Alps is not and cannot be a first-rate mountaineer. Let them graduate on the well known glacier passes, and on such peaks as Mont Blanc or Monte Rosa, but until they are able to go in the style and with the certainty of such men as Michel Croz it is unfair for them to venture up difficult summits.

I am, Sir, your obedient servant,

Leeds, July 25. THOMAS STUART KENNEDY.

4.10
J.J. COWELL – WHYMPER

41 Gloucester Terrace, Hyde Park.
Monday July 31. 1865.

Dear Whymper,

I am much concerned at reading your letter. It is possible I may, now that so few of our members are in England, be of some service to you in the way you suggest; and if I can be I assure you it will give me the greatest pleasure. Would not this be a good way? Summon an Extraordinary Gen. Meeting to consider "if any enquiry should be made into Hudson's death": move to "appoint a Committee of three to make inquiries of Mr Whymper": move that "the Committee commences its inquiries then before the meeting; and make a report".

I think a general Meeting would be the only body that would give a sanction to an inquiry in such a manner as to satisfy the public. If any members on their own authority undertook an inquiry it might not satisfy the public which might say it was not an impartial inquiry but was got up privately by your friends.

If you approve of calling an Extry. Gen. Meeting look at Rule 14. Wills is in England and could act in Grove's place. I could undertake to get the signatures in 3 days. The time spent would then be as follows

	Days
Getting 10 signatures	3
Writing to Wills, Midland Circuit	1
Time for him to consider	1
Sending draft circular to London	1
Printing and posting (perhaps only)	1
Delivery of circulars	1
Notice	10
Day of Meeting	1
	19

Nineteen days is a long time – but is it possible to do it quicker? I feel how very desirable it is for your comfort to lose no time.

Since I wrote to you I had (yesterday) an attack of spitting of blood and I cannot leave the house so I cannot come to call on you. But if you think my suggestion worth discussing will you call here to-morrow any time before 5 p.m.

We should be very glad if you will come to a quiet dinner with us two on Wednesday 7 p.m., no dressing.

Believe me
Very truly yours
J.JERMYN COWELL.

4.11
GLOVER – WHYMPER (see 4.40)

Christ Church Parsonage, Dover.
July 31 1865.

My Dear Whymper,

I should have written to you before but I did not know whether you had come home – and indeed I do not know even now but I shall take my chance and send this to your Club.

I wished first of all to offer you my sincere sympathy under the sad and painful circumstances attending your ascent of the Matterhorn – and secondly to present at the same time my congratulations on your own providential escape primarily and chiefly – and on your own successful achievement of your darling project. I took, as you will suppose, the deepest and most painful interest in all the tidings and was most thankful to find that one who had been so kind to myself was spared the awful fate of his companions. Poor Michel Croz – he little thought the day he was with us under the Matterhorn that he was standing so near his own grave. And we little thought that so painful an affliction was so soon to attend you there. I knew none of the rest of your party save Taugwald. My brother took an excursion or two with Lord Francis Douglas two years ago. The rest I only knew by name and repute.

I dare say you saw my letter in *The Times*. I could not help writing in your absence and I hope that nothing I said was at all displeasing to you. I foresaw that there would be much discussion about your *rope* and that was the chief point to which I wished to draw attention. And with respect to the points – subsequent letters and articles in the papers convinced me that I did well to speak on them. I am anxiously looking out for your own account.

I fancy I am indebted to your kindness for sending me a copy of the *Leisure Hour* with the most faithful and admirable sketches of the Matterhorn and Monte Rosa by your pencil. They are first rate and I shall greatly value them as sketched by you. Accept my best thanks.

I sincerely hope you are recovering from the shock and from all its effects of your trying position – and with kind regards

Believe me very faithfully yours,
RICHARD GLOVER.

Edward Whymper Esq.

4.12
BUXTON – *THE TIMES* (see 4.25)

TO THE EDITOR OF THE TIMES (published 31.7.65)

Sir,– I regret to see that in the leading article of the 27th inst, you repeat the sentiments that, in much more violent form, have been urged by your contemporaries against those who find pleasure in exploring the less accessible parts of the Alpine Districts. You ask concerning these expeditions, "Is it life? Is it duty? Is it common sense? Is it allowable?" And you imply that the danger involved forbids any answer but in the negative. But can any other answer be given to similar questions when put in reference to hunting, shooting, boating, or many other such sports?

To take the case of the first. No year passes without some fatal accident occurring in the hunting field. But do men on that account stigmatise it as reckless folly? Every man who has had any experience of hunting knows that there is an element of risk of accident, but it is a risk that ordinary care & horsemanship reduce to a *minimum*. Yet if ordinary care is wanting, if man and horse, ignorant of their duties, with rotten or loose saddle girths, attempt to keep up in a fast run across a stiff country, they certainly incur very unwarrantable risks. But will any man sell his hunter because such an one breaks his neck? There is besides in every sport that commands the love of Englishmen a danger that is unavoidable. Good and well-mounted riders have met with death. If we would avoid all chances of fatal accident we must cease to hunt, to shoot, to travel by train, or road, or boat; we must give up all at once and altogether. The question, then, as to mountaineering, is, how much of unavoidable danger is there in it compared with other sports and amusements? My own opinion is that there is no more necessary risk in a "grand course" than in a good run. If the danger could be reduced to an average, I feel sure that mountaineering would not stand worse than hunting. In each – perhaps in the Alps more than with hounds – care and experience are absolutely necessary, and the neglect of them involves a possibility of accident.

Mr. Glover in his letter on the Matterhorn accident says that Mr. Whymper, probably to some extent the leader of the party, was altogether prudent and experienced. If there was no want of prudence, then it shows that the accident was unavoidable, and the expedition one that it was morally wrong to undertake. It, in fact, involves a greater blame upon the party than if it occurred through a want of foresight.

It seems evident that on some points care was wanting. And first, as to the rope. Mr. Whymper and the two guides were able, in spite of the great jerk, to keep their foothold. The party were safe until the rope broke. With such a rope it was imprudent to undertake such an expedition.

On another point, too, greater foresight was desirable. Everybody knows how all-important it is to make such arrangements for the night previous to a long expedition as to insure the greatest amount of rest. For most men it is essential to husband and economise their strength through every hour of the day and night. And a night spent on nothing but hard rocks above the snow line is one of the most wearisome forms of rest that can well be imagined.

In the present case it appears that the party had not intended to sleep on the mountain, but were out only for the purpose of surveying. They therefore could not have been prepared with clothing or food sufficient for a bivouac and two days hard work. It would have been indeed surprising had not some of the party failed when the greatest call was made upon their strength and activity.

None can be more horrified at this terrible accident than those who are acquainted with the nature of the cliffs on which it occurred.

It is, indeed, an occasion for urging the absolute necessity and duty of using the well-known precautions upon all, especially upon those who are making their first expeditions; and I must regret that this opportunity should be thrown away in the general outcry against all ascents of the high Alps, an outcry that will not be regarded by any single member of the Alpine Club.

I am, Sir, your obedient servant,

T. FOWELL BUXTON.

Warlies, Waltham Abbey. July 29.

4.13
GLOVER – *THE TIMES*

TO THE EDITOR OF THE TIMES (published 1.8.65)

Sir,– A relative of the late Lord Francis Douglas has written to me expressing pain that I should have hazarded a conjecture as to the origin of the catastrophe on the Matterhorn which seems to reflect the cause of the accident on his departed cousin, and requests me to write to you on the subject. I beg accordingly to say that this was not a mere conjecture on my part, but was based on one of the published accounts in the *Journal de Genève*.

Perhaps it would have been imprudent to hazard such a conjecture unsupported by authority; and, as it has given pain to those already so sorely afflicted, I sincerely regret that I should have said anything on that part of the subject, although no reader could imagine for one moment that in a letter written with the avowed purpose of comforting the relatives I should have intended to impute any blame to the unfortunate and deeply-lamented young nobleman. Even if he did meet with the original slip, it was, of course, a pure accident, and could not possibly cast any greater responsibility upon him than on any other person who attempted such a perilous excursion.

It is but just, however, to state that, if Mr.Cormick's account is correct, Lord Francis Douglas was not next to Croz, but had Mr.Haddo and Mr.Hudson between him and Croz.

Mr.Whymper's account, which has not appeared, can be the only authentic one; but it really matters little by whom the false step was made.

Perhaps not even Mr.Whymper can tell us; and, if he can, no sort of blame can attach to the unfortunate subject of it, and no one would dream of imputing it.

I am, Sir, your obedient servant,

RICHARD GLOVER.

Christ Church Parsonage, Dover, July 29.

4.14
ADAMS REILLY – J.D.FORBES

Cabane on the Col St Theodule.
August 1 [1865].

My dear Mr.Forbes,

I am making a last effort to complete my survey, but, I am afraid in vain, as there is a tourment raging round us at this moment which threatens to lift this queer little deal box up bodily and cast it down on the Gorner Gl. I left Zermatt yesterday, and went to the top of the kleine Matterhorn, but though the early morning was fine, wind and mist were in full swing by the time I arrived at the top, so I could do nothing.

However I left my theodolite on the peak, intending to reach it again this morning as soon after sunrise as possible, the mornings being generally clear: but this has turned out an exception, for a tremendous storm of snow & wind raged all night, and appears inclined to continue through the day. I sleep here again to-night, but if next morning is unfavourable, I can do no more, my time is up, and I must get on towards England. I can at least conscientiously say that I have done all I could do.

The weather broke up on the 18th, and has been bad ever since, so that even had I been able, I could not have done any work. Ever since that, the Bies has been blowing steadily, and of course bringing heavy rain with it: besides, for the last fortnight there has been at Zermatt almost every day something to cause us great anxiety at least, if not grief, and it is difficult to look back upon those days, without thinking that they must have been a dream.

Mr.Hadow's Uncle, and the Marquis of Queensberry, poor Douglas' brother, arrived on Monday, and on Wednesday, as there was a slight clearance in the weather, a large party of us walked up to the Riffel Hotel and dined there: we were rather late in starting to return, and when I got down (some time after the rest, in consequence of my lameness) I found all in the greatest anxiety. Lord Queensberry and Mr.Hadow were both missing! They were lost in the forest (which is in some places very dangerous in the dark) and it was one oclock before the parties sent in search of them returned with them. Next day we went to a spot commanding a view of the Matterhorn to show Lord Queensberry & Mr.Hadow what had been done, and on our return were met by the news that a party going up Monte Rosa had been overwhelmed by an Avalanche, and one life, that of a porter, lost. The 6th death in 14 days.

Next morning we were awoke by the news that Lord Queensberry had started *alone* at one oclock the night before with the intention of actually searching the sides of the Matterhorn for traces of his brother! You may imagine our consternation, and the state of mind of Mr.Stephenson a friend of mine who had come out with Lord Queensberry and who had the very day before received a message from Queensberry's sister begging him for God's sake not let him do anything rash, or risk his life in any way. Stephenson and Mr.McCormack started at once with a party of guides, and I followed them to the top of the Hörnli. They found him at the end of the Hörnli arrete, happily safe, but the risks he had run were frightful. He had actually found his way to the Hörnli in the dark, gone straight up the E. face of it, and if he had gone much further would certainly have been killed. He was quite exhausted, and had almost to be carried down the last part of the way to Zermatt. Next day, Saturday, they left Zermatt...

Zermatt. Aug 2.

This morning I had a great fight with the powers of the air, and licked them. All night there was a storm which the proprietor of the cabane (a connoisseur in such matters) pronounced "épouvantable", and as it showed no sign of abatement, we set off up the little Mt Cervin to bring down my theodolite which I had left up there on Monday. We reached the top in a positive gale of wind, but I was determined not to be beaten if possible, and set up the theodolite. It was blown down twice, but I had stationed a man to catch it, and at last I got it firmly fixed, and did nearly all I wanted. We then rushed down and went up the Theodul Horn, where I had just time to finish my work before a snow storm came up. The base line is short, but it will do very well, as the next stations are not far from it.

I leave Zermatt tomorrow, and shall spend next Sunday at Chamounix. I will not forget your photographs.

Believe me with kindest remembrances to all,
Yours always affectionately,
A.ADAMS REILLY.

4.15
TIMES EDITOR – WHYMPER

Printing House Square, E.C.
August 2.

The Editor of *The Times* presents his compliments to Mr. Whymper and begs to suggest that the public will expect from him a much more detailed account of the lamentable catastrophe on the Matterhorn than the bare contradiction of one unimportant statement which at Mr. Whymper's request he has published to-day.

As the only English survivor, the only one capable of explaining what really occurred, the Editor trusts he will not appeal in vain to Mr. Whymper for the full explanation which is so anxiously expected.

Edward Whymper Esq.

4.16
WHYMPER – *TIMES* EDITOR (Whymper's copy)

[Undated. ?4.8.65]

Sir,

I regret that my absence from Haslemere has prevented an earlier reply to your note of the 2nd inst.

I had hoped that the letters of the Revd. J.McCormick would have been sufficient for the information of the public, although they were intentionally silent on certain points, including the exact cause of the accident, in order to spare the families of Messrs. Hadow & Hudson the additional pain they must feel if it is published.

It appears however that the cause of this silence has been misunderstood and I have, in consequence, requested an enquiry on the part of the Alpine Club into the causes of the accident. I cannot say if my request will be granted, but if it is the report cannot be presented in less time than three weeks.

As a matter of taste I should have preferred any information from myself coming before the public as the result of an enquiry on the part of the Alpine Club, but should you consider it undesirable to delay it for so long a time, I will at once forward a plain statement of the facts.

I am, Sir,
Yours very obediently,
EDWARD WHYMPER.

4.17
TIMES EDITOR – WHYMPER (see 4.24 and 4.26)

Printing House Square, E.C.
August 5.

The Editor of *The Times* presents his compliments to Mr. Whymper and has no hesitation in advising him to make a plain statement of the facts of the lamentable catastrophe on the Matterhorn without waiting for the intervention of the Alpine Club.
Edward Whymper Esq.

4.18
LEADER IN *THE TIMES* (see also 4.8 and 4.28)

SATURDAY, AUGUST 5, 1865.

This year will be remarkable in the annals of Alpine adventure. Another disastrous accident is added to that which has been the chief incident of the present summer. The frightful fall of the three Englishmen and their guide down the Matterhorn is now followed by another accident, which, though it has not proceeded from any undue rashness or culpable negligence, shows to the full the dangers of mountaineering. We have the particulars from Mr. M'CORMICK, the chaplain at Zermatt. Two Englishmen who were ascending Monte Rosa with two guides and three porters were swept away by an avalanche. The guides, as is usual, did their work with skill and courage, and succeeded in rescuing their employers, but one of the porters perished, and his body was found the next day buried six feet deep under the snow. Of course, it is of no use to read a homily on this fresh disaster. There is no liklihood that an end will be put to mountaineering, nor have we the smallest wish to accomplish such an object. We confess that in its most ambitious forms we do not see the use of it. To scale the highest and most difficult peaks of the Alps does not add to human happiness or knowledge; it does not contribute to health in any greater degree than an ascent to more modest and safer heights; the most bracing air and the most strengthening exercise can be had at a less elevation than from thirteen to fifteen thousand feet above the sea. We do not esteem very highly the courage which prompts these adventures, nor the skill which enables men to prosecute them successfully. But there will always be a certain number of people who will take a pleasure in such enterprises. What common sense seems to condemn will for that very reason have an attraction, as raising the successful climber out of the list of the staid and the sober, and surrounding him with the halo of adventure. Perhaps it is necessary that there should be an order of men to attempt what no one else will attempt, to show what can be done, and the feats which human courage and endurance can perform. We have no desire, therefore, to interfere with professed climbers, not one of whom, as we have been assured by their spokesmen in these columns, is likely to be turned from his pursuit by anything that can be urged against it.

But to the ordinary traveller who may be tempted to attack the more arduous peaks, passes, and glaciers of Switzerland, the narrative of the Chaplain at Zermatt may give a word of warning. One of the most successful and celebrated of Alpine climbers wrote to us the other day deprecating the ascent of difficult peaks by mere novices – that is, as he explained, by persons who have spent only three or four seasons in mountaineering. Such persons, he said, should accustom themselves by degrees to the difficulties of the work, and should graduate on Mont Blanc and Monte Rosa before trying really difficult peaks. To most people Monte Rosa, with the long ridge which leads to its summit, will appear a rather difficult examination for the degree of Bachelor of the Alps, and that it requires practised mountaineers is evident from this last accident. An avalanche is an enemy from which on many occasions no skill or courage can defend the climber. But there are ways of receiving the charge even of an avalanche. The guides were the first to extricate themselves, and it was well for the two Englishmen that their conductors were so successful, for one of our countrymen was wedged so tightly that he could not move, and the other was buried in the snow with his head downwards, and nothing visible but his heels. Of the three porters, one appears to have got out at once, the second was taken out nearly suffocated, while the third was not found until the next day, when, of course, he was quite dead.

We know not whether these Englishmen were expert climbers, but, if they were, the warning is all the more worthy of consideration by the ordinary tourist. If it had not been for their guides, both these Englishmen would have perished, and with nine out of ten who attempt the higher Alps it is the same. They cannot ascend, or, still more, descend, without the constant assistance of the guide, who cuts their steps in the ice, and fits in their feet, and by whom at times they are helped in a manner more convenient than dignified. When, therefore, the accounts of these perils inflame youthful ambition and urge the stream of travellers to follow in the steps of those who have so terribly perished or so narrowly escaped, the adventurers should have a due sense of their dependence on others for their safety. It is only by long experience of the Alps, and by acute and practised observation, that the mountaineer can tell which path to take, how he may most easily attain a point which he has in full view, where he can put his foot with the probability of finding a support, and how far he can move his body without danger of a slip or an overbalance. Not only must the unpractised tourist – that is, the man who has not been spending summer after summer in the Alps – be dependent on his guide for actually piloting him about the mountain, but he must in almost every difficult ascent trust his life wholly to him, for the amateur himself is at times wholly ignorant where he shall place hand or foot. By all means let climbing flourish, and its celebrities gain their due need of honour. But, as the travellers in Switzerland increase in numbers yearly, and Alpine ambition increases in a still larger ratio, the crowd should understand what it is they attempt, and the conditions under which alone the feats they aspire to must be performed.

4.19
QUEENSBERRY – WHYMPER (see also 4.23)

17 Cromwell Road
Saturday [5.8.65]

My dear Whymper,

If you are in town can I come down & see you this afternoon or meet you anywhere

I have just returned from Zermatt. I should like to see you very much if possible – will you send an answer by this cab – excuse my writing as if I know you – but after this dreadful accident it does not matter.

Yours sincerely
QUEENSBERRY

4.20
S.PARKER – J.D.FORBES

Bell Alp. Valais.
Aug. 5 1865.

My dear Sir,

I have been travelling in this country for the last fortnight. I intended to write to you from Zermatt but was prevented from doing so.

We found Zermatt in a very excited state from the numerous accidents which had occurred. I think no one will attempt the Matterhorn at present – as it would be a violation of good taste & look like bravado.

Poor Lord Francis Douglas' remains cannot be found. We went the other day up towards Zmutt, & watched carefully with an opera glass – soon observed 8 eagles together – but they were *leaving* the spot – so we agreed to camp at Staffel Alp at the foot of the Zmutt glacier, and watch their approach at dawn. The weather prevented our doing this for some days – and when we went to explore the snow fields above the Zmutt glacier we found that some guides of Zermatt had already made a thorough search there – & as there was considerable risk in getting to the spot we decided that it was better not to incur it.

The general belief now is that Ld. Douglas must have fallen on the upper part of the rocks, & his body be lodged there. Prof Tyndall has got 600 feet of rope, & sent to Geneva for 2000 feet more, & says he intends thoroughly to examine the face of the mountain. It will be very difficult to do this – as he will have to get to the place whence they fell: &, from what I hear, it was only the unusual absence of snow that enabled the party to cross the face of the pyramid above Zmutt gl.

At present Peter Taugwald would on no account attempt the ascent, as he says the snow renders the rocks quite impracticable.

Mr.Reilly was in Zermatt, but left for the Theodul just after our arrival. I fear he had wretched weather...

The other day we started alone for Monte Rosa. A gentleman with 3 guides was also to make the attempt but we kept our own counsel, started out of the house before him – & they did not discover us till we were on the snow slopes some hours after.

Unfortunately it blew up a perfect gale with clouds, & snow drift, & we were obliged to lie for 2 hours in a hollow below the Sattel in hopes of its abating. Here we were joined by our friend with the guides. The weather moderated a little, & we all pushed on together – but soon the other party gave it up, & we crossed the avalanche where the porter was killed last week. It is just below the saddle on the left as you ascend. Since then a small one had fallen to the right, & from what we cd. see there was no apparent reason why a third should not fall in the middle between the two. Arrived on the saddle, we were saluted with such violent gusts of wind as made our further progress out of the question. We had however the satisfaction of a good look down into the wild glacier basin at the back of the höchste Spitze – & on our way home snow, & distant thunder convinced us that we had acted wisely in coming down. The weather broke so thoroughly that we had to take the valley route to this place instead of crossing the Adler to Saas & making our way to Simplon, as we had intended. Now we are bound for Lucerne & home, hoping to do another high pass or two during the present week. This is a lovely spot, the view is across the Rhone to the Weisshorn, & Matterhorn & the other well known peaks which are all distinctly seen...

With kind regards to all your party. I am, dear Sir,

Yours sincerely

S.SANDBACH PARKER.

4.21
WILLS – WHYMPER

Midland Circuit.
6 Aug. 1865.

Dear Whymper,

I enclose a letter dated from the Temple which I append thus because – if you are disposed to accede to my request it may be expedient to publish the request as well as the answer.

Let me however in these lines which have no destination but yourself express my most deep and respectful and heartfelt sympathy – I would have liked to write to you before but I felt sure that would happen which Cowell tells me has happened and that you would be exposed to positive torture from the inquisitive and the rude and the thoughtless, and I almost feared to take up my pen and write to you.

There is, however, in my judgment only one way to put an end to all this. Give your own account; let it be truthful, manly and unflinching – wherever blame is due – if blame there be – let it rest – but don't let people go on conjecturing the worst and talking and writing in the feeblest and most ignorant and most uncharitable manner when you could silence the greater part of it all by your utterance. To some extent also the Club is on trial. People are daily writing to abuse us and our doings. I don't care greatly about it myself, but still it does not do for a body of men associated for any purpose to let needless aspersions fall thick and threefold upon them. It is a great deal better for us – as it always is for everybody under all circumstances as I venture to think – to have the whole truth known and *then* let people make what they will of it.

I think the same observations apply with tenfold force to yourself – you will be open to all sorts of misconstruction if you *don't* give an account. After all you have gone through, you will perhaps think this a very small matter, but let us your friends, whose judgment is not disturbed, as yours can hardly fail to be, by the mental suffering you have gone through, judge a little for you in this matter.

The A.C. Journal is published on the 1st September. What I would ask you to do, would be to give an account both of the ascent and the accident in that number – but meanwhile to write a somewhat more considered account of the accident itself in answer to my letter and let me send both my letter and your answer to the *Times*. If you approve of my suggestion, perhaps when you do write to me you will return my letter for I have no copy of it.

"Midland Circuit" is address enough. I hope quiet and employment will restore you gradually to health and tranquillity. I have myself experienced some awful shocks in my experience of life and if I might refer to my own history, I should say as far as possible be busy about things you *must* do.

Believe me Dear Whymper,
Ever very truly yours,
ALFRED WILLS.

4.22
WILLS – WHYMPER (see also 4.32)

Dear Whymper,

I cannot refrain from asking you to accept the assurance of my deep and heartfelt sympathy with you in the terrible and afflicting circumstances in which you have so lately been placed – and I advisedly name yourself first, for there are few men who would not feel that in many respects it were more tolerable to be of the lost than of the survivors. If the sympathy and confidence of your friends can be of any avail, I think I may assure you you will have it freely; for I think it will not be suspected by anyone who knows you that with two such mountaineers as yourself and Hudson of the party any reasonable precaution was likely to be neglected, so far as you and he at all events were concerned. I speak only of you and him, because I did not know the others. Hudson I did know, and therefore know that there never was a man who had a more active frame, a more steady hand or head or foot, a firmer mind in danger, or a more keen and scrupulous sense of right and wrong. A man more unlikely rashly or inconsiderately to put in jeopardy his own life and that of others I never knew – and this not because he feared danger when it came in a proper way but because he appreciated too highly the ties that bound him for the sake of himself and others to life and duty.

But may I make an appeal to you to relieve those who take an interest in this sad matter from the state of anxiety and suspense in which your own silence – a silence which I at once understand and respect – has kept us? It is impossible now to get together the Committee, and therefore I hope I am not taking too much on myself as President of the Alpine Club to make the request which I know the Committee would make – namely, that you should give us a full and detailed account of the accident and the causes which led to it. You will remember that once before when a fatal accident happened to one of a party of which a member of the Alpine Club was also one, the Committee took all the means in their power to investigate the affair, in the hope that from so lamentable an experience, warning and instruction for the future, if nothing more, might be gathered. I am sure you will feel that it is only right and proper that the Club should exercise this kind of friendly jurisdiction over its members, and will do justice to yourself and to your companions in misfortune by giving us a faithful and fearless narrative of this deplorable disaster.

Pray take this into your consideration and if you can sufficiently command your feelings to face the painful task of narration, I hope you will accede to my request.

Believe me, dear Whymper,

Yours most truly,

ALFRED WILLS.

Inner Temple.
7 August 1865.

4.23
QUEENSBERRY – WHYMPER (see also 4.39)

17 Cromwell Road
Monday 7th.[8.65]

My dear Whymper,

I quite forgot the other day to ask you if you had paid any thing for my dear brother at Zermatt. If you would kindly let me know I would send it to you.

You spoke also of some gloves & a belt which belonged to him being found – which I heard nothing of at Zermatt. If you can remember if any one had them as my Mother would like to have these things.

Believe me
Yours very sincerely
QUEENSBERRY

4.24
TIMES EDITOR – WHYMPER

Printing House Square, E.C.
August 7.

The Editor of *The Times* presents his compliments to Mr. Whymper and begs to congratulate him upon the very interesting and affecting narrative he has given of the catastrophe from which he has happily escaped.

He is sure that Mr. Whymper will have no reason to regret his compliance with the wish of the public.

Edward Whymper Esq.

4.25
WHYMPER – BUXTON (Whymper's copy; see also 4.31)

20, Canterbury Place.
Private Lambeth Rd S.
Aug. 8. 1865.

Sir,

Your letter that appeared in the *Times* of the 31st July relative to the sad accident on the Matterhorn, and which bears your signature, has given me great pain.

I wrote a reply to it on the following day but it accidentally remained unposted. I now beg to refer you to my letter in the *Times* of this day.

In my letter I scrupulously abstain from offering observations and casting blame on any one, and also from taking notice of the remarks that have been made on my personal capability for the expedition we undertook. There remains unanswered therefore your charge of want of prudence or inexperience in myself – for I imagine no mountaineer will venture to assert that the expedition was one that it was morally wrong to undertake. In answer to this charge I can only refer you to that which I have done previous to this last and most disastrous expedition and I think you will find that few people can point to more success than myself, and none to an equal list with fewer accidents.

If you included the Revd. Charles Hudson in your charge of want of prudence and experience, I can only say that you could not have known him, for a more prudent and a more experienced man could not I think be found.

Mr.Hadow was the sole cause of the accident. If any fault can be found with us it can only be for allowing him to go. If after what I have stated in the *Times* it is considered that I am to blame in the matter, I must bear the blame; but few men would have acted differently if they had been in the same position.

In conclusion I have to say that Mr.Glover is a gentleman whom I took over the Theodule in last June, and left in the hut while I and other guides examined the Matterhorn. I saw him afterwards for half an hour at Chamonix, but beyond this I know nothing of him. I must say I greatly regret that you wrote the letter to which I refer. Had it been done by one without position, or unknown as a mountaineer, I should not have cared but coming from yourself it was calculated to do considerable harm.

I trust you will excuse the freedom with which I have expressed myself and that you will in your own mind at least now that you are in possession of the facts, be just to myself and to the memory of my deeply lamented friend Charles Hudson.

I am, Sir, your obedient servant,
EDWARD WHYMPER.

Sir T.F.Buxton.

4.26
WHYMPER – *THE TIMES* (see also 4.28)

TO THE EDITOR OF THE TIMES (published 8.8.65)
Sir,– After the direct appeals which I have received from the President of the Alpine Club and from yourself to write an account of the accident on the Matterhorn, I feel it is impossible to remain silent any longer, and I therefore forward to you for publication a plain statement of the accident itself, and of the events that preceded it and followed it.

On Wednesday morning, the 12th of July, Lord Francis Douglas and myself crossed the Col Theodule to seek guides at Zermatt. After quitting the snow on the northern side we rounded the foot of the glacier, crossed the Furgge Glacier, and left my tent, ropes and other matters in the little chapel at the Lac Noir. We then descended to Zermatt, engaged Peter Taugwalder, and gave him permission to choose another guide. In the course of the evening the Rev. Charles Hudson came into our hotel with a friend, Mr.Hadow, and they, in answer to some inquiries, announced their intention of starting to attack the Matterhorn on the following morning. Lord Francis Douglas agreed with me it was undesirable that two independent parties should be on the mountain at the same time, with the same object. Mr.Hudson was therefore invited to join us, and he accepted our proposal. Before admitting Mr.Hadow I took the precaution to inquire what he had done in the Alps, and, as well as I remember, Mr.Hudson's reply was, "Mr.Hadow has done Mont Blanc in less time than most men." He then mentioned several other excursions that were unknown to me, and added, in answer to a further question, "I consider he is a sufficiently good man to go with us." This was an excellent certificate, given us as it was by a first-rate mountaineer, and Mr.Hadow was admitted without any further question. We then went into the matter of guides. Michel Croz was with Messrs. Hadow and Hudson, and the latter thought if Peter Taugwalder went as well that there would not be occasion for anyone else as well. The question was referred to the men themselves, and they made no objection.

We left Zermatt at 5 35 on Thursday morning, taking the two young Taugwalders as porters, by the desire of their father. They carried provisions amply sufficient for the whole party for three days, in case the ascent should prove more difficult than we anticipated. No rope was taken from Zermatt, because there was already more than enough in the chapel at the Lac Noir. It has been repeatedly asked, "Why was not the wire rope taken which Mr.Hudson brought to Zermatt?" I do not know; it was not mentioned by Mr.Hudson, and at that time I had not even seen it. My rope alone was used during the expedition, and there was – first, about 200 feet of Alpine Club rope; second, about 150 feet of a kind I believe to be stronger than the first; third, more than 200 feet of a lighter and weaker rope than the first, of a kind used by myself until the Club rope was produced.

It was our intention on leaving Zermatt to attack the mountain seriously – not, as it has been frequently stated, to explore or examine it, – and we were provided with everything that long experience has shown to be necessary for the most difficult mountains. On the first day, however, we did not intend to ascend to any great height, but to stop when we found a good position for placing the tent. We mounted accordingly very leisurely, left the Lac Noir at 8 20, and passed along the ridge connecting the Hörnli with the actual peak, at the foot of which we arrived at 11 20, having frequently halted on the way. We then quitted the ridge, went to the left, and ascended by the north-eastern face of the mountain. Before 12 o'clock we had found a good position for the tent, at a height of 11,000 feet; but Croz and the elder of Taugwalder's sons went on to look what was above, in order to save time on the following morning. The remainder constructed the platform on which the tent was to be placed, and by the time this was finished the two men returned, reported joyfully that as far as they had gone they had seen nothing but that which was good, and asserted positively that had we gone on with them on that day we could have ascended the mountain and have returned to the tent with facility. We passed the remaining hours of daylight – some basking in the sunshine, some sketching or collecting, and, when the sun went down, giving, as it departed, a glorious promise for the morrow we returned to the tent to arrange for the night. Hudson made tea, myself coffee, and we then retired each one to his blanket bag; the Taugwalders, Lord Francis Douglas, and myself occupying the tent, the others remaining, by preference, outside. But long after dusk the cliffs above echoed with our laughter and with the songs of the guides, for we were happy that night in camp, and did not dream of calamity.

We were astir long before daybreak on the morning of the 14th, and started directly it was possible to move, leaving the youngest of Taugwalder's sons behind. At 6 20 we had attained a height of 12,800 feet, and halted for half-an-hour, then continued without a break until 9 55, when we stopped for fifty minutes, at a height probably of about 14,000 feet. Thus far we had ascended by the north-eastern face of the mountain, and had not met with a single difficulty. For the greater part of the way there was, indeed, no occasion for the rope; and sometimes Hudson led, sometimes myself. We had now arrived at the foot of that part which from Zermatt seems perpendicular or overhanging, and we could no longer continue on the same side. By common consent, therefore, we ascended for some distance by the arête – that is by the ridge descending towards Zermatt – and then turned over to the right, or to the north-western face. Before doing so we made a change in the order of ascent; Croz went first, I followed, Hudson came third, Hadow and Old Taugwalder were last. The change was made because the work became difficult for a time, and required caution. In some places there was but little hold, and it was therefore desirable those should be in front who were least likely to slip. The general slope of the mountain at this part was less than forty degrees, and snow had consequently acccumulated and filled up the irregularities of the rock face, leaving only occasional fragments projecting here and there. These were at times coated with a thin glaze of ice, from the snow above having melted and frozen again during the night. Still it was a place over which any fair mountaineer might pass in safety. We found, however, that Mr.Hadow was not accustomed to this kind of work, and required continual assistance; but no one suggested that he should stop, and he was taken to the top. It is only fair to say that the difficulty experienced by Mr.Hadow at this part arose, not from fatigue or lack of courage, but simply and entirely from want of experience. Mr.Hudson, who followed me, passed over this part, and, as far as I know, ascended the entire mountain without having the slightest assistance rendered to him on any occasion. Sometimes, after I had taken a hand from Croz or received a pull, I turned to give the same to Hudson; but he inevitably declined, saying it was not necessary. This solitary difficult part was of no great extent, certainly not more than 300 feet high, and after it was passed the angles became less and less as we approached the summit; at last the slope was so moderate that Croz and myself detached ourselves from the others and ran on to the top. We arrived at 1 40 p.m., the others about 10 min. after us.

I have been requested to describe particularly the state of the party on the summit. No one showed any signs of fatigue, neither did I hear anything to lead me to suppose that anyone was at all tired. I remember Croz laughing at me when I asked him the question. Indeed, less than ten hours had elapsed since our starting, and during that time we had halted for nearly two. The only remark which I heard suggestive of danger was made by Croz, but it was quite casual, and probably meant nothing. He said, after I had remarked that we had come up very slowly, "Yes; I would rather go down with you and another guide alone than with those who are going." As to ourselves, we were arranging what we should do that night on our return to Zermatt.

We remained on the summit for one hour, and during that time Hudson and I consulted, as we had done all the day, as to the best and safest arrangement of the party. We agreed that it would be best for Croz to go first, as he was the most powerful, and Hadow second; Hudson, who was equal to a guide in sureness of foot, wished to be third; Lord F. Douglas was placed next, and old Taugwalder, the strongest of the remainder, behind him. I suggested to Hudson that we should attach a rope to the rocks on our arrival at the difficult bit, and hold it as we descended, as an additional protection. He approved the idea, but it was not definitely settled that it should be done. The party was being arranged in the above order while I was making a sketch of the summit, and they were waiting for me to be tied in my place, when some one remembered that we had not left our names in a bottle; they requested me to write them, and moved off while it was being done. A few minutes afterwards I tied myself to young Taugwalder and followed, catching them just as they were commencing the descent of the difficult part described above. The greatest care was being taken. Only one man was moving at a time; when he was firmly planted the next advanced, and so on. The average distance between each was probably 20 feet. They had not, however, attached the additional rope to rocks, and nothing was said about it. The suggestion was made entirely on account of Mr.Hadow, and I am not sure it even occurred to me again.

I was, as I have explained, detached from the others, and following them; but after about a quarter of an hour Lord F. Douglas asked me to tie on to old Taugwalder, as he feared, he said, that if there was a slip Taugwalder would not be able to hold him. This was done hardly ten minutes before the accident, and undoubtedly saved Taugwalder's life.

As far as I know, at the moment of the accident no one was actually moving. I cannot speak with certainty, neither can the Taugwalders, because the two leading men were partially hidden from our sight by an intervening mass of rock. Poor Croz had laid aside his axe, and in order to give Mr.Hadow greater security was absolutely taking hold of his legs and putting his feet, one by one, into their proper positions. From the movement of their shoulders it is my belief that Croz, having done as I have said, was in the act of turning round to go down a step or two himself; at this moment Mr.Hadow slipped, fell on him, and knocked him over. I heard one startled exclamation from Croz, then saw him and Mr.Hadow flying downwards; in another moment Hudson was dragged from his steps and Lord F. Douglas immediately after him. All this was the work of a moment; but immediately we heard Croz's exclamation Taugwalder and myself planted ourselves as firmly as the rocks would permit; *the rope was tight between us, and the shock came on us both as on one man.* We held; but the rope broke mid way between Taugwalder and Lord F. Douglas. For two or three seconds we saw our unfortunate companions sliding downwards on their backs, and spreading out their hands endeavouring to save themselves; they then disappeared one by one, and fell from precipice to precipice on to the Matterhorn glacier below, a distance of nearly 4,000 feet in height. From the moment the rope broke it was impossible to help them.

For the space of half an hour we remained on the spot without moving a single step. The two men, paralyzed by terror, cried like infants, and trembled in such a manner as to threaten us with the fate of the others. Immediately we had descended to a safe place I asked for the rope that had broken, and to my surprise – indeed, to my horror – found that it was the weakest of the three ropes. As the first five men had been tied while I was sketching I had not noticed the rope they employed, and now I could only conclude that they had seen fit to use this in preference to the others. It has been stated that the rope broke in consequence of its fraying over a rock; this is not the case, it broke in mid-air, and the end does not show any trace of previous injury.

For more than two hours afterwards I thought every moment that the next would be my last; for the Taugwalders, utterly unnerved, were not only incapable of giving assistance, but were in such a state that a slip might have been expected from one or the other at any moment. I do the younger man, moreover, no injustice when I say that immediately we got to the easy part of the descent he was able to laugh, smoke, and eat as if nothing had happened. There is no occasion to say more of the descent. I looked frequently, but in vain, for traces of my unfortunate companions, and we were in consequence surprised by the night when still at a height of 13,000ft. We arrived at Zermatt at 10 30 on Saturday morning.

Immediately on my arrival I sent to the President of the Commune, and requested him to send as many men as possible to ascend heights whence the spot could be commanded where I knew the four must have fallen. A number went and returned after six hours, reporting they had seen them, but that they could not reach them that day. They proposed starting on Sunday evening so as to reach the bodies at daybreak on Monday; but, unwilling to lose the slightest chance, the Rev.J.M'Cormick and myself resolved to start on Sunday morning. The guides of Zermatt, being threatened with excommunication if they did not attend the early mass, were unable to accompany us. To several, at least, I am sure this was a severe trial; for they assured me with tears that nothing but that which I have stated would have prevented them from going. The Rev. J. Robertson and Mr. J. Phillpotts, of Rugby, however, not only lent us their guide, Franz Andenmatten, but also accompanied us themselves. Mr.Puller lent us the brothers Lochmatter: F. Payot and J. Tairraz, of Chamounix, also volunteered. We started with these at 2 a.m. on Sunday, and followed the route we had taken on Thursday morning until we had passed the Hörnli, when we went down to the right of the ridge and mounted through the séracs of the Matterhorn Glacier. By 8 30 we had got on to the plateau at the top, and within sight of the corner in which we knew my companions must be. As we saw one weather-beaten man after another raise the telescope, turn deadly pale, and pass it on without a word to the next, we knew that all hope was gone. We approached; they had fallen below as they had fallen above – Croz a little in advance, Hadow near him, and Hudson some distance behind; but of Lord F. Douglas we could see nothing. To my astonishment, I saw that all of the three had been tied with the Club, or with the second and equally strong, rope, and consequently there was only one link – that between Taugwalder and Lord F. Douglas – in which the weaker rope had been used.

The letters of the Rev.J.M'Cormick have already informed you respecting the subsequent proceedings. The orders from the Government of the Valais to bring the bodies down were so positive, that four days after the events I have just related twenty-one guides accomplished that sad task. The thanks of all Englishmen are due to these brave men, for it was a work of no little difficulty and of great danger. Of the body of Lord F. Douglas they, too, saw nothing; it is probably arrested in the rocks above. No one can mourn his loss more deeply or more sincerely than myself. Although young, he was a most accomplished mountaineer, hardly ever required the slightest assistance, and did not make a single slip throughout the day. He had only a few days before we met made the ascent of the Gabelhorn – a summit considerably more difficult, I believe, to reach than the Matterhorn itself.

I was detained in Zermatt until the 22nd of July, to await the inquiry instituted by the Government. I was examined first, and at the close I handed into the Court a number of questions which I desired should be put to the elder Taugwalder; doing so because that which I had found out respecting the ropes was by no means satisfactory to me. The questions, I was told, were put and answered before I left Zermatt; but I was not allowed to be present at the inquiry and the answers although promised, have not yet reached me.

This, Sir, is the end of this sad story. A single slip, or a single false step, has been the sole cause of this frightful calamity, and has brought about misery never to be forgotten. I have only one observation to offer upon it. If the rope had not broken you would not have received this letter, for we could not possibly have held the four men, falling as they did, all at the same time, and with a severe jerk. But, at the same time, it is my belief no accident would have happened had the rope between those who fell been as tight, or nearly as tight, as it was between Taugwalder and myself. The rope, when used properly, is a great safeguard; but whether on rocks, or whether on snow or glacier, if two men approach each other so that the rope falls in a loop, the whole party is involved in danger, for should one slip or fall he may acquire, before he is stopped, a momentum that may drag down one man after another and bring destruction to all; but if the rope is tight this is all but impossible.

I am, Sir, your obedient servant,
Haslemere, Aug. 7. EDWARD WHYMPER.

4.27
WIGRAM – WHYMPER (see 4.29 and 4.30)

Furneaux Pelham, Buntingford.
8 August.

Dear Sir,

I have not the honour of your acquaintance and I have no wish to intrude upon you; still, I think that you ought to hear what has come to my knowledge.

I have received a letter from Jean Baptiste Croz (Michel's brother, and my tried companion during 3 Alpine campaigns), in which he speaks of a suspicion prevalant in the Valley of Chamonix, and I fear shared by himself that Taugwald *cut the rope* on the Matterhorn. The grounds for this dreadful charge are the improbability of such a rope breaking and the fact that young Taugwald had just come to Chamonix: whence it was assumed that he was escaping justice. You shall see Croz's letter if you wish to do so.

I am writing to Croz to represent the impossibility of such a thing being done without your knowledge; that the man who could plan it could not have joined in the expedition; & the want of connection between young T's coming to Chamonix & the deed attributed to his father.

Still I cannot think that anything from me is likely to have the effect in stopping this ghastly and indeed most blameworthy scandal, that a letter from yourself to Croz would have.

If you write I have of course no objection to your mentioning my name.

Yrs very truly
WOOLMORE WIGRAM.

E. Whymper Esq.

4.28
LEADER IN *THE TIMES* (see also 4.8 and 4.18)

WEDNESDAY, AUGUST 9, 1865.

Mr. WHYMPER'S interesting and affecting narrative of the accident on the Matterhorn has now been read by thousands, and no doubt remains as to the causes and circumstances of that grievous disaster. Not only the friends of those that have perished, but Englishmen in general, have reason to be grateful to Mr. WHYMPER for having overcome his natural repugnance to relate the melancholy history, and for having so clearly stated all that can be known. Every man of feeling will appreciate the unwillingness of the sole English survivor to give to the world a narrative which might seem to throw blame on any one of his unfortunate companions, but it will not the less be the general opinion that Mr. WHYMPER'S friends were right in requesting him to tell the tale, and that his compliance is in the highest degree creditable to himself. From his account it is plain that several inaccuracies have crept into the former statements. First, with regard to the preparations made for effecting the ascent. It had been said that the party had started with merely the intention of reconnoitring the Matterhorn, and that, finding the ascent easier than they had expected, they had continued their way until they reached the summit, without having strengthened themselves beforehand with proper sleep and food. This story, derived, no doubt, from some of the Zermatt guides, turns out to be wholly incorrect. Mr. WHYMPER had provided himself with all that was necessary for the ascent, including between 500 and 600 feet of rope. The four Englishmen were accomanied by four guides, three of whom actually made the whole ascent. They had a proper tent and blanket-bags, and passed a good night before attempting the more arduous part of their work, and we are told positively that they reached the top in full strength and spirits, and without exhaustion on the part of any one.

What, then, was the cause of the disaster? Mr. WHYMPER and Mr. HUDSON were known as two of the most expert mountaineers living; the former has this very summer accomplished the ascent of the Aiguille Verte, a peak which from beneath looks even more hopeless than the Matterhorn, and poor Mr. HUDSON was acknowledged by all who had accompanied him on his expeditions to have had marvellous strength, activity, and sureness of foot. Lord FRANCIS DOUGLAS, though but a boy, was a practised climber, he had made one or two very difficult ascents, and Mr. WHYMPER bears witness that during the whole of their arduous ascent and descent he did not make a single slip. The guides were first-rate. MICHEL CROZ was one of the celebrities of the Alps. He and his brother have for years been employed by the boldest and most enterprising of the English mountaineers, and MICHEL especially was looked upon as almost indispenable in new and difficult expeditions. His strength, courage, knowledge of ice and snow and rock, his skill in choosing the best points of attack, and finding a way where to other eyes the height appeared inaccessible, gained him the confidence of his adventurous patrons. TAUGWALDER also had a good reputation as a strong and tried mountaineer. It is reasonable to believe that if the Matterhorn had been attacked by experienced climbers alone the ascent and descent would have been made in safety. Such men as Messrs. HUDSON and WHYMPER and MICHEL CROZ would undoubtedly have done the work successfully on the 14th of July. Though the mountain looks precipitous from below, it is now proved to be accessible by at least one path, and Mr.WHYMPER states that it does not present any surpassing difficulty. But these things are comparative. Where a mountaineer of extraordinary natural aptitude for the work, developed by long and continuous practice, finds no very great difficulty, a less experienced climber is a helpless and nervous burden in the hands of his guide. Now, the Matterhorn, though accessible, has, by the description of Mr WHYMPER, a *mauvais pas* of the most serious kind. The Alpine Club has been assailing the mountain for several years without success. Mr.BALL in his *Alpine Guide*, speaks of three attempts. The first, described by Mr.VAUGHAN HAWKINS in *Vacation Tourists*, was made in 1860, from Breuil on the south side, but "three hours of very difficult climbing over rocks made slippery by a varnish of ice did not suffice to reach the summit of the left-hand buttress forming the watershed between Zmutt and Breuil." "In 1862" continues the same authority, "Mr.WHYMPER, with great boldness and perseverance, made several attempts, which were carried higher on the same ridge, and were terminated by an accident in which that gentleman had an extraordinary escape from destruction." Later in the same season Professor TYNDALL, with two guides, returned to the attack and overcame all the difficulties which had seemed so formidable from below; "but at a point a few hundred feet below the summit they were arrested by faces of rock that defied their utmost efforts." The conclusion at which Mr.BALL, writing two years ago, arrives is, that "after the failure of efforts in which the best mountaineers have pushed daring to the verge of temerity, it is allowable to believe that this, perhaps, alone among the great peaks of the Alps will preserve the epithet 'inaccessible.' "

Such was the enterprise on which these four Englishmen and their guides set forth on the present occasion. The attempt to ascend from Breuil was abandoned, and the party started from Zermatt and pursued their course by the Hörnli, and then by the ridge which connects it with the Matterhorn. The ascent is sufficiently described in Mr.WHYMPER'S letter. Suffice it to say that by the right of this ridge on the north-western face of the mountain it is possible to reach the summit. But to do this it is necessary to pass over a slope which no man, whatever his strength and courage, should attempt, or should be allowed by his companions to attempt, without having had long experience of the most difficult mountaineering. Such work was very well for Mr.WHYMPER or Mr.HUDSON, but for an unpractised youth like Mr.HADOW it was simply destruction. His companion, Mr.HUDSON, and the guide CROZ, acted incautiously in permitting him to go with them at all, and still more so in taking him up the dangerous slope when they found he was unequal to such work. The story, as told by

Mr. WHYMPER, is piteous in the extreme. Mr. HADOW evidently had no aptitude for such an expedition. In the ascent he had to be helped continually, and in coming down CROZ "had laid aside his axe, and, in order to give Mr. HADOW greater security, was absolutely taking hold of his legs, and putting his feet one by one into their proper positions." But all the care of this courageous and skilful guide was of no avail. HADOW slipped, knocked down CROZ, then HUDSON and Lord FRANCIS DOUGLAS were pulled from their feet, the rope broke, and all four were hurried to destruction.

The technicalities respecting the ropes and the proper means of using them we leave to others to discuss; but it is perhaps allowable to express a regret that Mr. WHYMPER'S suggestion to Mr. HUDSON, that they should attach a rope to the rocks on their arrival at the difficult part and hold it as they descended, was not acted upon. It was by this means that Professor TYNDALL and his guides were able to descend without accident in 1862.

It is, of course, futile to draw morals, particularly when the conclusion is such a truism as that no one ought to attempt Alpine ascents who is not thoroughly competent for them. But the chief guides of life are truisms of this kind, and we feel bound to impress on ambitious tourists, and almost equally on those who have the advising of them, that it is not given to every one to climb ice slopes, or even to walk across glaciers. Persons weak of lung or limb should not try such work at all, and even the strongest and most active should be aware that he can only attain to proficiency by long and gradual efforts. There is no exercise of bodily skill in which the difference between the unskilled and the expert is greater than in climbing an ice-glazed rock with an abyss beneath, and there is certainly none where the consequences of failure are so terrible. At a place where even an old sure-footed guide may become paralyzed with fear the mere novice in the Alps ought never to be found. The younger amateurs should mingle discretion with their courage, and the more experienced should make sure of the fitness of their companions before taking them on the more dangerous expeditions.

4.29
WIGRAM – WHYMPER

Furneaux Pelham, Buntingford.
9 August.

Dear Sir,

Since writing to you I have seen the *Times* of yesterday. I now propose to retain my letter to Croz and instead of it to forward to him a translation of the most important paragraphs of your account. You may depend upon this translation being well done & by an accomplished French scholar.

I would not have troubled you at all if I had known that you were about to give us the sad details.

Allow me in conclusion to add one word of sympathy; and to express my conviction that no mountaineer will impute to you either fault or rashness in connection with this terrible catastrophe.

Yrs sincerely

WOOLMORE WIGRAM.

E.Whymper Esq.

4.30

WHYMPER – WIGRAM (Whymper's copy; see also 4.33)

20 Canterbury Place
Lambeth Road. S.
Aug. 9. 1865.

Dear Mr. Wigram,

Unless I am mistaken I had the pleasure of meeting you at Zermatt 3 years ago when you were with T.S.Kennedy and you gave me a flask of spirits of wine which was used this year on the Matterhorn.

I cannot say that I am altogether surprised at the rumour to which you refer, as there is not amiable feeling (this year particularly) between the guides of Chamonix and the German guides, but the rumour is absolutely without foundation.

It occurred to me immediately after this fearful calamity that Taugwalder might be inclined to make away with the rope that broke, under the impression that it would save himself trouble, and I therefore asked him for it, and I have it here. It has not been tampered with since the accident, indeed it has hardly been handled and it is an absolute certainty that it broke fairly and was neither cut, nor as far as I can see, injured before it broke.

I can however express to you privately, but it ought not to go to Croz, as it could do no possible good and would only add to the ill feeling of which I have spoken, my extreme dissatisfaction with both the Taugwalders, but particularly with the younger man. They not only showed a most unmanly fear for their own lives, but directly we got to the easy part of the descent showed a heartlessness that was perfectly revolting. You will have seen the *Times* by this time and my letter. How it came to pass that the weakest rope was used between Taugwald and Lord Douglas I have no idea, that is, I have no idea why he did not use the stronger ropes. Still I have no reason to suspect even that this was done *intentionally*.

Although I have seen J.B.Croz we have never spoken to each other or travelled together, but I will write at once a short note to him to stop this horrible rumour. His poor brother I lament most deeply; we had made many expeditions together, and I think I may say we had the greatest confidence in and liking for each other. His loss is a public one, for he had the strength and courage of a lion, joined to a skill and sagacity rarely to [be] met with.

I think it would be desirable for you to write to Croz as well as myself, and pray give him my most positive assurance that there is not the slightest reason for suspecting that there was any foul play with the rope.

I am, dear Mr. Wigram,
Yours very faithfully
EDWARD WHYMPER.

4.31
BUXTON – WHYMPER (see 4.37)

Warlies, Waltham Abbey.
Aug 9 1865.

My Dear Sir,

I very deeply regret that my letter to the *Times* should have occasioned you pain, especially in reference to the accident with which you have so distressingly been connected. Allow me to assure you that nothing was further from my intention than to find fault with you or your party.

The fact was that on the news of the accident arriving there were several bitter attacks on the Alpine Club and all mountain climbers, attacks conveyed both by leading articles and letters in many different papers. The general sentiment was that all Alpine explorations were so far dangerous that it was morally wrong to undertake them, and I wrote for the purpose of showing that with care the danger was not greater than in hunting etc.

Mr.Glover's letter rather tended to confirm the general impression that no precautions could insure safety, and I pointed out where it appeared that precautions were wanting. From your most clear and graphic account I now see that I was misled by the then current accounts as to the imprudence of setting out without preparation and perhaps in some measure as to the rope.

Mr.Hadow was apparently the cause of the accident through his inexperience of difficult climbing, but I know how extremely difficult it is to object to a companion for any such reason.

I am most willing to say anything that would relieve your annoyance in reference to my letter, by pointing out my mistakes. I feel however I could hardly do so without attending to Mr.Hadow's inexperience, and the weaker ropes, or making it appear that the accident was unavoidable.

If any remember my letter, it must be clear to them that it was written under a mistaken impression of the facts. I am therefore of the opinion that it would be better to let it drop, though I am most willing to say anything that would be a satisfaction to yourself, if I can avoid giving any pain to Mr.Hadow's friends. I shall be very glad to hear your views on the subject; should it suit you to come to Warlies for a night on Monday or Tuesday in next week it would give Lady Victoria and myself great pleasure to see you. We might then arrange as to the best course to pursue.

I remain
Yours truly
T.FOWELL BUXTON.

Edward Whymper Esq.

4.32
WILLS – WHYMPER (see also 4.42)

Leeds.
9 Aug 1865.

Dear Whymper,

Thank you very much for your kind letter and for your prompt and effectual reply to my request. You have discharged a painful duty – and your narrative bears all the intrinsic marks of as much accuracy as possible under circumstances of such extremely painful excitement.

It is a sad story – and really becomes sadder by the knowledge we have gained – for it is impossible not to see that it was a good natured mistake, but still a mistake, on Hudson's part to take Hadow – and that in the second place, the slackened rope effectually did its deadly work. My brother and two others of our party would have lost their lives on the Col des Grandes Jorasses last year if we had allowed such length slack of rope [sic]. I know well the difficulty of being prudent when such a great success has been achieved – and I suppose our poor friend Hudson was not proof against excitement more than others.

Longman has asked me to write an art. for the Journal on this and some other of the late accidents. I shall try to do so – and may possibly ask you for a little more information. But I want you to busy yourself with other things and I will not do so if I can help it. I wish I could offer you anything more satisfactory than the expression of my sympathy – I do feel very deeply for you as must anyone who has a heart to feel – and I trust that though life looks bad enough to you just now, you may yet have happy and tranquil times in store, and may find returning peace and health as the vividness of this terrible experience becomes softened by time. I have passed myself scarcely less painful experiences – for I have known what it is to have the joy and the pride and the light of my life taken from me without warning and in an hour – and I have returned to the home I expected to find so bright and happy and on reaching it found that my joy was turned into mourning and sadness unutterable. I have lived through it, and by the mercy of God, have become, though a much older and very sobered man, yet I think more habitually cheerful than I was before. Pardon my troubling you with my own experience – I don't think – I hope it is not – that I do so in a spirit of egotism – but I could not help thinking that you might be glad to know from one who has gone through it all, that these things may be intensely and permanently felt and yet may not rob life in the end of its usefulness or its quieter and more abiding cheerfulness. No tinge of self reproach can mingle with your recollections of this sad catastrophe – and time and patience and trust will, I doubt not, work the cure they should do.

With every kind wish,
I remain, dear Whymper
Yours most truly
ALFRED WILLS.

E. Whymper Esq.
I would have written by the earlier post – but I have been extremely busy today.

4.33
WIGRAM – WHYMPER

Furneaux Pelham, Buntingford.
10 August.

Dear Mr. Whymper,

I made my former communications as brief as possible because I feel that in special times of either joy or sorrow none but an intimate friend has a right to intermeddle.

We did meet at Zermatt in 1862 just before my brother & I started with T.S. Kennedy to attack the Dent Blanche. Kennedy, who manages an ice axe better than a pen, gave an account of the ascent in the *Alpine Journal* but only a very indifferent narrative. During our absence on that expedition you had your fall on the Matterhorn. It was from my brother that you actually received the spirits of wine.

I never believed that there was any foundation whatever for the rumour I mentioned to you: and but that I think J.B. Croz believed it I should not have written. I regret much that he should have given ear to it; for the more one thinks of it the more improbable, not to say impossible, does it appear: and it is dreadful to entertain such suspicions & I like the man. I am not surprised at their using any rope you had with you: that you had brought it would be sufficient warrant in their eyes; and the best guides are too apt to think of a rope as a rope, even if it be an old rotten clothes line. I have absolutely known a man propose to take the line from the laundry ground at the Riffelberg.

My friend George Chater also was shocked at the indifference to human suffering & life displayed by the men employed by Jacomb and him on the occasion of the accident to wh. Mr. Wills refers. He believes that that porter's life was muddled away.

We know that Taugwalder's acquaintance with the pass from Zermatt to

Gressonay was acquired by smuggling: and if he has done much business of that kind he has probably drank hard so that his nerve is now failing or failed. He broke down altogether at the first attempt on la D.B. He returned to Kennedy from an attempt to surmount the last difficulties of the natural 'stoneman' on the crag arete of that mountn. pale, trembling and refusing to do anything but return immediately.

[There follows a lengthy paragraph reminiscing about Michel Croz]

I did not mean to gossip on at this length but perhaps being thrown out of the Alpine world my penchant for its life and the men who bustle [?] in it is stronger.

I will as far as possible reassure J.B.C.
Yours very faithfully,
WOOLMORE WIGRAM.

4.34
P.D.HADOW – McCORMICK

The Priory,
Sudbury, Middlesex,
August 10, 1865.

My dear Sir,

My brother tells me that you have probably now returned to London; I am very anxious to see you, if it were only to thank you in person for the kind and generous sympathy you have shewn in our own very sad and terrible bereavement; but I wish also to learn something more about the church proposed to be erected at Zermatt, and to have your advice as to the stone to be placed over the grave of my dear son and our friend Mr.Hudson.

We have been greatly distressed at Mr.Whymper's letter in the *Times*, and the leading article which I was sure would follow. I had thought from your published letter that all actually seen and known was there described as to the sad catastrophe, but Mr.Whymper now describes the details so minutely, as to lead people to suppose he must have seen it all, and the *Times* writes accordingly.

I think too that without keeping back anything material, he might have spared those unnecessary remarks about poor Mr.Hudson, which have brought blame on him for want of prudence and caution...

Yours very truly,
P.D.HADOW.

4.35
J.W. COWELL – WHYMPER (see 4.50-52)

41 Gloucester Terrace, Hyde Park.
Aug 11 1865.

Dear Sir,

I have repeatedly perused your account of the disaster on the Matterhorn and find it at last impossible for me to refrain from expressing the feelings of deep respect for you with which your narrative has impressed me. This can do no harm and I hope that you will not consider it intrusive. Perhaps however I might have repressed my desire to signify my sentiments on what to you must be so very painful a subject had I not observed that you had passed over in your narrative, some points in the demeanour of the Taugwalds which I venture to think it is due to yourself that you should consign to writing exactly in the manner in which you related them to my Son and myself at this house on Wednesday the 2nd of August.

You do not know what relations these men may endeavour to propagate – you were not permitted to be present at their examination at Zermatt – their answers to the questions which you proposed should be put to them have been withheld from you – there will be a strong *local* feeling at Zermatt to support any pretensions of these men to your detriment – you know what sort of men they are, and that their first thoughts after the dreadful disaster – and when, alone & unprotected you appeared almost at their mercy – were to urge you so to shape your account of it in such a manner as should turn to their pecuniary advantage.

You have yet to learn what they have said, and what impression it may make.

I submit to you that it would be prudent, not only as regards yourself, but also as regards the memory of those who are gone, to consign to writing exactly what you communicated to my Son & myself on the 2nd of August, so that we might, if the necessity for your making it public should arise hereafter, be in a condition to certify that what you may say regarding these men is no afterthought. And I think besides that some such step as this is called for in regard to the English who may visit Zermatt, & whose generous sympathies may be otherwise enlisted in favour of very undeserving persons in all respects.

Pardon this suggestion. My son is out of town and I cannot consult him regarding it.

Believe me
My dear Sir
With deepest respect
Your faithful humble servant
JOHN W.COWELL.

4.36
MRS. HUDSON – WHYMPER

Sharow Parsonage
Ripon. Au: 11th. 1865.

Dear Sir,

Having obtained your address from a friend, I feel I can no longer delay writing to you. I am at a loss to find words to express all the gratitude I feel towards one, who wd. have saved the life of my dear husband if he could.

When I think of how you started off again, after all the horror & fatigue of the previous days, – to look for those whom you *knew* no human help could avail, – I can only say, God bless you for it! – and I am sure you will undertand me when I say, that these are the only words I can find.

The blow has been a terrible one to me, but it has not shaken my faith in God's overruling Providence. I believe that it has been for some wise & good purpose of his own, that he has permitted this sad calamity to happen, and I trust good may come out of it to all concerned. It wd. be a sad pleasure to me to see you some day; as one of the last persons who saw my beloved husband in life. As my home will in future be at Norwood Street I may have this opportunity ere very long.

Believe me
Y'rs very truly
EMILY A. HUDSON.

4.37
WHYMPER – BUXTON (Whymper's copy)

Town House
Haslemere
Aug 12 1865

My dear Sir,

I am greatly obliged and relieved by your letter of the 9th and I quite agree with you that it is best to let the subject drop.

I regret that I am unable to accept your invitation but I shall doubtless have the opportunity one day of expressing my thanks for your very kind answer as I now quite understand the motive of your letter to the *Times*, and understand that which appeared to me to be objectionable arose entirely from the erroneous reports that were published at first.

I am, my dear Sir
Yours very truly
EDWARD WHYMPER

Sir T.F.Buxton.

4.38
WILLS – *THE TIMES*

TO THE EDITOR OF THE TIMES (published 14.8.65)

Sir,– The terribly simple and intelligible story of the Matterhorn disaster is now known to us all. Mr. Whymper's clear and manly narrative, told with a candour and honesty which give him an additional claim on the sympathy of every feeling heart, strips the calamity of all mystery or doubt. One lesson it inculcates with awful distinctness you have already pointed out. Young and inexperienced climbers should neither go nor be taken on expeditions of this kind. Another warning, hardly less distinctly uttered and hardly less important, but valuable chiefly to those who engage in similar undertakings, is against the slackened rope – the best friend of the climber converted only too easily into his most insidious and dangerous foe.

But I do not propose to enlarge on these topics. I have been urging prudence and caution, as the members of the Alpine Club well know, till I fancy some of my younger friends have almost begun to think that I was losing nerve and enterprise; and both at the Club and in private I have not ceased to express my conviction that the insulted majesty of nature would repudiate by some terrible example the notion that her grandest and most solemn fastnesses might be safely won by every novice in the mysteries of mountain craft. If the sad lessons she has read us in the untimely deaths of men whom to know was to admire and to love do not find their way home to those to whom they are addressed, it is certain that no words of mine can be of any avail. But it is, perhaps, not an unfitting moment to refer to another danger, less obvious and more insidious, but of which I think quite as seriously as of the actual risk of instant loss of life or limb which threatens many of our mountaineers, especially the younger ones, and that is the danger of over-exertion...

I did not pay much heed to such considerations when I was younger, and I have not too much expectation of being listened to myself; but if, by the kindness and confidence of my Alpine friends, I have been placed in a position of some influence among them, the least I can do is so far to justify their choice as to show that the rashness and folly which some persons who have little taste for mountain pleasures themselves are so fond of attributing to the members of the Alpine Club are not the qualities for which they have elected their principal officer. The Alpine Club has to answer for giving a new direction as well as some extension to that intense love for beautiful scenery which, I venture to think, is a good characteristic of our day. It has to answer for opening a new field – and, I venture to think, a glorious field – for the expenditure of that physical energy which active men, when they get their leisure, will work off in some way or other – in shooting, fishing, hunting, boating, or cricketing, if not in climbing. It has to answer for bringing together men of common tastes in these matters, and enabling them to compare their different experiences and to profit by one another's successes, difficulties, and failures; and by so doing it has, I believe, saved many a life and prevented many an accident, not only to its own members, but to those who benefit indirectly by a slow but definite improvement which is taking place in the race of guides, and which has already reached beyond the higher class of men who are brought more directly within the influence of the Alpine Club. But I say unhesitatingly that the Club has not only not given its sanction and encouragement to rash and ill-considered enterprises, but has done what it could to ascertain and make known the conditions under which a kind of enjoyment, blameless and elevating when pursued with due regard to safety and duty, may be properly and prudently indulged in, and to place within the reach of those who may be willing to profit by its labours information, appliances, and facilities without which the element of danger, from which no manly sport is wholly free, would have been infinitely greater and more calamitous.

I am, Sir, your most obedient servant,
ALFRED WILLS,
Inner Temple, Aug.11. President of the Alpine Club.

4.39
QUEENSBERRY – WHYMPER (see also 4.53)

Glen Stuart, Annan. NB.
Thursday 17th [August] 65.

My dear Whymper,

I heard a report of what you told me in your telegraph yesterday but I cannot think it is true, it is not in the *Times*. Besides they would surely have sent me the first new's

Thank you very much for offering yourself for anything but I hardly know yet what would be done if his poor body was found.

If there is anything to be done I will let you know.

Believe me
Yours sincerely
QUEENSBERRY

4.40
WHYMPER – GLOVER (see also 4.44)

20 Canterbury Place,
Lambeth Road S.
Aug. 18. 1865.

Dear Mr.Glover,

Your letter of July 31st has been forwarded to me by a friend who found it at the Club rooms; pray excuse my not having replied to it before as I have been overwhelmed by letters.

People talk of the vanity of human wishes and we have all felt at some time or another that they are vanity, but never have I felt it as I do at the present. For five years I have dreamt of the Matterhorn; I have spent much labour and time upon it – and I have done it. And now the very name of it is hateful to me. I am tempted to curse the hour I first saw it; congratulations on its achievement are bitterness and ashes and that which I hoped would yield pleasure produces alone the severest pain: it is a sermon I can never forget.

I saw your letter soon after its appearance and feel obliged for the pains you had taken to place me in a favourable light before the public. I could not however help regretting and I am sure you must do so yourself, the reference you made to poor Douglas. A more excellent walker and promising mountaineer I never came across, and had it not been for that final meeting with the others, as far as man can see, we should have made the ascent in perfect safety. What a series of accidents life is altogether. Last year I was at Zermatt intending to go by the same route as we followed this year. I was however obliged by business to return without trying. If it had not been for that I should doubtless have done it then, and we should not most likely have had to deplore this frightful calamity. If again, we had had our dinner on the 12th. only half an hour earlier, I should have missed seeing Hudson and Hadow and it might again have been prevented. So far as I am personally concerned I cannot feel myself in blame at all, except for allowing Hadow to go; in other respects if I had known what was to happen, I think I should have acted exactly as I did.

I write from my office, my time is divided between this and Haslemere, but I am principally here, therefore should you desire to write on any matter, please to address as above.

I am, dear Mr. Glover,
Yours very faithfully,
EDWARD WHYMPER.

4.41
H.HADOW – WHYMPER (see 4.43)

The Priory, Sudbury,
Middlesex.

Dear Sir,

My absence in Wiltshire since my return from Zermatt must be my apology for not having sooner requested you to let me know the amount of the bill you paid for my late nephew. If you will be so good as to inform me the amount at the above address it shall be remitted by return of post.

I beg to remain,
Dear Sir,
Yours faithfully,
HENRY HADOW.

19th August 1865.

4.42
WILLS – WHYMPER

Ruby Cottage,
Malvern Wells,
Worcestershire.
20 August 1865.

Dear Whymper,

I am much obliged by your note and very glad you have written about Croz. I enclose a subscription of £20 for them. Will you please add a stamp and put "A W 21 Aug" across it, as I have not one here and cannot get one to-day.

Mr.McCormick has been trying to improve the occasion just as a clergyman would do. He wrote – or rather got Reilly to write – a letter to me suggesting that 'the Club' should build his church as a memorial to Hudson. This I told him I thought was out of the question but said I would be pleased to subscribe myself to *a* memorial to Hudson and his companions and that from my knowledge of Hudson and his professional zeal, I was very much inclined to think the building of a church at Zermatt would be a sort of thing he would have liked himself though I added that in my opinion a church was very little use in a place where people evidently did not think it worthwhile to pay the moderate sum required for one – straightaway Mr.McCormick writes to the *Times*. There is no sort of propriety in inviting a *public* subscription. It is the thing for the friends of our friends to do – and for others to join in it would make the thing far less worth than it otherwise would be.

Now as to the statement you have so kindly forwarded to me. I take a little different view from you as to the desirability of saving the Taugwalders from the natural & proper consequences of their scandalous conduct. So much do *I* feel this that I was intending to write to you & say that your narrative left on my mind the strong impression that in this respect there was something behind wh. I intended to urge you when you wrote for the Journal to set forth. I think a great deal of mischief is done by shielding fellows like this. They get quite enough of that at Zermatt & amongst their own people, and it is greatly for the *public* benefit that people of this sort shd. be *exposed*. I crossed the Trift last yr. with a mixture of brag, bullying, selfishness & cowardice named Kronig: I have never hesitated to say what I thought of him, not I assure you from any revengeful feeling but because I felt it to be quite shocking that such a fellow should fall to the lot of others as he did to mine in consequence of a heap of laudatory writings concerning him wh. I am quite convinced he never *can* have deserved. These Taugwalders are not fit to be trusted – & the world ought to know it: & I think myself, if you will pardon me for saying so, that you will make a great mistake if you hesitate to speak of them as they should be spoken of.

As Mr.Cowell senr. has written you so kind & so judicious a letter if you are disposed to consult him on the matter again, I should be very glad if you would show him what I have said about it & see how it strikes him. I would suggest to you also to let him and his son write under your narrative that it is in substance or in any way they like to put it what you told them on the 2nd Aug. & let me write also that I read it on the 20th. Life is a very uncertain thing with the best of us & you may be glad (though it is not likely that what you say will ever be called in question) to have it in writing that so & so has seen it & that so & so knows it is what you told him at first...

Meanwhile believe me dear Whymper
Yours most faithfully
ALFRED WILLS.

4.43
WHYMPER – H.HADOW (Whymper's copy)

20 Canterbury Place
Lambeth Road. S.
Aug. 21. 1865.

Dear Sir,

In reply to yours of the 19th requesting me to state the amount of the bill I paid for your late nephew, I have to say that I cannot call to mind having paid any bill for him. Mr.McCormick repaid me your share of the amounts I paid to the guides after the search at the base of the mountain and also your share of the provision bill. I remitted 100 francs by Mr.Reilly to the family of Michel Croz as payment for the two days but paid nothing on account of the work he had previously done as I had no means of learning what was due. I paid Taugwalder 100, his son 80, and the porter 20.

We divided these amounts among the four and your share of the whole including provisions and for the searching expedition amounted to 114fr. 25 centimes.

This as I have said was repaid by Mr.McCormick & I have no note in my book of having made any other payments.

4.44
GLOVER – WHYMPER

Christ Church Parsonage, Dover.
23 August 1865.

My Dear Whymper,

Many thanks for your interesting letter. I was not surprised at your delay in answering it for I knew how you would be overwhelmed with letters, and could sympathise fully in the pain you must experience in writing on the subject.

I do not wonder at the nature of your feelings with regard to the Matterhorn *now*. It is as you very rightly say, another proof of the vanity of human wishes and of the disappointing character of human ambition however harmless or even laudable it may often be. There is only one hard climb concerning which he may cry "Excelsior" without any fear of ultimate disappointment and vain regret, and I trust you know something of *that* climb.

You are quite right in supposing that I now regret my allusion to poor Lord Francis Douglas in my letter. I do so most sincerely and I so expressed myself in my second letter to the *Times* which I dare say you saw at the time. I have very little leisure for such employments and I write too hastily – and so far foolishly. I have endeavoured to make the "amende honorable" but none the less regret hazarding such an unwise and useless conjecture. As to yourself no one *has* blamed and no one *can* blame you – and I hope you are allowing yourself freedom from self reproach.

May I be permitted to trouble you with a trifle for the Michel Croz fund. I wish I could make it more worthy of acceptance, but every little will help – and although I was with him so short a time I should like to have the satisfaction of just sending a mite of 5/-

Don't come into this neighbourhood without coming to see me. We shall at any time be glad to give you hospitality and a warm welcome.

Ever very faithfully,
RICHARD GLOVER.

4.45
P.D.HADOW – WHYMPER

Pacific and Oriental Steam Navigation Company,
Offices. 122 Leadenhall Street,
London EC. August 23 1865.

Dear Sir,

I have just been informed by Messrs. Goupil that it is their intention to publish a print of the catastrophe of the "Matterhorn" and that you are going to supply the drawing for it, while I am actually asked to supply a likeness of my dear son for the picture.

I can hardly say how much pain and distress such a proceeding would cause to ourselves and to Mrs.Hudson, who has written to us on the subject. I have no wish to interfere with parties who may wish to publish drawings of the scene of this sad accident, but they might surely spare the feelings of those relatives who have already suffered so much, and abstain from bringing forward again to notoriety the victims of this fatal occurrence.

I venture therefore to hope that you will exert your influence with the publishers and the artist to omit from the design any attempted likeness of

Mr.Hudson or of my son; their insertion could not in any way improve it, while it would be most distasteful to all the relatives and friends of the deceased. Glad indeed should we be if a veil could now be drawn over this distressing occurrence.

I am dear Sir,
Yours very truly,
P.D.HADOW.

4.46
WHYMPER – P.D.HADOW (Whymper's copy)

20 Canterbury Place,
Lambeth Road.
Aug 23 1865.

Dear Sir,

I take the earliest opportunity of replying to your letter of to-day.

You have either been misinformed by Messrs Goupil or else you have misunderstood their communication in as much as it regards myself.

For *several weeks* past Messrs. Goupil have exhibited in Paris, two large drawings by Gustave Doré, one of the accident and the other of the summit of the mountain. At the same time they publicly announced that they were going to publish these drawings, which I have been informed by a friend are grossly inaccurate in almost every particular.

On Friday last Messrs. Goupil sent me the enclosed letter by which you will see that I am a total stranger to their house.

On Saturday one of their employees called here by my desire and I found that they were determined to publish the drawing whether they had correct material or not. I imagined that I was neither offending against good taste or good feeling in promising to give a sketch of the spot; supposing indeed that you would prefer a correct to an incorrect representation of it. At the same time I expressed my opinion that it was bad taste to publish the drawing, declined to give them the slightest assistance in procuring the portraits of my unfortunate companions and said that I believed any application for them would be altogether useless.

I greatly regret that anything I have done should have caused you the slightest pain or annoyance and I shall immediately withdraw my promise to help Messrs. Goupil to produce a correct representation of the spot, and at the same time – with your permission, forward them a copy of your letter. I am sorry to say that I believe it will be of no use to endeavour to prevent them publishing the drawings.

I have endeavoured in all that I have done since this much lamentable accident, to avoid giving pain to yourself and to the relatives of Lord Douglas and Mr.Hudson.

I came home with a firm intention to print nothing and to say nothing. I found this was impossible. Most injurious rumours were circulated and I was forced – most unwillingly, to write to the *Times*; a more difficult and more painful task it is impossible to imagine.

It gives me the greatest pain to see from the tenor of your letter you have been led to believe that the idea of publishing these drawings was more or less originated or helped by myself but I trust that you will no longer entertain any such idea, as it is entirely without foundation.

I am overwhelmed by letters, and therefore I shall esteem it a great favour if you will forward this letter and its enclosure to Mrs.Hudson to save my writing in duplicate, and on their return I shall be obliged if you will forward the letter of Messrs Goupil to me.

I am dear Sir,
Yours very truly,
EDWARD WHYMPER.

P.D.Hadow Esq.

4.47
P.D.HADOW – WHYMPER

Sudbury Priory,
Middlesex.
Aug. 26 1865.

My dear Sir,

I beg to thank you for your prompt answer to my letter. I have forwarded it to Mrs.Hudson to whom I am sure it will be as satisfactory as to me.

I had no intention, nor do I now wish to interfere with your arrangements for supplying a correct sketch of the mountain or of the scene of this lamentable catastrophe, but gathering from Messrs. Goupil's letter that they proposed to introduce portraits or attempted likeness into the sketch you were to furnish, I ventured to solicit your influence to prevent that part of the work being done, for the reasons which must be obvious to any person of good taste.

With regard to your letter in the *Times* after Mr.McCormick's account, there were indeed some portions which caused us pain, as they appeared to enter into unnecessary details; I have however no desire to criticise these for I can well believe you had a difficult and painful [task]; I would much rather take the opportunity of sincerely thanking you for your gallant and successful exertions in recovering the remains of our dear boy and his companions, which at first seemed so improbable.

Yours very truly,
P.D.HADOW.

I will return Messrs. Goupil's letter.

4.48
ROBERTSON – McCORMICK

7 New Street,
Rugby.
[Undated. c.26.8.65.]

My dear McCormick,

We came back to our duties here yesterday. From your letter which was awaiting me, I gather that you have not had any communications with the Wilsons. Captain W. with a brother and a daughter started for Zermatt just after I went to see them at Windsor, and had hoped they might still find you there. I have not heard from them yet, but no doubt shall hear soon...

For a fortnight past I have been vegetating at Bangor and Llandudno alone and dreary. The weather was too bad for excursions & on the whole it is as well for me to begin work again, though one does not like it first...

I suppose you have seen and been a little pained by the villainous little paragraph in this week's *Punch*. But anyone who knows enough of the case to know that you are referred to, will be pretty sure to know also enough to see how utterly pointless vulgar & unfair the words are. So I don't think you need much mind it. I wrote off last night a very earnest letter about it to Mark Lennon, and even if the formalities of journalism do not admit of an apology, I trust he may fire the contributor a wigging for his pains. I am sure that all who had any thing to do with that week's events feel most warmly towards you for the way in which you bore your own share of the burden & helped them to bear theirs.

My visits to London are few & short but I hope to see you sometime either there or here. Perhaps you may be able to turn up at some of our great foot-ball matches. They are worth seeing.

Yours very sincerely
JAMES ROBERTSON.

I have no doubt Phillpotts will write to you himself soon. Let me know if I owe you any francs for anything that turned up after I left Zermatt.

4.49
WHYMPER – ROBERTSON

Town House,
Haslemere.
Aug 27. 1865.

Dear Robertson,

I am glad to see your handwriting, and gratefully acknowledge the receipt of your cheque for 2£ towards the Croz fund.

I was extremely sorry to miss you at Visp; I got in there very late (11.15) and was surprised to find my packet there although you were not. I did not like to call on you at the other place at midnight, and went off by the early diligence while, I suppose, you were still reposing. The manner in which I was persecuted by impertinent people on my way home passes all belief.

You were right in supposing that letter was a difficult one to write. It appears to have given satisfaction to most people, but not to all, as I will show you one day. I would have stuck to the resolution I made at Zermatt had it been possible, but it was not; all kinds of pleasant rumours were propagated and among them it was said that *I* cut the rope from fear of being pulled over. The amount of silly nonsense that was being written rendered it also desirable that I should write. Therefore after having recd two letters from Wills pressing me to write, two from the Ed. of *Times* and a score of others from friends whose opinion I value more or less, I gave way.

I do not know of any friends of Hudson's of the names you mention. Is it Gray? I know he has relatives of that name.

I have not seen the paragraph which you mention in *Punch*, but I will look for it. There was a tolerably strong and intolerably stupid article in *All the year round* of the week before last which irritated me somewhat. But really after all, abuse or condemnation by these kinds of people does not amount to much. Slander is another matter. I shall be due at Birmingham for the Assn about the 9th Septr, and as I should like to see you and Phillpotts, if only for five minutes, I will see if it is not possible to give you call about that date, but I will not occupy much of your valuable time.

I am dear Robertson
Yours very faithfully
EDWARD WHYMPER.

I had almost forgotten to tell you that the reason we started the Croz fund was, that we feared, and fear, Jean B.Croz will go out of his mind, and will probably have to be placed in confinement.

4.50
J.W.COWELL – WHYMPER

41 Gloucester Terrace, Hyde Park.
Sepr.4. 1865.

My dear Sir,

I return Mr.Wills letter [4.42] and your memorandum [4.51] – with mine and my son's certificate [4.52] as to its authenticity as we heard it from you on Aug 2.

If I may be permitted to pass an opinion upon anything you have done in this most painful affair it would be that you paid those Ruffians a farthing more than they were entitled to by agreement. I sympathize with the feeling which leads us as Englishmen on every occasion of service to us in disaster, to be over generous in reward or in compensation but on this occasion I think it was – if I may take the liberty of saying so – a duty devolving on you in the odious circumstances of the conduct of the Taugwalders, to have repressed every emotion of generosity. Any thing savouring of the character of reward, or of generosity to such men offers necessarily the very worst example to others like them, and really holds out a sort of inducement to guides to promote accidents and misfortunes when they see that in previous instances guides have received large pecuniary benefits from having been present at their occurrence.

I hope that a good collection will be made for poor Croz's family; I hope that a small tablet will be erected to his memory in the church at Chamouny.

But I also hope that you will be called upon to publish all you know about the Taugwalders, and I trust that the Club will, upon consideration of the matter, invite you to do so.

Excuse this expression of my sentiments, and since Mr. Wills in his letter to you, does me the honour of referring to my opinion I venture to hope that you will communicate this letter to him, and I remain my dear Sir, with the deepest respect

very faithfully yours
JOHN W. COWELL.

4.51
WHYMPER'S MEMORANDUM

Memorandum of a conversation between Peter Taugwalder fils and myself at 6.30 p.m. on July 14th 1865.

We had descended from the difficult part of the Matterhorn and were sitting eating on some snow at the commencement of the easy part. The Taugwalders, father and son, talked together in their patois for two or three minutes, and the son then said in French.

"Herr."

"Yes."

"We are poor men; we have lost our Herr; we shall not get paid, we can ill afford this."

"Stop", said I, interrupting him, "that is nonsense, I shall pay you of course, just as if Lord Douglas were here."

They talked together again for a short time and then the young man spoke again,

"We don't wish you to pay us; we wish you to write in the hotel book at Zermatt and to your journals that we have not been paid."

"What nonsense are you talking?" I said. "I don't understand you, what do you mean?"

The young man proceeded,

"Why next year there will be many travellers at Zermatt, and we shall get more voyageurs."

I was so disgusted with this heartless talk that for the whole distance down to Zermatt I did not speak, – excepting when I was obliged, and this probably gave rise to the rumour that I had not uttered a single word during the whole of that fearful night. And when the Taugwalders suggested that we should continue the descent by moonlight, and again that I should lay down and endeavour to sleep when we stopped, I objected, feeling that men who could view the loss of their fellow creatures with such commercial feelings as these, might not, possibly, be ill pleased if I also slipped. They seemed to understand that what they had said was displeasing to me, for during the whole of the time (8 days) that I remained at Zermatt after the accident, I did not even see either of them until the last two days. The son indeed left Zermatt for Chamonix soon after the accident and I did not see him at all excepting for half a minute. It is unnecessary to say that they *were* paid, and paid the highest price ever given for mountain ascents.

Aug. 17. 1865. EDWARD WHYMPER.

4.52
COWELL MEMORANDUM

London. Sepr 1. 1865. 41 Gloucester Terrace, Hyde Park.

The foregoing Memorandum [4.51] records the substance of a communication made to the Undersigned on Wednesday August 2. 1865 by Edward Whymper in answer to questions which they put to him. But it was fuller, more comprehensive and more significant than this Mem: exhibits it.

Edward Whymper informed us that upon the occurrence of the Catastrophe the Taugwalders displayed the most abject cowardice, entire want of resource – utter and helpless bewilderment – that after he had succeeded in rallying them and enabled them to reach a place of comparative safety, the young one broke out into frightful levity, displaying the most brutal insensibility – eating – drinking – smoking – laughing – vociferating – that then the two, after consulting together apart for some time, made to him the horrible proposal that he should enable them to make a more lucrative market of the Catastrophe by leaving them unpaid and publicly announcing that they would take no payment: so that he would save his money and they wd. profit by public esteem & sympathy – that their demeanour gradually became, and continued to be, suggestive of personal danger to himself – that at night they, as it were, hustled him to induce him to attempt the further descent *by Moonlight* – that thereafter they urged him to lie down in a manner so importunate and minatory as to induce him to place himself with his back to a rock and with his axe in his hand to order them to keep at a greater distance from him – and that he passed the night standing in that manner and prepared to defend himself.

The inferences which arose in our minds from what E.Whymper described were that the Taugwalders saw that the additional loss of E.Whymper would afford them an opening to a future notoriety of a very lucrative nature, and that they were prepared to avail themselves of any opportunity that might offer during the descent of bringing about that loss – and Edward Whymper did not deny to us that similar inferences suggested themselves to him during the whole of that dreadful night.

JOHN W.COWELL
JOHN JERMYN COWELL

4.53
QUEENSBERRY – WHYMPER

Glen Stuart, Annan. N.B.
Sunday 10th. [August 65]

My dear Whymper,

I enclose you a photo of my dear brother as I promised.

Yours very sincerely
QUEENSBERRY

4.54
C.PARKER – HIS FATHER

3 October 1865.

My dear Father,

...Am curious to hear what passed when Margt. & Sandbach met Whymper. If I had known they were to meet him I sd. have asked Sandbach to try to make out the truth about Peter Taugwalder. I am under engagement to write to him, and I am waiting to try to pick up something more. Of course nothing is easier than to tell him in writing, what he was not content to be told when I saw him, that there is no sort of truth in the belief (wh. at Zermatt is universal) that a money-reward was to be given for the first ascent of the Matterhorn.

But what I wanted also to ascertain for him is whether he had better make up his mind at once that the payment he rec'd. is final & cannot be reconsidered.

I want to ascertain this without letting it be mentioned in such a way as to give me the appearance of a meddler. It is very possible that the payment was just what was right under the circumstances. But all I yet know is this, that

Whymper and Taugwalder very possibly misunderstood each other, at any rate each is aggrieved at the other.

Whymper says that Taugwalder behaved ill, imperilled Whymper's life and was greedy about pay. Taugwalder says Whymper behaved ill, especially in the colouring he gave to his evidence at Zermatt wh. has damaged Taugwalder, that *he saved Whymper's life*, as it is certain if he had not held on that Whymper being tied to him by a strong rope must have fallen with him. He and his son were also the only guides in descending, & one cant expect guides to admit that he wd have got down alone, much less that he took them down as he wd have us believe. Taugwalder is a very good cragsman & Whymper is said to be a bad one. And as regards the payment Taugwalder says that he was *promised* a much larger sum, that he wd. never have run so much risk for the payment he recd. (120 francs, and his son 80), and that he has had no opportunity of being heard on this matter by anyone but Whymper, who had quarrelled with him.

I thought I cd. hardly refuse his request to make some inquiry for him in England. Perhaps the best way wd. be for me to see Whymper – casually if I can. But if I had known Sandbach was to meet him, I wd. have asked him to make out how the land lay. Will you show him this, wh. I fear may only bother you, and ask him if anything he heard throws light on the matter. Dont let it be talked about so as to come round to Whymper...

4.55
WHYMPER – LADY QUEENSBERRY (Whymper's copy)

20 Canterbury Place,
Lambeth Road,
Dec 16. 1865.

Dear Lady Queensberry,

I have endeavoured, but without success, to procure for you the best photograph of the Matterhorn that is published. I am afraid it is not to be had in London, and I have sent to Paris for it. I would have let you have my own copy willingly, but that some time since I sent it to Mrs Hudson.

I have not seen the lines to which you refer and should like to do so, for anything that refers to my poor companion has for me a sad interest. I am sure that all who met your son feel very deeply the loss you have sustained and no one more so than myself for he frequently spoke of going home to join you in a way that shewed even a stranger how much he loved you. It was terrible to have him taken away, and be powerless to help him. I shall ever feel his loss as that of a friend, although I had seen so little of him, for in those few days he shewed himself as kind & gentle as he was brave and skilful.

Pardon my writing these things; ...we may never meet and I may never have again the opportunity of expressing my sorrow and sympathy for your bereavement. Should you require my aid again in a matter like the present I will do whatever I can to further your wishes.

I am,
dear Lady Queensberry
yours very obediently
EDWD WHYMPER.

4.56
LADY QUEENSBERRY – WHYMPER

East Warriston
Friday

Dear Mr. Whymper,

Thank you I do *very* sincerely for this kindness. The photograph will be doubly valuable to me as coming from yourself. The Mark too wh. you have made to show the spot from wh. they fell is to *me* so interesting because I can imagine how very possible it was for my precious one to have remained somewhere above in the rocks, wh. I had *always* believed to be the case *most* firmly – tho' by the *first* spot pointed out to me as from whence they fell I cd. scarcely see how it cd. be so.

With repeated thanks I remain
Yrs. very sincerely
CAROLINE QUEENSBERRY.

4.57
MACKENZIE – *THE TIMES*

TO THE EDITOR OF THE TIMES (published 1?.9.66)

Sir,– *[the letter begins with a reference to Loppé]*

Before terminating this letter I may communicate another little matter which will interest some of your readers, in as much as it has reference to last year's melancholy event on the Mont Cervin at Zermatt.

A monument had been ordered to be erected over the graves of the deceased gentlemen who perished on that too memorable occasion, in the churchyard at Zermatt, and inquiries had been made whether any impediment existed or any steps were required to be taken to obtain the requisite permission from the competent authorities; the answer was that no difficulty existed, and no order required.

The workmen were sent up last week with the stone completed for putting up the monument, when suddenly the Communal Council made a demand of 5,000f. (200l.) for the ground.

I immediately put myself in communication with the Cantonal authorities of the Valais, informing them of what had occurred, and craving their protection from so preposterous and vexatious a demand upon our countrymen.

I am credibly informed that the Communal Council of Zermatt have based their exaction upon the fact of their having received a similar sum from a Russian family who lost a relation by accident on one of the Zermatt glaciers; but the money was a gift to the parish, and not paid in consequence of any demand or right of the parish authorities at Zermatt.

I have, however, taken the matter in hand, and we do not intend to pay any more for our ground than any other inhabitant of the Commune would have to pay under similar circumstances, and if we manage to agree upon this important point the relations of the deceased gentlemen can give what they choose voluntarily afterward; but on public grounds we are bound to resist such unwarrantable and unreasonable demands.

Begging you will excuse the length of this letter, I remain, Sir, yours faithfully,

A.M'KENZIE, Her Britannic Majesty's Consul, British Consulate,
Geneva, Sept, 7.

4.58
WHYMPER – ROBERTSON

20 Canterbury Place,
Lambeth Road S.
Sept. 29 1866.

My dear Robertson,

I want to ask your assistance and advice on these two points. And first as to the advice.

Do you think the enclosed inscription can be taken exception to, either in taste or truthfulness? or do you see any way in which it can be readily improved? It is intended to go on a tomb that is erected in Zermatt churchyard in memory of poor Croz, and I want to send it out as soon as possible, as the mason is waiting in Zermatt to cut it.

Now as to the assistance. I want to have it turned into French, and correct French. Of course I could do it myself, or get a translator in London to do it, but this won't do. I want it as well, and as elegantly (to use a word I detest) rendered as I can get it, and it has occurred to me that it might be accomplished by your intervention. I have a lively recollection of the kindness of M.Vecqueray, and I do not call to mind anyone who would be likely to do it as well as he, or who would take the pains that I think he would be likely to exercise.

What I wish then, and I ask it with hesitation, is, that you will endeavour to obtain the translation of this epitaph by M.Vecqueray. It should be scarcely becoming for myself, almost a stranger, to prefer the request, or I would not trouble you in the matter, and it will be doing me a genuine favour if you will make it. I have already mentioned that I wish to send the inscription out as soon as possible; therefore, should anything prevent the accomplishment of my wishes please to be so kind as to let me know without loss of time.

I have not heard whether you went Alpwards this year. My own time was only sixteen days away from England, and almost every day was favoured with rain, wind and snow, each in excess. I did not go out wishing to make ascents or passes, having, as you may suppose, not quite so much appetite for this sort of thing as I had, but I went out nevertheless for definite objects, and I got as hard scrambling and walking as ever I have had. I have done with the Alps now and am getting rid of my properties, which looks as if I meant it.

I am, my dear Robertson,
Yours very faithfully,
EDWARD WHYMPER.

[PS] I shall be glad of an early answer as Seiler, who is looking after the matter, leaves Zermatt shortly. "Not far from here" will render better in French. I shall be glad to have any suggestion as to the disposition of the lines, which is always difficult.

In Memory
of
Michel-Auguste Croz
of le Tour, valley of Chamounix
this monument is erected
as an expression of regret
for the loss
of
a brave man.

Beloved by his comrades
and esteemed by his employers
he died not far from here
trying to preserve the life
of another.

4.59
ROBERTSON – WHYMPER

7 New Street,
Rugby.
Octr. 14th.

My dear Whymper,

These should have been sent off to you yesterday; but Vecqueray had reckoned on meeting me last night at a party where I was not. I am sorry they are so late. He was glad to do it.

1 is a literal translation of yours.

2 a slight modification which Vecqueray and I both think better. The French runs nicely, and as Croz could only be said to die while saving another in so far as he was engaged with poor Hadow's helplessness throughout it might jar needlessly in some ears.

I thought 'voyageurs' as near 'employers' as would be courteous in French. I hope either 1 or 2 will do...

Everyone says you're going to Greenland. Is it so?

Yours sincerely
JAMES ROBERTSON.

1

A la Mémoire
de
Michel Auguste Croz
de le Tour (vallée de Chamounix)
cette tombe a été élevé
comme témoignage de regret
à la perte d'
un homme Brave.

Aimé de ses compagnons
et estimé des voyageurs
il périt non loin d'ici
en tâchant de sauver
la vie d'un autre

2

A la Mémoire
de
Michel Auguste Croz,
né à le Tour (vallée de Chamounix)
en témoignage de regret
à la perte d'un
homme brave et devoué.

Aimé de ses compagnons,
estimé des voyageurs,
il périt non loin d'ici
en homme de coeur et guide fidèle.

4.60
PENNELL – TYNDALL

Septr. 4th. 1871.
1, Powis Square,
Notting Hill.

Prof. Tyndall. F.R.S.
Sir,

I trust you will excuse me – (an utter stranger) writing to you – but I should feel much obliged if you would let me know whether you supposed Joseph Pierre Maquignaz went alone up the Matterhorn in the autumn of 67? I have just been reading yr. book with great interest but feel surprised at several statements in yr. last ascent on the Matterhorn. You speak of the ropes that I believe my brother spent many extra hours on the mountain for the purpose of arranging as – 'rope left by Maquignaz' – & also speak as though the guide knew nothing of the Zermatt side of the Matterhorn. I believe when my brother (Mr.Jordan) persuaded those two guides to attempt the ascent with him not having (for various reasons) been able to get a guide that knew anything of the mountain – that they *then* in 67 crossed over from Breuil to Zermatt being the first ascent after the fearful accident in 65 – & they found several vestiges [of] it – the ice axe of Michel Croz – I believe & other articles – & my brother felt confident that he could distinguish the missing body – hanging over a ledge of rock – but thought it wld only tend to harrow the feelings of his friends did he make it known. My brother unfortunately is in South America but I am sending your book – & perhaps he may write about it –

Trusting you will excuse my writing
I am yours truly
ELIZA PENNELL.

4.61
DIXIE – *DAILY GRAPHIC*

TO THE EDITOR OF THE DAILY GRAPHIC (published 1905)

Sir, I do not pretend to account for the following incident, but only know and vouch for the fact that it took place. When I was a very little child, my second brother (Lord Francis Douglas), then barely eighteen years of age, was killed in the first successful ascent of the Matterhorn. The accident took place on July 14th, my mother's birthday. That night my mother and myself were in London, passing through it en route for home. We stayed there one night to break the journey, and my brother was expected back early to take part in festivities arranged in Scotland for the coming-of-age of my eldest brother Queensberry.

My mother and myself occupied one room that night, and went early to bed. There was no apprehension about my brother in Switzerland. About 10.30 p.m.

the door of our bedroom opened, and my mother's maid appeared. Her name was Emily Whiting, but we both called her by the pet name of "Bengy", whereas my brother Francis always called her Whiting. She came in and asked my mother if she had called her, and on being replied to in the negative retired. About eleven o'clock she returned again, declaring that her name had been distinctly called, but was once more sent away. A third time (it was nearly twelve o'clock) she came back, assuring my mother that a voice had called her, and each time by the name of Whiting. She was certain the voice was near.

Annoyed at this frequent disturbance, my mother told her to go back to bed, and not to come again. Yet a fourth time she reappeared, and this time in a very agitated state. She declared that she had had a dream or vision, in which she saw my brother Francis lying on a rocky ledge on a great precipice, terribly wounded. He was dragging himself along. This dream seemed to startle my mother, but she tried to soothe the maid, and got her to go back to bed.

A few days later news came of the terrible accident on the Matterhorn, in which my brother, Mr.Hudson, Mr.Hadow, and Croz, the guide, were killed, Mr.Whymper and two other guides escaping. Of the four killed, Mr.Hudson's, Mr.Hadow's, and Croz's remains were found, but no trace of my brother has ever been discovered. The incident I have related is an indelible reminiscence of my childhood. The accident took place on 14th July, the very day of that night to which this account refers.

Yours faithfully,
FLORENCE DIXIE.

4.62

R. TAUGWALDER – MONTAGNIER (see also 4.63)

Zermatt, 8th May – 17.

Mr.Henry F. Montagnier!

Answering your letter of 23rd April. I am to explain you that there are no relations living consequently there can no books to be found of brothers Brantschen. That family quite died out.

As for Peter Taugwalder. I told him that a certain gentleman is offering him frs.50– if he would bee so kind to answer the questions yo wanted to know as good as he could and far and square. He answered them as follows:

I. Old Peter Taugwalder climed with Mr.Lord Douglas the Ober Gabel-Horn from the Mountet Hut before – it was the first accention.

II. Nor Mr.Hudson nor Mr.Wimper engaged the two Taugwalders, it was "Lord Douglas" though all these gentlemen united together in a single company under the comend of the chief Guide "Michel Croz".

III. Mr.Hadow whose slip caused the accident was a very bad climber, those who followed him always were compelled to place his feet into the right foothold.

IV. Old Peter Taugwalder felt at all anxious about the descent before they left the summit.

V. Old Peter also said the rope would not be strong enough but, Michel Croz wanted to have it so – and atachached Mr. Wimper between the two Taugwalders, father and son – for Miche Croz acted as commandeur of the Caravan.

VI. Peter Taugwalder never climbed with Michel Croz before.

VII. The father went to America – anno – 1874, and remained there till 1878.

VIII. His father (old Peter) day of death was July 11 – 1888.

Die 9te Frage wäre: Warum ging der alte Peter Taugwalder nach Amerika?...
[The letter was written in English, spelt as it appears above, until it suddenly and unaccountably switched into German for eight lines, written in the old style which is so very difficult for anyone unfamiliar with it to decipher. The German section has now been translated into English and this part appears below in inverted commas, the original letter having thereafter reverted to English for the final half-dozen lines or so.]
"The ninth question would be: why did old Peter Taugwalder go to America? Answer: After this accident and this success on the Matterhorn, all the guides of Chamonix and St.Niklaus were so envious and cunning that they did everything they could to make the lives of the Taugwalders as unbearable as possible. All sorts of jealousy and slander were used to weaken their good reputation in every respect. Both the guides of St.Niklaus and those of Chamonix caused thousands of francs loss by their shameful slanders. Peter Taugwalder eventually wanted to escape from these envious people and these slanders and so he went to America!"
If you would like to buy young Peter new Führerbuch he is willing to sell it you. He wants frs.125. If you like to buy it you may write and I shall send it you.
I hope you will receive these lines in your best health as also I and my family are.

Very Truly
Yours
RUDOLF TAUGWALDER.

N.B. Best regards of Matthew, Z.T.W.

4.63
MONTAGNIER'S QUESTIONS AND ANSWERS

The Matterhorn Accident.

Questions to be put to young Peter Taugwalder with his answers.

1. Had either his father or himself ever climbed with any of the party before the accident.

   Answer. Old Peter Taugwalder climbed with Mr. Lord Douglas the Ober Gabelhorn from the Mountet hut before (the accident) It was the first ascension.

2. Who engaged the two Taugwalders.
   Answer. Neither Mr.Hudson nor Mr.Wymper engaged the two Taugwalders. It was Lord Douglas, though all these gentlemen united together in a single company under the command of the chief guide Michel Croz.
3. His recollections of Mr.Hadow.
   Answer. Mr.Hadow whose slip caused the accident was a very bad climber, those who followed him always were compelled to place his feet into the right place.
4. Did old Peter feel any anxiety about the descent?
   Answer. Old Peter Taugwalder felt at all anxious about the descent before they left the summit.
5. Did old Peter choose the rope used to attach himself, his son and Mr. Whymper to the rest of the party?
   Answer. Old Peter also said the rope would not be strong enough but Michel Croz wanted to have it so and attached Mr.Whymper between the two Taugwalders father and son, for Michel Croz acted as commander of the caravan.
6. Had they ever climbed with Croz before.
   Answer. Peter Taugwalder had never climbed with Michel Croz before.
7. Date of the father's departure for America and that of his return to Zermatt.
   Answer. The father went to America anno 1875 [sic] and remained till 1878.
8. The date of the father's death.
   Answer. July 11th 1888.

[Note. Some of the above Answers do not accord exactly with Rudolf Taugwalder's letter above. The document is included here because it appears to be the only remaining record of the Questions, having been made on the same typewriter that Montagnier used for his correspondence with Farrar.]

4.64
P. TAUGWALDER – MONTAGNIER

[November 1917]

Dear Mr.Montagnier!

You want from me a description of the first ascent of the Matterhorn in the year 1865, when the great disaster occurred and four fine strong young men lost their lives. I am now 75 years of age, but I can still recall many of the details as clearly as if they had only taken place yesterday, despite the subsequent passage of 52 years. The terrible catastrophe made such an impression on me that I will never forget it as long as I live.

It was in the first half of July in the above-mentioned year that young Lord Douglas made several climbs at Zermatt accompanied by my late father, including the first ascent of the Ober Gabelhorn. He also intended to attempt the ascent of the Matterhorn. Then, on about the 10th or the 11th the Chamonix guide, Michel Cros, arrived at the Hotel Monte Rosa with the Englishmen Wymper, Hadow and Hudson, intent on forcing an ascent of the Matterhorn. Lord Douglas then decided to join them with his guide.

I was very young at that time, the first downy beard was just sprouting on my lips. But I had courage and no rock was too high and no glacier too steep. When only 16 I had done Monte Rosa with three English students and my father. My father did not want to let me go with him, as he was afraid I would get too cold. – Monte Rosa is well known as a very cold mountain and since then many have had their toes frost-bitten up there. – But I got my way, as I had lined up the three students for this expedition when they had been climbing the Gornergrat. They were therefore my clients, as it were, and I told my father that if he did not want to come along I would get another guide in his place. In short, I went and it was marvellous. My delight almost carried me up.

But to get back to the subject. I was no longer a novice in the mountains, having also done the Breithorn and various other climbs. So it came about that my father suggested taking me along. He had wanted them to take another two guides and form two parties, but Mr.Hudson did not approve as he thought they were all better than the guides.

On the morning of the 13th July we collected the necessary provisions from the Hotel Monte Rosa and set off at nine o'clock. The weather was wonderful, the Matterhorn was completely free of snow and it gave us a wink as it smiled in the morning sun.

We had lunch on the Hörnli. What a superb view! All around were the majestic mountain giants; below was the green valley and above it the dark pine forests, which reached up as far as the eternal ice.

My heart leapt with joy and I could scarcely wait for the morrow. Reaching the foot of the Matterhorn we made a platform for the tent to spend the night. But Cros and I climbed on quite a bit further, about as far as the spot where they built the so-called old hut. It went splendidly and we did not encounter the slightest difficulty. With this cheerful news we returned to our companions, enjoyed another good soup that someone had made in the meantime, put our sacks under our heads – and I slept like an angel.

All through the night I dreamt I was standing on the very top of the Matterhorn and that I gave a jubilant shout down into the valley and that I was heard as far away as Zermatt. And then all of a sudden I was almost alone on the summit. I could no longer see the others anywhere. I was frightened and I woke up. It was about 2 o'clock. The others were also awake. We quickly brewed some hot tea and set off up the giant mountain.

Naturally, we roped up right away. Cros led the way, followed by Hudson, Whymper, and Hadow. Then came my father, Lord Douglas and me. Daybreak came at about 3 o'clock and in the east the sky shone like pure gold. Not a cloud was to be seen. Not a sound was to be heard, except the tread of the seven mountain enthusiasts and the clang of ice axes on the hard rock.

We took the same route that Cros and I had reconnoitred the evening before. It went like a song until just above the site of the old hut, as it is now called. Thereafter the difficulties increased, but we were all in good heart and so we were still advancing fairly quickly. Some 50 metres above the present Solvay hut we stopped and had something to eat to fortify ourselves. The way now led up over the shoulder and Cros had to cut steps. But Douglas, who was in front of me, could not place his feet properly in the steps and slipped from time to time. With my hands I held his legs in the steps almost all the time. Eventually we were on the shoulder. Just above where the ropes start to-day we left the sacks containing the provisions. There was some discussion about the line to take as this was the most dangerous part. Once the roof was climbed it would get easier again. Cros decided. He thought we should climb over onto the west side, the so-called lee side. It was entirely free from snow. There were small rock ribs, between 2 and 4 cm wide. We climbed up on them. Beneath us the mountain, almost overhanging, fell away 2000 metres. Without a sound we climbed up in a state of intense excitement, reflecting the seriousness of the situation. It needed only one foothold or handhold to give way and we would all be lying smashed to pieces on the glacier below. I was young and agile and climbed like a cat. I had plenty of time to watch the others and to place Lord Douglas's feet. He was not a good climber. We advanced slowly but surely. At last we were on the Roof and at 2 o'clock we reached the summit.

We did not linger long. I felt so light I could have flown far away over all the mountains, heaven knows where. Down to my sweetheart in Zermatt. We then prepared for the descent.

Whymper changed places with Lord Douglas and was now in front of me. Cros again led. Thus we slowly descended the Roof, roughly where one descends it nowadays. At the bottom of the Roof we turned back onto the West face via a rock band. Everything was taken slowly and with extreme caution, as the descent was much more difficult than the ascent. We reached the end of the rock band and Cros and the three following him were descending the West wall. From time to time my father passed the rope round a projecting rock in order to safeguard those descending. Then! suddenly the four were projected into space like a small cloud. The rope broke like a piece of string and the four young men disappeared from our sight. It all happened as fast as a flash of lightning. No one made a sound. At a stroke they were off down into the terrible abyss.

Our feelings can be imagined. For a while we could not move for fright. Eventually we tried to proceed. But Whymper was trembling and could scarcely take another safe step. My father climbed in front, for ever turning round and placing Whymper's legs on the rock ledges. Time and again we had to stop and rest, as we did not feel well. Then we slowly pushed forward again and finally reached the Shoulder, utterly exhausted. Here we took a little refreshment, but the food did not want to go down. It was as if someone had tied our throats. Small wonder; we saw our poor comrades lying on the cold glacier far below. It almost broke my heart and great tears ran down my cheeks. Alas, our poor friends! This morning still so bright and active, and now torn corpses down there on the cold glacier. And that nice Mr.Douglas, if only he had not changed his place, he would now be safe instead of Whymper, and he would surely have proved a better and a kinder friend than this Whymper, who was quite alien to us and always remained alien to us although we saved his life. Without us he would also have been lost, even though he later boasted of being the lion of the party and reported various matters that simply are not true.

At least I noticed nothing whatever of the three crosses in the sky that he claimed to have seen. Likewise various phrases that he put into our mouths are quite false. Anyway how can Whymper have understood what we said, for at that time he did not understand a word of German and my father spoke nothing else but the Zermatt dialect of the German language.

But back to our descent. We collected the rucksacks and slowly and with difficulty we reached a place below the Shoulder which was free of snow and afforded us room to sit down. Here in a sitting position we spent the night. Towards dawn it got quite chilly although the temperature had been very mild. As soon as we had sufficient daylight we continued our descent. We encountered no difficulties and once on the move we regained our former agility. But we did not reach Zermatt before 3 o'clock.

In Zermatt we went straight to Papa Seiler at the Hotel Monte Rosa and reported the sad circumstances of our climb.

At once preparations were made to recover the victims. It was Saturday. It was known that they were all dead and so it was pointless setting off in the night. They waited till daybreak.

I did not go with the rescue party, I was too exhausted; likewise Whymper and my father. Our poor friends were found lying on the glacier as we had indicated. Only Lord Douglas was missing, but to this day nothing has ever been found of him. They were all terribly mutilated, especially Cros, and all had lost almost all their clothing. Some days later they were buried next to the simple little village church in Zermatt with everyone attending.

I have since climbed the Matterhorn more than a hundred times, but never without thinking of my dear unfortunate friends. My father and Whymper have already followed them to their eternal rest and the angel of death will soon summon me as well.

So now I have related to you simply my experience on the first ascent of the Matterhorn. Should you use it and hand it down to posterity, I leave my reputation in the hands of all those who will read it and hereby conclude my narrative.

PETER TAUGWALDER

[Translated from the original German]

4.65
P. TAUGWALDER'S CONSENT

I am quite agreeable to my description of the Matterhorn accident appearing in the *Alpine Journal* in any shortened form that may be necessary.

PETER TAUGWALDER
former mountain guide

[Translated from the original German, which is undated]

4.66
P. TAUGWALDER – MONTAGNIER

Zermatt, 27.XI.17.

Dear Mr.Montagnier,

Please accept my best and most sincere thanks for the 50frs, that you have been so good as to send me. It has reached me safely.

In such bad times one can have need of something special, as fate has unfortunately not made life a bed of roses for me. I am spending my latter days with two daughters from my second marriage in a small house some 30 minutes from Zermatt. We have a small cow and a couple of goats and live mainly off bread and milk. Yet the bread is starting to run out and what one can get is so expensive that one can no longer afford the money for it. So you see how welcome your gift was when it came. May the Almighty God, the creator of our splendid mountains, repay you a thousandfold.

Unfortunately I have no photographs taken in my youth, and there is only one available of my late father and it is in the Alpine Museum in Zermatt. If you still want them I will try and get one of me made in the summer and also try and obtain one of my father, but for the time being there is no photographer here.

So, once again thank you very much. With best wishes for your well-being.

Your grateful and respectful
PETER TAUGWALDER
former mountain guide.

[Translated from the original German]

4.67
SMYTHE – COOKE

Tenningshook
Abinger Hammer
Surrey
9.10.39

Dear Mr. Cooke,

Many thanks for your letter & the extracts. I return the latter with some marginal comments. It is not I think possible or justifiable for anyone to take sides. You have not seen Whymper's memorandum to Cowell Hon Sec. of the A.C. at that time. He was obviously greatly exercised in his mind over the conduct of the Taugwalders after the accident. Having read all Whymper's diaries through his life it is not possible to come to any conclusion other than that he was an absolutely honest & scrupulous man, of a hard & unsympathetic type. He accuses the Taugwalders of trying to encompass his death after the accident & states that he stood all night when bivouacking with his back to a wall prepared to defend himself as by their callous behaviour he suspected that they would prefer to be the sole survivors on account of the publicity it would give them. In their defence I have made it plain that in my opinion their nerves were unstrung & that between them & Whymper was a gulf of misunderstanding due to temperament etc. I believe it was this conduct of the Taugwalders revealed for the first time in the memoranda I found among W's papers that is responsible for the story that Whymper sought the advice of Bishop Browne. Lord Conway said that he did go to Browne and ask him whether he should divulge something & Browne advised him not to do so. If Whymper's statement is true & it bears, like all he wrote the impress of truth, the Taugwalders come out of it very badly, but as I say I prefer the explanation of nerves & in the case of the rope carelessness due to psychological & physical reasons – have we not all done some careless things on mountains due to the reaction following on physical stress & mental excitement?

Yours sincerely
FRANK SMYTHE

4.68
BIRKBECK'S LECTURE EXTRACT

[The following account of John Birkbeck's Matterhorn attempt on the 14th July 1866 is extracted from the handwritten text of a lecture that appears from the contents to have been written and delivered by him in about 1882. The text accompanied a letter from Rachel Birkbeck to Farrar of 12.3.1918]

The first time I attempted the M'horn was in '66. I wished to ascend it from the Swiss side & leaving Zermatt I slept at the actual foot of the mountain where the Hörnli ridge runs into it. Abroad one is apt to take little notice of the days of the month & without knowing it I had fallen upon the exact anniversary of the first ascent. In '66 there was believed to be an amount of ice on the upper rocks of the mountain which might make the ascent impossible. Nevertheless I was wishful to try it, intending to turn back at once if I found any real danger. Before I went to sleep my guides came to me & said that they had been talking about the mountain & that they did not wish anyone who was nervous to be of the party, would I agree not to mention afterwards which of them went with me to the top so that any of them might have no hesitation in remaining behind if he found himself at all afraid. I did not like the arrangement but agreed. The next morning when we started I noticed that the guides carefully crossed themselves. This did not look to me a very healthy sign. As I expected from Mr.Whymper's account of the first ascent we did not find the climbing up the part that looks so steep from Zermatt at all difficult and in course of time we reached the shoulder. Beyond this point I found it impossible to persuade the guides to go. I am not sure whether in any case we could have got to the top in the then state of the mountain, but as it was we turned back before we had found ourselves in the presence of any real difficulty. In fact I could have ascended the mountain to that point without any guides at all. I did not try the mountain again from various reasons until 1874.

4.69
DOUGLAS'S GABELHORN ACCOUNT

[An account by Lord Francis Douglas, found among his papers at Zermatt after his death, addressed to the Editor of the Alpine Journal. From AJ2, 221-2]

The Gabelhorn

We had made two previous attempts from Zermatt in vain. In the first attempt we ascended the Unter Gabelhorn, leaving Zermatt at 11 o'clock at night, but, at 3 o'clock on the following day, found ourselves only at the foot of the Gabelhorn, and had to return. In the second attempt, we reached the summit of another peak of the Gabelhorn, about 13,000 feet in height, which lies immediately to one's left in crossing the Trift pass from Zermatt, but the arête connecting this with the Gabelhorn was found impracticable. I cannot conceive why this mountain has no name. It is very often mistaken for the Gabelhorn.

Third attempt.—Left Zinal at 2.30 and reached the foot of Gabelhorn at 6 o'clock. Halted 30 minutes for breakfast. Left at 6.30; and, at 8.30, after traversing some steep slopes and cutting our way up some walls of ice, we arrived at the base of the rocks leading to the summit. In some places those rocks, intermingled as they are with steep ice slopes, presented greater difficulties than I have ever yet encountered. It took us 4 hours to mount these, and we arrived at the summit at 12.30 (10 hours including rests). There we found that someone had been the day before, at least to a point very little below it, where they had built a cairn; but they had not gone to the actual summit, as it was a peak of snow and there were no marks of footsteps. On this peak we sat down to dine, when, all of a sudden, I felt myself go, and the whole top fell with a crash thousands of feet below, and I with it as far as the rope allowed (some 12 feet). Here, like a flash of lightning, Taugwald came right by me some 12 feet more; but the other guide, who had only the minute before walked a few feet from the summit to pick up something, did not go down with the mass, and thus held us both. The weight on the rope must have been about 23 stone, and it is wonderful that, falling straight down without anything to break one's fall, it did not break too. Joseph Viennin then pulled us up, and we began the descent to Zermatt. Leaving at 1.30, we reached the foot of the rocks onto the glacier at 5.30, having been delayed an hour in leaving the arête to join the rocks where a wall of snow intervened, down which the guides cut a path while I sat on the arête and smoked. From thence it took us 4½ hours to reach Zermatt, as the guides wasted much time in eating as usual, and we reached Zermatt with a full moon at 10.30 p.m. The rocks on this side are not easy, but are nothing to those on the other, which, in addition to difficulty, present an undoubted danger from avalanches, as a tremendous glacier overhangs them nearly all the way to the summit. In some places we saw immense blocks of ice which had come across the very path we were going. Guides: Peter Taugwald of Zermatt and Joseph Viennin of Ayer. Peter Taugwald acted admirably, and really showed himself a first-rate guide. Joseph Viennin makes a good *second* guide in an expedition like this; but if he had been leader, I may safely say we never should have reached Zermatt.

This will make a capital pass for those who have already gone over the Trift Joch and Col de la Dent Blanche, and being much higher, commands far finer views. A good guide will be indispensable, and the descent to Zinal will always be found a matter of great difficulty.

FRANCIS DOUGLAS.

4.70
JORDAN'S TIMETABLE

October 1st 1867.	
Hotel Mont Cervin Breil	5.15 a.m.
Tent arr: 11.15. dept:	12.15 p.m.
Cabanne on the Cravate	3.45
October 2nd	
Cabanne departure	5.40 a.m.
Peak Tyndall	6.10
Arete Tyndall (End)	7.15
Col Félicité	7.45
Summit	9.50
Commenced descent on the Zermatt side	11.15
Commenced to reascend	1.00 p.m.
Summit regained	2.15
Cabanne on Cravate	5.40
October 3rd	
Cabanne dept.	6.35 a.m.
Tent	8.15
Hotel Mont Cervin Breil	11.00

4.71
ADAMS REILLY 1865 DIARY EXTRACTS AT ZERMATT

Tuesday July 18.
Whymper soon came back from an expedition on the Gorner.

Wednesday July 19.
A rumour came down that someone was missing from the Riffel. Whymper, McCormick & Charlet went up, and his body was found at the bottom of the Riffelhorn. He had strolled out with a book after dinner & never returned. His name was Wilson...

Thursday July 20.
A party of guides brought down the fragments of the bodies already found, but found no more...

Friday July 21.
Michel Croz interred at ½ past 8. Hudson, Haddo & Wilson at 10. The official came down, and said that the government wished everything to be done according to the wishes of the English. The three coffins, covered with palls, with a wreath laid on each were laid just below the church, & then carried to the grave by the guides. The service was read at the grave by Mr.McCormick assisted by Mr.Downton. Official inquiry held at 2. Sent Charlet over the Theodule for my things & Whymper's, with a porter. Day turned out wet and stormy with thunder.

Saturday July 22.
Mr.Vicary [sic] went. Charlet arrived. Phillpotts and Robertson went. Whymper went. (100frs for Croz's representatives given me by Whymper to bring to Chamounix). (given to J.B.Croz). Jean Baptiste Croz came in the evening, also Albrecht, gave Croz the 100 francs – he promised to give me Michel's hat.

Sunday July 23.
Jean Baptiste went in the morning.

Monday July 24.
...Arrival of Mr.Haddo's uncle and a brother of Lord Douglas the Marquiss of Queensberry with Stephenson.

Tuesday July 25.
At Zermatt – wet.

Wednesday July 26.
...In the afternoon started a project of going up to the Riffel to dine...dined at Riffel & started down rather late at 9...It soon got dark, but Charlet produced a candle end, which we lit & as there was no wind, I got through the forest by its light. At the foot of the forest met Stevenson & McCormick with a lantern looking for Queensberry and Hadow who were lost. A little further on met Mr.Sheepshanks [?] & went on with him, sending Charlet on in front to get my lantern & go & help. Parties sent out. Mr.Hadow found at the top of the forest above the Findelen torrent, Ld. Queensberry on the Gorner side of the River, and Mr.Frère had got the E side of the River & nearly fell into it. All got back at 1 a.m.

Thursday July 27.
...Just before the table d'hote heard that 2 Mr.Bayleys had tried Mte Rosa with the two Lochmatters & 2 porters, avalanche fell, burying all but the 2 guides. All dug out except one porter Inshof [?] of Möral. Arrival of Mr. & Mrs.Bright. Prof & Mrs.Sellar & Mr.Cross with Albrecht.

Friday July 28.
Stephenson knocked me up with the news that Queensberry had started alone for the Matterhorn at one o'clock the night before, leaving a letter explaining his purpose. Stephenson & McCormick got a party of guides & started after him. I followed with Hadow & Cross to the Hörnli, where I met the rest, who had found him on the end of the Hörnli arete. He had found his way to the Hörnli in the dark, clambered up the E face, had several narrow escapes, & slipped down an ice slope. He was completely done. Found a party of ladies at the Swatzsee where Hadow had stopped, bathed. Saw parties searching on Mte Rosa. Saw them again, coming down.

Saturday July 29.
Sketched the church. Queensberry & Stephenson went & Hadow & I walked part of the way with them. The body of the porter brought down. Arrival of 3 Parkers.

Sunday July 30.
Funeral of the porter.

Monday July 31.
Left Zermatt at about 4.30...for Theodule hut.

4.72 WHYMPER'S *GRAPHIC* ARTICLE EXTRACTS

The Graphic
The Alps revisited
By EDWARD WHYMPER

4.72.1 September 29. 1894 (*Extract from part I, on page 374*)

The death of Michel Auguste Croz, the finest guide the valley of Chamounix has produced in modern times, was even more tragic than that of Carrel. At the time he perished he was in the prime of life, at the maximum of his powers. He could take a man by the collar and hold him off the ground with one arm, or hew steps all day long without showing any signs of fatigue. "Chamounix! Oh, what will Chamounix say?" burst from old Peter Taugwalder as the doomed man disappeared over the edge of the precipice. He meant, Who would believe that Croz could fall. With axe in hand Croz might have averted the catastrophe, for the rope held during a fraction of a second. But he had laid it aside and was powerless. The next instant the rope parted in mid-air, the ends flew up and recoiled, and then it was all over.

Two incidents in connection with this Matterhorn catastrophe have recently come to my knowledge. The men who were lost fell over the great North cliff. It was an imperative duty to attempt to recover their remains, but to reach them was more hazardous than to ascend the mountain, for they were lying on the upper plateau of the Matterhorn Glacier, on a spot inaccessible except by passing through *séracs* – towers and pinnacles of ice – which tumbled about right and left, often without premonition. To minimise the peril, it was arranged to start at midnight so as to pass through the *séracs* before they were struck by the sun. When this became known, the Zermatt guides were threatened with excommunication if they failed to attend the early Mass, and were thus debarred from coming. Volunteers were then called for, and a sufficient number of men came forward. First to offer himself was Franz Andermatten, a first-rate mountaineer, who lived at Saas, beyond the jurisdiction of the priests of Zermatt; and under his leading the bodies were recovered and buried. Next Sunday Franz Andermatten went to Mass, and this was his reward. "I saw him," said my informant (who is now Head Master of one of our public schools), "turned out, *ejected*, from the church at Zermatt!"

The other incident relates to Peter Taugwalder, the father. No sooner had the survivors of the ill-fated expedition returned to Zermatt, than the baseless, monstrous rumour was circulated that the old man had *cut* the rope which broke. It passed from lip to lip, spreading like wildfire, and emanated in his own village amongst his neighbours. The calumniated man, walking about shunned like a murderer, met the returning volunteers. "Mr. R–," he said to one of them, "they say I *cut* the rope. Look at my fingers!" and, opening his hands, showed how they had been lacerated by the jerk which all but tore him from his grasp.

4.72.2 October 6. 1894 (*Extract from part II, on page 402*)

After the occurrence of the Matterhorn accident in 1865, much discussion took place as to the utility of rope in mountain climbing, and of the manner of its employment. Some persons entertained the opinion that it was not advisable to attach man to man. "Suppose," they said, "that none of this party had been tied together, and that Mr.Hadow had slipped and upset Croz, would not only two lives have been lost instead of four?" The answer to this was "Yes, only two lives would have been sacrificed." This led to another question. "Now, tell me, if the rope had *not* broken between the fourth and the fifth man, would not all the party have been swept away?" And as the answer to this question was also in the affirmative, it was concluded that upon this particular occasion, anyhow, it was exceedingly imprudent to be attached together.

I do not agree with this conclusion. When climbers are tied together, it is presupposed that everyone has acquired, to a reasonable extent, the art of *keeping on his legs*, and by that is meant not only a respectable amount of endurance, but some proficiency in *balancing*. It is presupposed that everyone will maintain his distance, that in difficult places only one will move at a time, and that the rest will be on the look out to render assistance. The loss of life in the Matterhorn catastrophe of 1865 did not arise from being tied together, but its occurrence was primarily due to the inexpertness of one of the party. There were two great faults committed on this occasion. The first was in allowing a very young and inexperienced man to go with us, who had not acquired the art of keeping on his legs. The second was the neglect of an ordinary measure of precaution.

It is the habit of mountaineers now, and it was customary with them long before 1865, besides being tied together, to fix ropes and to hold them, as an additional protection against the consequences of a slip, while descending difficult places. The accident took place on a spot where rope ought to have been fixed, and if it had been fixed no accident would have happened. There were more than four hundred feet of rope out of use, which had been brought for this express purpose. None of it was employed, and why it was not used I cannot tell. I have always regarded this accident as arising from divided responsibility, through no *one* person being in command of the party. Ever afterwards I have travelled alone. The persons in my employment have obeyed my directions; I have held myself responsible for *their* safety; and, in the twenty-eight years which have elapsed since that lamentable occasion, I have had *no* accidents.

On difficult rocks, when climbing directly upwards, it is, however, questionable whether the first man derives any advantage from being attached to those who follow. If he *should* slip and come down, it is more likely that he will drag some of the others off their legs than that he would be pulled up himself. The first man very seldom slips. He is alive to consequences, and exercises caution. Youthful impetuosity sometimes causes exceptions to the general rule, and the last accident that took place on the Matterhorn – one of the saddest that has occurred on the mountain – was of this description.

4.73
WHYMPER INTERVIEW IN *JOURNAL DE ZERMATT* (25 August 1895)

Chronique de Zermatt
La première ascension du Cervin.
Interview de M. Ed. Whymper. – Récit complet de la catastrophe de 1865. – Détails inédits.

M. Ed. Whymper, le premier ascensioniste du Cervin et l'auteur distingué des livres connus de tous les Alpinistes, se trouvant de passage à Zermatt, nous avons eu la bonne fortune de l'interviewer, et nous publions ci-dessous le récit complet et détaillé de la terrible catastrophe du 14 juillet 1865...
M. Ed. Whymper est un homme de cinquante-six ans, imberbe, à figure énergique; blond, avec une physionomie d'un grand caractère personnel, il a le regard d'un homme qui sait ce qu'il veut et comment il le veut. Enthousiaste de la montagne, savant dans toute l'expression du terme, M.Whymper, en tout et partout est quelqu'un. Nous lui laissons la parole:

"Vous savez que c'est par hasard que je me recontrai à Zermatt le 14 juillet 1865, avec M.le Révérend Ch.Hudson et son élève M.Hadow. J'étais accompagné du jeune lord Francis Douglas, frère cadet du marquis de Queensberry. Nous avions engagé les deux guides Taugwalder père et fils, et nous avions déja pris toutes nos dispositions pour tenter l'ascension du Cervin, que j'essayais pour la huitième fois, quand ces Messieurs, qui m'étaient inconnus, arrivèrent, avec le guide Michel Croz, de Chamonix, pour faire, eux aussi, une tentative d'ascension du Cervin par le côté nord. Michel Croz avait déja été avec moi, au commencement de la saison, comme guide-chef, mais il m'avait quitté vers la fin de juin, à Chamonix, pour attendre l'arrivé d'un M.Birkbeck, qui l'avait retenu. Croz connaissait mes idées; j'avais discuté souvent avec lui la possibilité de l'ascension du Cervin par le versant du nord, et il pensait, lui aussi, qu'elle était praticable, bien que l'opinion générale était qu'il fallait la tenter par le côté italien. Après avoir attendu plusieurs jours à Chamonix, il reçut une lettre de M.Birkbeck, lui disant que, pour cause de maladie, il ne pouvait venir. A ce moment, M.Hudson et son ami arrivèrent à Chamonix et, trouvant Croz libre, l'engagèrent immédiatement. Coïncidence curieuse, Croz leur communiqua mes projets sur le Cervin et ils decidèrent de suite de tenter l'ascension avec moi. Bien qu'au premier abord, je fusse un peu vexé de voir la conquête du pic sur le point d'être effectué par d'autres après tous les efforts que j'avais fait dans ce but, et la route que j'avais tracée, en partie, moi-même, je me consultai avec Douglas, et j'invitai MM. Hudson et Hadow à se joindre à nous, afin d'éviter les ennuies et les dangers d'une rivalité.

Nous partîmes de Zermatt, le 13 juillet et, après avoir traversé l'arête du Hoernli, très peu visité à cette époque et où il n'existait aucun sentier, nous trouvâmes un endroit favorable pour planter la tente et passer la nuit au pied du pic du Cervin. Il faisait un temps superbe. Croz monta en avant pour examiner la route et il revint, nous assurant du succès. Nous nous endormîmes sous la tente, qui ne contenait que quatre personnes; trois d'entre nous se couchèrent dehors.

Au point du jour, le 14, nous nous mîmes en route et, jusqu'à l'*Epaule*, nous ne trouvâmes aucune difficulté, ainsi que je l'avais présumé. Jusqu'à cet endroit, nous n'employâmes même pas la corde.

A 6½ heures du matin, nous arrivions sur l'emplacement où, quelques années plus tard, les frères Knubel, de Zermatt, bâtirent le seule cabane qui exista pendant longtemps et était située à moitié chemin du sommet. Après une halte, nous gravîmes l'*Epaule*, où nous nous arrêtâmes pour manger et étudier la route. Cet endroit n'avait encore jamais été atteint. Nous vîmes qu'il serait indispensable de passer sur la droite et de gravir la face qui domine le glacier de Z'mutt, parce que nous étions arrêtés partout par des parois à pic et des précipices effroyables. A ce moment, nous nous attachâmes pour la première fois.

– Maintenant, dit Croz, cela devient une toute autre affaire. La pente n'était pas excessivement rapide, mais elle était composée d'un mélange de glace, de neige et de rochers, qui exigeaient les plus grandes précautions.

Croz monta le premier, moi après; Hudson était le troisième. Je remarquai, à ce moment, le manque d'expérience de Hadow; toutefois je ne me serais jamais douté que c'était la première *grimpade* sérieuse qu'il faisait. Douglas et le fils Taugwalder n'étaient d'ailleurs guère plus expérimentés.

Après avoir monté pendant cent mètres environ, nous obliquâmes sur la gauche, vers l'arête par laquelle se font les ascensions actuelles. A 1½ h., nous étions sur le sommet, où nous jouîmes d'une vue incomparable. Je la revois encore, aussi nettement qu'à cette heure inoubliable, cette immense ceinture de cimes gigantesques, dominant tout un amoncellement de sommets et de pics inférieurs...

Après une heure d'admiration et d'extase, nous nous préparons à redescendre; nous décidâmes que Croz descendrait le premier, Hadow le second, Hudson le troisième, Douglas le quatrième, puis Taugwalder père. Ils s'attachèrent les uns aux autres, pendant que je prenais un croquis du sommet. Je ne remarquai pas s'ils avaient été attachés par Taugwalder ou Croz, et de quelle manière ils l'avaient été. Ils étaient prêts à partir, quand nous remarquâmes que nous n'avions pas, comme c'est l'usage, mis nos noms dans une bouteille. On me demanda de faire la chose, et pendant que je la faisais, ils partirent les premiers, me laissant sur le sommet, avec le fils Taugwalder. Quelques minutes après, je m'attachai avec le jeune homme et suivis la caravane. Quand je les rattrapai, ils étaient sur la pente, du côté de Z'mutt; ils descendaient très lentement, prenant les plus grandes précautions. Je les suivis pendant cinq minutes environ, sans me lier à eux, ayant l'intention de continuer ainsi la descente. Mais lord Douglas me demanda de me faire attacher à Taugwalder père, avec eux, parce que, dit-il: "Si quelqu'un glisse, il ne sera pas assez fort pour le retenir." De plus, il était inquiété par la démarche chancelante de Hadow. Alors je m'attachai au père Taugwalder, faisant ainsi corps avec le reste de la caravane.

A peu près cinq minutes après, voici ce qui arriva: Croz avait lâché son piolet et s'occupait de placer les pieds de Hadow à l'endroit le plus sûr. Il se tournait pour faire lui-même un pas en avant, quand Hadow glissa, tomba sur le dos et avec ses pieds, frappa violemment Croz dans les reins et le projeta sur la déclivеté, la tête en avant. Hudson fut entrainé à leur suite, puis Douglas. La secousse effroyable atteignit Taugwalder père, qui leur faisait suite; heureusement qu'ayant vu la glissade de Hadow, il put se tourner sur lui-même, les jambes croisées, et embrasser convulsivement un grand rocher qui se trouvait à côté de lui. Pendant une seconde, il soutint ainsi les autres qui étaient pêle-mêle, sur le dos, le long de la pente, mais la corde se rompit brusquement, à moitié de la distance entre Douglas et Taugwalder, soit à 2m.50 de ce dernier, les deux extrémités se repliant violemment, en sens inverse, comme un fouet. Les quatre malheureux descendirent alors, précipités sur le dos, faisant des efforts désespérés pour se retenir aux aspérités et conservant à peu près leurs distances respectives, sur une pente de 45 degrés, toutefois sans jeter un seul cris. Arrivés au bord de l'abîme effroyable, ils culbutèrent l'un après l'autre et disparurent dans le vide, au milieu d'un grand tourbillon de pierres.

Nous restâmes plusieurs instants dans l'horreur et la stupéfaction, sans pouvoir prononcer une parole, inertes, anéantis. Puis, je demandai à Taugwalder père de me faire passer le bout de corde qui l'attachait à nos amis. J'avais, en effet, apporté trois espèces de cordes, celle du Club alpin Anglais, faite exprès pour les ascensions, très résistante et capable de supporter un poids de 2000 kilos, une seconde de l'égale grosseur, mais moins forte, et enfin une troisième, plus faible, d'un centimetre de diamètre, destinée à être coupée et abandonnée, après la descente, dans les endroits trop à pic, et qui n'était pas fait pour supporter un homme.

Il me la donna sans hésitation, et je vis que c'était justement la plus faible avec laquelle avaient été attachés nos amis, sans savoir par qui, comme je l'ai expliqué plus haut.

Que devions-nous faire? Il était inutile de chercher à descendre à la recherche des malheureux, parce qu'il était évident qu'ils étaient tombés dans le grand précipice de 1200 mêtres, qui aboutit au glacier du Cervin. Néanmoins, pendant quelque minutes, nous poussâmes des cris d'appel, mais personne ne nous répondit; seul, le silence effrayant et profond! Alors nous continuâmes la descente, pas à pas, suivant le chemin que nous avions pris en montant, et dont les traces étaient encore visibles. De temps en temps nous fixions la corde aux rochers pour nous soutenir, et en coupions les extrémités que nous laissons en arrière. Les fragments en sont restées une douzaine d'années parce que personne ne voulut plus passer par là: ils ont marqué ainsi longtemps les traces de notre ascension. Plus tard, un Anglais les recueillit comme souvenir de la catastrophe.

Arrivés sur l'*Epaule*, nous appelâmes encore et regardâmes de tous côtés, pendant une demi-heure, mais sans résultat. A ce moment, nous nous préparions à descendre de nouveau, quand nous vîmes un arc immense, avec deux grandes croix lumineuses, qui se dessinaient dans le ciel, à une très grande hauteur, au-dessus du Lyskamm. Cette vision mystérieuse et extraordinaire nous causa une impression d'une grande intensité. Ce n'était point un mirage, puisque nos différents mouvements n'y apportaient aucun changement. Je n'explique pas ce phénomène terrible et merveilleux, que je n'ai vu nulle part, et que les circonstances où nous nous trouvions rendaient surnaturel; je dis seulement, et j'affirme ce que j'ai vu; d'ailleurs les deux Taugwalder en ont été également frappé, et lui ont attribué même une corrélation avec l'accident. L'impression qui nous en est restée est inoubliable. J'en ai donné une reproduction exacte dans mon ouvrage: *Scrambles amongst the Alps*, et aucun savant n'a jamais pu le définir.

Nous fûmes surpris par la nuit à peu prés au milieu de la grande pente, et dûmes rester plusieurs heures, blottis sur un rocher surplombant, à moitiés transis et nous serrant les uns contre les autres. Au point du jour, nous continuâmes à descendre, et arrivâmes à l'arête du Hoernli. Je quittais alors les deux Taugwalder, et descendis à Zermatt au pas du course. J'arrivai à 10 heures du matin, et rencontrai M.Alexandre Seiler père, à la porte de l'hotel du Mont-Rose: "Où sont les autres?" me demanda-t-il. Je répondis: "Moi et les Taugwalder sommes revenus!" Il comprit. Nous montâmes dans ma chambre, et tînmes conseil. Une demi-heure après, une grande caravane de guides partait du côté du Hohlicht, pour découvrir les corps de nos amis. Vers le soir, ils revinrent, disant qu'ils avaient vu quelque chose sur la neige, au pied du grand précipice du Cervin. Pour arriver à cet endroit, il était nécessaire de passer entre les séracs du glacier, tentative très dangereuse, parce que ces séracs tombent presque continuellement, quand ils sont frappés par les rayons du soleil. Il était donc indispensable de partir vers minuit, pour éviter ce danger. Comme le lendemain était un dimanche, M.le curé de Zermatt meneça d'excommunier les guides qui partiraient sans avoir entendu la messe, qui avait lieu à 5h.½. J'étais, par conséquent, privé de l'aide des guides de Zermatt, dont pas un ne voulut venir. Comme on ne pouvait retarder le départ, je demandai, par l'entremise de M. Seiler, des hommes de bonne volonté. Le premier qui s'offrit était Franz Andermatten, de Saas, puis les deux frères Joseph-Marie et Alexandre Lochmatter, de St-Nicolas, Frédéric Payot et A.Tairraz, de Chamonix, plus trois Anglais, qui se mirent à ma disposition d'eux-mêmes, le Révérend Cormick, chanoine de York, Révérend J.Robertson, de Cambridge, et Phillpotts, Recteur de l'école de Bedford. Partis à minuit, nous franchîmes les séracs avant le jour; il ne fut pas difficile d'atteindre, par des pentes de neige, le plateau supérieur. Là, dans un coin, au pied de la grande paroi, nous trouvâmes les corps de nos amis, placés dans le même ordre que pendant la descente. Le spectacle était affreux. Enfoncé dans la neige d'un demi-mètre, les cadavres étaient absolument nus, décapités et horriblement mutilés; les tendons et les os saillaient dans les chairs déchhiquetées; ils étaient exsangues, le sang ayant jailli complètement au cours de la chute. Croz était le premier, je le reconnus à sa longue barbe, qui était resté fixée à un debris du cou; puis, vingt mètres plus loin, Hadow, puis, à la même distance, Hudson. Autour d'eux, leurs habits dispersés de tous côtés; les pantalons de Croz étaient déposés près de lui, intacts, ainsi son chapeau, qui portait une large déchirure, et que j'ai conservé; puis ça et là, huit souliers. On aurait dit qu'un géant avait pris les corps par les pieds et les avait frappés avec violence contre les rochers. Je n'aperçus pas de trace de Douglas, à part ses chaussures, que je reconnus de suite, parce qu'étant trop petites il les avait coupées et fait rajuster avant de partir. Je cherchai partout, sur le plateau et jusqu'au fond de l'abîme, mais sans résultat. Un examen approfondi, au moyen de mes lunettes, ne me permit pas d'apercevoir quelque indice. Comme il était impossible de supposer que, plus léger que les autres, il se fût enfoncé dans la neige, il faut croire qu'il a été complètement déchiqueté ou qu'il est resté accroché par un bout de corde, à un rocher à pic. En tout cas, on n'a jamais rien retrouvé de lui.

Nous rassemblâmes les restes de nos amis, et les enterrâmes dans la neige, mais quelques jours après ils furent exhumés, par ordre officiel, et ensevelis sur la face Nord de l'église de Zermatt. Lorsque j'eus accompli ce triste devoir, je me décidai de partir de Zermatt, mais je fus retenu par l'enquête faite sur cette affaire. Bien qu'il me fût pénible de revenir sur ce terrible événement, je donnai à M. le juge Clémenz, chargé de l'enquête, tous les renseignements et détails qu'il me demanda, comprenant, entr'autres choses, un questionnaire rédigé par môi-même, signé de ma main, et destiné à faire une lumière complète sur l'accident, appuyant entr'autres sur le fait que la corde la plus faible avait été employée à attacher Douglas à Taugwalder père. Le questionnaire devait m'être retourné par M.Clemenz, mais je ne l'ai jamais revu. Quelques heures après notre retour, il se répondit dans Zermatt une accusation abominable; on prétendait que la corde avait été *coupée* par Taugwalder père. Cette assertion est absolument fausse; comme je l'ai expliqué, la corde n'a pas été coupée et je l'ai vue moi-même se casser. Ce bruit causa tant de chagrin et d'ennuis à Taugwalder qu'il partit pour l'Amerique où il resta une dizaine d'années. Je déclare que je tiens Taugwalder pour un homme de toute confiance et de bon caractère; je regrette de n'avoir pas appris, par la lecture du questionnaire précité, la réponse qu'il fit lui-même aux demandes de M. le juge Clemenz.

C'est seulement après la catastrophe que j'entendis dire que le Cervin était la première ascension sérieuse de Hadow. Cela n'était pas exactement vrai; il avait déjà fait le Mont-Blanc et quelques autres petites excursions, mais jamais une montagne où il faille affronter le rocher. C'était une imprudence incroyable de la part de Hudson de l'avoir laissé venir avec nous. Le malheureux a, d'ailleurs, payé de sa vie cette inconséquence.

La route que nous avons tracée, ce jour, est celle que l'on suit aujourd'hui; seul, le trajet suivi à partir du *Toit* est un peu différent. Pour éviter cet endroit fatal, on monte directement sur l'arête, au moyen de chaînes et de cordes, mais si l'on regarde vers la droite, on peut voir la place exacte où s'est produit la catastrophe, environ à 120 mètres du sommet.

Le retentissement fut si grand qu'une foule de personnes voulurent voir le Cervin, et cet affreux malheur contribua à faire le renom de Zermatt. Je fus harcelé par les journalistes, mais je donnai seulement au *Times* un récit qui tint environ deux colonnes, et qui fut reproduit par tous les journaux anglais d'abord, puis par ceux du monde entier. Depuis ce jour, je suis revenu souvent à Zermatt, que j'aime beaucoup, mais je n'ai plus voulu faire l'ascension du Cervin, tant le souvenir de la mort de mes compagnons est resté profondément gravé dans mon esprit.

Pour copie conforme,
Jules MONOD.

4.74
ENQUIRY REPORT IN GERMAN

[The Official Enquiry Report written mostly in German, but partly in French and with even a few words in English, has been reproduced as closely to the original as possible, preserving the original errors. Some may have been careless spelling errors and others merely typographical, but most of them seem to have resulted from language difficulties. Thus the German Clerk seems to have had difficulty in transcribing Whymper's French evidence, just as Jullien's clerk from Geneva had similar problems half a century later transcribing some of the German documents. In the English translation of the Enquiry Report evidence in section 5.2, some minor errors in Whymper's evidence have been corrected by taking account of the occasional word in the Vecqueray document which the Clerk to the Enquiry omitted.]

4.74.0 COPIE
DE LA PROCEDURE DE L'ACCIDENT DU MONT CERVIN.
– 1865 –

Sitzung des Einleitungsgerichtes des Bezirks von Visp zu Zermatt im Hotel Mont Cervin unter dem Vorsitze des Hr. Einleitungsrichters Jos. Ant. Clemenz in Visp, Berichtsteller Subst. Cesar Clemenz, Aktuar Don. Andenmatten in Visp, und Weibel ad hoc Joh. Julen, den 21 Juli 1865.

4.74.1 Monsieur Wimper, touriste

Question 1. Quel est votre nom, âge, condition, et votre domicile?

Rép. Edouard Whimper, 25 ans, domicilié à Londres, artiste dessinateur, pas marié.
2. Avez vous fait partie de l'expédition qui a eu lieu le 13 courant aux fins d'opérer l'ascension du Mont Cervin?
Rép. Oui.
3. De combien de personnes a été composé le personnel de cette expédition?
Rép. A partir de Zermatt nous étions 8 personnes, savoir 4 voyageurs, 2 guides et deux porteurs. Un des porteur fils de Pierre Taugwalder est reparti pour Zermatt le 14 au matin de l'endroit où nous avons pris le quartier de nuit.
Q.4. Quel est le nom des 4 voyageurs, des deux guides et du porteur?
Rép. Rev. Charles Hudson, M.Hadon, Lord François Donglas, et moi-même, guides: Michel Cropt de Chamonix, Pierre Taugwalder père de Zermatt et porteur: Pierre Taugwalder fils.
Q.5. Quel est le domicile de Mr. Donglas, Hudson et Hadou?
Rép. Mr. Hudson a été vécaire à Skillington-Angleterre, le domicile des autres m'est inconnu.
Q.6. A quelle heure vous-êtes parti le 14 pour continuer votre chemin pour arriver à la pointe du Mont-Cervin?
Rép. Nous sommes parti de notre quartier du 13 au 14 à 3.40 du matin.
Q.7. A quelle heure êtes-vous arrivé au sommet du Mont-Cervin?
Rép. A 1.40 de l'aprés-midi.
Q.8. Combien du temps avez vous séjourné au sommet du Mont-Cervin?
Rép. Une heure.
Q.9. Est-ce que vous avez pris en descendant la même direction qu'en montant?
Rép. Exactement la même.
Q.10. Est-ce que les 4 voyageurs et les guides ont été liés par des cordes entre eux?
Rép. Oui, dans l'ordre et conditions suivantes:
à la tête de la colonne a été le guide Michel Cropt, venait ensuite M.Hadon, Hudson, Lord Duglas, Taugwalder père guide, moi-même et enfin Taugwalder fils. Entre Lord Donglas et Taugwalder père la corde a été moins épaisse qu'entre Michel Cropt et Lord Donglas d'un côté et Taugwalder père et Taugwalder fils de l'autre côté.
Q.11. De quelle manière est arrivé la malheureuse catastrophe?
Rép. Nous descendions dans l'ordre indiqué plus haut. A une distance d'environ 300 p. du sommet nous arrivions a un endroit difficil composé de rochers et de neige. Pour autant que je sache au moment où l'accident eut lieu, M.Hadou était le seul qui fut en mouvement. Ce même M.Hadou éprouvait évidemment beaucoup de difficultés à faire la descente et Michel Cropt pour plus de securité prenait et placait lui-même l'un après l'autre les pieds de M.Hadou. Je ne saurais dire avec certaineté qu'elle était la véritable cause de l'accident. Mais je crois que Michel Cropt avait placé les pieds de M.Hadou sur des points de rochers et venait de se retourner pour faire un pas en avant lui-même lorsque M.Hadou glissa dans sa chute renversa Michel Cropt. Ce double poids entraina M.Hudson et après lui

Lord Donglas. Les quelques instants que cela dura donnenent temps aux 3 qui étaient en arrière de prendre pied ferme, si bien en effet que la corde se brisa entre Lord Donglas et Taugwalder père. Pendant 2 ou 3 moments nous vimes les 4 malheureux glisser sur le dos et tendre les mains pour se sauver et puis ils disparurent entièrement. Pas un cri n'a été entendu. Après le premier cri de surprise poussé par Michel Cropt. Moi-même et les 2 Taugwalder nous sommes descendu sans autre accident par le même chemin que nous étions monté usant de toute la prudence possible et cherchan partout des traces de nos malheureux compagnons. Mais nous n'avons vu que deux haches enfoncées dans la neige. Par suite de ces précautions et de ces recherches nous fumes surpris par la nuit à une hauteur d'environ 13.000 pieds anglais. Là nous primes cartier sur une espace d'environ 12 pieds de superficie et le lendemain matin samedi le 15 nous nous remimes en route, arrivant à Termatt à 10½ h. du matin.
Q.12. N'êtes vous pas remonté au pied du Mont-Cervin pour chercher les malheureuses victimes de cet accident?
Rép. Oui, dimanche matin le 16 crt.
Q.13. Etiez vous seul ou étiez vous en compagnie? Dans le cas que vous n'étiez pas seul, veuillez désigner les personnes qui vous ont accompagné?
Rép. J'étais accompagné du Rév. Joseph Mr.Cormick, ami de M.Hudso ainsi que du Rd. M.Robertson et de M. Phillpots et des guides Lochmatter Alexandre et un de des frères Maurice Andenmatten de Saas, François Payot de Chamonix et un autre guide de Chamonix dont le nom m'est inconnu.
Q.14. Avez-vous trouvé les 4 victimes?
Rép. Seulement les cadavres de trois: savoir: M.Hudson M.Hadou et Michel Cropt.
Q.15. N'avez-vous pas donné connaissance à l'autorité de la commune de Zermatt que vous avez retrouvé les cadavres de 3 victimes?
Rép. Non, pas officiellement, mais à mon retour à Zermatt le samedi matin, j'ai donné connaissance du triste accident au président de la commune de Zermatt le priant en même temps d'envoyer des hommes sur le lieu de la catastrophe; en cas qu'après tout l'un ou l'autre de mes malheureux compagnons fut encore en vie. Cette demande fut accordée et bon nombre des guides se mirent aussitôt en route. Ils revinrent six heures plus tard, disant qu'ils avaient entrevus les cadavres, mais qu'il est impossible de parvenir jusqu'à là ce jour. D'un autre côté ces mêmes guides de Zermatt refusèrent en masse d'aller à la recherche des cadavres le lendemain dimanche et c'est pour celà même que je mis en route sans autorité officielle pour retrouver les cadavres et qu'à mon retour je ne crus pas devoir faire un rapport officiel. Cependant le fait que 3 des cadavres avaient été retrouvés fut communiqué non officiellement à quiconque prenait intérèt dans cette triste affaire.
Q.16. Est-ce que vous n'avez pas trouvé des traces de Lord Douglas?
Rép. J'ai rencontré une paire de gants que je lui avait donné moi-même à Zermatt et la ceinture de cuir qu'il portait pendant l'ascension.

Q.17. Avez-vous à votre déposition quelque chose à changer ou à ajouter?
Rép. J'ajouterai qu'à partir du 14 au matin Taugwalder fils qui nous avait d'abord accompagné comme porteur, nous servit de guide.

Le protocole prelu et approuvé.
Sig. Edouard Whymper.

Le Juge-instructeur:
J.A. Clemenz.

Le Greffier ad hoc:
Donat Andenmatten.

Denselben Tag und vor denselben

4.74.2 Verhör des Peter Taugwalder, Vater

Fr. 18. Wie heisset Ihr? etc.
Ant. Ich heisse Peter Taugwalder, 45 jährig, verheiratet, Bergführer wohnhaft in Zermatt.
Fr. 19. Habt Ihr am 14. dieses das Matterhorn bestiegen?
Ant. Ja.
Fr. 20. In welcher Eigenschaft habt Ihr diese Besteigung gemacht?
Ant. Als Bergführer.
Fr. 21. Von wem wurdet Ihr zur Besteigung des Matterhorns als Führer bestellt?
Ant. Von Lord Douglas und Whymper.
Fr. 22. Hattet Ihr schon Gebirgsreisen mit Lord Douglas vor der Ersteigung des Matterhorns gemacht?
Ant. Ja, ich habe den Lord Douglas als Führer begleitet, nach dem Zinal und auf das Gabelhorn.
Fr. 23. Hat man Euch vor der Abreise (zur Besteigung des Matterhorns) mitgeteilt aus welchen Herren die Gesellschaft eigentlich bestehen soll, und hattet Ihr irgend einen Einwurf gemacht entweder gegen den einen oder den andern von diesen Herren oder auch gegen die verhältnissmassige Anzahl der Reissenden und Führer?
Ant. Sie haben mir allerdings gesagt aus wie viel Personen die Gesellschaft bestehe. Ich habe keinen Einwurf gemacht gegen irgend eine Person dieser Gesellschaft. Nur bemerkte ich, dass in Verhältnis zu den Reisenden zu wenig Führer wären. H. Whymper und Hudson bemerkten mir, dass sie so gut gehen als Führer, worauf ich keine Bemerkung mehr machte.
Fr. 24. Wer hat die Männer zusammen gebunden als Ihr wieder vom Cipfel herabkamet?
Ant. die 4 ersten Männer der Colonne bestehend aus dem Führer Cropt, Hadon, Hudson und Lord Douglas wurden vom Führer Cropt gebunden und ich habe mich mit einem besonderen Seil an Lord Douglas angebunden.
25 Fr. Wer ist zuerst angebunden worden?

Ant. Wer von den 3 Herren von Cropt zuerst ist angebunden worden, erinnere ich micht nicht bestimmt.
Fr. 26. Was für Seil ist dazu gebraucht worden?
Ant. Das Seil woran Cropt und die 3 Herren gebunden waren, war ein festes und ganz neues Seil.
Fr. 27. Wer hat Euch an Lord Douglas angebunden?
Ant. Ich mich selbst.
Fr. 28. Warum ist zwischen Lord Douglas und Euch ein anderes Seil angewendet worden?
Ant. Weil das erste Seil zu wenig lang war um auch mich daran binden zu können.
Fr. 29. War das Seil das zwischen Lord Douglas und Euch angewendet worden in Eurer Meinung von hinreichender Stärke?
Ant. Wenn ich das Seil so zwischen Lord Douglas und mir angewendet wurde zu schwach gefunden hätte so hätte mich wohl gehütet mich mit demselben an Lord Douglas anbinden zu lassen, und hätte auch diesen eben so wenig in Gefahr bringen wollen als mich. Hätte ich das Seil zu schwach gefunden so hätte ich es vor der Besteigung des Matterhorns als solches bezeichnet und verworfen.
Fr. 30. Beschreibt den Punkt, wo das Unglück vorgefallen ist?
Ant. Als wir zwischen 200 und 300 Schuhe von der Spitze des Matterhorns herunter waren kamen wir zur 2ten. der gefährlichsten Stellen, wo die Felsen von glatten Platten sich verfindet und wo es sehr schwierig war ein Fuss einzustellen. Es geschah dann auch da, wo der erste Herr nach dem Führer Cropt ausglitschte und dieser die nach ihm kommenden Herren mitriss und diese dann den Führer Cropt nachdem das Seil zwischen Lord Douglas und mir zerriss.
Fr. 31. War nach Ihrer Meinung alle gehörige Vorsicht auf diesem Punkte genommen?
Ant. Ja. Zu bedauern war, dass das erste Herr nach Cropt ein sehr schlechte Gänger war.
Fr. 32. Wie hat das Unglück stattgefunden?
Ant. Ich habe bereits schon oben erwähnt nur habe ich beizufügen, dass nachdem das Seil zwischen Lord Douglas und mir zerrissen blieben Whymper ich und mein Sohn auf der Stelle, aus der wir uns so bald möglich herauszuwinden suchten. Wir gingen hinunter bis wir eine Stelle antrafen, wo wir übernachteten. Den folgenden Morgen kamen wir dann glücklich in Zermatt an.
Fr. 33. War das Seil gespannt oder nicht im Augenblick wo die Männer gefallen sind?
Ant. Es war gespannt.
Fr. 34. Woher kommt es in Eurer Meinung, dass das Seil zerbrach?
Ant. Ich weiss es nicht, aber das Gewicht der 3 Herren mit der Heftigkeit ihres Falles konnten auch ein festes Seil zerreissen.
Fr. 35. War es möglich die 4 Männer aufzuhalten nachdem das Seil zerbrach?
Ant. Unmöglich.
Fr.36. Wenn das Seil zwischen H. Douglas und Ihnen nicht gebrochen wäre, hättet Ihr die Herren retten können?

Ant. Ich bin fest überzeugt, dass wenn das Seil zwischen Lord Douglas und mir nicht gebrochen wäre, ich vereint mit Führer Cropt die Herren hätte retten können.

Verlesen und bestätigt.
Peter Zaugwalder.

Der Verhörrichter:
Clemenz.
Der Aktuar ad hoc:
Donat Andenmatten.

– – – – – – – – – – –

Denselben Tag und vor denselben

4.74.3 Verhör des Franz Jos. Andenmatten

Fr. 37. Wie heisset Ihr?
Ant. Ich heisse Franz Andenmatten, 40 jährig, verheiratet, Bergführer, wohnhaft in Allmagel.
Fr. 38. Seid Ihr nicht in jüngster Zeit vereint mit andern Führeren nach dem Zmuttal gegangen um allda die auf dem Matterhorn verunglückten Männer aufzusuchen?
Ant. Jawohl zweimal. Den ersten Mal ging ich und 4 andere Führer in Begleitschaft von 4 Herren dahin, und wir fanden 3 der Verunglückten sogleich. Diese 3 befanden sich auf einer Schneefläche wo in einer grossen Strecke weder Schründe noch Bergrisse vorkommen.
Fr. 39. Wo glaubt Ihr, dass der Körper des vierten Verunglückten wohl magh hingekommen sein?
Ant. Der wird wahrscheinlich weiter hinauf im Felsen geblieben sein.
Fr. 40. Wie heissen die Herren, die das erstemal mit Ihnen gegangen sind?
Ant. Maac Cormick, Whymper, Robertson, Philpots.
Fr. 41. Was habt Ihr mit diesen 3 Todten angefangen?
Ant. Ich war in einiger Entfernung von den Verunglückten allein ich glaube man habe sie zusammen getragen, sie mit Schnee bedeckt und wie ich bemerkte hat der englische Pastor Gebete verrichtet. Das 2te. Mal ging ich nach der Stelle des Verunglückten, um sie abholen zu lassen.
Fr. 42. Wer war von den Führern das erstemal mit Euch?
Ant. Alexander und Josef Maria Lochmatter und 2 Chamonix Füheren wovon einer Payot heisst, der Name des anderen ist mir unbekannt.

Deponent kann nicht schreiben.

Der Verhörrichter:
Clemenz.
Der Aktuar ad hoc:
Donat Andenmatten.

– – – – – – – – – – –

Fortsetzung den 22. Juli am gleichen Orte und vor denselben
4.74.4 Verhör des Alexander Lochmatter

Fr. 43. Wie heisset Ihr etc.?
Ant. Ich heisse Alexander Lochmatter, 27 jährig, ledig, Bergführer und Uhrmacher, wohnhaft in St. Niklaus.
Fr. 44. Seid Ihr nicht mit Begleitschaft von mehreren Herren und Füheren an den Fuss des Matterhorn's gegangen, um die 4 Verunglückten aufzusuchen?
Ant. Ja.
Fr. 45. Wie viele habt Ihr allda der Verunglückten gefunden?
Ant. Ja, drei derselben.
Fr. 46. Wisst Ihr, welchen man vermisste?
Ant. Ja, wie die Herren mir sagten, Lord Douglas.
Fr. 47. Waren die 3, so aufgefunden wurden, bei einander oder von einander entfernt?
Ant. Sie lagen in einer ganz geringen Entfernung von einander.
Fr. 48. Hat man die 3 Körper nicht auf eine Stelle zusammengebracht und Schnee darauf gelegt?
Ant. Ja wohl.
Fr. 49. War es die Absicht um sie dort als begraben zu betrachten?
Ant. Ja ich betrachtete, wie die Uebrigen auch, dieselben für dort begraben, umsomehr als der englische Pastor aus einem Buch Gebete ablas.
50 Fr, Habt Ihr von Lord Douglas keine Ueberbleibsel sei es vom Körper sei es von seinen Kleidungstücken gefunden?
Ant. Nichts, das ich weiss.
Fr. 51. Wo glaubt Ihr, dass Douglas möchte aufzufinden sein?
Ant. Ich vermute, er müsse in dem Felsengebiete sein. Denn unten hätte er unmöglich weiter als die Uebrigen fallen können.
Fr. 52. Sind die 3 Leichname nicht untersucht worden und haben sich da keine Effekte vorgefunden?
Ant. Die Herren Whymper, Robertson und der Pastor haben die Leichname untersucht und die darauf befindlichen Effekten zu Hand genommen.

Verlesen und bestätigt. Der Einleitungsrichter:
Alexander Lochmatter. J.A. Clemenz.
Der Aktuar ad hoc:
Donat Andenmatten.

– – – – – – – – – – –

Sitzung des Einleitungsrichters vom 23. Juli am gleichen Orte und vor denselben.
4.74.5 2tes. Verhör des Peter Taugwalder

Fr. 53. Was habt Ihr Euch seit dem letzten Verhöre über den Unglücksfall auf

Matterhorn besonnen, habt Ihr Ihren frühern Aussagen etwas beizusetzen oder abzuändern?
Ant. Weiters nicht, als ich dem Führer Cropt, bevor wir auf die gefährliche Stelle gekommen sind, sagte, man solle zur grössern Sicherheit ein Seil spannen, Cropt gab mir zur Antwort es sei nicht notwendig.
Fr. 54. Hat Eure Sohn gesehen, auf welche Weise sich das Unglück zugetragen?
Ant. Ich glaube nicht, weil er mich oben noch fragte: seid Ihr Vater noch da?
Fr. 55. Wie kam es, dass zwischen Cropt und Euch 3 Herren waren, dagegen zwischen Euch und Euerm Sohne nur einer. Es will den Verhörrichter scheinen, dass eine solche Einteilung eine fehlerhafte gewesen sei, was sagt Ihr dazu?
Ant. Der erste vom Zug war der Führer Cropt. Dann kam H. Handou, sodann Hudson, der sich als Führer stellte, nach diesem kam Lord Douglas, sodann ich Whymper und mein Sohn. Wenn Sie also Verhörrichter den Hudson als Führer annehmen, so werden Sie sehen, dass jeder Reisender zwischen zwei Führer war.
Fr. 56. Sah die Reisegesellschaft den Hudson als Führer an?
Ant. Hudson sagte selbst, er brauche keinen Führer und könne selbst als Führer dienen.
Fr. 57. Wer hat das Seil geliefert an dem Lord Douglas und Ihr gebunden waret?
Ant. Das Seil wurde von den Herren Reisenden geliefert.
Fr. 58. War Ihr Sohn mit Euch als Führer oder als Träger?
Ant. Am ersten Tag als Träger und den folgenden Tag als Führer. Die Herren wollten anfänglich meinen Sohn zurückschicken, weil sie behaupteten Cropt und ich genügen als Führer. Auf mein dringendes Ansuchen meinen Sohn als Führer mitzunehmen, willigten dann die Herren in meinen Antrag.
59.Fr. Um welche Zeit seid Ihr am 13ten. von Zermatt verreisst?
Ant. Zwischen 5 und 6 Uhr Morgens.
Fr. 60. Um welche Stunde seid Ihr auf die Stelle angekommen, wo Ihr das Nachlager bezogen?
Ant. Gegen 12 Uhr Mittags.
Fr. 61. Um welche Zeit seid am 14ten. wieder auf gebrochen?
Ant. Gegen 2 Uhr und sind da etwa über eine halbe Stunde geblieben. Die Herren waren guten Mutes und jauchzten.
Fr. 63. Herr Whymper sagte in seiner Aussage, dass Hadou zuerst ausglitschte und den Führer Cropt mit sich zog und diese dann den Hudson und Donglas. Während dieses geschah habe er Whymper und seine Führer Taugwalder Vater und Sohn Zeit gehabt festen Fuss zu fassen. In diesem Moment sei dann auch das Seil zwischen Douglas und Taugwalder zerrissen. Ihr aber sagtet in Eurer Antwort auf die 30te. Frage, dass zuerst Hr. Hadou ausglitschte, sodann Hudson und Lord Douglas und erst nach diesen 3 der Führer Cropt. Da die Aussage des Hr. Whymper und die Ihrige nicht ganz übereinstimmt, so seid Ihr aufgefordert zu erklären, ob Ihr auf Euerer frühern Aussage beharrt?
Ant. Da Hr. Whymper ob mir war in einer Stellung wo er den unglücklichen Vorgang besser sehen konnte als ich, so mag seine Aussage richtiger sein, sozwar,

dass ich nicht darauf beharren könnte, dass Cropt erst nach den 3 Herren gefallen sei. Alles ging in einem Moment vorbei, und man war so überrascht, dass eine genaue Kenntniss des Vorfalles beinahe unmöglich wurde.
Fr. 64. Habt Ihr obigen Aussagen noch etwas beizusetzen oder abzuändern?
Ant. Beizusetzen habe ich, dass ich um fester zu sein, mich gegen den Felsen gekehrt war, und da das Seil, welches zwischen Whymper und mir war, nicht gespannt war, so konnte ich es glücklicher Weise an einem Felsenvorsprung umwickeln, welcher mir dann die notwendige und rettende Festigkeit gab; das Seil welches mich mit Douglas und der Vorhergehenden anschluss hat mir durch ihren Fall solche Züge gegeben, dass ich noch jetzt an der Stelle, wo mein Körper mit dem Seile gebunden war, sehr leidend bin.

Verlesen und bestätigt.
Peter Taugwalder.

Der Verhörrichter:
Clemenz.
Der Aktuar ad hoc
Donat Andenmatten.

– – – – – – – – – – –

4.74.6

Der Untersuchungs-Ausschluss des Bezirkes Visp gebildet aus dem Einleitungsrichter Josef-Anton Clemenz und Aktuar C.Clemenz, beide wohnhaft in Visp hat bezüglich der amtswegen eingeleiteten Untersuchung wegen dem bei der Besteigung des Matterhorns ereigneten Unglückes folgende Nichtstatthaftigkeitsbescheid getragen.

Sachbestand.

Den 13ten. Juli Morgens 5 Uhr verreisste eine Karavanne, gebildet aus Herrn Lord Douglas, Hudson, Edouard Whymper und Hadou und den Füheren Michel Cropt von Chamonix, Peter Taugwalder Vater und dessen Sohn Peter, beide von Zermatt von Zermatt um die Besteigung des Matterhorns zu versuchen. Sie übernachteten den 13. Abends am Fusse desselben. Den folgenden Tag verliessen sie ihr Nachtquartier Morgens 3.40 und gelangten um 1.40 auf dem Gipfel des Horns an. Im Heruntersteigen befolgten sie die gleiche Richtung als beim Hinaufgehen und zwar waren sie in folgender Ordnung an miteinander gebunden. An der Spitze der Colonne war Führer Cropt, es folgten dann Hadou, Hudson, Lord Douglas, Taugwalder Vater und Whymper und Taugwalder Sohn. In einer Entfernung von ungefähr 300 Schuh von der Spitze kamen sie an einer Stelle mit Felsen und Schnee bedeckt, so dass es sehr schwer war den Fuss festzusetzen. Bei Ueberschreitung dieses gefährlichen Ortes glitschte H. Hadou aus und zog in seinem Falle den Führer Cropt mit. Dieses doppelte Gewicht riess nun auch Hr. Hudson hinunter und nach ihm Lord Douglas. Die wenigen

Augenblicke während obiges dauerte, gaben den Hinterstehenden Zeit festen Fuss zu fassen und zwar so gut, dass das Seil zwischen L. Douglas und Taugwalder Vater in zwei ging. Die Uebriggebliebenen stiegen mit aller möglichen Klugheit den Berg hinunter und kamen ohne weitere Unfälle Samstag den 15. um 10½ Uhr in Zermatt, nachdem sie die Nacht 14/15. in einer Höhe von 13.000 englischen Fuss auf einem auf einem Felsglied von ungefähr 12' Oberfläche zugebracht hatten.

In Erwägung:

1. dass aus obigen Tatbestande gegen Niemanden eine Schuldbarkeit hervorfliesst.
2. dass H. Hadou die Ursache des Unglückes war.

dass aus obigen Tatbestande Niemand einer Schuld und Verbrechen bezogen werden kann

wird

beschlossen:

a. es sei der vorliegenden Untersuchung keine fernere Folge zu geben und die Nichtstatthaftigkeit zu bescheiden mit Verurteilung des Fiskus zu den Kosten.

4.75 ENQUIRY REPORT INVENTORIES IN GERMAN

4.75.1 Inventar des H. Hadou's Habschaften

vorgenommen den 22ten. Juli zu Zermatt in der Wohnung des H. Hauptm. Alexander Seiler, Gasthof Monte-Rosa auf Instanz der öffentlichen Partei vorgestellt durch H-Berichtsteller Subst. Cesar Clemenz, vor H.Bezirksrichter Alois Biner von Randa verbeiständet von Aktuar ad hoc Donat Andenmatten.

1. Billet circulaire 1 à 10 L.W.St.	ff. 250.–
2. Napoleon d'or 14 à 20 ff.	280.–
3. Münze	2,70

4. Zwei Goldringe.
5. Ein Portmonnaie, mit einer Silberuhr und Goldkette.

Diese obigen Artikel hat der verunglückte Hadou vor seiner Besteigung des Mont-Cervin dem H.Gastwirt Seiler hinterlegt.

6. In den Säcken desselben beim vorgefundenen Leichnam hat H.Pastor und seine Freunde gefunden–

a. gefärbte Brillen.

4.75.2 Inventar des H. Hudson

1. Eine Banknote von England von Franken hundert fünf und zwanzig	125.–
2. Sechs lib. St. von Franken hundert und fünfzig	150.–

3. Napoleon zwei von zwanzig Franken)
id einen von fünf Franken) 45.–
4. Ein silbernes Bleistiftheft.
Obige Artikel wurden bei H. Gastwirt Seiler von Hudson vor seiner unglücklichen Besteigung des Matterhorns hinterlegt.
In den Taschen des verunglückten Leichnams fanden sich nachstehende Gegenstände vor:
a. Eine goldene Sackuhr, gebrochen, zeigt 3¾ Uhr.
b. Zwei Sackmesser
c. Goldenes Uhrenketteheft.
d. Ein Zweifrankenstück.
In einer Schachtel befinden sich, ein Felleisen, Reisebücher Kleider und Haarbürste, Landkarte und Kleidungsstücke zugehörend dem verunglückten Hadou und Hudson und ihrem Reisefreunde Campbcl. Obige den H.H. Hadou und Hudson behörenden und inventarisierten Artikel hat H. Pastor Mr. Cormick in Empfang genommen, nachdem er sich dem Gerichte vorläufig für selbe und selber gewissenhaften Anhandstellung persönlich verantwortlich stellte.
Zermatt den 22 Juli 1865.

Joseph Mce. Cormick.
Englich Chaplan at Zermatt.

4.75.3 Inventar des Michel Cropt

vorgefunden auf dem Leichname.
1. an Gold hundert fünf und zwanzig Franken 125.–
2. drei Zweifrankenstücke 6.–
3. Münze Franken drei und Rappen ein und dreissig 3.31
4. Eine silberne Sackuhr mit silbernem Schlüssel.
5. Ein Nasstuch, ein Bleistift, und 1 Hut.
Bei H. Gastwirt Seiler hat Cropt vor seiner Bergbesteigung hinterlegt:
a. 1 Flanelhemd.
b. 1 parr Strümpfe wollene.
c. 1 Portfeuille.
d. 1 Gurt.
e. oben schon bezeichnet.
Obige dem verunglückten Michel Cropt zugehörend Artikel wurden dem H. Gastwirte Alexander Seiler hinterlegt, der sich persönlich für deren Erhaltung und Sicherheit verantwortlich stellt und sich dafur eigenhändig unterschreibt.
Zermatt den 22. Juli 1865.
Alle in obigem Inventar bezneichneten Gegenstände sind seinem Bruder Jean-Baptiste Cropt eingehändigt worden.
Zermatt, den 23. Juli 1865.

Cropt Jean-Baptiste.

4.75.4 Inventar des Edouard Wilson

Inventar vorgenommen den 22. Juli 1865, zu Zermatt in dem Gasthofe Monte Rosa auf Instanz der öffentlichen Parthei vorgestellt durch Berichtsteller Substitut Cesar Clemenz vor dem H. Bezirksrichter Alois Biner in Randa, verbeiständet von dem gefertigten Aktuar ad hoc Donat Andenmatten in Visp.
1. Hut, weiser, mit blauem Schleier.
2. Verschiedene Toilettensachen, wie Seife, Schwam, Nastuch, 2 Flanelhemden, Oelmittel, Handschuh 2 paar.
3. Drei Taschentücher.
4. 2 Gesprächbücher, und 2 Gebetbücher.
5. Portefeuille.
6. Eine kleine Schachtel.
7. Ein paar Hosen.
8. Ein paar Zimmerschuhe, eine Weste.
9. An Wert sind da vier Billets circulaire von zweihundert fünfzig Franken, also Franken tausend.
An Geld Franken zweihundert vier und siebenzig.
10. Eine silberne Uhr.
11. Ein Sackmesser.
12. Ein Federrohr.
13. Ein Bleistift.

Zu Glaub alles Obigen

Der Bezirksrichter:
Alois Biner, Richter.
Der Aktuar ad hoc:
Donat Andenmatten.

Obige inventarisierte Artikel wurden den Herrn Professor J.S.Philpotts und Rev. James Robertson aus England, Freunden des verunglückten Edouard Wilson, unter Solidarbürgschaft und Verantwortlichkeit des H. Hauptmann Alexander Seiler überlassen, die deren Empfang mit ihrer Handschrift bescheinen.
Zermatt, den 22 Juli 1865.

J.S.Philpotts.
James Robertson.
Alexander Seiler.

4.75.5 Inventar der Effekte Lord Douglas

zu Zermatt im Gasthof H. Staatsrats J.A. Clemenz, Hotel Mont-Cervin, vorgenommen den 22. Juli 1865 auf Instanz der öffentlichen Parthei vorgestellt durch H. Berichtsteller Substitut H. Cesar Clemenz, vor H. Bezirksrichter Alois Biner in Randa, mit Zutug des gefertigten Aktuars ad hoc Donat Andenmatten in Visp.

1. Brieftasche enthaltend mehrere Briefkorrespondenzen und eine Banknote

Englands von 10 L.St. oder	250 Frk.
und eine dit. Englands von 5 L.W.St. oder	125 Frk.
mehr 1 Frankenstück Geld	1.–

und mehrere Rechnungen von Gasthöfen.
2. Ein Habersack, enthaltend:
a. Ein Palteau.
b. Ein Flanelhemd.
c. Ein paar weisse Strümpfe–
d. ein paar lederne Gueten.
e. ein paar Zimmerschuhe.
f. Zwei Reisebücher.
g. Landkarte.
h. eine Scheere.
i. Schüsselchen mit Pomade.
k. Knotenlöser.
l. Schachtelchen mit Pillen.
m. Zahn und Haarbürste und andere Kämme.
n. Graue wollene Strümpfe und Handschuh.

Auf dem Platze wo die Leichname Hadou, Hudson und Cropt gefunden wurden, fand man auch ein Schuh, den man dem Lord Douglas zugehörend angibt und gebrochen ist, so wie auch ein zerrissenen Aermel von dem Palteau desselben.

Zermatt den 22. Juli 1865.

Der Bezirksrichter:
Alois Biner.

une
Sig. ilisible.

Der Aktuar ad hoc:
Donat Andenmaten.

4.76
QUESTIONS À FAIRE À PIERRE TAUGWALD, PÈRE, AU NOM DE MR. WHYMPER

1. Aviez-vous fait des excursions avec Lord Douglas avant l'ascension du Matterhorn?
2. Vous avait-on dit avant le départ de qui la partie devait consister, et aviez vous fait des objections à l'égard de l'un ou de l'autre des voyageurs proposés, ou au nombre proposé de guides en proportion avec celui des voyageurs?
3. Qui a lié les hommes ensemble au moment de quitter le sommet?
4. Qui fut lié le premier?
5. Quelle espèce de corde fut employée?
6. Qui vous à lié à Douglas?

7. Pourquoi s'est-on servi d'une différente espèce de corde entre Lord Douglas et vous-même?
8. La corde employée entre Lord Douglas et vous-même était-elle, dans votre opinion suffisament forte?
9. Faites une description de l'endroit où l'accident est arrivé?
10. Est-ce que dans votre opinion tout le soin nécessaire a été pris à la descente de ce point?
11. Comment l'accident est-il arrivé?
12. Au moment où les hommes sont tombés, est-ce que la corde était bien tendue ou lâche?
13. Quelle était dans votre opinion la cause que la corde s'est rompue?
14. Etait-ce possible de retenir les quatres hommes, après que la corde fut rompue?

Le juge d'instruction est prié d'addresser les questions ci-contre au guide Taugwald, père.
Zermatt, ce 21 Juillet 65.

Edouard Whymper.

5
THE ENQUIRY

5.1
THE ENQUIRY DOCUMENTS

Thanks to the efforts of Montagnier, the Report of the Enquiry, or rather a variety of documents relating to it, was finally released in 1920. The documents appear to have been obtained from Visp, or more likely copied there, by an employee of Librairie A.Jullien of Geneva, who published the French edition of Whymper's *Guide to Zermatt and the Matterhorn* in 1911 and who had been preparing a new French edition of *Scrambles* before Whymper died. The documents are not in fact limited to the extracts published by J.P.Farrar in *AJ33*, 234-47, but consist of the following:

1. Evidence of Whymper, in French.
2. Evidence of Taugwalder, in German.
3. Evidence of Andenmatten, in German.
4. Evidence of Lochmatter, in German.
5. Further evidence of Taugwalder, in German.
6. Verdict in German.
7. Undated extract from Whymper's evidence, in French.
8. List of names of 15th July search party, in French.
9. List of names of 20th July recovery party, in French.
10. Transcript of various receipts relating to 8 & 9 above.
11. List of Court fees etc, in German.
12. Copy (incomplete) of summons to Whymper to attend Enquiry, in French.
13. Inventory of possessions of Hadow & Hudson, in German.
14. Inventory of possessions of Croz, in German.
15. Inventory of possessions of Edouard Wilson [sic – killed on Riffelhorn].
16. Inventory of possessions of Lord Douglas, in German.
17. Questions to put to Taugwalder 'in the name of Mr. Whymper', in French.
18. Official French translations of 2-6 & 13-16 above.

5.1.1 Comments on the above

7. This appears to be the brief resumé referred to by Ronald Clark in *The Day the Rope Broke*, 191.

8. The list confirms Whymper's figure of 20 in *Scrambles*. It includes the President of the Commune Welschen, Peter Perren and the two Lochmatters. For full details see section 3.15 (Search parties).

9. Once again Whymper got the number right; this time 21 participated, including the President Welschen and 'M. le juge Louis Julen', whose name does not appear elsewhere in connection with the Enquiry but who seems to have played a prominent part behind the scenes as Taugwalder's lawyer or adviser. Peter Perren took part again amongst at least fifteen inhabitants of Zermatt including Young Peter Taugwalder and his brother Joseph, but not Old Peter.

12. The Court copy of Whymper's summons, correctly dated 21st July, omits the words 'à 2 heures de cet aprés midi', which appear in the original.

13. Hudson's broken watch with the hands at 3.45, together with his other possessions and those of Hadow were handed to McCormick on the Saturday.

14. Croz' possessions were handed over to his brother on Sunday 23rd July.

15. Wilson's inventory raises the possibility that a separate enquiry was held into his death. His possessions were handed to Phillpotts and Robertson, who signed for them on the Saturday, the day they left Zermatt.

16. Lord Douglas's possessions, unlike those of the other victims, which each mention Seiler or the Monte Rosa hotel, are recorded as being in the Hotel Mont Cervin of State counsellor J.A.Clemenz. There is no record of anyone signing for them, although Lord Queensberry did arrive in Zermatt on Monday 24th July.

17. This document dated 21st July and signed by Whymper sets out his fourteen questions for Taugwalder and concludes that the presiding judge is asked to address the above questions to the guide Taugwalder, father.

It would seem as though whoever copied the documents copied just about everything in the Court file, regardless of its nature or relevance. It looks as though someone from Geneva actually made the copies, rather than a German speaking person and that he made two trips to Visp, having to go there a second time in order to take a copy of the French translations (item 18 above). As he did not therefore copy everything the first time and only added French translations the second time, there is a possibility that the Court file, if it still exists, will contain some of the other documents that did once exist, such as the list of Whymper's own questions and answers, which he must have handed to Clemenz at the start of the Enquiry and the similar list of Taugwalder's written answers alongside a German translation of Whymper's list of questions for him in French. The 18 items listed above are all in the possession of the Alpine Club and there is currently on display in the Zermatt museum an identical copy of the evidence of Whymper in French and of Taugwalder in German.

5.2
THE MATTERHORN ACCIDENT PROCEEDINGS. 1865

Session of the Court of Enquiry for the district of Visp held at Zermatt in the Hotel Mont Cervin under the presidency of the examining magistrate Jos. Ant. Clemenz of Visp, the deputy recorder César Clemenz, the clerk of the court Don. Andenmatten of Visp, and the ad hoc bailiff Joh. Julen, on the 21st July 1865.

5.2.1 Mr. Whymper tourist

Q 1. What is your name, age, status and domicile?
A 1. Edward Whymper, 25 years old, single, artistic draughtsman, living in London.

Q 2. Did you participate in the expedition that took place on the 13th inst.?
A 2. Yes.

Q 3. How many people constituted the personnel of the expedition?
A 3. When we left Zermatt there were eight people, that is four tourists, two guides and two porters. One of the porters, a son of Peter Taugwalder, set off again for Zermatt on the morning of the 14th from the place where we camped for the night.

Q 4. What are the names of the tourists, the two guides and the porter?
A 4. The Rev Charles Hudson, Mr. Hadow, Lord Francis Douglas and myself; guides, Michel Croz of Chamonix, Peter Taugwalder father of Zermatt and porter, Peter Taugwalder son.

Q 5. What is the domicile of Messrs. Douglas, Hudson and Hadow?
A 5. Mr. Hudson was vicar of Skillington, England; the domicile of the others I do not know.

Q 6. At what time did you set off on the 14th to continue your route to reach the top of the Matterhorn?
A 6. We left our camp of the 13th/14th at 3.40a.m.

Q 7. At what time did you arrive at the summit of the Matterhorn?
A 7. At 1.40p.m.

Q 8. How much time did you stop on the top of the Matterhorn?
A 8. One hour.

Q 9. Did you take the same route on the descent as on the ascent?
A 9. Exactly the same.

Q 10. Were the four tourists and the guides tied by ropes between them?
A 10. Yes, in the following order and manner: at the head of the column was the guide Croz, then came Messrs. Hadow, Hudson, Lord Douglas, the guide Taugwalder father, myself and finally Taugwalder son. Between Lord Douglas and Taugwalder father the rope was less thick than between Michel Croz and Lord Douglas on the one side and between Taugwalder father and Taugwalder son on the other side.

Q 11. How did the unfortunate catastrophe come about?
A 11. We were going down in the order indicated higher up. At a distance of about 300 feet from the summit we came to a difficult place composed of rock and snow. As far as I know at the moment the accident occurred Mr.Hadow was the only one moving. The same Mr.Hadow experienced considerable difficulty in coming down, and Michel Croz in order to give greater security was taking Mr.Hadow's legs one after another and placing them. I cannot say with certainty what was the real cause of the accident but my belief is that Michel Croz had placed the feet of Mr.Hadow on some rock holds and was turning round to go down a step himself when Mr.Hadow slipped and in his fall knocked over Michel Croz. This double weight dragged down Mr.Hudson and after him Lord Douglas. The few instants that this lasted afforded sufficient time for the three at the rear to plant themselves firmly, so firmly indeed that the rope broke between Lord Douglas and Taugwalder father. For two or three moments we saw the unfortunate four sliding on their backs and spreading out their hands to save themselves and then they disappeared altogether. Not a cry was heard after the initial cry of surprise uttered by Michel Croz. I myself and the two Taugwalders descended without further accident by the same route as we had ascended, using all possible care and looking everywhere for traces of our unfortunate companions. But we saw nothing beyond two axes stuck in the snow. Consequent on these precautions and searches, we were surprised by the night at a height of about 13,000 English feet. We made camp there in an area of about 12 feet and the following morning, Saturday the 15th, we resumed the descent arriving at Zermatt at 10.30a.m.

Q 12. Did you not return to the foot of the Matterhorn to seek the unfortunate victims of the accident?
A 12. Yes, on Sunday morning, the 16th instant.

Q 13. Were you alone or accompanied? In the latter event, please indicate the names of those who accompanied you.
A 13. I was accompanied by the Rev Joseph McCormick, a friend of Mr.

Hudson, as well as by the Rev Mr. Robertson and by Mr. Phillpotts and by the guides, Lochmatter, Alexander and one of the brothers of Maurice Andenmatten of Saas, François Payot of Chamonix and another guide from Chamonix whose name I do not know. *[see note A13 in section 5.4.1 below for the confusion over this answer]*

Q 14. Did you find the four victims?
A 14. No, only the bodies of three, namely Mr.Hudson, Mr.Hadow and Michel Croz.

Q 15. Did you not inform the authority of the Commune of Zermatt that you had found the bodies of three victims?
A 15. No, not officially, but on my return to Zermatt on the Saturday morning I informed the President of the Zermatt Commune of the sad accident and at the same time asked him to send some men to the scene of the catastrophe, in case after all one or other of my unfortunate companions was still alive. This request was granted and a good number of guides set off immediately. They returned six hours later, saying that they had caught sight of the bodies but that it was impossible to reach them that day. On the other hand these same Zermatt guides refused en masse to go in search of the bodies the following morning, Sunday, and it was on this account that I set out without official authority to recover the bodies and that on my return I did not think I had to make an official report. Nevertheless the fact that three of the bodies had been discovered was made known unofficially to anyone who took an interest in this sad affair.

Q 16. Did you not find any trace of Lord Douglas?
A 16. I came across a pair of gloves that I had given him myself in Zermatt and the leather belt that he wore during the ascent.

Q 17. Have you anything to alter or add to your deposition?
A 17. I will add that Taugwalder son who accompanied us at first as porter served us as guide from the morning of the 14th onwards.

Protocol read and approved.
Sig. Edward Whymper.

The examining magistrate:
J.A.Clemenz.

The ad hoc clerk:
Donat Andenmatten.

————————————

The same day and before the same

5.2.2 Examination of Peter Taugwalder father

Q 18. What is your name? etc.
A 18. My name is Peter Taugwalder, 45 years old, married, mountain guide living in Zermatt.

Q 19. Did you climb the Matterhorn on the 14th instant?
A 19. Yes.

Q 20. In what capacity did you make the ascent?
A 20. As mountain guide.

Q 21. By whom were you engaged as guide for the ascent?
A 21. By Lord Douglas and Whymper.

Q 22. Had you already made some mountain excursions with Lord Douglas before the ascent of the Matterhorn?
A 22. Yes, I accompanied Lord Douglas as guide to Zinal and on the Gabelhorn.

Q 23. Were you informed before starting (for the ascent of the Matterhorn) of which tourists the party was actually to consist and did you make any objection to any of these tourists or even to the relative number of travellers to guides?
A 23. I was certainly told of how many persons the party consisted. I did not make any objection to any person in the party. But I did remark that in proportion to the number of tourists there were too few guides. Messrs. Whymper and Hudson replied to me that they went just as well as guides, whereupon I made no further remark.

Q 24. Who tied the men up on leaving the summit?
A 24. The first four men of the party, consisting of the guide Croz, Hadow, Hudson and Lord Douglas, were tied up by the guide Croz and I tied myself to Lord Douglas with a special rope.

Q 25. Who was tied up first?
A 25. I do not recall for certain which of the three tourists was tied up first by Croz.

Q 26. What kind of rope was used for that?
A 26. The rope to which Croz and the three tourists were tied was a strong and brand-new rope.

Q 27. Who tied you to Lord Douglas?
A 27. I did, myself.

Q 28. Why was another rope used between Lord Douglas and you?
A 28. Because the first rope was not long enough to be able to tie me on it as well.

Q 29. Was the rope used between yourself and Lord Douglas in your opinion of sufficient strength?
A 29. If I had found the rope used between Lord Douglas and myself was too weak, I would have taken good care not to tie myself to Lord Douglas with it and I would not have wished to endanger him any more than myself. If I had found the rope too weak, I would have recognised it as such before the ascent of the Matterhorn and would have rejected it.

Q 30. Describe the place where the accident occurred.
A 30. Having descended about two to three hundred feet from the summit of the Matterhorn, we arrived at the second of the most dangerous places where the rocks are composed of smooth slabs and where it was very difficult to get a footing. It was there it happened, where the first tourist after the guide Croz slipped and he dragged off the tourists above him and they in turn dragged off the guide Croz after the rope between Lord Douglas and myself broke.

Q 31. In your opinion was all necessary caution exercised at this place?
A 31. Yes. It was regrettable that the first tourist after Croz was a very bad climber.

Q 32. How did the accident occur?
A 32. I have already described it above and have only to add that after the rope between Lord Douglas and myself broke Whymper, my son and I remained at the spot from where we tried to extricate ourselves as soon as possible. We descended until we found a place where we spent the night. The following morning we arrived safely in Zermatt.

Q 33. Was the rope tight or not at the moment when the men fell?
A 33. It was tight.

Q 34. How is it in your opinion that the rope broke?
A 34. I do not know but the weight of the three tourists with the force of their fall could even have broken a strong rope.

Q 35. Was it possible to hold back the four men after the rope broke?
A 35. Impossible.

Q 36. If the rope between Mr.Douglas and you had not broken, would you have been able to save the tourists?

A 36. I am firmly convinced that if the rope between Lord Douglas and me had not broken, I together with the guide Croz would have been able to save the tourists.

Read and confirmed.
Peter Taugwalder.

The examining magistrate:
Clemenz.
The ad hoc clerk:
Donat Andenmatten.

The same day and before the same

5.2.3 Examination of Franz Jos. Andenmatten

Q 37. What is your name?
A 37. My name is Franz Andenmatten, 40 years old, married, mountain guide, living in Almagell.

Q 38. Did you not go recently along with other guides into the valley of Zmutt in search of the victims of the accident on the Matterhorn?
A 38. Yes, twice. The first time I went with four other guides accompanied by four tourists and we found three of the victims at once. These three were on a level snowfield where for a great distance there were neither crevasses nor couloirs.

Q 39. Where do you believe the body of the fourth victim may have got to?
A 39. It is probably lodged higher up in the rocks.

Q 40. What are the names of the tourists who went with you the first time?
A 40. McCormick, Whymper, Robertson, Phillpotts.

Q 41. What did you do with the three bodies?
A 41. I was on my own some distance from the victims; I believe that they were placed together and covered with snow and I noticed the English minister conducted prayers. The second time I went to the place where the bodies were buried to have them brought down.

Q 42. Which guides were with you on the first occasion?
A 42. Alexander and Joseph-Marie Lochmatter and two guides from Chamonix, one of whom was called Payot. The name of the other I do not know.

The deponent cannot write.

The examining magistrate:
Clemenz.
The ad hoc clerk:
Donat Andenmatten.

Continuation on the 22nd July in the same place and before the same

5.2.4 Examination of Alexander Lochmatter

Q 43. What is your name etc?
A 43. My name is Alexander Lochmatter, 27 years old, single, mountain guide and clockmaker living in St.Niklaus.

Q 44. Did you not go in company with several tourists and guides to the foot of the Matterhorn in search of the four victims?
A 44. Yes.

Q 45. How many of the victims did you find there?
A 45. Just three of them.

Q 46. Do you know which was missing?
A 46. Yes, the tourists told me it was Lord Douglas.

Q 47. Were the three that were found together or some distance apart?
A 47. They were lying at quite a short distance from one another.

Q 48. Were not the three bodies collected together in one place and covered with snow?
A 48. Yes, indeed.

Q 49. Was it the intention to regard them as buried there?
A 49. Yes, like the rest I regarded them as buried there, all the more so when the English minister recited some prayers from a book.

Q 50. Did you find no remains of Lord Douglas, either of his body or of his clothes?
A 50. Nothing, that I know of.

Q 51. Where do you believe that Douglas might be found?
A 51. I think he must be in the rocky part as he could not possibly have fallen further than the others.

Q 52. Were not the three bodies searched and were not objects found on them?
A 52. Messrs Whymper, Robertson and the minister did search the bodies and took possession of the objects they found on them.

Read and confirmed.
Alexander Lochmatter.

The examining magistrate:
J.A. Clemenz.
The ad hoc clerk:
Donat Andenmatten.

———————————

Session of the examining magistrate on the 23rd July at the same place and before the same.

5.2.5 Second examination of Peter Taugwalder

Q 53. What have you remembered about the accident on the Matterhorn since your last examination; have you something to add or to alter in your previous deposition?
A 53. Nothing except that I said to the guide Croz before we reached the dangerous place that one ought for greater safety to stretch a rope. Croz replied that it was not necessary.

Q 54. Did your son see how the accident occurred?
A 54. I do not think so for he asked me at once 'are you still there father?'

Q 55. How was it that there were three tourists between Croz and yourself as against only one between yourself and your son? Such a division appears to the Examining Magistrate to have been an incorrect one. What do you say about it?
A 55. The first in the column was the guide Croz. Then came Mr.Hadow, then Hudson who regarded himself as a guide, and after him Lord Douglas, then myself, Whymper and my son. So if you, the Examining Magistrate, accept that Hudson was acting as guide you will see that each traveller was between two guides.

Q 56. Did the party of travellers regard Hudson as a guide?
A 56. Hudson himself said he did not need a guide and that he could act as a guide.

Q 57. Who supplied the rope to which you and Lord Douglas were tied?
A 57. The rope was supplied by the tourists.

Q 58. Was your son with you as guide or as porter?
A 58. On the first day as porter and the following day as guide. Initially the tourists wanted to send my son back as they claimed that Croz and I sufficed as guides. On my pressing my request to take my son as guide the tourists then agreed to my proposal.

Q 59. At what time did you set off from Zermatt on the 13th?
A 59. Between 5 and 6 in the morning.

Q 60. At what hour did you reach the place where you camped for the night?
A 60. About midday.

Q 61. At what time did you set off again on the 14th?
A 61. About 2, and stayed there for just over half an hour. The tourists were in good spirits and shouting with joy.

[The Official Report omits Q&A62 altogether. It seems probable, however, that it was A61 & Q62 that got lost and that A61 as quoted above, which does not answer Q61, should in fact be A62. See note Q59-62 in section 5.4.3 below.]

Q 63. In his deposition Mr.Whymper said that Hadow slipped first and dragged off the guide Croz with him and that these two then dragged off Hudson and Douglas. While this was happening he, Whymper, and his guides Taugwalder father and son had time to secure their footing. At this very moment the rope between Douglas and Taugwalder broke. But you said in your reply to Question 30 that at first Mr.Hadow slipped, then Hudson and Lord Douglas and only after these three the guide Croz. As Mr.Whymper's deposition and yours do not entirely correspond you are asked to declare whether you stick to your earlier statement?
A 63. As Mr.Whymper was above me in a place where he could see the unfortunate course of events better than I could, his deposition may be more correct so much so that I could not insist that Croz only fell after the three tourists. It was all over in a moment and we were so taken by surprise that precise knowledge of the occurrence became almost impossible.

Q 64. Have you anything else to add or alter in your above deposition?
A 64. I have to add that to be more secure I turned towards the rocks and as the rope which was between Whymper and myself was not taut I was fortunately able to wind it round a projecting rock, which then gave me the necessary and life saving anchorage; the rope that connected me with Douglas and those ahead gave me such a pull from their fall that I am still suffering a lot at the place where my body was tied with the rope.

Read and confirmed.

Peter Taugwalder.

The examining magistrate:
Clemenz.
The ad hoc clerk:
Donat Andenmatten.

5.3
[VERDICT]

The committee of enquiry for the district of Visp made up of the examining magistrate Josef-Anton Clemenz and recorder C.Clemenz, both living in Visp, have reached the following decision that there are no grounds for prosecution with regard to the enquiry officially conducted into the accident that occurred on the ascent of the Matterhorn.

Facts.

At 5 o'clock on the morning of 13th July a caravan consisting of Messrs. Lord Douglas, Hudson, Edward Whymper and Hadow and the guides Michel Croz of Chamonix, Peter Taugwalder father and his son Peter, both of Zermatt, set off from Zermatt to attempt the ascent of the Matterhorn. They spent the night of the 13th at the foot of the mountain. The following day they left their sleeping place at 3.40 in the morning and reached the summit of the Horn at 1.40. They followed exactly the same route on the descent as they had on the ascent, and they were roped to one another in the following order. At the head of the column was the guide Croz, then came Hadow, Hudson, Lord Douglas, Taugwalder father and Whymper and Taugwalder son. At a distance of about 300 feet from the summit they came to a place composed of rock and snow, so that it was very difficult to get firm footing. Whilst crossing this dangerous place Mr.Hadow slipped and in his fall knocked over the guide Croz. This double weight dragged down Mr.Hudson as well and after him Lord Douglas. The few instants that this lasted gave those at the rear time to secure firm foothold, so firmly indeed that the rope between L.Douglas and Taugwalder father broke in two. Those that were left descended the mountain with all possible prudence and reached Zermatt without further accident at 10.30 on Saturday the 15th, after having spent the night of the 14th/15th at a height of 13,000 feet on a rocky ledge with a surface of about 12 feet.

Considering:

1. that guilt attaches to no one on the above facts;
2. that Mr.Hadow was the cause of the accident;

that on the facts of the case set out above no one can be accused of a fault or of a crime it is decided

a. [sic] there is to be no sequel to the foregoing enquiry, but a decision of no grounds for prosecution with an order that the Treasury bear the costs.

5.4
NOTES ON THE EVIDENCE

5.4.1 Edward Whymper Questions 1-17

Q 2. This is the first question that appears in the document in Vecqueray's handwriting, translating Whymper's answers into French.

A 3. Vecqueray's entry here suggests that he had second thoughts about his original translation and later made a number of alterations. His final version, which coincides with the wording in the Official Report in all but minor details, deletes his original last three lines and replaces a number of words with others written in above the line.

Q 4. It seems most unlikely for the reasons stated below that this records Clemenz' precise wording, rather than an improvement made by Vecqueray in the course of his translation, as there is almost no sign of Clemenz heeding the answers, having merely recited in French the questions he had previously put to Whymper in writing, to which Whymper then recited his written answers.

Q 6. Vecqueray seems to have amended this question in the course of writing it out in French (suggesting that Clemenz provided it in German), by deleting after 'chemin' the words 'conduisant au sommet etc', and replacing them with 'pour arriver etc', which appear on the line below. Apart from some minor details in the initial words his amended version again agrees with that in the Official Report.

Q&A 8. Whymper's own note of the Enquiry includes an extra question [8½] 'Was there any difficulty in remaining on the top?' together with his answer, 'No'. Like Q16½ referred to below it does not appear in the Official Report, suggesting that whilst Clemenz could not resist following up the previous answer that they spent an hour on the top, (it being a feature of Whymper's and Taugwalder's evidence on the Friday, apart from three minor instances which are noted, that none of the answers ever leads to a fresh question) the Clerk was not recording the answers as they were given but intended to transcribe them later from the document Whymper had handed in, from which Clemenz was reciting the questions.

A 10. Vecqueray again altered his translation as he went along, deleting his initial reference to the less thick rope and bringing it back a few lines further on. This reference to the rope between Douglas and Taugwalder being less thick than the other ropes constitutes the only evidence before the Court of there being any difference at all between the ropes, apart from A24 in which Taugwalder spoke of tying himself to Douglas with a special rope. In neither case was the witness asked to elaborate.

A 11. This is the only occasion when Whymper referred to the 'double weight' of Hadow and Croz dragging down Hudson, apart from stating in 1909 in the *Strand Magazine* that the strain of these two falling men pulled Hudson off his legs. It is hardly consistent with Hadow slipping and knocking Croz off, unless Hudson had held Hadow for some time before Croz' weight was added to the rope. The reference in the first sentence to 'higher up' seems to confirm that the answers were already written out, quite apart from the actual words in Vecqueray's translation also appearing in the Report. Taugwalder's reply A32 'I have already described it above' is also consistent with his answers being written out in advance. Some of Whymper's phrases here reappear in almost identical words in the accounts he gave subsequently, but not the double weight.

A 13. It is apparent that Whymper was mistaken as to the identity of the guide Andenmatten, probably believing him to be Moritz Andenmatten of Visp, rather than Franz Andenmatten of Saas. His confusion seems to have been appreciated both by Vecqueray and by the Enquiry Clerk, who was also an Andenmatten, although neither went so far as to correct the mistake altogether. Whymper recorded 'the guides Alexandre Lochmatter & his brother, Moritz Andermatten de Saas, François Payot...' Vecqueray who was probably climbing with Franz Andenmatten, Robertson and others that week and knew his correct name, initially wrote 'Lochmatter Alexandre et son frère, Moritz Andermatten', but then he seems to have had second thoughts and altered Moritz to Maurice and continued on the next line with 'Franz Anderm'. But before completing the surname with the letters 'atten' he seems to have had another change of mind, deciding that he should translate precisely what Whymper had written, crossing out 'Franz Anderm' and continuing with 'de Saas, François Payot de Chamouny...' The Clerk Donat Andenmatten of Visp clearly knew Moritz Andenmatten, who was also President of the Commune of Visp, and by the time he wrote out his record of the evidence the Enquiry had actually heard evidence from Franz Andenmatten. He seems therefore to have tried to reconcile Whymper's mistake with his own knowledge in order to make some sense of it, by switching the word 'brother' from Lochmatter to Andenmatten, thereby losing a Lochmatter and making it read as though the guide in question came from Saas and was one of Maurice's brothers. The Report records 'et des guides Lochmatter Alexandre et un des frères Maurice Andenmatten de Saas, François Payot de Chamonix...'

Q&A 16. Whymper's own note of the Enquiry includes an extra question here from Clemenz [16½] 'What was my opinion about Douglas body? Gave it'. The Clerk did not record this, which again tends to confirm that Whymper handed in to Clemenz a copy of the questions and answers, which the Clerk later transcribed.

A 17. Whymper's own note of A17 begins with 'Nothing to change but to elicit further information I hand in further questions'. A further paragraph then

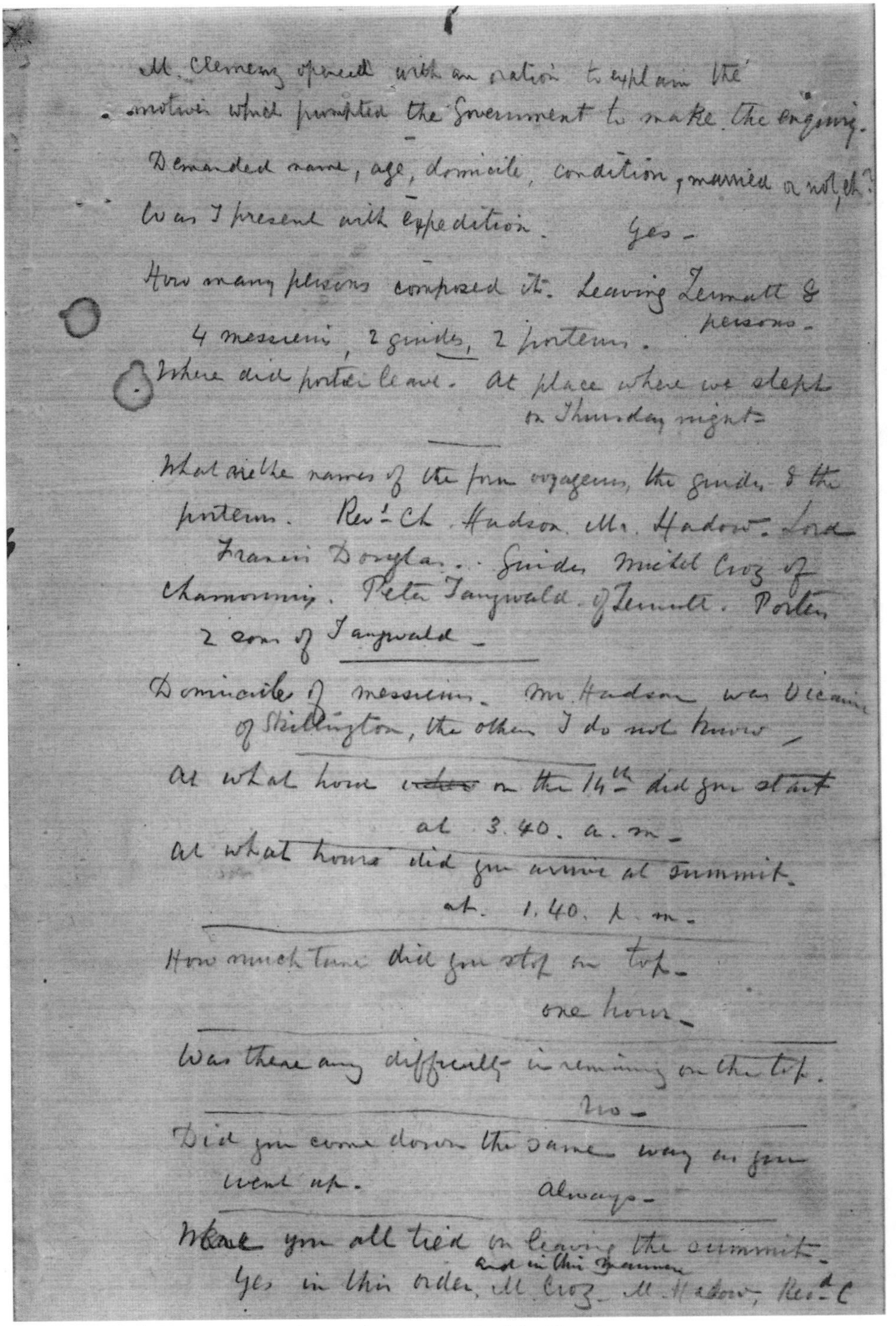

M. Clemenz opened with an oration to explain the motives which prompted the Government to make the enquiry.

Demanded name, age, domicile, condition, married or not, etc?

Was I present with expedition. Yes –

How many persons composed it. Leaving Zermatt 8 persons –
4 messieurs, 2 guides, 2 porters.

Where did porters leave. At place where we slept on Thursday night –

What are the names of the four voyageurs, the guides & the porters. Revd Ch. Hudson. Mr. Hadow. Lord Francis Douglas. Guides Michel Croz of Chamonix. Peter Taugwald of Zermatt. Porters 2 sons of Taugwald –

Domicile of messieurs. Mr. Hudson was Vicar of Skillington, the others I do not know –

At what hour ~~when~~ on the 14th did you start
at 3.40. a. m –

At what hours did you arrive at summit.
at. 1.40. p. m.

How much time did you stop on top –
one hour –

Was there any difficulty in remaining on the top.
No –

Did you come down the same way as you went up. Always –

Were you all tied on leaving the summit –
Yes in this order, and in this manner M. Croz. M. Hadow, Revd C

Whymper's own record of the Enquiry

Hudson, Douglas, Taugwald père, Whymper, Taugwald fils., but the cord between Taugwald pere & Lord Douglas was less thick than that between Michel Croz and Ld Douglas on one side and the two Taugwalds on the other.

How did the accident occur. We were going down in the order mentioned, about 2 or 300 feet from the summit, and arrived at a difficult place, composed of rocks and snow, as far as I know at the moment the accident occurred Hadow was the only one moving. Hadow experienced considerable difficulty in coming down, and Michel Croz in order to give greater security was taking his legs one after another and placing them in their exact position. I cannot speak with certainty, but my belief is that Michel Croz had placed the feet of M. Hadow on some rocks, and was turning round to go down a step or two himself, when M. Hadow slipped and knocked over in his fall Croz. The two falling dragged Hudson out of his steps and after him Lord Douglas. The few moments that passed, allowed those above to plant themselves firmly, so firmly indeed that the cord broke between Lord Douglas & Taugwalder pere.

Go on with narration. For two or three moments we saw them sliding on their backs, and spreading out their hands endeavouring to save themselves, they were then lost to our sight. No cry was uttered after the first exclamation of surprise by Croz. We came down with

A10 – A11

(the Taugwalds & myself) without any further accident by the way we had ascended, using all possible care, and looking everywhere for our unfortunate companions – but seeing nothing beyond 2 of their axes stuck in the snow. We were consequently surprised by the night at a height of about 13000 English feet, and had to remain there until day break, when we continued the descent and arrived at Zermatt at 10.30 a. m.

Did you not return to the foot of the Mont Cervin to seek for your unfortunate companions.

Yes on Sunday morning the 16.

Were you alone, or were you accompanied by others, if so please to name them.

I was accompanied by the Revd Joseph McCormick a friend of Mr Hudson's, the Revd Mr Robertson, & Mr Philpots, also by the following guides. Alexander Lochmatter & his brother, Moritz Andermatten de Saas, Francois Payot de Chamounix et another guide of Chamounix who I do not know.

Did you find the four victims.

No, only the bodies of Michel Croz, Hadow & Hudson.

Did you not inform the authority of the commune of Zermatt that you had found the dead bodies of the three victims. No I did not do so officially on my return on Sunday but I informed the president of the commune of the sad accident immediately on my arrival at Zermatt on Saturday morning, and desired him to despatch men immediately to search for ~~their bodies~~ thinking it was possible some one might remain alive. This ~~was~~ request was complied with and a number of guides immediately set out to search for the bodies; they returned, but reported that they

A11 – A15

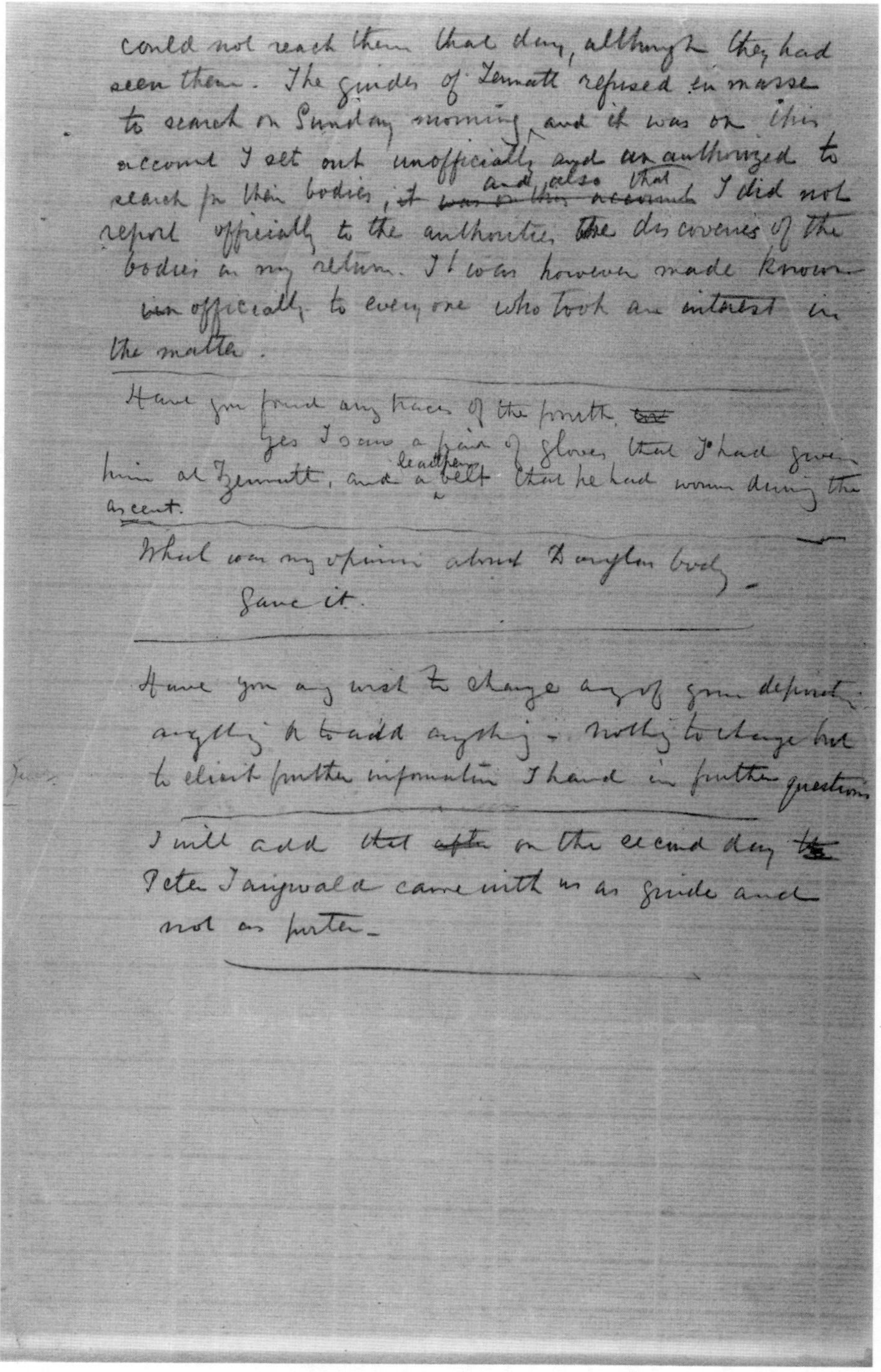
could not reach them that day, although they had seen them. The guides of Zermatt refused en masse to search on Sunday morning and it was on this account I set out unofficially and unauthorized to search for their bodies, and also that I did not report officially to the authorities the discoveries of the bodies on my return. It was however made known unofficially to every one who took an interest in the matter.

Have you found any traces of the fourth?

Yes I saw a pair of gloves that I had given him at Zermatt, and a leather belt that he had worn during the ascent.

What was my opinion about Douglas body –

Gave it.

Have you any wish to change any of your deposition anything or to add anything – nothing to change but to elicit further information I hand in further questions

I will add that on the second day Peter Taugwalder came with us as guide and not as porter –

A15 – A17

follows 'I will add that on the second day Peter Taugwald came with us as guide...' It seems probable that Whymper's formality over the questions for Taugwalder was for the benefit of the other members of the Tribunal, and that Clemenz not only knew what was coming but had probably asked Whymper to prepare such a list to relieve himself of the need to draft questions. Indeed it looks very much as though Clemenz must have given Whymper a short list of questions for Taugwalder, including such as Q22, 23, 30, 31, 32 & 35 and that he must have asked him to supplement it with questions relating to the use of the rope, as otherwise Clemenz did not on the first day seek any information from Taugwalder about the accident other than the ambiguous Q36, as from Q22 to Q35 inclusive every single question comes from Whymper's list and appears on the face of it to have been asked by him.

5.4.2 Peter Taugwalder Questions 18-36

Q 22. Although this might look like a Clemenz question to Taugwalder, asked by the hotelier familiar with his guest's activities (as Douglas had stayed at the Mont Cervin for a fortnight), it comes in fact from Whymper's list, as do all those that follow up to and including Q35. Nevertheless it may have originated with Clemenz for the reason stated in the note to A17 above. It seems as though the only purpose in Whymper asking such a question, the only one to which he knew Taugwalder's answer, would be to enable him to establish his link with and consequent loyalty to Douglas, but this hardly seems likely.

Q 23. Also from Whymper's list, but drafted perhaps by Clemenz (see note to A17). The Tribunal took it up again in Q55 & 56. The German translation first introduced the bracketed reference to the Matterhorn as though to exclude any possible ambiguity following on A22, and it is interesting to note how several of the German versions of the questions have been treated as though they relate back to previous answers, whereas it is a feature of both Whymper's original questions for Taugwalder and of Clemenz questions for Whymper that they disregarded previous answers, for the obvious reason that they were all drafted before the Enquiry even started. This again seems to confirm that the questions were answered in writing, although both questions and answers were later recited, as the Clerk would hardly have recorded such a verbal phrase in brackets. It is not known who translated Whymper's questions into German, the list he handed to Clemenz having been already translated into French. The translator, whoever he was, must have known that all the questions had been written out in a list in advance, as there is no evidence whatsoever to suggest that an interpreter translated them one by one as Taugwalder gave his evidence to the Tribunal. The amendment of Q23 on account of A22 is particularly interesting in the light of the way Q26 was amended so that it related, wrongly and nonsensically, to A25. If Clemenz did not translate and ask each question orally one at a time (and it is virtually certain that he did not, judging from such things as the superfluous questions Q27 & Q32, which Taugwalder had already answered in A24 & A30), and if Clemenz did not present Taugwalder in advance with the list of questions in their final German form (which would be inconsistent with adding German words to Whymper's Q23 & Q26 in order to relate the questions to the previous answers) the only alternative seems to be that each question was translated from French into German as and when it was put to Old Peter for him to prepare his answer. We know that Old Peter could not speak French and the probability is that his cousin Alois Julen, who was a mountain guide as well as a judge, not only translated the questions into German but also helped him to draft his answers.

A 24. If Croz tied up the first four, it might be expected that someone else would have tied up 'the last four' with another rope, until it was decided that Whymper should write down their names, put them in a bottle and then follow on with Young Peter and catch the others up. Taugwalder made no mention of this nor of his son and Whymper. His reference to tying himself on to Lord Douglas with a special rope seems to have passed unnoticed by the critics, just as Clemenz and the other members of the Tribunal appear not to have noticed it, or not to have considered it to be of any relevance. But even without any further elaboration from Taugwalder, we can confidently draw the conclusion that he knew the special rope had been taken and was intended for use as fixed rope, which they could attach to the rocks and leave behind. The fact that he had in mind the likely need to leave fixed rope is confirmed by his comment in A53.

A 25. Taugwalder chose to confine his answer here to which of the tourists was tied up first *by Croz*, although Whymper's question was in more general terms and was almost certainly intended to reveal whether he tied on to Douglas before or after Croz tied on to Douglas. Had the examination been oral and had the answer not already been committed to writing by Taugwalder, the questioner would surely have sought a fuller answer. Even so Taugwalder's answer throws no light on whether any excess length of rope, beyond what was necessary to tie the four men in the circumstances, was carried by Croz or was available at the Douglas end, although he seems to exclude the latter in A28. As with the next question, Q26, it is remarkable that Taugwalder in his answer should have been able and allowed to concentrate the Enquiry's attention on the rope that did *not* break.

Q 26. Whymper's French wording of the question was in general terms, asking what kind of rope was used (Quelle espèce de corde fut employée?). He did not relate it to Q25 or limit it in any other way. But in the course of translating it into German someone has added the word 'dazu' (for that) confining the question to the irrelevant rope mentioned in A25, instead of asking about the ropes in general or, more sensibly the 'special' rope that broke. It is understandable that by the time the question reached Taugwalder he should have regarded it as referring to the rope between Douglas and Croz, particularly if he was unaware of the German amendment to Whymper's French.

A 26. Clemenz appears to have accepted Taugwalder's answer as though the question related solely to the irrelevant Croz rope. He did not put a similar question about the Taugwalder – Douglas rope either when he first heard the answer or during Taugwalder's second examination on the Sunday after the Tribunal had had the opportunity of considering the adequacy of the evidence. It would be easier to understand Clemenz' neglect if Taugwalder's replies had been submitted in writing and merely recited by him in response to Clemenz recital of the questions (which appears to have been the case) than it would be if Taugwalder had only been questioned orally. But it is hard to avoid the conclusion that, whoever meddled with this Whymper question, Clemenz was happy to condone it and to concentrate on the irrelevant. Even though Taugwalder said nothing in evidence about the special rope mentioned in A24 and even though Whymper's reference to the same rope being less thick than the Croz rope (A10) may have passed unnoticed by Clemenz initially, one would have thought that he would have appreciated the significance of the quality, strength and condition of the rope that actually broke. Whymper's questions Q26, 28 & 29 in fact provided three clear opportunities for Taugwalder to describe the rope and say how it came to be used. On two occasions, Q26 & 28, someone altered the question so that Taugwalder did not need to refer to the use of a weaker rope, and in A29, as in A24, Clemenz accepted an answer which skirted round the issue and he failed to seek clarification or amplification.

Q 27. This Whymper question, already answered by Taugwalder in A24 by the time it was put to him, seems to have been intended to confirm or to exclude the possibility that Croz or someone else other than Taugwalder chose to use the sashline. One would expect a competent, experienced and wide awake judge to have realised the witness had already answered the question, the same situation recurring with Q32. The only feasible explanation is that of Taugwalder having been given the list of questions in advance with time to prepare his answers in writing.

Q 28. Taugwalder gave a straightforward answer to this futile question, which was phrased in German in such a way as to distort and miss the whole point of Whymper's original question. Even so the answer fails to reveal anything about the overall length of the first rope and does not mean that it was not long enough for five men. In A25 Taugwalder said he could not recall which of the tourists Croz tied up first. Had Croz tied Douglas first there might have been plenty of spare rope at Croz' end, and all Taugwalder's answer means is that there was insufficient rope for him to attach himself at the Douglas end. No regard was ever had as to whether it was intended all along that they should descend in one long column of seven.

This question is the most extreme instance of distortion in the course of translation into German. Whymper's French version asked why 'une différente espèce de corde' was used. 'Why was a different kind of rope used between Lord Douglas and yourself?' was his original consistent draft in English. In Q26 the same words 'espèce de corde' were correctly translated into German as, what 'kind of rope' was used. It seems therefore that to ask Taugwalder merely why 'another rope' was used between him and Douglas was deliberate distortion and not just the result of misunderstanding the French. But that does not explain why Clemenz condoned it nor why he failed to ask for some elaboration. Whereas both Whymper and Taugwalder seem to have had the same thing in mind, one referring to a different kind of rope and the other to a special rope, Clemenz avoided the subject and failed to elicit any evidence from Taugwalder, firstly as to the way in which the rope was special or different and secondly as to why such a rope was used. Whereas the original question might seem to have been a leading question, it did in fact relate to the last words of A24 even though it had been drafted earlier, and furthermore the Tribunal had already heard evidence from Whymper in A10 about a less thick rope. It has been widely supposed that Taugwalder had something to hide, whereas his frank reference to the rope that broke being a special rope (A24) suggests that he might well have been able to provide an excusable explanation for using it, if only he had been given the opportunity and been asked the proper questions.

Graham Brown observed, and recorded in his copious notes on the '1865 Matterhorn accident' now in the National Library of Scotland, how in the List of Illustrations in *Scrambles* (but not in the actual captions in the text) Whymper described each of the three kinds of rope depicted as 'broken on the Matterhorn'. This is so in all five editions published by John Murray in Whymper's lifetime and must have been deliberate. Indeed it gives meaning to the tattered ends of the twisted ropes that fell to the glacier in contrast to the broken end of the plaited one, and to the presence of twine whipping on all three above the damaged strands, revealing much more than a comparison of the diameter of the three ropes. It suggests that two ropes were employed between Croz and Douglas, that Croz must have carried one of them with the end tied to Hudson via Hadow, and that Hudson carried the other with a short length uncoiled and tied to Douglas. This would not completely invalidate Taugwalder's answer A28, but would mean that extra twisted rope could readily have been made available to him by Hudson and Douglas. It would also partly undermine Taugwalder's answers A24-A26, as it is hardly likely that Croz had to tie Hudson's rope on to Douglas. It also suggests that the party was much more flexible than it seemed to be with four men tied on a single rope, but it raises many more questions than it answers! The three ropes shown in *Scrambles* are now on display in the Zermatt Museum.

A 29. Taugwalder could have answered this question with a simple 'yes', but chose instead the far more elaborate indirect response of stating what different action he would have taken had he found the rope to be of insufficient strength. The answer looks much more like the pleading of a lawyer than the response of a peasant and there would seem to be a distinct possibility that it was drafted by a lawyer. Taugwalder would not have known that Whymper had said in evidence merely that this rope was less thick than the others (it is even open to doubt whether the Tribunal realised what Whymper had said prior to considering the evidence and drawing up their verdict) but as this was the sixth question he had been asked about the rope and he had still been asked nothing and had said nothing about its age, quality, condition or specification beyond saying that it was a special rope, he may have begun to realise that the Tribunal was regarding it simply as another rope like the strong and brand-new rope he mentioned in A26, in which they seemed to be more interested. Graham Brown made a note to the effect that Taugwalder's reference to rejecting the rope if he had found it too weak as he 'would have recognised it as such before the ascent' suggests that he had examined all the ropes at the Schwarzsee. When one adds this to his appreciation of the likely need to leave fixed rope on the mountain and his evidence that he tied himself to Douglas with a special rope, it seems certain that he knew the sashline was being taken for use as fixed rope. However it still leaves open the question as to whether Taugwalder himself regarded it as quite adequate for use as a climbing rope.

A 30. This account of the events after Hadow slipped is fundamentally different from that given by Whymper in A11 describing how Hadow knocked Croz over and the double weight dragged down Hudson and after him Lord Douglas. But, when Taugwalder was confronted with the inconsistency in Q63 during his second examination on the Sunday, he conceded that Whymper's version might be more correct, as Whymper was in a position where he could see the unfortunate course of events better than he could. Once again the Tribunal's failure to appreciate at the time that Taugwalder's reply was inconsistent with what they had already been told by Whymper suggests not so much an extraordinary lack of concentration or of competence on their part, but that the evidence of both witnesses was primarily given in writing. Otherwise there would have been plenty of time for Clemenz to appreciate the inconsistency whilst waiting for the Clerk to record Taugwalder's answer. Whereas it is almost certain from Whymper's own note of the hearing that he must have handed in his completed list of questions & answers 2-17 on the Friday afternoon and that Clemenz then read out the questions one by one whilst Whymper interposed his answers, it seems more likely that Taugwalder did not hand in his answers until the Saturday morning. This would give him the necessary time to write out his answers and would also account for Whymper not being told until at least mid-morning on the Saturday that he was free to leave Zermatt. He wrote in his letter to *The Times* how 'The questions, I was told, were put and answered before I left Zermatt', which rather implies that Taugwalder did not answer them immediately on the Friday afternoon.

A 31. Despite saying here that all necessary caution was exercised at the scene of the accident, Taugwalder subsequently recalled in A53 having suggested to Croz that they should fix a rope. Although this question (Q31) appears in Whymper's list, it is an unlikely one for him to have drafted yet exactly what one might expect from Clemenz, particularly in the light of the finding that there had been no culpable negligence. Bearing in mind that all the questions of substance put to Taugwalder on the first day came from Whymper's list, it is hard to find any other explanation than that Clemenz drafted half a dozen general questions for Taugwalder and gave them to Whymper asking him to add some appropriate questions about the ropes. (see notes to A17 and Q22 above)

Q 32. Taugwalder seems on the face of it to have appreciated better than the lawyer Clemenz that he had already answered this question, whereas the explanation must be that Clemenz did not receive Taugwalders answer A30 before Taugwalder had already replied in writing to A32. The word 'above' seems to confirm that he was giving a written answer; compare Whymper's reference in the first sentence of A11 to 'higher up'.

Q 33. This is another example of a question drafted by Whymper having lost its point by the time it reached Taugwalder, but this time the fault seems to lie with Whymper. His original English version read 'Was the rope tight, that is, not in loops, between the men at the time they fell?', but his French version omitted the words 'between the men' so that there was no knowing which rope Taugwalder was referring to in his reply. The probability is that he was referring to the rope between him and Douglas, and we do not therefore know whether he noticed any slack between Hudson and Hadow, which is likely to have been one of the principal causes of the catastrophe.

A 34. The official French translation refers to 'une corde bien solide', a really strong rope, but this is incorrect as Taugwalder's German reply was to the effect that the load on the rope could have – 'auch ein festes Seil zerreissen' – even broken a strong rope. It is difficult to reconcile Taugwalder's answer with the impression given by his Answer 29, when he said he would have rejected the rope had he found it too weak. The word 'auch' meaning 'even' or 'also' seems significant, as it draws a distinction between a strong rope and the one that actually broke; without it he would have left open the possibility that it was in fact a strong rope. This reply reverting to the use of the rope after four general questions about the happening of the accident has something in common with A24 when he drew a distinction between the Croz – Douglas rope, which he later described in A26 as a strong brand-new rope, and the special rope between him and Douglas. Once again Clemenz did not seek any clarification, even on the Sunday.

Q 35. Whymper presumably put in this question so that the layman would realise that there was nothing whatever that Taugwalder could have done after the rope broke, or was it really a Clemenz question in a list Whymper was asked to expand?

Q 36. This was not a Whymper question but one of Clemenz own. It is doubtful if there was ever any merit in it, and it is in fact confusing and open to a number of different interpretations. It has been suggested that it is based on Taugwalder's initial assertion in A30, but subsequently abandoned in A63, that Croz was the last of the four to lose his footing. It seems however that it was probably nothing more than an attempt by Clemenz to show that he was alert after Taugwalder had handed in his written answers to the fourteen Whymper questions. Apart from not featuring in the Whymper list, it stands out as something different from what has gone before on account of the reference to Mr.Douglas. It also refers to the tourists (die Herren), whereas Q35 referred to the men (die Männer), the difference being that the former would include Whymper and the latter Croz. Clemenz also introduced the word 'save' or rescue, in place of the previous reference to stopping the fall of the four men, suggesting that he was raising an entirely new aspect and in effect asking Taugwalder if he would subsequently have been able to get the four tourists safely down the mountain if this incident had been checked and if the rope had not broken. If Taugwalder had misunderstood Clemenz or otherwise thought he was being asked whether he would have been able to retain his footing with the weight of three or four men on the rope, he would surely have introduced the further qualification that Whymper and his son would have had to be able to stand firm and hold him. As Dangar & Blakeney pointed out in *AJ70*, 160, if Taugwalder was right that he and Croz could have held up the three falling men, then it was the weak link between Douglas and Taugwalder that led to the fatality.

5.4.3 Peter Taugwalder Questions 53-64

Q 53. The wording suggests that Taugwalder may have let it be known that he had remembered something else about the accident.

Q 54. Although Young Peter was a member of the party that recovered the bodies on 19th/20th July, it seems that he had left Zermatt by Sunday 23rd, and probably as early as the 21st, to go to Chamonix. Clemenz must have asked the question for the sake of completing the record, already knowing the answer as otherwise the completion of the Enquiry might have been delayed for a week or two, pending Young Peter's return.

Q 55. This reveals some serious consideration of the evidence on the part of the Tribunal, although the question appears to have been put by someone other than Clemenz, in view of it referring to Clemenz by his title. Clemenz may possibly not have sat on the Sunday, leaving it to other members of the Tribunal to deal with these further questions. In such circumstances Julen might well have attended with his cousin Taugwalder and helped him to give his answers.

A 55. This reply, somewhat reminiscent of A29, may be impressive and logical, but its sophisticated form seems more likely to have been drafted by someone well versed in legal procedures, such as Alois Julen, rather than by a simple mountain guide.

Q 56. This question clearly arose out of A55, suggesting that at this stage of the hearing the answers were being given orally, with the Tribunal paying attention. But this does not mean that Taugwalder was not given advance notice of Q55, or that Julen did not help him give his answer in some other way.

Q 59-62. These questions seem to have been intended to fill a gap in the times given by Whymper, albeit with some duplication. The Official Report omitted altogether Q62 as well as A62, for no apparent reason, but as A61 does not really fit in with Q61 there is a likely explanation. Q61 is virtually the same as Q6, but Taugwalder's recorded answer A61 is inappropriate. His real answer is therefore missing, suggesting a clerical error. Q62 is also missing but it could well have been a combination of Q7 & Q8, namely 'At what time did you arrive at the summit and how long did you stay there?' An appropriate answer to this double question can then be found at A61, which is not far out of line with Whymper's own answers.

A 63. There are some material differences between the original German spoken by Taugwalder, as recorded in the Report, and the official French translation, which is clearly wrong. He expressly stated that Whymper was above him 'in a place where he could see the unfortunate course of events better than I could'. There is also another reason why Whymper should have seen more of the events following Hadow's initial slip, in that if Taugwalder turned towards the rocks and wound the rope round a projecting rock (A64), or more likely hugged the rock, the vital thing for his own safety would have been to ensure that the rope or his hands did not come off the rock. It is therefore hardly likely that he would have been watching Croz, whereas Whymper had no cause to look away from the falling men.

A 64. Doubt has been expressed as to which rope, if any, Taugwalder wound round the rock (see Montandon in *Die Alpen 5*, 1929, 220). It would seem more likely to have been the Douglas rope as it is difficult to imagine how he would have been able to obtain any purchase with the Whymper rope. Whereas Whymper said that the rope between him and Taugwalder was taut, and some critics have sought to rely on Taugwalder's evidence here as indicating fault on the part of Whymper, it should be remembered that Taugwalder must have had the opportunity of belaying the rope before the accident and that it was then up to him to decide, before letting Douglas descend further, whether he himself would descend the full length of the rope between him and Whymper, whether he would belay that rope or the Douglas rope round the rock or whether he would retain enough slack to be able to belay either rope later.

However the probability is that the report of Taugwalder winding the rope round the rock, which first appeared in the *Journal de Genève* of 18.7.65, was based on an error by Young Peter; the reason being that for half an hour after the accident the Taugwalders could not see each other (A54) and only after Old Peter had finally 'summoned up courage, and changed his position to a rock to which he could attach the rope' (see *Scrambles*) did Young Peter descend. Seeing his father with the 'Whymper' rope then belayed round a rock he would not have known that he had not secured it before the other rope broke. In any event, the idea of Old Peter winding the rope round a rock before the Douglas rope broke, is not only out of line with the report in *Der Bund* on 19th July, 'the elder Taugwalder managed to throw his weight upon a rock', which shows several signs of being based on an interview with Old Peter, but it is wholly inconsistent with what Whymper wrote in *Scrambles* about being fixed between the two guides, unable to move up or down.

He 'begged Young Peter to descend, but he dared not. Unless he did we could not advance.' For as long as Young Peter dared not descend, Old Peter could not secure the taut rope between him and Whymper to the rock he was hugging, and there was nothing Whymper could do to provide any slack, fixed as he was between the two unable to move up or down, except beg the son to descend. Ultimately Old Peter must have taken the only other course available, short of Whymper cutting his way free, and he climbed up a few feet, created some slack and 'changed his position to a rock to which he could fix the rope'. He presumably then shouted up to his son that it was safe to descend, and he did so. It is not as though Old Peter's A64 came in a direct or spontaneous reply to a specific question, and whether or not he had a clear recollection of what he did and whether A64 originated with him or with his lawyer, it may simply have been a matter of taking advantage of the report in the *Journal de Genève*, of which a copy would have reached Zermatt by Friday 21st July, if not before.

5.5
WHYMPER'S QUESTIONS FOR TAUGWALDER

The three versions compared; Whymper's original English, the French version he handed in to Clemenz, and the questions actually put to Taugwalder in German.

Q 22.
Had you made excursions with Lord Douglas before the ascent of the Matterhorn?
Aviez-vous fait des excursions avec Lord Douglas avant l'ascension du Matterhorn?
Hattet Ihr schon Gebirgsreisen mit Lord Douglas vor der Ersteigung des Matterhorn gemacht?

Q 23.
Were you told before starting of [whom] the party was to consist and did you make any objection to any of those proposed, or to the proportion of guides to travellers?
Vous avait-on dit avant le départ de qui la partie devait consister, et aviez vous fait des objections à l'égard de l'un ou de l'autre des voyageurs proposés, ou au nombre proposé de guides en proportion avec celui des voyageurs?
Hat man Euch vor der Abreise (*zur Besteigung des Matterhorns*) mitgeteilt aus welchen Herren die Gesellschaft eigentlich bestehen soll, und hattet Ihr irgend einen Einwurf gemacht entweder gegen den einen oder den andern von diesen Herren oder auch gegen die verhältnismässige Anzahl der Reisenden und Führer?

Q 24.
Who tied the men up on leaving the summit?
Qui a lié les hommes ensemble au moment de quitter le sommet?
Wer hat die Männer zusammen gebunden als Ihr wieder vom Gipfel herabkamet?

Q 25.
Who was tied up first?
Qui fut lié le premier?
Wer ist zuerst angebunden worden?

Q 26.
What rope was used?
Quelle espèce de corde fut employée?
Was für Seil ist *dazu* gebraucht worden?

Q 27.
Who tied you to Lord Douglas?
Qui vous a lié à Douglas?
Wer hat Euch an Lord Douglas angebunden?

Q 28.
Why was a different kind of rope used between Lord Douglas and yourself?
Pourquoi s'est on servi d'une différente espèce de corde entre Lord Douglas et vous-même?
Warum ist zwischen Lord Douglas und Euch ein *anderes* Seil angewendet worden?

Q 29.
Was the rope used between yourself and Lord Douglas, in your opinion, sufficiently strong for the purpose?
La corde employée entre Lord Douglas et vous-même était elle, dans votre opinion suffisament forte?
War das Seil das zwischen Lord Douglas und Euch angewendet worden in Eurer Meinung von hinreichender Stärke?

Q 30.
Describe the place at which the accident occurred?
Faites une description de l'endroit où l'accident est arrivé?
Beschreibt den Punkt, wo das Unglück vorgefallen ist?

Q 31.
In your opinion, was sufficient care used in the descent of that part?
Est-ce que dans votre opinion tout le soin nécessaire a été pris à la descente de ce point?
War nach Ihrer Meinung alle gehörige Vorsicht auf diesen Punkte genommen?

Q 32.
How did the accident occur?
Comment l'accident est-il arrivé?
Wie hat das Unglück stattgefunden?

Q 33.
Was the rope tight, that is, not in loops, between the men at the time they fell?
Au moment ou les hommes sont tombés, est-ce que la corde était bien tendue ou lache?
War das Seil gespannt oder nicht im Augenblick wo die Männer gefallen sind?

Q 34.
In your opinion what was the cause of the rope breaking?
Quelle était dans votre opinion la cause que la corde s'est rompue?
Woher kommt es in Eurer Meinung, dass das Seil zerbrach?

Q 35.
Was it possible to have stopped the four falling men after the rope broke?
Etait-ce possible de retenir les quatre hommes, après que la corde fut rompue?
War es möglich die 4 Männer aufzuhalten nachdem das Seil zerbrach?

6
THE CRITICS

6.0
THE PRINCIPAL BOOKS AND ARTICLES

1865. Abraham Roth. *Sonntagspost*. 30th July, 13th and 20th August.
1865. Eugène Rambert. *Journal de Genéve*. 28th July.
1866. Eugène Rambert. *Les Alpes suisses*. Genève. (Gos. *Le Cervin* 1, 198-202)
1876. Stéphen d'Arve. *Les fastes du Mont Blanc*. Genève.
[1896] Theodor Wundt. *Das Matterhorn und seine Geschichte*. Berlin.
1907. Guido Rey. *The Matterhorn*. (Original Italian edition 1904)
1911. Heinrich Dübi. Zur Erinnerung an Edward Whymper. *SACJ 47*. 183-216.
1911. Georges Casella. Comment le Cervin fut conquis – les dernières paroles de Whymper. *L'Auto*. Paris. 18 septembre.
1914. Arnold Lunn. *The Alps*. 147-84.
1917. [H.F.Montagnier] Early ascents of the Matterhorn. *AJ31*, 87-94.
1918. J.P.Farrar. Days of long ago. *AJ32*, 2-36.
1920. J.P.Farrar. His comments on the Enquiry Report. *AJ33*, 247-50.
1922. Charles Gos. *Propos d'un Alpiniste*.
1923. G.W.Young. Mountaineering and its prophets. (In *Cornhill Magazine*; see also *AJ54*, 102-6)
1929. H.Dübi & P.Montandon. Zum Matterhornunglück vom 14.7.1865. *Die Alpen V*, 203-23.
1932. T.Graham Brown. The Great Matterhorn Disaster of 1865. *The Field*, February 13.
[1932] W.H.Lewin. *Climbs*. 130-45.
1933. H.Edwards. The Ropes in the Matterhorn Accident of 1865. *AJ45*, 319-327.
1934. Charles Gos. *Alpinisme anecdotique*.
1936. H.E.G.Tyndale. (Editor of) 6th edn. of Whymper's *Scrambles*.
1940. Frank Smythe. *Edward Whymper*.
1940. Egmond d'Arcis. Edward Whymper. *Die Alpen 16*, 272-5 & 279-80.
1940. [C.Schuster] Review of *Edward Whymper. AJ52,* 147-51.
1940. Carl Egger. Les Taugwalders du Cervin. *Die Alpen 16*, 275-8.
1943. A.Lunn. *Mountain Jubilee*. 189-214. (& *The British Ski Year Book* 1940).

1944. A.Lunn. *Switzerland and the English*. 131 & 169.
1946. Carl Egger. *Pioniere der Alpen*. 178-200.
1946. A.Lunn. Taugwalder and the Matterhorn. *AJ55*, 290-6.
1947. A.Lunn. *Switzerland in English prose and poetry*. 108-12.
1948. C.Gos. *Alpine Tragedy*. 24-34. (Original French edition 1940)
1949. F.Smythe. (Editor of) New edn. of Whymper's *Andes*. Introduction, 5-20.
1950. T.G.Brown. Girdlestone & the Matterhorn accident 1865. *AJ57*, 369-84.
1950. C-E.Engel. *A History of Mountaineering in the Alps*. 126-33 & 138-42.
1952. C-E.Engel. *They came to the Hills*. 110-32.
1954. Karlrobert Schäfer. Schicksaltag am Matterhorn. *Die Alpen 30*, 111-12.
1954. A.Lunn. Whymper's engravings for *Scrambles*. *AJ59*, 344.
1954. D.F.O.Dangar. The Führerbuch of Young Peter Taugwalder. *AJ59*, 436-41.
1955. A.Lunn. *Zermatt and the Valais*.
1956. Ronald W.Clark. *Six Great Mountaineers*. 11-51. (Edward Whymper)
1957. A.Lunn. *A Century of Mountaineering*. 51-61.
1957. Dangar & Blakeney. The first ascent of the Matterhorn. The narrative of 'Young' Peter Taugwalder. *AJ61*, 484-506.
1960. T.S.Blakeney. Whymper and the Taugwalders. *AJ65*, 94. (Note)
1963. Alfonso Bernardi. *Il Gran Cervino*. (Anthology)
1963. D.F.O.Dangar. The Parkers and the Matterhorn. *AJ68*, 285-90.
1964. W.Schmid. *Menschen am Matterhorn*.
1964. Cicely Williams. *Zermatt Saga*.
1965. Ronald W.Clark. *The Day the Rope Broke*.
1865. A.Lunn. *Matterhorn Centenary*. 37-75.
1965. Walter Unsworth. *Matterhorn man*.
1965. A.D.M.Cox. The Matterhorn Centenary. *AJ70*, 7-26.
1965. Dangar & Blakeney. Old Peter Taugwalder. *AJ70*, 26-37 & 323.
1965. Dangar & Blakeney. The Matterhorn. A diary of events. *AJ70*, 199-204.
1965. Dangar & Blakeney. Review of *The Day the Rope Broke*. *AJ70*, 159-61.
1965. G.Grosjean. La première ascension du Cervin le 14 juillet 1865. *Les Alpes 41,* 89-100.
1966. Dangar & Blakeney. A word for Whymper. *AJ71*, 111-32.
1966. A.Lunn. Whymper again. *AJ71*, 228-33.
Dangar & Blakeney. Comments on Lunn's article. *AJ71*, 233-5.
1966. H.R.Müller. The first ascent of the Matterhorn in the light of contemporary reports. *MW64/65,* 1-28.
1966. T.S.Blakeney. Review of Müller's article. *AJ71*, 334-5.
1967. Gaston Rébuffat. *Men and the Matterhorn*. (French & German edns.1865).
1986. Max Chamson. *Whymper le fou du Cervin*.
1990. Hannes Taugwalder und Martin Jaggi. *Der Wahrheit näher*.

6.1
D'ARCIS, CHARLES EGMOND (1887 – 1971)

Although d'Arcis lived in Geneva, where for many years he was the *Times* Swiss correspondent, he was very familiar with Zermatt and its history as a mountaineering centre and he played a part in the development of its Museum. He was one of several contributors of special articles to *Die Alpen* in 1940, the centenary year of Whymper's birth, although his article describing an encounter with Whymper at the age of ten had previously appeared elsewhere. His main article refers to Smythe's biography, which had been published not long before, and it amounts to a short biography of Whymper. It contains nothing of particular significance apart from the last paragraph, which refers to Whymper as '...brusque parfois avec les autres, mais bon, généreux pour les humbles, surtout pour les guides dont il appréciait le dévouement et les conversations tout empreintes de naïveté et de bon sens...'

1. Edward Whymper. *Die Alpen. XVI.* 1940, 272-5.
2. Avec Whymper à Zermatt. Ibid, 279-80.

6.2
D'ARVE, STÉPHEN (VICOMTE EDMOND DE CATELIN)

Claire Engel once described d'Arve as 'the garrulous and inaccurate historian of Mont Blanc'. Charles Gos recorded that he was a publicity agent and wrote in *Le Cervin*, after quoting from d'Arve's book *Les Fastes du Mont-Blanc* an extract about the Taugwalders, that one cannot take his texts seriously. Judging from the many obvious inaccuracies and the extraordinary and original nature of some of d'Arve's observations, this could well be true. Nevertheless there may be grains of truth in some of the details that he alone has recorded, the only problem being how to recognize them.

In 1865 d'Arve appears to have been living in Chamonix and to have been the Editor in chief of *L'Abeille de Chamonix*, the small weekly newspaper serving the spas of Savoy. The issue of the 23rd July recorded ascents of Mont Blanc on the 7th by F.A.Y.Brown and by 'Sir Thomas Kennedy, lord Douglas, Rd.J.Cormik et C.Hudson, Anglais'. It published a letter from Gabriel Loppé to the Editor about the search for the bodies on the Matterhorn glacier and it included an account of the Matterhorn accident written by d'Arve himself. In it Lord Douglas is referred to as the son of the Marquess of Huntley and is said to have slipped and fallen on to one of Croz' hands and dragged down Hudson, whom Croz managed to hold with his other hand, until the third tourist Mr.Haddo fell in turn, causing the rope tying him to the last two (sic) to break. The account goes on to refer to the rope breaking on a sharp rock. The accident is also referred to in some later issues of *L'Abeille de Chamonix*.

In 1876 d'Arve published in Geneva his book *Les Fastes* [Annals] *du Mont Blanc* and incorporated in it a revised version of the Matterhorn accounts from *L'Abeille*. He also referred to the Taugwalders and to such things as the Enquiry. He wrote of tests being carried out on one of the rope ends establishing that it took at least three minutes to bring about complete disintegration of the hemp filaments by violent and sustained chafing on a sharp rock. He referred to there having been another explanation circulating right from the start, adding 'impartially' that it found favour throughout the valley and amongst the Chamonix guides. He then mentioned Old Peter's axe and his predicament, comparing it to the survivors of a shipwreck sailing away from the burning vessel on a life raft, when they know there are men still aboard facing certain death when the powder magazine explodes.

d'Arve states that Whymper in his account adopted the sudden breaking of the rope and, whilst not doubting Whymper's good faith, goes on to suggest that he was in no position to see Old Peter. He then backs up his opinion by citing an incident a fortnight after the accident, when he saw the two Taugwalders in Chamonix. A Swiss cabinet maker introduced him to Old Peter as a journalist, saying that he was writing about him and asking if he would furnish some more details; ' "You cut the rope didn't you? The axe worked well didn't it?" "Yes! yes!" echoed the voices of fifteen [Valais] guides sitting at the same table.' It is not clear whether d'Arve had ever published this prior to 1876, but it is quite possible. In any event it must have been far more potentially damaging to Old Peter's reputation as a guide than any of the true facts recorded by Whymper in *Scrambles*, particularly in view of its publication being in Geneva.

Charles Gos refers to and quotes from d'Arve's writings in his books, *Propos d'un Alpiniste, Alpinisme anecdotique* and *Le Cervin*.

1. *L'Abeille de Chamonix*. Dimanche. 23 juillet 1865.
2. *Les Fastes du Mont-Blanc*. Genève. 1876.

6.3
BERNARDI, ALFONSO

Bernardi's Matterhorn anthology, *Il Gran Cervino*, is written in Italian but nevertheless is of interest to those who do not understand the language, as it is well illustrated with photographs and drawings of the pioneers and of many of the classic views from Zermatt and Breuil. There are extracts from the writings of such pioneers as Forbes, Whymper, Tyndall and Leighton Jordan, from those of the Italians Amé Gorret and Canon Carrel and also from articles in the *Alpine Journal*. All the foreign extracts have been translated into Italian, but certain documents like Jordan's entries in the Führerbuch of J-J Maquignaz are reproduced in facsimile. The principal items of interest to the English reader with no understanding of Italian are as follows:

Facsimile of Jordan's arrival times at various stages of his climb between 1st and 3rd October 1867. p129.
Gustave Doré's 'Arrival at the summit', in colour. p145.
Facsimile extracts from *Journal de Genève* of 16 & 18 July 1865. pp 158 & 168.
F.C.Grove's entries in S.Meynet's Führerbuch. 6.8.67 & 16.8.67. p182.
Photograph of Félicité Carrel. p184.
Jordan's entries in J-J Maquignaz' Führerbuch in September 1868, referring to his 1867 Matterhorn ascent and other expeditions. pp188-9.

Bernardi's collected writings of Amé Gorret, which are entirely in French, are closely linked with the early history of the Matterhorn in view of Gorret's own achievements as a pioneer climber and mountain writer and include the account which he wrote of the first ascent from Breuil, in which he played such a prominent part.

1. *Il Gran Cervino*. Antologia di Alfonso Bernardi. Bologna. 1963.
2. *Ecrits de l'Abbé Gorret*, recueillis par Alfonso Bernardi. Vallée d'Aoste. 1965.

6.4
BROWN, THOMAS GRAHAM (1882 – 1965)

Graham Brown's exceptional climbing career is fully detailed in his obituary in *AJ71*, 191-194 and elsewhere. His exceptional interest in mountaineering literature led to an even greater achievement, which future generations will share with him, his collection of an extensive library of mountaineering books. The Graham Brown collection was bequeathed to the National Library of Scotland in Edinburgh in 1965. In 1982 the Library held an exhibition to mark the centenary of Graham Brown's birth, and the Exhibition Catalogue included three articles on him, one of which reviews 'The Graham Brown Collection' in considerable detail. The National Library of Scotland also published in 1994 a splendid catalogue *Mountaineering*, which covers both the Graham Brown and Lloyd collections in the Library and runs to some 450 pages.

As a writer Graham Brown is best known for the authoritative work he produced with Gavin de Beer for the Alpine Club centenary in 1957, *The first ascent of Mont Blanc*. There seems to be a possibility that he had intended, some 30 years earlier, to write something of a comparable nature about the first ascent of the Matterhorn or about Edward Whymper, as his papers in the National Library of Scotland include copious notes on the subject as well as his own hand-written copies of, and extracts from, various rare pamphlets, climbers' diaries,

Führerbücher and letters etc. making reference to the early history of the Matterhorn. Graham Brown may even have intended to write a joint work with Frank Smythe, his climbing partner on the Brenva face routes, until they fell out. Why else did Graham Brown do so much research work and publish so little? He drew up lists of the movements of the likes of Whymper, Hudson, McCormick, Girdlestone and Lord Francis Douglas in the summer of 1865 and even a record of the weather in the vicinity of the Matterhorn during the first half of July, and his lists of documentary sources for pre- and post-accident events relating to the Matterhorn and to those directly or even indirectly involved in the first ascent run into many pages. He made a detailed analysis of the contents of *Scrambles* and also a line by line comparison of Whymper's three main accounts of the accident, in his letters to von Fellenberg and to *The Times* and in *Scrambles*. Apart from the Whymper diaries, which were seen by both Smythe and Graham Brown, the two men seem to have complemented each other's research on Whymper and the Matterhorn.

Included in his notes is an important observation that seems to have escaped the attention of all other critics. It helps to establish that the plaited rope with the broken end displayed in the Zermatt Museum is in fact the Taugwalder half of the rope that broke between him and Douglas in the accident and not merely a sample of the rope intended for use as fixed rope. Graham Brown observed how in the List of Illustrations in *Scrambles*, but not in the actual captions in the text, Whymper described the Manilla and second ropes depicted as 'broken on the Matterhorn', which must mean that they were used and got broken somewhere between Croz and Douglas and that Whymper recovered them from the glacier. There can be little doubt from the distinctive nature of the frayed ends of the two twisted ropes displayed in the same glass case in the Museum that all three ropes must be the ones shown in *Scrambles* and that at some stage Whymper must have presented them to the Museum in Zermatt. This is confirmed by a photograph in Gindraux' book, page 62 number 4.

But apart from one or two Notes on matters relating to the Matterhorn accident, which Graham Brown wrote as Editor of the *Alpine Journal*, he does not seem to have published more than a single page article in *The Field* in 1932 and one major article in the *Alpine Journal* in 1950. These two articles were:

1. The Great Matterhorn Disaster of 1865. p227. *The Field*. February 13, 1932.
2. Girdlestone and the Matterhorn accident, 1865. *AJ57*, 369-84, 1950.

6.4.1 The Great Matterhorn Disaster of 1865

para 2. Farrar in his article 'Days of long ago' also expressed the opinion that the Matterhorn was no more difficult then than now, and he seems to have been wrong on both counts. The presence of ropes and chains to-day must mean that the Matterhorn was more difficult then than now. But the justification, if any, for taking Hadow must also take account of the difficulties that were anticipated but never materialised. The mediocre climber of to-day, or more likely his leader, knows from the guidebook or from the experience of others that, apart

from the weather, the traffic and the snow conditions, the difficulties will not exceed a certain level, whereas Hudson hardly knew what to expect, which accounts for his taking to Zermatt 'a kind of ladder for scaling precipices', as well as a wire-rope.
para 11. 'He can have had little or no opportunity to discuss the Matterhorn attempt before he left for home'. This overlooks the ample opportunity afforded by Hudson driving with Kennedy, his wife and presumably his dog, from Chamonix to Les Ouches on the morning of his departure for England (*AJ3*, 76). The probable explanation for Hudson taking Hadow is not that he was unaware of his problems descending Mont Blanc, any more than he would have forgotten Hadow's problems descending Pennyghent in about 1864, but that until McCormick arrived at Zermatt he intended nothing more than a reconnaissance. The sudden arrival of Whymper, whom Hudson would know to be determined to overcome extreme difficulties in order to reach the top before Carrel, seems not to have changed Hudson's plan to take Hadow, presumably because he did not think they would succeed without his ladder or wire-rope.
para 12. 'Hudson and Croz were now left with...no chance of knowing anything of [Hadow's] actual ability'. This overlooks the presence of Peter Perren, who could speak French and communicate with Croz as well as with Hudson, and of whom Kennedy had written on the descent of Mont Blanc: 'I left Perren to bring up the rear and afford Hadow support'.

6.4.2 Girdlestone and the Matterhorn accident, 1865

370/2. Charles Hudson's preparations for an attempt on the Matterhorn seem to have been rather overrated by Graham Brown as, apart from the rope and the ladder, we know little more than that he lined up Kennedy, Birkbeck and McCormick. The first two then had to go home and instead of waiting for the third, who had been delayed for a day or so by bad weather, he set off with Hadow instead.
373/5. Whymper's narrative seems to suggest correctly that Douglas was not contemplating a Matterhorn attempt before they met. He had originally intended to try it after the Gabelhorn, according to the *Dumfries Courier*, but by July 11th he no longer had the time or the inclination, he was ready to leave Zermatt and was simply planning an attempt for the following year.
374/2. There does not seem to be any evidence to support the statements that Old Peter was still in Douglas's employ and that Douglas had sent him to reconnoitre. The only pre-Matterhorn fees outstanding after the accident were those of Joseph for going to Breuil. As for the unliklihood of Old Peter making any reconnaissance of the Hörnli, see 2.52.5 (Old Peter) or 2.14.3 (Douglas).
375/1. Whereas Whymper, Hudson and Hadow were all staying at the Monte Rosa, and Douglas spent the night of 12th July there as well despite having stayed at the Mont Cervin for most of the previous fortnight, it seems probable that Girdlestone merely dined with them and spent the night at the Mont Cervin, where he certainly stayed on 16th July.
376/2. The earliest extant account by Whymper himself (any letter he wrote to his father on about 17th July has not survived) must be the Vecqueray translation of his answers to the questions Clemenz was to put to him a day or two later at the Enquiry (on 21st July). This may have been about the same time as Girdlestone put pen to paper.
376/3. Graham Brown's copious notes refer from time to time to the question of Whymper suppressing Hudson's contribution, but he seems to have been biased against Whymper on this, as he did not have any real evidence.
377/2. Further doubt about Old Peter passing the rope between him and Whymper round a rock arises from it hardly being able to afford him any purchase. For the likely origin of the

mistaken idea that Old Peter belayed the Whymper rope before the Douglas rope broke, see end of section 3.12.4 (The rope in 1865).
377/3. The relative viewpoints of Old Peter and Whymper are affected by a mistake in the official French translation of Answer 63. The German version in fact begins: 'As Mr. Whymper was above me in a place where he could see the unfortunate course of events better than I could...'
378/2. (footnote 13). Old Peter's questions and answers, as translated into English in the 6th edition of *Scrambles*, do not always accord with the original German, on account of some French translation errors in the answers and a number of differences between Whymper's original English version of his questions for Old Peter, the French version he handed in and the questions actually asked in German; see sections 5.4 & 5.5.
378/2 line 9. The record of Old Peter's German evidence does still exist, although for some reason Farrar chose not to reveal the fact.
378/2. lines 10-12. This was Clemenz' only question of substance to Old Peter on the first day. For comment on it, see section 5.4.2.
378/3. 'At that time, no peasant-guide would have contradicted the direct statement of a "Herr" '. Perhaps not, but Old Peter's answers hardly read like those of a peasant-guide.
379/1. Whymper must have gone over to the Mont Cervin to see Girdlestone where he may also have bumped into Clemenz!
379. footnote 15. He seems to be referring to the person who acted as chaplain in McCormick's absence, either the Rev Warr or the Rev Sanders (see McCormick. *A sad holiday*, 14).
381. line 9. Whymper's letter to von Fellenberg was incorporated in the *Berner Sonntagspost* on 13.8.65, the delay being due to von Fellenberg's absence in the Oberland. Its publication was therefore overtaken by his letter to *The Times*, but had it appeared towards the end of July the probability is that *The Times* would have published an English translation of it and that Whymper would have been spared the pain of writing his letter to *The Times*.
381/4. The clearest evidence of Whymper's motives in climbing the Alps comes at the beginning of chapter 13 of *Scrambles*, in which he states that his rather ambitious programme for 1865 was undertaken to find out to what extent he was capable to select a way over mountainous country, with a view to travelling further afield.
382/2. Another potential source of information about Hadow's climbing experience was McCormick. Hadow's stay at the Monte Rosa in September 1864 seems to have been with another private tutor, the Rev Robert Bolton or Mansford. They also spent a night at the Riffel hotel, but the weather seems to have been so bad that they did not do anything at Zermatt.
382/4. It is in fact possible, although unlikely, that Girdlestone saw the Douglas manuscript at the Mont Cervin on the 16th July, when he spent the night there, if Clemenz, who had custody of Douglas's valuables and rucksack, asked him to check his belongings.
383/1. line 8. Graham Brown seems not to have been aware of the correspondence which Whymper retained during the month or so following his return to London, from which it is apparent that he did everything he could to avoid giving pain to the relatives of Hudson, Hadow and Douglas. Whatever Whymper's state of mind may have been in 1909, or even in 1895 when he seems first to have criticised Hudson in public in the *Journal de Zermatt*, there does not seem to be any justification for Graham Brown faulting him by stating that 'For many years after the Matterhorn accident, Whymper's adverse criticism of Hudson was implied rather than openly stated, at least in print...' For, as Dangar & Blakeney pointed out in *AJ71*, 235, Graham Brown's opinion 'seems to be completely outweighed' by those of Hudson's

contemporaries. 'Graham Brown's opinion...that Whymper made an unfair attack on Hudson later in life, by blaming him for taking Hadow on the climb, does not impress us...But that Hudson was too easy-going in the way he invited people to join him on the Matterhorn seems beyond dispute.'

383/2. Whymper was blaming the experienced mountaineer for taking the inexperienced on a difficult climb, a climb which had previously been avoided by all the leading guided pioneers during their long summer holidays, on account of its forbidding appearance. The fact is that Hadow had difficulties on Mont Blanc and had needed help to descend Pennyghent the previous year. The points that Graham Brown makes do not carry any weight, particularly when it is remembered that Hudson like everyone else was expecting the climb to be far more difficult than it turned out to be. Hudson had not taken Hadow on the Aiguille Verte the week before, even though he was available with him at Chamonix.

383/2. lines 15-16. It is hardly true to say that Douglas had done very little climbing in the Alps before the season of 1865, as it was at least his fourth season – see section 2.14.1.

384/3 & 4. The matter of Douglas's pipe throws no light on his visit to Breuil, and although one might guess that he lost it with the cornice on the Gabelhorn, his account of that climb did in fact refer to his smoking on the descent, whilst the guides were busy cutting a path down a wall of snow.

6.5 CASELLA, GEORGES

Charles Gos, in his book *Le Cervin* (vol 2, 277-8 & 290-6), drew attention to Casella's admiration for Whymper and to the fact that he had written a newspaper article about Whymper after encountering him only a few days before his death. Gos described Casella as a charming man, an excellent mountaineer and a very fine writer and experienced journalist. He seems to have lived in Paris and his most interesting and fascinating article on Whymper appeared in a Parisian daily called *L'Auto* on 18th September 1911, two days after Whymper's death. It tells of a chance meeting with Whymper on the evening of 13th September when Casella and some friends were sitting on the terrace of the Hotel de Paris in Chamonix. They had just climbed the Aiguille Verte and were talking of the energy and the courage of the pioneers who had to bivouac, instead of staying in comfortable huts. 'That's true' said a voice from the shadows and they soon discovered that it was Whymper. Gos expressed the opinion that the ensuing conversation with Whymper was apocryphal or rather knowingly contrived and presented. He quoted a reference to the conversation in Casella's book *Pèlerinages*, which rather implies that Whymper confided in Casella his thoughts about the 1865 accident, whereas the article suggests that Casella's friends also took an active part in the conversation. But whatever the circumstances in which the two men met, there is little doubt that Casella was able to record details about the accident and other matters that he could only have learnt direct from Whymper himself, such as his father attaining the age of 90, his devotion to Mme.Seiler and the fact that he had been able to attend her funeral in September 1895. Another article by Casella,

'Edward Whymper', reveals how at Whymper's funeral, after tributes on behalf of various Alpine clubs and others, he himself spoke on behalf of some old Chamoniard friends including Frédéric Payot of Whymper's generosity and friendship.

Gos refers (*Le Cervin* 2, 277 & 296) to Casella's book *Pèlerinages* [not seen] being published in 1910, yet quoting an event in 1911! There is however no reason to doubt that Gos was correct in stating that it contains a chapter devoted to Whymper, which includes reference to Alphonse Daudet's *Tartarin sur les Alpes* and to it being due to Whymper that Tartarin set off from Tarascon for the four-thousanders! Gos himself vouches for Whymper having stayed with Daudet in Paris.

1. Comment le Cervin fut conquis – les dernières paroles de Whymper. *L'Auto*. Paris. 18 septembre 1911.
2. Edward Whymper. *Les sports d'hiver & l'alpinisme*. Paris. 1911. pp9-13.
3. *Pèlerinages*. Payot, Lausanne et Paris [Not seen].

6.6
CHAMSON, MAX

Whymper le fou du Cervin is the title of his book published in Paris in 1986. It is carefully written, pays attention to detail and reproduces a good range of illustrations mostly by, of, or relating to Whymper. The book traces Whymper's climbing career and relates it to some of the other pioneers. It quotes a number of extracts from Whymper's diaries and, although there is not much that is new about his climbing, Chamson makes a number of fresh observations. He quotes an amusing Swiss entry in the guestbook of the original Lauber Inn by someone who states that they will be pleased to come again 'if there are a few more chairs and a few less English'. Chamson inevitably inherits a few of the regular factual errors, but there is one particularly serious and unusual misstatement that ought to be mentioned.

6.6.1 *Whymper le fou du Cervin*

186. When Whymper was asked to write down the names of the party and leave them in a bottle, Young Peter Taugwalder stayed behind with him while the other five started their descent, all roped together. It is therefore wrong to state that both the Taugwalders waited behind with Whymper, that Whymper tied himself in between the two Taugwalders whilst the others were beginning the real descent, and that when Douglas later remarked that it would be better for the two ropes to join together, Old Peter Taugwalder then tied himself on to Douglas.

6.7
CLARK, RONALD WILLIAM (1916 – 1987)

Clark wrote many books on mountaineering, and those such as *The Early Alpine Guides* and *The Victorian Mountaineers* include material relating to the climbers and guides involved in the first ascent and other early ascents of the Matterhorn. He also included a biography of Whymper in *Six Great Mountaineers*, but it is his book *The Day the Rope Broke* that concentrates on the Matterhorn accident and its aftermath, and it must be by far the most readable book on the subject. His considerable experience as a mountaineering historian and as a journalist put Clark in a strong position to present a new and accurate account of the disaster. He seems to have had a better understanding of the subject than most writers and he related the sashline or plaited rope to the 1864 report of the AC Committee on Ropes etc., despite allowing a broken twisted rope to appear on the dust-jacket of his book! He also recognised the failure of the Tribunal to ask the vital questions (see 178/4, 179/4, and 183/2). Although he did not have access to Whymper's scrapbook or diaries, he ought perhaps to have realised from Tyndale's editing of the 6th edn. of *Scrambles* that Whymper's questions for Old Peter were all put to him on the first day in one form or another. But, as Dangar & Blakeney pointed out in their review in *AJ70*, 159-61, certain imaginary scenes and conversations which Clark introduces into the story do occasionally lead to minor inaccuracies. There are also quite a number of other factual errors, which for the most part are minor. The comments that follow, whilst by no means exhaustive, are intended to supplement the facts in the text, reveal serious errors and identify the source of some of the less well-known allusions. The book, which unfortunately has no index, was reviewed in *AJ70*, 159-61. Ronald Clark's obituary appears in *AJ93*, 316-18.

1. 1956. *Six Great Mountaineers*. Edward Whymper. 11-51.
2. 1965. *The Day the Rope Broke*. 'The story of a great Victorian tragedy'. (German and Italian translations were published in 1965 in Zürich and Milan respectively, entitled *Als das Seil riss* and *Quando la corda si ruppe*.)

6.7.1 *Six Great Mountaineers* (see above)

6.7.2 *The Day the Rope Broke*

12/2. Whymper was not so obsessed with climbing the Matterhorn that he could not contemplate anyone else getting there first (like Adams Reilly in 1864) and his eight unsuccessful attempts compare favourably with Dent's nineteen on the Dru.

13. line 10. 3 p.m. was the time Young Peter gave in his 'Narrative' more than 50 years later and it is clearly wrong, as are many details he gave.

15/1. Based on Long. *Echo des Alpes* 1867, 52.

17/3&4. McCormick. *A sad holiday*, 12; but see 42/2 below for Campbell.

18/3. The small cloud appears in Young Peter's 'Narrative', para 12.

18/5. The Wilberforce story comes from Browning's *Memories of sixty years*, but did not involve Seiler who only purchased the Hotel Mont Cervin in 1867.

36/1. Douglas seems to have made his first Alpine ascent in 1862. In 1865 he had to be home by the 19th July and would need to leave Zermatt by the 15th at the very latest. He no longer intended to try the Matterhorn in 1865.
37/1. It is often said that only Taugwalder believed that the Matterhorn might be climbed, but this is open to doubt despite what Douglas told Whymper. Whereas Douglas may well have had the Matterhorn from Breuil in mind when he arrived at Zermatt, they had spent so long trying to get up the Gabelhorn that he seems to have decided to postpone it until 1866.
38/2. Douglas was not staying in the same hotel as Walker & Moore and as they would have known of his unsuccessful attempts to find the Gabelhorn and did not 'discuss possibilities' with him before setting off for it, there is no reason to suppose they would have wanted to invite a relative novice to join in an attempt on the Matterhorn; they did not attempt it without him!
38/4. For Douglas's account, see *AJ2*, 221-2.
40/2. Douglas spent the weekend at the Clemenz' Mont Cervin, not at Seiler's Monte Rosa, before moving up to the Riffel on his way to Breuil. For his movements and intentions, see section 2.14.3.
40/2&3. There is no reason to suppose he had set his heart on the Matterhorn for 1865, nor evidence that he sent Taugwalder to reconnoitre, quite apart from the unsuitable weather.
41/2. Douglas set out from the Riffel, his probable intention being to investigate the prospects of engaging Carrel or someone else for 1866.
42/2. There does not seem to be any reason to suppose that Campbell was a former pupil of McCormick or indeed travelling with him. He was one of Hudson's current pupils (*A sad holiday*, 4).
47/1&4. See note above (42/2). There is no reason why Campbell should have gone to Grindelwald with McCormick (ibid, p4 para 3), particularly when his luggage was with that of Hadow & Hudson (see Enquiry Inventories).
47/4. According to Preston-Thomas Hudson was not going to take Hadow climbing that year.
54/2. Whereas Robertson had climbed Mont Blanc on 4th July and was probably still in or around Chamonix on the 7th, there is no reason to suppose that he was a friend ofYeats Brown (who wrote of first meeting him on the 10th), or that Hudson invited him to join him on the Matterhorn.
56/2. It is open to doubt whether Yeats Brown saw Whymper at Chamonix.
69/1. It is doubtful whether Whymper's suppression of Girdlestone's name as the sick Englishman and of his accompanying him and Douglas to Zermatt was due to Girdlestone's book, rather than to his being a stickler for the proprieties, as suggested by Graham Brown.
87/5. There does not seem to be any evidence or good reason for supposing that on 11th July Whymper already knew Joseph Taugwalder by sight.
88/6&7. It is almost certain that Douglas did not send Old Peter on a reconnaissance; see 2.14.3.
89/5. The evidence is all against Douglas having had any such plans.
90/1. There is no reason to suppose that Old Peter had been anywhere near the upper slopes of the mountain or even, at that stage, that he would necessarily have been available to accompany Whymper & Douglas.
94/2. Whymper did not in fact say that the stronger rope was in one length of 150 feet. As for the sashline, it seems as though he was one of those who had regarded plaited ropes as particularly strong, until the results of the 1864 tests were made known.
95/1. 'A rope was a rope' – maybe – but to Old Peter the sashline, plaited rope or lighter rope which he was carrying was 'a special rope' (A24).
95/2. Douglas did not already have a room at the Monte Rosa, having stayed the last fortnight

or so at the Mont Cervin, where the rest of his luggage was and remained, ready packed for his departure. Whereas Whymper & Douglas spent the night at the Monte Rosa, it is probable but not certain that Girdlestone stayed at the Mont Cervin although he too dined at the Monte Rosa.

101/2. It would be unwise to attach too much importance to anything in Young Peter's 'Narrative', as his recollection of many details is faulty.

101/3. Whymper wrote to *The Times* of the steel cable: 'it was not mentioned by Mr.Hudson, and at that time I had not even seen it'.

106/3. There is no evidence of Douglas handing anything to Seiler, as his valuables were still deposited with Clemenz at the Mont Cervin.

108/2. Douglas did wear boots, one of which is in the Zermatt Museum.

111/2&3. These two paragraphs help to emphasise the unliklihood of Old Peter having carried out any reconnaissance for Douglas; likewise 114/2.

121/2. Clark is almost certainly correct in suggesting that Young Peter got the two Douglases confused, despite Dangar & Blakeney not being convinced (see *AJ70*, 160).

128/3. Clark is by no means alone in underrating Girdlestone, but to compare him with Hadow is unrealistic. Not only did he take part in the sixth ascent of the Hörnli ridge in 1868 along with Grove, the arch-critic of guideless climbing, but he made a further guided ascent from Breuil in 1871.

130. line 1. He gave it to the Alpine Club in 1866, see *AJ50*, 330.

130/2&3. It is amusing to contrast Clark's comment on Whymper's description of the view from the summit with that of Arnold Lunn, who wrote in *Mountain Jubilee* (p210) that it read 'like an auctioneer's catalogue of peaks for sale'.

132. The first sentence is misleading in that they did not all leave together.

133/4. There is no justification for Clark's comment about 'that rough treatment which in the aftermath of events he was apt to give Hudson'. It was not until 1895 (*Journal de Zermatt*) that Whymper first criticised Hudson in public, his earlier writings being consistent with his statement to Hadow's father in August 1865: 'I have endeavoured in all that I have done since this much lamentable accident, to avoid giving pain to yourself and to the relatives of Lord Douglas and Mr.Hudson'.

133/6. '150 ft.' – see note 94/2 above.

134/1. There is no evidence to support this order of roping up (see Old Peter's answer A25).

134/6. There is no basis for Clark asserting that there was some of the Croz rope to spare at the Douglas end. Had all seven left the summit together the probability must be (subject to Graham Brown's observation – see section 6.9.3 item 505/3) that, with Douglas as middleman, both ropes would have been attached from him outwards with the guide at each end carrying any spare.

135/1. For considerations bearing on Old Peter's use of the sashline see section 3.16 (The special rope).

136/4. Clark must be wrong here, as apart from any special considerations over Hadow, he seems to place all five on one stance before they each descend one at a time to regroup on the next stance. The more probable mode, which is consistent with Whymper's complaint after the accident that 'Fixed between the two [Taugwalders], I could neither move up nor down' until Young Peter descended, is that they descended in file one at a time with each new pitch initiated by Old Peter from the back, like the advance of a caterpillar.

139/2. It is extremely doubtful whether Old Peter took hold of the Whymper rope, as well as grasping the rock with both arms.

139/4. There is no evidence of the Douglas rope being slack. Old Peter was probably referring to it in A33, when answering an ambiguous question.

140/3&4. Whymper was hardly describing the Taugwalders' behaviour in 'the blackest possible terms' but recording the facts, and Clark has certainly misjudged 'the reason for this attitude' in para 4.
140/7. There is no evidence of Whymper *then* attributing the use of the weakest rope to Old Peter. Referring in his letter to *The Times* to the first five men, he wrote: 'I had not noticed the rope they employed, and now I could only conclude that they had seen fit to use this in preference to the others'. It was only two days later that he discovered 'there was only one link – that between Taugwalder and Lord F. Douglas – in which the weaker rope had been used.'
141/2. The first public reference by Whymper to the possibility of Old Peter using the thinnest rope deliberately does not come for another six years when, in the long Taugwalder footnote in *Scrambles* and in the text above it in relation to Clemenz' failure to disclose the answers to the 'questions which were framed so as to afford old Peter an opportunity of exculpating himself', he referred to such things as 'the grave suspicions which at once fell on him'. Whymper was not referring to his own suspicions ('I have no reason to suspect even that this was done intentionally', he wrote to Wigram), but was recording objectively the facts.
141/5. As already stated (140/7 above), Whymper did not at that time know that Old Peter alone had selected the weak rope.
142/3. Once more Young Peter's account made 50 years later cannot be preferred to Whymper's almost contemporary record, particularly when comparison is made between Old Peter's incapacity with Kennedy on the Dent Blanche in 1862 and Whymper's ability the same year to descend part of the Italian ridge of the Matterhorn on his own, after falling 200 feet, sustaining head injuries and losing consciousness.
146/2. At the Enquiry Whymper confined his answers to the questions put to him, but his letter to *The Times* did refer obliquely to the incident with the words 'There is no occasion to say more of the descent', meaning that that was not the occasion to do so. 'His version' was not written some years later for the first time, but was then transcribed from the original memorandum dated 17.8.65, which he had made on the advice of others.
146/4. It was not an 'accusation', but a record of a conversation. Like other critics Clark has overlooked Whymper writing in the long footnote in *Scrambles* of what he later learnt, probably in about September 1869, about Young Peter: 'The odious idea that he propounded (which I believe emanated from him) he has endeavoured to trade upon, in spite of the fact that his father was paid (for both) in the presence of witnesses'.
147/3. Clark does not seem to have appreciated the reason for Whymper's silence; see Whymper's private letter of c.4.8.65 to the *Times* Editor (4.16).
148/2. The last sentence relates to one of the subjects in the Cowell memorandum.
148/4. There is no reason whatever to doubt Whymper's evidence of arriving back in Zermatt at 10.30, in view of its acceptance by Clemenz in his statement of the facts.
154. line 3. It seems likely that the Randa correspondent was a tourist rather than a local, particularly as the second report looks as though it was based on an interview with Young Peter who, unlike his father, could speak French.
154. lines 29-31. The 'best course' was the belief of McCormick and Whymper, and no doubt others staying at the Monte Rosa, see note 147/3 above. As for experience in the ways of the world, see for example Whymper's letters to Buxton and to father Hadow.
154/2. It is misleading to attribute the growth of rumours to Whymper's silence, which presumably means his reluctance to write to *The Times*, as this would have had no influence on those circulating in Zermatt and Chamonix. He did write to von Fellenberg on the 25th and to Rimini on 26th July and he was not to know for some weeks of the delay in the former receiving his letter. Whymper was not 'utterly alone' following the arrival of McCormick, Robertson & others on the Saturday afternoon.

155/5. For Campbell being Hudson's pupil etc see notes to 42 & 47 above.
156/4. Whymper's accuracy in virtually everthing he recorded is well shown by the first search party consisting of exactly 20 men, and the recovery party of 21 men, as he stated in *Scrambles*.
156/5. It seems probable that the men originally went to the Stöckli hoping to be able to reach the glacier from there, as they would have been back much sooner had they gone straight to the Hohlicht.
158/3. Much of this appears to be Clark's invention. McCormick wrote to Hadow's father on the Sunday and almost certainly to Mrs.Hudson at the same time. There is no record of how the Queensberry family was informed, although there is in Whymper's scrapbook a curious undated note from Clemenz asking him for the address of 'Madame Douglas'. There is no evidence about any 'semi-official statement', nor was there any question of Whymper not wanting to mention the Taugwalders' name.
159/160. This paragraph is mere supposition by Clark and is inconsistent with the facts; see section 3.5 (Excommunication).
160/2. There is no basis for Clark seeking to contradict the threat of excommunication and pretending that it was a misunderstanding on the part of Whymper. Even Arnold Lunn did not go that far! Clark expresses surprise that Whymper believed it in the company of McCormick, Robertson, Phillpotts and Girdlestone and says that they cannot 'have believed the tale'. Girdlestone was not even in Zermatt but at the Riffel at the time. However there is good reason to conclude that Robertson had as clear an understanding as Whymper in view of his later report to Whymper of the sequel to the threat of excommunication. If the fact that the priests prevented the Zermatt guides going to the scene on the Sunday is to be doubted, and presumably also that 'Peter Perrn declared with tears that nothing else would have prevented him from joining in the search for his old comrades', although Clark does not even mention this, a further look at the evidence is called for. But as in the case of some unjustified claims made on behalf of Old Peter by certain critics vainly trying to discredit Whymper, this makes it necessary to draw attention to matters that might have been better left unmentioned. So if anyone should think that the priests' conduct was above reproach and that they did not threaten excommunication in order to prevent the men going on the search, they should look at the *Graphic* of 1894 and ask what other explanation there could be for the disgraceful way in which Franz Andenmatten of Saas, who was the first to volunteer and who led the search party, was ejected from the church at Zermatt the next time he tried to attend Mass! On p164 Clark refers to a second incident reported by Robertson, which Whymper also mentioned in the same *Graphic* article, but Clark seems to have turned a blind eye to Andenmatten being ejected from the church.
165/3. If this is supposed to implicate Whymper in the origin of the mischievous rumours that the rope was cut, it does seem rather far-fetched and contrived, quite apart from Whymper having no time for talking before the rumours started and the fact that no details of the accident percolated out of the Monte Rosa hotel, as appears from the errors in the newspaper reports. But it must be sheer invention by Clark to state that 'Whymper openly criticised the fact that the thinner rope had been used'. Compare with this Clark's comment on p166, para 2, 4th sentence.
166/3&4. There is no evidence whatever to support this invention.
167/3. It is almost certain that Whymper liaised with McCormick in writing the letter and the 'gap' to which Clark refers was deliberate, see Whymper's private letter of c.4.8.65 to *Times* Editor (4.16).
167/4. There is no reason to suppose the hotel account contained anything that would give pain to any of the relatives of the victims.
168/3. It is more likely to have been made shortly before leaving on the 22nd. Campbell's entry made on the 18th has survived.

175/2. There were 21 men in the recovery party, as Whymper recorded.
176/2. It is doubtful whether Clark had any evidence of Robertson & Phillpotts being at the Riffel and not at the funerals, as this would be most extraordinary in view of the fact that their colleague Knyvet Wilson was being buried at the same time. He seems to rely on Yeats Brown, whose recollection 50 years later was far from reliable.
176/4. The new Hotel Mont Cervin, as Clark calls it, had been opened in 1854 by Clemenz, who conducted the Enquiry. It may have been 'neutral ground' in one sense, but one of Clemenz' guests for most of the past fortnight had been Lord Francis Douglas and Clemenz may even have introduced him to Old Peter.
177/2. Clemenz cannot have arrived on 21st July, and was probably there already in his capacity as hotelier. Johann (Jean) Julen, the bailiff was a cousin of Old Peter. Whether Clemenz was 'innocent of any specialist knowledge of mountaineering' is open to doubt, as according to the Centenary publication of the Monte Rosa section of the SAC (p17), he appears to have succeeded Seiler as vice-president of the section at the end of 1866.
177/3. The circumstances in which the Enquiry was conducted now appear to have been very different from what had been thought. Whymper had been given his questions in advance of the hearing, and almost certainly handed in his written answers, already translated into French.
178/3. Whymper actually said 'less thick'.
178/4. The Court never asked for any explanation of any answer on the first day.
178/5. Whymper gave his evidence in French.
179/2. Whymper's actual words referred to the Zermatt guides refusing 'en masse' to go in search of the bodies!
179/6. For the circumstances in which Old Peter probably gave his answers in writing after his cousin Alois Julen, who was a fellow guide and also the Zermatt district judge, had helped with both the questions and the answers, see sections 3.4 & 5.4.2 dealing with The Enquiry .
179/6&7. With the exception of the amiguous Q36, all the questions of substance put to Old Peter on the first day (Q22-35) originated with Whymper. Clark was apparently unaware of this and was therefore wrong in the inferences he sought to draw from the questioning.
180/2. Clark omits that Old Peter said it was a special rope (A24).
180/3. For the apparently deliberate distortion in Q28 of 'a different kind of rope' so that it became 'another rope', see section 5.4.2.
181/7. Although Clark knew nothing of the involvement of Vecqueray or Julen or of the questions being in writing, he seems to have recognized the unreality of some of the answers.
182/3. This was a Clemenz question (Q36), the only one of substance he asked Old Peter on the first day.
183/2. Clark would no doubt have deleted this paragraph, had he appreciated the way in which the Enquiry was actually conducted.
183/3. This is completely wrong. As Tyndale revealed in an appendix in the 6th edn. of *Scrambles*, Whymper's questions were put to Old Peter on the Friday and not on the Sunday.
184/2. It seems quite likely that Clemenz had asked Whymper to draft some questions for Old Peter to answer.
184/3. Whymper's original questions have survived in English, also a copy of the French translation he handed in, as well as the actual questions put in German; see section 5.5. As for a question asking 'why the rope was chosen on the summit', this had been covered by Whymper in what was to become Q28, until someone distorted it.
185/7. Old Peter's German answer translates: 'as Mr. Whymper was above me in a place where he could see the unfortunate course of events better than I could, his deposition may be more correct...'

186/5. Whymper had left Zermatt on the Saturday. Old Peter's protesting as Clark calls it (see 195/3) seems to have occurred a month later.
188/2. Young Peter cannot have left Zermatt before Thursday afternoon, having gone on the recovery party.
192/1. The 'local comment' comes from the *Dumfries Courier*, quoted in *The Times* of 28.7.65; that from Zermatt comes via Coolidge's aunt.
192/3. The first word in the penultimate line should read 'Tyndall'.
193/2. Queensberry could well have stayed at St.Niklaus on the 29th on his way home from Zermatt, as his brother had stayed there several times.
194/3. Clark seems to have taken this quote from de Beer's *Travellers in Switzerland* p310.
195/3. It seems more likely that Charles Parker saw Old Peter on about 28th August, when he climbed Monte Rosa, possibly with Old Peter.
198/2. There can be no justification for the last two lines.
200/1. Whymper did not 'put the statement on record'.
200/3. He dined with Cowell and his father on Wednesday 2nd August. The circumstances in which the Cowell memorandum came into existence on 1st September, following the creation of Whymper's own memorandum of 17.8.65 and also Wills' advice to Whymper, were never appreciated or disclosed by Smythe, when he published it.
201/2. There is no reason to suppose the Cowells breached Whymper's confidence over anything recorded in their memorandum, as there were many other things omitted from his letter to *The Times*. It must be wrong to refer to libel 'seeping out over the years'.
201/4. Clark's presumption is wrong; furthermore such a long and detailed account must have been in preparation for some time.
202/3. Clark is mistaken to keep suggesting some sort of malice on the part of Whymper towards the Taugwalders. He did several things to benefit them.
202. last line. Whymper was not making any 'accusation', but relating the facts. Even Clark himself has referred more than once (e.g. p178/4 and 184/3) to expecting Old Peter to be asked why the weaker rope was chosen on the summit, which is tantamount to asking why, when the others were tied with strong brand-new rope (as Old Peter called it A26), there was a weak link between him and Douglas. As for having little chance for effective reply, Whymper had already provided such a chance for Old Peter to reply by including the question, 'Why was a different kind of rope used between Lord Douglas and yourself' (Q28), in the list for Old Peter to answer. He was informing the Editor that although the questions were put and answered before he left Zermatt, the answers although promised had not yet reached him. It seems that in 1865 everyone else wanted to know the answer to the same question that Clark himself was to emphasise a century later, and he can hardly maintain that Whymper's recital of the material facts constituted some sort of accusation.
208/1. Clark says of Young Peter that 'Whymper's comments made singularly little impression on possible employers', and the same would be true of Old Peter, so far as those comments were concerned. But it is not right to state that Young Peter *quickly* became the acknowledged expert of the Swiss face, when he avoided the climb for seven years after the accident.
208/2. Clark does not indicate what he is referring to by 'the libellous implications of Whymper's story'. He cannot presumably have had in mind anything he wrote in *Scrambles*, as it was not published until 1871 and could hardly have affected Old Peter's career during the six year gap following the accident. The *Times* letter may have drawn a minute fraction of the public's attention to the lack of any explanation for the use of the weak rope, but the public memory is notoriously short and we know that Old Peter had no lack of opportunity of repeating the ascent but instead declined all requests to climb the Hörnli. The reason why he seems never to have led another successful climb after 1865, and even failed by losing the way

whilst descending a pass with Güssfeldt after insisting that no one else should accompany them, must be found elsewhere and it is nothing to do with anything Whymper ever wrote or said. Old Peter left Zermatt in 1874, according to Young Peter, and returned in 1878, and he did not therefore die for another 10 years.

210/2. The 2nd edition of *Scrambles* appeared in Autumn 1871.

211/1. There is no reason to suppose that Douglas still intended to attempt the Matterhorn in 1865 by the time he met Whymper. The footnotes in *Scrambles* supplemented his previous account to *The Times*, but Whymper did still avoid saying anything that might cause pain to the relatives.

211/2. The inconsistency Clark supposes does not exist. The relevant memorandum was made only a month and not six years after the accident. As for what Whymper told Prior (p146-7 above) there is no reason why he should have told him all the details, particularly as that was the subject he had some doubts about revealing in full, as is shown by his seeking the advice of the Cowells and of Browne. The last two sentences relate to statements of fact by Whymper, and both stemmed from Clemenz' failure to disclose the answers he had promised.

212/1. 15 words have been omitted after 'Douglas', see section 2.48 (Leslie Stephen). The essential difference between Whymper denouncing the idea that Old Peter cut the rope and not rejecting the less serious accusation that he intentionally used a weak rope is that Whymper knew all the material facts relating to the former but not to the latter. He did not suspect even that Old Peter used the weakest rope intentionally (section 4.30, letter to Wigram) but he did not have the information necessary to refute it as a fact.

212/3. The first sentence is ill-founded for, like Clark, Lunn certainly had no inkling of the circumstances in which the Cowell memorandum came into existence.

216/1. The Enquiry records that were released were far more extensive than Farrar revealed; see section 5.1. Old Peter never answered the question Clark and everyone else has asked about the use of the weak rope, because someone distorted Whymper's question before it reached him.

216/2. The original of Young Peter's Narrative is not lost! It seems likely that it was written by one of his daughters and certainly not by Montagnier's man! The literary trimmings must be Peter's own.

217/218. There is no direct evidence to favour the theory of deliberate choice by Old Peter of the weak rope and Whymper himself had no reason even to suspect it was done intentionally, but it did call for an explanation in 1865 as it still did in 1965, when Clark considered the questions that were put to Old Peter at the Enquiry. It is most unlikely that some unknown document will yet be revealed with the answer, but it may be possible, by considering all the facts and circumstances in their proper context, to reconstruct Old Peter's probable state of mind at the time and finally dispel the suspicions which his lawyer inadvertently did so much to foster by preventing him from answering Whymper's questions; see section 3.16 (The special rope).

6.8
COX, ANTHONY DAVID MACHELL (1913 – 1994)

As Editor of the *Alpine Journal*, David Cox seems to have been responsible for the first two of five articles that appeared in the 1865 *Journal* dealing with 'The Matterhorn Centenary'.

1. Some dates in the history of the Matterhorn, 1865-1965. *AJ70*, 8-15.
2. Some documents relating to the first ascent of the Matterhorn. *AJ70*, 15-26.

6.8.1 Some Dates

9. Item 5. This ascent has an additional special interest as, although Whymper recorded that the second guide was Victor Maquignaz, he was in fact J-Pierre who with his brother J-Joseph had made the first traverse from Breuil with Tyndall a few days before. They were both still in Zermatt when Thioly, who with his eccentric friend Hoiler had virtually decided to make the ascent without guides as none of the Swiss guides would go with them, discovered them and suggested that they might like to return home by traversing the Matterhorn in the opposite direction. They agreed and after waiting for the weather to improve they completed the first double traverse of the mountain, despite Hoiler producing and playing his clarinet on the summit!
15. Illustration No. 9. The photograph was taken from the Hohbalm-Schönbühl path, see correction on page 323 of *AJ70.*

6.8.2 Some Documents

15. Documents, para 2. Whymper's concurrence in McCormick's letter to *The Times*, if not his participation in it, is confirmed by a private letter he wrote to the Editor on about the 4th August 1865, referring to his having hoped that it would have been sufficient for the information of the public, having been intentionally silent on the exact cause of the accident in order to spare the families of Hudson and Hadow.
16. No. II. The telegram from Lady Queensberry seems to have reached Brig on the same day that her son the Marquess reached Zermatt. Her seemingly irrational message was probably related to the dream or vision by her maid on the night of the catastrophe, when she saw Lord Francis Douglas 'lying on a rocky ledge on a great precipice, terribly wounded'; see sections 2.44 (Queensberry) and 4.61 (Dixie's letter).
16. No. III. McCormick's letter of 16th July to Hadow, which Hadow was acknowledging, must have been one of the very earliest written accounts, but there is nothing to suggest that it or any similar letter McCormick sent to Mrs.Hudson has survived, any more than a letter that Whymper must have sent to his father at about the same time.
22. Last paragraph. Kennedy certainly wrote as though he appreciated better than Hudson and Whymper the potential danger of a cumbersome party etc. It must however be open to doubt as to whether he would have acted any differently had he been of the party, in view of what he wrote of the descent of the Aiguille Verte on the 5th July: 'We left the top...all [six, +dog?] tied to one long rope, a mode of proceeding which was certainly not the best one. Croz led the way...'
26. para 3. The contents of Whymper's letter to von Fellenberg were largely published as reported speech in the *Sonntagspost*, a Bern Sunday paper, on 13.8.65. It therefore saw the light of day before the Italian version, which was not published before the end of August. It was however behind *The Times*.

6.9
DANGAR, DUDLEY FREDERICK OLIPHANT (1902 – 1992) BLAKENEY, THOMAS SYDNEY BLAKENEY (1903 – 1976)

It is convenient and appropriate to list 'Dangar & Blakeney' together, as although they wrote a number of separate articles, book reviews or Notes in the *Alpine*

Journal on various aspects of the Matterhorn accident, it is for their several joint works on the subject that they will be chiefly remembered. Mention should also be made of their joint article 'The first ascent of the Trifthorn' (*AJ61*, 348-51), which helps to clarify some of Douglas and Taugwalder's earlier activities in July 1865.

Their three principal articles concern Young Peter Taugwalder's 'Narrative', the career of Old Peter Taugwalder and a 20 page review of Arnold Lunn's book *Matterhorn Centenary*, entitled 'A word for Whymper'. Ronald Clark described their article and annotations on Young Peter's 'Narrative' as 'a work of scholarship which is a masterpiece of its kind'. Although there is a very marked contrast between the accuracy of what they wrote and of what Arnold Lunn wrote about the accident and its aftermath, it could be said that their main achievement vis-à-vis Arnold Lunn was to draw attention to his campaign against Whymper, to put an end to it and to restore the truth. In 1966 they wrote: 'It is hardly an exaggeration to say that [Lunn] appears ready to impugn Whymper's veracity on everything he wrote about the events of July 13 to 15, 1865'.

Their principal writings on the Matterhorn and on Whymper, either individually (D) or (B) or jointly (D&B) are as follows:

1. (B) Whymper and Mummery. *AJ57*, 339-40.
2. (D) The Führerbuch of young Peter Taugalder [1860-1883]. *AJ59*, 436-41.
3. (D&B) The first ascent of the Matterhorn. The Narrative of 'Young' Peter Taugwalder. *AJ61*, 484-506.
4. (B) Note. Hadow's boots. *AJ63*, 124.
5. (B) Note. Whymper and the Taugwalders. *AJ65*, 94-5.
6. (D) The Parkers and the Matterhorn. *AJ68*, 285-90.
7. (D&B) 'Old' Peter Taugwalder, 1820-88. *AJ70*, 26-37.
8. (B) Note. Whymper and Southend, *AJ70*, 135-6.
9. (D&B) Review. *The Day the Rope Broke*. By Ronald W. Clark. *AJ70*, 159-61.
10. (D&B) The Matterhorn: a diary of events after the disaster of 1865. *AJ70*, 199-204.
11. (D&B) A word for Whymper: a reply to Sir Arnold Lunn. *AJ71*, 111-32.
12. (D&B) Their comments on Lunn's article, 'Whymper again'. *AJ71*, 233-5.
13. (B) Note. Whymper and the Royal Society. *AJ71*, 308-9.
14. (B) Review. *The Mountain World, 1964/65*. [Article by Müller] *AJ71*, 334-5.

6.9.1 Whymper and Mummery

Blakeney no doubt regretted having written this piece about Whymper's review of Mummery's book by the time Lunn got hold of it, but it can hardly have helped Lunn's case coming so late in Whymper's life, when his health was already failing and his state of mind was completely different from what it had been in the days when he was writing his letter to *The Times* or when he was writing *Scrambles*.

6.9.2 The Führerbuch of 'Young' Peter Taugwalder

437/3. The gap between June 26 and August 13 1865 is not immediately apparent, but a whole section of the book appears to have been removed.
437/5. Thioly went to Zermatt in 1866 with the intention of climbing the Matterhorn, but could find no guide willing to go.
438/7. On 30th July 1869 Young Peter, Peter Perren and Joseph Maquignaz had to turn back with Heathcote in a storm on the Italian ridge of the Matterhorn, within 500 feet of the summit. Although Heathcote completed the ascent on 27th August the same year, he did so with four of the Maquignaz, who fixed the Jordan ladder at the same time. Young Peter was otherwise engaged with a Frenchman, Desmousseaux, for several days.
439. lines 2-3. According to a letter written by Rudolf Taugwalder on Young Peter's behalf to Montagnier, Old Peter went to America in 1874, until 1878.
439/3. Young Peter had been on the Italian ridge before, see 438/7 above.

6.9.3 The first ascent of the Matterhorn. The Narrative of 'Young' Peter Taugwalder

484/1. The AC Archives do in fact contain the document in question. It is in German, typewritten and undated, but has been signed by Taugwalder in a rather shaky hand.
484/2. The AC does have what seems to be the original copy. It is written on eight full sheets of paper slightly smaller than A4, mostly bearing 31 or 32 lines of German script, written in a fairly large, legible hand including a number of deletions and additions in smaller writing but probably the same hand. There is also a ninth sheet, only half as long and of a different type of paper, bearing eight lines of large script in the same hand followed by Young Peter's signature. This is fairly similar to the one already referred to above, but even more shaky. The writer was probably one of Young Peter's daughters by his second marriage, either Salomena or Balbina, most likely the latter, and it was certainly not Montagnier's 'man', as suggested in Footnote 3, as the same handwriting appears in a 'thank you' letter of 27th November 1917, written on Young Peter's behalf to Montagnier. He did not sign it himself, possibly because there was too little space at the bottom of the page for his shaky hand!
485. lines 2-4. It is necessary to bear in mind the distinction between these accusations under which Old Peter suffered, which were not made by Whymper but only recorded by him, and what Lunn repeatedly referred to as Whymper's 'accusations' against Old Peter, which seem in fact never to have existed!
485/2 last sentence. See D&B's later comment on this in *AJ71*, 124-5.
486. line 3. Whymper wanted the AC to hold an Enquiry and, had he been properly questioned by it or even by Clemenz, he would have been relieved of the burden of having to decide which details he ought to withhold for the sake of not causing further suffering to the relatives.
487/2. Gos seems to have been relying on *AJ21*, 538. It is not very clear and the writer of Robertson's obituary probably got it wrong.
487/4 last sentence. For the reasons why Douglas probably no longer intended to try in 1865 by the time he met Whymper, see section 2.14.3.
488. Note 27. The von Fellenberg letter was in fact quoted very fully in the Berner *Sonntagspost* of 13.8.65.
491. lines 4-5. It seems probable that Young Peter was confused by there being two Douglases in the party.

493. Note 2. The St.Niklaus hotel entry facsimile has subsequently also been reproduced in *Mountain World 1964/65,* 25.
493. Note 4. Whereas Douglas clearly had his eye on the Matterhorn at the start of his holiday, he had not expected it to take so long to reach the top of the Gabelhorn. For the reasons why he probably no longer intended to try the Matterhorn in 1865, rather than the following year, see section 2.14.3.
493. last 2 lines. Friedrich was the sharp-eyed lad who saw the accident from Zermatt. He probably accompanied his father to America in 1874.
494/1. Confirmation that it was Joseph and not Young Peter who accompanied Douglas to Breuil comes from the fees Whymper paid to Old Peter. Likewise the outstanding fees prove that Douglas had already paid off Old Peter (with a loan from Clemenz!).
494. Note 6. Young Peter's experience by 1865 included more than 25 ascents of Monte Rosa and there is little doubt that he and Kennedy could have safely climbed the Dent Blanche, had Old Peter not been with them.
494. Note 11. Old Peter's '2' in A61 was almost certainly 2 p.m. and should have appeared as part of his answer to Q62, which must have asked what time they arrived at the summit and how long they stayed there. Someone seems to have mislaid A61 & Q62!
495. Note 12 (v). It should be borne in mind that Young Peter was probably confused by the two Douglases, see 491 above and section 3.9 (Newspapers).
496. Note 14 (i). see 495 & 491 above.
497. Note 19. Between 3.05 and 3.10 may be a little early for the happening of the accident, as progress would have been exceedingly slow with a rope of five descending one at a time, and slower still when two more were added. If the accident happened only minutes after Old Peter tied himself on to Whymper's rope, Whymper and Young Peter could not have descended any further before the accident occurred. One possible indicator of the exact time is Hudson's watch which had stopped at 3.45, according to the Inventory of his possessions in the Enquiry Report.
498. Note 21 (ii). last sentence. Young Peter may furthermore have confused his father's position at the time of the accident (when he could not see him) with that more than half an hour later, by which time his father had 'changed his position to a rock to which he could attach the rope'.
498. Note 22 (ii). There is even more reason to accept Old Peter's retraction when one realises what he actually said, as this was incorrectly translated into French. Furthermore, he must surely have kept his eyes glued to the rock he was hugging!
498. Note 22 (iii). Studer's editors may perhaps have spoken to Alois Julen at some stage.
499. Note 23. Whymper could not move, being stuck between the two Taugwalders, until one of them moved. But comparing his performance in 1862, when he got himself down to Breuil in the dark after falling 200 feet, sustaining head injuries and losing consciousness, with that of Old Peter the same year on the Dent Blanche, 'his nerve being entirely destroyed by...fright' without even sustaining an accident, it hardly seems possible that Whymper should have needed and have received help from Old Peter!
500. Note 27 (iii). The reference in *Western Alps* to Peter zum Taugwald must have been meant for Old Peter, as there was no one else of that name and some of Ball's comments reappear for Old Peter in the 1870 edition.
501/3. Old Peter fell short of the criterion for selection in *The Pioneers of the Alps*, see its Preface or section 6.9.7 below, page 26.
502. para (vii). Old Peter's pre-1865 climbing career is in *SACJ 1865*, 535.
502. para (viii). D&B appear to have overlooked (like everyone else!) that Whymper recorded how Young Peter had endeavoured to trade upon the idea of non-payment, which seems to

exclude any possibility of misunderstanding. As for the circumstances in which the Cowell memorandum came to be written, see section 3.2 (The Cowell memorandum).
503. Note 31. Young Peter and his brother Joseph were members of the third search party that recovered the bodies.
503. Note 34. 'This footnote to Taugwalder's Narrative' is the half page (the ninth page) referred to above (484/2), the original German copy of which Young Peter signed. As for the efforts at 'fine' writing this seems to be consistent with Young Peter's character and further instances appear in the letter of 27.11.1917.
504/3. Despite what Charlton wrote, there can be no doubt from the terms in which McCormick wrote of Hadow in *A sad holiday* (page 4 in particular), that he was a former pupil of Hudson.
505/3. It would hardly be strange that Whymper did not distinguish between the Manilla and the 'second and equally strong rope' if in fact he recovered pieces of both ropes from the glacier. He was making the point that the victims had not been tied with the sashline, but with one of the stronger ropes – and to him it did not matter which – unlike those critics who have tried to determine where each particular length of rope was at the time of the accident! Graham Brown seems to have been the only one to observe (as recorded in his copious notes on the '1865 Matterhorn accident' now in the National Library of Scotland) that in the List of Illustrations in *Scrambles*, but not in the actual captions in the text, Whymper described the pieces of the Manilla rope and of the 'second' rope as 'broken on the Matterhorn'. The tattered ends of the twisted ropes depicted are exactly what might be expected of a rope that broke during the 4,000ft fall to the glacier and, if the ropes had become detached from the victims' bodies like their boots, there would be no way of knowing who had used which one. It seems probable that Croz carried one of the ropes with an end tied to Hudson via Hadow, and that Hudson carried the other with a short length uncoiled and tied to Douglas. But it is difficult to understand why Hudson's rope extended only as far as Douglas unless it was originally intended that the last three should descend separately, or why Taugwalder did not ask Hudson to release some rope, retie Douglas and then tie himself to the end, and the realisation that three different kinds of rope were probably involved in the four links between the leading five seems to raise more questions than it answers! All three broken rope ends are now on display in the Zermatt Museum.
506/2 penultimate sentence. For a possible explanation for Old Peter honestly, albeit mistakenly, believing that the sashline was strong enough, see section 3.16 (The special rope).
506/2 last sentence. Whymper would not have got within 15 or 20 feet of Old Peter when he threw him down the end of the rope.

6.9.4 Hadow's boots

For consideration of the Montandon article, see section 3.7 (Hadow's boots).

6.9.5 Whymper and the Taugwalders

Without seeing exactly what Lunn wrote in the Journal referred to, it is not possible to comment except to draw attention to the possibility that when Charles Parker climbed Monte Rosa on 28th August 1865 with W.H.Gladstone, he may have employed Old Peter as guide.

6.9.6 The Parkers and the Matterhorn

286/5. It now seems probable that Charles Parker met Old Peter on about 28th August 1865, when he and W.H.Gladstone climbed Monte Rosa, and it is even possible that he employed Old Peter as guide. As for Whymper behaving ill in the colouring he gave to his evidence, it is possible that Old Peter had in mind something he learnt from one of his cousins, either the Enquiry bailiff Johannes Julen or the Zermatt judge, Alois Julen. Perhaps it was the tenor of the questions Whymper drafted for him to answer, and Old Peter did not realise that it was probably Alois Julen and not Whymper who had acted to his detriment by preventing him from giving the answers that might have exonerated him altogether. There can therefore be no question of Whymper's evidence having damaged Old Peter although, if Clemenz should have reacted to the restrictions imposed on his handling of the Enquiry by no longer recommending Old Peter to his hotel guests, it is understandable that Old Peter might have been misled into thinking that this was Whymper's fault.
287/2 It seems clear from Parker's account that Old Peter must have pocketed the whole of the tip, which Whymper bore entirely himself and did not share with the families of the victims like the guides' fees etc.
289/6 lines 4-6. This extraordinary remark about the strong rope seems to have something in common with Old Peter's A34 and to be implying that the Douglas – Taugwalder rope was less than 'strong'.

6.9.7 'Old' Peter Taugwalder

26/2. Old Peter's Führerbuch is mentioned again in a note at the very end of the article suggesting that some member of the Taugwalder family in Zermatt should institute a house search for the missing volume. It seems that this brought no response and a more recent enquiry directed through someone living in Zermatt produced the reaction that even if the book was still in existence no one was going to see it. The criterion for inclusion in *The Pioneers of the Alps* was selection by eight leading mountaineers from a list of guides, deleting those who should not be included, adding any others who should and writing 'D' against any considered to be doubtful. The fact is that Old Peter was little more than a Monte Rosa guide of considerable experience and ability.
29/5. It is necessary to cast doubt on much of this paragraph, including Old Peter's reconnaissance. It is unlikely he made it and it certainly did not achieve anything. It may also be asked whether Old Peter was the right man to make a reconnaissance on his own, judging from the consequences of his 'exploration' on the Dent Blanche. He would have needed to go further than Kennedy or the Parkers and indeed beyond the shoulder to learn anything new. As for the last sentence, Whymper had already decided in 1864 to try from Zermatt, without Carrel he had no other option on the 11th July 1865, and he had already decided to cross the Theodule to Zermatt before Douglas hove in sight.
30/2. Whymper's diary also tends to confirm this, as Douglas's only outstanding fees were for Joseph, apart from reimbursement of an advance by Clemenz for guide's fees.
31/2. Young Peter did in fact go on the third search party, the one that recovered the bodies, as did his brother Joseph.
31/3 lines 8-10. For consideration of his reputation as a guide, see Old Peter Taugwalder, section 2.52.3.
31/4. For his opportunities to climb the Matterhorn in 1866 & 1867, see sections 2.52.10 & 11. The Matterhorn ascent seems to have been a watershed in his guiding career as instead of

insisting that Young Peter should be taken as second guide he himself seems thereafter to have been taken as second guide to his son. In fact there is no evidence of Old Peter having led any successful climb after the accident, disregarding the Stogden and Parker possibilities.

32/1. According to information supplied by Young Peter to Montagnier, Old Peter went to America in 1874 and returned in 1878.

32/2. It should be borne in mind that Kennedy's 'attack' on Old Peter in *AJ1*, 33, when writing of the Dent Blanche fiasco, seems not to have damaged his career, although it related far more closely to his competence as a guide than did Whymper's account of his reaction to the shock of a real catastrophe.

32/4. lines 1-3. Pre-1864 Old Peter had made some 85 ascents of Monte Rosa and three of the Lyskamm, as well as frequent ascents of the Breithorn. He had crossed many passes but all his peaks had been in the south-eastern sector from Zermatt.

33/2. lines 2-8. In 1865 many climbers seem to have referred to Old Peter as 'Taugwald', and Leslie Stephen was still doing so in 1871 in his Review of *Scrambles* in *Macmillan's Magazine*, so it is hardly surprising that Ball should have mistakenly referred to him as Peter zum Taugwald in *Western Alps, 1863*.

33/2 line 9. Eccentric seems to cover such conduct as that described by Thioly and by Stephen and there may also be something in Stogden's description of 'the somewhat coarse, dirty old beggar'!

33/4. 'a very good cragsman' seems likely to be based on Ball's 1863 entry for Old Peter in *Western Alps*, if not Parker's own experience.

34/4. Hadow's fault seems to have been not so much that he slipped, but that he slipped at the wrong moment, when he should have stood still to let Croz go down a step or two. They were supposed to be climbing one at a time.

35/1. Girdlestone! There does not appear to be any reason for supposing that he was any less sure-footed or competent than the leading climbers of his day, whatever mistakes he may have made on his guideless ventures. Even his arch-critic Grove wrote of his 'exceptionally large experience', and with ascents of the Hörnli in 1868 (with Grove!) and of the Italian ridge in 1871, it can be said that he and Kelso were the first tourists after Grove himself to make the ascent and descent of both ridges of the Matterhorn.

35/4. Old Peter was not asked about the sashline as such and apart from Whymper saying that the Douglas – Old Peter rope was less thick than the others (A10), and Old Peter saying that it was a special rope (A24), there was no evidence before the Enquiry that it was any different. To Clemenz, in his public capacity, it was simply 'another' rope.

36/2. For Old Peter's pre-1864 climbs, see also *SAC Jahrbuch 1865* p535 and page 323 of *AJ70*.

37. '1866'. One could add after 'this year.' 'Nor could Birkbeck, who had to engage seven guides from St.Niklaus.'

6.9.8 Whymper and Southend

This short note by Blakeney is of no great importance.

6.9.9 Review. *The Day the Rope Broke*

para 2. Asking not to be paid may sound improbable, but it seems to have been true judging from what Whymper learnt (probably in about September 1869) and wrote in the long footnote in *Scrambles* about Young Peter: 'The odious idea that he propounded (which I believe

emanated from him) he has endeavoured to trade upon, in spite of the fact that his father was paid (for both) in the presence of witnesses'.
160. lines 1-3. D&B state that Clark's suggestion of confusion between the two Douglases is not convincing, yet there are two documents that support it. Firstly the *Journal de Genève* of 18.7.65 said it was Lord Francis Douglas who slipped, which seems to have been based on an interview with Young Peter and could never have come even indirectly from Whymper or from Old Peter. The other document is Rudolf Taugwalder's letter of 8.5.1917 to Montagnier, relaying on Young Peter's behalf the answers to some questions he had asked. Rudolf may have made some use of his own knowledge as custodian of the Zermatt Museum, but he actually wrote: 'Mr. Hadow whose slip caused the accident was a very bad climber. Those who followed him always were compelled to place his feet into the right foothold'.
161. 2nd sentence. The other possibility is that he wished to spare the families of Hudson and Hadow, and that he and McCormick had hoped the latter's letter of 17th July to *The Times* 'would have been sufficient for the public', as stated in his private lettter to the *Times* editor of c.4.8.65.

6.9.10 The Matterhorn. A diary of events after the disaster of 1865

201. Saturday July 15. They seem to have 'set out' for the Matterhorn glacier via the Stöckli, but retreated to the Hohlicht on account of wide crevasses.
201. Monday July 17. Whymper's account in the Visitors' Book is likely to have been made on 21st or 22nd, as several double sided pages are missing from 18th or 19th, resuming on the 28th July.
201. Friday, July 21. The Enquiry opened at 2 pm.
201. Sunday, July 23. Whymper's questions for Old Peter were put on the Friday and not on the Sunday, as they were Questions 22 to 35 inclusive.
201. Tuesday, July 25. The contents of the von Fellenberg letter were quoted at some length in the *Berner Sonntagspost* on 13.8.65.
202. Wednesday, July 26. The Rimini letter was published no earlier than September 1865.

6.9.11 A word for Whymper

This excellent article, prompted by Arnold Lunn's book, *Matterhorn Centenary* and by his reiteration on the occasion of the centenary of the first ascent of the Matterhorn 'of his well-known adverse criticisms of Whymper', said everything that needed to be said and there is nothing to add to it!

6.9.12 Comments on Lunn's 'Whymper again'

Again, there is nothing to add to Dangar & Blakeney's further comments.

6.9.13 Whymper and the Royal Society

A short note by Blakeney.

6.9.14 Review. *Mountain World 1964/65*

Mountain World contained an article by Hans Richard Müller, 'The first ascent of the Matterhorn in the light of contemporary reports', which included a number of interesting extracts from contemporary newspapers etc. Blakeney sought to correct a number of distortions made by Müller and it should also be pointed out that there is no evidence to support Müller's statement (p5) that Douglas had crossed the Theodule 'in search of a guide with whom to attempt the Matterhorn' in 1865.

6.10
DÜBI, HEINRICH (1848 – 1942)

Dübi was for more than 30 years editor of the *SAC Jahrbuch* and had a wide interest in Alpine history. His two articles relating to the first ascent of the Matterhorn are amongst the most reliable ever written. They were written in German, and it seems as though they have never been translated into English. He was a friend of Edward Whymper and his article in the 1911 *Jahrbuch* must constitute the most comprehensive review there has ever been of Whymper's climbing record.

Dübi was also one of the editors of the 1898 edition of Studer's *Über Eis und Schnee*, which refers in volume 2, page 173, to the inconsistency between the evidence of Whymper and that of Taugwalder at the Enquiry as to when Croz fell (see A11, A30 & Q&A63). Dangar & Blakeney commented on this in *AJ61*, 498 (22) (ii) & (iii), and there is no obvious explanation as to how Dübi or his co-editor Wäber could have known of the evidence, when it had not then been released, unless one of them had learnt it from someone like Alois Julen.

1. Zur Erinnerung an Edward Whymper. *SAC Jahrbuch 47*. 1911, 183-216. (The Matterhorn accident and its aftermath is dealt with at pages 192-200.)
2. Zum Matterhornunglück vom 14. Juli 1865. (With Paul Montandon). *Die Alpen V*. 1929, 203-23.

6.10.1 Zur Erinnerung an Edward Whymper

192. For the probability that the *Journal de Genève* report was based primarily on Young Peter's account and the account in *Der Bund* on that of Old Peter, see section 3.9 (Newspapers).
193/2. For the letter extracts see sections 2.36 (Martin) and 6.13.2 (Engel).
193/3. There is in fact no evidence of Whymper wanting Young Peter to answer any questions.
195. Dübi was unable to establish the date of the Meissner article or quote from it. There still seems to be no full account published other than the original, which according to *Der Wahrheit näher* by Hannes Taugwalder (which contains extracts) was published on the front page of the Vienna *Neue freie Presse* No.336 for 4th August 1865, as a report despatched by Meissner from Interlaken on 31st July.

203/3. In 1868 Whymper went to Grindelwald in November.

6.10.2 Zum Matterhornunglück vom 14 Juli 1865

This well written article is divided into four main parts: a) the preparation and the competence of the participants; b) the direction and execution of the first ascent; c) proximate and immmediate causes of the accident; d) liabilities and the question of the rope. It takes into consideration virtually all the evidence available in 1929, and it is therefore unfortunate that the existence of the original German evidence given by Taugwalder to the Enquiry and of the list of questions Whymper handed in for Taugwalder to answer had not been revealed by Farrar, and that Dübi and Montandon never therefore had the opportunity of taking them into account. They, therefore, quoted Taugwalder's evidence in French or translated it back into German.

211/3. Whilst there is no reason to suppose that Lord Douglas had ever been a pupil of Hudson, there is no doubt that Hadow was a former pupil, as McCormick recorded (*A sad holiday* p4).

211/5. The authors appear to have been misled by Farrar's reference to Taugwalder being the best Zermatt guide, although they do disregard Farrar's comment on his boldness.

211/212. Like Farrar they refer to Taugwalder being the only guide (apart from Carrel) who did not believe in the inaccessibility of the Matterhorn, but like Farrar they offer no evidence in support.

212/3. It is not correct that entries for the whole of 1865 were torn out of Young Taugwalder's Führerbuch; only a few weeks are missing.

219/2. last four to seven lines. Hudson may not have had to bear the double weight, but only that of Hadow if there was slack between him and Croz.

220. The problem with Taugwalder passing the Whymper rope round a rock may be explained by this account originating with Young Peter, who could not see his father when the accident occurred, and did not realise that his father had 'changed his position to a rock to which he could fix the rope' (as Whymper wrote in *Scrambles*) before he himself descended far enough to be able to see his father.

221. Last para. Despite the reference to the Tribunal finding fault in that there were too few guides, there does not appear to have been any such finding.

223. Note 8. Güssfeldt's attempt in September from the south was made with Old Peter and his son Joseph, and not Young Peter. (see *In den Hochalpen*, 22).

6.11
EDWARDS, HENRY (1859 – 1934)

An Alpine climber as well as a Welsh pioneer, Edwards appears to have made three ascents of the Matterhorn, the first from Zermatt, the second from Breuil with Archer Thompson and the third via the Zmutt ridge. His contribution to Matterhorn literature, an article in *AJ45*, 319-27, 'The Ropes in the Matterhorn

Accident of 1865', deals not only with the ropes but also includes extracts from the 1895 *Journal de Zermatt* 'Whymper' article as well as comment on the Official Enquiry Report. Edwards' obituary appears in *AJ46*, 380-2.

6.11.1 The Ropes in the Matterhorn Accident of 1865

320/7. There does not seem to be any justification for the assumption that some of the rope was not taken up the mountain. It is most unlikely that the guides' report of the reconnaissance threw any light on the conditions they were likely to encounter above the shoulder, which was where the ropes were most likely to be needed. It would not, therefore, have enabled Whymper and Hudson to dismiss the fears which had previously deterred anyone from making a serious assault from Zermatt.
325. end of para 4. The Report is in fact mainly in German, Whymper's evidence in French being the sole exception, although Farrar chose to disclose only the French translation.
326. footnote 3. The French translation is at fault, as Taugwalder actually said in German that 'the weight of the three tourists with the force of their fall could even have broken a strong rope'.
327/4. In the course of commenting on 'The Ropes' and on Edwards' article, Dangar & Blakeney wrote in 1957 (*AJ61*, 505): 'Edwards seems quite out of order in doubting Whymper's figure of 250ft'.
327/5. The *Journal de Zermatt* article error was probably made by the interviewer Monod rather than by Whymper. For a likely explanation, see section 2.57.12(e).

6.12
EGGER, CARL (1872 – 1952)

Egger like Arnold Lunn was a pioneer ski-mountaineer, and there is little doubt that they collaborated to some extent in their attempts to denigrate Whymper. They chose to do this by seeking to defend Old Peter Taugwalder from 'attacks' and 'accusations' that Whymper never in fact made, and in so doing they have unnecessarily, unwisely and even perhaps inadvertently highlighted the limitations and weaknesses of Old Peter, as well as certain faults of Young Peter. Egger's mistake seems to have been to take Whymper's sentences out of their proper context and distort them in such a way as to try and rewrite history. Take for example the contemporary reaction to the fact that it was the weakest rope that broke. This was obviously widely known in July 1865 but, because Whymper was the only one to chronicle it in August that year, Egger writes as though Whymper was the only one who ever asked himself why Old Peter did not use one of the stronger ropes. Furthermore he does so in such a way as to imply that Whymper was voicing his own suspicion that he used the weak rope intentionally when he later wrote that 'if Taugwalder thought that an accident was likely to happen, it was to his interest to have the weaker rope where it was placed'. Egger even refers to it as an 'accusation' by Whymper. But Whymper was only recording the facts, the public reaction (including that of the friends and relatives of the victims) and most of all the fact that Clemenz' failure to disclose Old Peter's answers as promised caused him 'to remain under unwarranted suspicion'. Whymper's own view of Taugwalder's use of the weakest rope appears in a letter he wrote to Wigram: 'I have no reason to suspect even that this was done *intentionally*'.

On his return to London Whymper wanted the Alpine Club to hold an Enquiry, because he did not want to be the one who had to decide how much the public should be told. Had this been done, or had a proper Enquiry been conducted at Zermatt and the evidence made known, things would no doubt have been kept in their proper perspective and Egger would not have been able to treat Whymper's chronicle as though it had no basis in fact but was merely his own attempt to discredit Old Peter. Egger often ignored or distorted the circumstances surrounding the accident and its aftermath, and there is now some fresh evidence of which he was unaware. Sections 2 and 3 above, particularly those parts that deal with Whymper and the Taugwalders, try and put things back into their proper perspective, and the comments below are intended to draw attention to Egger's distortions and to the evidence that he did not heed.

Whymper's concern for the truth was tempered by the wish to avoid aggravating any misunderstanding and to spare the families of Hudson and Hadow. There is therefore a distinction to be drawn between what he wrote or otherwise communicated to friends in the days and weeks following the accident and what he allowed to be made public. This is particularly so in the case of the Taugwalders and he disregarded advice that he should publish all he knew about them. Egger unfortunately recognised no such distinction and after Smythe had taken the Cowell memorandum out of its context and published part of it in 1940, Egger reacted as if Whymper had accused the Taugwalders of conspiring to murder him and had done so publicly.

Egger's two contributions to the literature of the Matterhorn accident are:

1. Les Taugwalder du Cervin. *Die Alpen. XVI.* 1940, 275-8.
2. *Pioniere der Alpen.* Peter Taugwalder. 178-200. 1946.

6.12.1 Les Taugwalder du Cervin

275/2. To say that Young Peter was no longer a novice in 1865 hardly does him justice; see *SAC Jahrbuch* 1865, 535-6.

276/1 last 3 lines. Correct, but the main reason seems to have been his reluctance to repeat the climb despite ample opportunity, particularly in 1866, 1867 & 1868. Seiler seems to have recognised the potential immediately, or at least after Jordan had in 1867 trodden the whole of the Swiss and Italian ridges, but he seems to have had to look to the stonemasons and guides of St.Niklaus firstly to build the hut and secondly to take his guests up the Matterhorn. The extent of Young Peter's fear of repeating the Hörnli ridge can be judged from the fact that he did not even attempt it again until 1872, the year after Peter Perren made the second Zermatt guide ascent, although with Perren and Maquignaz he had almost reached the summit via the Italian ridge in 1869, until turned back by a thunderstorm.

276/2. Old Peter was a well established Monte Rosa guide with some 85 ascents by 1865, and Egger is right to disregard Farrar's error stating he was the best guide in Zermatt. But there is no evidence of his making a reconnaissance of the Matterhorn for Douglas.

276/3. In referring to the Taugwalders as Whymper's life-savers, Egger seems to have missed the point Whymper was making about the two men being paralysed by terror, crying like infants and trembling in such a manner as to threaten another accident. Egger cannot contradict Whymper's statement of fact, which amplified the statement in McCormick's letter of 17.7.65, and there is not the slightest reason to doubt it. The probability that Whymper was perfectly capable of acting safely and continuing the descent without endangering the lives of the other two, gains support from the way he was able to save himself in 1862, after falling 200ft., sustaining head injuries and losing consciousness. Old Peter by contrast lost his nerve on the Dent Blanche 'his face as white as that of a frightened girl' without there even being any accident. If 'life-saving' has to be brought into it, one can only conclude that it was Whymper who saved the lives of the Taugwalders by keeping his nerve, whilst for more than two hours they were utterly helpless. Old Peter's skill in hugging the rock is a separate matter in which Young Peter played no part.

276/3. lines 6-7. The subject of the phrase, which Egger says Whymper omitted from his book, reappears in the Cowell memorandum. Whymper had been appalled by its heartlessness, which is something he appears to have been able to forgive with the passage of time. His memorandum of 17.8.65 also recorded related matters and there are many references in contemporary documents to the question as to how much he should disclose about the Taugwalders.

276/3 line 8. There is no evidence of the Taugwalders having or expressing any fears for the future – quite the opposite – Young Peter recognised immediately he had recovered from the shock the opportunities it offered, particularly with a bit of help from Whymper.

277. line 6-7. Whereas it is true that misunderstandings cannot be ruled out, Egger's approach seems to be to rule out any understanding between Whymper and the Taugwalders. But fortunately in his next lines Egger highlights something that excludes any misunderstanding about the idea that Whymper should not pay them. He criticises Whymper for saying that he would never trust his life to Young Peter, but omits altogether the reason Whymper gave, namely: 'The odious idea that he propounded (which I believe emanated from *him*) he has endeavoured to trade upon, in spite of the fact that his father was paid (for both) in the presence of witnesses. Whatever may be his abilities as a guide, he is not one to whom I would trust my life...' Critics seem never to have commented on Young Peter actually endeavouring to trade upon the idea of not being paid, presumably because they realised they could not contradict it. But it does exclude any possibility of Whymper having misunderstood Young Peter when he first put forward the odious idea.

277. lines 11-13. Egger suddenly changes the subject to suspicions about Old Peter's use of the weak rope and this is followed by the rumours of his cutting the rope, culminating in his reputation and career being ruined so that he had to emigrate to America. He implies that these matters which span some nine years are Whymper's fault in some way, he complains that Whymper keeps coming back to the 'suspicion' and yet he never mentions Clemenz' 'failure to give up the answers that he promised', which underlies most of the footnote about the Taugwalders. These issues must each be looked at separately, when it will be seen that Whymper was merely recording facts and was not making 'attacks' or 'accusations' against the Taugwalders. It seems to have been the consequence of the inadequacy of the Enquiry that Old Peter was allowed 'to remain under unmerited suspicion'. Whymper seems to have been expected to explain everything about the accident, but he did not know why Old Peter used the weak rope, and he seems to have felt compelled to restate the issues and the underlying facts as far as he knew them, but without speculating on the explanation or otherwise expressing his own views.

277. lines 19-20. The only evidence of Old Peter's hands being injured, as opposed to his chest

or body (Enquiry) or wrist (Güssfeldt), is the account given by Robertson to Whymper some 30 years later (the *Graphic*), of Old Peter complaining to him on 16th July 1865 that the Zermatters were saying he had cut the rope.
277. line 29. Egger could not appreciate from the limited Enquiry documents revealed by Farrar, and in particular without seeing Taugwalder's original German questions and answers, the inadequacy of Clemenz' investigation. He could not know that the important issues were avoided or side-stepped; see sections 3.4 and 5.4.2 (Enquiry).
278. lines 10-11. There is no reason to suppose that Whymper had to tie the rope on to Old Peter for him. In all probability he merely threw the end down to him.
278. lines 14-16. Whymper was not the only one who knew the thinnest rope was a reserve. Old Peter even described it in A24 as a special rope.
278/2. Hudson did nothing and contributed nothing without which Whymper and Douglas and the Taugwalders would not have made a successful ascent.
278/3. Egger seems to have been the first to suggest that the disaster resulted from the fault of the Taugwalders, and he deserves no credit for then dismissing the suggestion that no one else ever made. Whymper's adverse comments on the Taugwalders related solely to their post-accident behaviour. In his letter to von Fellenberg he wrote of their being utterly unnerved etc so as to threaten him and them with the fate of the others, but more importantly he said in the final paragraph: 'No blame can be attached to any of the guides; they all did their duty manfully...' Whymper did write to Wigram of his extreme dissatisfaction with both the Taugwalders but particularly with the younger man, stating how when they got to the easy part they showed a heartlessness that was perfectly revolting. But he never intended that this should be published, nor could he ever have anticipated that someone like Egger would seek to suggest that he had blamed the Taugwalders for the accident. Egger's negative approach prevented him from highlighting something far more important, which is what Whymper wrote about Old Peter in the same footnote: 'Not only was his act at the critical moment wonderful as a feat of strength, but it was admirable in its performance at the right time.'

6.12.2 *Pioniere der Alpen*. Peter Taugwalder

Egger quotes the sources upon which he relies, which are all English books, chiefly the *Alpine Journal*, but they do include *Ich gedenke der Berge*, the Swiss edition of Lunn's *Mountain Jubilee*. He overlooks mentioning Güssfeldt's *In den Hochalpen*.

178. Egger begins badly with a paragraph that is full of errors and inaccurate generalities of a prejudicial nature. Old Peter's career as a guide seems to have been in decline prior to 14.7.65. He was eccentric and his nerve was already beginning to fail and, having never made any mountain ascents other than in the sector to the south-east of Zermatt prior to 1865, he clearly had no ambition but to continue his career as a good Monte Rosa guide. As Dangar & Blakeney wrote in 1965, 'Looking to his past record, one is inclined to think that it was unfortunate that Old Peter was engaged by Douglas in 1865, for it took him out of his class'. Egger now quotes Farrar's error of his being one of the boldest guides in the Alps (which must be nonsense) and much the best of the Zermatt men (which ignores Peter Perren and others). Old Peter's pre-1865 record appears in *SACJ 1865*, 535.
Lines 11-14 give notice of Egger's intention of attacking Whymper in supposed vindication of Old Peter's good name, and he no doubt convinced himself that the end justified the means. The only snag is that the whole concerted approach of Lunn and Egger towards Whymper

seems from the start to have been misconceived and fundamentally flawed, because the 'attacks' and 'accusations' of which they frequently wrote were never made by Whymper. They may have misunderstood the circumstances prevailing during the aftermath of the accident and they have certainly distorted the perspective by disregarding a number of relevant considerations, but their greatest mistake was to have taken up arms to defend Old Peter against an imaginary foe.

181. Egger recites the Dent Blanche fiasco in much fuller detail than most critics, yet he fails to realise its inconsistency with his initial paragraph stating that Old Peter was one of the boldest guides. Kennedy and Young Peter could easily have made the ascent without him, as Kennedy did with J-B Croz a few days later.

184. lines 4-5. Like many others, Egger misunderstood Douglas's remark that 'Old Peter had lately been beyond the Hörnli'. There was no time for such an expedition in 1865, but even if he had made it previously he certainly cannot have achieved anything to justify the belief that an ascent was possible from the Zermatt side.

184. lines 9-10. There is no evidence whatever that Douglas intended to climb the Matterhorn with the Taugwalders in 1865, before he met up with Whymper.

184/2 line 3. Whymper used the plural to denote himself and his guide.

184/5. Parker's record of Old Peter's complaint that he would never have run so much risk for the payment he received (120frs) for the Matterhorn is consistent with his wanting 200frs for the Italian ridge, and there can be no justification for Egger saying that Whymper wanted to make him look ridiculous. As for referring to Whymper's exaggerations, what does he mean? As for doubting that Old Peter even named the high price, this is unrealistic. To state that Old Peter was the only one who maintained from the start that the Matterhorn could be climbed, is again unsupported by any evidence.

185. line 3. There is no justification for suggesting that Whymper owed his life to both Taugwalders; Egger cannot have been referring to Old Peter hugging the rock.

185/3. It is significant, for reasons referred to below, that these lengthy quotations of what Whymper wrote in *Scrambles*, extending through to page 187, are not taken from the Steger German translation of 1872, but are Egger's own (improved) translation of Whymper's original English text.

187/2. Egger was not aware of the circumstances in which Whymper came to record his memorandum of 17.8.65. Although it was first published in full by Smythe, Egger does not indicate this in the footnote (as he does with the Cowell memo), but implies falsely that Whymper published the whole of it.

188/2. Egger was not aware of the circumstances in which the Cowell memorandum came to be made following advice from Cowell and Wills, and Egger should have shaken his head in disbelief at Smythe for having taken it out of its context and for having misled him! Smythe even omitted the first five lines and the heading.

189/1. Egger seems now to be relying on Lunn with statements for which there is no justification, such as needing a Hudson to show him the easy way. There is no similarity between the guides wanting to make a business out of the accident and Whymper's Zermatt guidebook. Whymper was disgusted by Young Peter's heartless talk and, according to his memorandum by the fact that the guides could view the loss of their fellow creatures with such commercial feelings. It seems as though Whymper was later prepared to forgive Young Peter's heartless conduct until in about September 1869 he learnt that he had endeavoured to trade upon the idea of non-payment, and added reference to it in *Scrambles*. For Lunn's unfounded reference to Whymper not liking Taugwalder etc, see section 6.18.3 (Lunn) page 198 below.

190. Egger had to translate Old Peter's Questions & Answers into German, as Farrar never revealed the original. For this and comment on the complicated issues arising from the extraordinary way Clemenz conducted the Enquiry, see section 3.4 (The Enquiry).
191/2. Whymper did not write 'not the first occasion' but, 'not the only occasion', the second occasion being in 1869 when Clemenz presided over the Lyskamm Enquiry. Egger was again making his own new translation and his version of the Taugwalder footnote is of particular interest because it contains a most extraordinary error. It is of such importance in judging whether Egger is any more reliable as a historian than Lunn, when it comes to Whymper and the Matterhorn, that it will be detailed in full.

191 paragraph 2 to 192 paragraph 3 inclusive.
Whymper's footnote consisted of four paragraphs and so does Egger's version. The 1872 German translation was made by Friedrich Steger. The following table shows the English origin of each paragraph (P) and of each sentence (S) in the footnote, as it is set out by Egger, and it also names the German translator of each sentence in the Egger version. Thus the first line indicates that the first sentence of Egger's paragraph 1 comes from the 1st English edition of *Scrambles* and that it was translated into German by Egger himself. Egger was clearly very familiar with the English editions of *Scrambles* and must have had both the 1st and 4th English editions as well as the Steger German edition before him as he wrote the chapter.

Egger Para & Sentence	English origin	German translator
P1/S1	1st edn.	Egger
P1/S2	4th edn.	Egger
P1/S3	1st edn.	Egger
P2/S1	4th edn.	Egger
P2/S2	4th edn.	Egger
P2/S3	1st or 4th edn.	Egger
P2/S4	1st or 4th edn.	Egger
P2/S5	1st or 4th edn.	Egger
P3/S1	1st or 4th edn.	Egger
P3/S2	1st or 4th edn.	Egger
P3/S3	1st edn.	Steger
P3/S4	1st edn.	Steger
P4/S1	1st edn.	Steger
P4/S2	1st edn.	Steger and also Egger *
P4/S3	1st edn.	Egger

Translating the above into words means that Egger made his own new improved translation of each sentence up to and including the second sentence in the third paragraph, some of it being a translation of Whymper's 1st edn. and sometimes a translation of Whymper's 4th edn. He then gave up doing his own translation and used the original Steger German translation of Whymper's 1st edn. for the last two sentences of paragraph 3 and the first two sentences of paragraph 4. However in the second sentence in paragraph 4 he did make an improvement in the ten words that appear in brackets in the Steger German translation. But when he came to the third and final sentence of paragraph 4 Egger abandoned the Steger German translation and reverted to making his own improved translation of Whymper's 1st edition.

Taking the analysis a stage further it is apparent that for the most part Egger made his own new translation, having, as noted above, also made his own new translation of the earlier extensive extracts quoted from Whymper's original English. He only relied on the Steger 1872 German translation for four out of several dozen sentences. But even in one of those four sentences he made a slight alteration to some of the words in brackets, which would have entailed referring to Whymper's English 1st edn.

The question therefore arises as to why he was not consistent throughout and, secondly, as to what difference it makes anyway. It is not possible to answer the first question except by suggesting that Egger wanted to take advantage of a fundamental difference between the Whymper and the Steger versions of the second sentence in the fourth paragraph. That difference was between the good sense that Whymper wrote in the 1st edn. of *Scrambles* and the 'nonsense' that appeared in the Steger German translation of that sentence. Instead of making his own new German translation of Whymper's original English wording: 'The odious idea that he propounded (which I believe emanated from *him*) he has endeavoured to trade upon, in spite of the fact that his father was paid (for both) in the presence of witnesses', Egger used the defective Steger German translation, whilst making a slight improvement in the words in brackets:

'Er machte mir seinen hässlichen Vorschlag (von dem ich glaube, dass er von ihm ausgegangen ist), obgleich sein Vater (für beide) in Gegenwart von Zeugen bezahlt worden war.'

The 'nonsense' in the Steger version stems from the omission of the six words that form the crux of Whymper's original English sentence. *'he has endeavoured to trade upon'*. It seems as though the words may initially have been removed from the German translation deliberately and that someone subsequently forgot to rectify the resulting defect. It is interesting to note in passing, that this defect seems never to have been corrected in the German editions, as it is still there in the 3rd edn. in 1909. But why should Egger have wanted to incorporate such nonsense into his book, when he had been making his own new translation of Whymper's original English, which was undoubtedly an improvement on the Steger translation? Fortunately Egger seems to provide the answer, or at least an easy clue to it, in his very next sentence:

'Nebenbei bemerkt: den Vorschlag und die Zahlung in zeitlichen Kausalzusammenhang zu setzen, ist ein unbegreiflicher Schachzug Whympers'! – which means that 'to set the proposition and the payment together in time as cause and effect is an incomprehensible chessmove by Whymper'! Is there any possible explanation other than that Egger deliberately used the defective translation in order to mislead his readers into thinking that was what Whymper himself had written, so that he could then make that malicious remark about Whymper? It seems not to have been an incomprehensible chessmove by Whymper, but an incredible own goal by Egger, which does at least help to clarify his motive and some of the other dubious things he wrote.

192/3 line 7. Egger's comment that Clemenz may not have wanted to publish any details of the evidence 'so as not to cause even more unrest in the community' is an interesting one. Perhaps Egger did carry out some research and discovered that the successful ascent or the accident did cause some unrest in Zermatt (presumably involving the Taugwalders), but if so, why did he not disclose it?
192-193. Whymper deleted or altered some sentences in the Taugwalder footnote in the 4th edn. of *Scrambles* to take account of Old Peter's death. Critics have often remarked on the remarkable consistency in Whymper's accounts, the minor variations about the Taugwalders in such things as the *Times* letter being due to the considerations which culminated in the Cowell memorandum.
193. lines 3-5. It is mere invention by Egger for him to suggest that the memorandum shows how the Taugwalders' conduct was directed at his welfare!
193. lines 6-14. Egger had no appreciation of how Whymper confined himself to the facts. He was not referring to his own suspicion, but to 'the grave suspicions which at once fell upon [Old Peter]', and he was not prepared to publish his own opinions. Egger appears to have been unaware of the AC's 1864 report on Ropes etc, the origin of the sashline, the reason Whymper ceased using it as a climbing rope in 1865 or even, it would seem, that 'it was intended as a reserve, in case we had to leave much rope behind, attached to rocks'.
193. lines 16-19. On the dubious question of Old Peter belaying the rope, see section 3.12.4 (The rope in 1865).
193/2 – 194/1. Egger distorts many of the details here, like Croz' laying aside of his axe being hypothetical, and Whymper only being able to see their heads instead of 'the movements of their shoulders'. Old Peter's German A63 stated Whymper *could* see better than he could.
194/2. Egger has by now introduced almost 40 errors or distortions of the truth and it is therefore hardly surprising that he should have come to a conclusion inconsistent with the real evidence.
194/2 lines 5-6. These two questions are incompatible, as the qualities of the ropes were not known to Whymper alone. Even Old Peter referred to the sashline as 'a special rope' (A24).
194/2 lines 7-8. As already stated above, Old Peter must have been capable of tying himself on to the rope, after Whymper threw the end down.
194/3. The indirect causes of the accident present complex questions but Egger's distorted comment about literary editing of the course of events is particularly inappropriate coming from someone prepared to seize the typographical error of a translator, dress it up as though Whymper himself had written it and then accuse him of 'an incomprehensible chessmove'! (see 191/2 to 192/3 above).
195. line 15. The second guide was, as Güssfeldt stated, Old Peter's younger son Joseph and not Young Peter, as is generally believed.
196/2. lines 4-5. Güssfeldt's 1868 reference to Old Peter's troubles since the catastrophe is consistent with Whymper being told in about September 1869 that he was 'now nearly

incapable for work', and is obviously inconsistent with what Egger would have us believe; e.g. p199 lines 7-9.
196/4. Any non-realisation of Old Peter's expectations for the future, whatever they may have been, can have had nothing to do with Whymper. He had many opportunities of climbing the Matterhorn in the three years following the accident, but turned them all down, and he seems even to have abandoned his former role as a Monte Rosa guide. The cause of his deterioration may have been his inability to cope with the jealousy and spite of his fellow guides and neighbours in Zermatt, or it may have been something of which we have yet to learn, but it certainly cannot have been the publication of *Scrambles*, which did not take place until 1871.
199/3. It is disappointing that Egger did not discover or reveal more about Old Peter's emigration to America. He attributes it to 'the old suspicions', but he did not go until 1874, according to Young Peter, and he returned in 1878. He did not therefore die *soon* after his return, but 10 years later. Egger might also have been expected to discover something more about Joseph's drowning in the Schwarzsee in 1867.
199/4. Egger refers to Young Peter's 1873 ascent of the Weisshorn still being regarded then as a major undertaking, seemingly unaware that he had first climbed it in 1863!
200. line 6. Egger refers to Young Peter being included in Whymper's drawing 'The Clubroom of Zermatt', without any regard for its inconsistency with the malice which he himself contrives to see in almost every aspect of Whymper's dealings with the Taugwalders.

6.13
ENGEL, CLAIRE ELIANE (– 1977)

Engel was a prolific writer on mountaineering and she discovered much fresh material. She also wrote several books in English which, as Graham Brown remarked in *AJ58*, 138, was a considerable *tour de force* for a Frenchwoman resident in Switzerland, but, as his lengthy review of *A History of Mountaineering in the Alps* revealed, 'the value of the book is seriously affected by inaccuracies of many sorts'. The next volume of the *Alpine Journal* contained a review by Dangar of her next book, *They came to the Hills*. Dangar quoted Engel's comments on a nineteenth century book and said that the same words applied with equal force to her own book: 'When reading [the] book now, one is impressed by the large number of erroneous statements, and by the evidence of a careless reading of documents...' There is even a footnote to the review, which quotes Blakeney writing to her publishers after they had sent him a set of page proofs with a view to making last-minute corrections: 'the extent of the corrections is becoming so great that a really meticulous dealing with them is her work, and not mine. I never agreed to do formal proof-reading... There are a lot more corrections I could have put in, but I have no time or inclination to do more; it is her job to get the book reasonably accurate in the first place.'

The two books already mentioned devote several pages to the Matterhorn accident and to Whymper, but it is hardly worthwhile attempting to detail all the errors here. Graham Brown, without making a deliberate search or bothering about such things as *Roger* Hadow, filled over four pages of the *Alpine Journal* with

Engel's errors, and said that it was a matter for deep regret that inaccuracies of many sorts seriously affected the value of the book, which was, by and large, of great interest. A new 'totally revised and enlarged edition' appeared in 1971 under a different title.

Typical of Engel's discovery and publication of fresh material is her article 'Autour de la première ascension du Cervin', revealing the diary entries made by A-J Martin at Zermatt for the days immediately following the Matterhorn accident. She also quoted some extracts from it in *They came to the Hills*. In about 1944 she published her own new and abridged French translation of *Scrambles*, *Escalades*, including in the book four chapters from the *Great Andes*. She wrote of the need to update the original Joanne translation, as his English was not very good and many technical mountaineering terms did not then exist in French. But a cursory glance at the two suggests that much of Joanne remains and that Engel may have worked from Joanne rather than from Whymper and so preserved some of Joanne's errors and omissions, such as the translation of Whymper's reference to the broken rope. Whereas Whymper wrote how he found 'to my surprise – indeed to my horror – that it was the weakest of the three ropes', both Engel and Joanne elaborately translated the word 'it' as 'la corde maudite', causing Gos to write in *Le Cervin* 1, 183 that 'the accursed rope' was Whymper's own expression, and then devote a whole chapter to it.

Engel's major contributions to the literature of the Matterhorn are:
1. *Edward Whymper. Escalades*. Introduction de Claire-Eliane Engel. 1944.
2. Autour de la première ascension du Cervin. *Die Alpen. XXV.* 1949, 129-32.
3. *A History of Mountaineering in the Alps*. 1950. (See pages 126-33 & 138-42 in particular) Reviewed *AJ58*, 138-45.

'New edition, totally revised and enlarged 1971', entitled *Mountaineering in the Alps*. An historical survey.' (See pages 118-24 & 128-32 in particular)
4. *They came to the Hills*. 1952. (See pages 110-32 in particular) Reviewed *AJ59*, 98-100.

6.13.1 *Escalades*

11/1. Whymper wrote one such letter to *The Times*, published on 8.8.65.
11/3. Whymper never traversed the Matterhorn.
23/5. The first edition of Joanne's translation was published in 1873.
177/2. line 15. Whymper's word 'lately' is wrongly translated as 'peu de jours auparavant'.
195. line 1. Whymper did not use the words 'the accursed rope', merely 'it'.
200. line 3. The translations of both Joanne and Engel omit Whymper's words 'at once' before 'pesaient'.
200. paras 2-4. Apart from 'son engagement' in place of 'sa promesse' in the second line, the whole of the long footnote appears to come from Joanne.

6.13.2 Autour de la première ascension du Cervin

The following amendments are necessary:
130. line 7. 'Zermatt' should read 'Zermatt!'
130. line 9. 'ça' should read 'Cela'.
130/4. line 3. Delete 'couvert'.
130/5. line 4. Insert 'cette nuit' after 'réparti'.
130/6. line 6. Delete ¼ and insert '¾. Nous sommes à Zermatt à midi et demi'.
130/6. line 8. In the last word, delete 're'.
131/4. The letters were not published in full, only some extracts.
131/8. Gautier said that Croz was the first, and then three Englishmen, but she did not name them, as Engel implies.
132. line 2. 'le poids' should read 'ce poids'.
132. line 3. 'des roches' should read 'du rocher'.
132 last para. Mme.Gautier was quite right, in as much as the next attempt by an AC member, Birkbeck, was made on the 14th July 1866.

6.13.3 *A History of Mountaineering in the Alps*

For a wide range of errors see the review by Graham Brown (*AJ58*, 138-45). There is little purpose in noting here all the erroneous statements, of which good examples appear in paragraph 3 on page 140. It states that 'during the inquests both Whymper and Taugwalder lost their heads', and that Whymper's 'depositions are contradictory in certain places'. It then goes on to imply that Taugwalder may in fact have cut the rope! This paragraph remains unchanged in the 'totally revised' 1971 edition. Graham Brown's list of errors seems to have been heeded only perfunctorily, so that the sentence 'Hudson agreed to lend Michel Croz to Whymper and join the party' becomes 'Hudson agreed to invite Whymper to join the party'. The same minimum revision occurs with the name of the peak on which the cornice broke under Douglas and the words 'which was later to be known as the Wellenkuppe' become 'which was later to be known as the Obergabelhorn'. Even 'Roger Hadow' survived the total revision!

6.13.4 *They came to the Hills*

111/1. Whymper had intended to try the Hörnli in 1864 with Adams Reilly and Croz, and in 1865 with Carrel.
113/3. Hudson climbed Mont Blanc on July 7th. Hadow's first name was Douglas. The Matterhorn accident was on July 14th.
117/1. Lines 5-7 misquote Barnard. According to some notes compiled by Graham Brown, the article on p593 of the Dec. 25 1858 number of *The Illustrated London News* included: 'If ever this vast crag is climbed by Hudson, Kennedy or other brave hands, it will be from this side...' Whereas the article started in Zermatt and Barnard then went on to describe the view from the Riffelberg, Engel appears to have overlooked the fact that he then crossed the Monte Moro and made his way up Valtournanche to Breuil, so that he had Breuil, and not Zermatt, in mind as 'this side'. This is confirmed by the full account Barnard gave of the same trip in *Drawing from Nature* (p258), when he stated in relation to Breuil, 'From this side the mountain certainly does not look quite so impossible to climb...' There is no reason to suppose that

Hudson or Kennedy reconnoitred the Swiss ridge, apart from the latter's 1862 winter attempt. The Kennedy referred to by Barnard in 1858 must have been E.S.K. and not T.S.K., who was then only a lad of 17! The two articles to which Engel refers relate to the same holiday, the detailed account in *Drawing from Nature* being from a lecture he gave in 1858, judging by its opening words.

118/2. There is no reason to suppose Hudson intended anything more than a reconnaissance, pending the arrival of McCormick.

121/2. lines 10-12. There does not appear to be any evidence of a bad temper, nor – despite what Lunn has written – of any lack of friends; see end of next but one to final paragraph of *Scrambles*.

123/ 2. lines 8-11. Engel once more misquotes and is wrong about Barnard, see p117 above.

126. lines 1-4. Hudson did not take Croz from Whymper. It was Birkbeck who had engaged him for some weeks and Hudson only took him over after illness forced Birkbeck to return home.

126/1. last sentence. See *Scrambles* chapter 13, paragraph one.

126/2. Whymper did not traverse the Matterhorn in 1874, but ascended and descended via the Hörnli.

128/5. Whymper first published his Chamonix and Zermatt guidebooks in 1896 and 1897 respectively.

6.14 FARRAR, JOHN PERCY (1857 – 1929)

Educated in Germany and in Lausanne, it is a pity that Farrar's fluency in French and German did not cause him to take a closer look at the 'Minutes of the Enquiry' before publishing entirely in French (in *AJ33*, 234-47) the Report containing the evidence of the witnesses, the verdict of the Tribunal and the inventories of the four victims' possessions. Farrar followed up the Report with three pages of his own comments on it, dated October 8, 1920. He referred to one of Taugwalder's answers being 'peculiar' and another 'remarkable', but it seems as though he only looked at the French translation of his evidence and that he failed to notice one or two small but significant errors in it, compared with the original answers given by Taugwalder in German. Nor did he even disclose that the documents released included Taugwalder's original German answers, and others as well, an oversight that has led more than one critic to comment that it was a matter for regret that there was no record of Taugwalder's actual words. Farrar also failed to notice or reveal that the list of questions Whymper handed in for Clemenz to put to Taugwalder contained almost all the questions put to Taugwalder during his first examination on the Friday, something that has continued to baffle almost all the critics ever since, despite Tyndale discovering the truth from a different source in the 1930's and revealing it somewhat secretively in an appendix to the 6th edition of *Scrambles*.

Although Farrar never saw the original list of Whymper's questions in English, he could and should have seen the typewritten copy of the French version

Whymper handed to Clemenz and had he compared it with the questions actually put to Taugwalder in German, he might have noticed certain slight but subtle and significant changes, sufficient to defeat Whymper's object. It might then have been pertinent for Farrar to comment that had Whymper ever been provided with Taugwalder's answers he would have been very disappointed to discover that they did not answer, but sidestepped, the vital issues about the rope.

Farrar nevertheless played a leading role, albeit secondary to that of Montagnier, in securing, preserving and in some instances publishing documents and other information that might otherwise in the course of time have disappeared without trace. His principal works relating to the Matterhorn are:

1. An attempt on the East Face and an Ascent of the Italian Face of the Matterhorn in 1867. *AJ30*, 316-23. (Wm. Leighton Jordan's accounts)
2. Days of long ago. Charles Hudson... *AJ32*, 21-36.
3. Report of the Official Enquiry into the Accident on the Mont Cervin, in July 1865. *AJ33*, 234-50.

6.14.1 Jordan's accounts

These require no comment.

6.14.2 Days of long ago. Charles Hudson...

6. Last para. note 3. Disregarding the first ascent, Young Peter did not start guiding on the Swiss side of the Matterhorn until 1872. He ceased in about 1900.
21. note 16. Whereas there is no evidence that Lord Francis Douglas had ever been a pupil of Hudson's, despite Lunn's brief and unsupported statement to that effect (*Matterhorn Centenary* 54), there is no doubt that Hadow was a former pupil. (McCormick, *A sad holiday*, 4)
22. last para. 'almost the sole great master'. No! see D&B *AJ71*, 119/2.
25. line 9. Should be Joseph and not Peter Taugwalder.
26. note 30. 'He was certainly at the time one of the boldest guides in the Alps, and probably much the best of the Zermatt men'. No! see D&B *AJ70*, 34/1
26. note 30. last sentence. There is no evidence whatever to support this.
27/1. May there not be a very simple explanation for Croz' change in attitude? If Birkbeck had told him in confidence of the plan to attempt the east face, he would not have wanted to encourage Whymper to get there first.
28/2. There can be no justification for stating that the party of 'Hudson and Hadow with Croz' was quite competent to make the ascent of the Matterhorn, particularly when regard is had to the difficulties anticipated but never encountered.
28/4. 'I say distinctly that Hudson and Croz were fully qualified to conduct [Hadow] on the proposed expedition.' This may be so in the sense in which it is said that the modern Zermatt guides could take a cow up the Matterhorn, but this was a pioneering expedition on which no one knew what difficulties and dangers lay ahead. Furthermore no one seems ever to have given any consideration to the problem of getting the cow back down again!
28/7. 'no more difficult then than now' completely disregards the fixed ropes and chains.
29. line 23. 'Taugwalder cannot properly be blamed for the use of this rope... The intention to use this rope only as a "spare" rope had not been explained to him.' This is pure speculation on

Farrar's part; not only did Taugwalder take an interest in the quality of the ropes (A29), he also had in mind the need to fix a rope for greater security (A53) and he actually referred to the sashline as 'a special rope' (A24).

31. note 24. 'Young Peter Taugwalder can scarcely have been the mere porter'. He had in fact already climbed Monte Rosa 26 times and the Weisshorn once.

32. line 5. 'The ban of the Matterhorn was broken'. For mountaineers in general perhaps, but not for the guides of Zermatt who promptly gave it a new lease of life, that was to last six years.

32. penult. para. '...Charles Hudson, its first systematic assailant whose just appreciation overcame it.' Hudson in fact contributed nothing to the climb without which Whymper, Douglas and the Taugwalders would not have made a safe ascent, quite apart from a safe descent.

6.14.3 Report of the Official Enquiry

R 29. There is an error in the French.

R 34. There is an error in the French.

R 41. Several words are omitted from the French.

Q 55. There is an error in the French.

R 63. There is an error in the French.

Inventory of Lord Douglas. 1. 'and several hotel bills' omitted from French.

Inventory of Croz. Item 4, & item 5 including his hat, are omitted.

247. line 10. Montagnier does indeed deserve credit, but so do others and something on the following lines ought to appear after 'Mr.Montagnier': 'and to the efforts of M.Alexandre Jullien of Geneva, as well as the intervention of the Cantonal Judge at Sion, M. Jean-Ch. de Courten,'.

lines 14 & 15. 'There is remarkably little in them, and they throw practically no further light on the matter.' Unfortunately this statement made by Farrar in 1920 is both misleading and inaccurate. There may not be all that much in the documents that Farrrar published although close study reveals rather more than he observed, but when one includes the other documents from the Court file, of which Farrar makes no mention whatever, there is a wealth of information revealed for the first time. German writers have up to now been forced to retranslate Old Peter's evidence from French back into German, not realising that his original German answers had survived. Whymper's questions for Taugwalder, on which Q22-Q35 are based, appear in French in the form in which Whymper actually handed them to Clemenz before some of them were distorted.

6.15
GOS, CHARLES (1885 – 1949)

Born in Geneva, the son of Albert Gos the painter, Charles Gos lived for a long time in St.Niklaus prior to his death in April 1949 after many years of illness and suffering. He started climbing early and in 1906 at the age of 20 he and a friend made the first guideless ascent of the Zmutt ridge. The same year he was going to make an attempt on the North face, but after setting off from the Hörnli they were forced to abandon the climb by a storm which struck as soon as they reached the Matterhorn glacier.

Winthrop Young, who first met Gos in 1906 on the summit of the Matterhorn, wrote of him in one of two obituaries in *AJ57*, 235-8:

> 'He devoted every gift to the service of the mountains. The mountains were, literally, the breath of daily life to him; and I have known no mountain lover to whom they meant quite so much...During the tedious years of illness, that prevented him from climbing and kept him for long periods a complete invalid, he lived upon his window views of the high peaks, winter and summer; any lower prospect he detested, it was "poached-egg scenery!"...he fought disease and depression with an equal ardour, writing his books and newspaper articles and a large correspondence, collating literary material and interviewing innumerable friends, as he lay in bed...'

Gos was by far the most enterprising, industrious and entertaining writer and researcher of almost everything relating to the early history of the Matterhorn. Although there is much in *Propos d'un Alpiniste* and also in *Alpinisme anecdotique*, his principal work on the subject is the two volume *Le Cervin*, published in the autumn of 1948, some six months before his death. It is a mine of information, but is only available in French and unfortunately it does not have an index. Like other Swiss writers Gos relied primarily on English publications and documents, although he also traced entries in hotel guestbooks, in Führerbücher and in newspapers. But there seems to be one aspect of the Matterhorn accident to which he turned a blind eye or, more likely, on which he maintained a deliberate and resolute silence – Old Peter Taugwalder. Such an omission might be of little consequence in normal objective criticism, but when he descended to the level of Egger and Lunn in the chapter 'La corde maudite' in *Le Cervin*, seeking to attribute all Taugwalder's post-accident problems to Whymper without producing any evidence in support, he should have addressed the important questions of Old Peter's family life and history, his emigration to America, his record as a guide and his influence in the commune of Zermatt. As a journalist, Gos would be familiar with the local newspapers, yet the only obituary of Old Peter to which he makes any reference comes from the *Alpine Journal*. His enquiring mind must have led him to find out how Joseph came to drown in the Schwarzsee in 1867 and to judge whether his death and the circumstances leading to it had any influence on his father's post-accident problems, yet we are told nothing. One does not need suspicious circumstances like those surrounding the death of Pfarrer Imseng in the Mattmarksee in 1869 to justify some investigation, and Gos seems to have had a fascination for the tragic, the dramatic and the sensational, as his book *Alpine Tragedy* bears out.

His three major contributions to the literature of the Matterhorn are detailed below, in addition to which he included individual chapters on the Matterhorn catastrophe, on Carrel and on Maquignaz in *Alpine Tragedy*.

1. *Propos d'un Alpiniste*. 1922. Reviewed *AJ34*, 332.
2. *Alpinisme anecdotique*. 1934. Reviewed *AJ47*, 180.
3. *Alpine Tragedy*. 1948. Reviewed *AJ57*, 115. (First published 1940 as *Tragédies Alpestres*.)
4. *Le Cervin*. 1948. Reviewed *AJ57*, 106.

6.15.1 *Propos d'un Alpiniste*

The book contains many short chapters relating to the circumstances surrounding the Matterhorn accident, including details of the Alpine careers of Whymper, Croz and Carrel, but not Taugwalder. It also quotes Gorret's account of the first Italian ascent, as well as an appeal leaflet about the Croz family, which it seems did not form part of the September 1865 *Alpine Journal*, as Gos states, but must have been sent out to members at the same time.

39. There is no evidence to suggest that Douglas had sent Old Peter on a reconnaissance of the Matterhorn on his return from the Gabelhorn. 'Peu de jours auparavant' were Joanne's words; Whymper actually wrote 'lately'.
41. Farrar's remarks about Old Peter being one of the boldest guides in the Alps and probably the best in Zermatt simply are not true.
42. There is no evidence to suggest that Old Peter did not share the general opinion that the Matterhorn was inaccessible. See section 2.52.5 (Taugwalder).
42. Young Peter's climbing career, like that of his father, was detailed in the Gletscherführer article in *SACJ 1865* 535-6. He did not make the first ascent of the Dom a month after the accident, although it was probably *his* first ascent of the Dom.
51. The text which Gos has translated into French does not in fact appear in *AJ2*, although there may be some volumes which have the originally loose leaflet bound in.
76. It was Joseph Taugwalder and not Young Peter, who accompanied Douglas to Breuil.

6.15.2 *Alpinisme anecdotique*

This book contains more than a hundred pages relating to the Matterhorn accident and includes the Official Enquiry Report and Whymper's letter to *The Times*, in French, as well as extracts from such things as *L'Abeille de Chamonix*.

242 & 247. 'La corde *maudite*' was not Whymper's expression, as Gos states elsewhere, but seems to have been introduced by Joanne who first translated *Scrambles* into French.
243. Gos writes of Old Peter's incomprehension and fright when confronted by members of the Tribunal, but his answers to the questions suggest the exact opposite. The self-confidence, clear thinking, logic and literacy they reveal would do credit to a modern business man unfamiliar with Court procedures, quite apart from Old Peter appearing at times to have a better grasp of the situation than his principal questioner Clemenz. The likely explanation is that Old Peter had the assistance of his cousin and fellow guide, the Zermatt district judge Alois Julen, when he answered the questions in writing.
247-9. For Old Peter's appreciation of the sashline being intended as a reserve rope in case they had to leave much rope behind, attached to rocks, and for a possible explanation of his using it to tie on to Douglas, see section 3.16 (The special rope). Gos' use of the words 'murderer' and 'assassin' seem somewhat over the top.
250. Gos says that after returning to Zermatt from America Old Peter resumed guiding for a time, but he provides no evidence of this, and there does not appear to be any elsewhere.
251. Whymper was not voicing his suspicions about the use of the weak rope, but simply stating the fact that it remained unexplained. His own personal view was that Old Peter did not use it intentionally; see section 4.30.

6.15.3 *Alpine Tragedy*

Chapter 4. The Matterhorn Catastrophe pp24-34.
Chapter 17. The disappearance of J-J Maquignaz on Mont Blanc in 1890 pp204-217.
Chapter 18, Carrel the Great. The death of Jean-Antoine Carrel. pp218-28.

6.15.4 *Le Cervin*

Volume 1.
46/2. Kennedy engaged Perren the first day, and it was only after they had got down safely after a number of problems that they met Taugwalder 'evidently wishing for work' and Kennedy engaged him as well for the next day.
77/1. Gos provides no evidence to support his contention that Douglas sent Taugwalder on a Matterhorn reconnaissance on his return from the Gabelhorn and there is none elsewhere.
83. 4 lines from end. 'quand une voix s'écria' and 84/2. 'la corde, subitement tendue' provide examples of the weakness of the French translation upon which Gos relied (see footnote p81). In the first, Whymper actually wrote 'when someone remembered' and in the second, 'the rope was taut between us'.
85. line 4. Another translation change in which Whymper's reference to the rope as 'it' becomes 'cette corde maudite' – this accursed rope!
86/1. 'alpinistes tous deux'. Although McCormick seems to have been a very able walker, nothing seems to be known of his mountaineering apart from the fact that he accompanied Hudson and others up Mont Blanc in July 1865 and that he had been invited by Hudson to join him on the Aiguille Verte and Matterhorn attempts.
102/2. Long's account in 1867 is not the only record by an eye witness, but it is certainly more detailed than the 1865 account of McCormick (*A sad holiday* p13). See also Girdlestone – *AJ57*, 375.
111/1. It was probably not Whymper's fault, but that of Monod the interviewer, that the *Journal de Zermatt* article stated that he had never wanted to climb the Matterhorn again; see section 2.57.12.(e). It was not Franz Biner, but his son.
111/2. This reference to Gustave Doré shows just how observant and thorough Gos was in his consideration of every detail he could lay his hands on. It is almost certain that he was right and that the four falling bodies were based on a sketch provided to Doré by Whymper. (see *AJ100*, 215-21.)
122. last para. There is no doubt that McCormick conducted the service. He was the summer chaplain at Zermatt; Robertson was just on holiday.
123. Robertson did not in fact join the Alpine Club until 1864. Gos seems to have been misled by Robertson's obituary in *AJ21*, as there is no basis for suggesting that on 12th July he was in Zermatt and that Hudson invited him to join the Matterhorn attempt. Robertson did not reach Zermatt until 15th.
126. Gos sends Tyndall to Zermatt on about Monday 17th July, whereas he did not in fact get there until 31st July, after both Whymper and Queensberry had left.
147/2 & 3. Whereas para 2 is in *Scrambles* chapter 8, para 3 is in chapter 13.
148-9. Whymper did not in fact write the sentence starting 'Nous laissâmes...', nor the next one, which appear to be paraphrases by Claire Engel (*Whymper Escalades*). Gos' first sentence comes from her fourth paragraph and his second from her first! The intervening 37 lines in

Engel (pp159 & 160) are not relevant, but such a misquotation presented as though Whymper had written it himself has all the makings of distorted history.
149/1. Birkbeck did in fact arrive at Chamonix, but due to ill-health, he had to return to England; see *Scrambles* chapter 20 or Kennedy *AJ3*, 69.
149. last para. For the circumstances in which Vecqueray helped with the translation and also the way he helped Whymper with the Enquiry, see section 2.56.
150. Robertson deserves some of the credit for the inscription. The portrait was a photograph of the Calkin portrait, and is now at the Alpine Club.
159. The Parker's 1865 visit to Zermatt is referred to in Dangar's 1963 article 'The Parkers and the Matterhorn'; *AJ68*, 285-90.
163. Charlton's letter is somewhat misleading, as Hadow had undoubtedly been a pupil of Hudson, perhaps in 1864, and the link between them was obviously based on that relationship, even though it had probably terminated 6 months or more before. See McCormick, *A sad holiday* p4.
164-175. The Whymper-Tyndall misundertanding hardly has any relevance to the accident and its aftermath except for two things:
1. It shows Whymper's precise and thorough attention to detail, and the availability of additional material to support what he had written, so that one cannot necessarily assert or dispute a fact simply because he did not refer expressly to it.
2. It also shows his thoroughness in preparing the text of *Scrambles*, by reading portions of it to Carrel in 1869; see 170/2, lines 13-17.

177-191. La corde maudite.

This lengthy section is uncharacteristic of Charles Gos and may perhaps be explained in one of two ways. Firstly it is probably one of the last sections that he wrote or completed towards the end of his long and fatal illness, as it relies in part on the 1944 French edition of Smythe's *Whymper* and also on Egger's *Pioniere der Alpen* published in mid-1946. Secondly, it looks as though it was in part inspired by Carl Egger, as it exhibits the inaccuracy, distortion, extravagance and almost hysterical protests to which only Egger had previously resorted. It may also have been influenced by Lunn's May 1946 article in the *Alpine Journal* (*AJ55*, 290-6), which supported Egger and had no sounder basis of fact. It is also inconsistent with some of the things Gos wrote in the same book prior to being exposed to such negative influences. Lunn prided himself in having influenced Smythe to write his uncharacteristic Introduction to the 1949 edition of Whymper's *Andes*, and Egger may perhaps have felt the same about Gos.

177. Gos gets off to a bad start with the dramatic chapter heading 'La corde maudite', perhaps, 'the accursed rope'! Five lines from the bottom of p183 he states as a fact that 'la corde maudite' was Whymper's expression. But both Joanne and Engel, in their French translations, used the expression in place of Whymper's word 'it'. (see 1st French p398 & Engel 1944 edn. p195). Gos' chapter combines invention, distortion and muddle, and it is necessary to highlight the details because of the cumulative effect of such false accounting in causing the reader to prejudge the more important issues.
177/1. Gos does not state what he is referring to, the nature of the crime nor how immediately it arose, nor does he explain the basis for the story of the cut rope being born of Whymper's attitude to the two Taugwalders. Is he referring to the Taugwalder footnote in *Scrambles*, hardly published 'immediately' but six years after the accident? Or is he perhaps referring to what

Whymper wrote in his letter to *The Times* on 8.8.65 or to what McCormick had said in his letter published on 22.7.65 about the Taugwalders being so completely unnerved by the calamity that Whymper found it difficult to descend with them?

177/1. 'A guide is not an assassin.' No one else has ever made any such suggestion although Gos did play with the idea, only to dismiss it, in *Alpinisme anecdotique* (p249). In the same article (p244) Gos wrote of people still referring to-day to the story of the cut rope 'despite the emphatic and immediate denials by Whymper himself'. In 1934 Gos did not have the temerity even to suggest, let alone assert, that some undisclosed conduct on the part of Whymper gave rise to the story of the cut rope. It is quite clear that no such thought had ever entered his head and that he would have refuted any such idea that anyone else might put forward. So why did he change in 1946, unless his better judgment was distorted by Egger?

177/2. Taugwalder did not take one of five or six lengths of rope at random; he used the rope round his shoulder, and the one most readily to hand, seemingly without regard to its quality. The words in italics are true in themselves, but not in the misleading context into which Gos seeks to put them.

177-8. Gos insists that Taugwalder knew nothing of the weak rope being intended as a reserve yet fails to tell us the supposed basis for his groundless statement. Not only is there no evidence elsewhere to support his contention but there is in fact evidence to show that Taugwalder fully understood why he was carrying the rope that could not be described as 'brand-new and strong', his description of the Croz – Douglas rope. He knew of the intention to use fixed ropes to overcome difficulties and increase security and he knew that the rope which he had been carrying at the ready both on the ascent and on the descent was for that purpose. He even referred to it as a special rope (A24).

178. line 6. It is not right to describe Douglas as an elite mountaineer. Despite his undoubted intelligence and the promising start to his climbing career, he seems to have misjudged Old Peter's exploits on the Gabelhorn and he clearly had never addressed his mind to the best route to take, leaving it to Old Peter to try and find a way up.

178. line 10. There is no justification for anyone presuming that Old Peter murdered Douglas, on any interpretation of the circumstances in which he came to use the weakest rope.

178. lines 15-19. see section 3.16 (The special rope).

178. lines 20-21. 'Et comment expliquer ce rôle bizarre d'accusateur pris par Whymper'. Gos accuses Whymper of accusing without any indication of what he is relying on.

178. The conclusions of the Tribunal have no bearing on Gos' insinuations, and in any event it is doubtful whether the Enquiry was conducted properly, having regard to Clemenz delegating to Whymper the task of questioning Taugwalder.

179/3. Old Peter was certainly not in Chamonix a fortnight after the accident and it is odd that Gos should have omitted from the second paragraph of the d'Arve extract the most important sentence: 'N'est ce pas que tu as coupé la corde?' He also omits to tell his readers of two previous pages which d'Arve devoted to Old Peter cutting the rope. The book published in Geneva in 1876 must have done far more harm to Old Peter's reputation than anything Whymper ever published.

180-1. On the subject of J-B Croz' return to Chamonix from Zermatt, see the Whymper-Wigram correspondence.

182. lines 3-4. Famous mountaineers – Güssfeldt, Kennedy etc – engaged Old Peter, says Gos, but there is no evidence apart from Güssfeldt on one occasion in 1868, when Old Peter insisted that no one else should accompany them and then lost the way on the descent. This dubious generality seems to have been inspired by Egger's unsupported assertion (*Pioņiere* 199) that Old Peter frequently participated in expeditions for at least 5 years after the accident.

182. lines 4-5. What was the blow to his reputation from Whymper's suspicions? Does Gos

mean something Whymper published six years after the event? Is he somehow relying on the questions for Old Peter to answer at the Enquiry or is he simply trying to adopt the general anti-Whymper prejudice expressed by Egger in *Pioniere*? It was not until 1874 that Old Peter went to America and there is no evidence to suggest that he tried to resume guiding on his return in 1878 and certainly none that the tourists avoided him.

182/2. Gos' analysis of veiled accusations by Whymper does not seem to accord with the facts, see section 2.57.10 (Whymper).

182. footnote 1. It is not true to say that Whymper had a very bad understanding of French. This was no doubt based on what Farrar had said (*AJ33*, 247). Even Arnold Lunn, who claimed that Whymper's knowledge of French was almost non-existent, ultimately conceded to Dangar & Blakeney (*AJ71*, 232) that he had been wrong.

183. The circumstances in which Whymper came to draft questions for Old Peter to answer at the Enquiry are not as straightforward as Gos would suppose. He also omits Whymper's words 'at once' from the end of line 8, which should read 'at once fell upon him'.

183. lines 9-10. Whymper was not the author of the suspicions, which seem to have been shared by most of those who knew that it was the weakest rope that broke. He was merely recording the facts. Nor was he an 'accuser'.

183. lines 13-16. This pageless reference to the 12th edition of Whymper's *Zermatt Guide* is impossible to understand, implying as it does that whatever Gos had in mind had not featured in the previous eleven editions. Gos seems to be getting more and more muddled, culminating in the extraordinary display of heavy print and capital letters on p188. The only feasible explanation for Gos' misleading succession of errors about the 1908 12th edn. is that he must have assumed wrongly and without reading it properly that the Taugwalder footnote in 1908 was still in the original wording that Whymper must have drafted in about 1869, and that he was unaware of the 1893 revision of the wording that appears in every edition of the *Guide* including the French one.

183. lines 17-19. This is a misquotation. Whymper wrote of Taugwalder 'he could not do so at the moment of the slip, and...the end of the rope in my possession shows that he did not do so beforehand'. Gos seems to have failed to notice the word 'beforehand' (although Engel included it), and he repeats his error twice in different types of emphatic print on p188.

183. lines 19-21. There is no evidence of Taugwalder's mental troubles on his return from America and Whymper certainly did not refer to them. The four line quote is based on what Whymper wrote in the first three editions of *Scrambles*, publishing it for the last time in 1879/80. He deleted it from the 4th edition in 1893 and it is hard to understand how Gos purports to quote it from the 1908 edn. of the *Guide to Zermatt*, when it is not even there! (see Note on lines 13-16 above.)

183. last line first para. 'la corde maudite'. This was not Whymper's own expression, but a French translation of Whymper's word 'it'!

184/2. The answer to Gos' false question is that the rope was not almost useless, as was proved by its use as fixed rope after the accident. In the circumstances it was almost ideal for the job and was a necessary and valuable part of the equipment taken on the climb.

184/3 last sentence. Not only was Whymper not the leader, but Gos' language is more reminiscent of the journalistic style in which he wrote *Alpine Tragedy*, than that of the reliable and objective historian who wrote most of the rest of his present book.

184/4. This hardly merits comment, except to suggest that it seems to have been inspired by Egger.

186. lines 29-30. The reason why the Rimini – and the von Fellenberg – letter did not refer to the weak rope, must be that Whymper expected Clemenz to keep his promise and send him

Taugwalder's answers. The letter was intended to correct inaccuracies in the numerous versions of the accident already published.

187/2, last line. The murderer is back! But any deliberate use of a weak link would not be creating danger so much as withdrawing the benefit of a safeguard, which in 1865 still seemed to be regarded by some as of dubious value.

187/5. Gos himself raised the idea of criminal intent and murder.

188/2. The word 'redire' in line 4 is incorrect, as Whymper's original word was 'asserting'. But Gos is guilty of a far more serious defect, which is the entire omission of Whymper's last word in the sentence, 'beforehand'. The word 'avant' is not there, and for good measure Gos repeats it all in para 4 with the same omission, putting everything into capital letters!

188-9. Gos seeks to attribute the Cowell memorandum to a frightful misunderstanding between Whymper and his guides, although he has no knowledge of the circumstances in which it came to be made. There does not seem to be any justification for Gos' invention of a second copy. In a footnote he acknowledges the works of Egger and Lunn, describing them as two important studies, and he was obviously influenced by them. As for attributing Whymper's account of the Taugwalder's conduct to the shock he sustained in the accident, it should not be forgotten that he survived a far more desperate and frightening experience in 1862, when alone he fell some 200ft., sustained head injuries and lost consciousness for a while, but nevertheless managed to find his way down the mountain in the dark, and to be back climbing it again within a week.

190-191. It is perhaps fitting that Gos should have chosen or chanced to conclude this erratic chapter by taking another Whymper quotation out of its context. He quotes four lines out of some fourteen, mistaking Wednesday for Friday and omitting ten lines between the two sentences which he quotes in such a way as to make them appear consecutive. His object appears to have been to complain that Whymper noted the Col du Géant accident without making 'the slightest comment'. But Whymper's lack of comment in his own diary on something about which he had insufficient information stands out in marked contrast to the willingness of Gos, Lunn and Egger to criticise Whymper in public, by pronouncing on the Cowell memorandum of which 'too little is known...for it to be wise for anyone to pronounce upon it' (in the words of Dangar & Blakeney). But the most remarkable thing about Gos' final quotation and his remarks about Whymper's lack of comment, is the way he misleads his readers by failing to quote the explanation given by Whymper in his very next sentence. 'There are many details in connection with this melancholy accident which I have yet to learn...'

192-3. On the question of Whymper's relationship with G.F.Browne and Conway's comments, see section 2.5 (Browne).

196/4. Although Gos states that he submitted 'La corde maudite' to Winthrop Young, he does not publish his reply!

211/2. This quotation, which Gos states expressly comes from Güssfeldt's book *In den Hochalpen* does not in fact come from there. It bears a close resemblance, for the most part, to the text of a note in *AJ37,* 386, although if this is its origin Gos must on occasions have switched from the first person to the third.

302/1. The 29.7.62 entry was by Tyndall. see Rey's *The Matterhorn* 1st edn. p311 n.34 or 1946 edn. 269 n.20.

303. para 2. lines 6-7. Rey quotes a Whymper entry of 11.8.63. Ibid 311 n.37 or 269 n.21.

Volume 2.

197. footnote. The illustration referred to in Manning is almost certainly not by Whymper, see section 3.8.4 (Illustrations).

6.16
GROSJEAN, GEORGES

Grosjean states in his centenary article 'La première ascension du Cervin le 14 juillet 1865' that it is not an easy task for the historian to retell the story of the first ascent a century later, in view of the constraints imposed by the original documents and by the fact that all the narratives emanate from Whymper's own account which, he adds, 'cannot and should not be regarded by the historian as objective'. But, he says, the historian 'can perhaps attempt...to throw a slightly more objective light on at least one or two points'. Yet Grosjean does not in fact quote any historical authority for contradicting many of the established facts, such as the arrival of Lord Francis Douglas at Breuil with Old Peter Taugwalder's second son Joseph. According to Grosjean Douglas arrived with Old Peter as guide and Young Peter as porter, and Old Peter offered to transport Whymper's baggage across the Theodule. Another example is his rejection of Whymper's account of his 1862 fall, when he fell 200 feet, sustaining head injuries and losing consciousness. Grosjean tells us initially, that 'he fell on a harmless slope', and on the next page, that 'On the descent...he hurt himself in a slight fall'. It is therefore of particular interest to read Whymper's letter of 1st August 1862 to his father, describing the fall (see section 2.57.3), as it once again confirms the reliability of what Whymper later published.

La première ascension du Cervin le 14 juillet 1865. *Les Alpes. XLI.* 1965, 89-100.

6.16.1 La première ascension du Cervin le 14 juillet 1865

90/5. lines 8-10. Kennedy did not regard the Matterhorn as feasible from the Italian side, but wrote (*AJ1*, 77) of his observations in 1858 and 1860: 'From Breuil all access to the summit appeared to me to be out of the question'.

91/5. In the present context, the point about Coolidge's mischievous letters to Gos is, surely, not merely that he was stating that Whymper had lied in standing up for Old Peter by denying that he cut the rope, but that if Grosjean wants to accept the statement of 'someone as important as Coolidge' on this instead of supporting Guido Rey's emphatic rejection, he must wrongly believe that Old Peter did cut the rope; (but see 97/3 below).

92/2 lines 17-18. A slope of 52° is hardly 'une pente inoffensive' (see Whymper's letter to his father in section 2.57.3).

92/5 last sentence. Whymper explains in *Scrambles* why he had no local guide. He also declined Old Peter's exorbitant demand of 200frs.

93/3 last line. Striking one's head four or five times in the course of a 200ft. fall, as one whirls downwards in a series of bounds each longer than the last, coming to a halt only ten feet from an 800 ft. precipice, is hardly 'a slight fall'!

93. last para. Whymper had intended to try the Hörnli in 1864, with Reilly.

94/2 line 13. Croz did not abandon Whymper but accompanied him to Chamonix, making first ascents of the Grandes Jorasses and the Col Dolent on the way.
94/3 lines 3-5. Whymper's engagement with Carrel is corroborated by Gorret's account (*AJ2*, 238) and elsewhere.
94/5. Whymper had decided to cross to Zermatt and try the Hörnli before Douglas arrived at Breuil. The latter was not accompanied by Old Peter or by Young Peter Taugwalder; his only companion was Joseph Taugwalder.
95. lines 5-8. Old Peter and Young Peter did not accompany Whymper and Douglas across the Theodule. Douglas did not even have two guides.
95. line 16. Hadow's correct name was Douglas Robert Hadow.
95. lines 20-21. It was not Friedrich the youngest son, but Joseph, Old Peter's second son, who went as porter, and, contrary to what Grosjean states at the end of para 3, he did not descend to Zermatt until the following day.
95/4. Whymper and Croz did not unrope when they reached the 'Roof', but only on the very last stretch, where the slope eased off.
97/2 lines 5-7. Grosjean provides no evidence whatever to support this.
97/3. This is hardly consistent with the inference to be drawn from the earlier mention of Coolidge (see 91/5 above).
97/4. Taugwalder told the Tribunal that he tied himself on to Douglas with 'a special rope' (A24). He was not asked what he meant by this, but it must be of some significance that he said the rope between Douglas and Croz 'was a strong and brand-new rope' (A26). As for the possibility of Old Peter having belayed the Whymper rope, rather than merely hugging the rock with both arms, see sections 2.52.8 (Taugwalder) and 3.12.4 (The rope in 1865).
98/2. Croz, Hudson and Hadow were *not* still roped together, see McCormick's letter to *The Times*.
99/5. There is no evidence of Whymper regarding Hudson and Douglas as rivals rather than as friends.
100/2. Whymper had seriously intended to try the Hörnli in 1864 and in 1865, before he ever met Douglas or Hudson. There is no evidence that Hudson had profited from the opinion or experience of Kennedy, who never attempted the Matterhorn again after January 1862, despite going to Zermatt again in 1866 and in 1867. There is no reason to suppose that Whymper and Douglas would not have made a successful ascent without Hudson. Grosjean is wrong in his belief that Whymper joined himself to the Taugwalders in Breuil, when they were both in Zermatt.
100/3. Grosjean alleges that Old Peter's reputation as a guide was destroyed partly through the fault of Whymper, but he does not refer to the evidence of his career ending long before *Scrambles* was published, nor does he seem to have any appreciation of how in his first three written accounts Whymper was merely recording the facts and was not expressing his own opinion.
100/4. Grosjean has not in fact provided any contemporary evidence that justifies casting any doubt on Dübi's or Guido Rey's belief in Whymper, to which he previously referred at 91/5.

6.17
LEWIN, WALTER HENRY

Lewin wrote in his privately published book *Climbs* that he only took up climbing in his fifties. He was a friend of Noel Odell, with whom he made a number of climbs in North Wales, and he became a member of the Climbers Club. His book, limited to 250 signed and numbered copies, consists mainly of essays previously published elsewhere, but it also includes a lecture he gave on behalf of some hospital on 'The first ascent of the Matterhorn'. How he came to be so interested in the subject is not revealed, although he seems to have written a previous book about the North Pole, but it is just possible that he may have been related to Miss Edith Mary Lewin, who married Edward Whymper in 1906. The book was never reviewed in the *Alpine Journal*, but it was mentioned by Dangar & Blakeney in *AJ61*, 487 and it was brought to the attention of Frank Smythe in October 1939 by Herbert E.Cooke, but this was after *Edward Whymper* had gone to press. An extract from pages 134-136 sent to Smythe by Cooke now appears in the AC Archives with some marginal comments from Smythe, but they are of no particular interest. The chapter as a whole seems to be based on a series of incorrect assumptions and misunderstandings by Lewin and is almost devoid of all detail in such matters as the use of the ropes. It is possible that it inspired Lunn and Egger, as it seems to have been the first serious attempt to attribute all Taugwalder's problems to Whymper!

Climbs. Published privately by the Author. [1932] 'The First Ascent of the Matterhorn. With an analysis of the causes of the disaster that followed. A lecture given by the Author on behalf of Letchworth hospital.' 130-45.

6.17.1 The First Ascent of the Matterhorn

130/2. Lewin refers to attempting 'to discover new causes for a disaster which differ appreciably from those tradition has handed down to us'.
131/2. It is hardly correct to state that in the early 1860's 'friction between [Whymper & Carrel] was not infrequent' or that at that time Whymper 'had the reputation of being a rather difficult man to get on with: in fact a somewhat temperamental character'. Lewin offers no evidence in support.
132. line 10. Douglas was not yet 'a well known English climber', even though his brother the Marquess of Queensberry was well known and he himself climbed.
133/3. Taugwalder senior was hardly 'the strongest man'. Croz was.
134/3. This paragraph is simply not true. Whymper made no such declaration as to the cause of the accident. The last paragraph of his letter to *The Times* included: 'A single slip, or a single false step, has been the sole cause of this frightful calamity...'
134/4. It may be 'a monstrous suggestion' for Lewin to make, that 'upon old Taugwalder was heaped all the responsibility for the disaster', implying that this was done by Whymper, but this is due to Lewin's inability to judge what Whymper wrote within the context of 1865 or 1871. But like Lunn and Egger, who were probably inspired directly or indirectly by him, Lewin does not quote chapter and verse or indicate the date Whymper is supposed to have made his accusation or suggestion. The six year gap between the only two possibilities of 1865 or 1871, when *Scrambles* was published, is such a relatively long time that one might think that Lewin's accusation must date from 1865, were it not virtually impossible to find anything that Whymper wrote in 1865 that could be remotely linked to Lewin's complaint. Lewin seems not to have appreciated the extent to which Whymper confined himself to the facts and even abstained from making observations, never mind accusations. So far as Lewin appointing

himself as counsel for the defence is concerned, it seems quite probable that Taugwalder was legally represented at the Enquiry, or at least that he was allowed to confer with and seek advice from his 'lawyer' before answering the questions at the Enquiry, his lawyer being his cousin the guide and Zermatt district judge Alois Julen.
134. last three lines. Lewin's reference to being assumed guilty 65 years ago seems to indicate he had in mind something Whymper wrote in 1865, rather than 1871 when *Scrambles* was published.
135/1. Whymper was 'one hundred feet or more from the others whilst they were being tied up' and he was unable to throw any light on the matter. He may have had an opportunity of noticing the weak rope round Taugwalder's waist, but the fact is that he did not see it. There is no reason to suppose that the reference to Whymper tying on to Taugwalder means any more than that he threw the end of the rope down to him, for him to tie it round himself.
135/3. 'To create and foster the unworthy suspicion...'? Lewin does not reveal what he has in mind that Whymper did, but he may have meant that Whymper wrote in *Scrambles* of such things as 'the suspicious fact'. But Whymper was not voicing his own suspicions, only the general public reaction, such as 'the grave suspicions that at once fell upon him'. The six year gap before the publication of *Scrambles* once again casts doubt on cause and effect. As for Machiavelli, Lewin ought surely to have been aware of the several incidents in the 1860's of guides holding a rope so as to be able to let go if necessary, including the Stogden story related by Lunn.
136/1. Lewin has provided no evidence to justify relating 'the unmerited fate of this old guide' to Edward Whymper, particularly in view of the fact that Taugwalder's fate must have been sealed very early in the six year gap and long before *Scrambles* appeared. There is no question of Whymper seeking or even needing a scapegoat.
136/2. The possibility that seven instead of four might have lost their lives was not overlooked by Whymper; see last paragraph of his letter to *The Times*.

6.18
LUNN, ARNOLD (1888 – 1974)

It is surprising to find less than half a page devoted to Lunn's main obituary in the *Alpine Journal*, despite his published books and articles on mountaineering spanning more than half a century. He may have largely given up climbing soon after breaking his leg on Cader Idris at the age of 21 and concentrated on ski-mountaineering thereafter, but the Swiss Foundation for Alpine Research chose him to write its Centenary Tribute to the Alpine Club, *A Century of Mountaineering. 1857–1957*, and he was undoubtedly one of the leading English mountaineering writers of his day.

His first book *The Alps* was published in 1914 and it contains a chapter of some forty pages, 'The story of the Matterhorn', which relates the history of the attempts to scale it and comments on the various aspects of the accident on the first ascent that have given rise to so much controversy. Unlike his return to the same subject a quarter of a century later, *The Alps* displays none of the anti-Whymper prejudice that was to taint and dominate his Matterhorn writing for a further twenty five years, although he did state in it that 'Whymper, in his classic book, suggested the possibility of criminal dealings by publishing photographs of the three ropes showing that the rope broken was far the weakest'.

Lunn returned to the scene in 1943 with a twenty six page chapter 'Edward Whymper' in his book *Mountain Jubilee*, which was essentially a review of Smythe's book of the same name and had already appeared in *The British Ski Year Book* of 1940. This recycling of earlier writings was to become the hallmark of Lunn's allergy to Whymper with anything from a sentence to several paragraphs appearing again and again, as though they had been stored away in the memory of some very early word processor. Lunn's friendship with another pioneer of ski-mountaineering, Carl Egger, who lived in Bern not so very far away from Lunn's own residence in Grindelwald, accounts for the admiration that each was quick to express for the anti-Whymper writings of the other. In the 1940's and the 1950's Lunn was repeating himself fairly regularly in books and articles but it was only when he came to publish his book *Matterhorn Centenary* in 1965 that Dangar & Blakeney, the assistant editors of the *Alpine Journal*, decided that the time had come to challenge him.

Their twenty page article in *AJ71*, 'A word for Whymper: a reply to Sir Arnold Lunn', took the form of a review of his book, and began by stating how it had

> 'afforded him the opportunity for a reiteration of his well-known adverse criticisms of Whymper. For many years Lunn has used his talents to voice his dislike or his distrust of Whymper: it would scarcely be worth while to attempt an exhaustive scrutiny of his former books, in order to see how often he has said the same things...'

The article went on to express their view that Lunn had distorted the facts in his presentation of them:

> 'In fact, one cannot avoid an uneasy feeling that Lunn has used the prestige that he rightly enjoys, as an interpreter of Anglo-Swiss relationships, to foster and propagate error as regards Whymper.
> This accusation, which clearly must be justified, comprises both specific charges of inaccuracy on particular points, and a general disposition on Lunn's part to run down Whymper by use of petty charges that, collectively, would damage his reputation. In the handling of these charges Lunn, as it seems, drops the historian for the journalist, and fails to distinguish between gossip and evidence.'

Halfway through their article (on p120) and after dealing with various points, they comment: 'But really one can scarcely any longer be surprised by anything Lunn writes in his campaign against Whymper; it is hardly an exaggeration to say that he appears ready to impugn Whymper's veracity on everything he wrote about the events of July 13 to 15, 1865...'

Lunn in his reply 'Whymper again' in the next number did concede that he had been wrong on one or two minor details, as he called them, but for the most part he stood by what he had written and it was necessary for Dangar & Blakeney to respond with two further pages of argument. That seems to have been Lunn's last published pronouncement on the subject, but because he wrote and repeated so much over a period of twenty five years, there is still a lot of it around and it is likely to continue to mislead people for many years to come. But thanks to Dangar & Blakeney there is now a growing realisation that Lunn was allergic to Whymper and that he cannot be trusted on the subject of the Matterhorn accident or its aftermath. It is particularly unfortunate that *A Century of Mountaineering*, which was intended to be a serious history of mountaineering, should have been partially tainted as a result of virtually the whole of the section relating to Whymper being a reiteration of Lunn's multi-cycled prejudices and distortions.

Lunn's principal Matterhorn/Whymper publications were as follows:

1. 1914. *The Alps*. 147-84.
2. 1940. *The British Ski Year Book*. 370-95.
3. 1943. *Mountain Jubilee*. 189-214.
4. 1944. *Switzerland and the English*. 131 & 169.
5. 1946. Taugwalder and the Matterhorn. *AJ55*, 290-6.
6. 1947. *Switzerland in English prose and poetry*. 108-12.
7. 1954. Whymper's engravings for *Scrambles*. A note. *AJ59*, 344.
8. 1955. *Zermatt and the Valais*. 18-45.
9. 1957. *A Century of Mountaineering*. 51-61.
10. 1958. *The Bernese Oberland*. 85.
11. 1965. *Matterhorn Centenary*. 37-75.
12. 1966. Whymper again. *AJ71*, 228-33.

6.18.1 *The Alps*

A nice little book of Alpine history with a bibliography and an index.

177/2. 'Taugwalder ultimately left the valley for America, returning only to die.' In fact he returned in 1878, according to Young Peter, and died in 1888.

177/2. It is surprising to find that Lunn's statement that 'Whymper, in his classic book, suggested the possibility of criminal dealings by publishing photographs of the three ropes showing that the rope broken was far the weakest' seems never to have been recycled in his later works!

179/2. Young Lunn seems to have been capable of taking an objective view, and it is interesting to find him volunteering Stogden's account of Old Peter taking the rope off so that he could choose whether or not to hold on in the event of an accident. He did in fact refer to this again in *AJ55*, 291.

6.18.2 *The British Ski Year Book*. 1940

'Edward Whymper and the Matterhorn. A study in Alpine revaluation'. Apart from one short unimportant paragraph, the whole article was repeated in *Mountain Jubilee*.

6.18.3 *Mountain Jubilee*

Chapter 18 is essentially a 25 page critical review of Smythe's book *Edward Whymper*. It is also the origin of much that Lunn was to recycle in other books and articles for the next 25 years.

195/5. 'His persistent neglect of what is now the normal route from Zermatt is difficult to explain'; but see Leslie Stephen's view in *Macmillan's* (section 2.48).

197. line 5. There is no evidence to suggest that Douglas had already decided to attempt the ascent later that week, rather than the following year.

197/3. Lunn says Hudson had not wasted years in exploring the more difficult routes but went straight for the easiest route. But Hudson had wasted 13 years not making any attempt, having first crossed the Theodule pass from Breuil to Zermatt in 1852. He hardly went straight for it and cannot have expected the Hörnli to be easy, needing a special ladder and wire-rope. As for Croz' reluctance with Whymper, see section 6.14.2 (Farrar) 27/1 above.

198/3. 'He left his native valley for America, returning only to die.' His years away appear to have been 1874-8, according to Young Peter, but he did not die till 1888.

198/4. Whymper related the fact, which was true, and he could hardly have concealed it, even though he had no reason to suspect he did it intentionally.

198/5 last 4 lines. It is hardly likely that Whymper had to tie the rope on to Taugwalder himself, rather than throw an end down.

198. last para. A typical generality from Lunn. There is no reason to suppose Whymper disliked Taugwalder and there is no truth in the last three words, even if Lunn intended them to apply to the day he himself met Whymper rather than to 1865.

199/1. Lunn was misled by Smythe over the Cowell memorandum. It was not made by Whymper. Smythe failed to realise this or to reveal the circumstances in which it came to be made.

199/2. It simply is not true to talk of 'Whymper's gross libel', nor even of 'the accusation'. It was Lunn who got it all wrong and who is 'unsupported by a shred of evidence' and it is nonsense for him to write of 'the criminal irresponsibility with which Whymper committed to paper a charge of attempted murder', when he did no such thing!

201/4. lines 13-14. Lunn was not there at the time and cannot contradict what Whymper wrote! Lunn may have thought it was an idle threat, but the guides did not, and it worked!

202/2. This further reference to an accusation of attempted murder is typical of Lunn's recycling of his errors and distortions.

204/2. lines 12-13. This is not true for amateurs or guides, although as he rarely climbed with an amateur after the 1865 accident and gave up serious climbing in the Alps, the scope is rather limited.

6.18.4 *Switzerland and the English*

There is very little reference to Whymper or the Matterhorn in this general book, nevertheless Lunn could not resist sniping at Whymper, although he was only repeating what he had already published the year before. Two examples:

131/2. It is not true to say that the conquest of the Matterhorn from Zermatt was due to the mountaineering insight of Hudson. There is no reason to suppose that Whymper and Douglas would not have made the ascent without him. As for wasting time, see *Mountain Jubilee* above, 197/3, where Lunn made the same bad point the year before.

169. line 3. This is also a repeat from *Mountain Jubilee*, 213. One of Lunn's favourites, he kept

on and on about Mahoney for over 20 years. See Graham Brown, *AJ57*, 369 and Dangar & Blakeney, *AJ71*, 119-20.

6.18.5 Taugwalder and the Matterhorn

This article by Lunn, his first in the *Alpine Journal* on the subject, appears intended to draw attention to the chapter in Egger's book, *Pioniere der Alpen*, attacking Whymper and praising Taugwalder. The article is so lacking in detail and inconsistent with the evidence that it grossly distorts history, but it was never challenged at the time and this seems to have encouraged Lunn to go even further in his subsequent writings, until he was finally challenged by Dangar & Blakeney in 1966. It is not possible, for want of space, to deal fully or even at all with some of Lunn's pejorative remarks. Take for example the reference to Knubel in paragraph one. Which Knubel is he referring to? The son Josef, whom Lunn first met two years after Whymper's death and who was then aged 32, or the father Peter a contemporary of Whymper's who did not die until 1919? Josef would have been 19 in 1900 and may well have known Whymper by sight for the last ten years of his life, or does Lunn's remark date back to the 1860's so that even if Lunn heard it from Josef it must have come via Peter? Lunn would no doubt have been surprised had he heard what Peter Knubel had to say about the two Taugwalders. He might have told him that Young Peter Taugwalder was 'nicht beliebt', to put it mildly, having regard to the incident in the Schönbühl hut in 1876 (reported by Gardiner in *AJ8*, 382), and some further research in the Alpine Club Archives could well reveal the source of a comment Farrar made to Montagnier in a letter of 17.10.1917: 'I will be sure to tell Gardiner what old Knubel says about him. I read his opinion of the Matterhorn accident with considerable astonishment. He does not give old T [sic] much credit!' It is neccesary to go back to the sources rather than rely on hearsay, and in view of what is known of Lunn's unreliability as a Matterhorn historian, anything he says that is not supported by the necessary evidence ought to be disregarded.

290/1. Lunn's oft repeated compliment from Otto Furrer is unsatisfactory coming from himself as, whatever he said in his 1945 speech, the reference to what he had written could only mean his chapter in *Mountain Jubilee*. But this wartime book had only been published in 1943 and even the Zürich translation only appeared first in 1945.

290. lines 8-10. Knubel has already been mentioned above, and even if there were any justification for the remark it is unlikely that it would be attributable to Whymper's attitude to guides. A more likely origin might be his friendship with Alexander Seiler and the fact that the Zermatters went to extraordinary lengths to try and destroy Seiler's business. They were jealous of the St.Niklaus guides including Peter Knubel as they had almost acquired a monopoly of taking local tourists up the Matterhorn. In 1917 Young Peter Taugwalder expressed great bitterness about the envy and cunning of the St.Niklaus guides (and those of Chamonix) and even attributed to them his father's emigration to America.

290. line 11. What attack on the Taugwalders? And when was it made?

290/2. Lunn's comparison of the two books appears misconceived, as the big weakness of Egger's is that he carried out virtually no original research and rarely saw the Swiss guides

other than through English eyes, as he relied almost entirely on English sources. The high standard of the criterion for inclusion in *The Pioneers of the Alps* inevitably excluded Taugwalder.
290/3. For detailed consideration of the unsuccessful outcome of Egger's attempted 'vindication', see Egger, *Pioniere der Alpen* in section 6.12.2.
290/4. Taugwalder was certainly not in the class of leading guides like Almer, Anderegg or Croz, nor even Peter Perren of Zermatt. He was a sound second class guide, a Monte Rosa guide with over 85 ascents to his credit, who rarely ventured beyond the peaks and passes to the south-east of his own doorstep. Even Leslie Stephen referred to him as 'comparatively incompetent', in the *Macmillan's* article Lunn was so fond of quoting from.
290/4. 'He led the first determined attack on the Dent Blanche'! True, although determined may not be the right word to associate with him, as it was his loss of nerve that caused Kennedy and Young Peter to have to retreat not far from the summit. Kennedy climbed it with a more competent guide a day or two later.
290/4. Lunn provides no evidence in support of the myth that Taugwalder believed the Matterhorn could be climbed. Taugwalder did not lead Kennedy's winter attempt, but Peter Perren. There is no evidence of his making a solitary exploration on his own initiative. If Lunn had in mind what Douglas said to Whymper, which seems likely to have been no more than salesmanship by Taugwalder, it cannot in any event have been in 1865; see section 2.52.5. It is false to credit him with some sort of super-judgment transcending that of all others, particularly when he did not apparently believe that it could be climbed by him again after the accident.
291/1. To say Taugwalder was fully qualified to take part in the expedition is inconsistent with Stephen's view, which Lunn ignored. The reason why he never received more credit for the ascent must have been his inability to repeat it, or any of his other first ascents in 1865, and show that he really was more than a good Monte Rosa guide. Clemenz' secrecy cannot have helped him.
291. Part 3. Whymper did not make any 'charges' against Taugwalder. He reported the facts, and for Lunn to quote the Stogden incident in such detail seems in itself to justify a similar reaction amongst those who knew that Taugwalder had used the weaker rope. Whymper did not say '*I* thought this had a very ugly look etc', but was reporting the contemporary reaction. Lunn's mention of the two fatal accidents cited by Longman and of Furrer's tale about Burgener is appropriate, yet it is about the only occasion he ever put an issue into its proper perspective.
292. The Egger quote. There is a typographical error in the second line and should be a full stop after Taugwalder, and then the word 'For'. Egger adopts a strange technique for prejudice by asking a series of dubious questions, some of which are fundamentally flawed. The several answers are not Whymper, as Egger supposed. Whymper was not alone in knowing the characteristics of the rope and even Taugwalder described it as a special rope (A24). Taugwalder must have been capable of tying the rope for himself, and the probability is that when Whymper approached him he threw the end of the rope down, having no cause to inspect Taugwalder as he stood 20 feet below.
292. last para. This is from Whymper's memorandum of 17.8.65, of which Lunn did not know the origin, as Smythe never revealed it.
293/3. Lunn's speculation is inconsistent with the facts, and the possibility of any misunderstanding seems to have been excluded by Young Peter subsequently endeavouring to trade upon the idea of not being paid. This is something that both Lunn and Egger tried to ignore, although it is there in the long Taugwalder footnote in *Scrambles* on which they so often

relied. Egger in fact went to extraordinary lengths to pretend that it was not there (see *Pioniere*, 191-2 in section 6.12.2 above).
293/4&5. The wording 'memorandum of a communication made to...Cowell by... Whymper' is ambiguous, and there is no reason to suppose that Lunn knew more than Smythe, who misled himself by taking the Cowell memorandum out of its context. As in *Mountain Jubilee* (p199), and in *Zermatt & the Valais* (p39), Lunn must therefore have regarded the memorandum as having been made by Whymper, which it was not. It came into existence following advice from Cowell senior and Wills, and was written out by Cowell after he took the view that Whymper's own memo. of 17.8.65 did not go far enough. Lunn was wrong in his conclusions, as the disservice to Whymper's memory stemmed only from Smythe's failure to notice and make known the circumstances in which the document came to be made. Distorting it was no service to truth.
295. The first sentence is interesting as it had seemed as though it was only Whymper's reputation which certain people had sought to undermine since his death. But by choosing his supposedly unfair treatment of the Taugwalders as the means of attack, they have drawn far more attention to Taugwalder's faults than Whymper ever did in *The Times* or *Scrambles*. They have imagined 'charges' and 'accusations' that Whymper never made and the danger is that, after it has been shown that Whymper did not make them, the impression may remain that Taugwalder is still 'guilty'. It would have been far better had these negative critics taken a more positive attitude, put things back into their proper perspective and sought an explanation instead of another victim. Too many people have interfered and thereby distorted the truth, whereas the truth would never have caused any lasting harm to Taugwalder had it been published, instead of being concealed.
295/2. Lunn seems to have overlooked what W.H.Lewin wrote.
295/3. Lunn does not specify what 'gross injustice to a guide' he has in mind.
295/5. It is wrong for Lunn to be writing about 'conspiracy to murder'. As for the final sentence, Lunn's recycled version in *Zermatt and the Valais* (p41) is far more amusing!
295-296. Lunn omits fifteen important words after 'Lord F. Douglas'. For comment on *Macmillan's* review, see section 2.48 (Leslie Stephen).
296/2. lines 1&2. Unfortunately Lunn does not specify the years to which he refers nor the evidence upon which he relies. The explanation is probably that he did not know and was simply recycling what Egger had written (*Pioniere*, 199). There is no sign of Egger having any evidence either.
296/2. Lunn states that Taugwalder's reputation suffered from Whymper's attack, but he does not specify the date nor identify the 'attack' he has in mind. It must presumably be one of the three 'charges' detailed by Lunn, but it cannot be the third one, the Cowell memorandum, as it did not come to light until 1940. There is hardly anything in the second one and Whymper's brief indirect reference to its subject matter in his letter to *The Times* was quite harmless, so he must be relying on something in *Scrambles*, published in 1871. It seems therefore, quite apart from the lack of evidence supporting Lunn's charges, that he reckoned Old Peter's reputation suffered following publication of *Scrambles* and that for some years he became unemployed. Disregarding 1865, when Old Peter may have suffered from the aftermath of two near fatal shocks within a week, and also 1871, despite few mountaineers having read *Scrambles* by then or been able to react adversely to Old Peter's part in it before embarking for Zermatt, we are still left with five full seasons from 1866 until 1870, which not even Lunn could relate to an 1871 publication. But there is next to no evidence of Old Peter making any ascents after 1866 and even then he seems to have been led by his son, instead of vice versa. Something had gone seriously wrong long before *Scrambles* was published. He was incapable of repeating the Matterhorn ascent, for which there was a considerable demand, and he seems never to have

gone near the Gabelhorn or Wellenkuppe again. But the oddest thing is that he seems even to have turned his back on Monte Rosa and in 1866 to have been led by his son up the Dom and Mont Blanc, which he had never climbed before. And that cannot have been Whymper's fault!

6.18.6 *Switzerland in English prose and poetry*

Although this was an anthology, Lunn took the opportunity of including five pages on Whymper repeating much that he had written before. He repeated many of his regular errors and introduced a few new ones that he followed up later.

109-110. A repeat of pp197-8 of *Mountain Jubilee* almost word for word.

112. For consideration of Stephen's review in *Macmillan's* see section 2.48.

112/3. The Zermatter referred to appears to be Karl Lehner, although later references by Lunn reduced his special study to local traditions rather than Matterhorn history (e.g. *Zermatt and the Valais*, 39). It is however idle to suppose that any Zermatter could speak 75 years later for the belief of hundreds of Taugwalders 'comrades and neighbours at Zermatt', and there is further evidence apart from what Whymper recorded. Lunn's third sentence appears mischievous, as no one had ever suggested that any 'responsible mountaineer' made the charge, and his previous sentence does not dispose of the fact recorded by Whymper that: 'Notwithstanding repeated denials, even his comrades and neighbours at Zermatt persist in asserting or insinuating that he cut the rope which led from him to Lord F. Douglas.' Lunn did not even attempt to explain what was implied by 'equally absurd accusations which originated with Whymper'. As for the fourth sentence see section 3.3 (Emigration to America by Zermatters).

112/4. Whymper did not allege 'in his book that old Taugwalder suggested' etc. He quoted from his memorandum of a conversation with Young Taugwalder and, elsewhere in a footnote, he reverted to the suggestion of non-payment with: 'In respect to young Peter, it is not possible to speak in the same manner. The odious idea that he propounded (which I believe emanated from him) he has endeavoured to trade upon, in spite of the fact that his father was paid (for both) in the presence of witnesses.' Lunn, like the other hostile critics, seems always to have turned a blind eye to this reference by Whymper to Young Peter endeavouring to trade upon the idea of non-payment, presumably because it undermined any possibility of a misunderstanding.

6.18.7 Whymper's engravings for *Scrambles*

This reaction to Graham Brown's article adds almost nothing to what Lunn wrote elsewhere and is mentioned only for the sake of completeness.

6.18.8 *Zermatt and the Valais*

Some 35 pages of this book, which deals primarily with the history of the various villages and their people, relate to Zermatt and the Matterhorn. For the most part Lunn recycled his previous Matterhorn writings and subsequently used the outcome to help fill a chapter on Whymper in *A Century of Mountaineering*.

18/2. Lunn's references to 'Whymper's bitter attack' on the Taugwalders, to it being 'bitterly resented' by the Zermatters and to 'Taugwalder himself remained silent under accusations which he knew to be false', are groundless.

19/1. Prejudice is introduced by reference to the Zermatters recording their 'dissent from

Whymper's verdict', without divulging the verdict or stating when, how and where it was given. For comment on Lunn's repeat of this in slightly different form, see *Matterhorn Centenary* (6.18.11) p68 below.
27/3. Whymper actually wrote 'M.le Curé Ruden required' etc. Lunn goes on to refer three times to another 'attack', this time on the parish priest, by which he must mean Whymper reporting that the guides were threatened with excommunication if they did not attend early Mass. Lunn states that Whymper never removed from *Scrambles* the statement that the Curé threatened them with excommunication, not realising that he could not remove what was not there in the first place! In *Scrambles* he did not mention the Curé but wrote of the men being 'threatened by their priests'.
35/2. lines 9-15. Both Graham Brown and Lunn seem to have jumped to the wrong conclusion here; see section 2.14.3 (Lord Francis Douglas).
35/3. lines 9-12. Lunn's oft repeated error of Hudson not wasting time but 'realising from the first [i.e. in 1852!] the weak points in the Eastern face', is still an error.
37/2. Further repetition of priests having no power of excommunication does not alter the fact that their threat achieved its object.
37/2. There were no guides from Täsch in Whymper's search party.
39/1. Another Lunn repeat, which was to crop up yet again, until he finally conceded (*AJ71*, 232) that he had been wrong.
39/2. Lunn has ignored the evidence of McCormick and of Long.
39/3. Lunn is wrong to refer to three accusations by Whymper. The three points Lunn tries to make can be summarised:
1. Whymper recorded the fact that the use of the weaker rope had an ugly look for Taugwalder.
2. He reported a conversation on the way down, in which Young Taugwalder had propounded 'an odious suggestion', Whymper having first recorded it on 17.8.65 on the advice of J.W.Cowell.
3. Lunn did not know what he was talking about on this issue, having been misled by Smythe, who also confused himself. Whymper wrote no such memorandum. Cowell senior wrote the Cowell memorandum.
40. penult. para. Lunn is being mischievous in suggesting relevant evidence may have been suppressed. Any such shortening of one rope (of which the Mason hearsay story is hardly reliable evidence) would no more have caused Old Peter to have to use the sashline than it would have prevented him from using it double or would have prevented the first five from delaying their departure for a few more minutes until Whymper was ready.
40. last 2 lines. Lunn conceded to Dangar & Blakeney (*AJ71*, 232) that this was wrong.
41/2. The charge of plotting murder was Lunn's own and he should have investigated the Cowell memorandum for himself, if he wanted to keep referring to murder on the basis of the sketchy, inadequate, inaccurate and misleading information provided by Smythe. He was not to know that Smythe had confused himself over its origin, but he should have appreciated as well as Dangar & Blakeney that so far as Whymper's conversations with the Cowell were concerned: 'too little is known on the latter subject for it to be wise for anyone to pronounce upon it' (*AJ71*, 234-5).
41/3. Lunn seems to have abandoned all prospect of credibility as a Matterhorn historian when he writes of Whymper's 'bogus pretence of scrupulous partiality'.
41/4. Lunn had nothing to be proud of in having misled Smythe.
42/3. Lunn's *AJ* article appeared *after* Furrer complimented Lunn, as the article itself indicates! Had Stephen's article reached Zermatt the Taugwalders would not have been at all pleased to find themselves described as 'comparatively incompetent', quite apart from the fact that Stephen did not attribute the 'accusation' to Whymper, as Lunn would have us believe, but

'rather regretted that he should not reject decidedly another grave, though less serious accusation' etc.
42/4. Another example of an unsubstantiated statement by Lunn intended to undermine what Whymper wrote.
42/5. Another 'uninformed verdict' by Lunn. He cannot have given any thought at all to why it should suddenly have seemed attractive to Old Peter to leave his wife and family at the age of 54 and go to America, when he could speak no language other than the Zermatt German dialect!
43. line 10. Once again Lunn provides no time scale. For many years Whymper's main source of income was the family business.
43/3. Lunn's unsympathetic first sentence is simply not true and almost on a par with what he condemns in Whymper on the next page (44/4). There is furthermore the distinction that (in the 44/4 quote) Whymper was only making a private note for himself some two years before his death, when his health was already failing, whereas Lunn was publishing a book. For Whymper's attitude towards Hudson and his death, see his correspondence and that of Montagnier.
44/1. As for Lunn's suggestion that Whymper knew he had attached himself to Hudson's expedition and that this rankled with him, there is nothing to say but that Hudson contributed nothing to the expedition, without which Whymper and Douglas would not have succeeded on their own. For the 'unfair attack' see *AJ71*, 235 (d).

6.18.9 *A Century of Mountaineering*

This book was commissioned by the Swiss Foundaton for Alpine Research in order to commemorate the Centenary of the Alpine Club and one might have expected Lunn to have honoured his role as author by writing an objective account. Surprising though it may seem, the major part of the section relating to Whymper (pp51-61) comes word for word from a book Lunn had published two years earlier, *Zermatt and the Valais*, in which he had accumulated many of the distortions and errors that he had been repeating since the early 1940's and was to continue to repeat until 1966. The most appropriate comment on Lunn's short cut, offering almost nothing new, is probably an extract from the Preface by Othmar Gurtner, who mistakenly believed that in choosing Lunn as author the Foundation would 'combine the factual approach of the historian with the personal interpretation of an essayist'. But so far as the section on Whymper is concerned, their worst fear seems to have been realised by Lunn, the fear that if they gave preference to an essayist, 'he might open too many windows onto his favourite foregrounds and the resultant draught might sweep away too many essential facts'. It is interesting to note from Lunn's Introduction that the typescript was in fact seen by T.S.Blakeney and that both he and D.F.O.Dangar, amongst others, read the proofs. Lunn did say that those who had helped him and made suggestions did not necessarily agree with everything he had written, but it would be interesting to learn Dangar & Blakeney's reaction to the Whymper section having regard to their forthright comments some ten years later, when most of it had been repeated yet again in Lunn's *Matterhorn Centenary* (see the extracts from *AJ71*, 111 quoted in 6.18 above). In view of the close similarity between the Whymper section here and what Lunn had written only two years before in *Zermatt and the Valais*, there is little purpose in repeating the comments already made above.

6.18.10 *The Bernese Oberland*

The Matterhorn has nothing to do with the Oberland but, in a chapter headed 'The Mountain Way of Life', Lunn took the opportunity of trying to denigrate Whymper by repeating that 'no member of the Alpine Club was ever given the slightest hint of how bitterly the Berglers of Zermatt resented Whymper's unjust attack on the Taugwalders'. As on previous occasions when Lunn wrote much the same, he made no attempt to explain what he was referring to as the 'unjust attack' nor when it was made. The ever closer unity between Taugwalder and 'his comrades and neighbours at Zermatt', suggested by Lunn each time he repeated this distortion, is wholly inconsistent with the evidence from various sources, not least that of Bernard Biner, as recorded in 1965 by Lunn himself in *Matterhorn Centenary* p142 below.

6.18.11 *Matterhorn Centenary*

This rehash of the errors and distortions of twenty five years, which in fact takes up less than a quarter of the book, the rest being devoted to various historical aspects of Zermatt and the Matterhorn as well as other early ascents and the first ascents of other routes on the mountain, was the subject of a twenty page review by Dangar & Blakeney in *AJ71* and there is little purpose in covering much of the same ground again here. The following notes are therefore confined to certain matters that Lunn raised for the first time in this book.

54. The penultimate sentence of the footnote about Hadow is interesting. It is wrong in stating that Hudson was tutoring him at the time of the accident, as he was then a former pupil (see McCormick, *A sad holiday* p4), but a number of writers have got the Hudson/Hadow status wrong. Lunn then goes on to state that Hudson had previously tutored Lord Francis Douglas and that the Queensberry and Hadow families were close friends and neighbours. Whereas there is no reason to suppose that Douglas was a former pupil, particularly when Lunn got Hadow's pupillage wrong, there is no knowing about the friends and neighbours. But either fact, if it were true, would have far-reaching implications. There is no hint anywhere, not even from Girdlestone, that Douglas knew either Hudson or Hadow, apart from the Vevey priest Ceresole stating in his *Führer von Zermatt* (p27) that Hadow's mother was a Douglas but without providing any evidence, and coming from Lunn it must be assumed that it is wrong.

64/1. Whymper had written to von Fellenberg on July 25.

64/2. It is not true to state that Whymper wrote with great bitterness of the Taugwalders in either letter. Lunn refers a little later to Whymper's original attacks on the Taugwalders being amplified in *Scrambles*, but he still does not clarify what he is referring to as the attacks.

66/3. It is misleading to state that Stephen 'defended Taugwalder against Whymper's charges'. Stephen did not even imply that Whymper had made the 'accusation', but simply expressed regret that he had not rejected decidedly 'another grave, though less serious accusation'. For the reason why Whymper probably shared Stephen's regret see section 2.48 (Leslie Stephen).

66/5. The reason 'no Swiss amateur...defended the Taugwalders' is that there was nothing to defend them against! See also Dangar & Blakeney in *AJ71*, 124, end of para 3. Had Egger been writing in 1870, he would have had no difficulty in keeping things in their proper perspective and would never have written such a distorted article.
68. last 2 lines. Albert Julen, born in 1895, would know nothing first hand of the events and was probably giving Lunn the answer he thought he wanted. Whymper's mild criticisms of the Taugwalders, such as they appear in *The Times* and in *Scrambles*, relate only to their post-accident conduct. In his letter to von Fellenberg, which was later related in the *Berner Sonntagspost*, Whymper actually stated : 'No blame can be attached to any of the guides; they all did their duty manfully'. There seems therefore to be no difference of opinion between Albert Julen and Edward Whymper and there is no reason to suppose that Julen initiated the monument to the Taugwalders simply as a result of reading too much Lunn!
70/3. Lunn conceded to Dangar & Blakeney (*AJ71*, 232) that he himself, rather than 'popular acclaim', was guilty of the 'uninformed verdict'.
141-2. Lunn's report of a conversation with Bernard Biner is interesting, as although the first part concentrates on the unspecified attack by Whymper and also refers to the idea of non-payment, whilst ignoring Whymper's statement that Young Peter had endeavoured to trade upon it, the second paragraph on p142 introduces something new. It refers to many guides being jealous of Taugwalder and states that 'some of them were really unpleasant about him. There were one or two disagreeable incidents. And then he drank a little too much and was criticised on that account by serious people. All of which explains why he emigrated to America.'

6.18.12 Whymper again

This relatively short article, Lunn's last on the subject, makes some concessions to Dangar & Blakeney, but tries to outwit them. It is hardly necessary to comment further here in view of their reply, which is published at the end of the article.

6.19
MONTAGNIER, HENRY FAIRBANKS (1877 – 1933)

Montagnier was a Europeanised American, whose friendship with Whymper and other celebrities inspired him to undertake laborious investigation into matters of early Alpine history. Although his research bore plentiful fruit in relation to the Balmat – Paccard first ascent and other early ascents of Mont Blanc in the form of articles in the *Alpine* and other *Journals*, an equally valuable achievement was Montagnier's collecting of Führerbücher and other records relating to the early history of the Matterhorn and other peaks in the Zermatt area. Not only did he ultimately secure an official copy of the numerous documents relating to the Enquiry that followed the accident on the first ascent of the Matterhorn, something Whymper himself had been unable to achieve, but his correspondence with Rudolf Taugwalder, the first custodian of the Zermatt Museum, enabled him to communicate indirectly with Young Peter Taugwalder and subsequently directly with him and to place on record his (none too reliable!) recollection of some of the details surrounding the first ascent.

As early as 1899 or 1900 he had made contact with Young Peter, trying the Zinal Rothorn with him, and in 1917 he wrote to Farrar of that occasion: 'I tried my best to make him talk but even with the aid of a few glasses of schnapps I found it almost impossible to pump him. It may be pure imagination on my part but that time I really fancied that there were details of the accident which he was determined not to divulge.' There is a letter of 8th May 1917 from Rudolf Taugwalder to Montagnier, which refers initially to the Brantschen family and then goes on to set out the answers to eight questions that Montagnier had asked Rudolf in an earlier letter of 23rd April to put to Young Peter. Rudolf refers to Peter being paid 50frs if he answers the questions. For a copy of Rudolf's letter and of Montagnier's typewritten note of the questions, both of which are in the Alpine Club Archives, see section 4.62 & 63.

Young Peter's 'Narrative' of the first ascent of the Matterhorn was published in 1957 (*AJ61*, 489-92), annotated by Dangar & Blakeney. On p484 there is reference to it being obtained by Montagnier and sent to Farrar, who intended to publish it in the *Journal*, but he never did so, and when it was eventually published there seems to have been some confusion over the whereabouts of the original. In 1992 it was possible to trace in the AC Archives one German version and an English translation, and it seems that this is the original German version, not written by Young Peter but signed by him on the last half page. The handwriting of the eight full page document is the same as that of a short (ninth?) page which concludes with Peter Taugwalder's signature. The fact that the signature is in Peter's hand gains support from the fact that another short typewritten document bears the same signature in the same rather shaky hand. The latter document (see 4.65) is the one mentioned by Dangar & Blakeney (*AJ61*, 484 para 1), in which Peter agrees to any shortening necessary for the purpose of publication. The AC Archives also include two handwritten copies of the 'Narrative' in a separate file, one in German and the other in French.

The 'Narrative' was written out by the same person who wrote to Montagnier on Peter's behalf on 27th November 1917, when the 'signature' was in the same writing as the letter and was not Young Peter's own. It was certainly not written by Rudolf and he does not, therefore, seem to have been involved with the 'Narrative'. It seems probable that the writer was one of two daughters with whom Peter was then living, probably Balbina born in 1894. The letter was thanking Montagnier for 50frs he had sent him and as it seems unlikely that this was late payment for the Answers in May, the explanation must be that it related to the 'Narrative', despite there being considerably more work involved in an eight and a half page account than in eight short answers.

So far as the content of the 'Narrative' is concerned it could be said that it contains virtually nothing that is new, apart from inaccuracies. Dangar & Blakeney dealt sympathetically with it and referred to only a few of the discrepancies, but the fact is that it is riddled with errors and it would serve no purpose to detail them all here. Nevertheless the document is of considerable interest and it does indirectly help to resolve one or two matters, such as the origin of the false report almost immediately after the accident that it was Lord Francis Douglas who slipped.

Montagnier's correspondence with Farrar, now in the AC Archives, contains some useful information about Whymper. A letter of 4th May 1917 includes:

> 'The one thing that impressed me in Whymper's chats with me about the accident was his attitude towards Hudson. He spoke of him as a man many years his senior who had had vastly more experience in mountaineering than he had had. In arranging the party Whymper told me that he relied mainly on Hudson's judgement, as the oldest man in the party and the most experienced climber. But he insisted that Hudson made a very grave mistake in admitting to the party an inexperienced youth of 18.'

Another letter of 9th April 1917 includes:

> 'Whymper whom I knew about as well as one can know a man about 40 years one's senior, often talked to me about the accident with the utmost frankness. I remember one evening in 1907 he came to dine with me...He regarded Hudson as an exceptionally competent mountaineer but blamed him severely for admitting such an inexperienced youth as Hadow to the party; in fact he maintained that the entire responsibility for the tragedy fell upon Hudson and that had Hadow been left in Zermatt they would have effected the descent without the least difficulty.'

Whymper had tried in 1910 to obtain a copy of the Enquiry Report with the assistance of Librairie Alexandre Jullien of Geneva, with whom he worked in close association prior to their publishing in 1911 the French edition of his *Zermatt Guide, Guide à Zermatt et au Cervin*. But his attempt proved unsuccessful and following his death Jullien did not pursue it further until Montagnier revived the matter some years later. Thanks to the intervention of the Cantonal Judge at Sion, M. Jean-Ch. de Courten, Jullien succeeded in May 1920 in obtaining a copy of the Official Enquiry Report, and extracts were published in French in *AJ33*, 234-47, followed by the comments of J.P.Farrar, one of the Editors of the *Journal*, dated October 8, 1920. For a complete list of the documents released, and now in the AC Archives, see section 5.1.

6.19.1 Early ascents of the Matterhorn

These extracts from the 'Travellers' Book' of the Hôtel du Mont Rose made by Montagnier, appear in *AJ31*, 87-94, (1917) and are of particular value now that the original book that included the years 1867 and 1868 can no longer be found.

6.20
MONTANDON, PAUL (1858 – 1948)

A very active Swiss climber, who made many first guideless ascents in the late 1870's and 1880's as well as some fifty first ascents above 3,000 metres, Montandon was the author of numerous articles in mountaineering journals, and he and Heinrich Dübi together wrote the important article on the 1865 accident, which appeared in *Die Alpen* in 1929. Montandon was an Honorary Member of the Alpine Club for thirty years, and his obituary appears in *AJ56*, 390-3.

Zum Matterhornunglück vom 14. Juli 1865. (With Heinrich Dübi) *Die Alpen V*. 1929, 203-23. For notes on the article see Dübi, section 6.10.2 above.

6.21
MÜLLER, HANS RICHARD

Müller appears to have been the Swiss Editor of *Berge der Welt 1964/65* and his Matterhorn Centenary article featured in the English version *The Mountain World* with the title 'The first ascent of the Matterhorn in the light of contemporary reports'. The book was reviewed by Blakeney in *AJ71*, 334-5, more than half of the review being devoted to the article so that there is little need to comment further on it here, as its real value lies not in Müller's commentary but in the documents and other extracts that accompany it. It is however necessary to point out that the extract from the *Sonntagspost* article of August 13, 1865 is but a very small part of the whole and that in the *Journal de Genève* of July 16 extract quoted on p17 John Tyndall's name should expressly appear in line four after the word 'climbers', as in the original French, instead of being relegated to a footnote.

The documents include facsimiles of the entry by Lord Francis Douglas in the St.Niklaus hotel guestbook on 26.6.65 and of two pages from Whymper's letter to von Fellenberg, as well as various newspaper extracts relating to the accident and several relating to the rumoured reward for making the first ascent.

The first ascent of the Matterhorn in the light of contemporary reports. *The Mountain World 1964/65*, 1-28.

6.22
RAMBERT, EUGÈNE (1830 – 1886)

Professor of literature at the Académie de Lausanne for six years before moving to the Ecole polytechnique fédérale in Zürich, Rambert wrote many books on mountains, his principal work being *Les Alpes suisses*. Despite his enthusiasm for the mountains he does not seem to have made many, if any, ascents of the major peaks, preferring the lesser limestone ranges.

The *Journal de Genève* published a letter from him on 28th July 1865 referring to the Matterhorn accident and in particular to the use of the rope, and after Whymper's letter had been published in *The Times* he amplified this and included a twenty page chapter in the first volume of *Les Alpes suisses*, which was published in 1866. He pointed out the risk of a multiple accident to a party roped together for the purpose of avoiding an individual accident, of which the risk might perhaps be ten times greater, and he emphasised the need to fix a baton in the snow or create some other form of fixed point. He specified a maximum of four on a rope and warned that there was nothing more illusory than the confidence inspired by a large number of climbers. He cast doubt on some of Whymper's statements and went into great detail to try and prove that it could not be right to state that 'the rope was tight between us, and the shock came on us both as on one man'. But he admitted that he did not know many relevant details and could not therefore apply his observations to the Matterhorn accident. He made the point that had it not been for Hadow's inexperience and the need for Croz to take hold of his legs and put his feet into their proper positions, then, if someone had found the climbing really difficult, he would not have forgotten at the critical moment to fix some rope to the rocks.

1. *Journal de Genève*. 28th July 1865.
2. *Les Alpes suisses*. Genève. 1866. A propos de l'accident du Cervin. Vol 1, 273-94.

6.23
RÉBUFFAT, GASTON (1921 – 1985)

Men and the Matterhorn is far more than a fine picture book by a great mountaineer, who really knew what he was writing about. It is a history book ranging from de Saussure's crossing of the Theodule pass in 1789 to the first winter ascent of the North face in 1962, with a final chapter describing some of Rébuffat's own experiences on the mountain. The first ascent and the catastrophe in 1865 are particularly well illustrated with many much enlarged, high quality details from Whymper's engravings, and a double page enlargement of Hadow's fall as depicted by Gustave Doré. Michel Croz' head fills another page with a mirror image based on the painting by Lance Calkin, and there is a fine double page enlargement of 'The Clubroom of Zermatt in 1864'. The quality of the reproduction of Bradford Washburn's superb aerial photographs is excellent.

Rébuffat's account of the events leading up to the first ascent is reliable, apart from the common error (attributable to the French translation of *Scrambles*) of stating that 'old Peter Taugwalder had climbed beyond the Hörnli a few days before'. Almost four pages are devoted to the ascent and more than six to the descent including Rébuffat's own original and pertinent comments on the issues that have given rise to so much controversy. However he does not seem to have appreciated that, following on Clemenz' failure to disclose Old Peter's answers to the questions he had handed in, Whymper was only recording the facts and was not making his own 'accusations' against Old Peter. Rébuffat's obituary, written by John Hunt, appears in *AJ91*, 282-3.

Men and the Matterhorn. London. 1967. (The book was originally published in 1965 in Paris as *Cervin: cime exemplair*, and also in Rüschlikon as *Das Matterhorn. Epos eines Zauberberges*)

6.23.1 *Men and the Matterhorn*

128/1&2. Whymper was neither making an accusation nor an insinuation. He was drawing attention to the fact that 'the suspicious fact' remained, and that Clemenz failure 'to give up answers that he has promised' allowed Old Peter 'to remain under unwarranted suspicion'. The suspicion was nothing new but had existed ever since it was realised, initially by those in Zermatt and subsequently by those beyond, that the rope that broke between Old Peter and Douglas was the thinnest and weakest rope they had. Whymper had 'handed in a number of questions which were framed so as to afford Old Peter an opportunity of exculpating himself from the grave suspicions which at once fell upon him'. Q28 in particular, until it became distorted in the course of being translated into German, asked 'Why was a different kind of rope used between Lord Douglas and yourself?' We now know that Clemenz probably did not dare to disclose to Whymper the answers he had promised, because he had allowed Q28 to be distorted and become 'Why was another rope used between Lord Douglas and yourself'. Publication of Old Peter's answers would never have allayed the suspicions, but Whymper was not to know this.

128/3. Rébuffat seems again to have been confused, although he might have realised from Tyndale's editing of the 6th edition of *Scrambles* had he seen it that Whymper's Q28 wording had never been put to Old Peter by the Tribunal. But it is misleading to imply that Whymper 'uttered the most terrible insinuations' and that he did so *before* the Tribunal's failure to conduct a proper and thorough Enquiry. If the questions had been asked and the answers published, Whymper would not have had to write the long footnote, and Old Peter might never even have become 'nearly incapable for work – not absolutely mad, but with intellect gone and almost crazy'.

128/4. Any omission must have been deliberate to the extent that the Tribunal never addressed the important issues. It relied entirely on Whymper to put Questions 22-35 to Old Peter on the first day, when apart from the ambiguous Q36 it did not ask him a single question of substance of its own.

128/5. The answer must be 'yes', judging from Old Peter's answers. In A24 he said the rope between him and Douglas was a special rope, whereas in A26 he described the Croz – Douglas rope as 'strong and brand-new'. A53 shows that he had in mind fixing rope.

133/1. The tired looking sashline now in the Zermatt Museum hardly seems capable of rivalling any 'strong and brand-new' thicker rope in anyone's thoughts, unless it should have had some special quality that was not apparent to the eye.

133/8. There are several grounds for doubting whether this answer can have been correct. Old Peter seems to have hugged a rock with both arms, but he is unlikely to have belayed the rope, see the note about A64 in section 5.4.3.

6.24
REY, GUIDO (1861 – 1935)

Rey's name will for ever be associated with the Matterhorn on account of his great book that bears its name, first published in Milan in 1904. The equally splendid English edition appeared in 1907, and there were also French and German translations. The book is full of interesting historical details and extends from the pioneers who first explored the valleys and passes at the foot of the mountain to Rey's own pioneering attempts to climb the Furggen ridge in the 1890's. The *Alpine Journal*'s review of the original Italian edition (*AJ22*, 86-7) commented how: 'The book has all the charm which thorough knowledge of the subjects treated of, warm appreciation of the good points of others, a genial sense of humour, kindly sympathy, and generous enthusiasm can give'.

Rey, whose lengthy obituary appears in *AJ48*, 149-56, was a nephew of Quintino Sella who had hoped to climb the Matterhorn with Giordano in 1865, and the book contains extracts from a good deal of original material including letters Sella received from Giordano, as well as from the latter's diaries. A new less elaborate English edition appeared in 1946, with the text revised by R.L.G.Irving and with two additional chapters by him, bringing the history of the mountain up to date. The book itself certainly lacks the splendour of the early editions with their fine drawings, but it contains a wide range of interesting photographs which like the text are not confined to the Italian side, but do justice to Zermatt as well.

In his book *Le Cervin* (vol 1, 194-6) Charles Gos published a letter he had received from Guido Rey in 1921, after sending Rey a couple of letters he had received from Coolidge purporting to tell Gos in great secrecy that he had just heard from a most reliable source, Conway, that the rope had been cut on the Matterhorn in 1865. The second letter referred indirectly to G.F.Browne, to whom Whymper had told everything in 1865, and to this proving that Whymper was a liar, although Coolidge himself had been convinced of it for a long time! It is hard to understand how anyone could have doubted, particularly from the abundance of exclamation marks in the first letter, but that Coolidge was being mischievous and that there could be no substance whatever in his secret. We do not know exactly what Gos wrote to Rey, but he gives the impression in his book that he added credence to the absurdity, when he talks of his dilemma as to whether he should betray Coolidge's trust by confiding the secret to one of his best friends. Rey's reply certainly implies that Gos had communicated an indisputable fact, as he questions the value of such a revelation that could benefit no one, even if he himself was not going to let it affect his judgment. It is rather pathetic that Gos should have acted as he did and that he should then have followed it up by publishing Rey's reply, particularly when Rey had replied to him in good faith, giving his word of honour that he would not tell anyone what Gos had confided in him. But it is to the great credit of Guido Rey, and a tribute to his generous and warm-hearted nature, that he should have expressed to Charles Gos his own belief:

> 'No! There is in all this something mean and evil which troubles me deeply. For me, despite everything, the figure of Whymper still stands high and very noble. He is an artist, he is a creator – you should understand me, you who live by art and for art. – The others are nothing but archivists, little library rats who do not know how to create and who love to destroy.'

The Matterhorn. London. 1907. Revised edition. (Edited by R.L.G.Irving) Oxford. 1946.

6.25
ROTH, ABRAHAM (1823 – 1880)

A journalist by profession, Roth was one of the founders of the Bern newspaper *Der Bund* and, until he resigned in 1865, he spent 15 years on the editorial staff. Roth then founded the *Sonntagspost* which he himself edited. Details of his other journalistic enterprises appear in a short biography by Paul Sieber in *Les Alpes. XXXIX*. 1963, 103-4. *Der Bund* was one of the newspapers in which Whymper had hoped his letter of 25th July 1865 to von Fellenberg might be published, not knowing that von Fellenberg was already away climbing in the Oberland. There was therefore some delay in his receiving the letter which he ultimately passed to Roth.

Roth and von Fellenberg were founder members of the SAC and some of their climbs together are described in Roth's book *The Doldenhorn and Weisse Frau*. Roth reported what Whymper had written to von Fellenberg, in an article in the *Sonntagspost* of 13th August. The article had been in the press when Whymper's letter appeared in *The Times* on 8th August and, as a French translation of the *Times* letter had also appeared in the *Journal de Genève* on 12th August, it inevitably lost some of the impact it might otherwise have had. Roth's own comments on the Matterhorn disaster are remarkable for their constructive approach and for the knowledge and experience on which they were so obviously based. He had also written about the accident at some length on 30th July, an extract from this appearing in *The Mountain World 1964/65*. In the August 20th number Roth wrote of the fresh details disclosed in Whymper's letter to *The Times* and, although he made some errors in relation to the ropes, he seems to have written far more common sense than was to be found elsewhere. He referred to Whymper being dissatisfied about the ropes and having handed in to the Examining Magistrate in Zermatt a list of questions which should be put to Taugwalder, and to his still being in ignorance of the answers although they had been promised. Roth went on to emphasise the need to publish the evidence, in view of the malicious nonsense doing the rounds of the European press, and he quoted a long extract from the *Anzeiger von Interlaken*, which is believed to have been written by Peter Ober, denouncing the Meissner article.

Sonntagspost. 30.7.65. Extract in *MW64/65*, 20-2. Referred to by Dübi in *SACJ 47* (1911) 194.

Sonntagspost. 13.8.65. Very short extract in *MW64/65*, 25. Long extract quoted by Dübi in *SACJ 47* (1911) 195-8.

Sonntagspost. 20.8.65. Long extracts in *MW64/65*, 25-8 and Dübi 198-200.

6.26
SCHÄFER, KARLROBERT (1894 – 1970)

Schäfer appears to have been a Swiss Matterhorn enthusiast, writing two articles in *Die Alpen* on the huts on the mountain and another with the title 'Day of destiny on the Matterhorn'. Charles Gos referred to him as the founder of the 'Archives du Cervin' at Basel [later given to the Zermatt Museum], and he must be the one referred to by Cicely Williams in her book, *Zermatt Saga* (p169), as the keeper of the Matterhorn archives in Basel who was present at a dinner given in honour of Ethel Blandy in Zermatt in 1949. But despite his enthusiasm, Schäfer's Matterhorn article rather implies that he was not too familiar with the finer details of his subject. His articles are:

1. Die Solvayhütte am Matterhorn. *Die Alpen. XX*. 1944, 177-85.
2. Hütten am Matterhorn. *Die Alpen. XXIV*. 1948, 275-82.
3. Schicksaltag am Matterhorn. *Die Alpen. XXX*. 1954, 111-12.

6.26.1 and 6.26.2 are beyond the scope of this book.

6.26.3 Schicksaltag am Matterhorn

111/3. Schäfer attributes Old Peter's emigration to America to the rumours about cutting the rope and says that after a while homesickness and longing drove him to return to his mountains. Unfortunately he does not quote any evidence in support, and he may merely be repeating other writers.

111/3. lines 11-13. He refers to being able to read about Old Peter in the reports of contemporary mountaineers who saw him in Zermatt and over in Valtournanche, but unfortunately he does not identify either the reports or the mountaineers.

111/4 line 1. Clemenz did not hold the Enquiry in the Hotel Monte Rosa, but in his own Hotel Mont Cervin.

111/4 line 3. It is hardly true to say that the Enquiry produced a faultless clarification of the subject, particularly now that it appears as though some of Whymper's questions for Old Peter were deliberately altered and that Clemenz himself only asked Old Peter one question of substance on his first examination. It is also open to doubt as to whether prompt publication would have led to Old Peter's early rehabilitation and put a stop to the rumours, as Clemenz so obviously failed to clear up the questions relating to the use of the weakest rope. Furthermore Carl Egger, whom Schäfer goes on to praise at inordinate length, wrote in *Pioniere* (p192) that publication might have caused 'even more unrest in the community', and presumably even more trouble for Old Peter.

111/4 lines 11-14. Schäfer bemoans the unavailiblity of the original protocol, but the Alpine Club has a copy of the German original and for many years the Zermatt Museum has also had a copy of Old Peter's German evidence.

112/3 lines 1-5. It seems to have been the Zermatters themselves who first said that Old Peter had cut the rope. See the *Graphic* 1894 and also Egger's article apparently accepting this evidence in *Die Alpen XVI*, 277.
112/3 line 7 to end. The long final paragraph gives the impression that Schäfer may have known far less about the subject than one might have expected. His unstinted praise for Egger, as a passionate seeker of truth and for his Matterhorn (sic!) book, suggests that he himself can have had only a superficial knowledge of the subject. There is certainly no justification for writing of Egger's objectivity and sense of justice in relation to the Taugwalder chapter in *Pioniere der Alpen*, and one wonders whether Schäfer would still have thought and written of Carl Egger with such 'deep respect and gratitude', if he had considered all the evidence!

6.27
SCHMID, WALTER

Menschen am Matterhorn was published in 1964 in anticipation of the centenary of the first ascent. It details the history of the mountain from the earliest attempts and devotes some forty pages to the 1865 ascent, the accident and its aftermath. Schmid wrote a number of books about mountaineering and seems to have been particularly fond of the Zermatt area. He does not however reveal anything new about the accident or its aftermath apart from confirming the probability that Old Peter was accompanied by his youngest son Friedrich when he went to America.

Menschen am Matterhorn. Bern. 1964.

6.27.1 *Menschen am Matterhorn*

47/2. Douglas was accompanied by Joseph and not Peter Taugwalder. Carrel was hardly a legendary figure before he succeeded in making the first Italian ascent.
59/1. For the Coolidge mischief, see his letter of 24.1.1921 to Charles Gos in the latter's book, *Le Cervin* 1, 192.
67/2. There is no evidence of Birkbeck's attempt on 14th July 1866 having to be abandoned on account of the weather rather than the nervousness of his seven guides; see section 2.3 (Birkbeck).
69/2. There is no reason to suppose that Grove was a naval officer, although he did go to sea for a while before he took up mountaineering. It seems to have been Canon Carrel who instigated the idea of breaking J-A Carrel's monopoly.
71/2&3. Jordan deserves some of the credit for opening up the Hörnli as, although he got no further than the scene of the accident climbing from Zermatt in August and September 1867, he reached the summit from Breuil that October, spent three hours exploring the upper part of the Hörnli route that he did not already know and then wrote a detailed account in the Monte Rosa guestbook which clearly inspired Elliott the following year.
83/4. Emigration to America may have been nothing unusual for someone like 24 year old Friedrich Taugwalder at that time, although this is not free from doubt, but it can hardly have been so for a married man of 54, who could speak no language other than the Zermatt dialect of German! There is no evidence of Old Peter leading any successful ascents after the accident, other than that with Stogden.
84/1. It is difficult to determine the number of guides in the valley in 1865, but the SAC

article on glacier guides published that year suggests there were many more experienced guides at Zermatt than at St.Niklaus. The Zermatt guides certainly became jealous of the Knubels and of J-M Lochmatter a few years later, after allowing them to acquire a local monopoly of the Matterhorn.

6.28
SCHUSTER, CLAUD (1869 – 1956)

A member of the Alpine Club for more than 60 years, Lord Schuster distinguished himself in public life. He also made a considerable contribution to mountaineering literature with such books as *Peaks and Pleasant Pastures*, but is included here for the review of Smythe's *Edward Whymper* in the *Alpine Journal*, which is generally believed to have been written by him. E.H.Stevens referred to it in *AJ53*, 156 as 'surely one of the the best things ever written about Whymper'.

Review. *Edward Whymper*. By Frank S.Smythe. *AJ52*, 147-51, 1940.

6.29
SMYTHE, FRANCIS SYDNEY (1900 – 1949)

One of the leading Alpine and Himalayan climbers of his generation and also an accomplished writer and photographer, Frank Smythe was probably the most successful of the early British professional mountaineers. He helped to introduce mountains to the general public with his many books about climbs, ski runs and Himalayan expeditions, and also with his books of mountain photographs and his lectures.

His biography of *Edward Whymper*, published in 1940, is unrivalled and has been translated into German, French and Japanese. Chapters 8, 9 & 10 deal with the Matterhorn ascent, the disaster and the repercussions, but there is much else besides that has a bearing on the aftermath. There would seem to be a distinct possibility that if Smythe had not fallen out with Graham Brown they might have produced some sort of joint work on Whymper and the Matterhorn, as Graham Brown carried out a far greater amount of research on aspects to which Smythe makes no reference than could ever be justified by his one fifteen page article in the *Alpine Journal* published some fifteen or twenty years later.

It is sad to recall Arnold Lunn's proud belief (see *Zermatt and the Valais*, 41) that his article 'Taugwalder and the Matterhorn' in *AJ55*, 290-6 influenced Smythe and led him to write some of the extraordinary things that appear in his Introduction to the 1949 edition of Whymper's *Travels amongst the Great Andes of the Equator*. Smythe had inexplicably but innocently taken the Cowell memorandum out of its context, when he revealed it's existence in *Edward Whymper*, and this misled both Lunn and Egger to seize upon it with relish. Lunn compounded Smythe's error and in so doing seems to have induced him to tell his *Andes* readers, wrongly, that 'Whymper wrote an extraordinary letter to the Secretary of the Alpine Club in which he accused the Taugwalders of wanting to murder him'.

In addition to the Whymper biography and the *Andes* Introduction, there is in the Alpine Club Archives a letter that Smythe wrote to Herbert E.Cooke in October 1939, replying to a letter enclosing some extracts from W.H.Lewin's lecture on 'The First Ascent of the Matterhorn'. Smythe's reply and his marginal notes on the Lewin extracts which he returned to Cooke are of interest, particularly the former, as it helps in tracing his confusion over the Cowell memorandum and it is therefore included below, as if it were a published work. His three Whymper/Matterhorn 'works' are therefore:

1. A letter dated 9.10.39 addressed to Herbert E. Cooke.
2. *Edward Whymper*. Published in 1940.
3. Whymper. *Travels amongst the Great Andes of the Equator*; edited with an Introduction by F.S.Smythe. 5-20. 1949.

6.29.1 Letter to H.E.Cooke. 9.10.39 (see section 4.67)

This letter helps to exclude the possibility of a typographical error in the *Andes* Introduction (see below). The fact that Smythe got the two memoranda so confused suggests that he paid no attention to the Cowell and Wills correspondence with Whymper about them and could not therefore tell his readers how either memorandum came into existence.

Extracts from the first page: 'You have not seen Whymper's memorandum to Cowell Hon sec. of the A.C at that time. He was obviously greatly exercised in his mind over the conduct of the Taugwalders after the accident...He accuses the Taugwalders of trying to encompass his death after the accident & states that he *stood* all night when bivouacking with his back to a wall prepared to defend himself as by their callous behaviour he suspected that they would prefer to be the sole survivors on account of the publicity it would give them.'

6.29.2 *Edward Whymper*

174/4. The 11th July should be the 10th.
176. line 1. The guide was not young Peter Taugwalder, but his brother Joseph, the porter on the Matterhorn on 13th July.
176. lines 11-15. There is in fact no evidence of Old Peter prospecting the east face of the Matterhorn from the Hörnli, unless this extends to the 1862 winter attempt with Kennedy.
176. lines 15-16. Smythe's paraphrase of what Whymper wrote in *Scrambles* rather implies that Douglas was already intending to attempt the ascent that week, but this cannot have been so.
187. penultimate line. 'little more than a sash-line'. It was in fact one of 'those plaited ropes which are generally supposed to be so strong' which, in the 1864 Alpine Club Committee's initial test of the strain produced by twelve stone falling five feet, 'gave way in such a manner as was very startling to some of our number, who had been in the habit of using these treacherous cords with perfect and most unfounded confidence'.
188. lines 1-3. It is most unlikely that these two ropes were each of a single length in view of

Whymper stating in the tenth paragraph of chapter 20 of *Scrambles* that 'In 1865 we carried two 100 feet lengths of the Manilla rope'.
189/3. Unfortunately the question itself was rather misleading.
191. four lines from end. The sharp-eyed boy was Taugwalder's youngest son.
194. line 14. The memorandum was in fact written out by Whymper on the advice of J.W.Cowell.
195/4. The wording of the first line was unfortunate and no doubt contributed to Smythe's confusion as it was the Cowell memorandum itself which began: 'The foregoing Memorandum [written by Whymper and dated 17.8.65] records the substance of a communication to the Undersigned on Wednesday August 2. 1865 by Edward Whymper in answer to questions which they put to him...' But Smythe went on to say that in the memorandum 'it is stated that after the accident the Taugwalders "displayed the most abject cowardice, entire want of resource..."' But this comes from the memorandum drawn up by Cowell from which Smythe quotes 22 lines, and not from the 'foregoing' Whymper memorandum. But Smythe's major error was to take the Cowell memorandum out of its context, omit the heading and the first five lines and not tell his readers how it came to be made after Wills had advised Whymper to get the Cowells to endorse his own memorandum of 17th August. Had Smythe quoted the Cowell memorandum in its entirety, he might have avoided his subsequent blunder of stating in the *Andes* Introduction, that 'Whymper wrote an extraordinary letter to the Secretary of the Alpine Club in which he accused the Taugwalders of wanting to murder him'! For further consideration of the subject see section 3.2 (The Cowell memorandum).
196. footnote. The memorandum, or certificate, was in fact an enclosure accompanying Cowell's letter to Whymper of 4.9.65.
205. lines 1-2. Farrar's mistake about Old Peter being the best guide in Zermatt is repeated by many of the critics, but there is no doubt that Peter Perren was streets ahead of him.
205/5. The leading article in question was published on 27.7.65. This would make Whymper's arrival in England the 26th July, but that was the date he left Interlaken to return via Bern, Neuchatel and Paris.
215. line 2. Whymper's same use of the word 'pleasant' recurs on pp218 & 236.
215. line 4. The word 'rumour' should read 'nonsense'.
226-227. Smythe did not apparently see any 1869 diary and it may not have survived. Whymper certainly engaged Carrel for eight days until 3rd August; a week later he left London for Turin, and he was in Zermatt on 1st September!
232. footnote. The portrait on p316 is not the right one – see *AJ26*, 58.
233/2 line 3. The 2nd edn. of *Scrambles* appeared in the autumn of 1871.

6.29.3 Smythe's Introduction to Whymper's *Andes*

9/4. Douglas's guide was not Young Peter but Joseph Taugwalder.
10/1. Old Peter Taugwalder was not engaged as an additional guide, but had been engaged by Douglas and Whymper before they met Hudson.
11/3. For Dangar & Blakeney's comments on the 'vile insinuation' see *AJ71*, 234 para (b). Smythe also used the word vile in *Edward Whymper*, p214.
12/3. 'Later, Whymper wrote an extraordinary letter to the Secretary of the Alpine Club in which he accused the Taugwalders of wanting to murder him. He wrote that he had to protect himself from them by standing all night on the ledge with his back to the rocks and ice axe in hand.' Whymper wrote no such letter, nor was J.J.Cowell the Secretary in 1865, but in 1863-4.

Had Smythe fully appreciated the circumstances in which the Cowell memorandum came into existence following the advice of Cowell senior and of Alfred Wills, and had he made this known to his readers, a great deal of unnecessary and unjust criticism of Whymper would have been avoided. Arnold Lunn responded almost immediately with comments like 'this monstrous suggestion', 'a charge of attempted murder' and 'this fantastic absurdity', and he later wrote in his article 'Taugwalder and the Matterhorn' in *AJ55*, 293: 'Mr.Smythe has done a disservice to Whymper's memory by publishing this document, but a real service to truth and to justice'. Lunn's 'uninformed verdict' may not on this occasion have been entirely his own fault, although it was published three years before Smythe made his *Andes* blunder. But Dangar & Blakeney's comment on Whymper's meeting with the Cowells, made in 1966 (*AJ71*, 234) when Lunn was still criticising Whymper about 'fearing that the Taugwalders might murder him', would have applied equally to the years immediately following Smythe's publication of Cowell: 'As regards...Whymper's conversations with the Cowells, we think too little is known on the latter subject for it to be wise for anyone to pronounce upon it.'

6.30
TAUGWALDER, HANNES (1910 –)
JAGGI, MARTIN (– 1987)

It appears as though most of the research for their book, *Der Wahrheit näher*, was carried out by Jaggi, whereas most of the book was actually written or put together by Taugwalder after Jaggi's death. In the process a large number of errors and distortions have found their way into the book and prevented it from living up to its title, 'Nearer to the truth'. It would be impracticable to attempt to detail them all here.

Der Wahrheit näher. Aarau. 1990. (Review in *AJ97*, 311-2)

6.31
TYNDALE, HARRY EDWARD GUISE (1888 – 1948)

An able mountaineer and a schoolmaster, Tyndale translated a number of German mountaineering books into English, he edited the Blackwell's Mountaineering Library re-issue of various Alpine classics and for ten years he was Editor of the *Alpine Journal*. His book *Mountain Paths* refers in chapter 5 to the Matterhorn, describing one of his ascents, from Breuil, and also commenting on the historical associations of the route. But his main literary connection with the mountain comes from the 6th edition of Whymper's '*Scrambles*', which he edited and John Murray published in 1936.

Edward Whymper. *Scrambles amongst the Alps*. With additional illustrations and material from the Author's unpublished diaries. Revised and Edited by H.E.G.Tyndale'. [6th edition] 1936.

6.31.1 6th edition of *Scrambles*

Preface p.VII lines 6-9. Tyndale states that if Whymper had realised 'how greatly feeling in England was stirred by the disaster...he would assuredly have made public his own account at the earliest possible moment', but this does seem to be contrary to the weight of the evidence. Whymper was reluctant to give a full account for several reasons. McCormick's letter to *The Times* 'was intentionally silent on certain points, including the exact cause of the accident, in order to spare the families of Messrs Hadow and Hudson the additional pain they must feel if it is published', and even after writing his own letter to *The Times* Whymper seems to have remained unconvinced that it was right for him to say anything.

Chapter 3, The Mont Cenis etc., was omitted from the 6th edition, as was also the tenth paragraph of the old chapter 20, referring to 'A committee of the English Alpine Club...appointed in 1864 to test and to report upon, the most suitable ropes for mountaineering purposes'. The same paragraph also referred to Whymper using in 1865 'two 100 feet lengths of the Manilla rope' approved by the Committee. The report highlighted the question of suitable ropes and showed how plaited ropes like those formerly used by Whymper were not suitable. Had Whymper realised that the likes of Egger would suggest that he made too much of the difference between the sashline and the Manilla, he would doubtless have quoted some extracts from the Committee's report.

323. footnote 1. This answer by Young Peter to one of the questions posed by Montagnier in his letter of 23.4.1917 (which has not survived) serves to undermine completely his 'Narrative' written some six months later. It is inconsistent with almost everything else that has ever been written on the subject and its only possible value is to confirm Young Peter's unreliability and prejudice. The word 'also' has been omitted from 'Old Peter also said...'

330/5. Tyndale's footnote, 'The questions, with old Peter's answers, are shown in Appendix H', has largely escaped the critics' notice, as have pages 374-6.

367. Appendix F. A modern view of the 1865 accident. There are unfortunately a number of errors in Farrar's article – see section 6.14.2 above.

374. Appendix H. Interrogation of Old Peter Taugwalder. This gives an English translation of the French translation of Taugwalder's German answers, and in one or two instances it differs significantly from what he actually said. As for the questions, Tyndale distinguished between those handed in by Whymper (22-35) and those asked by Clemenz (36 & 53-64), but he allowed himself to be confused by the existence of Whymper's original English draft as well as the French version he actually handed in, quite apart from the actual questions put to Taugwalder in German. As a result he sometimes quoted an answer against a question that was never asked in so many words – see sections 5.2.2, 5.4.2 and 5.5.

377. footnote. Old Peter's reply was distorted in the course of being translated into French. He actually stated that Whymper was 'in a place where he could see the unfortunate course of events better than I could'.

381. Whymper–Robertson 27.8.65. This letter appears to be quoted in full, but there are omissions, one of which involves the penultimate sentence. After the word 'propagated' Whymper actually wrote 'and among them it was said that *I* cut the rope from fear of being pulled over', see section 4.49.

383. line 4. Despite Whymper's concern about the disposition of the lines, something subsequently went awry, as not only did the mason disregard the lines when cutting the stone but many words are interrupted with a hyphen in the most unlikely places!

383. lines 6-16. The two French verses are not those sent by Whymper, which were in English, but come from Robertson's reply suggesting some modifications to the second verse.

Whymper adopted them, although the wording underwent some further minor alterations before it finally reached the stone.

6.32
UNSWORTH, WALTER (1928 –)

Best known perhaps for his highly acclaimed definitive work on Everest, Walt Unsworth has been writing books about mountaineering and its history for more than thirty years, including the life and adventures of both Whymper and Mummery. *Matterhorn man* was published in 1965, coinciding with the centenary of the first ascent of the Matterhorn, and it seems to have been aimed at the growing number of young people taking an interest in mountaineering at that time. It gives a reliable, straightforward account of the Matterhorn's early history, the first ascent and the accident, as well as Whymper's other mountaineering achievements. Based mainly on *Scrambles*, Rey's *The Matterhorn* and Smythe's biography *Edward Whymper* it is refreshingly free from the distortions and 'uninformed verdicts' too often found elsewhere.

Matterhorn man. The Life and Adventures of Edward Whymper. London. 1965.

6.33
WILLIAMS, CICELY (– 1985)

Cicely Williams was for very many years a regular visitor to Zermatt where her husband, who became Bishop of Leicester, was Summer Chaplain at the English Church from 1946 until 1978. She wrote several books including *Women on the Rope*, but her first mountain book was *Zermatt Saga*, published in 1964. This nice book gives a general and personal account of the development of Zermatt; it is neither a history book nor a guide book, and there is no need to detail here a number of errors in what was designed 'to give enjoyment to ordinary readers', in the words of its reviewer in the *Alpine Journal* (*AJ70*, 173). However it should be pointed out that amongst several entries quoted from the guestbook of the Hotel Monte Rosa are those in fact made in the Riffelhaus book in July 1865 by Lord Francis Douglas and by Townsend. There seems to have been some general confusion between the books for a number of years.

Cicely Williams also wrote a booklet for the Commonwealth and Continental Church Society on the occasion of the centenary of the English Church in Zermatt. Again there are some minor inaccuracies and in one of the illustrations the Matterhorn appears back to front, a fault by no means uncommon in brochures for skiing holidays!

1. *Zermatt Saga*. London, 1964. Brig, 1970. (There have also been two editions in German)
2. *A Church in the Alps*. 1970.

6.34
WUNDT, THEODOR (1858 – 1929)

A high-ranking officer in the German army, Wundt wrote a number of mountaineering books, but appears to have had a particular interest in the Matterhorn. The text of his profusely illustrated book on the Matterhorn and its history (*Das Matterhorn und seine Geschichte*) pays no very special attention to the 1865 first ascent and accident but gives a general account of the mountain and its historical associations. There is a very detailed description of the ascent from Breuil and a shorter one of the Hörnli. Most of the mountain's fatalities are mentioned including Carrel, Brantschen, Moseley, Borckhardt, Göhrs and Seiler.

Wundt seems to have been one of the first to take an interest in the old hotel guestbooks and he included in facsimile the entry that Whymper made in the Monte Rosa book on 1st September 1869 and the names of many well-known mountaineers, as well as photographs of some of Alexander Seiler's relics of mountaineering accidents. The photograph of Douglas's boot is useful in resolving the recent confusion between it and another said to have belonged to Hadow. Wundt quotes the wording on the Croz memorial stone and refers to another stone commemorating Douglas.

Although he has quite a bit to say about Seiler's problems with the Zermatters, Wundt says nothing more contentious about the 1865 accident than that it is not known whether Old Peter's use of the weakest rope resulted from carelessness or the deliberate intention of safeguarding himself. He seems however to be the only writer who has ever quoted the account in the *Graphic* of 29th September 1894 of Franz Andenmatten being ejected from the church at Zermatt when, after successfully leading Whymper's search party, he next attended Mass.

A revised edition with a new title, published in 1930 after Wundt's death, is more of a general guide to climbs and excursions in the Zermatt area and although much of the original text is retained the facsimile guestbook names, the relics and the fine reproductions of Gustave Doré's 1865 lithographs are omitted. Wundt also wrote a very readable Matterhorn novel, which seems to have sold well in its day.

1. *Das Matterhorn und seine Geschichte*. Berlin. [1896]
2. *Zermatt und seine Berge*. Zürich. 1930.
3. *Matterhorn. Ein Hochgebirgs Roman*. Berlin. [1918]

6.35
YOUNG, GEOFFREY WINTHROP (1876 – 1958)

A distinguished mountaineer and writer of mountaineering prose and verse, Young exercised a profound influence on all aspects of British mountaineering during the first half of the twentieth century, despite losing a leg in the First World

War. Aside from his own experiences on the Matterhorn, however, he wrote very little about the mountain, but he did include Whymper as one of his subjects in two articles he wrote on 'Mountain Prophets', the first appearing in the *Cornhill Magazine* in 1923, the second in the *Alpine Journal* in 1943.

Young first met Charles Gos on the summit of the Matterhorn, when Gos had just completed the first guideless ascent of the Zmutt ridge, and they seem to have corresponded at intervals thereafter. Gos submitted to Young the chapter 'La corde maudite' in his book *Le Cervin*, but the only extracts he quoted from Young's reply (vol 1, 196-7) related to some mischievous letters Gos received from Coolidge and to the supposed 'secret' that Whymper confided in G.F.Browne after the accident. It would have been interesting to learn Young's reaction to the chapter as a whole, as it was so uncharacteristic of Gos and contained numerous errors and distortions.

1. Mountaineering and its Prophets. *Cornhill Magazine*. 1923. (See extract in Smythe's *Edward Whymper*, 230-3. Smythe in fact made an error over the second Whymper portrait to which Young referred, which is not the one he included on page 316 but that in *AJ26*, 58)

2. Mountain Prophets. *AJ54*, 102-6, 1943.

7
SOURCES

7.1
HOW TO USE THEM

The sources are intended to provide the origin of, or the authority for, any significant, dubious or obscure facts and statements in sections 2 and 3, to draw the attention of historians to other documents and publications that may be relevant and to make known the whereabouts of original or copy correspondence and other archive material. Reference is also made to some of the principal works of a biographical nature.

Whereas the reader familiar with a particular subject may be able to go straight to the sources and use them to determine what further reading matter may be relevant or available, they are primarily intended to justify the text and are therefore sometimes dependent on it. A single quotation or reference in the text to an author may be backed up in the sources by the author's name, the title of the work and the page number without any reference to the topic concerned, but when two or more references in the text relate to different topics in the same work the page numbers in the sources are distinguished by explanatory words. There is some duplication amongst the various characters' and subjects' sources in order to reduce the need to look elsewhere, so that something as important as Whymper's letter to *The Times* may perhaps feature a dozen times or more. But not all the books or articles in which a document or quotation has been reproduced may be quoted every time, in order to save space. If, therefore, it is not possible to get access to any of the publications quoted, it may sometimes be worth looking elsewhere in the sources for an alternative, preferably under the name of the person or subject most directly related to the document or topic in question.

For the most part, Whymper's *Guide to Zermatt and the Matterhorn* has been excluded from the sources as it follows so closely the chapters in *Scrambles* that cover the first ascent and the subsequent accident, and it has a very good index of its own. As for *Scrambles*, the many different editions pose a problem as it would be far too complicated to quote against each subject each of the four different number sequences used in the first six English editions. *Scrambles* 1 (the 1st edn) shares its numbering with *Scrambles* 2 (2nd edn) and *Scrambles* 4 & 5 share a separate sequence. *Scrambles* 6 is different again but is equally important, being probably the most common edition in use to-day. *Scrambles* 3, the abridged edition entitled *The Ascent of the Matterhorn*, is completely different again and it has been necessary to disregard it for the most part on account of its rarity and the fact that it does have an index of its own. At the end of section 7.3.14 (the sources for *Scrambles amongst the Alps*) will be found a table in which the page numbers in *Scrambles* 1 (or 2), *Scrambles* 4 (or 5) and *Scrambles* 6 are compared, making it possible to convert from one edition or numbering sequence to another, assuming that the particular subject features in both editions. But this will not always be the case with the additions and deletions that Whymper himself introduced in *Scrambles* 4 any more than with the amendments made by Tyndale in *Scrambles* 6.

The present whereabouts of archive material is recorded where it is known and in one or two instances this extends to identifying a library that has a copy of a particularly rare or obscure leaflet or periodical, such as the 1895 issue of the *Journal de Zermatt* containing the text of the interview with Whymper in which he recounted the first ascent of the Matterhorn. As for the books, almost all of them appear in one or more of the comprehensive catalogues of the three principal Alpine libraries, the Alpine Club Library in London, the National Library of Scotland in Edinburgh and the Swiss Alpine Club Library in Zürich, and the sources do not therefore include any reference to where a particular book may be found.

The sources are primarily based on the literature available in the English language, but a number of French, German and even Italian sources are quoted as well when they are considered to be of sufficient importance, particularly when there is no English version available. The title of a book, if not quoted in full, may be determined from the bibliography below. Several of the more frequently quoted books are occasionally referred to solely by the author's name or by only one word from the title, and these can be identified from the list of abbreviations. The distinguishing feature between a photocopy or typewritten copy of an original letter and a copy of the same letter made and retained by its writer is also explained in the list of abbreviations.

7.2
THE PRINCIPAL CHARACTERS

7.2.1 Andenmatten, F

(a) Biography

Obituary. AJ11, 345.
Biographical note. AJ70, 202.
Cunningham & Abney. The Pioneers of the Alps. 235-9 (Conway).
Egger. Pioniere der Alpen. 156-66.
SAC Jahrbuch 1865, 537-8.
Photograph AJ30, 69.

(b) Letters & archives
Enquiry Report. ACA. 8 & 26 and AJ33, 240 (his evidence). 16 (search pty).

(c) Books & articles etc
Conway. see Cunninham & Abney above.
Dent. Above the snowline. 11-12, 68 & 79.
Slingsby. AJ31, 80-1.
Stephen. see Galton, Vacation Tourists...in 1860. 272.

Graphic. 29.9.94. p374 (Whymper's article).
The Times. 22.7.65. McCormick's letter of 17.7.65. AJ70, 19. MW64/65, 10-12.

7.2.2 Biner, F

(a) Biography
Obituary. AJ31, 253-60 (photograph).
Egger. Pioniere der Alpen. 294-300.
Elliott testimonial. see AJ31, 257 (facsimile).
Ruden No.96 p30. Kronig No.553 p45. No.96 p44.
SAC Jahrbuch 1864, 578. 1865, 536.

(b) Letters & archives
Führerbuch. ACA. see note AJ31, 96. & AJ31, 253-60 (extracts & facsimiles). 255 (name 'Weisshorn'). 256 (Whymper facs). 257 (Elliott facs).

(c) Books & articles etc
Kronig. Familien-Statistik. 45 & 255.
Tyndall. Hours of exercise in the Alps. 91-113 (Weisshorn 1st ascent).
Whymper. Scrambles. 1, 378 (7.7.65). 426-8 (1866). 4, 420 (tent platform).

Elliott conversation. see AJ28, 284.
1876 Stockje incident. see AJ8, 382.
1892 visit to Whymper's tent platform. see AJ32, 28. and Scrambles 4, 420.

7.2.3 Birkbeck, J

(a) Biography
Mumm 1, 35-6.

(b) Letters & archives
10.6.65. Reilly – Whymper. SPRI. cACA.
15.7.66. Seiler – Thioly. see Die Alpen 25 (1949) 349-50.
27.9.66. Hodgkinson – Reilly. ACA.
12.3.18. Rachel Birkbeck – Farrar. (enclosing lecture notes) cNLS.
20.3.18. Rachel Birkbeck – Farrar. (Hadow & Pennyghent) ACA. cNLS. AJ70, 18.

Girdlestone's letter journal. 29.7.66. ACA.
Whymper diary entry c.31.7.66. (Birkbeck attempt). SPRI.
Young Peter Taugwalder Führerbuch. ACA. and see AJ59, 437.

(c) Books & articles etc
Gos. Le Cervin 1, 214-16 (1966 attempt).

Farrar's notes on 1866 attempt. AJ32, 108 & 273.
Hudson's article. Col de Miage. Peaks, passes & glaciers 2 vol 1, 208-24.
Weisshorn account in Hotel Monte Rosa book 17.8.63. see AJ32, 217.

Journal de Genève 26.7.66. Report of attempt. see AJ32, 108 & 273.

7.2.4 Brown, F.A.Y

(a) Biography
Mumm 2, 27-8.
Biographical note. AJ70, 202.

(b) Letters & archives
Adams Reilly 1865 journal. ?ACA. cNLS in Graham Brown Papers.
Enquiry Report. ACA. 16 & 17 (recovery party – Devouassoud).
Riffelhaus guestbook entry. 17.7.65. Zermatt Museum.

(c) Books & articles etc
Brown, F.A.Y. Family Notes. Printed at Genoa 1917. 273 & 277 (funeral). 273, 274 & 276 (Payot). 274 (Hadow a novice). 276 (1st & 3rd search parties). 277 (rope broke & summit rock). 278 (safety valve). 287 (Monte Rosa).
Tuckett. A pioneer in the high Alps. 250.

Dangar & Blakeney references. AJ61, 485-6, 496 & 502-3. also AJ70, 31.
Kennedy. AJ3, 75-6 (Mont Blanc ascent 7.7.65).
(Yeats Brown) 1828 Jungfrau attempt see AJ5, 374.

L'Abeille de Chamonix. 23.7.65. SPRI.

7.2.5 Browne, G.F

(a) Biography
Mumm 2, 29-30.
Obituary AJ42, 295-7.

(b) Letters & archives
24.1.21. Coolidge – Gos. see Gos Le Cervin 1, 192.
29.1.21. Coolidge – Gos. see Gos Le Cervin 1, 193.

Whymper's 1895 diary (30 Aug & 2 Sep). SPRI.

(c) Books & articles etc

Browne,G.F. The recollections of a bishop. London. 1915. 104-5.
Reviewed. AJ30, 84-5. Extract. AJ53, 366.
Clark. An eccentric in the Alps. 211-12. The Day the Rope Broke. 198-200.
Conway. Episodes in a varied life. 1932. 28-9.
Gos. Le Cervin 1, 127-8, 192-7. Le Cervin 2, 270.
Smythe. Edward Whymper. 194-6.
Tyndale. Note in Scrambles 6th edn 1936. p vii. Footnote in AJ53, 366.
Whymper. Scrambles. 1, 404 (Taugwalder footnote).
Young,G.W. see Gos Le Cervin 1, 196-7.

Cooke. Whymper again. AJ53, 366.
Dangar & Blakeney. Note AJ61, 485n.
Graham Brown. Note AJ57, 108.
Schuster. Footnote. AJ54, 82.

7.2.6 Campbell, A.J

(b) Letters & archives

[13.7.65] Hudson – McCormick. (5am note) ACA. Smythe 180. McCormick 12.

Monte Rosa guestbook entry. 18.7.65. p258. Seiler Hotels Zermatt.

(c) Books & articles etc

McCormick. A sad holiday. 4, 5, 12 & 13.

7.2.7 Carrel, Canon

(a) Biography

Obituary. AJ5, 270. and AJ7, 398 (monument).
Bernardi. Il Gran Cervino. 59 (in Italian).
Gorret. Il Canonico Carrel di Aosta. see Bernardi. Ecrits de l'Abbé Amé Gorret 109-10 and Bollettino del CAI n.17 (1870), 155 (in French).
Lunn. Matterhorn Centenary. 34-5.
Rey. The Matterhorn. 1st & 2nd edns 108-13, 1946 edn 75-80.
Tuckett. Peaks, passes, and glaciers. 2nd series. 2, 261.

(b) Letters & archives

14. 7.65. L'abbé Chasseur – G.Carrel. see AJ51, 330 and Gos Le Cervin 1, 103.
16. 7.65. L'abbé Chasseur – G.Carrel. see AJ51, 330 and Gos Le Cervin 1, 104.
19. 7.65. L'abbé Chasseur – G.Carrel. see AJ51, 331 and Gos Le Cervin 1, 105.
19. 7.65. L'abbé Gorret – G.Carrel. see AJ51, 331 and Gos Le Cervin 1, 106.
14.10.65. G.Carrel – Gastaldi (CAI). see Gos Le Cervin 1, 113-16.
16. 6.66. L'abbé Chasseur – G.Carrel. see Gos Le Cervin 1, 291-2.
24. 6.66. J.J.Maquignaz – G.Carrel. see Gos Le Cervin 1, 292-3.
29. 7.66. J.J.Maquignaz – G.Carrel. see Gos Le Cervin 1, 217.

5. 8.67. Rimini [CAI] – G.Carrel. see Gos Le Cervin 1, 293-7.
28. 8.67. L'abbé Gorret – G.Carrel. see Gos Le Cervin 1, 297-8.
18. 9.67. G.Carrel – Tyndall. see Gos Le Cervin 1, 256-8.
12.10.67. Giordano – G.Carrel. see Gos Le Cervin 1, 241-2.
22.10.67. Tyndall – G.Carrel. see Gos Le Cervin 1, 258-9.
1.11.67. Gastaldi [CAI] – G.Carrel. see Gos Le Cervin 1, 298-300.

For photograph of Matterhorn taken by Carrel, marked by Jordan (together with note of Jordan's times) see Bernardi Il Gran Cervino 128-9.

(c) Books & articles etc

Ball. A guide to the Western Alps. 1863, 153-4. Panorama facing p151.
Bernardi. Il Gran Cervino. 1963. (makes various references in Italian).
Carrel, G. La Vallée de Valtornenche en 1867. (Bollettino del Club Alpino Italiano, numero 12. 1 Semestre 1868). 50-2 (hut contributors). 52 & 67 (Jordan). 61 (Tyndall). 63 (Whymper).

7.2.8 Carrel, J-A

(a) Biography

Obituary by Whymper. AJ15, 284-9. see also Scrambles 4, 415 & 418 and Daily Graphic, Sept. 20, 1890.
Bernardi. Il Gran Cervino. 92-3.
Clark. The early Alpine Guides. 139-55.
Cunningham & Abney. The Pioneers of the Alps. 197-205 (portrait 197).
Gos. Propos d'un Alpiniste. 64-9.

(b) Letters & archives

21.12.65. Elijah Walton – Whymper. SPRI.
30. 8.90. Sinigaglia – Cainer. see Bernardi Il Gran Cervino, 93-5.

Führerbuch. In Alpine Museum, Turin. (per Gos Le Cervin 1, 302)
Führerbuch. see 3.8.69 for Dauphiné, and Gos Le Cervin 1, 303-4.
Führerbuch. see 24.8.74 for Whymper Hörnli ascent, and Gos Le Cervin 1, 305.
Giordano diary. see Rey The Matterhorn, 1st edn 140. 1946 edn 103.
Unsigned guides declaration. see Gos Le Cervin 1, 106.

(c) Books & articles etc

Carrel. La Vallée de Valtornenche en 1867, 61-4 (monopoly). 63 (Whymper).
Gos. Alpine Tragedy. 'Carrel the great'. 218-28.
Lunn. Matterhorn Centenary. 76-80.
Rey. The Matterhorn. see chapter 3.
Sinigaglia's account. see Scrambles 4, 416-18.
Tyndall. Hours of exercise in the Alps. 2, 166-7 (1862 'Note'). 1, 268-70 (1867). & see Gos Le Cervin 1, 254-9 (1867).
Whymper. Scrambles 1, 380 (bamboozled). 391 (*the* man). 415-17 (1st Italian ascent). 418-20 (Grove).

Whymper. Travels amongst the Great Andes of the Equator.

Davidson/Farrar. Notes on the Ascent of the Matterhorn by Carrel's Galerie. AJ37, 221-35.
Gorret. The Italian ascent of the Matterhorn. see AJ2, 239 (237-45).
(Sella). First winter ascent. see AJ10, 494.
Whymper. Letter to editor re Tyndall. see AJ5, 333 (329-36).
Whymper. Carrel fund appeal. Daily Graphic. 20.9.90.
Whymper. Carrel fund list of contributors. see AJ15, c.396 (leaflet).

7.2.9 Clemenz, J.A

(a) Biography
Coolidge. Swiss travel and Swiss guidebooks. 298 (History of Zermatt).
Engelhardt. Das Monte Rosa- und Matterhorn-Gebirg. 125.
Hallenbarter. Staatsrat Clemenz. Walliser Jahrbuch 1941, 54-67. Picture 58.

(b) Letters & archives
22.7.65. P.D.Hadow – McCormick. ACA. AJ70, 16-17.
25.7.65. Whymper – McCormick. Smythe, 205.

Undated. Clemenz – Whymper. (note re Mme Douglas) SPRI.
21.7.65. Clemenz summons to Whymper. SPRI. cACA in Enquiry Report, p18.
Enquiry Report. ACA. and see AJ33, 234-47.
Girdlestone's letter journal. ACA.
Whymper. Questionnaire for Taugwalder. (English) SPRI. (French) cACA in Enquiry Report 22-3.
Monte Rosa guestbook entry. 29.7.65 (Queensberry). 31.7.65 (Hadow). Seiler Hotels Zermatt.
Riffelhaus guestbook entry. c.10.7.65 (Douglas). Zermatt Museum.

(c) Books & articles etc
Clark. The Day the Rope Broke. 191 (British Mission).
Coolidge. Swiss travel & Swiss guidebooks. 321 (disturbances).
Lunn. The Swiss and their mountains. 152-3 (Seiler).
(SAC) Monte Rosa 1865 | 1965. 17 & 21.
Whymper. Guide to Zermatt. 15 & 17 (hotels). 173-4 (Lyskamm accident).
Whymper. Scrambles, 1, 404 (Clemenz footnote). 4, 125n (hotels).
Wundt. Das Matterhorn und seine Geschichte. 118-19.

Davies, J.Llewelyn. Peaks, passes & glaciers 1, 196.
Graham Brown. Girdlestone & the Matterhorn accident, 1865. AJ57, 375-9.
Hall. The fatal accident on the Lyskamm. AJ5, 23-32.
Monod. (Whymper interview) Journal de Zermatt 25.8.95. ACA. SPRI.

The Times. 8.8.65. Whymper's letter of 7.8.65. AJ2, 148-53.
Sonntagspost. 20.8.65. see MW64/65, 27. and Dübi. Zur Erinnerung an Edward Whymper. SACJ47, (1911) 198-9.

7.2.10 Coolidge, W.A.B

(a) Biography

Mumm 2, 54-79.
Obituary. AJ38, 278-89.
Clark. An eccentric in the Alps. 1959. (Contains a note on sources pp13-14)
Clark. The Victorian Mountaineers. 1953. 145-73.

(b) Letters & archives

24. 1.21.	Coolidge – Gos.	see Gos Le Cervin	1, 192.
29. 1.21.	Coolidge – Gos.	see Gos Le Cervin	1, 193.
21. 3.21.	Rey – Gos.	see Gos Le Cervin	1, 194-6.
25.12.46.	Young – Gos.	see Gos Le Cervin	1, 196-7.

Brevoort diary entry. see Clark 'Eccentric' 21, & The Day the Rope Broke 192.
Coolidge archives. (SAC Library) Zentralbibliothek, Zürich.
Monte Rosa guestbook entry. (Queensberry) 29.7.65 p260. Seiler Hotels Zermatt.

(c) Books & articles etc

Clark. An eccentric in the Alps. 21 (Brevoort diary maid's account). 54 (1869 attempt). 71 (1870). 84 (Straton attempt). 84-5 & 87-8 (1871). 211-12 (re letters to Gos).
Coolidge. Swiss travel and Swiss guide-books. 251-322 (History of Zermatt).
Coolidge. The Alps in nature & history. 240 (Elliott's ascent).
Coolidge. Alpine studies. 192-223 (The history of the St.Théodule pass). 252-62 (The Matterhorn & its names).
Gos. Le Cervin 1, 192-7 (Coolidge, Rey & Young letters).

7.2.11 Cowell, J.W and J.J

(a) Biography

Mumm 1, 80-81.

(b) Letters & archives

c.29.7.65.	Whymper – J.J.Cowell. Not known to have survived.
31.7.65.	J.J.Cowell – Whymper. SPRI. cACA.
3.8.65.	Wm. Mathews – Whymper. SPRI. cACA.
? 4.8.65.	cWhymper – Editor of The Times. SPRI. cACA.
7.8.65.	Wills – Whymper. SPRI. & in The Times 8.8.65.
11.8.65.	J.W.Cowell – Whymper. SPRI. cACA.
c.17.8.65.	Whymper – Wills. Not known to have survived.
20.8.65.	Wills – Whymper. SPRI. cACA (extract).
? 21-31.8.	Whymper – J.W.Cowell. Not known to have survived.
4.9.65.	J.W.Cowell – Whymper. SPRI. cACA.

17.8.65. Whymper 'Memorandum of a conversation...' SPRI. Smythe 194-5. and Scrambles 1, 400-1 (omitting last paragraph).

1.9.65. Cowell memorandum or certificate of authenticity. SPRI. cACA (extract). Incomplete extract in Smythe 195-6.

(c) Books & articles etc

Browning. Memories of sixty years. 94-6.
Clark. The Day the Rope Broke. 200-1 & 212.
Smythe. Edward Whymper. 194-6. and see 'Andes' below.
Whymper. Scrambles 1, 400-1.
Whymper. Travels amongst the Great Andes of the Equator. 1949 edn. 12 (5-20).

Dangar & Blakeney comment. AJ71, 234.
[Ropes] 1864 Report of the Special Committee on ropes etc. AJ1, 321-6. and see Scrambles 1, 373-4.

The Times. 29.7.65. J.J.Cowell's letter of 28.7.65.
The Times. 8.8.65. Whymper's letter of 7.8.65. AJ2, 148-53.
The Times. 8.8.65. Wills' letter of 7.8.65.

See also 7.3.2 (The Cowell memorandum)

7.2.12 Croz, J-B

(b) Letters & archives

8.8.65. Wigram – Whymper. SPRI. cACA.
9.8.65. cWhymper – Wigram. SPRI. cACA.
9.8.65. Wigram – Whymper. SPRI. cACA.
10.8.65. Wigram – Whymper. SPRI. cACA.
13.8.65. Wills – Whymper. SPRI.
13.8.65. Reilly – Whymper. SPRI.
21.8.65. cWhymper – H.Hadow. SPRI. cACA. (M.Croz payment)
24.8.65. Whymper – Glover. cZermatt Museum.
27.8.65. Whymper – Robertson. ACA.

Adams Reilly journal. 23.7.65. ?ACA. cNLS in Graham Brown Papers.
Croz fund appeal leaflet. SPRI. and see Gos, Propos d'un Alpiniste below.
Croz fund list of contributors. 31.10.65. SPRI.
Enquiry Report. ACA. 19-20 & 31 (inventory). and see AJ33, 245-6.

(c) Books & articles etc

Ball. Guide to the Western Alps. 1863. xxxv.
Gos. Le Cervin 1, 180-1 (Buxton's account).
Gos. Alpinisme anecdotique. 254-8 (hat) and see AJ47, 180.
Gos. Propos d'un Alpiniste. 51-2 (Croz fund appeal September 1865).
Maclean. Three weeks amongst the upper regions of the Alps. 1865.
Whymper. Guide to Zermatt. 175 (Breithorn).
Wigram, Woolmore. Memoirs of. 1908. 83.

Buxton. AJ2, 332 (J-B Croz' return to Chamonix).

Kennedy. Ascent of the Dent Blanche. AJ1, 33-9.
Mathews. Letter re Croz fund. AJ2, 422-3.

L'Abeille de Chamonix. 23.7.65. SPRI.
The Times. 2. 8.65. Anneçy paper report.
The Times. 19. 8.65. Whymper's & Mathews' letters re Croz fund.
The Times. 21.11.65. re closure of fund.

7.2.13 Croz, M-A

(a) Biography

Clark. The early Alpine Guides. 87-94.
Cunningham & Abney. The Pioneers of the Alps. 221-5.
Gos. Propos d'un Alpiniste. 48-50 & 54-5.
Whymper. 'Of all the guides etc', see Scrambles 1, 181.
Portrait. see Whymper's Scrambles 1, 180.
Portrait by Lance Calkin at the Alpine Club. see Whymper's Guide to Zermatt, 65. and Rebuffat, Men and the Matterhorn, 83.

(b) Letters & archives

22.4.65. Whymper – Reilly. ACA. Scrambles 6, 378-9.
1.5.65. Whymper – Reilly. ACA. Scrambles 6, 379-80.
20.6.65. Whymper – Reilly. ACA. Scrambles 6, 380-1.
13.8.65. Reilly – Whymper. SPRI.
3.8.66. Seiler – Whymper. SPRI.
22.8.66. Welschen – Whymper. SPRI. (plus Whymper's note)
16.9.66. Seiler – Whymper. SPRI.
29.9.66. Whymper – Robertson. ACA. Scrambles 6, 382.
14.10.66. Robertson – Whymper. SPRI. (see Vecqueray sources for enclosures)
12.4.67. Seiler – Whymper. SPRI.
8.5.17. Rudolf Taugwalder – Montagnier. ACA. (Young Peter Taugwalder's answers to Montagnier's questions)

Adams Reilly journal 1865. ?ACA. cNLS in Graham Brown Papers.
Enquiry Report. ACA. 19-20 & 31 (inventory) and see AJ33, 245-6.
Montagnier questions with Young Peter answers. cACA. and see Scrambles 6, 305n & 323n.
Robertson's sonnet. ?SPRI. and see Smythe, 201. & Gos Le Cervin 1, 150 (French).
Robertson's copy of Croz inscription. ACA.
Whymper's diaries. 1865 & 1866. SPRI.
Whymper's draft Croz inscription. SPRI.

(c) Books & articles etc

Gos. Alpinisme anecdotique. 254-8 & 284 (Croz hat). see also AJ47, 180.
Whymper. Scrambles 1, 181 (Of all the guides). 267n (note about B engaging Croz, with Croz letter). 293 (Croz declines Hörnli).

Farrar. AJ33, 250. (Note about relations between Croz & Whymper)

L'Abeille de Chamonix. 23.7.65. SPRI.
The Times. Mackenzie's letter of 7.9.66.

Tomb inscriptions. Bernardi. Il Gran Cervino. 176.
Cunningham & Abney. The Pioneers of the Alps. 225.
Gos,C. Le Cervin 1, 150.
Gos,F. Zermatt and its valley. 71.
Rébuffat. Men and the Matterhorn. 128.
Whymper. Guide to Zermatt. 71.
Yung. Zermatt & the valley of the Viège. 50.

7.2.14. Douglas, Lord F

(a) Biography
Mumm 2, 118-19.
Photograph AJ28, 281.

(b) Letters & archives
31.7.65. Glover – Whymper. SPRI.
5.8.65. Sandbach Parker – J.D.Forbes. USA. (eagles)
9.8.65. cWhymper – Wigram. SPRI. cACA.
18.8.65. Whymper – Glover. cZermatt Museum.
(3.10.65. Charles Parker – his father) cACA. see AJ68, 288.
4.9.71. Eliza Pennell – Tyndall. ACA. & see AJ61, 499 note 24 ii-iv (?body seen by Jordan).
see also Carrel below.

Alpine Club. Candidates book. ACA.
Douglas. Poem. 'At Zermatt when the sun is low'. (Whymper's copy) SPRI. cACA.
Enquiry Report. ACA. 6, 10, 24 & 27 (Taugwalder A24 & A53). 21-2 & 32-3 (Douglas inventory). & see AJ33, 246.
Führerbuch. Peter Inäbnit. AJ61, 349 (Trifthorn).
Führerbuch. Joseph Lauber. AJ73, 255 (Breithorn & Adler pass).
Führerbuch. Joseph Viannin. see AJ57, 62. & Gos Le Cervin 1, 67.
Whymper. 1865 diary. SPRI.
Guestbooks. Zermatt. Hotel Monte Rosa. 29.7.65 p260 (Queensberry). 24-31.7.65 p260 (H.Hadow). Seiler Hotels Zermatt.
Zermatt. Riffelhaus. c.8.63 (H.Glover). 16.7.63, 24.8.63 & c.10.7.65 (Douglas). Zermatt Museum.
St.Niklaus. Hotel Monte Rosa. 26.6.65 (Douglas). MW64/65, 25. & Gos Le Cervin 1, 225.
Zinal. Hotel Durand. 6.7.65. AJ32, 25n. AJ41, 227. Gos Le Cervin 1, 65. L'Echo des Alpes 1872-3, 105.

(c) Books & articles etc
Ball. Guide to the Western Alps. 1863, xxxiii (rope). 1877, 307 (Bruneggjoch).
Carrel. La Vallée de Valtornenche en 1867. 64.
Ceresole. Führer von Zermatt. 27.
Clark. An eccentric in the Alps. 21 (Brevoort).
Clark. The Day the Rope Broke. 192 (Brevoort). & 194 (Hall).

Gos. Le Cervin 1, 65 (Durand). 67 (Viannin facs). 225 (St.Niklaus facs).
Lunn. Matterhorn Centenary. 54. (compare AJ61, 504)
Maclean. Three weeks amongst the upper regions of the Alps. 22.
Mumm. The Alpine Club register. 1, 70 (Carr). 183-4 (Latham).
McCormick. A sad holiday. 4 (Hadow former pupil).
Whymper. Scrambles 1, 385n (nimble as a deer).
Wundt. Das Matterhorn und seine Geschichte. 126 (photograph of boot).

Dangar. Note. AJ73, 255 (Adler & Breithorn). AJ61, 548 (Bruneggh orn).
Dangar & Blakeney. AJ61, 348-51 (Trifthorn). 496 (his climbing). 499 note 24 ii-iv & see AJ60, 381 (body). AJ70, 27 (Old Peter in 1851). 32 (out of his class). 159-60 (2 Douglases).
Douglas. The Gabelhorn. AJ2, 221-2.
Dübi. SACJ 47 (1911) 200 (owed money).
Farrar. see AJ32, 25n (Inäbnit).
Graham Brown. see AJ57, 374.
Hawkins. Partial ascent of the Matterhorn. see Galton's Vacation Tourists. 282-304.
Kennedy. Zermatt & the Matterhorn in winter. AJ1, 77-82.
Mears. Experience with climbing ropes. AJ58, 81.
Moore. The first ascent of the Ober-Gabelhorn. AJ28, 273-81.
[Ropes] 1864 Report of the Special Committee on ropes etc. AJ1, 321-6. and see Scrambles 1, 373-4.
SAC Jahrbuch 1865, 535 (Bruneggjoch).
Stephen. Macmillan's Magazine. August 1871, 304-11.
Taugwalder. Young Peter's Narrative. AJ61, 490-1 ('Douglas' difficulties).
Whymper. Camping out. AJ2, 1-11. see 8-9 (Matterhorn).

Athenaeum. (Matterhorn attempts) see 16 & 23.8.62, 29.8.63 and elsewhere.
L'Abeille de Chamonix. 23.7.65 (Douglas on Mont Blanc!). SPRI.
Der Bund. 19.7.65. see Dübi. SAC47 (1911) 192-3. MW64/65, 18-20.
Journal de Genève. 18.7.65. Facsimile in Bernardi. 168. and see Dübi ibid 192. & MW64/65, 17-18.
The Times. 28.7.65. Dumfries Courier extract.
The Times. 2.8.65. Note (Douglas did not slip).
The Times. 8.8.65. Whymper's letter of 7.8.65. AJ2, 148-53.
The Times. 18.4.05. Florence Dixie's letter of 15.4.05. For her other letters see under Queensberry.

7.2.15 Downton, H

(a) Biography
Biographical note. AJ70, 202-3.

(b) Letters & archives
20.7.65. Downton's report to Geneva (?Mackenzie). PRO. see Clark, 172-4.

Adams Reilly 1865 diary. ?ACA. cNLS in Graham Brown Papers (burial service).

(c) Books & articles etc
Clark. The Day the Rope Broke. 172-5 & 186.
McCormick. A sad holiday. 20.

Hudson. Col de Miage. Peaks, passes and glaciers 2 vol 1, 213 & 217.

7.2.16 Elliott, J.M

(a) Biography
Mumm 2, 125.
Biographical note. AJ28, 281.
Memoir of the Rev.Julius M.Elliott. [c.1870]
Bateman, J. The life of Rev.H.V.Elliott (includes the above).

(b) Letters & archives
25.7.68. Elliott – Wood. For long extract see AJ28, 289-96.
18.1.17. Farrar – Montagnier. ACA.

Hotel Monte Rosa guestbook. 1867. Jordan's account. see AJ31, 90-2.
Riffelhaus guestbook entry. p54. July 1865. Zermatt Museum.

(c) Books & articles etc
Clark. The early Alpine Guides. 164-5.
Coolidge. The Alps in nature and history. 240.
[Elliott] Memoir of the Rev.Julius M.Elliott. c.1870. and see AJ28, 282-9.
Engel. A History of Mountaineering in the Alps. 146 (Gautier).
Gautier, Theophile. Les vacances de lundi. 1881. and see Engel above.
Gos. Le Cervin 1, 260-5.
Gos. Voyageurs illustres en Suisse. 101 (Gautier).
Lunn. Matterhorn Centenary. 84-7.
Thioly. Ascension du Mont Cervin. Genève. 1871. p5.

Contemporary note of ascent. AJ4, 158.
Elliott. The Second Ascent of the Matterhorn by the East Face. AJ28, 281-96.
Long. L'Echo des Alpes. 1867, 52 & 67 (Rev.R.Wood).
The Field 1910. Elliott's letter of 25.7.68 to Mr.Wood.

For Gustave Doré see 7.3.8 (Illustrations).

7.2.17 Fellenberg, E von

(a) Biography
Mumm 1, 95-102.
Biographical note. AJ70, 26.
Jenny, E. see Der Ruf der Berge (below) 340-57.
Les Alpes 39 (1963), 120-2.

(b) Letters & archives

25.7.65. Whymper – von Fellenberg. SAC Section Bern (manuscript No.779). cZM. cACA. AJ70, 23-6. MW64/65, 13-16 plus two pages in facsimile.

26.7.65. Whymper – von Fellenberg. cACA. Alpina 1911. & see Scrambles 6, 319n.

26.7.65. Hawker – von Fellenberg. cACA. see AJ70, 323 & Bergsteiger 7/65. German translation in Alpina 1911.

26.7.65. Whymper – Rimini. see CIA Bollettino No 1 of 1865, 20-5. also in Bernardi. Il Gran Cervino. 161-3.

(c) Books & articles etc

Der Ruf der Berge. Die Erschliessung der Berner Hochalpen von Edmund von Fellenberg. Mit Lebensbild von Ernst Jenny. 340-57.

Roth. The Doldenhorn and Weisse Frau. 1863.

Dübi. (re von Fellenberg getting letter) see Alpina 1911, 225-6.

Sonntagspost 13.8.65. see Dübi SACJ 47 (1911) 195-8. Extract MW64/65, 25.
Sonntagspost 20.8.65. see Dübi SACJ 47 (1911) 198-200. Extract MW64/65, 25-8.

7.2.18 Giordano, F

(b) Letters & archives

7. 7.65. Giordano – Sella.)
11. 7.65. Giordano – Sella.) see Rey. The Matterhorn. 1907, 132-7. 1946 edn. 97-100.
14. 7.65. Giordano – Sella.) or Scrambles 6, 339-43.
15. 7.65. Giordano – Sella.)
29. 7.66. Maquignaz – Canon Carrel. see Gos Le Cervin 1, 216-17 (1866 attempt).
12.10.67. Giordano – Canon Carrel. see Gos. ibid, 241-2 (Maquignaz ascent).
31.12.68. Giordano – Tyndall. see Hours of exercise in the Alps. 1, 294.

Hotel Monte Rosa guestbook account by Giordano. see AJ31, 93.
Giordano 1864 notebook. see Rey. The Matterhorn. 127-8. 1946 edn. 92.

(c) Books & articles etc

Giordano. Ascensione al Gran Cervino 1868. Milano 1868.

Rey. The Matterhorn. see Chapter 3 for comment, letters & notebook quotes.

Tyndall. Hours of exercise in the Alps. 1, 294 (letter extract).

Whymper. Scrambles 1, 380 (family of distinction). 415-16 (1865). 421 (1868 ascent). 424-5 (geology section & note). 4, 435 (death).

7.2.19 Girdlestone, A.G

(a) Biography

Obituary by W.H.Glover. AJ24, 504.
Biographical note by Dangar & Blakeney. AJ70, 203.
Tyndale. 'First affections'. AJ53, 305.
The Alpine Club has a fine large framed photograph of Girdlestone.

(b) Letters & archives

Girdlestone's letter journal. ACA. and see AJ57, 369-84.

(c) Books & articles etc

Coolidge. The Alps in nature and history. 1908. 248.

Girdlestone. The high Alps without guides. 19 (guides fees). 20 (selected adventures). 167 (ropes). 167-8 (cause of Matterhorn accident).

Hort. Life and letters. vol 2, 40.

Whymper. Scrambles 1, 367 (Montanvert). 378 (sick Englishman). 4, 425 & 426 (Matterhorn ascents).

Dangar & Blakeney comment. AJ70, 35.

Graham Brown. Girdlestone and the Matterhorn accident, 1865. AJ57, 369-84.

Grove. The Comparative Skill of Travellers and Guides. AJ5, 87-95.

Editor's note of Alpine Club discussion of above. AJ5, 96.

7.2.20 Glover, R

(b) Letters & archives

31.7.65. Glover – Whymper. SPRI.
8.8.65. cWhymper – Buxton. SPRI.
18.8.65. Whymper – Glover. cZermatt Museum.
23.8.65. Glover – Whymper. SPRI. (Contributing to Croz fund)
24.8.65. Whymper – Glover. cZermatt Museum. (Acknowledging above)

Riffelhaus guestbook entries. Small book, pp314 & 351 (Douglas 1863). 358 (H.Glover 1863). 371 (17.6.65). Zermatt Museum.

Whymper's 1865 diary (19 & 20 June). SPRI.

(c) Books & articles etc

The Times. 27.7.65. Glover's letter of 25.7.65.
The Times. 1.8.65. Glover's letter of 29.7.65.
The Times. 2.8.65. Note about Lord Douglas.

7.2.21 Gorret, A

(a) Biography

Obituary by H.Ferrand in Revue Alpine de la Section Lyonnaise du CAF. 1907. also in (Bernardi) Ecrits de l'Abbé Gorret, 19-26.

Bernardi. Il Gran Cervino. 147.

Deffreyes, A. (Article on Gorret's writings) see 'Ecrits' 53-62.

Lunn. Matterhorn Centenary. 35-6.

Rey. The Matterhorn. 1st & 2nd edns 58, 72-3. 1946 edn 33, 45-6.

(b) Letters & archives

19. 7.65. L'abbé Gorret – G.Carrel. see AJ51, 331 and Gos Le Cervin 1, 106.
28. 8.67. L'abbé Gorret – G.Carrel. see Gos Le Cervin 1, 297-8.
7. 9.07. L'abbé Gorret – Gos. see Gos Le Cervin 2, 177-8 (Cervin railway).

(c) Books & articles etc

Bernardi. Il Gran Cervino. 1963. 147-53.
Bernardi. Ecrits de l'Abbé Amé Gorret. 1965.
Gorret. Guide de la vallée d'Aoste. 1876. and see Gos Le Cervin 1, 206-10.
Gorret. Victor-Emmanuel sur les Alpes. 1879. see Ecrits (above), 196-221.

Gorret. Ascension du Cervin. Feuille D'Aoste. October 1865, No's 41, 43 & 44. also in AJ2, 237-45 (French). Die Alpen 11 (1935), 94-101 (German). Bernardi, Il Gran Cervino, 148-153 (Italian). and in Ecrits 65-74.
Gos. Amé Gorret, "der Bär der Berge". Die Alpen 11 (1935), 140-5.

7.2.22 Grove, F.C

(a) Biography

Mumm 1, 125-7 & 2, 369.
Obituary. AJ21, 244-6.

(b) Letters & archives

31. 7.65. J.J.Cowell – Whymper. SPRI. cACA.
22.10.67. Tyndall – G.Carrel. see Gos. Le Cervin 1, 258-9.

Bich Führerbuch entry. 1867. see Bernardi Il Gran Cervino. 182.
Hotel Monte Rosa guestbook entry. 1867. see AJ31, 88-90.

(c) Books & articles etc

Bernardi. Il Gran Cervino. 181-2.
Carrel. La Vallée de Valtornenche en 1867. 60.
Girdlestone. The high Alps without guides.
Gos. Le Cervin 1, 229-38.
Tyndall. Hours of exercise in the Alps. 1, 269-70.
Whymper. Scrambles. 1, 418-20.

Buxton. The Glacier du Dôme. AJ2, 332.
Grove. The Comparative Skill of Travellers and Guides. AJ5, 87-95.
Grove. The Northern and Southern Ascents of the Matterhorn. AJ4, 185-93.
For Grove's Matterhorn ascents see also AJ4, 56. Saturday Review, 7.3.68 (also in AJ37, 235-241). and CAI Boll. ii, 391-2 & iii, 73-80.
Report of the Special Committee on ropes etc. AJ1, 321-6.

The Times. 29.7.65. Cowell's letter of 28.7.65.

7.2.23 Güssfeldt, P

(a) Biography

Obituary. AJ33, 144.
Elected Honorary Member of Alpine Club in 1909, see AJ25, 95.
Photograph. see Wundt. Das Matterhorn und seine Geschichte. 52.

(b) Letters & archives

Young Peter Taugwalder's Führerbuch. ACA.
Peter Knubel's Führerbuch. ACA. and see AJ32, 97-8.

(c) Books & articles etc

His book. In den Hochalpen. Berlin 1886. 2nd edn. 21-3 (1865 attempt). 23-4 (1868 ascent). 24-7 (Old Weissthor). Review of book. AJ13, 49-51.
Egger. Pioniere der Alpen. 194-6.
Gos. Le Cervin 1, 211 (French translation of Alpenrosen extract in AJ37).
Whymper. Scrambles 1, 423 (1868 ascent listed).

Die Alpenrosen. Bern. 1876 [not seen]. For extract in English with note by Farrar, see AJ37, 386. Same extract in French, see Gos Le Cervin 1, 211.
Farrar. An attempt on the Matterhorn in 1865. AJ37, 386.
Farrar. (Peter Knubel's Führerbuch) AJ32, 97-8.

7.2.24 Hadow, D.R

(a) Biography

Ceresole. Führer von Zermatt. 27.
Dangar & Blakeney. Note on Hadow family. AJ61, 504 (1).
Lunn. Matterhorn Centenary. 54.
Photograph. AJ61, 488.

(b) Letters & archives

16. 7.65. McCormick – P.D.Hadow. Not known to have survived.
22. 7.65. P.D.Hadow – McCormick. ACA. AJ70, 16-17.
3. 8.65. Mathews – Whymper. SPRI. cACA (extract).
?4. 8.65. cWhymper – Times Editor. SPRI. cACA.
7. 8.65. Longman – Whymper. SPRI. cACA.
8. 8.65. cWhymper – Buxton. SPRI.
9. 8.65. Buxton – Whymper. SPRI.
9. 8.65. Wills – Whymper. SPRI.
10. 8.65. P.D.Hadow – McCormick. ACA. AJ70, 17-18.
18. 8.65. Whymper – Glover. cZermatt Museum.
19. 8.65. Henry Hadow – Whymper. SPRI. cACA.
21. 8.65. cWhymper – Henry Hadow. SPRI. cACA.
23. 8.65. P.D.Hadow – Whymper. SPRI.
23. 8.65. cWhymper – P.D.Hadow. SPRI.
26. 8.65. P.D.Hadow – Whymper. SPRI.
20. 3.18. Mrs.Rachel Birkbeck – J.P.Farrar. ACA. cNLS. AJ70, 18.

Adams Reilly 1865 journal. ?ACA. cNLS in Graham Brown Papers.
Enquiry Report. ACA. 19 & 30 (spectacles). and see AJ33, 245.
Girdlestone's letter journal. ACA. and see AJ57, 375.
Hotel Monte Rosa guestbook entry. 3.9.64 p236. 24-31.7.65 p260. Seiler Hotels.
Riffelhaus guestbook entry. 3.9.64. Zermatt Museum.

(c) Books & articles etc
Brown. Family Notes. 274 & 277-8.
Ceresole. Führer von Zermatt. 27.
Gos. Le Cervin 1, 160-3.
Hort. Life & letters. 1896. vol 2, 39.
Lunn. Matterhorn Centenary. 54.
McCormick. A sad holiday. 4, 16 & 19.
Preston-Thomas. The work and play of a Government Inspector. 97-8.
Whymper. Scrambles 1, 383, 385n & 389.
Wundt. Das Matterhorn und seine Geschichte. 122.

Dangar & Blakeney. AJ61, 486 & 496 (14) ii & iii. AJ70, 34.
Farrar. AJ32, 28.
Graham Brown. AJ57, 382 (1864 visit).
Kennedy. Ascent of the Aiguille Verte. AJ3, 69 & 76.
Taugwalder. Young Peter's Narrative. AJ61, 490 (484-503).

L'Abeille de Chamonix. Dimanche 23.7.65. SPRI.
Journal de Genève. 18.7.65. see Bernardi, Il Gran Cervino 168. MW64/65, 17-18.
Journal de Zermatt. 25.8.95. ACA. SPRI.
The Field. 13.2.32. Graham Brown. The great Matterhorn disaster of 1865. 227.
The Times. 22.7.65. McCormick' letter of 17.7.65. AJ70, 19-21. MW64/65, 10-12.
The Times. 26.7.65. Charlton's letter of 21.7.65. AJ32, 21n. also in Gos Le Cervin 1, 163 (French).
The Times. 27.7.65. Glover's letter of 25.7.65.

See also 7.3.7 (Hadow's boots).

7.2.25 Hawker, W.H

(a) Biography
Mumm 1, 139-40.

(b) Letters & archives
26.7.65. Hawker – von Fellenberg. cACA. see AJ70, 323.

(c) Books & articles etc
Whymper. Scrambles 1, 266 (Ebnefluh). see 6, 224-6 for Whymper's diary account.

Hawker. 'A chamois hunt in the Oberland.' AJ4, 129.

7.2.26 Hudson, C

(a) Biography
Mumm 1, 160-2.
Chaix. (His letter to The Times) see AJ32, 9n-11n.
Farrar. Days of long ago. Charles Hudson. AJ32, 2-35.

Gos. Le Cervin 1, 86-98.
McCormick. A sad holiday.
Whymper. Scrambles 1, 384n-5n.

(b) Letters & archives

26.4.65. Hudson – McCormick. ACA. and see AJ70, 15-16.
10.6.65. Reilly – Whymper. SPRI. cACA.
13.7.65. Hudson – McCormick. ACA. and see Smythe, 180 or McCormick, 12.
?4.8.65. cWhymper – Editor of Times. SPRI. cACA.
8.8.65. cWhymper – Buxton. SPRI.
10.8.65. P.D.Hadow – McCormick. ACA. and see AJ70, 17-18.
11.8.65. Emily Hudson – Whymper. SPRI.
9.4.17. Montagnier – Farrar. ACA.
4.5.17. Montagnier – Farrar. ACA.
20.3.18. Rachel Birkbeck – Farrar. ACA. cNLS. and see AJ70, 18.

Girdlestone letter journal. ACA. and see AJ57, 375.
Graham Brown Papers. NLS. (Acc4338/206 No 21)

(c) Books & articles etc

Barnard. Drawing from nature. 258.
Coleman. Scenes from the snow-fields. 28.
Gos. Le Cervin 2, 290-6. (Casella article in Auto of 18.9.1911)
Hudson & L.S.Kennedy. Where there's a will there's a way. 1856.
Lunn. Matterhorn Centenary. 69 (Coolidge). 70 ('uninformed verdict' and Graham Brown re 'bitterness').
McCormick. A sad holiday. (contains many references to Hudson)
Preston-Thomas. The work and play of a Government Inspector. 97-8.
Whymper. Scrambles 1, 382-3 (meeting Croz & Hudson). 396 (Croz placing feet). 397n (rope not taut, and 'easy part').

Barnard. Article in Illustrated London News of 25.12.58 p593. and see Graham Brown Papers NLS, above.
Casella. 'Auto' article. see Gos above.
Dangar & Blakeney. A word for Whymper. AJ71, 117-19 (Whymper & Hudson). 235 (Graham Brown's opinion).
Farrar. Days of long ago. AJ32, 2-35. 22 (rock-climbing master).
Gorret. The Italian ascent of the Matterhorn. AJ2, 237-45.
Graham Brown. Girdlestone and the Matterhorn accident 1865. AJ57, 369-84. 370 & 376-7 (suppression of Hudson). 383 (bitterness).
Graham Brown. The great Matterhorn disaster of 1865. The Field 13.2.32, p227.
Kennedy. Ascent of the Dent Blanche. AJ1, 34.
Kennedy. Ascent of the Aiguille verte. AJ3, 68 (visited Hudson at Easter). 73 (almost as great as a guide).
Long. L'Echo des Alpes 1867. No.2 p67.
Lunn. Whymper again. AJ71, 232 (Whymper record better than Hudson).
Monod. (Whymper interview) Journal de Zermatt. 25.8.95. ACA. SPRI.
Morshead. see AJ32, 63 (Perren's view of Hörnli).

Stephen. see Macmillan's Magazine. August 1871 p306 (Taugwalder's view of Hörnli).
Whymper. Mountaineering Tragedies. Strand Magazine, vol 37 p55. 1909.

The Times. 22.7.65. McCormick's letter of 17.7.65. AJ70, 19-21. MW64/65, 10-12.
The Times. 31.7.65. Buxton's letter of 29.7.65.
The Times. 1.8.65. Chaix' letter of 26.7.65. AJ32, 9n-11n.
The Times. 8.8.65. Whymper's letter of 7.8.65. AJ2, 148-53.

7.2.27 Jordan, W.L

(a) Biography
Mumm 2, 206-8.

(b) Letters & archives
5.8.65. Sandbach Parker – J.D.Forbes. USA. (eagles)
25.7.68. Elliott – Wood. see AJ28, 289-96.
4.9.71. Eliza Pennell – Tyndall. ACA. see AJ61, 499.

28.9.65. Photograph of Matterhorn taken by G.Carrel, later marked by Jordan, plus timetable of Jordan's ascent & diversions. 1-3.10.67. see Bernardi below.
Knubel's Führerbuch. ACA. and see AJ32, 96.
Maquignaz' Führerbuch. see Bernardi. 188-9.
Breuil. Hotel Mont Cervin guestbook. Jordan's account see AJ30, 321-3.
Zermatt. Hotel Monte Rosa guestbook. Jordan's account see AJ31, 90-2.

(c) Books & articles etc
Bernardi. Il Gran Cervino. 1963. 128-9 (photo & timetable). 185 (ladder). 188-9 (Maquignaz Führerbuch entries).
Carrel. La Vallée de Valtornenche en 1867. 59 (attempts). 62 (Félicité). 64 (ascent). 65 (relative difficulties). 67 (cable/ladder).
Gos. Le Cervin 1, 242-53.

Dangar & Blakeney. AJ61, 499. Footnote. (24)ii-iv (Pennell's letter).
Farrar's footnote to Elliott letter. see AJ28, 289n.
Jordan's 1916 accounts to Farrar etc. AJ30, 316-23. 320 (handpulls). and see Farrar's note about Galerie Carrel, AJ31, 139-40.
Note of 1867 ascent. see AJ4, 56.

7.2.28 Julen, A

(a) Biography
Ruden No.186 p48. and see No.190 for 'Alois Julen, Richter' (judge).
Kronig No.186 p75. No.190 p78.
SAC Jahrbuch 1864, 578. 1865, 537.

(b) Archives
Enquiry Report. ACA. 16 (search party). 18-22 & 30-33 (inventories). and see AJ33, 244-7 (inventories).

(c) Books & articles etc
Hinchliff. Summer months among the Alps. 88, 125-6 & 153.
Kronig. Familien-Statistik. 75, 78, 134 & 148.
Ruden. Familien-Statistik. 48, 81 & 93.

7.2.29 Kennedy, T.S

(a) Biography
Mumm 1, 175-7 & 2, 370.
Obituary AJ17, 331-4.

(b) Letters & archives
3.8.65. Mathews – Whymper. SPRI. cACA.

Riffelhaus guestbook entry. 1866. Zermatt Museum.
St.Niklaus hotel guestbook entry 1865. see Gos Le Cervin 1, 225 & MW 64/65, 25.

(c) Books & articles etc
Whymper. Scrambles 1, 96-7, 365, 385n and 4, 370n.

Dangar & Blakeney. Comment, see AJ70, 21-2.
Elliott. The Second Ascent of the Matterhorn by the East Face. AJ28, 295.
Kennedy. Zermatt & the Matterhorn in winter. AJ1, 77-82.
Kennedy. Ascent of the Dent Blanche. AJ1, 33-5.
Kennedy. Ascent of the Aiguille Verte. AJ3, 73-6.

The Times. 28.7.65. Kennedy's letter of 25.7.65. AJ70, 21-2.

7.2.30 Knubel, P

(a) Biography
Ruppen. Familien-Statistik...von St. Niklaus. 79.
SAC Jahrbuch 1865, 537.
Clark. The early Alpine Guides. 162-6.
Cunningham & Abney. The Pioneers of the Alps. 151-3.
Egger. Pioniere der Alpen. 302-7.
For portraits, see 'The Pioneers' 151, and AJ32, 96, 97, 100 & 368.

(b) Letters & archives
His Führerbuch. ACA. and see AJ32, 94-109.

(c) Books & articles etc
Elliott's ascent. see AJ28, 293 & 295.
Farrar. Article on Knubel's Führerbücher. AJ32, 94-109.
Gardiner. Stockje incident. see AJ8, 382.
Note re Birkbeck. AJ32, 273.

7.2.31 Lochmatter, A

(a) Biography
Ruppen. Familien-Statistik...von St. Niklaus. 84.
SAC Jahrbuch 1865, 537.
Biographical note. AJ70, 203.
Charles Gos note. AJ52, 134. and see Die Alpen (1940) 16, 478.

(b) Letters & archives
Enquiry Report. ACA. 9 & 26-7 & see AJ33, 240 (evidence). 15 & 17 (search party).
Adams Reilly 1865 journal. ?ACA. cNLS in Graham Brown Papers. (avalanche)

(c) Books & articles etc
Whymper. Scrambles 1, 402 (search). 4, 427 & 429 (ascents).

Puller. Note of Monte Rosa tour 1864. AJ1, 377-8.

The Times. 22.7.65. McCormick's letter of 17.7.65. AJ70, 19-21. MW64/65, 10-12.
The Times. 8.8.65. J.R.Bailey's letter. (Monte Rosa avalanche)

7.2.32 Lochmatter, J-M

(a) Biography
Ruppen. Familien-Statistik...von St.Niklaus. 84.
SAC Jahrbuch 1865, 537.
Biographical note. AJ70, 203.
Charles Gos note. AJ52, 134-5. and see Die Alpen (1940) 16, 478-9.
Memorial card. see AJ52, 134.

(b) Letters & archives
Enquiry Report. ACA. 15 & 17 (Hohlicht search party).
Adams Reilly 1865 journal. ?ACA. cNLS in Graham Brown Papers (avalanche).

(c) Books & articles etc
Clark. The Day the Rope Broke. 193-4 (Tyndall).
Gos. Alpine Tragedy. 142-51 (Dent Blanche).
Gos. Le Cervin 1, 126. (Tyndall)
Tyndall. Hours of exercise in the Alps. 1, 253.
Whymper. Scrambles 1, 402 (search). 4, 425-9 & 431-3 (ascents).

For attempts & ascents. see AJ28, 284 (Elliott). & AJ30, 318 (Jordan).
Dent Blanche accident. see AJ11, 98. and Gos 'Alpine Tragedy', above.

The Times. 22.7.65. McCormick's letter of 17.7.65. AJ70, 19. MW64/65, 10-12.
The Times. 8.8.65. J.R.Bailey's letter. (Monte Rosa avalanche)

7.2.33 Long, C

(b) Letters & archives
25.7.68. Elliott – Wood. see AJ28, 289, 290 & 291.

(c) Books & articles etc
Clark. The Day the Rope Broke. 174 (Downton).
Gos. Le Cervin 1, 99-102 (Extracts from Long's account).
McCormick. A sad holiday. 13.
Whymper. Scrambles 1, 396 (sharp-eyed lad).

Dangar & Blakeney. AJ61, 486 (Wood). AJ71, 122-3 (Lunn's invention).
Lunn. AJ71, 232 (I was wrong).
L'Echo des Alpes 1867 – No.2. pp49-53 & 67 (Long's account).
Mountain World 1964/65, 16-17 (Extract from Long's account).

7.2.34 McCormick, J

(a) Biography
Notes by Alpine Journal Editor. see AJ30, 161 & AJ70, 15.
Note by Dangar & Blakeney. AJ70, 35n.
Also mentioned in AJ30, 161 (A.T.Parker) & AJ32, 21 (Farrar).

(b) Letters & archives
26. 4.65. Hudson – McCormick. ACA. AJ70, 15-16.
13. 7.65. Hudson – McCormick. (5am Note) ACA. Smythe, 180. McCormick, 12.
15. 7 65. Whymper – McCormick. ACA. Smythe 198. McCormick, 13.
16. 7.65. McCormick – P.D.Hadow. Not known to have survived.
22. 7.65. P.D.Hadow – McCormick. ACA. AJ70, 16-17.
24. 7.65. Telegram. Lady Queensberry – McCormick. ACA. AJ70, 16.
25. 7.65. Whymper – McCormick. Smythe, 205.
?4. 8.65. cWhymper – Times editor. SPRI. cACA.
10. 8.65. P.D.Hadow – McCormick. ACA. AJ70, 17-18.
c.26.8.65. Robertson – McCormick. ACA.
28. 8.65. Punch – Robertson. ACA. (apology)
31.10.65. McCormick – Whymper. SPRI.
9.12.65. Whymper – McCormick. Smythe, 216.
11.12.65. McCormick – Whymper. SPRI.

Adams Reilly 1865 journal. ?ACA. cNLS in Graham Brown Papers.

(c) Books & articles etc
Hort. Life and letters. vol 2, 40.
McCormick. A sad holiday. A Lecture delivered before the Liverpool College. London. [1865]. 20 pages. Extracts are quoted in French in Gos Le Cervin 1, 86-98.

The Times. 22.7.65. McCormick's letter of 17.7.65. AJ70, 19-21. MW64/65, 10-12.
The Times. 24.7.65. McCormick's letter of 19.7.65. (Riffelhorn) see AJ2, 153-4.
The Times. 28.7.65. McCormick's letter of 22.7.65. (bodies recovered)
The Times. 5.8.65. McCormick's letter of 1.8.65. (Monte Rosa accident)

The Times. 14.8.65. McCormick's letter of 11.8.65. (Zermatt church appeal)
The Times. 22.8.65. McCormick's letter of ?.8.65. (Zermatt church appeal)

7.2.35 Maquignaz, J-J

(a) Biography

Short obituary. AJ15, 274.
Bernardi. Il Gran Cervino. 186.
Clark. The early Alpine Guides. 155-9.
Cunningham & Abney. The Pioneers of the Alps. 191-5. (portrait 191)
Portrait, see 'The Clubroom of Zermatt in 1864' in Scrambles.

(b) Letters & archives

24. 6.66. Joseph Maquignaz – G.Carrel. see Gos Le Cervin 1, 292-3.
29. 7.66. Joseph Maquignaz – G.Carrel. see Gos Le Cervin 1, 217.
18. 9.67. G.Carrel – Tyndall. see Gos Le Cervin 1, 256-8.
22.10.67. Tyndall – G.Carrel. see Gos Le Cervin 1, 258-9.

Führerbuch. for Jordan's entries see Bernardi. Il Gran Cervino, 188-9.
Giordano's diary. see Rey below.

(c) Books & articles etc

Bernardi. Il Gran Cervino. 186-90.
Carrel. La Vallée de Valtornenche en 1867. 61-4.
Gos. Le Cervin 1, 238-9 (1867 ascent).
Rey. The Matterhorn. 1st edn. note 51 p312 / 1946 edn. note 29 p269 (14.7.65 retreat). 151-153 / 112-14 (Giordano 1866 attempt). 154-5 / 115-16 (1867 ascent). 155 / 116 (the heroic age).
Tyndall. Hours of exercise in the Alps. 1, 268-70 (Carrel in 1867). 274-93 (1868 ascent). 288-289 (boiling point).
Whymper. Scrambles 1, 414-15 (struck by lightning). 415 (14.7.65 attempt). 420 (1867 ascent). 423 (various ascents by Joseph).

Gorret. Ascension du Mont Cervin. see AJ2, 237-45. (and elsewhere)
Jordan. for details of their climbs together see 'Jordan'.
Thioly. see Seylaz article in Die Alpen 25 (1949) 351-3.

7.2.36 Martin, A.J

(b) Letters & archives

1865 Diary of Alexandre Jules Martin. Geneva. Privately owned.
Riffelhaus guestbook entry. 15.7.65. Zermatt Museum.

(c) Books & articles etc

Engel. They came to the Hills. London. 1952. 124-5.
McCormick. A sad holiday. 13-14.

Engel. Autour de la première ascension du Cervin. Die Alpen 25 (1949) 129-32.

Journal de Genève. 20.7.65. Extracts from the anonymous letters of Mme.Gautier and another; see Die Alpen 25 (1949) 131-2.

7.2.37 Ober, P

(b) Letters & archives

26.7.65. Hawker – von Fellenberg. cACA. see AJ70, 323.

(c) Books & articles etc

Dübi. Zur Erinnerung an Edward Whymper. SACJ47 (1911) 199-200 (Anzeiger).
Dübi & Montandon. Zum Matterhorn Unglück vom 14.7.65. Die Alpen V (1929) 205.
Meissner. Neue freie Presse. 4.8.65. see MW64/65, 25 & 27-8. and Taugwalder, Der Wahrheit näher, 143-5 (extracts).

Anzeiger von Interlaken. 1?.8.65. quoted in Sonntagspost 20.8.65.
Sonntagspost. 20.8.65. Extracts in Dübi (1911) 198-200 & MW64/65, 25-8.

7.2.38 Parker, C.S, A.T and S.S

(a) Biography

Mumm 1, 253-4 (Alfred) & 254-5 (Sandbach).
Comments by Farrar. AJ30, 25 & 184. and AJ32, 22 (including portraits).

(b) Letters & archives

10. 5.60. Alfred – Charles. cACA. AJ32, 22.
12. 7.61. Charles – Margaret. cACA. AJ68, 287-8.
30. 7.65. Alfred – father. cACA. AJ30, 159-61.
5. 8.65. Alfred – father. cACA. AJ30, 162.
5. 8.65. Sandbach – J.D.Forbes. USA.
13. 8.65. Alfred – father. cACA. AJ30, 162-4.
(3.10.65. Charles – father.) cACA. AJ68, 288-90.

Hotel Monte Rosa guestbook entry. 29.7-3.8.65. p261. Seiler Hotels Zermatt.
Riffelhaus guestbook. 4.8.65. & 27-29.8.65. Zermatt Museum.
Whymper's 1865 diary. SPRI.

(c) Books & articles etc

Clark. The Day the Rope Broke. 195.
Gos. Le Cervin 1, 42-5.
Ruden. Familien-Statistik. 164-5 (Guides tariff).
Whymper. Scrambles 1, 84-5, 87 & 422 (Parker attempts). 81 & 88 (1861 fees).
Whymper. Scrambles 1&2, 404. 3, 294. 4&5, 392. 6, 329 (Taugwalder footnote).

Blakeney note. AJ65, 94-5.
Dangar. The Parkers & the Matterhorn. AJ68, 285-90.
Farrar. For his comments etc. see 'Biography' above.
Parker, A.T. Triftjoch and Finsteraarhorn in 1865 without guides. AJ30, 159-64.
Parker, C.S. Passages in 1860. AJ30, 26-43 (extracts from letters).

7.2.39 Payot, F

(a) Biography
Biographical note. AJ70, 203.
Whymper's Guide to Chamonix and Mont Blanc. Introduction, page v.

(b) Books & articles etc
Whymper. Scrambles 1, 402.

Whymper. Graphic. 20.10.1894. pp467-9 (incl. portraits).

7.2.40 Perren, J.P

(a) Biography
Ruden No.263 p62. Kronig No.263 p102. see also p331.
SAC Jahrbuch 1864, 578. 1865, 534.
Photograph AJ28, 276. and see Whymper's Clubroom of Zermatt in Scrambles.

(b) Archives
Enquiry Report. ACA. 15 & 16 (search parties).
Monte Rosa guestbook. Morshead entry 10.7.63. see AJ32, 63.

(c) Books & articles etc
Ball. Guide to the Western Alps. 1863. xxxvi.
Ball. Introduction to The Alpine Guide. New edn. 1873.
Whymper. Scrambles 1, 402 (excommunication). 414-5 (lightning). 4, 426 & 430 (his Matterhorn ascents).

1862 Matterhorn winter attempt with Kennedy, see AJ1, 77-82.
1869 Lyskamm incident, see AJ5, 30.

7.2.41 Phillpotts, J.S

(a) Biography
Biographical note. AJ63, 123-4.
Mentioned in Mumm 2, 260 & 284. and see AJ32, 101, 227 & 391.

(b) Archives
Riffelhaus guestbook entry. 27.7.63. Zermatt Museum.

(c) Books & articles etc
Whymper. Scrambles 1, 402 (mentioned).

The Times. 22.7.65. McCormick's letter of 17.7.65. AJ70, 20 (mentioned).

7.2.42 Prior, W.P.

(b) Letters & archives
18.7.65. Prior – Mackenzie. PRO. Extracts in Clark, 146-7 & 176.

Hotel Monte Rosa guestbook entry. 18.7.65 p258. Seiler Hotels Zermatt.
Riffelhaus guestbook entries. 19.7.65 (small book). see also p53 (large book). Zermatt Museum.

(c) Books & articles etc

Clark. The Day the Rope Broke. 146-7 (Taugwalders). 176 (Whymper).

7.2.43 Puller, A.G

(a) Biography

Mumm 1, 261.

(b) Archives

Riffelhaus guestbook entries. 1 & 8.8.64. p14 (large book). Zermatt Museum.

(c) Books & articles etc

Clark. The Day the Rope Broke. 161.
Whymper. Scrambles 1, 402 (Lochmatters). 4, 147n (Dent d'Herens). 427 (Matterhorn).

7.2.44 Queensberry, Lord

(b) Letters & archives

24. 7.65. Lady Caroline's telegram to McCormick. ACA. AJ70, 16.
1. 8.65. Adams Reilly – Forbes. USA.
5. 8.65. Queensberry – Whymper. SPRI. (requesting meeting)
7. 8.65. Queensberry – Whymper. SPRI. (brother's debts at Zermatt)
17. 8.65. Queensberry – Whymper. SPRI. (rumour of finding body)
10. 9.65. Queensberry – Whymper. SPRI. (enclosing photograph of brother)
7.12.65. Lady Caroline – Whymper. SPRI. (requesting photo of Matterhorn)
16.12.65. cWhymper – Lady Caroline. SPRI.
22.12.65. Lady Caroline – Whymper. SPRI. (enclosing verses)
27.12.65. cWhymper – Lady Caroline. SPRI. (returning verses)
[Friday] Lady Caroline – Whymper. SPRI. (thanking for photo of Matterhorn)

Adams Reilly 1865 journal. ?ACA. cNLS in Graham Brown Papers.
Coolidge archives. (SAC) Zentralbibliothek, Zürich. and see Clark below.
Enquiry Report. ACA. 13-15 (extract from Whymper's evidence). 18-22 & 30-3 (inventories) and see AJ33, 244-7.
Monte Rosa guestbook entry. 29.7.65. p260. Seiler Hotels Zermatt.
Matterhorn verses. cACA.
Young Peter Taugwalder's Führerbuch. ACA. and see AJ59, 438-9.

(c) Books & articles etc

Clark. The Day the Rope Broke. 192. lines 12-17.
Clark. An eccentric in the Alps. 21.
Dixie, Florence. Across Patagonia. London 1880.
Hall, Newman. Autobiography 1898. Quoted by de Beer in Travellers in Switzerland. 310.
Queensberry. The spirit of the Matterhorn. 1881.

Tyndall. Hours of exercise in the Alps. 1, 252-4 (search on Matterhorn).
Zsigmondy. Im Hochgebirge. 282. In the High Mountains. 281.

Dangar. The Führerbuch of Young Peter Taugwalder. AJ59, 438-9.
Dangar & Blakeney. re Queensberry's 1871 visit to Zermatt. AJ70, 32.
Douglas, J.S. Piz Linard. Zeitschrift des D. u. Oe. Alpenvereins 1874.
Peck, E. Pioneers of the Paine. AJ97, 222-5.

Dumfries Courier. see The Times below.
Daily Graphic 1905. cACA. (Dixie's letter)
Tatler. No.201 of 3rd May 1905. cSPRI.
The Times. 28.7.65. Dumfries Courier extract.
The Times. 14.8.65. McCormick's letter of 11.8.65. (Zermatt church appeal)
The Times. 18.4.05. Florence Dixie's letter of 15.4.05.

7.2.45 Reilly, A.M.W. Adams

(a) Biography

Mumm 1, 268-71.
Obituary. AJ12, 256-9.
Whymper. Scrambles 4, 239n.

(b) Letters & archives

18.1.64. Whymper – Reilly. ACA.
22.4.65. Whymper – Reilly. ACA. Scrambles 6, 378-9.
1.5.65. Whymper – Reilly. ACA. Scrambles 6, 379-80.
10.6.65. Reilly – Whymper. SPRI. cACA.
20.6.65. Whymper – Reilly. ACA. Scrambles 6, 380-1.
19.7.65. Reilly – Forbes. USA.
1.8.65. Reilly – Forbes. USA.
?4.8.65. cWhymper – Times editor. SPRI. cACA.
13.8.65. Reilly – Whymper. SPRI.
27.8.65. Whymper – Robertson. ACA.
12.9.65. Forbes – his wife. USA. (Whymper)
27.9.66. Hodgkinson – Reilly. ACA. (Birkbeck Matterhorn attempt)

Girdlestone's letter journal. ACA. and see AJ57, 373-9.
Reilly's journals of 1864 & 1865. ?ACA per AJ32, 109. cNLS in Graham Brown Papers.

(c) Books & articles etc

Clark. The Day the Rope Broke. 192.
McCormick. A sad holiday. 12 (Visp).
Whymper. Scrambles 1, 262 & 289. For correspondence in 6th edn. see above.

Farrar. 1864 notebook extract. see AJ32, 24n.

The Times. 22.7.65. McCormick's letter of 17.7.65. AJ70, 19. MW64/65, 11.

7.2.46 Robertson, J

(a) Biography
Mumm 2, 284.
Obituary. AJ21, 537-9.
Biographical note. AJ70, 203-4.
Portrait, see The Clubroom of Zermatt in Scrambles.

(b) Letters & archives
27. 8.65. Whymper – Robertson. ACA. (The extracts in Smythe, 214-15 and in Scrambles 6, 381 contain some errors)
c.26.8.65. Robertson – McCormick. ACA.
28. 8.65. Punch – Robertson. ACA. (apology)
27.10.65. Emily Hudson – Robertson. ACA. (re lock of hair)
29. 9.66. Whymper – Robertson. ACA. Scrambles 6, 382. (Croz inscription)
14.10.66. Robertson – Whymper. SPRI. (see under Vecqueray for enclosures)
2. 3.69. Whymper – Robertson. ACA. (club rope)
9. 6.69. Whymper – Robertson. ACA. (Clubroom of Zermatt)
23. 6.69. Whymper – Robertson. ACA. Smythe, 225. (comment on Scrambles)

Croz sonnet. ?SPRI. and see Smythe 201. & Gos Le Cervin 1, 150 (in French).
Enquiry Report. ACA. 20-1 & 31-2 (Wilson inventory).
Riffelhaus guestbook entries. (small book) 4.8.62 & 27.7.63. Zermatt Museum.
Robertson's photograph of Calkin portrait of Croz. ACA.
His verses on the death of Knyvet Wilson. ACA.

(c) Books & articles etc
Brown. Family Notes. 275 & 277. also 276 (search party).
Clark. The Day the Rope Broke. 54 (Brown and Hudson). 164 (rumours).
Gos. Le Cervin 1, 123 (121-4). also 150 (Croz sonnet in French).
Smythe. Edward Whymper. 201 (Croz sonnet). 200-1 (inscription).
Whymper. Scrambles 1, 402 (excommunication & search party).

Dangar & Blakeney notes. AJ61, 498 (21) iv ("Mr. R-"). 503 (32) (Ainslie J).
Heathcote, C.G. The Laquin Joch. AJ3, 44-9.

Graphic. 29.9.94. p374 (Whymper's article).

7.2.47 Seiler, A

(a) Biography
Anthamatten, G. Alexander Seiler. 1819-1891. (English) Seiler Hotels Zermatt.
Kämpfen. Alexander Seiler der jüngere. 9-32.
Kronig. Familien Statistik. 155.
Lunn. Matterhorn Centenary. 31-2.
Lunn. The Swiss and their mountains. 152-3.
Stephen. Alexander Seiler: reminiscences. AJ15, 491-3.
Whymper. A guide to Zermatt and the Matterhorn. 15-17.

Wundt. Zermatt und seine Berge. 5-7.
Death of Madame Seiler. Note AJ17, 568.

(b) Letters & archives

22.9.65. Seiler – Whymper. SPRI. cACA. (tent & ropes)
15.7.66. Seiler – Thioly. see Die Alpen 25 (1949) 349-50.
3.8.66. Seiler – Whymper. SPRI. (Croz memorial)
22.8.66. Welschen – Whymper. SPRI. (plus Whymper's note)
16.9.66. Seiler – Whymper. SPRI. (re Curé Welschen)
12.4.67. Seiler – Whymper. SPRI. (acknowledging 400frs for Curé)
8.5.17. Rudolf Taugwalder – Montagnier. ACA.

Monte Rosa guestbook entry. Jordan's account, see AJ31, 90-2.
Privatsammlung der Briefschaften Alexander Seilers, Vater und Sohn von 1840-1920. see Kämpfen. Ein Burgerrechtsstreit im Wallis. vii.
Whymper. 1895 diary (Mme.Seiler funeral 15.9). SPRI.

(c) Books & articles etc

Coolidge. Swiss travel & Swiss guide-books. 306, 321. (History of Zermatt)
Kämpfen. Ein Burgerrechtsstreit im Wallis. 1942. 154-5.
Kronig. Familien Statistik und Geschichtliches über Zermatt. 233-7 (Einbürgerung – A.Seiler). 286-90 (Die Gasthöfe). 291-2 (Zermatterhof).
Ruden. Familien Statistik. 149-53 (Die Gasthöfe in Zermatt).
(SAC) Monte Rosa 1865 | 1965. 17-19.
Wundt. Das Matterhorn und seine Geschichte. 118-19 (lifelong fight).
Wundt. Zermatt und seine Berge. 5-7.

Gardiner. Expeditions round Zermatt...in 1876. AJ8, 382-3.
Seylaz. François Thioly. Die Alpen 25 (1949). 292-3, 349-50.

The Times. Mackenzie's letter of 7.9.66.

7.2.48 Stephen, L

(a) Biography

Mumm 1, 304-12 & 2, 373.
Obituary. AJ22, 141-6.

(b) Letters & archives

31.7.65. Stephen – Whymper. SPRI. (letter of sympathy)
9.8.65. cWhymper – Wigram. SPRI. cACA.
23.2.66. Stephen – [America] see Maitland below.

(c) Books & articles etc

Berlepsch. The Alps; translated by Leslie Stephen. 1861.
Maitland, F.W. The life & letters of Leslie Stephen. Duckworth. 1906.
Stephen. The playground of Europe. 1871.

Dangar & Blakeney. Old Peter Taugwalder. AJ70, 32 (26-37).
Lunn. Taugwalder and the Matterhorn. AJ55, 290-6.
Stephen. Alexander Seiler: reminiscences. AJ15, 491-3.
Stephen. The Allalein-Horn. see Galton. Vacation Tourists in 1860, 272.
Stephen. Note as AJ Editor, The fatal accident on the Lyskamm. AJ5, 33-4.
Stephen. Review of Whymper's Scrambles. AJ5, 234-40.
Stephen. Review in Macmillan's Magazine. August 1871, 304-11. 306 (Taugwalder & Anderegg remarks). 308 (comparatively incompetent). 309 (weak rope accusation). For a defective (15 words missing) extract about the 'weak rope', see AJ55, 295-6. & Clark, 212.
Stephen. 'Alpine Dangers', for list of his articles see Mumm 1, 312.

Journal de Genève. 26.7.66 (Birkbeck) and see AJ32, 108 & 273.

7.2.49 Tairraz, J

(a) Biography
Biographical note. AJ70, 204.

(b) Letters & archives
Enquiry Report. ACA. 17.

(c) Books & articles etc
Whymper. Scrambles 1, 402.

7.2.50 Taugwalder, F

(a) Biography
Ruden No.354 p82.
Kronig No.354 p135. See No.701 p135 for Kamil.

(b) Letters & archives
20.7.65. Downton's report to Geneva (?Mackenzie). PRO. see Clark below.

(c) Books & articles etc
Clark. The Day the Rope Broke. 174 (Downton).
Gos. Le Cervin 1, 101 (Long's account).
McCormick. A sad holiday. 13.
Schmid. Menschen am Matterhorn. 83.
Taugwalder,H. Der Wahrheit näher. 165.
Whymper. Scrambles 1, 396.

Dangar & Blakeney. re Lunn. see AJ71, 122-3 & 232.
Long. L'Echo des Alpes 1867, 53. and see MW 64/65, 17. and Gos above.
Lunn. 'I was wrong'. see AJ71, 232.

7.2.51 Taugwalder, J

(a) Biography

Ruden. No.354 p82.
Kronig. No.354 p135.

(b) Letters & archives

Recovery party. see Enquiry Report. ACA. 16.
Führerbuch of Young Peter Taugwalder. ACA.
Riffelhaus guestbook. 1.8.64. Puller Monte Rosa ascent. Zermatt Museum.

(c) Books & articles etc

Güssfeldt. In den Hochalpen. 22.
Whymper. Scrambles 1, 381, 385-7. 1&2, 404 and 3, 294 (Taugwalder footnote).

7.2.52 Taugwalder, Old Peter

(a) Biography

Ruden. No.351 p81 & see No.354 p82 for children & No's. 186, 188 & 190 p48 for cousins Johannes & Alois Julen.
Kronig. No.351 p134 & see No.354 p135 for children & No's. 186 p75, 188 p76, & 190 p78 for cousins. For Old Peter's ghost, see p328(b).
SAC Jahrbuch 1865, 535.
Dangar & Blakeney. Old Peter Taugwalder. AJ70, 26-37.
Egger. Pioniere der Alpen. 178-99.
Obituary. AJ14, 169.
Portrait see Egger ibid 179.
Photographs see AJ32, 232; AJ59, 440 and Clark, The Alps, 65.
Taugwalder family tree. see AJ31, 338 & Die Alpen XXX (1954) special supplement biography of Alexander Taugwalder p7.

(b) Letters & archives

25.7.65. Whymper – von Fellenberg. SAC Bern. cZM. cACA. AJ70, 23-6. MW64/65, 13-16.
31.7.65. J.J.Cowell – Whymper. SPRI. cACA. (Alpine Club enquiry)
5.8.65. Sandbach Parker – J.D.Forbes. USA.
8.8.65. Wigram – Whymper. SPRI. cACA. (J-B Croz & cut rope)
8.8.65. cWhymper – Buxton. SPRI.
9.8.65. cWhymper – Wigram. SPRI. cACA. (ill feeling at Chamonix) see also Scrambles 1, 364-5.
10.8.65. Wigram – Whymper. SPRI. cACA. (smuggling)
20.8.65. Wills – Whymper. SPRI. cACA (extract).
21.8.65. cWhymper – Henry Hadow. SPRI. cACA.
27.8.65. Whymper – Robertson. ACA. and see extracts in Smythe, 214-5 & in Scrambles 6, 381.
22.9.65. Seiler – Whymper. SPRI. cACA.
(3.10.65. Charles Parker – to his father.) cACA. and see AJ68, 288-90.
25.7.68. Elliott – Wood. see AJ28, 289 & 290.
8.5.17. Rudolf Taugwalder – Montagnier. ACA. (Young Peter's answers to questions)

Monte Rosa guestbook. Parkers' entry 3.8.65. p261. Seiler Hotels Zermatt. For Jordan 7.10.67 see AJ31, 90. For Morshead 10.7.63 see AJ32, 63.
Riffelhaus guestbook entry. C.S.Parker. 27-29.8.65. Zermatt Museum.
Search party names. see Enquiry Report. ACA. 15-17.
Whymper climbing diary for 1865. SPRI.
Whymper memorandum. 17.8.65. SPRI. and see Smythe, 194-5, also in Scrambles 1, 400-1 omitting last paragraph.

(c) Books & articles etc

Arve, Stéphen d'. Les fastes du Mont Blanc. 1876. 230-3.
Ball. Guide to the Western Alps. 1863. xxxvi. 1870, see AJ70, 33.
Carrel. La Vallée de Valtornenche en 1867. 47.
Cunningham & Abney. The Pioneers of the Alps. 1887. Preface, vi.
Egger. Pioniere der Alpen. 178-99.
Gos. Le Cervin 1, 179 (S.d'Arve). 182 (Gos following Egger).
Güssfeldt. In den Hochalpen. 21-7.
Kämpfen. Ein Burgerrechtstreit im Wallis. 1942.
Lunn. Matterhorn Centenary. 142 (Bernard Biner).
Lunn. The Alps. 179. see also AJ55, 291 (Stogden).
Lunn. The Swiss and their mountains. 152-3 (Seiler).
Maclean. Three weeks amongst the upper regions of the Alps. 22.
Ruden. Familien-Statistik. 164-5 (guides fees).
(Seiler) see Kämpfen and Lunn. (Burger application)
Taugwalder, H. Der Wahrheit näher. 143-5 (Meissner). 164 (America).
Thioly. Voyage en Suisse et ascension du Mont Rose 1860. 36 & see Die Alpen 25 (1949) 294.
Thioly. Ascension du Mont Cervin. 1871. p5.
Tuckett. A pioneer in the High Alps. 283.
Whymper. Scrambles 1, 81 (Carrel's 1861 fees). 88 (Old Peter's 1861 fees). 397n (position of the victims). 1&2, 404n. 3, 294n (Old Peter footnote). Later amended in 4&5, 392n & 6, 329n.

Buxton. The glacier du Dôme. AJ2, 332-3.
Dangar & Blakeney. The first ascent of the Matterhorn. The Narrative of Young Peter Taugwalder. AJ61, 484-503. NB p501 note 27 para vi.
Dangar & Blakeney. Old Peter Taugwalder. AJ70, 32 & 26-37.
Dangar & Blakeney. A word for Whymper. AJ71, 124 (75 years to defend).
Douglas. The Gabelhorn. AJ2, 221-2.
Dübi & Montandon. Zum Matterhornunglück von 14 Juli 1865. Die Alpen V (1929) 220 (203-23).
Farrar. Days of long ago. AJ32, 26 (one of the boldest guides).
Graham Brown. Girdlestone & the Matterhorn accident, 1865. AJ57, 369-84.
Jordan. ...the Matterhorn in 1867. AJ30, 316-23.
Jordan. Monte Rosa guestbook entry of 7.10.67. see AJ31, 90-2.
Kennedy. Ascent of the Dent Blanche. AJ1, 33-5.
Kennedy. Zermatt & the Matterhorn in winter. AJ1, 80-2.
Kennedy. Ascent of the Aiguille Verte. AJ3, 73 (rope of 6 + dog!).
Lunn. Taugwalder and the Matterhorn. AJ55, 290-6.
SAC Jahrbuch 1865. Gletscherführer. 534-5. (Perren & Zumtaugwalds)
Stephen. Allalein-Horn. see Galton Vacation Tourists in 1860. 272.
Thioly. see Seylaz in Die Alpen 25 (1949) 294 & 349-51.

Journal de Genève. 18.7.65. see MW64/65, 17-18. Bernardi Il Gran Cervino 168.
Der Bund. 19.7.65. see MW64/65, 18-20. & Dübi in SACJ47 (1911) 192-3.
Neue freie Presse. 4.8.65. (Meissner article) see MW64/65, 27 & 28. and see Taugwalder,H. (above).

Macmillan's Magazine. August 1871, 304-11 (Stephen review). & see AJ55, 295-6.
Graphic. 29.9.94. p374.
The Times. 22.7.65. McCormick's letter of 17.7.65. AJ70, 19-21. MW64/65, 10-12.
The Times. 28.7.65. Dumfries Courier extract.
The Times. 8.8.65. Whymper's letter of 7.8.65. AJ2, 148-53.

For 'cover up' after other accidents, see AJ13, 170 etc (Borckhardt). AJ5, 23-32 (Chesters). AJ6, 306-15 (Fedchenko).

7.2.53 Taugwalder, Young Peter

(a) Biography

Ruden No.354 p82.
Kronig No.354 p135 & see No's. 701 & 702 p135.
SAC Jahrbuch 1865, 535-6.
Portrait, see The Clubroom of Zermatt in 1864 in Scrambles, or in Rebuffat's Men and the Matterhorn, 86-7 & 99.
Photographs see Clark. The Alps, 64. Lunn. Matterhorn Centenary, 80. Wundt. Das Matterhorn und seine Geschichte, 134. Yung. Zermatt & the valley of the Viège, 48. and AJ59, 440-1.

(b) Letters & archives

18.7.65. Prior – Mackenzie. see Clark. The Day the Rope Broke. 146-7.
25.7.65. Whymper – von Fellenberg. see 7.2.17 (von Fellenberg sources).
9.8.65. cWhymper – Wigram. SPRI. cACA.
10.8.65. Wigram – Whymper. SPRI. cACA.
11.8.65. J.W.Cowell – Whymper. SPRI. cACA.
20.8.65. Wills – Whymper. SPRI. cACA (extract).
22.9.65. Seiler – Whymper. SPRI. cACA.

4. 5.17. Montagnier – Farrar. ACA.
8. 5.17. Rudolf Taugwalder – Montagnier. ACA.
5. 9.17. Young Peter – Montagnier. ACA.
17.11.17. 50frs posting receipt. ACA.
27.11.17. Young Peter – Montagnier. ACA.
17.12.17. Montagnier – Farrar. ACA. (encl. 'consent', see below)
16. 1.18. cMontagnier – Young Peter. ACA.
18. 1.18. cYoung Peter – Montagnier. ACA.

(November 1917) Young Peter's Narrative. ACA. and see AJ61, 489-92.
Undated. Consent to shortening above. ACA.
17.8.65. Whymper's memorandum. SPRI. and see Smythe 194-5. also in Scrambles 1, 400-1 omitting last paragraph.

1. 9.65. Cowell memorandum or certificate. SPRI. cACA (extract) and see incomplete extract in Smythe 195-6.

Enquiry Report. ACA. 10 & 27 (Q & A 54). see also AJ33, 242.
Führerbuch, 1859-83. ACA. (see Dangar below). Note of gift, see AJ40, 408.
Montagnier questions with Peter's answers. cACA. and see Scrambles 6, 305n. & 323n.

(c) Books & articles etc
Clark. The Day the Rope Broke. 146-7 (Prior). 199 (slightly out of focus).
Egger. Pioniere der Alpen. 192 (Egger's chessmove).
Gos. Alpinisme anecdotique. 303-6 (Un guide historique).
Güssfeldt. In den Hochalpen. Berlin 1886. 2nd edn. 22 (Joseph Taugwalder).
Jegerlehner. Die Todesfahrt auf das Matterhorn. Berlin. 1928. (AJ40, 406).
Taugwalder,H. Der Wahrheit näher.
Thioly. Ascension du Mont Cervin. Geneva. 1871. p5 (Zermatt guides trembling).
Whymper. Scrambles 1, 404 (Taugwalder footnote). 414-15 (Heathcote).

Buxton. The Glacier du Dôme. AJ2, 332-3.
Dangar. The Führerbuch of young Peter Taugwalder. AJ59, 436-41.
Dangar & Blakeney. The first ascent of the Matterhorn. The Narrative of young Peter Taugwalder. (With foreword and notes) AJ61, 484-503.
Egger. Les Taugwalders du Cervin. Die Alpen 16 (1940) 275-8.
Elliott. AJ28. 290 (Zermatt guides). AJ31, 257 (Biner testimonial).
Gardiner. AJ8, 382 (Knubel incident).
Jordan. AJ30, 319 (Taugwalders at Breuil).
Kennedy. Ascent of the Dent Blanche. AJ1, 34.
Seylaz. François Thioly. Die Alpen 25 (1949), 350-1 (1866 & 1867).

(Borckhardt death) see AJ13, 170 etc.
(Lyskamm death) see AJ5, 23-32.
(Mer de Glace death) see AJ6, 306-15.

Journal de Genève. 18.7.65. see Bernardi, Il Gran Cervino 168 & MW64/65, 17&18.
Journal de Genève. 26.7.66. see AJ32, 108-9.
The Times. 22.7.65. McCormick's letter of 17.7.65. AJ70, 19-21. MW64/65, 10-12.
The Times. 8.8.65. Whymper's letter of 7.8.65. AJ2, 148-53.

7.2.54 Thioly, F

(a) Biography
Seylaz. François Thioly. Un pionnier oublié de l'alpinisme suisse. Die Alpen 25 (1949) 290-4 & 347-54, with a photograph 296, and a Thioly bibliography 354.
Seylaz. Les Alpes 39 (1963) 116.

(b) Letters & archives
15.7.66. Seiler – Thioly. M.P.Thioly archives Geneva. and see Die Alpen 25, (1949) 349-50.

Whymper memorandum 17.8.65. (Matterhorn fees) SPRI. and see Smythe, 195.

(c) Books & articles etc

Gos. Le Cervin 1, 272-80.
Lunn. Matterhorn Centenary. 90.
Rey. The Matterhorn. 1st edn. 309. 1946 edn. 267.
Ruden. Familien Statistik. 164-5 (guides tariff).
Thioly. Ascension du Mont Cervin. Genève. 1871. and see SACJ6, 169-98.
Thioly. Voyage en Suisse et ascension du Mont Rose. 36. (Taugwalder)

Seylaz. François Thioly. Die Alpen 25 (1949) 290-4 & 347-54.

7.2.55 Tyndall, J

(a) Biography

Mumm 1, 339-49.
Obituary. AJ17, 25-7.
Schuster. John Tyndall as a mountaineer. see Postscript to adventure. 126-81.

(b) Letters & archives

22. 9.65. Seiler – Whymper. SPRI. cACA. (Tyndall's use of Whymper's tent)
18. 9.67. G.Carrel – Tyndall. see Gos Le Cervin 1, 256-8. & Bernardi 183 (Ital)
12.10.67. Giordano – G.Carrel. see Gos Le Cervin 1, 241-2.
22.10.67. Tyndall – G.Carrel. see Gos Le Cervin 1, 258-9. & Bernardi 184 (Ital)
25. 7.68. Elliott – Wood. see AJ28, 294.
31.12.68. Giordano – Tyndall. see Hours of exercise in the Alps. 1, 294.
4. 9.71. Eliza Pennell – Tyndall. ACA. see AJ61, 499. (re Jordan and body)

Diaries of John Tyndall. Royal Institution, London.
Breuil, Hotel du Mont Cervin guestbook. see Carrel below p60.

(c) Books & articles etc

Carrel. La Vallée de Valtornenche en 1867. (being Bollettino del Club Alpino Italiano No.12 1868). 60-1.
Clark. The Day the Rope Broke. 192-4.
Gos. Le Cervin 1, 254-9 (problem with Carrel). 256-9 (letters, see above). 265-72 (1868 traverse).
Tyndall. Hours of exercise in the Alps. 1, 252-4 (1865). 268-70 (1867). 273-93 (1868). 2, 166-167 (re Scrambles).

Hawkins, F.V. Partial ascent of the Matterhorn. see Galton. Vacation Tourists in 1860. 282-304. also in Hours of exercise, chapter 3.
Whymper's letter to Alpine Journal editor. see AJ5, 329-36. also in Gos Le Cervin 1, 164-75 (in French).

For Florence Dixie, Graphic and the telegram (re body) see 7.2.44 (Queensberry).

7.2.56 Vecqueray, J.W.J

(b) Letters & archives

29. 9.66. Whymper – Robertson. ACA. Scrambles 6, 382.
14.10.66. Robertson – Whymper. SPRI. (enclosing Croz inscriptions)
[Note re the Croz' inscriptions.
A. Whymper's suggested inscription (encl.29.9) ACA. cSPRI.
B. French translation of A (encl.14.10) in Vecqueray's writing. SPRI.
C. Slight modification of B (encl.14.10) in Vecqueray's writing. SPRI.
D. Further copy of C in Robertson's writing, retained by him. ACA. and see Smythe, Whymper 201 for contents of 'C'.]

Vecqueray translation of Enquiry Questions & Answers. SPRI.
Enquiry Q's & A's 2-17. ACA. see Report 1-4. also AJ33, 235-7.
Adams Reilly 1865 journal. ?ACA. cNLS in Graham Brown Papers.
Riffelhaus guestbook entry. July 1863. (small book) p321. Zermatt Museum.

(c) Books & articles etc

Smythe. Edward Whymper. 200-1.

Anderegg fund contributors. AJ6, 317.

7.2.57 Whymper, E

(a) Biography

Mumm 1, 373-80 & 2, 374-5.
Obituary. AJ26, 54-61 & 104-5.
Arcis, E.d'. Edward Whymper. Die Alpen 16 (1940) 272-5.
Chamson, Max. Whymper le fou du Cervin. 1986.
Clark. Six great mountaineers. 9 & 11-51.
Dübi. Zur Erinnerung an Edward Whymper. SAC Jahrbuch 47 (1911) 183-216.
Kernahan, C. In good company. 2nd edn. 1917, 149-88.
Smythe. Edward Whymper. 1940. (and see Smythe Andes Introduction 5-20 below)
(?Schuster) Review of above. AJ52, 147-51.
Unsworth, W. Matterhorn man. 1965.
Young, G.W. Mountaineering & its Prophets. Cornhill Magazine 1923. see Smythe 230-3.
Young, G.W. Mountain prophets. AJ54, 102-6.
Blakeney. Note. AJ70, 135 (Southend).
'An interesting sidelight'. AJ46, 164-5 (Journal of Michael Field).
Photographs. see AJ26, 55 & 58, and AJ32, 220. Also Smythe's Edward Whymper, and see Stevens below.

(b) Letters & archives

1. 8.62. E.Whymper – J.W.Whymper. JMA. (account of fall)
8. 8.62. J.W.Whymper – J.Murray. JMA. (enclosing above)
18. 1.64. E.Whymper – Reilly. ACA. (a route I should like to try)
22. 4.65. Whymper – Reilly. ACA. Scrambles 6, 378-9.
1. 5.65. Whymper – Reilly. ACA. Scrambles 6, 379-80.
10. 6.65. Reilly – Whymper. SPRI. cACA.

20. 6.65.	Whymper – Reilly. ACA. Scrambles 6, 380-1.
11. 7.65.	Giordano – Sella. see Rey The Matterhorn. 133. 1946 edn. 97. & Scrambles 6, 340.
15. 7.65.	Whymper – McCormick. ACA. Smythe, 198. McCormick, 13.
16. 7.65.	McCormick – P.D.Hadow. Not known to have survived.
Undated	Clemenz – Whymper. (note re Mme Douglas) SPRI.
18. 7.65.	Prior – Mackenzie. Extracts in Clark, 146-7 & 176.
19. 7.65.	Reilly – J.D.Forbes. USA.
20. 7.65.	Downton's report to Geneva (?Mackenzie). PRO. see Clark below.
24. 7.65.	H.B.George – Whymper. SPRI. cACA
25. 7.65.	Whymper – McCormick. Smythe, 205.
25. 7.65.	Whymper – von Fellenberg. SAC Bern. cACA. cZM. AJ70, 23-6. MW64/65, 13-16.
26. 7.65.	Whymper – von Fellenberg. cACA. see Scrambles 6, 319n. Alpina 1911.
26. 7.65.	Hawker – von Fellenberg. cACA. see AJ70, 323. Bergsteiger 7/65. Alpina 1911.
26. 7.65.	Whymper – Rimini. CAI Bollettino No.1 of 1865.
31. 7.65.	J.J.Cowell – Whymper. SPRI. cACA.
31. 7.65.	Glover – Whymper. SPRI.
31. 7.65.	L.Stephen – Whymper. SPRI.
1. 8.65.	Hort – his wife. see AJ57, 381 and F.J.A.Hort 'Life...' below.
2. 8.65.	Times editor – Whymper. SPRI. cACA.
3. 8.65.	Mathews – Whymper. SPRI. cACA.
?4. 8.65.	cWhymper – Times editor. SPRI. cACA.
[5. 8.65]	Queensberry – Whymper. SPRI. (dated Saturday)
5. 8.65.	Times editor – Whymper. SPRI. cACA.
6. 8.65.	Wills – Whymper. SPRI.
7. 8.65.	Wills – Whymper. SPRI. See The Times and Smythe, 210-11 (extract).
7. 8.65.	Times editor – Whymper. SPRI. cACA.
7. 8.65.	Longman – Whymper. SPRI. cACA.
7. 8.65.	Queensberry – Whymper. SPRI.
8. 8.65.	Wigram – Whymper. SPRI. cACA.
8. 8.65.	cWhymper – Buxton. SPRI.
9. 8.65.	Longman – Whymper. SPRI. cACA.
9. 8.65.	cWhymper – Wigram. SPRI. cACA. (weak rope not used intentionally)
9. 8.65.	Wills – Whymper. SPRI.
9. 8.65.	Buxton – Whymper. SPRI.
9. 8.65.	Wigram – Whymper. SPRI. cACA.
10. 8.65.	Wigram – Whymper. SPRI. cACA.
10. 8.65.	Mathews – Whymper. SPRI.
11. 8.65.	J.W.Cowell – Whymper. SPRI. cACA.
11. 8.65.	Emily Hudson – Whymper. SPRI.
12. 8.65.	cWhymper – Buxton. SPRI.
13. 8.65.	Reilly – Whymper. SPRI.
17. 8.65.	Queensberry – Whymper. SPRI.
18. 8.65.	Whymper – Glover. cZermatt Museum.
19. 8.65.	H.Hadow – Whymper. SPRI. cACA.
20. 8.65.	Wills – Whymper. SPRI. cACA.
21. 8.65.	cWhymper – H.Hadow. SPRI. cACA.
23. 8.65.	P.D.Hadow – Whymper. SPRI.
23. 8.65.	cWhymper – P.D.Hadow. SPRI.
26. 8.65.	P.D.Hadow – Whymper. SPRI.

c.26.8.65. Robertson – McCormick. ACA.
27. 8.65. Whymper – Robertson. ACA. (see Robertson sources for extracts)
28. 8.65. Punch – Robertson. ACA.
29. 8.65. Obach (Goupil) – Whymper. SPRI.
1. 9.65. Goupil – Whymper. SPRI. (in French)
4. 9.65. Obach (Goupil) – Whymper. SPRI. (encl. the above)
4. 9.65. J.W.Cowell – Whymper. SPRI. cACA. (encl. memorandum)
10. 9.65. Queensberry – Whymper. SPRI. (encl. photo of brother)
12. 9.65. J.D.Forbes – his wife. USA. (met Whymper)
22. 9.65. Seiler – Whymper. SPRI. cACA.
7.12.65. Lady Queensberry – Whymper. SPRI.
9.12.65. Whymper – McCormick. see Smythe, 216.
11.12.65. McCormick – Whymper. SPRI.
16.12.65. cWhymper – Lady Queensberry. SPRI.
21.12.65. Elijah Walton – Whymper. SPRI. (encl. Carrel portrait)
22.12.65. Lady Queensberry – Whymper. SPRI. (encl. verses)
27.12.65. cWhymper – Lady Queensberry. SPRI.
[Friday] Lady Queensberry – Whymper. SPRI. (?written Jan. 1866)
2. 1.66. Forbes – Wills. ?USA. (see Shairp below)
3. 8.66. Seiler – Whymper. SPRI. (Croz memorial)
22. 8.66. Welschen – Whymper. SPRI. (plus Whymper's note)
16. 9.66. Seiler – Whymper. SPRI. (re Curé Welschen)
29. 9.66. Whymper – Robertson. ACA. Scrambles 6, 382 (Croz inscription).
14.10.66. Robertson – Whymper. SPRI. (see under Vecqueray for enclosures)
12. 4.67. Seiler – Whymper. SPRI. (acknowledging 400frs for Curé)
2. 3.69. Whymper – Robertson. ACA. (club rope)
9. 6.69. Whymper – Robertson. ACA. (Clubroom of Zermatt)
23. 6.69. Whymper – Robertson. ACA. Smythe, 225 (extract about Scrambles).
9. 8.69. Whymper – [John Murray] JMA. (first instalment of Scrambles)
6.10.02. J.W.Whymper – Murray. JMA. (refers to age 90)
7. 4.03. Annette Whymper – Murray. JMA. (father died)
22. 7.11. E.Whymper – E.H.Stevens. AJ53, 157.
9.10.39. Smythe – Cook. ACA.

Adams Reilly journals of 1864 & 1865. ?ACA. cNLS in Graham Brown Papers.
Cowell memorandum. 1.9.65. SPRI. Extract in Smythe, 195-6. and see cACA.
Douglas. Matterhorn verses written c.10.7.65. SPRI. cACA.
Enquiry Report. ACA. and see AJ33, 234-47.
Girdlestone's letter journal. ACA. and see Graham Brown article AJ57, 369-84.
Graham Brown Papers. NLS.
Monte Rosa guestbook entry. 1.9.69. p285 (Matterhorn 1st ascent). Seiler Hotels Zermatt. see also AJ31, 88. and Wundt, Williams & Lunn below.
Riffelhaus guestbook entry. Douglas. c.10.7.65. Zermatt Museum.
Whymper. Climbing diaries. SPRI.
Whymper. His note of Enquiry. SPRI.
Whymper. His questions for Taugwalder (in English). SPRI. For French version dated 21.7.65. see Enquiry Report at ACA 22-3.
Whymper. Reilly receipt for Croz money. 22.7.65. SPRI.

Whymper. Memorandum of 17.8.65. SPRI. Smythe, 194-5. Also in Scrambles 1, 400-1, omitting last paragraph.
Whymper. Vecqueray's translation of his Questions & Answers. SPRI.
Whymper. Summons from Clemenz 21.7.65. SPRI. cACA in Enquiry Report, 18.
Whymper. 1894 lecture leaflet. ACA.

(c) Books & articles etc

Browne. The recollections of a bishop. 104-5.
Carrel. La Vallée de Valtornenche en 1867. 47.
Clark. The Day the Rope Broke. 146-7 (Prior letter). 172-3 (Downton letter).
Egger. Pioniere der Alpen. 184 (sarcasm & ridicule over 200frs). 191-2 (Taugwalder footnote, and chessmove).
[Field,M.] Works and days; from the Journal of Michael Field. see AJ46, 164-5.
[Forbes,J.D.] see Shairp below.
Gos. Le Cervin 1, 177-91 (La corde maudite). 183 (Whymper's expression!). 183 (Zermatt Guide, 12th edn). 198-202 (Rambert).
Gos. Le Cervin 2, 197 (Manning illustration). 290-6 (Casella).
Hort,F.J.A. Life and letters. vol 2, 39-40.
Kernahan,C. In good company. 2nd edn 1917. 149-88. see AJ71, 235n.
Lunn. The Alps. 1914. 174 (ropes exist to be cut).
Lunn. Mountain Jubilee. 189-214 (Edward Whymper).
Lunn. Zermatt and the Valais. 39 (3 accusations for 1). 40 (A.E.W.Mason). 41 (pride in Smythe). 42 (a good word).
Lunn. A Century of Mountaineering. 5 (Gurtner preface). 56-7 (3 for 1). 58 (a good word).
Lunn. Matterhorn Centenary. 64-5 (3 for 1) [& see AJ55, 291]. 64 (A.E.W.Mason). 67 (unfair attack). 72 (guestbook entry of 1.9.69).
McCormick. A sad holiday. 13 (Whymper note). 19 (say not they were rash).
Rambert. Les Alpes suisses. 1866. 1, 273-94. 'L'accident du Cervin'. and see Gos above & Journal de Genève 28.7.65.
Ruden. Familien-Statistik. 164-5 (Matterhorn tariff).
Shairp & others. Life and letters of J.D.Forbes. 1873. 426 (Studer). 429 (Wills).
Smythe. Edward Whymper. 153 (Reilly in 1864). 290-1 (1895 attempt). 291 (Mme Seiler funeral). 292, 298-300 & 315 (lectures; see also L'Echo below).
Smythe. see his Introduction to 1949 edn of Whymper's Andes. 5-15.
Whymper. A guide to Zermatt and the Matterhorn. 1897-1911.
Whymper. Guide à Zermatt et au Cervin (ou Matterhorn). 1911.
Whymper. 'Scrambles'. Original Taugwalder footnote, 1st & 2nd edns, 404. 3rd, 294. Revised footnote, 4th & 5th, 392. 6th, 329. The Clubroom of Zermatt in 1864. In all six John Murray edns. Old Peter Taugwalder's 1861 fees. Scrambles 1, 88.
Whymper. Berg und Gletscherfahrten. Braunschweig. 1872 1st edn, 495 and 1909 3rd edn, 493-4 (Taugwalder footnote).
Whymper. Escalades dans les Alpes. Paris. 1873. 398 (cette corde maudite). 403-4 (Taugwalder footnote).
Whymper. Escalades. [1944] Engel. 195 (corde maudite).
Williams,C. Women on the rope. 117 (Ethel's climbs).
Williams,C. Zermatt Saga. 48 (Monte Rosa guestbook entry 1.9.69).
Wundt. Das Matterhorn und seine Geschichte. 2nd edn. 123 (Monte Rosa guestbook entry 1.9.69).

Casella. L'Auto. 1911. 18th September. and see Gos, Le Cervin 2, 290-6.

Casella. Les sports d'hiver & l'alpinisme. Paris 1911. 12 (La Liberté).

Dangar & Blakeney. AJ61, 503 (Croz crucifix). AJ61, 485 & AJ71, 124-5 (ugly look). AJ61, 485n (the suspicious fact). AJ61, 485n & AJ71, 126 (A.E.W.Mason). AJ70, 32 (Old Peter out of his class). AJ71, 125 (Stephen's defence). AJ71, 234 (comment on Cowell and on speaking up for Taugwalder). AJ71, 235 (Kernahan).

Dauzat.A. La Liberté. 19.9.1911. (Douglas rumour). see Casella above & Dübi.

[Dickens] All the year round. 19.8.65 & 2.9.65 see AJ53, 363-5.

Dübi. Zur Erinnerung an Edward Whymper. SACJ 47 (1911) 183-216. 194 (Liberté).

Dübi & Montandon. Zum Matterhornunglück vom 14.7.65. Die Alpen V (1929) 203-23.

L'Echo des Alpes. 1893, 368-9 (lectures).

Egger. Les Taugwalders du Cervin. Die Alpen 16 (1940) 275-8.

Farrar. AJ33, 248 (the suspicious fact).

Gorret. (Matterhorn account). see AJ2, 237-45 (French), Die Alpen 11 (1935) 94-101 (German) or Feuille d'Aoste. October 1865, No's 41, 43 & 44.

Graham Brown. Girdlestone & the Matterhorn accident, 1865. AJ57, 369-84. 370 (a stickler).

Graham Brown. The great Matterhorn disaster of 1865. The Field. 13.2.32. 227.

Hall. The fatal accident on the Lyskamm. AJ5, 23-32.

Loppé. L'Abeille de Chamonix. 23.7.65. SPRI. and see Gos, Alpinisme anecdotique, 281-4.

Lunn. Taugwalder and the Matterhorn. AJ55, 290-6. 293 (service to truth).

Lyall, A. Gustave Doré and his links with Edward Whymper. AJ100, 215-21.

[Mason, A.E.W.] see AJ61, 485n & AJ71, 126. also Lunn Centenary 57 & Zermatt 40.

Meissner. Neue freie Presse. 4.8.65. see MW64/65, 25 & 27-8. and Taugwalder, Der Wahrheit näher, 143-5 (extracts).

Monod. (Whymper interview) Journal de Zermatt. 25.8.95. ACA. SPRI. and see AJ45, 321-7 & Gos Le Cervin 1, 108-9.

[Parker & Taugwalder] see AJ68, 289-90.

[Ropes] Report of the Special Committee (1864). AJ1, 321-6. and see AJ2, 95.

Roth, A. Sonntagspost 13.8.65. see Dübi SACJ 47 (1911) 195-8. MW64/65, 25.

Roth, A. Sonntagspost 20.8.65. see Dübi ibid 198-200. Extract MW64/65, 25-8.

Stephen. Macmillan's Magazine. August 1871, 306-7 (inaccessible). 308-9 (use of weak rope).

Stevens, E.H. Portraits of Whymper. AJ53, 156-8. and see AJ91, 294-5.

Whymper. 1862 lone excursion. see AJ2, 8-9.

Whymper. Strand Magazine. 1909. vol 37, 55-6.

Whymper. Graphic. 29.9 & 6.10. 1894. pp374 & 402. 'The Alps revisited.'

Journal de Genève. 20.7.65 [Gautier]. 28.7.65 (Rambert).

The Times. 22.7.65. McCormick's letter of 17.7.65. AJ70, 19-21. MW64/65, 10-12.

The Times. 31.7.65. Buxton's letter of 29.7.65.

The Times. 8.8.65. Whymper's letter of 7.8.65. AJ2, 148-53. also in Gos, Alpinisme anecdotique, 205-17.

The Times. 8.8.65. Wills letter of 7.8.65. to Whymper. Smythe, 210-11 extract.

The Times. 19.8.65. Whymper's letter about Croz fund.

The Times. ?.9.66. Mackenzie's letter of 7.9.66.

The Times. 24.7.97. Whymper's letter about Cooper. see AJ46, 164-5.

The Times. 27.7.65. Leading article.

The Times. 2.8.65. Report from Berne, July 29. (Based on Loppé's account)

The Times. 2.8.65. Note re Douglas.

The Times. 9.8.65. Leading article.
The Times. 2.5.94. Report of Whymper lecture on mountaineering.

7.2.58 Wigram, W

(a) Biography
Mumm 1, 380-2 & 2, 375.

(b) Letters & archives
8.8.65. Wigram – Whymper. SPRI. cACA. (J-B Croz & cut rope)
9.8.65. cWhymper – Wigram. SPRI. cACA. (weak rope not used intentionally)
9.8.65. Wigram – Whymper. SPRI. cACA.
10.8.65. Wigram – Whymper. SPRI. cACA. (Taugwalder on Dent Blanche)

Croz fund appeal leaflet. SPRI. and see Gos, below.

(c) Books & articles etc
Gos. Propos d'un Alpiniste. 51 (reference to Wigram furnishing details of Croz family for the appeal).
Memoirs of Canon Wigram. Privately printed 1908. 83 (Kennedy's Dent Blanche attempt with Taugwalders, followed by the first ascent with J-B Croz).

7.2.59 Wills, A

(a) Biography
Mumm 1, 383-8 & 2, 375.
Obituary. AJ27, 47-54 with photographs.
1865 portrait. see Leisure Hour 1896, 152.

(b) Letters & archives
6.8.65. Wills – Whymper. SPRI. (enclosing 7.8.65 below)
7.8.65. Wills – Whymper. SPRI. Smythe, 210-11 (extract). The Times 8.8.65.
?8.8.65. Whymper – Wills. Not known to have survived.
9.8.65. Wills – Whymper. SPRI. (expressing sympathy)
13.8.65. Wills – Whymper. SPRI. (suggesting Croz fund)
c.17.8.65. Whymper – Wills. Enclosing Cowell/Whymper letter of 11.8.65 & memo. of 17.8.65. Letter is not known to have survived.
20.8.65. Wills – Whymper. SPRI. cACA (extract).

Cowell memorandum. 1.9.65. SPRI. Extract in Smythe, 195-6. and see cACA.
Whymper memorandum. 17.8.65. SPRI. and see Smythe, 194-5, also in Scrambles 1, 400-1, omitting last paragraph.

(c) Books & articles etc
Smythe. Edward Whymper. 194-5 (17.8.65 memorandum). 195-6 (Cowell memorandum extract). 210-11 (Wills 7.8.65 extract).
Whymper. Scrambles 1, 400-1 (extract from 17.8.65 memorandum).

The Times. 8.8.65. Wills' letter to Whymper of 7.8.65. (extract Smythe, 210)
The Times. 8.8.65. Whymper's letter of 7.8.65. AJ2, 148-53.
The Times. 14.8.65. Wills' letter of 11.8.65.

7.2.60 Wilson, W.K

(a) Biography
Biographical note. AJ70, 204.

(b) Letters & archives
19.7.65. Reilly – J.D.Forbes. USA.
20.7.65. Downton's report to Geneva (?Mackenzie). PRO. see Clark, 174.
[c.26.8.65.] Robertson – McCormick. ACA. (reference to Wilson's family)

Adams Reilly 1865 journal. ?ACA. cNLS in Graham Brown Papers. (the search and the burial)
Enquiry Report. ACA. 20-1 & 31-2 (inventory of Wilson's possessions).
Riffelhaus guestbook note. (small book) 18.7.65. Zermatt Museum.
Robertson. Verses written August 1865, after the death of his friend. ACA.

(c) Books & articles etc
Brown. Family Notes. 278-80.
Hort. Life and letters. vol 2, 40.
McCormick. A sad holiday. 17-18.

Riffelhorn accident. AJ2, 153-4.

The Times. 24.7.65. McCormick's letter of 19.7.65. (Riffelhorn accident)

7.3
THE SUBJECTS

7.3.1 The Alpine Journal. No sources

7.3.2 The Cowell memorandum

(a) Letters & archives
18. 7.65. Prior – Mackenzie. Extract in Clark, 146-7.
20. 7.65. Downton's report to Geneva (?Mackenzie) PRO. and see Clark below.
25. 7.65. Whymper – von Fellenberg. cACA. AJ70, 23-6. MW64/65, 13-16.
31. 7.65. J.J.Cowell – Whymper. SPRI. cACA.
8. 8.65. cWhymper – Buxton. SPRI.
11. 8.65. J.W.Cowell – Whymper. SPRI. cACA.
20. 8.65. Wills – Whymper. SPRI. cACA (extract).
4. 9.65. J.W.Cowell – Whymper. SPRI. cACA.
9.10.39. Smythe – Cook. ACA.

17.8.65. Whymper. 'Memorandum of a conversation...' SPRI. Smythe 194-5. also in Scrambles 1, 400-1 omitting last paragraph.
1.9.65. Cowell memorandum or certificate of authenticity. SPRI. cACA (extract). Incomplete extract in Smythe, 195-6.
Enquiry Report. ACA. and see AJ33, 234-47.
Hotel Monte Rosa guestbook entry. Prior. 18.7.65. p258. Seiler Hotels Zermatt.

(b) Books & articles etc

Browne. The recollections of a bishop. 105. and see AJ53, 366.
Clark. The Day the Rope Broke. 172-3 (Downton). 146-7 (Prior).
Egger. Pioniere der Alpen. 187-8.
Gos. Le Cervin 1, 188-9.
Lunn. Mountain Jubilee. 199.
Smythe. Edward Whymper. 194-5 (17.8.65 memo). 195-6 (Cowell extract).
Smythe. see his Introduction to 1949 edn of Whymper's Andes. p12.
Whymper. Scrambles. Original Taugwalder footnote, 1st & 2nd, 404. 3rd, 294.

Dangar & Blakeney. AJ71, 234-5.
Lunn. AJ55, 293. (Cowell memorandum extract)
Whymper. Journal de Zermatt. 25.8.95. ACA. SPRI.

Journal de Genève. 20.7.65. (Gautier letter) and see Martin.
The Times. 22.7.65. McCormick's letter of 17.7.65. AJ70, 19. MW64/65, 10-12.
The Times. 8.8.65. Whymper's letter of 7.8.65. AJ2, 148-53.

7.3.3 Emigration to America by Zermatters

(a) Books & articles etc

Kronig. Familien-Statistik und Geschichtliches über die Gemeinde Zermatt. 1927. New edition. Visp. 1982.
Lunn. Switzerland in English prose and poetry. 1947. 112.
Lunn. Zermatt and the Valais. 1955. 42.
Ruden. Familien-Statistik der löblichen Pfarrei von Zermatt. 1869.
Schmid, W. Menschen am Matterhorn. Bern. 1964. 83.
Taugwalder, H. Der Wahrheit näher. Aarau. 1990. 165.

7.3.4 The Enquiry. Introduction

(a) Letters & archives

29. 9.66. Whymper – Robertson. ACA. Scrambles 6, 382.
14.10.66. Robertson – Whymper. SPRI. (encl. two inscriptions by Vecqueray)
2. 3.69. Whymper – Robertson. ACA.

Adams Reilly 1865 journal. ?ACA. cNLS in Graham Brown Papers.
Enquiry Report. ACA. and see AJ33, 234-47.
Vecqueray's translation of Whymper's Questions & Answers. SPRI.
Whymper's note of the Enquiry. SPRI.

Whymper's questions for Taugwalder. (in English) SPRI. (in French dated 21.7.65) see Enquiry Report. ACA. 22-3.
Whymper's summons from Clemenz 21.7.65. SPRI. cACA in Enquiry Report, 18.

(b) Books & articles etc
Wundt. Das Matterhorn und seine Geschichte. 118-19.

Davies, J.Llewelyn. Peaks, passes & glaciers 1, 196.
Hall. The fatal accident on the Lyskamm. AJ5, 32.
Tyndale. (Editor of) Scrambles 6th edn. 374-8 (Old Peter's interrogation).
Whymper. Journal de Zermatt. 25.8.95. ACA. SPRI.

The Times. 8.8.65. Whymper's letter of 7.8.65. AJ2, 148-53.

7.3.5 The excommunication threat

(a) Letters & archives
29.8.95. Zurbriggen – Monod. see Journal de Zermatt below.

Enquiry Report. ACA. 3-4 also AJ33, 237 (Whymper's evidence). and 15-16 (search party names).
Hotel Monte Rosa guestbook. 1.9.69. p285. Seiler Hotels Zermatt. and see AJ31, 88 and also Wundt, Lunn or Williams below.
Zermatt Commune archives. ?

(b) Books & articles etc
Clark. The Day the Rope Broke. 159-60.
Gos. Le Cervin 1, 226-8.
Lunn. Matterhorn Centenary. 72 (Monte Rosa guestbook 1.9.69).
Lunn. Mountain Jubilee. 201-2.
Lunn. Zermatt and the Valais. 26-7 & 37. (repeat)
Lunn. A Century of Mountaineering. 55. (repeat)
McCormick. A sad holiday. 14.
Mumm. The Alpine Club Register 1, 160. (Mrs.Hudson)
Ruden. Familien Statistik. 84 (Welschen cousins). 151 (Riffel hotel).
Tyndall. Hours of exercise in the Alps. 1, 275-6.
Whymper. Scrambles 1, 402.
Williams,C. Zermatt saga. 48 (Monte Rosa guestbook 1.9.69).
Wundt. Das Matterhorn und seine Geschichte. 123 (facsimile of 1.9.69). 126 (Andenmatten ejection).

Journal de Zermatt. 25.8.95 (Monod interview). Next edn (Zurbriggen letter). SPRI.
Whymper. Graphic. 29.9.1894. 374. 'The Alps revisited.'

The Times. 22.7.65. McCormick's letter of 17.7.65. AJ70, 19-21.
The Times. 8.8.65. Whymper's letter of 7.8.65. AJ2, 148-53.

7.3.6. Guides

(1) Fees

(a) Letters & archives

22. 4.65. Whymper – Reilly. ACA. and Scrambles 6, 378-9 (Croz/Birkbeck).
21. 8.65. cWhymper – H.Hadow. SPRI. cACA. (guides fees paid)
(3.10.65. Parker – His father.) cACA. and see AJ68, 289.
18. 9.67. G.Carrel – Tyndall. see Gos Le Cervin 1, 256-8.
22.10.67. Tyndall – G.Carrel. see Gos Le Cervin 1, 258-9.

Breuil hotel book. 1867 account by Jordan. see AJ30, 321.
Whymper's diary 1864. SPRI. and see Smythe, 153n (Croz tip).
Whymper's diary 1865. SPRI. and see AJ63, 255 (fees paid).
Whymper's memorandum of 17.8.65. SPRI. and see Smythe, 195.

(b) Books & articles etc

Carrel. La Vallée de Valtornenche en 1867. 67. see also 38.
Girdlestone. The high Alps without guides. 1870. 19.
Ruden. Familien-Statistik. 164-5.
Smythe. Edward Whymper. 153n (Croz 1864 tip).
Tyndall. Hours of exercise in the Alps. 1, 268.
Whymper. Scrambles 1, 81 (20frs). 88 (200frs).

Seylaz. François Thioly. Die Alpen 25 (1949) 290.
Zermatt tariff of 1858. see Die Alpen 30 (1954) p28 in Taugwalder supplement.

(2) Rivalry between Zermatt and Chamonix

(a) Letters & archives

8.8.65. Wigram – Whymper. SPRI. cACA.
9.8.65. cWhymper – Wigram. SPRI. cACA.
8.5.17. Rudolf Taugwalder – Montagnier. ACA.

Adams Reilly 1865 journal. (J-B Croz arrival & departure) ?ACA. cNLS in Graham Brown Papers.
Michel Croz inventory. see Enquiry Report 19-20 & 31. ACA. & AJ33, 245-6.
Search party names. see Enquiry Report 15-17. ACA.

(b) Books & articles etc

Arve, Stéphen d'. Les fastes du Mont-Blanc. Genève. 1876. 232-3.
Gos. Le Cervin 1, 179. (S.d'Arve, as above)
Gos. Propos d'un Alpiniste. 97. (as above)
Whymper. Scrambles 1, 364-5 (Aiguille Verte). 402 (search party).

Buxton. The glacier du Dôme. AJ2, 332-3.
Kennedy. Ascent of the Aiguille Verte. AJ3, 68.

(3) Rivalry between Zermatt and St.Niklaus

(a) Letters & archives

8.5.17. Rudolf Taugwalder – Montagnier. ACA.
12.3.18. Rachel Birkbeck – Farrar. cNLS. (encl. lecture notes of 1866 attempt)

Biner's Führerbuch. ACA. see also AJ31, 257 for Elliott entry.
Jordan's account in Hotel Monte Rosa guestbook. see AJ31, 90-2.

(b) Books & articles etc

SAC Jahrbuch 1865, 534-7.

Elliott's 1868 ascent. see AJ28, 293 & 295. (criticism in 1868)
Gardiner. AJ8, 382-3 (Knubel and Seiler incidents).

Journal de Genève 26.7.66. see AJ32, 108-9 & 273.

7.3.7 Hadow's boots

(a) Books & articles etc

Gos. Alpine Tragedy. London. 1948. 31 (reference to boot).
Gos. Alpinisme anecdotique. 1934. Le soulier de Hadow. 259-64.
Gos. Le Cervin 2, 160. (Extract from Echo des Alpes 1872)
Whymper. Scrambles 1, 397 (Hadow slipped). 397n (rope not taut).
Wundt. Das Matterhorn und seine Geschichte. 126 (photograph of Lord Francis Douglas boot).

Blakeney. Note on Hadow's boots. AJ63, 124.
Bruel,F. L'Echo des Alpes 1872. see Gos Le Cervin 2 above.
(Enquiry Report) AJ33, 236. lines 7-9. (Whymper's Answer 11)
Dangar & Blakeney. Comment. see AJ61, 496 note (14) (iv).
Fry, Frederick M. see photograph AJ60, 381.
Montandon,F. Les talons de Hadow. Die Alpen 26 (1950) 288-91. 288 (photograph of 'Hadow' boot).
Stevens,E.H. His comments in review of Gos, Alpinisme anecdotique. AJ47, 181.

Journal de Zermatt. 25.8.95. La première ascension du Cervin. Interview de M. Ed. Whymper. Fourth column: reference to eight boots.

7.3.8 Illustrations of the accident

(a) Reproductions

Doré. see Rébuffat, Men and the Matterhorn, 123 & 125. Bernardi, Il Gran Cervino, 160. Gattlen, Das Matterhorn im Bild, 103. Wundt, Das Matterhorn und seine Geschichte, frontispiece. AJ100, 340-1 and elsewhere.
Hodler. see Die Alpen. 10 (1934) 137. Walter Flaig. Lawinen! Leipzig 1935. 32. see also extracts in MW64/65, 9. and Berge, June 1983. 73.

(b) Letters & archives (relating to Gustave Doré)
13.8.65. Reilly – Whymper. SPRI.
18.8.65. Obach/Goupil – Whymper. Not known to have survived.
23.8.65. P.D.Hadow – Whymper. SPRI.
23.8.65. cWhymper – P.D.Hadow. SPRI.
26.8.65. P.D.Hadow – Whymper. SPRI.
29.8.65. Obach/Goupil – Whymper. SPRI.
1.9.65. Goupil – Whymper. SPRI.
4.9.65. Obach/Goupil – Whymper. SPRI.

[Aug.65] French newspaper cutting re Montmartre display. SPRI.

(c) Books & articles etc

[Aosta, Valtournenche & Zermatt] The Conquest of the Matterhorn in historical engravings. 1990. 57 [D] & 92 (Seiler).
Clark. Quando la corda si ruppe. Longanesi & C. Milano. 1865. 129 [C].
Feierabend, A. Die schweizerische Alpenwelt. 1873. Heyn u. Specht. [F]
Gattlen. Das Matterhorn im Bild. Brig. 1979. see plates 74 [D], 92 [G], 111 [F] & 151 (Seiler).
Gos. Le Cervin 1, 111. (Doré/Whymper account similarity) 112 [D].
Gos. Le Cervin 2, 195-7. Gustave Doré et le Cervin. 196-7 (Hodler). 197n (error about Whymper).
Javelle. Alpine Memories. 162 (text & note refer to Doré).
Manning, S. Swiss pictures drawn with pen & pencil. 1891. New edn. 134 [F].
Zurcher et Margollé. Les ascensions celèbres. Paris 1869. 108 [G].

Lyall, A. Gustave Doré and his links with Edward Whymper. AJ100, 215-21 [D].
Müller, Werner. Ferdinand Hodler: "Aufstieg" und "Absturz". Die Alpen 10 (1934) 140 [H].
Reichen, Q. Die erste Besteigung in der Malerei. Bergsteiger Juli 1990. 38-9 [F] [G] [L].
Uehlinger, W.M. Das Matterhornunglück von 1865 bei Doré und Hodler. Neue Zürcher Zeitung 4.9.24.
Whymper. Journal de Zermatt. 25.8.95. and see AJ45, 322.
Whymper. Graphic. 1894. 403 (Seiler).
Whymper. Strand Magazine vol 37 (1909). 56 (Doré).

A New Year's tract, by Rev. William Ritchie. SPRI.
Leipziger Illustrierte Zeitung. 26.10.65. [L]
Le Monde illustré. 5.8.65. SPRI. (Pajot's drawing)

7.3.9 Newspaper reports and letters

(a) Letters & archives
25.7.65. Whymper – von Fellenberg letter. cACA. AJ70, 23-6. MW64/65, 13-16.

Various newspaper cuttings. ACA and/or SPRI.
Young Peter Taugwalder's Narrative. ACA. and see AJ61, 489-92.

(b) Books & articles etc

Butler, A.G. Zermatt churchyard. Privately printed. Cambridge. 1909.

Irving. The mountain way. 496-7 (Butler verse extract).
McCormick. A sad holiday. 13.
Merrick. The perpetual hills. 234 (Butler verse extract).
Rambert. Les Alpes suisses. 1866. 1, 273-4. (see Gos Le Cervin 1, 198-202)

Arve, Stéphen d'. L'Abeille de Chamonix. 23.7.65. see also Les Fastes du Mont Blanc. Genève 1876. and Gos, Alpinisme anecdotique, 272-80.
Engel. Die Alpen 25 (1949) 129-132. (Martin & Gautier)

(c) Newspapers

L'Abeille de Chamonix. 23.7.65. see Gos, Alpinisme anecdotique, 272-4 & 281-4.
Anzeiger von Interlaken. 1?.8.65. quoted in Sonntagspost 20.8.65. see below.
Der Bund. 16.7.65. see Dübi SACJ 47 (1911) 192 and MW64/65, 17.
Der Bund. 19.7.65. see Dübi SACJ 192-3. MW64/65, 18-20.
Journal de Genève. 16.7.65. Facsimile in Bernardi 158. and see Dübi ibid 192 & MW64/65, 17.
Journal de Genève. 18.7.65. Facsimile in Bernardi 168. and see Dübi ibid 192 & MW64/65, 17-18.
Journal de Genève. 20.7.65. Zermatt letters see Dübi ibid 193 & Engel above.
Journal de Genève. 28.7.65. Rambert 'Accident du Cervin'. and see Gos Le Cervin 1, 198-202. and Rambert above.
Journal de Genève. 1.8.65. Zermatt correspondent see Dübi ibid 194.
Journal de Genève. 12.8.65. Whymper's Times letter (in French).
Sonntagspost. 30.7.65. Extract in MW64/65, 20-22 & see Dübi ibid 194.
Sonntagspost. 13.8.65. Extracts in Dübi ibid 195-8 & MW64/65, 25.
Sonntagspost. 20.8.65. Extracts in Dübi ibid 198-200 & MW64/65, 25-8.

The Times. 22.7.65. McCormick's letter of 17.7.65. AJ70, 19-21. & MW64/65, 10.
The Times. 26.7.65. Charlton's letter of 21.7.65. AJ32, 21.
The Times. 28.7.65. Kennedy's letter of 25.7.65. AJ70, 21-2.
The Times. 1.8.65. Chaix letter of 26.7.65. AJ32, 9n-11n.
The Times. 8.8.65. Whymper's letter of 7.8.65. AJ2, 148-53.
The Times. 30.8.66. Butler's Zermatt churchyard verse. see Merrick, & Irving.

7.3.10 Poems

(a) Letters & archives

7.12.65. Lady Queensberry – Whymper. SPRI.
22.12.65. Lady Queensberry – Whymper. SPRI.
27.12.65. cWhymper – Lady Queensberry. SPRI.

Douglas. 'At Zermatt when the sun is low'. cSPRI (Whymper's copy). cACA.(typed).
Horner, S.S. 'The Matterhorn'. August 1865. cSPRI (Whymper's copy).
Queensberry. July 1865 poem. cACA (typed).
Robertson. Croz sonnet. ?SPRI. (and see Gos & Smythe below).

Calkin painting of Croz. ACA. see also Whymper's Zermatt Guide, 65. or Rebuffat, Men and the Matterhorn, 83 (much enlarged!).

(b) Books & articles etc

Butler,A.G. Zermatt Churchyard. Privately printed, Cambridge. 1909. (Listed in AJ57, 392 & AJ96, 198)
Gos. Le Cervin 1, 150 (L.Seylaz French translation of Croz sonnet).
Irving. The mountain way. 496-7 (extract from Zermatt Churchyard).
Merrick. The perpetual hills. 234 (another extract Zermatt Churchyard).
Queensberry, Lord. The spirit of the Matterhorn. London. 1881.
Smythe. Edward Whymper. 1940. 201 (Croz sonnet).

The Times. 30.8.66. Zermatt Churchyard by B. [A.G.Butler]

7.3.11 Reward for the first ascent

(a) Letters & archives

(3.10.65. Charles Parker to his father.) cACA. see AJ68, 288-90.

(b) Books & articles etc

Carrel. La Vallée de Valtornenche en 1867. 42-3.
Girdlestone. The high Alps without guides. 164 (holiday cost).
Gos. Alpinisme anecdotique. 292-4 (newspaper reports).
Gos. Le Cervin. 1, 35 (Carrel & Tuckett).
Graham Brown & Gavin de Beer. The first ascent of Mont Blanc. 4 & 63.

L'Abeille de Chamonix. see Gos, Alpinisme anecdotique above.
Mountain World 1964/65. 22-4.

7.3.12 The rope in 1865

(a) Letters & archives

25.7.65. Whymper – von Fellenberg. cACA. AJ70, 23-6. MW64/65, 13-16.
9.8.65. cWhymper – Wigram. SPRI. cACA. (weak rope not used intentionally)
9.8.65. Wills – Whymper. SPRI.
10.8.65. Wigram – Whymper. SPRI. cACA.

Enquiry Report. ACA. and see AJ33, 234-43.
Taugwalder, Young Peter's Narrative. ACA. and see AJ61, 491.
Whymper. Questions for Taugwalder. (English) SPRI. (French) cACA in Enquiry Report, 22-3.

(b) Books & articles etc

Ball. A guide to the Western Alps. 1863. xxxiii, xlviii & liv.
Brown. Family Notes. 277-8 (taut rope).
Carrel. La vallée de Valtornenche en 1867. 66-7.
Egger. Pioniere der Alpen. 193-4.
Gindraux. La folle histoire du Cervin. 62 photo 4 (Ropes broken on the Matterhorn July 14 1865).
Girdlestone. The high Alps without guides. 16 (average guides). 167 (ropes).
Gorret. Guide de la vallée d'Aoste. 1876. see extract Gos Le Cervin 1, 209.
Lunn. The Alps. 179-80. see also AJ55, 291-2.

Rambert. Les Alpes suisses. 1866. 1, 273-94. & see Gos Le Cervin 1, 198-202
Whymper. Scrambles 1, 372-7 (use of rope). 373-4 (1864 report). 374 (keep rope taut). 382 (three kinds of rope). 397n (taut rope). 398 (the weakest).
Wilson,C. Mountaineering. 1893. 29.

Ball. Suggestions for Alpine travellers. Peaks, passes & glaciers 1, 492-3.
Dangar & Blakeney. Review. The Day the Rope Broke. AJ70, 161.
Dangar & Blakeney. The Narrative of Young Peter Taugwalder. AJ61, 491.
Douglas. The Gabelhorn. AJ2, 222.
Dübi u. Montandon. Zum Matterhornunglück... Die Alpen V (1929) 220.
Edwards. The ropes in the Matterhorn accident of 1865. AJ45, 321 & 324.
Elliott. The second ascent of the Matterhorn by the east face. AJ28, 293.
Jordan. ...the Matterhorn in 1867. AJ30, 319.
Kennedy. Ascent of the Aiguille Verte. AJ3, 68.
Longman. Accident on the Aletsch glacier. AJ1, 20-6. 21 (von Grote).
[A.E.W.Mason] see AJ71, 126 & AJ61, 485n. also Lunn, Centenary 57 & Zermatt 40.
Mears. The climbing rope defined. AJ57, 326.
Mears. Experience with climbing ropes. AJ58, 84.
[Ropes] Report of the Special Committee (1864). AJ1, 321-6. and see AJ2, 95.
(Schuster). Review of Smythe's 'Edward Whymper'. AJ52, 149.
Whymper. Graphic. 6.10.1894. p402.

Journal de Genève. 18.7.65. MW64/65, 17-18. Bernardi, Il Gran Cervino 168. and see SACJ47 (1911) 192.
Der Bund. 19.7.65. MW64/65, 18-20. and see SACJ47 (1911) 192-3.
The Times. 28.7.65. Kennedy's letter of 25.7.65. AJ70, 21-2.
The Times. 8.8.65. Whymper's letter of 7.8.65. AJ2, 148-53.
The Times. 14.8.65. Wills' letter of 11.8.65.

7.3.13 Ropes, chains & ladders

(a) Letters & archives

7.7.65. Giordano – Sella. see Rey, The Matterhorn. 1st edn, 132 or 1946, 97 (300m. rope etc).

Giordano 1864 notebook. see Rey, The Matterhorn. 1st edn, 127 or 1946, 92.

(b) Books & articles etc

Bernardi. Il Gran Cervino. 1963. 185 (Jordan ladder). 200-1 (rope photos).
Carrel. La Vallée de Valtornenche en 1867. 67 (money for cable/ladder).
Cunningham & Abney. The Pioneers of the Alps 1887. 39-40.
Gos. Le Cervin 2, 147-54. Les cordes.
(SAC) Monte Rosa 1865|1965. 21 (1870 ropes).
Whymper. Scrambles 1, 399 (rope fixed after accident).

1868. AJ4, 158 (chains unnecessary) and (Tyndall 1868 chains).
1875. AJ7, 390 & 408 (Wethered paper & discussion on it).
1923. AJ35, 303 (guides inclined to remove ropes).
1955. AJ60, 381 (rope given by Seiler to Fry).

Echo des Alpes. Dec. 1875. Extract (London chains) in Gos Le Cervin 2, 150.
Jordan. (repositioning rope in 1867) see AJ30, 320-1.

The Times. 8.8.65. Whymper's letter of 7.8.65. AJ2, 148-53.

7.3.14 Scrambles amongst the Alps

(1) Sources

(a) Reviews

Leslie Stephen in Alpine Journal. May 1871. AJ5, 234-40.
Leslie Stephen in Macmillan's Magazine. August 1871, 304-11.

(b) Letters & archives

25.7.65. Whymper – von Fellenberg. SAC Section Bern (manuscript No.779). cZM cACA. AJ70, 23-6. MW64/65, 13-16 plus two pages in facsimile.
4.7.05. Whymper – H.Murray. JMA.

Whymper's note of his Enquiry evidence. SPRI.
Whymper's diaries. SPRI. Extracts in Scrambles 6th edn & in Smythe.
17.8.65. Whymper memorandum. SPRI. and see Smythe 194-5. also Scrambles 1, 400-1 omitting last paragraph.
Graham Brown. His notes on Scrambles etc. NLS 4338/206 (21) & (22).

(c) Books & articles etc

Egger. Pioniere der Alpen. 192 (relying on error in Whymper's Berg- und Gletscherfahrten... Braunschweig 1872, 495).
Ceresole. Führer von Zermatt. 46.
Gos. Le Cervin 1, 183, (177-191). (La corde maudite)
Gos. Le Cervin 1, 189n. (Note re Lunn, AJ55, 290-6 & re Egger, Pioniere)
Whymper. Scrambles. Footnote re Clemenz & Taugwalders. Ist & 2nd edn, 404. 3rd edn, 294. German 1st edn, 495. French 1st edn, 403-4.

Graham Brown. Girdlestone and the Matterhorn accident, 1865. AJ57, 369-70.
Graham Brown. The great Matterhorn disaster of 1865. The Field, 13.2.32.
Lyall, A. Gustave Doré and his links with Edward Whymper. AJ100, 215-21.
[Ropes] Report of the Special Committee (1864). AJ1, 321-6.
Whymper. Ascent of the Pointe des Ecrins. AJ2, 225-36.
Whymper. Letter to Editor (re Carrel & Tyndall). see AJ5, 333 (329-36).
[Whymper] Note about abridged edition. AJ6, 320.

The Times. 8.8.65. Whymper's letter of 7.8.65. AJ2, 148-53.

(2) Comparison of page numbers

The page numbers vary in the different editions of Scrambles, an asterisk (*) denoting the absence of a passage or significantly different wording.

1st or 2nd edn	4th or 5th edn	6th edn
81	73	49
84-85	76	52-53
87	79	55
88	80	56
96-97	88-89	65-66
*	125-126	105
*	147	115
181	168	136
*	239	206
262	249	218-219
266	253	224
289	276	250
364-365	351-352	285
365	352	286-287
367	354	289
372-377	359-364	294-298
373-374	360-361	*
374	361	296
378	365	299-300
380	367	301
381	368	303
382	370	304
382-383	370	305-306
383	370	305
*	370n	*
384-385n	372-373n	307-308n
385-387	373-375	308-310
385n	373n	308n
389	377	312
391	379	314
396	384	320 or 321
397	385	321
397n	385n	321n or 322n
398	386	323
399	387	324
400-401	388-389	325-326
401-404	389-393	326-330
402	390	327
404n	392n*	329n-330*
414-415	401-402	*
415	402	343
415-417	402-404	343-345
418-420	405-407	347-349
420	407-409	350
421	410	*
*	415	363
*	416-418	364-366

1st or 2nd edn	4th or 5th edn	6th edn
*	418	366-367
422	424	*
423	425+426	*
423*	425-429	*
*	426+430	*
*	427	*
*	431-433	*
424-425	434-436	*
*	435	*
426-428	437-439	383-386

7.3.15 The search and recovery parties

(a) Letters & archives

20.7.65. Downton's report to Geneva (?Mackenzie). PRO. see Clark, 173.

Girdlestone's letter journal. ACA. and see Graham Brown article AJ57, 375.
Search party names etc. see Enquiry Report 15-17. ACA.
Enquiry Report, evidence & inventories. ACA. & see AJ33, 234-47 & Gos, below.
Zermatt Council meeting minutes etc. ?

(b) Books & articles etc

Brown. Family Notes. 1917. 276. see also AJ61, 502-3 (re party **A**).
Gos. Alpinisme anecdotique. 1934. 218-37 (Enquiry Report). 281-4 (Loppé).
Gos. Le Cervin 1, 129-46 (Enquiry Report).
Kronig. Familien-Statistik und Geschichtliches über Zermatt. 1927. also 1982.
McCormick. A sad holiday. 1865. 14-17.
Ruden. Familien-Statistik der löblichen Pfarrei von Zermatt. 1869.
Whymper. Scrambles, 1, 401-4.

Dangar & Blakeney. Notes on F.A.Y.Brown & party **A**. see AJ61, 502-3.

Journal de Zermatt. 25.8.1895. ACA. SPRI.
L'Abeille de Chamonix. 23.7.1865. SPRI. and see Gos, Alpinisme, 281-4.
Graphic. 29.9.94. p374. ACA.
Strand Magazine. 1909. vol 37, 55-6.
The Times. 22.7.65. McCormick's letter of 17.7.65. AJ70, 19-21. MW64/65, 10.
The Times. 2.8.65. Anneçy account, based on Loppé's letter in L'Abeille de Chamonix.

7.3.16 The special rope

(a) Letters & archives

25.7.65. Whymper – McCormick. Smythe, 205.
9.8.65. cWhymper – Wigram. SPRI. cACA.

Enquiry Report. ACA. 15-17 (search parties) & see AJ33, 234-47.
Vecqueray's French translation of Whymper's questions and answers. SPRI.
Whymper's questions for Taugwalder. (in English) SPRI. (For French version dated 21.7.65. see Enquiry Report 22-3. ACA.)
Whymper's 1865 diary. SPRI. (Douglas hotel bill)
Zermatt Council meeting minutes etc. ?

(b) Books & articles etc

Ball. A guide to the Western Alps. 1863. xxxiii (rope). xlviii (sashline).
Gindraux. La folle histoire du Cervin. 62 photo 4 (Ropes broken on the Matterhorn July 14 1865).
Ruden. Familien-Statistik. 48 (Alois Julen, Richter).
SAC Jahrbuch 1865, 534-7.

Dangar & Blakeney. AJ70, 32 (out of his class).
Douglas. The Gabelhorn. AJ2, 221-2.
Monod. (Whymper interview) Journal de Zermatt. 25.8.95. ACA. SPRI.
[Ropes] Report of the Special Committee (1864). AJ1, 321-6 and see AJ2, 95.
Stephen. Macmillan's Magazine. 1871. 308 (comparatively incompetent).

The Times. 8.8.65. Whymper's letter of 7.8.65. AJ2, 148-53.

7.3.17 Zermatt and the Matterhorn. No sources

7.3.18 Is there anything new to be found? No sources

ABBREVIATIONS

A = Answer. A24 = The answer to Question 24 (Q24) at the Enquiry.
AC = Alpine Club, 55/56 Charlotte Rd, London, EC2A 3QT. (0171 613 0755)
ACA = Alpine Club Archives. (see AC above)
ACL = Alpine Club Library. (see AC above)
AJ = Alpine Journal. AJ2, 332 = page 332 of the second volume.
Andes = 1949 edition of Travels amongst the Great Andes of the Equator, by Edward Whymper; edited with an Introduction by Frank Smythe.
Bernardi = Il Gran Cervino, by G.Bernardi. 1963.
Blakeney = T.S.Blakeney, assistant editor of the Alpine Journal, 1956-1969.
c = copy. A letter denoted as 'cWhymper – Wills. SPRI. cACA.' means that a copy retained by Whymper (not the original sent to Wills) is at the SPRI and a copy of Whymper's copy is in the Alpine Club Archives.
c. = circa (about), usually of a date that is uncertain.
CAI = Club Alpino Italiano (Italian Alpine Club).
Carrel = La Vallée de Valtornenche en 1867, by Canon G.Carrel.
Century = A Century of Mountaineering, by Arnold Lunn.
Clark = The Day the Rope Broke, by Ronald Clark. 1965.
Dangar = D.F.O.Dangar, assistant editor of the Alpine Journal, 1956-1974.
D & B = D.F.O.Dangar and T.S.Blakeney.
Eccentric = An eccentric in the Alps, by Ronald Clark. 1959.
Facs = a facsimile copy.
Guide = The valley of Zermatt and the Matterhorn: a guide, by Edward Whymper.
JMA = The archives of John Murray, Edward Whymper's London publishers.
Kronig = Familien-Statistik...über Zermatt, by Stanislaus Kronig. 1927.
McCormick = A sad holiday, by J.McCormick. [1865]
Mumm = The Alpine Club Register [1857-90], by A.L.Mumm (3 vols).
MW = The Mountain World, the English edition of Berge der Welt.
n. = footnote. 21n. = a note at the foot of page 21.
NLS = National Library of Scotland, George IV Bridge, Edinburgh, EH1 1EW.
Old Peter = Peter Taugwalder, father, 1820-88.
Pioniere = Pioniere der Alpen, by C.Egger. 1946.
Pioneers = The Pioneers of the Alps, by Cunningham & Abney. 1877.
PRO = Public Record Office, London. (Foreign Office files)
Q = Question. Q24 = Question 24 at the Enquiry, answered by A24.
Q's & A's = Questions and Answers at the Official Enquiry into the accident.
Ruden = Familien-Statistik der löblichen Pfarrei von Zermatt, by J.Ruden. 1869.
SAC = Schweizer Alpen-Club. (Swiss Alpine Club) Monbijoustrasse 61, 3000 Bern.
SACJ = Schweizer Alpenclub Jahrbuch. (Swiss Alpine Club Yearbook)
Scrambles = Scrambles amongst the Alps, by Edward Whymper. 1871.
Scrambles 1, 2, 4, 5 or 6 = 1st, 2nd, 4th, 5th or 6th edition of Scrambles.

Scrambles 3 = The ascent of the Matterhorn, by Whymper. (The abridged edition)
Seiler Hotels = Seiler Hotels Zermatt AG, CH-3920 Zermatt.
Smythe = Edward Whymper, by Frank Smythe. 1940.
SPRI = Scott Polar Research Institute, University of Cambridge, Lensfield Road, Cambridge, CB2 1ER. (Whymper archives)
USA = University of St Andrews. University Library, St Andrews, KY16 9TR, Scotland. (Correspondence and Papers of J.D.Forbes)
Young Peter = Peter Taugwalder, son. 1843-1923.
Zermatt = Zermatt and the Valais, by Arnold Lunn.
ZM = The Zermatt Alpine Museum. Vereinigung Alpines Museum, CH-3920 Zermatt.

SELECT BIBLIOGRAPHY

Alpine Club. *The Alpine Journal*. 1863 –
Peaks, passes and glaciers. 1859.
Peaks, passes and glaciers. 2nd series. 2v. 1862.
Alpine Club Library catalogue. *London*. 1982.
Anthamatten, G. *Alexander Seiler. 1819–1891*. Zermatt, 1991.
Arcis, E. d'. 'Avec Whymper à Zermatt.' *Die Alpen XVI*. 1940.
'Edward Whymper.' *Die Alpen XVI*. 1940.
Arve, S. d'. *Les Fastes du Mont Blanc*. Genève, 1876.

Ball, J. *A guide to the Western Alps*. London, 1863.
Introduction to 'The Alpine Guide'. New edition. London, 1873.
Barnard, G. *Drawing from nature*. London, 1865.
Beattie, W. *Switzerland*. 2v. London, 1836.
Berlepsch, H. von. *The Alps*. London, 1861.
Bernardi, A. *Ecrits de l'Abbé Amé Gorret*. Val d'Aosta, 1965.
Il Gran Cervino. Bologna, 1963.
Blakeney, T.S. see Dangar below.
Brown, F.A.Y. *Family Notes*. [Printed] Genoa, 1917.
Brown, T.Graham & de Beer, G. *The first ascent of Mont Blanc*. London, 1957.
Brown, T.Graham. 'Girdlestone and the Matterhorn accident, 1865.' *AJ57*, 1950.
'The Great Matterhorn Disaster of 1865.' *The Field*, 13.2.1932.
His mountaineering library; see Scotland, National Library of.
Browne, G.F. *The recollections of a bishop*. London, 1915.
Browning, O. *Memories of sixty years*. London, 1910.
Butler, A.G. *Zermatt churchyard*. Privately printed. Cambridge, 1909.

Carrel, G. *La Vallée de Valtornenche en 1867*. Turin, 1868.
Casella, G. 'Comment le Cervin fut conquis – les dernières paroles de Whymper.' *L'Auto*. Paris, 18.9.1911.
'Edward Whymper.' *Les sports d'hiver & l'alpinisme*. Paris, 1911.
Pèlerinages. Lausanne et Paris. [191?]
Ceresole, A. *Führer von Zermatt*. Zürich. [c.1890]
Chamson, M. *Whymper le fou du Cervin*. Paris, 1986.
Clark, R.W. *The Alps*. London. 1973.
The Day the Rope Broke. London, 1965. [*Als das Seil riss*. Zürich, 1965. *Quando la corda si ruppe*. Milano, 1965]
The early Alpine guides. London, 1949.
An eccentric in the Alps. London, 1959.
Six great mountaineers. London, 1956.
The Victorian mountaineers. London, 1953.
Club Alpino Italiano. *Bollettino*. 1865–1936.

Coleman, E.T. *Scenes from the snow-fields*. London, 1859.
Conway, W.M. *Zermatt pocket book*. London, 1881.
Coolidge, W.A.B. *Alpine studies*. London, 1912.
The Alps in nature and history. London, 1908.
Swiss travel and Swiss guide-books. London, 1889.
Coxe, H. *The Traveller's Guide in Switzerland*. London, 1816.
Cunningham, C.D. & Abney, W. de W. *The Pioneers of the Alps*. London, 1877.

Dangar, D.F.O. 'The Führerbuch of young Peter Taugwalder.' *AJ59*, 1954.
'The Parkers and the Matterhorn.' *AJ68*, 1963.
Dangar, D.F.O. & Blakeney, T.S. 'The first ascent of the Matterhorn. The Narrative of "Young" Peter Taugwalder.' *AJ61*, 1957.
' "Old" Peter Taugwalder.' *AJ70*, 1965.
'A word for Whymper: a reply to Sir Arnold Lunn.' *AJ71*, 1966.
de Beer, G.R. *Travellers in Switzerland*. London. 1949.
Dent, C. *Above the snow line: mountaineering sketches between 1870 and 1880*. London, 1885.
Dixie, F. *Across Patagonia*. London, 1880.
Douglas, F. 'The Gabelhorn.' *AJ2*, 1866.
Dübi, H. & Montandon, P. 'Zum Matterhornunglück vom 14. Juli 1865.' *Die Alpen V*. 1929.
Dübi, H. 'Zur Erinnerung an Edward Whymper.' *SAC Jahrbuch 47*. 1911.

Ebel, J.G. *Anleitung auf die nützlichste und genussvollste Art in der Schweiz zu reisen*. Zürich, 1793.
Edwards, H. 'The ropes in the Matterhorn Accident of 1865.' *AJ45*, 1933.
Egger, C. 'Les Taugwalders du Cervin.' *Die Alpen XVI*. 1940.
Pioniere der Alpen. Zürich, 1946.
Elliott, J.M. 'The Second Ascent of the Matterhorn by the East Face.' *AJ28*, 1914.
Memoir of the Rev. Julius M. Elliott. Privately printed. [c.1870]
Engel, C-E. *A History of Mountaineering in the Alps*. London, 1950.
'Autour de la première ascension du Cervin.' *Die Alpen XXV*. 1949.
They came to the Hills. London, 1952.
Engelhardt, C.M. *Das Monte Rosa- und Matterhorn-Gebirg*. Paris, 1852.
Naturschilderungen, Sittenzüge und wissenschaftliche Bemerkungen aus den höchsten Schweizer-Alpen, besonders in Sud-Wallis und Graubünden. Basel, 1840.
Escher, H.C. *Views and panoramas of Switzerland*. Zürich, 1975.

Farrar, J.P. 'An Attempt on the East Face and an Ascent of the Italian Face of the Matterhorn in 1867.' *AJ30*, 1916. [Jordan's climbs]
'Days of long ago.' *AJ32*, 1918.
'Report of the Official Enquiry into the accident on the Mont Cervin, in July 1865.' *AJ33*, 1920.

Feierabend, A. *Die schweizerische Alpenwelt.* Bielefeld, 1873.
[Field, M] *Works and Days; from the Journal of Michael Field.* London, 1933.
Flaig, W. *Lawinen!* Leipzig, 1935.

Galton, F. *Vacation Tourists and notes of travel in 1860.* Cambridge, 1861.
Gattlen, A. *Das Matterhorn im Bild.* Brig, 1979.
Gautier, T. *Les vacances de lundi.* Paris, 1881.
Gindraux, P. *La folle histoire du Cervin.* Genève, 1990.
Giordano, F. *Ascensione al Gran Cervino 1868.* Milano, 1868.
Girdlestone, A.G. *The High Alps without guides, being a narrative of adventures in Switzerland.* London, 1870.
Gorret, A. 'Ascension du Cervin.' *Feuille d'Aoste.* 1865.
Ecrits de l'Abbé Amé Gorret, see Bernardi above.
Guide de la vallée d'Aoste. Turin, 1876.
'The Italian ascent of the Matterhorn.' *AJ2*, 1866.
Victor-Emmanuel sur les Alpes. Turin, 1879.
Gos, C. *Alpine Tragedy.* London, 1948. [*Tragédies Alpestres.* Paris, 1940]
Alpinisme anecdotique. Neuchâtel. [1934]
Le Cervin. 2v. Neuchâtel, 1948.
Propos d'un Alpiniste. Lausanne, 1922.
Voyageurs illustres en Suisse. Berne, 1937.
Gos, F. *Zermatt and its Valley.* London, 1926.
Grosjean, G. 'La première ascension du Cervin le 14 juillet 1865.' *Die Alpen XLI.* 1965.
Güssfeldt, P. *In den Hochalpen.* 2. Aufl. Berlin, 1886.

Hall, N. *Autobiography.* London, 1898.
Hallenbarter. 'Staatsrat Clemenz.' *Walliser Jahrbuch* 1941.
Hawkins, F.V. 'Partial Ascent of the Matterhorn.' Galton's, *Vacation Tourists*; see above.
Hinchliff, T.W. *Summer months among the Alps.* London, 1857.
Hort, F.A.J. *Life and letters of Fenton John Anthony Hort.* 2v. London, 1896.
Hudson, C. & Kennedy, E.S. *Where there's a will there's a way.* London, 1856.

Irving, R.L.G. *The mountain way.* London, 1938.

Javelle, E. *Alpine Memories.* London, 1899.
Jegerlehner, J. *Die Todesfahrt auf das Matterhorn.* Berlin, 1928.
[Jordan, W.L.] see Farrar above.

Kämpfen, W. *Alexander Seiler der Jüngere.* Zürich, 1945.
Ein Burgerrechtsstreit im Wallis. Zürich, 1942.
Kennedy, T.S. 'Zermatt and the Matterhorn in winter.' *AJ1*, 1863.

Kernahan, C. *In good company.* 2nd ed. 1917.
Kronig, S. *Familien-Statistik und Geschichtliches über die Gemeinde Zermatt.* Ingenbohl, 1927. Nachdruck (Faksimile) Visp, 1982.
Kurz, M. Bibliographie du Cervin. see *Guide des Alpes Valaisannes* vol 2 1947, 389-93, 397 & 430.

Lewin, W.H. *Climbs.* Published privately. [1932]
Long, C. 'Ascension du Dom des Mischabel.' *L'Echo des Alpes 1867.* No.2.
Lory, G. *Voyage pittoresque de Genève à Milan par le Simplon.* Paris, 1811.
Lunn, A. *The Alps.* London, 1914.
The Bernese Oberland. London, 1958.
A Century of Mountaineering. 1857–1957. London, 1957.
'Edward Whymper and the Matterhorn. A study in Alpine revaluation.' *The British Ski Year Book.* 1940. Vol X. No.21.
Matterhorn Centenary. London, 1965.
Mountain Jubilee. London, 1943.
The Swiss and their Mountains. London, 1963.
Switzerland and the English. London, 1944.
Switzerland in English prose and poetry. London, 1947.
'Taugwalder and the Matterhorn.' *AJ55*, 1946.
'Whymper again.' *AJ71*, 1966.
Zermatt and the Valais. London, 1955.

McCormick, J. *A sad holiday.* London. [1865]
Maclean, F.W. *Three weeks amongst the upper regions of the Alps, with a few comments on "Mountaineering" and the "Matterhorn catastrophe".* [Printed] Hampstead, 1865.
Maitland, F.W. *The life and letters of Leslie Stephen.* London, 1906.
Manning, S. *Swiss pictures drawn with pen and pencil.* London, 1891.
Merrick, H. *The perpetual hills.* London, 1964.
Monod, J. 'La première ascension du Cervin. Interview de M. Ed. Whymper.' *Journal de Zermatt.* 25.8.1895.
[Montagnier, H.F.] 'Early ascents of the Matterhorn.' *AJ31*, 1917.
Montandon, F. 'Les talons de Hadow'. *Die Alpen XXVI.* 1950.
Montandon, P. see Dübi above.
Mountain World 1964/65, The. London, 1966.
Mumm, A.L. *The Alpine Club register. 1857–1890.* 3v. London, 1923-28.
Murith, L.J. *Le guide du botaniste qui voyage dans le Valais.* Lausanne, 1810.

[Parkers, The] see Dangar above.
Perren, B.H. *Matterhorn.* Zürich, 1990.
Preston-Thomas, H. *The Work and Play of a Government Inspector.* London, 1909.

Queensberry, Lord. *The spirit of the Matterhorn.* London, 1881.

Rambert, E. *Les Alpes suisses*. Vol 1. Genève, 1866.

Rébuffat, G. *Men and the Matterhorn*. London, 1967.

Reichen, Q. 'Die erste Besteigung in der Malerei.' *Bergsteiger*, Juli 1990.

Rey, G. *The Matterhorn*. London, 1907. Revised by R.L.G.Irving. Oxford, 1946.

Roth, A. *The Doldenhorn and Weisse Frau*. Coblenz, 1863.

[Roth, A.] 'Gletscherführer.' *SAC Jahrbuch 1*, 1864 and *2*, 1865.

Ruden, J. *Familien-Statistik der löblichen Pfarrei von Zermatt, mit Beilagen*. Ingenbohl, 1869.

Ruppen, P.J. *Familien-Statistik der löblichen Pfarrei von St. Niklaus*. Sitten, 1861.

Saussure, H.B. de. *Voyages dans les Alpes*. Vol 4. Neuchâtel, 1796.

Schmid, W. *Menschen am Matterhorn*. Bern, 1964.

Schweizer Alpen-Club. Bibliographie du Cervin. see Kurz, M. above.

(SAC) *Les Alpes/Die Alpen*. 1925 –

L'Echo des Alpes. Genève. 1865–1924.

Jahrbuch. 1864–1923.

Katalog der Zentralbibliothek. [Zähringerplatz 6, Zürich] Bern, 1990.

[Sektion] *Monte Rosa 1865/1965*. Sion, 1965.

Scotland, National Library of. *Mountaineering. Catalogue of the Graham Brown and Lloyd collections*. Edinburgh, 1994.

Seylaz, L. 'François Thioly. (1831–1911) Un pionnier oublié de l'alpinisme suisse.' *Die Alpen XXV*. 1949.

Shairp, J.C., Tait, P.G. & Adams-Reilly, A. *Life and letters of James David Forbes, F.R.S.* London. 1873.

Smythe, F.S. *Edward Whymper*. London, 1940.

Stephen, L.'Mr. Whymper's "Scrambles amongst the Alps".' *Macmillan's Magazine*. August 1871.

The playground of Europe. London, 1871.

Studer, G. *Über Eis und Schnee*. Vol 2. Bern, 1898.

Taugwalder, H. *Das verlorene Tal*. Aarau, 1979. [*The Lost Valley*. Aarau, c.1996]

Taugwalder, H. & Jaggi, M. *Der Wahrheit näher*. Aarau, 1990.

Thioly, F. *Ascension du Mont-Cervin (Matterhorn)*. [Printed] Genève, 1871.

Voyage en Suisse et ascension du Mont Rose. Ms. facsimile, 1860.

Tuckett, F.F. *A pioneer in the High Alps*. London, 1920.

Tyndall, J. *Hours of exercise in the Alps*. London, 1871.

Tyndale, H.E.G. *Mountain paths*. London, 1948.

Unsworth, W. *Matterhorn man*. London. 1965.

[Wall, D.] *The Swiss Tourist*. London, 1816.

Whymper, E. 'The Alps revisited.' *Graphic*, 29.9 & 6.10.1894.

The ascent of the Matterhorn. London, 1880.

Berg- und Gletscherfahrten in den Alpen in den Jahren 1860 bis 1869. Autorisirte deutsche Bearbeitung von Dr. Friedrich Steger. Braunschweig, 1872.
Chamonix and the range of Mont Blanc: a guide, London, 1896.
Escalades dans les Alpes de 1860 à 1869. Traduit par Adolphe Joanne. Paris, 1873.
Escalades. Introduction de Claire-Eliane Engel. Neuchâtel. [c.1944]
Guide à Zermatt et au Cervin. Genève. [1911]
'Mountaineering Tragedies.' *Strand Magazine*. 1909.
Scrambles amongst the Alps in the years 1860–69. London, 1871.
Travels amongst the Great Andes of the Equator; edited with an introduction by F.S.Smythe. London, 1949.
The valley of Zermatt and the Matterhorn: a guide. London, 1897.
Wigram, H.M. *Memoirs of Woolmore Wigram, Canon of St. Albans, by his wife*. London, 1908.
Williams, C. *A Church in the Alps*. London, 1970.
Women on the rope. London, 1973.
Zermatt Saga. London, 1964.
Wilson, C. *Mountaineering*. London, 1893.
Wundt, T. *Das Matterhorn und seine Geschichte*. Berlin. [1896]
Zermatt und seine Berge. Zürich, 1930.

Young, G.W. 'Mountaineering and its Prophets.' *Cornhill Magazine*, 1923.
'Mountain Prophets.' *AJ54*, 1943.
Yung, E. *Zermatt and the Valley of the Viège*. Geneva & London, 1894. [*Zermatt et la vallée de la Viège*. Genève, 1894]

Zsigmondy, E. *In the High Mountains*. London, 1992. [*Im Hochgebirge*. Leipzig, 1889]
Zurcher, F. & Margollé, E. *Les ascensions célèbres aux plus hautes montagnes du globe*. 2e éd. Paris, 1869.

INDEX

Page numbers in italics indicate an illustration and those in bold indicate a document reproduced in whole or in part. Brackets round such a document page number indicate that the document in question appears in its original French or German version rather than in an English translation.